# Dictionary of Prisons and Punishment

# Dictionary of Prisons and Punishment

Edited by

**Yvonne Jewkes and Jamie Bennett**

WILLAN
PUBLISHING

Published by

Willan Publishing
Culmcott House
Mill Street, Uffculme
Cullompton, Devon
EX15 3AT, UK
Tel: +44(0)1884 840337
Fax: +44(0)1884 840251
e-mail: info@willanpublishing.co.uk
website: www.willanpublishing.co.uk

Published simultaneously in the USA and Canada by

Willan Publishing
c/o ISBS, 920 NE 58th Ave, Suite 300,
Portland, Oregon 97213-3786, USA
Tel: +001(0)503 287 3093
Fax: +001(0)503 280 8832
e-mail: info@isbs.com
website: www.isbs.com

First published 2008

ISBN  978-1-84392-291-9 paperback
      978-1-84392-292-6 hardback

British Library Cataloguing-in-Publication Data

A catalogue record for this book is available from the British Library

Project managed by Deer Park Productions, Tavistock, Devon
Typeset by Pantek Arts Ltd, Maidstone, Kent
Printed and bound by T.J. International Ltd, Padstow, Cornwall

# Contents

# List of entries

# List of contributors

Jenny Adams Young, National Mother and Baby Unit Co-ordinator, HM Prison Service.
Rob Allen, Director, International Centre of Prison Studies.
Helen Arnold, University of Cambridge.
Lorraine Atkinson, Project Manager, Howard League for Penal Reform.
Dr Christie Barron, Simon Fraser University, Canada.
Chris Bath, Head of Projects, UNLOCK, the National Association of Ex-offenders.
Jamie Bennett, Prison Manager, HM Prison Service.
Hindpal Singh Bhui, Inspection Team Leader, HM Inspectorate of Prisons.
Simon Boddis, Head of Regimes Services, HM Prison Service.
Gill Brigden, Safer Custody Group, NOMS.
Dr Shane Bryans, Assistant Director of the Government Office for the West Midlands, former Prison Governor.
Carol Buckland, Voluntary Sector Unit, NOMS.
Dr Ros Burnett, University of Oxford.
Dr Jonathan Burnside, University of Bristol.
Michelle Butler, Dublin Institute of Technology.
Professor Rob Canton, De Montfort University, Leicester.
Dr Eamonn Carrabine, Dublin Institute of Technology.
Michael Cavadino, University of Central Lancashire.
Paul Cavadino, Chief Executive, Nacro.
Leonidas Cheliotis, University of Cambridge and University of London (Queen Mary and Westfield College).
Helen Codd, University of Central Lancashire.
Dr Roy Coleman, University of Liverpool.
Professor Andrew Coyle, King's College London.
Dr Elaine Crawley, University of Salford.
Simon Creighton, Human Rights Lawyer and Partner, Bhatt Murphy.
Dr Ben Crewe, University of Cambridge.
David Crighton, Deputy Chief Psychologist, NOMS.
Frances Crook, Director, Howard League for Penal Reform.
Jennifer DiCastro, American University, Washington, DC.
James Dignan, University of Leeds.
Anita Dockley, Assistant Director, Howard League for Penal Reform.
Dr Deb Drake, Open University.
Joyce Drummond Hill, Head of Internal Audit, HM Prison Service.
Dr Clare Dwyer, Queen's University, Belfast.
Kimmett Edgar, Prison Reform Trust.

Dr Tomer Einat, Emek Yezreel College, Israel.

Charles Elliott, Economist, formerly University of Cambridge.

Damian Evans, Governor, HMP The Mount.

Dr Stephen Farrall, Keele University.

Finola Farrant, University of the West of England.

David Faulkner, NOMS Research Associate, University of Oxford.

Dr Laurie Feehan, Edge Hill University.

Martina Feilzer, University of Oxford.

Dr Michael Fiddler, University of Greenwich.

Richard Garside, Director, Centre for Crime and Justice Studies, King's College London.

Dr Elaine Genders, University College London.

Steve Gillespie, Strategy and Performance Group, HM Prison Service.

Professor Barry Goldson, University of Liverpool.

Laura Graham, Safer Custody Group, NOMS.

Simon Green, University of Hull.

Jim Haines, International Centre for Prison Studies, KCL, and Independent Monitoring Board, HMP Wymott.

Peter Hammersley, Chaplain, HMP Hewell Grange.

Nigel Hancock, Safer Custody Group, NOMS.

Professor Craig Haney, University of California.

Sinead Hanks, SmartJustice.

Chris Hartley, Land-based Activities, HM Prison Service.

Dr Joel Harvey, London Metropolitan University.

Sophie Holmes, University of Lancaster.

Keir Hopley, Head of Sentencing Policy and Penalties Unit, Ministry of Justice.

Professor Yvonne Jewkes, University of Leicester.

Professor Robert Johnson, American University, Washington, DC.

Dr Helen Johnston, University of Hull.

Martin Kettle, Head of Case Management, HMP Whitemoor.

Professor Roy King, University of Cambridge.

Professor Alison Liebling, University of Cambridge.

Monica Lloyd, Inspection Team Leader, HM Inspectorate of Prisons.

Nancy Loucks, Independent Criminologist.

Juliet Lyon, Director Prison Reform Trust.

Professor Morag MacDonald, University of Central England.

Ruth Mann, Head of Sex Offender Treatment and Domestic Violence, HM Prison Service.

Dr Paul Mason, University of Cardiff.

Dr Shadd Maruna, Queen's University, Belfast.

Simon Matthews, Area Drug Strategy Co-ordinator, High Security Prisons, HM Prison Service.

Kirsten McConnachie, Queen's University, Belfast.

Professor Diana Medlicott, Buckinghamshire Chilterns University College.

James Mehigan, Open University.

Dr Alice Mills, University of Southampton.

Professor Rod Morgan, University of Bristol and former Chair, Youth Justice Board.

Professor John Muncie, Open University.

Professor Mike Nellis, University of Strathclyde.

Nigel Newcomen, Deputy Chief Inspector, HM Inspectorate of Prisons.

Tim Newell, Butler Trust Development Consultant, Butler Trust, and former Prison Governor.

William Payne, Office of the Children's Champion, Home Office, Border and Immigration Agency, former Prison Governor.

Dr Coretta Phillips, London School of Economics.

Professor John Pratt, Victoria University of Wellington, New Zealand.

Stephen Pryor, former Prison Governor.

Abigail Rowe, Open University.

Professor Mick Ryan, University of Greenwich.

Dr David Scott, University of Central Lancashire.

Jane Senior, Manager, Prison Health Research Network and the North West Forensic Academic Network.

Dr Mairead Seymour, Dublin Institute of Technology.

Stephen Shaw, Prisons and Probation Ombudsman.

Professor Joe Sim, Liverpool John Moores University.

Andy Simpson, Control and Restraint Training Centre, HM Prison Service.

Dr Roger Smith, De Montfort University, Leicester.

Enver Solomon, Centre for Crime and Justice Studies, King's College London.

Emeritus Professor Keith Soothill, University of Lancaster.

Professor Richard Sparks, University of Edinburgh.

Baroness Vivien Stern CBE, International Centre of Prison Studies.

Alisa Stevens, University of Oxford.

Duncan Stewart, Senior Research Officer, Research, Development and Statistics, NOMS.

Graham Towl, Chief Psychologist, NOMS.

Alan Tuckwood, HM Prison Service Head of Catering and PE (AT).

John Wagstaffe, Legal Adviser to the Criminal Cases Review Commission.

Dr Azrini Wahidin, University of Central England.

Roy Walmsley, International Centre of Prison Studies.

Michael Wheatley, Head of Reducing Reoffending Unit, High Security Prisons, HM Prison Service.

Sue Wilkinson, Librarian, HMP Birmingham.

Glynis Williams, Family Services Manager, HMP Styal.

Professor David Wilson, University of Central England.

Emeritus Professor Philip Zimbardo, Stanford University, California.

*The above list of contributors shows the position they held at the time of writing their entry.*

# About this book

The *Dictionary of Prisons and Punishment* is the first book of its kind in two important respects. Not only does it represent the first definitive cataloguing of key terms, concepts, theoretical approaches, institutions and policies associated with prisons and punishment, but it is also a unique collaboration between scholars and practitioners working in the fields of prisons and penology. Specifically, the Dictionary brings together contributions from academics; personnel within the Prison Service, Home Office, Ministry of Justice and National Offender Management Service; prison psychologists; health professionals; chaplains, members of prison charities and reform groups; and prison officers, managers and governors. The book's editors also combine academic and professional experience and, given this joint enterprise, it is perhaps unsurprising that the Dictionary has been compiled with two main readerships in mind.

First, it is aimed at people who work in prisons or who work with offenders in other capacities and environments. Contemporary prison practice is undergoing many challenges and is developing rapidly. In addition to the organizational and structural changes that have occurred in the past decade, there have been numerous developments in the ways that those who work in and around prisons understand and undertake their professional duties. This not only brings an increased emphasis on skills and qualifications but it has also introduced a new set of ideas and concepts into the established prisons and penal lexicon. At the same time, courses on prisons and penology remain important components of criminology and criminal justice degrees, and the second core readership are likely to be students on such programmes. It is arguable that those keen to further their knowledge of imprisonment are not as well served as students in other areas of criminology and criminal justice (although see recent contributions by Coyle 2005b; Jewkes and Johnston 2006; Bennett *et al.* 2007; Jewkes 2007c for useful introductions to prisons). The *Dictionary of Prisons and Punishment* is intended to be an essential compendium for undergraduate and postgraduate students seeking to pursue intellectual inquiry in this fascinating and fast-moving area.

As the spheres of prison scholarship and prison practice increasingly merge, it is probable that most of the contributors to this Dictionary will themselves use it as a source of reference. The brief to contributors was a challenging one. Dictionary definitions are, by their very nature, required to be thorough and wide ranging while, at the same time, succinct and to the point. The entries are thus intended to be comprehensive yet easily digestible, sophisticated yet accessible. It is also hoped that they stimulate further interest and research. Each entry concludes with a list of 'related entries' and 'key texts and sources' to which reference can be made and further inquiry followed up. At the same time, however, we have encouraged writers to express their own views in their own way, and we recognize the possibility of inconsistency – particularly, perhaps, between the contributions of an academic author and a practitioner writing on similar themes. Indeed, in some cases we have deliberately set up debates between approaches that differ theoretically or methodologically, or have invited contributors with divergent points of view to write on similar subjects. We believe that such an approach accurately reflects the complex and stimulating nature of prison studies and the breadth of contemporary penology. We think that scholars and practitioners (and, indeed, those who count themselves as *both*, as many contributors to this volume can rightly claim) greatly inform and enhance each other's work. Moreover, readers who follow up the suggested 'related entries' should be able to form their own opinions, while recognizing the diversity of knowledge, experience and understandings that underpin the writing of the definitions contained within these pages. As editors, we may not endorse all the opinions and views expressed in this volume, but we do maintain that our contributors are, in their different ways, ideally – in some cases, uniquely – placed to *have* an opinion on the topics they have been asked to write about.

While the focus is very much on prisons, it is a *Dictionary of Prisons **and Punishment*** in recognition of the changing nature of the criminal justice system: the restructuring of the Prison Service and Probation Service into an integrated system called the National Offender Management Service (NOMS); the splitting of the Home Office into two separate departments, with a new 'Ministry of Justice' taking responsibility for prisons, probation, criminal justice and sentencing; and the current political and penal rhetoric promising a 'joined-up' approach to punishing offenders and reducing rates of reoffending. The focus on punishment in the title is also intended to convey the notion that this Dictionary offers accessible definitions of penological terms – concepts, ideas and policies – that take us beyond the prison gates to the community and society at large.

The Dictionary's primary geographical focus is England and Wales, although many contributors refer to prison systems, research, practice and policy in other parts of the UK and internationally. While we can make no claim to have considered punishment in other countries in any systematic or comprehensive sense, we do believe that this Dictionary represents the first time a single book has covered all the major aspects of penology in a format that conveys the complexities of prisons and punishment in a clear, concise and engaging manner. It should be noted, however, that the decision to split the Home Office and to create a new Ministry of Justice came into being after most of the entries had been written. While every effort has been made to amend and replace all references to the Home Office, some of the developments are still in transition. Readers need to be aware that the Prison Service and NOMS are now the responsibility of the new ministry (which has an entry here) and to bear this in mind, especially where there is a reference to the role of the Home Office.

This volume is part of a new series of Dictionaries published by Willan that cover key aspects of the criminal justice system, providing an indispensable resource for reference and research. We sincerely hope that the *Dictionary of Prisons and Punishment* will meet the diverse needs of people studying penology, working in prisons, professionally interacting with prisoners and shaping penal policy, for many years to come.

*Yvonne Jewkes*
*Jamie Bennett*

# Introduction and overview

Prison today has such a central position in the criminal justice system that, for many, it is difficult to conceive that this has not always been the case. Prisons have been a feature of the criminal justice system since ancient times when they were administrative bodies for the collection of fines and also provided a holding place for offenders during trial or awaiting corporal or capital punishment. The emergence of prisons as we think of them today – as places explicitly designed for the infliction of punishment – was a relatively late development, taking place in the nineteenth century.

So how did prisons come to occupy their current position as the primary form of punishment (symbolically if not literally)? Pragmatically, the disappearance of transportation in the mid-nineteenth century following the loss of the American colonies and the emergence of Australia as a thriving and prosperous nation which no longer wanted the 'contaminating' influence of Britain's convicts meant that alternative punishments had to be sought. It has been argued by some writers that the shaping of prison into a practical institution for this purpose arose from the influence of campaigning reformers, such as John Howard (1726–90), who visited prisons throughout the UK and Europe, documenting conditions and lobbying for improvements. Managing prisons became a respectable profession, attracting altruistic, publicly minded men capable of speaking out and influencing reform (Coyle 2005a; Emsley 2005). From this rather optimistic perspective, then, prisons were seen as humanitarian, hygienic and progressive institutions, replacing the disorder and squalor of the old gaols and bridewells, and the barbaric practices of transportation and public execution. A less positive interpretation of these developments is that prisons were the product of a practical and moral crisis following the American Revolution of the 1770s (McGowen 1995). The loss of the main destination for transportation, the humiliating defeat of Britain in the War of Independence and the rise of revolutionary, democratic ideals in the face of an outdated and oppressive power all combined to force Britons to rethink how social institutions, including criminal justice, were managed.

These accounts, however, provide only a partial explanation for the transformations in the criminal justice system. In particular, they do not separate out the disappearance of one mode of punishment with the emergence of another. The decline in transportation can be understood on pragmatic grounds in as much as the loss of the American colonies and eventually the growth of national identity in the Australasian colonies meant that this form of punishment became progressively less available. In addition, the spectacles of torture and execution came to be seen as undesirable, and their disappearance from the public gaze was widely viewed as part of the 'civilizing process'.

The question still remains, however: given the gap that emerged in criminal justice when transportation and public execution 'disappeared', why did the prison become the preferred method to fill it? It is here that the French sociologist, Michel Foucault, and his book *Discipline and Punish: The Birth of the Prison* (1977), has been so influential. Foucault argues that the prison as a regimented, routinized, regulated and closely observed institution provided a form of punishment that fitted with the emerging values and methods of control employed in the industrial age. Prisons – like schools, hospitals and factories – can be viewed as sites of control and regulation designed to subdue their occupants while operating in the economic interests of the governing class. They are thus a product of the socio-economic conditions of the time. Furthermore, while imprisonment (as compared with transportation or execution) might be regarded as initiating 'the gentle way in punishment' (Foucault 1977: 104), the retreat of punishment from public spectacle to hidden practice might itself be called into question as a civilizing force. This tension between the perceived civilizing movement and the desire to control crime and criminals has been a constant feature in the history of imprisonment, and is central to understanding the development of prisons. It is a tension that frequently erupts in inquiries, public debates, changing policies and practices, and has been described as so deeply embedded in our prison system that it is 'one of its conditions of functioning' (Foucault 1977: 235).

## THE EMERGENCE OF THE MODERN PRISON

In the first half of the nineteenth century, many new prisons were built, including Millbank (1816) and Pentonville (1842). With their innovative architectural designs and regimes, they exemplified the experimentation and intellectual engagement of the era (Jewkes and Johnston 2006). Although the nineteenth century was a period in which conditions generally improved, and legislation was passed to standardize facilities, there was also public debate about whether prisoners were being treated with excessive leniency. This debate was played out in Parliament until the end of the century when the famous Gladstone Committee (1895) concluded that there should be a duality of purpose, achieving both deterrence and reform. The prison experience of the era reflected this dichotomy, with its mixture of uniformity, tight regulation and silence creating a punitive environment, underpinned by a mission to break the habits of the past and encourage prisoners to repent and reform.

The second half of the Victorian era saw the nationalization of the prison system under the Prisons Act 1877, put into effect under the leadership of Edmund Du Cane. The new structure was motivated by financial expediency achieved through rationalizing the estate and improving consistency and effectiveness, although it also reflected the development of a more extensive centralized state apparatus for managing social policy during that era (McConville 1998a). The system of penal servitude initiated by Du Cane and legitimized by the Carnarvon Report imposed a brutal uniformity on the prison experience, including hard labour, minimal contact with those inside and outside, poor diet and unsatisfactory sleeping conditions. However, the retirement of Du Cane and the publication of the Gladstone Report in 1895 marked a turning tide. Gradually, conditions of separation and the use of hard labour dwindled and, indeed, from 1908, the use of imprisonment itself entered a period of sharp and sustained decline which saw a reduction from over 20,000 prisoners to less than 10,000. Ushered in as part of New Liberalism, heralded by the 1906 general election, the early decades of the twentieth century have been described as a prototype welfare state due to extensive reforms of social policy and the redistribution of wealth

(Hennessy 1992). This period included Winston Churchill's dramatic 18 months as Home Secretary (1910–11), during which he personally intervened in cases where he considered disproportionate sentences had been awarded; undermined and curtailed the use of preventative detention; introduced legislative changes that limited the imprisonment of children and young adults; and initiated legislation that gave offenders time to pay fines, so dramatically reducing imprisonment for default (Bennett 2003). This era marked a determined attempt to limit the use of imprisonment that was sustained until after the Second World War.

The interwar years saw further improvements in prison conditions, the elimination of the last vestiges of the separate and silent systems, and greater efforts to allow prisoners to retain community contact and prepare them for release. Emblematic of the reforms of this period was the establishment of the first open prison at New Hall in Wakefield, Yorkshire, in 1933. Arguments for the introduction of an open prison system – and the consensus regarding minimal use of imprisonment more generally – were robust enough to be sustained despite a major riot at Dartmoor in 1932 and the inevitable public debate and backlash that followed (Brown 2006).

Following the Second World War, the welfare state was created, marking a fundamental shift in the role of the state and leading to a redistribution of wealth. Despite the radical nature of these reforms, they received wide public support and were quickly assimilated into political consensus (Hennessy 1992). In criminal justice, 'welfarism' was led by experts, including social workers, psychologists and academics, and was characterized by an emphasis on the responsibility of the state to care for and reform prisoners as well as punish them, although arguably this velvet glove concealed an iron fist, in as much as the failure to reform could be used to legitimate the use of punishment in individual cases (Garland 2001). In other respects, too, this was not quite a golden age. First, it was a period of prolonged and extensive expansion in the prison population, with a doubling of numbers incarcerated between 1945 and 1960. Secondly, penal policy was widely debated, both from within, as staff grew concerned about increasing levels of violence (Thomas 1972), and externally, as public concern intensified about crime rates generally and juvenile delinquency in particular (Sandbrook 2005). In short, while the first half of the twentieth century is often characterized as the epoch of welfarism, it was also the era in which cracks began to show and the consensus started to weaken.

Throughout the 1960s those cracks continued to widen in the face of popular concern about crime and imprisonment, particularly following a series of high-profile escapes, including that of the spy, George Blake (Mountbatten 1966), the intense media interest in crimes such as the great train robbery and the Moors murders, and the widely debated abolition of capital punishment. Already listing heavily, the rehabilitative ideal was finally sunk by Martinson's famous research commonly paraphrased as concluding that 'nothing works' (Martinson 1974).

It has been argued that the collapse of the rehabilitative ideal, along with an acceptance of high crime rates and limited power effectively to reduce them, led to the emergence of a new form of criminal justice management, described as 'the culture of control' (Garland 2001). Characterized by the re-emergence of traditional forms of punishment, particularly the use of imprisonment, and an expanding infrastructure of control throughout society (often supported by commercial organizations), this movement also implies an increasingly emotional tone to public and political debate about crime and punishment. The 'new punitiveness', as it has been coined, can be seen in the massive growth of the prison population in the UK and other Western democracies, and the adoption of punitive approaches to policing and sentencing, such as zero tolerance and three strikes (Pratt *et al.* 2005). In these conditions, the penal network has expanded dramatically, supported by a criminal justice infrastructure that includes more tightly controlled public spaces (Coleman 2004); more intensive community penalties, including electronic monitoring (Roberts 2004); and the criminalization of anti-social behaviour (Donoghue 2006). Public discourse has diversified, and punitiveness has become popularized in the media (Pratt 2007) and embedded in political discourse (Sparks 2003).

The brief history of prisons offered here illustrates how imprisonment is not only a long-established but also a central and expanding part of the criminal justice system. There has been a continuing tension between punitive and security values, on the one hand, and more compassionate and rehabilitative values on the other. This friction is a central feature of the prison and continues to play out to this day. In the section that follows we will look more closely at the 'compassion' end of the penal spectrum, and consider the extent to which prisons have been made more humane environments for the punishment of offenders. We will also discuss the new penal ideologies that came to the fore in the 1980s and 1990s – including privatization and managerialism – and examine whether these principles pose new threats to the humanizing of imprisonment.

## THE 1980s AND 1990s: COMPETING TENSIONS

The purpose of prison as punishment is self-evident, as is the desire of many to ensure that prisoners receive harsh punishment. However, appeals for compassion and humanity have been voiced since the earliest days of prison reform and, in modern times, notable statesmen from Winston Churchill to Nelson Mandela have articulated the view that the nature of imprisonment is a reflection of the fairness and humanity of the society in which it is located (Gilbert 1991; Mandela 1994). In contemporary penal discourse and practice, the Woolf Report, published following extensive rioting in prisons in April 1990, had a far-reaching impact on the way that those managing and staffing prisons are expected to carry out their professional duties. Encapsulating the notion that prisons should maintain a balance between security, control and justice, Woolf emphasizes the balance required between keeping prisoners in prison, maintaining order and regulating their activities, on the one hand, and recognizing prisoners' rights and respecting their dignity on the other (Woolf and Tumin 1991). This dynamic goes to the heart of debates about the legitimacy of prison; in other words, the creation of conditions where a prison is viewed *by the imprisoned* as morally justified (Sparks *et al.* 1996). The delicate balance implied by prisons' legitimacy has been institutionalized by the Prison Service in England and Wales in its *Statement of Purpose*, which places equal value on security, care and rehabilitation:

> *Her Majesty's Prison service serves the public by keeping in custody those committed by the courts.*

*Our duty is to look after them with humanity and help them to lead law abiding and useful lives in custody and after release (http://www.hmprisonservice.gov.uk/ abouttheservice/statementofpurpose/).*

In recent years, population increases and the emergence of punitive discourses have led to calls for an erosion of facilities available to prisoners that may be seen as luxuries (Jewkes 2002) – a belief enshrined in the principle of 'less eligibility' – and the introduction of conditions that make imprisonment more onerous (Whitman 2003; Pratt *et al.* 2005; Pratt 2007). Given that the UK has so enthusiastically embraced punitive measures in relation to sentencing and is rapidly moving closer to a state of mass imprisonment, it might further be anticipated that this country will adopt some of the other popular, punitive prison conditions emerging in America, including punishing physical routines, distinctive uniforms and petty rules. In the UK, however, the situation is arguably more complex than proponents of the new punitiveness sometimes suggest. For example, Matthews (2005) argues that quite different penal developments – sanctions that involve the infliction of pain, on the one hand, and the emergence of emotive (but non-punitive) punishments on the other – are frequently, and erroneously, regarded as two sides of the same coin. The reality of current penal policy is that it is characterized by plurality and diversity and, although punitiveness is inarguably a dominant contemporary discourse, there remains a tension between retributive and vengeful punishments, and more compassionate values. For example, the Woolf Report resulted in major improvements in prison conditions, including limiting cell-sharing and introducing in-cell sanitation (Woolf and Tumin 1991). It also briefly led to a reduction in the prison population, although this turned out to be a blip that was subsequently eradicated by the dramatic rise in numbers from 1992.

In prisons, there has also been professional resistance to unrelenting punitiveness, including a reinvigoration of professional advocacy of the humane treatment of prisoners. This was formalized by the current Director General of the Prison Service in 2002 when he defined the concept of 'decency', setting seven specific elements, but also asking the general question: 'whether or not staff would be happy with their relatives being held there' (cited in Coyle 2003). Subsequently, a tool was developed to assess the humane aspects of imprisonment, known as Measuring the Quality of Prison Life (MQPL) (Liebling assisted by Arnold 2004). This resistance to harsh, and frequently humiliating, penal practices in the face of popular media pressure and developing global professional practice remains a distinctive aspect of prison management in the UK.

A further 'compassionate' influence in UK prisons exists in the form of official bodies, including HM Inspectorate of Prisons and the European Committee for the Prevention of Torture, which act to protect human rights, and non-governmental organizations, such as the Howard League and Prison Reform Trust, both of which work for humane, effective and rational reform of the penal system. Yet some criminologists and penologists maintain that the prison reform movement is not a solution to the problems associated with imprisonment (which include social exclusion, overcrowding, drugs, mental illness and high rates of self-harm and suicide) but is part of the problem itself. Central to the position known as 'abolitionism' (see, for example, Mathiesen 1974; Ignatieff 1978; Fitzgerald and Sim 1979) is a critique of the penal reform lobby and its 'detrimental and deadening impact on the debates around prisons' (Ryan and Sim 2007). Ryan and Sim (2007: 701) offer this assessment:

> *Abolitionists, while recognising that **some** reforms at **some** historical moments may have enhanced the position of the confined, would also maintain that the prison reform movement more broadly has, however unintentionally, helped to reproduce the dominant discourses that the prison is the **natural** response to crime and deviance.*

Ryan and Sim (2007) further note that, by the early 1980s, there was an 'enlarged, diverse and fractured policy network in England and Wales around imprisonment' with some lobby groups campaigning for improvements in prisons to deliver reform, while other groups vigorously campaigned against prisons, arguing instead for alternatives to custody.

The abolitionist movement and academic intervention in debates about prison reform were gathering momentum just as a new approach to politics was being ushered in. The New Right ideology of the 1980s promoted the private sector, market discipline and small government, and marked a decisive split with the post-war consensus and the primacy of the publicly funded welfare state. For public sector organizations, this ideology advocated 'new public management' (NPM) – a set of principles borrowed from the private sector that embrace competition, privatization and managerialism.

Since coming to power in 1997, New Labour's policy on prisons has only further entrenched the NPM ideals of its predecessors, and there is now an even greater emphasis on auditing and setting performance targets. Perhaps most significantly, in 2004, the National Offender Management Service (NOMS) was established, a commissioning body for criminal justice services, including prisons and probation, which also has a stake in sentencing guidelines. This organization proposes to expand commercial competition, or 'contestability', as it is termed (Carter 2003: 34), including the award of contracts to all prisons for a fixed period, after which there would be an open competition. Although the first attempt to achieve this by market testing three prisons on the Isle of Sheppey in Kent was aborted, the government's commitment to contestability is evidence of the blurring of public and private boundaries in the delivery of punishment (Bennett 2007).

Privatization is further manifested in several ways, including the contracting out of prison escort services, prison work programmes, electronic monitoring of offenders released from prison, the financing of prison construction and – most controversially of all – the management and operation of prisons (Mehigan and Rowe 2007). Objections to private prisons are wide ranging and include fears that the drive for profit can result in cuts in staffing costs (e.g. paying staff less money, employing fewer staff, employing less qualified staff and offering less job security), with commensurate reductions in officer–prisoner interaction, time out of cell for prisoners and security for both staff and prisoners. Above all, many people believe that it is morally and ethically unacceptable for private individuals to profit from the delivery of pain to others and, despite voicing objections along these lines when in opposition, since coming to power the Labour government has continued to encourage private investment and has announced that all new prison building for the foreseeable future will rely on private contractors.

More generally, managerialist approaches – with their emphasis on meeting per-formance targets and doing well in prison 'league tables' – arguably move the focus away from meeting the needs of individual offenders to matching them to macro-needs – for example, employing actuarial methods of assessment of risk and providing structured offending behaviour courses to reduce potential risk. These developments have come in for criticism on a number of grounds. First, some prison managers considered the new measures a bureaucratic distraction from the manage-ment of people (Selby 1994). Secondly, there have been general criticisms that such measures cannot meaningfully reflect complex social institutions and the measure becomes more important than the outcome (Hennessy 1990; Smith and Goddard 2002). Thirdly, it is argued that, by making prisons more business-like, the unique moral aspects of imprisonment are marginalized (Wilson 1995). In essence, it is fre-quently argued that managerialism has a profoundly depersonalizing and dehumanizing effect on an organization – not just for prisoners but also for the man-agement and staff, causing Ryan and Sim (2007) to comment that prison staff have come to be far more worried by efficiency audits than they ever had been about visits from the Chief Inspector of Prisons. Managerialism has wide-reaching consequences for those who work in prisons, including potentially less supportive or collegiate pro-fessional relationships and a leaning towards compliance at the cost of innovation (Bryans 2007). There are also concerns that, in relation to prisoners, managerialist processes support trends such as 'new penology' (Feeley and Simon 1992) and prac-tices such as responsibilization (Hannah-Moffat 2000).

However, not all prison personnel are against managerialism; some practitioners have noted that the development of NPM has had a beneficial impact and has suc-ceeded in turning the good intentions of prison managers into reality (Wheatley 2005). NOMS has also pledged to place a greater focus on achieving a reduction in recidivism, and it has been suggested that, in the future, this will play a more signifi-cant role in performance measurement. Certainly in very recent years there has been a re-emergence of discourses around rehabilitation – refocused as 'reducing reoffend-ing' – including access to education, employment, drug treatment, offending behaviour programmes and family contact (NOMS 2006).

It must not be forgotten, therefore, that, while prisons are highly organized, rou-tinized and regulated environments, they are also social spaces. The development of managerialism has expanded the techniques of control and structure and, arguably, may have enfeebled the moral culture and craftsmanship of prison management. However, there is still scope for prison managers and staff to use their discretion and to avoid the insensitivity and injustices of rigid structures (Cheliotis 2006b). With that in mind, let us now turn to the main group of people who inhabit prisons: the prison population.

## PRISON POPULATION

Figure 1  The expansion of the prison population, 1900–2004

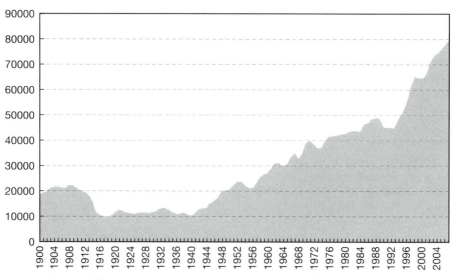

*Sources*: Home Office (2003b, 2006b); NOMS (2006, 2007a)[1]

Figure 1 illustrates the sustained expansion in prison population numbers (particularly from 1940), and the dramatic acceleration since 1992. A simple explanation that the general public and politicians often adhere to is that there is a direct relationship between crime rates and imprisonment – i.e. when crime increases, so does imprisonment, and high levels of imprisonment then lead to a reduction in crime. However, this does not accord with reality: crime rates and imprisonment rates show no straightforward correspondence:

> *Imprisonment rates and severity of punishment move independently from changes in crime rates, patterns and trends. Governments decide how much punishment they want, and these decisions are in no simple way related to crime rates, patterns and trends. This can be seen by comparing crime and punishment trends in Finland, Germany and the United States between 1960 and 1990. The trends are close to identical...yet the US imprisonment rate quadrupled in that period. The Finnish rate fell by 60 percent and the German rate was broadly stable* (Tonry 2004: 14; see also Mathiesen 2006; King 2007a; Sparks 2007).

If changes in levels of imprisonment cannot be explained in terms of crime rates, then what is the explanation? The rises over the last 15 years, and even as far back as the early 1970s, have been attributed to changes in public discourse, attitudes, policy and practice. In relation to public discourse, some commentators argue there has been a growth in 'penal populism' (Pratt 2007). There has been some debate about whether this has been a bottom-up initiative, driven by public concern, or whether that concern has been generated by established interests, such as the media and politicians (Jewkes 2007a), with some empirical evidence produced to support the latter view (Beckett 1997). While little research has been conducted on public opinion about prisons (though sweeping generalizations about punitive attitudes hold a great deal of currency), some commentators have suggested that better education and communication can play a role in changing public attitudes and building support for reducing the prison population (Mathiesen 2006). Today, however, there does not appear to be any public or political appetite for a change in direction in the UK. Any future reverse is more likely to arise from concerns about cost or operating pressures rather than from a change of heart.

In 2007, the prison population reached over 80,000, a new record in the UK. Increasing prison populations inevitably lead to overcrowding in many prisons. The pressure on accommodation can lead to greater numbers of prisoners being held in unsuitable conditions, including more prisoners being confined in a cell than it is designed to hold. Overcrowding can reduce the quality of life of prisoners, can reduce access to services and can increase tensions, ultimately leading to the loss of legitimacy and even the loss of control (Woolf and Tumin 1991).

The prison population comprises sentenced, remand and non-criminal prisoners. In 2005, they represented 81.7 per cent, 16.9 per cent and 1.4 per cent, respectively, of the prison population (Home Office 2006b). The sentenced prisoners were serving a range of sentences: 13.3 per cent were serving sentences of less than 12 months; 34.7 per cent were serving sentences of between 12 months and less than four years; 42.5 per cent were serving determinate sentences of four years or more; and 9.4 per cent were serving indeterminate sentences (Home Office 2006b). The last ten years have seen a significantly faster growth in the percentage of prisoners serving indeterminate sentences or sentences of four years and more (Home Office 2006b). The people in prison have committed a wide rage of offences, although the most prevalent are violence against the person (24.4 per cent), drugs offences (17.1 per cent), robbery (13.4 per cent), burglary (13 per cent) and sexual offences (9.9 per cent).

It has for a long time been recognized that crime is closely linked to social exclusion. Such themes were a staple of Charles Dickens' novels (Johnston 2006) and were the justification for many of the liberal reforms of the early twentieth century. People in prison are more likely than the general population to experience problems related to housing, education, employment, health, drug misuse and families (Social Exclusion Unit 2002). For example, prisoners are 13 times as likely to have been in care as a child and 13 times as likely to be unemployed as non-prisoners. Some 60–70 per cent of prisoners were using drugs before imprisonment, and many prisoners' basic skills are very poor, with 80 per cent having the writing skills, 65 per cent the numeracy skills and 50 per cent the reading skills at or below the level of an 11-year-old child (Social Exclusion Unit 2002). For many, the experience of imprisonment can further jeopardize employment, housing and family contacts, so making desistance from crime more difficult (Farrall and Calverley 2006). The link between exclusion and prison has also led to discussion about the appropriate boundary between criminal justice and social policy, essentially questioning whether mass imprisonment is simply punishing the consequences of social problems (for example, see Hillyard *et al.* 2005).

The prison population, then, is not one that directly mirrors the community, in the sense that certain groups of people are more or less likely to experience imprisonment. Furthermore, as countless criminologists have noted, the fact that the burdens of criminality fall disproportionately on certain groups reveals much about prevailing power structures and inequalities. This point can be illustrated by examining the demographics of the prison population. In 2005, the composition of the prison population included 24.7 per cent of prisoners from black and minority ethnic communities, a growth from 17.3 per cent in 1995 (Home Office 2006b). This compares with the general community, where 8.7 per cent of the population are non-white (Office for National Statistics n.d.). In addition, 13 per cent of the population are foreign nationals – again, an expanding group – with an increase in receptions of 182 per cent over a decade (Home Office 2006b).

Similarly, young people have long been the subject of moral panics about crime. People under 21 years of age make up 12.4 per cent of the prison population, with over 11,000 people of these ages being held in custody, including over 1,500 who are aged under 18 (NOMS 2007a). There has been much criticism of the UK's policy towards the imprisonment of children and young people, in particular that custody is used excessively (Coyle 2005a). Attempts to curb the imprisonment of children and young people over the last ten years had some temporary success, particularly in 2002–3 after responsibility passed to a dedicated Youth Justice Board (Morgan 2007), but this has now been eroded.

Women are disproportionately under-represented in prisons, making up 5.5 per cent of the prison population (NOMS 2007a). They are generally convicted of less serious offences than men (in particular, violence and sexual offending is less prevalent, while drugs and acquisitive offending, including theft, are more common). Since 1995, there has been an accelerated expansion of the female prison population, with a 126 per cent growth in the decade from 1995. This dramatic rise has occurred against a backdrop of campaigning groups (e.g. SmartJustice) arguing that *most* of the women who are incarcerated should not be in prison at all (Medlicott 2007).

## THE 'OTHER PRISON POPULATION'

The other significant group of people in prison, sometimes called the 'other prisoners', are prison staff (Hawkins 1976: 81). At the end of 2005, there were 48,425 directly employed staff in public sector prisons in England and Wales, including 25,971 unified grades (i.e. officers and governors). There is also a wide range of other staff working in prisons, including operational support grades (15.2 per cent) who carry out work including staffing the gate, perimeter security and driving escort vehicles, and administrative staff (15.3 per cent). There are also other smaller professional groups, including instructors (7 per cent), psychologists (1.9 per cent), chaplains (0.6 per cent) and healthcare professionals (2.2 per cent). This total figure does not include all the staff working in prison (for example, contracted staff will work in areas including education, healthcare and the prison shop). Prison officers are the largest group and have also been subject to the most extensive research. Many of these studies reflect the fact that prison officers have a long-standing sense of grievance regarding a perceived lack of recognition from the public, politicians and managers (e.g. Thomas 1972; Liebling and Price 2001; Crawley 2004). This has fuelled poor industrial relations and led the Prison Officers' Association to be criticized as militant and outdated (Arnold *et al.* 2007; Bennett and Wahidin 2007).

However, recent studies have also started to uncover that prison work involves complex skills, including the management of relationships and the use of discretion, and that the work is carried out in a particularly taxing physical and emotional arena (Liebling and Price 2001; Crawley 2004). As Arnold *et al.* (2007) observe, talk is central to everything prison officers do, and they are called upon to build up and maintain close relationships with those in their charge. Among their many and varied custodial duties are carrying out security checks and searching procedures; supervising prisoners and maintaining order; taking care of prisoners and their property, taking account of their rights and dignity; writing fair and perceptive reports on prisoners; taking an active part in rehabilitation programmes for prisoners; promoting anti-bullying and suicide prevention policies; providing appropriate care and support for prisoners at risk of self-harm; and employing authorized physical control and restraint procedures where necessary. These can all be complex challenges and require the ability to balance authority with understanding and compassion (www.hmprisonservice.gov.uk/careersandjobs/typeswork/prisonofficer; Arnold *et al.* 2007).

## CONCLUSION

It is hoped that this potted history of English prisons and brief outline of those who live and work in them today have conveyed some sense of the extraordinary complexity of the history of prisons and punishment. The contributors to this Dictionary further illuminate some of the tensions and contradictions that have informed countless and sometimes conflicting penal ideologies, especially over the course of the last century. While the chaotic and often incoherent approach to policy – sometimes called the 'penal merry-go-round' (Scott 2007) – suggests an underlying failure to find a sustainable and legitimate set of principles to guide what prisons are actually for, it is important to remember that mass incarceration is not inevitable, nor has the growth of imprisonment been unchallenged and unchecked throughout history. Prisons have always been subjected to some degree of external scrutiny, in particular through nationally appointed inspectors and local visiting boards, which have provided a degree of accountability in a frequently hidden world. It is also important to remember that prisons are not only physical institutions but are also social worlds in which it is necessary to understand the people, power and politics that shape the experience of everyday life. Despite the discourses of punitiveness and managerialism which permeate penal policy (and also pervade academic discussions of prisons and punishment), there is still scope for people to exercise decency and humanity within the prison world.

## NOTE

1. In the figure and in the text, the population figures from 1900 to 2002 are the mean average prison population for the year. The figures from 2003 to 2006 are the median average, taken on 30 June for those years. The 2007 figure is that on 27 April 2007.

# Prisons and punishment timeline

Some major events in the history of prisons and punishment.

| Date | Event |
| --- | --- |
| 892–3 | Law of Alfred mentions imprisonment |
| 1020–30s | Law of Cnut on imprisonment |
| 1166 | Assize of Clarendon orders building of county gaols |
| 1188 | King Henry II buys land next to Newgate (the gate looking west from the City of London towards Westminster) for a prison. Newgate Prison occupied this site until 1881. The Old Bailey (Central Criminal Court) now stands there |
| 1219 | Henry III's ordinance on imprisonment of suspect felons |
| 1275 | Statute of Westminster overhauls aspects of, and makes considerable use of, imprisonment |
| 1295 | Statute of Breaking Prisons |
| 1503 | Sheriffs' powers to keep gaols confirmed |
| 1531 | Act concerning construction of gaols and justice's powers |
| 1544 | First appointment of prison clergyman at Newgate |
| 1556 | Bridewell receives its first inmates |
| 1597 | Act for punishment of vagabonds allows transportation and galleys |
| 1605 | Charges for conveyance of offenders to gaol |
| 1609 | Houses of correction to be provided in all counties |
| 1666 | Act for relief of poor prisoners and setting them to work |
| 1679 | Habeas Corpus Act |
| 1681 | Regular inspection of Newgate Prison commences |
| 1692 | Surgeon from St Bartholomew's starts to visit Newgate |
| 1699 | Act enables justices of the peace to build and repair prisons |
| 1716 | Act details sheriffs' power and control of sale and gaoler's office |
| 1717 | Act permits transportation of felons |
| 1719 | Act covering prison building and justices of the peace's power to send offenders to houses of correction |
| 1751 | Sale of spirits in gaols forbidden |

| Date | Event |
|------|-------|
| 1774 | House of Commons Committee on Gaols leads to Discharged Prisoners Act and Health of Prisoners Act |
| 1776–83 | Loss of American colonies leads to temporary halt to transportation |
| 1777 | Publication of John Howard's *The State of the Prisons in England and Wales*. It becomes a major catalyst for UK prison reform |
| 1779 | Penitentiary Act passed – the first English Act authorizing state prisons (although only Millbank was built under the Act) |
| 1783 | Public hangings moved from Tyburn to Newgate |
| 1787 | First transportation to Australia |
| 1787–91 | Bentham draws up plans for the Panopticon prison |
| 1789 | First prisons opened incorporating separate cells |
| 1803 | Having been told nine years earlier that the government approved his plans for a Panopticon prison and wanted him to run it under contract, Jeremy Bentham is informed that the funds are no longer available |
| 1810 | Holford Committee recommends the building of a national penitentiary |
| 1813 | Elizabeth Fry's first visit to the women prisoners in Newgate |
| 1815 | Gaol Fees Abolition Act |
| 1816 | Millbank Penitentiary opens |
| 1823 | The Gaols Act introduces regular visits by prison chaplains, the payment of warders and the prohibition of irons or manacles. It also makes it mandatory to put women warders in charge of women prisoners for the first time |
| 1835 | Prison Act establishes a Prison Inspectorate |
| 1837–8 | Molesworth Committee recommends the abolition of transportation |
| 1839 | Prison Act incorporates idea of religious reformation |
| 1842 | Pentonville Penitentiary opens |
| 1849 | Elizabeth Fry's Refuge for Repentant Females opens, as does Winson Green Prison, Birmingham |
| 1851 | Wandsworth Prison opens |
| 1853 | Penal Servitude Act ends short periods of transportation |
| 1857 | Last hulk goes out of service and transportation abolished as a judicial punishment |
| 1861 | Act abolishes death penalty for all offences except murder, treason and piracy |
| 1863 | Carnarvon Committee recommends tougher prisons |
| 1865 | Prisons Act |
| 1867 | Formal end of transportation |
| 1868 | End to public hangings |

| Date | Event |
|---|---|
| 1877 | Prisons Act brings all prisons within central control of Prison Commission under Edmund Du Cane |
| 1879 | Summary Jurisdiction Act increases the availability of non-custodial penalties |
| 1887 | Probation of First Offenders Act – a further diversionary measure |
| 1895 | Gladstone Committee proposes that prisons maintain a balance between punishment and rehabilitation |
| 1898 | Prison Act gives effect to Gladstone's recommendations |
| 1902 | First Borstal established |
| 1907 | Probation of Offenders Act means the first probation officers are appointed, which enables courts to assist and advise offenders towards rehabilitation |
| 1908 | Prevention of Crime Act introduces preventative detention and enacts the Borstal system. Children Act restricts the imprisonment of children |
| 1913 | Mental Deficiency Act leads to diversion of mentally ill people from prison |
| 1932 | Dartmoor Prison mutiny |
| 1933 | Children and Young Persons Act leads to the replacement of reformatory and industrial schools with approved schools |
| 1936 | First adult open prison established |
| 1939 | Prison Officers' Association recognized |
| 1948 | Criminal Justice Act abolishes penal servitude and hard labour, while new sentences of preventative detention and corrective training are introduced. Detention centres established |
| 1952 | Prison Act consolidates prison legislation and sets out rules for managing prisons and rights of prisoners. This also formalizes the role of boards of visitors to oversee the work of each prison |
| 1959 | Mental Health Act leads to hospital orders and guardianship orders being introduced |
| 1963 | The Home Office begins running the Prison Service. It was previously run by the Prison Commission |
| 1964 | Probation Service made responsible for prison welfare |
| 1965 | Murder (Abolition of Death Penalty) Act suspends capital punishment for murder for a period of five years. This time limitation is subsequently removed and capital punishment for murder is abolished |
| 1966 | Escape of George Blake leads to Mountbatten Report on prison security |
| 1967 | Criminal Justice Act introduces suspended prison sentences and the availability of parole. Preventative detention, corrective training and corporal punishment abolished |
| 1969 | Children and Young Persons Act  introduces care and supervision orders and replaces approved schools and remand homes with community homes |

| Date | Event |
| --- | --- |
| 1970 | Administration of Justice Act removes imprisonment for debt |
| 1972 | Criminal Justice Act introduces further non-custodial penalties, including community service |
| 1978 | Decision in *R* v. *Board of Visitors of Hull Prison ex parte St Germain* establishes the principle that prison decisions, including adjudications, are subject to the rules of natural justice and open to judicial review |
| 1979 | Report of May Committee following a number of prison disturbances |
| 1982 | Criminal Justice Act removes imprisonment for all people under 21 and abolishes Borstals, replacing them with youth custody. It also introduces an independent HM Inspectorate of Prisons. In the case of *Raymond* v. *Honey*, Lord Wilberforce makes an important statement of legal principle: 'Under English law a convicted prisoner retains all civil rights which are not taken away expressly or by necessary implication' |
| 1986 | Widespread riots follow industrial action by prison officers |
| 1987 | 'Fresh Start' introduces a new pay and grading system for prison staff and abolishes paid overtime |
| 1990 | Riot at Strangeways spreads to other prisons, leading to the most serious and widespread disorder experienced in prisons in the UK |
| 1991 | Woolf Report published on the causes of prison disorder. It proposes that greater attention is given to improving conditions and meeting the legitimate needs of prisoners. In *Thynne, Wilson and Gunnell* v. *UK*, the European Court decides that the tariff for discretionary life sentences should be set by judges, not the Home Secretary |
| 1992 | Criminal Justice Act introduces new system for early release and parole and establishes that prison sentences should be commensurate with the seriousness of the offence, enshrining 'just deserts' as the main principle of sentencing. First privately operated remand centre opens at The Wolds in Humberside |
| 1993 | The Prison Service becomes an executive agency, providing a degree of operating independence |
| 1994 | Private prisons start to hold convicted prisoners. Prisons Ombudsman established; it was expanded in 2004 to also cover Probation. Criminal Justice and Public Order Act makes it illegal for prison officers to take industrial action. Escape of six prisoners from the Special Secure Unit at Whitemoor leads to concerns about security in prisons |
| 1995 | Escape of three Category A prisoner from Parkhurst leads to the dismissal of the Director General of the Prison Service and precipitates a major crisis in public confidence |
| 1996 | Mandatory drug testing introduced into prisons |
| 1997 | Two-strikes sentencing introduced, providing for a life sentence to be imposed automatically on conviction of a second sexual or violent offence |

| Date | Event |
|------|-------|
| 1998 | Human Rights Act introduced. This formally abolished capital punishment for high treason. Crime and Disorder Act establishes the Youth Justice Board to monitor and develop the management of offenders under 18 years of age. In 2000, its work is expanded to include commissioning of services |
| 1999 | Home detention curfew introduced, leading to a temporary drop in the prison population |
| 2000 | Zahid Mubarek murdered by racist cellmate at Feltham Young Offender Institution |
| 2001 | Prisoner Learning and Skills Unit established, starting the process of transferring responsibility for prisoner education and training to the Department for Education and Skills. The National Probation Service is launched under the control of the National Directorate of Probation |
| 2002 | In *R* v. *Secretary of State for the Home Department ex parte Anderson*, the European Court decides that the tariff for mandatory life sentences should be set by judges, not the Home Secretary |
| 2003 | Criminal Justice Act introduces wide-ranging reforms to sentencing, including changing the purpose of sentencing to meet a diversity of aims. Two-strikes legislation replaced by indeterminate public protection sentences that can be awarded for a first conviction for a sexual or violent offence. Boards of visitors change their name to independent monitoring boards as part of modernization |
| 2004 | National Offender Management Service (NOMS) introduced. Responsibility for private prisons removed from the Prison Service and transferred to NOMS. In *Hirst* v. *UK*, the European Court of Human Rights rules that a blanket ban on prisoners voting is unlawful |
| 2005 | Prison officers' right to strike reinstated, although the Prison Officers' Association enters into a binding 'no strike' agreement |
| 2006 | Transition of prison health facilities to NHS responsibility completed. Public inquiry into the murder of Zahid Mubarek is critical of race relations in prisons |
| 2007 | Prison population exceeds 80,000 for the first time, leading to a population crisis. Responsibility for prisons transfers from the Home Office to the newly created Ministry of Justice |

*Source:* Adapted from Harding *et al.* (1985). See also
http://www.citizenshipfoundation.org.uk and
http://www.mdx.ac.uk/WWW/STUDY/crimtim.htm.

# ABOLITIONISM

A term used to describe a number of positions and movements that seek to challenge the existence of prison as the answer to problems of crime. Abolitionists argue that prison has failed, is beyond reform and needs to be eradicated. They further contend that prisons sustain existing social and racial inequality and division. More broadly, abolitionism argues that crime is a social construct, a consequence of the structure of society, and it advocates the correction of the dominant culture rather than the prisoner.

Abolitionism questions the need for prison and asks whether it is the answer to protection for the public and to the problem of crime. Further, it seeks to promote a system in which crime is recognized as a social construct and in which the discourse of those supporting prison must be challenged. Thus, to refer to prisoners as 'inmates' and to speak of imprisonment as 'treatment' is to shift the focus away from the realities of prison. The Dutch abolitionist, Willem de Haan, notes that abolitionism aims for 'compensation rather than retaliation; reconciliation rather than blame allocation' (1991: 211).

Abolitionists argue that the traditional justifications for prison – deterrence, rehabilitation, incapacitation and retribution – do nothing more than justify the existence of institutions of pain delivery and social control. The abolitionist position contends that prisons fail those incarcerated within them and have a devastating effect on prisoners' families and friends. Fundamentally, prison abolition chal-

lenges the taken-for-granted nature of prisons' existence. Angela Davis, founder of the American abolition movement, Critical Resistance, has noted that:

> *people tend to take prisons for granted. It is difficult to imagine life without them. At the same time, there is a reluctance to face the realities hidden within them, a fear of thinking about what happens inside them. Thus the prison is present in our lives and, at the same time, it is absent from our lives*
>
> (2003: 15).

Abolitionism is not a monolithic term however, and some have considered it unhelpful in attempting to challenge the prison industrial complex in late modernity, allowing detractors simply to label such a movement as a long-range goal in the face of a prison crisis firmly located in the here and now. As a movement, abolitionism includes academic writers from the UK and Europe – Thomas Mathiesen, Nils Christie, Willem de Haan, Mick Ryan, Joe Sim among others – as well as activist groups such as Radical Alternatives to Prison in the UK in 1970s and 1980s and, more recently, No More Prison. In the USA, Critical Resistance is the largest abolitionist movement with ten 'chapters' across America.

The abolitionist movement draws a clear distinction between itself and prison reform. It contends that the notion of improvement, restructuring and/or modifying the prison is based upon the premise that prisons, fundamentally, should exist and can perform socially useful functions in a criminal justice system. Consequently, reform groups help to bolster and reinforce the prison system. In response to this position, critics of abolitionism argue that it is preferable to work with, reform and challenge existing state structures rather than attempt to remove them. This is closely linked to the accusation that abolitionists are unrealistic idealists and dreamers, preoccupied with large-scale fundamental ideologies that can never deliver tangible or practical solutions to crime in society. Often, the abolitionist is faced with the reductive argument about public safety from dangerous prisoners. The essence of such an argument is: 'what are you going to do with the rapists and paedophiles?'

This criticism, steeped in populist media-generated fear, shifts the justification for prison away from fundamental questions, and from the vast majority of the crimes committed by the prison population, to a small minority of prisoners. However, and in response to feminist disquiet about male violence, abolitionists would point to the socially situated nature of dangerousness as a construct and suggest that prison as a response to such crimes does nothing more than exacerbate misogyny and hegemonic masculine culture. In countering suggestions of the impracticalities of abolitionism, and as Ryan and Sim have regularly noted, abolitionist positions have had a number of successes – for example, in forcing accountability for deaths in custody through the organization Inquest and preventing at least one new prison wing from being built.

The challenge for abolitionism in the 'new punitive' climate of populist punishment, screaming tabloid headlines and a crime-obsessed media ecology, is to offer radical alternatives to the failures of the present system. With politicians and publics in agreement that fundamental changes must be made to the current system, abolitionists need to carve out a space to promote such a position.

*Paul Mason*

### Related entries

*Dangerousness; Deaths in custody; Families of prisoners; New punitiveness; Public perceptions.*

**Key texts and sources**

Davis, A. (2003) *Are Prisons Obselete?* London: Open Media.
De Haan, W. (1991) 'Abolitionism and crime control: a contradiction in terms', in K. Stenson and D. Cowell (Eds.) *The Politics of Crime Control*, London: Sage.
Mathiesen, T. (2000) *Prisons on Trial.* Winchester: Waterside Press.
Prison Research Action Project (1976) *Instead of Prisons: A Handbook for Abolitionists.* Syracuse, NY: Prison Research Action Project (available online at **http://www.prisonpolicy.org/scans/instead_of_prisons**).
Ryan, M. and Sim, J. (2007) 'Campaigning for and campaigning against prisons: excavating and re-affirming the case for prison abolitition', in Y. Jewkes (ed.) Handbook on Prisons. Cullompton: Willan.
See also the websites of No More Prison (**http://www.alternatives2prisons.ik.com/**) and Critical Resistance (http://www.criticalresistance.org/).

## ACCOUNTABILITY

Accountability refers both to the responsibility prisons have to deliver punishment for the state – or democratic accountability – and to their responsibility for meeting standards and targets set regarding the quality and quantity of that work – operational accountability.

Accountability is important in good governance and in the legitimacy of public power. It is associated with such concepts as democracy and the rule of law. In Britain, accountability has been identified as one of the 'seven principles of public life' by the Committee on Standards in Public Life. Accountability may come in two forms: democratic accountability and operational accountability.

*Democratic* accountability concerns the authority to punish. Some people argue that punishment is the quintessential function of government. To delegate this task impoverishes the public sphere and weakens the bond between citizen and state. Others argue that a distinction can be made between the allocation of punishment (which, under social contract theory, is one of the core state powers) and the administration of punishment (which is not a core power and can therefore be delegated).

However, the devil of this is in the detail. How exactly does one distinguish between the allocation and administration of punishment? Does the allocation of punishment begin and end in the court? Are prisons only concerned with the administration of punishment? Arguably not, when one considers adjudications, parole reports, sentence planning and categorization. All these affect prisoners' experience of imprisonment and may be seen as part of the allocation and not simply the administration of punishment. A contemporary concern is how far the authority to punish can be delegated to the private sector before democratic accountability is undermined (Harding 1997; Genders 2002).

*Operational* accountability concerns the administration of punishment. Prisons operate within a legal framework that derives from the Prison Act 1952. Section 47 of the Act allows the Secretary of State to issue more detailed Prison Rules. Prisons must also comply with legal requirements, including health and safety, employment, race relations and data protection.

Other mechanisms exist to promote good governance in prisons, including HM Inspectorate of Prisons and the independent monitoring boards, which provide independent, external scrutiny. The move to new public management in the 1990s saw the introduction of additional mechanisms of operational accountability, including audit, key performance indicators and key performance targets. In the case of contracted-out prisons, supplementary means of accountability compensate for the fact that they are not under the direct line management of the public sector. The main additional mechanisms for ensuring the accountability of private sector prisons are through the contract and through the Home Office Controller, whose duty to monitor and to report to the Secretary of State derives from the Criminal Justice Act 1991 (s. 85).

Advocates of the privatization of prisons argue that the separation of the day-to-day administration of prisons from the state's supervisory responsibilities leads to an enhanced system of accountability and higher standards of service. An alternative view is that this separation of functions removes public accountability from the private sector, and this is what enables it to cut corners in pursuit of efficiency and increased profits.

*Elaine Genders*

### Related entries

*HM Inspectorate of Prisons, Independent monitoring boards; Legitimacy; New public management (NPM); Performance management; Power; Privatization.*

**Key texts and sources**

Genders, E. (2002) 'Legitimacy, accountability and private prisons', *Punishment and Society*, 4: 285–303.
Harding, R. (1997) *Private Prisons and Public Accountability*. Buckingham: Open University Press.

## ACTIVITIES

Prisons provide a range of activities for prisoners, including activities that are considered 'purposeful' because they provide some benefit in terms of health, well-being and personal development or in reducing reoffending.

Prisons provide a range of activities for prisoners in custody. These include recreational activities, association with other prisoners and what are classified as 'purposeful' activities. Keeping prisoners engaged in activity is important for their individual well-being, to help reduce reoffending, for managing security and for manitaining order and control. The amount of time spent in these activities is monitored and recorded. Each establishment has key performance targets for the amount of time each prisoner spends on average in purposeful activity and the amount of time prisoners are unlocked on average each day.

HM Prison Service groups purposeful activities under four headings: work, education, resettlement and other. Work covers all forms of prison industries and employment in other areas, such as catering, farms and gardens, and cleaning. Education covers assessment and teaching, and physical education. Resettlement covers such issues as sentence planning, offending behaviour programmes, work to tackle problems with drugs, bullying and self-harm. This heading also includes visits and temporary release. The 'other' category includes health promotion, religion and voluntary work. Activities that are also recorded but that are not considered 'purposeful' include exercise, association, medical treatment, drug testing, legal visits and time visiting court.

Prisons have not performed well in terms of the level of purposeful activity over the last ten years. In 1994–5, almost 26 activity hours were achieved per prisoner per week. However, this steadily declined until it reached 23.2 hours per prisoner per week in 2003–4. During that period, the national target was missed for eight consecutive years (HM Prison Service 2004). In 2004–5, this was dropped as a national target and, as a result, figures are now only reported for each individual prison. The level of purposeful activity hours varies across different prisons. Local prisons generally have the lowest levels of activity. For example, in 2005–6 the prison with the lowest reported hours was a local prison, Pentonville, with 13.3 hours per prisoner per week. High-security prisons also generally have lower levels of activity due to security restrictions. Training prisons have a higher level of activity, although it is open prisons that have the highest. For example, in 2005–6 the highest reported hours were at Latchmere House, an open prison, with 58.6 hours per prisoner per week.

HM Inspectorate of Prisons assesses purposeful activity as part of its 'healthy prison' criteria. It describes a healthy prison as one which provides prisoners with access to activities that are likely to benefit them, although it distinguishes this from resettlement, which covers activities aimed at preparing prisoners for release and at reducing reoffending. For HM Chief Inspector of Prisons, purposeful activity includes education, library access, physical exercise, health promotion, work, religious activities and association. Its perspective is more qualitative and it has frequently criticized the

recording of purposeful activity hours and the activities that are included – in particular, the high level of employment in domestic cleaning.

In summary, activities are an important and potentially beneficial aspect of prison life. However, access varies across different prisons, activity hours have declined and the focus on quantity has sometimes been at the cost of quality.

*Jamie Bennett*

## Related entries

*Education and training; Employment and industries; Farms and gardens; HM Inspectorate of Prisons; Offending behaviour programmes.*

### Key texts and sources

HM Prison Service (2003) *Regime Monitoring Guidance Notes, 2003–04* (PSO 7100). London: HM Prison Service.

HM Prison Service (2004) *HM Prison Service (Public Sector Prisons): Annual Report and Accounts, April 2003–March 2004.* London: HMSO.

See also the websites of the European Prison Education Association (**http://www.epea.org/**) and the Prisoners Education Trust (**http://www.prisonerseducation.org.uk/**). The Home Office's 'Offender learning and skills' website is at **http://www.dfes.gov.uk/offenderlearning/index.cfm?flash=1.** The Rideout (creative arts for rehabilition) website is at **http://www.rideout.org.uk/**.

# ADJUDICATIONS

Adjudications in prisons are internal disciplinary hearings for breaches of the Prison Rules. A prison governor is responsible for conducting adjudications and for deciding on any punishment that may be imposed, again according to the available punishments outlined in the rules.

HM Prison Service provides detailed written guidance regarding how adjudications should be conducted (HM Prison Service 2005), though no equivalent detailed advice has been written for prisoners (Loucks 2000). The prisoner charged is allowed to sit at a table and be provided with writing material. Those who have difficulty hearing or understanding English should receive assistance to enable them to participate fully in the proceedings. Prison instructions allow prisoners to consult a solicitor before or after an adjudication. Adjudications will not necessarily be adjourned for this unless the prisoner has not had adequate time to contact the solicitor. Prisoners are allowed a minimum of two hours to prepare for an adjudication following notice of a disciplinary charge.

Governors are required to ask prisoners whether they wish to have any assistance or legal representation during an adjudication, though ultimately this is at the governor's discretion. If legal representation is refused, as is most often the case (see Loucks 2000), prisoners may go on to request a 'McKenzie friend' – a lay adviser or assistant, which can include a solicitor, friend or, indeed, another prisoner. The prisoner and reporting officer may also request witnesses for adjudications, and the governors conducting adjudications may call additional witnesses if they wish.

The European Court ruling in *Ezeh and Connors* v. *UK* (2003) ECHR 485 declared that adjudications were not adequately impartial hearings in order to impose punishments of additional days on a prisoner's sentence. More serious infractions that previously incurred punishments of additional days can now be heard in front of district court judges specially assigned to hear prison disciplinary cases. Alleged breaches of criminal law may be referred to the police and dealt with in outside courts, in which case no adjudication takes place in the prison.

Arguably one of the more controversial aspects of prison disciplinary procedures is the fact that prisoners are likely to be segregated prior to adjudication. This is not meant to take place without justification (i.e. risk of collusion or intimidation of witnesses) but may nevertheless interfere with a prisoner's ability to prepare a defence. Initially this segregation takes place prior to the governor's first inquiry under Rule 53(4), though segregation may be prolonged after this under Rule 45 regarding removal from association. Continued segregation should be reviewed at least every 14 days, and governors should consider temporary transfers of prisoners to other establishments so the prisoner can remain on normal location (unsegregated) pending the adjudication (HM Prison Service 2005).

During adjudications, governors must prove cases 'beyond a reasonable doubt', and their decisions are subject to judicial review.

*Nancy Loucks*

### Related entries

*Discipline; Discretion; Fairness; Governors; Legitimacy; Prison Rules.*

---

**Key texts and sources**

HM Prison Service (2005) *The Prison Discipline Manual: Adjudications* (PSO 2000). London: HM Prison Service.
Loucks, N. (2000) *Prison Rules: A Working Guide.* London: Prison Reform Trust.
See also the Legal Services Commission's website (http://www.legalservices.gov.uk/criminal/contracting/prison.asp).

---

## ADJUSTING TO RELEASE

Adjusting to release can be as difficult as adjusting to incarceration. The released ex-prisoner has to relearn how to succeed in society with substantial handicaps, including stigma, social isolation and a lack of resources.

Considerable criminological research has focused on the difficulties involved in coping with imprisonment and all the adjustments this requires. Yet, ironically, some ex-prisoners suggest that the process of adjustment to release from prison can be as difficult as adjusting to imprisonment itself. Ex-prisoners turned academic criminologists, Alan Mobley and Chuck Terry (2001: 2), eloquently describe the lived experience of re-entry from prison:

*Prison, we submit, is an absorbing, surreal, exhausting arena of the absurd. The intensity of the experience varies among facilities and individuals, surely, but it never entirely lets up. After some time in captivity one does adjust, and your bodily frequency will come into a kind of harmony with your fellows and your surroundings. Eventually you become like the fish that doesn't know it is living in water. A realization of what you are going through often doesn't begin to dawn until the ordeal is over, until you are released. Re-entry, aptly named to approximate an astronaut's return from outer space, is then, both an end point and a beginning. It is a slippery space where time slides, meanings blur, and your very being squirms in a sea of panic. It's all you can do to hold yourself together.*

Although under-researched, adjusting to release is clearly a serious and substantial problem for ex-prisoners and for wider society. In the UK, 57.6 per cent of prisoners released in both 2003 and 2000 were reconvicted within two years of their release. Young people aged 18–20 re-offended at a rate close to 70 per cent. In fact, released ex-prisoners are thought to commit at least 1 million crimes in the UK every year, costing an estimated £11 billion annually.

The released offender frequently confronts a situation that virtually ensures his or her failure. The lethal combination of stigma, social exclusion, social learning, temptation, addiction, lack of social bonds and dangerously low levels of human and social capital (not to mention financial capital) certainly makes a smooth adjustment to release difficult to say the least. The problems of reintegration may be exacerbated by the record-high numbers of individuals being processed through probation and the prison system in the UK and the USA. This strain on the system of release and parole, combined with recent high-profile scandals in England and elsewhere involving released prisoners under community supervision, gives the impression of a resettlement establishment in a period of crisis (Padfield and Maruna 2006). None the less, it is clear that the problems ex-prisoners face are anything but 'new'.

Perhaps the most frequently researched issue regarding adjustment to release is the process of institutionalization or prisonization. This is the process whereby inmates assume 'the folkways, mores, customs, and general culture of the penitentiary,' including 'the criminalistic ideology in the prison community' (Clemmer 1940/1958: 299). More contemporary research has framed the issue of the effects of imprisonment in terms of post-traumatic stress disorder (Jamieson and Grounds 2005). Characteristic symptoms of post-traumatic stress disorder include restlessness, irritability and severe difficulties in forming or restoring close relationships; fear and distress in response to reminders of the traumatic event; avoidance behaviour; diminished interest or participation in significant activities; feelings of detachment and estrangement from others; loss of motivation and a restricted range of affect (for example, an inability to feel warmth); and anxiety and depression. There may also be physical symptoms: increased physiological arousal, outbursts of anger, difficulties in concentration and hyper-vigilance. Such symptoms can be associated with increased alcohol and drug use.

Efforts at prisoner resettlement are intended to help ameliorate some of these problems by assisting in the process of adjusting to release, although this is not always the case (see Maguire and Raynor 2006). Sometimes the added stigma and perceptions of paternalistic coercion involved in post-release supervision can exacerbate rather than alleviate the difficulties of coping with release. According to ex-prisoners Mobley and Terry:

*When offenders 'get out' they want to be out. Any compromise or half-measure, any 'hoops' or hassles placed in their path, breeds resentment. Certainly ex-cons need access to social services and community resources, but they should not have to engage with law officers to get them. After years of being thrown together, battling through a struggle that neither could win, the two sides should be allowed to drift apart. Each stands to benefit (2001: 3).*

Shadd Maruna

*Related entries*

*Alcohol; Families of prisoners; Prisonization; Probation Service; Reoffending.*

**Key texts and sources**

Clemmer, D. (1940/1958, 2nd edn) *The Prison Community*. New York, NY: Holt, Rinehart & Winston.

Jamieson, R. and Grounds, A. (2005) 'Release and adjustment: perspectives from studies of wrongly convicted and politically motivated prisoners', in A. Liebling and S. Maruna (eds) *The Effects of Imprisonment*. Cullompton: Willan Publishing.

Maguire, M. and Raynor, P. (2006) 'How the resettlement of prisoners promotes desistance from crime: or does it?', *Criminology and Criminal Justice*, 6: 19–38.

Mobley, A. and Terry, C. (2001) 'Guess who's coming to dinner? A prisoner perspective on the possibilities of re-entry.' Paper presented at the Bureau of Justice Statistics Program workshop on prisoner re-entry, Ann Arbor, Michigan.

Padfield, N. and Maruna, S. (2006) 'The revolving door: exploring the rise in recalls to prison', *Criminology and Criminal Justice*, 6: 329–52.

Bridging the Gap helps offenders to settle after release from prison (**http://www.btguk.org/**). NACRO's website is at **http://www.nacro.org.uk/**. See also the website of Unlock, the association for

# AGEING PRISONERS

The term 'ageing prisoners' refers to that section of the prison population that is significantly older than the average. In the UK, men aged 60 plus are the fastest-growing prisoner group.

The number of prisoners over the age of 60 continues to increase on both sides of the Atlantic. It is important to recognize, however, that this increase does not reflect an upsurge of offending among older people. Rather, the growth in the numbers of ageing prisoners is a direct consequence of recent changes in sentencing and parole practices, including the incremental extension of the life sentence over recent years, the increasing number of life sentences and the phenomenon of the 'natural life' sentence for certain prisoners. In the UK, the relatively recent determination to pursue 'historic' (usually sexual) offences – committed up to three, four and even five decades earlier – has been a significant contributor to the increasing numbers of men serving a first prison sentence late in life (Crawley 2007).

In the UK, the population of older prisoners has increased significantly over the past decade. In 1990 the number of prisoners under sentence aged 60+ years was 365; by 2002 the number sentenced had almost quadrupled to 1,359. Of these prisoners, 80 per cent were serving sentences of longer than four years and around 20 per cent were serving life sentences (Prison Reform Trust 2003). According to the latest statistics provided by Age Concern, in January 2006 the number of prisoners aged 60 and above was 2,012; of these, 421 were aged 70+.

Although the economic implications of rising numbers of ageing prisoners – in particular, the expanding cost of prison healthcare – have been widely recognized (especially by prison managers), the practical and policy responses to ageing prisoners' needs contrast markedly across jurisdictions. In the USA the so-called 'greying' of the prison population is now an acknowledged consequence of mass incarceration, and the sheer scale of the problem has demanded that the Federal Bureau of Prisons turn its attention to developing programmes and regimes specific to the needs of its ageing prisoner population (Aday 2003). In the 1970s, the US correctional system started to develop specialist units for elderly infirm inmates, and by the end of 2000 there were over 15 such units in 13 different states.

In the UK, in contrast, the long-standing presumption that imprisonment is 'a young man's game' has continued to mask the dimensions of age at the level of both prison policy and practice. Almost five years on from the publication of a joint report by HM Inspectorates of Prisons and Probation, which recommended the development of a national strategy for dealing with ageing prisoners, the Prison Service of England and Wales, as an executive agency of the Home Office, still does not have such a strategy. In consequence, the

Prison Service has made relatively little progress in terms of the development of appropriate regimes for ageing and infirm prisoners, even for those serving a life sentence and for whom the need for palliative care is likely to become increasingly pressing. Despite the relatively small numbers of older women in prison (of the prisoners aged 60 and above, only 45 are female), there is evidence that their health and social care needs are also marginalized (Wahidin 2004).

That is not to say, however, that there have been no developments in individual prisons; on the contrary, at establishment level there have been a number of notable achievements. In the main, however, these have occurred because of on-the-ground concerns and because of prison staff goodwill and innovations. Such initiatives include an occupational therapy group and a social club for the over 60s run by staff at Wymott Prison (the latter is run by volunteers from the Salvation Army) and the opening of a unit for elderly life-sentence prisoners in Norwich Prison. In 2003, Age Concern (Leicestershire and Rutland) set up an older prisoner advocacy and support project at Gartree Prison and has since developed a *Good Practice Guide* for the training of prison officers working with this prisoner group. Such training is essential: not only do ageing prisoners – especially those aged 70 and above – suffer from physical ailments such as poor eyesight and hearing, respiratory and heart problems, cancer, diabetes, arthritis, bladder problems, Alzheimer's, Parkinson's and hypertension, but mental illness, notably depression, is also commonplace. Learning how to understand – and ultimately manage – the needs of ageing prisoners, however, does not feature in basic training.

In recent research into the experiences and 'survival' strategies of ageing prisoners, Crawley and Sparks (2005) refer to the 'institutional thoughtlessness' commonly found in many prisons holding elderly men. When Crawley and Sparks use this term they do so in relation to the traditional prison principle that 'one-size-fits-all'; in other words, the principle that 'everybody gets treated the same'. Treating the elderly the same as the young – largely because of an institutional failure to recognize that the former have specific health and social care needs – may not constitute fair treatment. On the contrary, a regime of 'one-size-fits-all' is decidedly unfair in that it fails to meet the legitimacy expectations of the ageing prisoner group. Indeed, one-size-fits-all regimes restrict ageing prisoners' participation in even the most basic of the prison's social activities (such as attending a chapel service, visiting the library or going outside for fresh air), not least because participation invariably requires them to walk long distances or climb several flights of stairs.

Except in the small number of prisons which have made 'on the hoof' innovations (noted above), ageing and infirm prisoners are generally subjected to the same regime (same timetable, same diet, same physical layout, same practices, same rules and same activities) as fit, active and often confrontational young men in prison. The development of a range of facilities in both criminal justice and health services is crucial – and pressing – if elderly and infirm prisoners do not continue to be stuck in inappropriate facilities with nowhere else to go.

*Elaine Crawley*

### Related entries

*Alternatives to imprisonment; Healthcare; Home Office; Legitimacy; Life-sentence prisoners; Young men in prison.*

**Key texts and sources**

Aday, R.H. (2003) *Aging Prisoners: Crisis in American Corrections.* Westport, CT: Praeger.

Crawley, E. (2007) 'Imprisonment in old age', in Y. Jewkes (ed.) *Handbook on Prisons.* Cullompton: Willan Publishing.

Crawley, E. and Sparks, R. (2005) 'Older men in prison: survival, coping and identity', in A. Liebling and S. Maruna (eds) *The Effects of Imprisonment.* Cullompton: Willan Publishing.

Prison Reform Trust (2003) *Growing Old in Prison: A Scoping Study on Older Prisoners.* London: Centre for Policy on Ageing/Prison Reform Trust.

Wahidin, A. (2004) *Older Women in the Criminal Justice System: Running Out of Time.* London: Jessica Kingsley.

See also the websites of Older Prisoners (http://www.olderprisoners.co.uk/?pageid=144) and the Prison Reform Trust (http://www.prisonreformtrust.org.uk/subsection.asp?id=592).

# ALCOHOL

> Prisoners are not allowed to drink alcohol while they are in prison; however, many of them arrive in prison with alcohol use problems. Prisons have an important part to play in contributing to the government's strategy to reduce the impact of alcohol misuse.

As a population we are drinking more and more often. As consumption increases, so does the risk of certain types of offending. Moreover, alcohol problems among offenders have been identified as a factor preventing successful resettlement. It is estimated that alcohol misuse costs around £20 billion a year in relation to alcohol-related health problems, crime and anti-social behaviour. Around half of all violent incidents are related to alcohol misuse, as are a third of incidents of domestic violence; almost 60 per cent of rapists report drinking before committing the offence (Prime Minister's Strategy Unit 2004).

A study conducted by the Office for National Statistics revealed that 63 per cent of men and 39 per cent of women in prison were classed as hazardous drinkers in the year before coming into prison (Singleton *et al.* 1999). Those most likely to report hazardous drinking before their imprisonment were young (aged 16–24) and identified themselves as white and single. They were more likely to be held for violent offences and to have more previous convictions. Furthermore, hazardous drinkers generally experienced a range of other problems, such as mental illness, drug misuse and homelessness. Nevertheless, tackling alcohol use and offending has not attracted the same attention or resources that drug-related offending has. For example, the HM Prison Service *Alcohol Strategy* (HM Prison Service 2004) was published six years after the strategy for drugs.

The *Alcohol Strategy* has a number of aims and objectives, including to reduce the harm associated with alcohol misuse (including that related to offending) by offering treatment and support to prisoners, and to prevent the use of alcohol in prisons. The strategy aims to achieve this by improving education and communica-tion; by improving the identification of prisoners who have a drinking problem; by improving both the capacity and quality of alcohol treatment interventions available to prisoners; by spreading good practice to ensure greater consistency; and by reducing the supply and use of alcohol by prisoners within prison establishments. However, whereas addressing drug misuse has led to increased funding, new treatment approaches and a raft of measures to encourage drug-misusing offenders into treatment, the same cannot be said for the current approach to alcohol.

Although the relationship between alcohol and crime is complex and the subject of continued debate, one recent study on young adult prisoners found that young men in prison were more likely to report that their offending was related to alcohol, rather than drug, use. Over half the young men in the study linked their offending to alcohol (Farrant 2006). It was also found that many of the young men did not think that they were dependent upon alcohol, nor did they wish to abstain from alcohol in the future. What the young men sought were techniques, strategies and the appropriate support to help them control their alcohol intake when they were released. However, the research evidence about the effectiveness of various initiatives and treatment modalities to tackle alcohol-related crime, both in prison and the community, remains limited.

It is generally accepted that there are insufficient prison-based alcohol interventions to meet the level of need. Interventions for women, black and minority ethnic prisoners, and children and young people are particularly lacking. The Prison Service is, however, in a unique position to raise awareness of alcohol misuse among a population that is at high risk of developing alcohol problems and committing alcohol-related crimes. Although prisoners are banned from drinking alcohol, it may be smuggled in or made in prison ('hooch'). Therefore, prison staff can test prisoners for alcohol through breath-testing.

All prisoners should be screened for alcohol-related needs, should receive basic information on alcohol misuse and should have access to detoxification if needed. The various interventions available in prison include general awareness sessions, one-to-one motivation sessions, groupwork, Alcoholics Anonymous, structured treatment programmes, pre-release programmes and post-release access to community services. Despite the range of interventions, few, if any, prisons provide the whole range of possible services. To improve the skills base and knowledge of prison staff about how best to work with those who misuse alcohol, DANOS, the Drugs and Alcohol National Occupational Standards, have been introduced. These set out the occupational competencies needed to work with people with drug and alcohol problems. Using the DANOS approach should ensure that staff with the necessary knowledge, skills and experience are recruited. It is also hoped that it will help to bring new workers quickly up to speed with relevant issues for working with prisoners who misuse alcohol.

Without additional funding, however, it is likely that access to alcohol support will remain *ad hoc*, partial and inadequate for the majority of prisoners. For example, despite the significant risk of reoffending, high levels of alcohol use and the correlation between alcohol and offending, few young prisoners are able to access the prison-based offending behaviour programmes which seek to tackle alcohol use – such as PASRO (Prisons Addressing Substance Related Offending). Many of those who wish to attend such courses cannot do so due to the length of their sentence or waiting lists being in operation. Given these shortcomings, it is unsurprising, perhaps, that a quarter of young ex-prisoners report they have been involved in some type of alcohol-related offending following their release from prison (Farrant 2006).

Following on from the *Alcohol Strategy* for prisoners, a staff alcohol policy was introduced in 2005. This outlined that all members of staff should be fit to carry out the full range of their duties while they are at work, and that those staff with an alcohol dependency are identified and managed appropriately. The policy also introduced breathalyser testing where there is reasonable cause to believe a member of staff may have breached the alcohol standard. The policy does not ban drinking by prison staff completely; however, if tested, they must be under the current limit used under drink-driving legislation to be considered fit for work.

*Finola Farrant*

### Related entries

*Drugs; Offending behaviour programmes; Prison officers; Subcultures; Young men in prison.*

**Key texts and sources**

Farrant, F. (2006) *Out for Good: The Resettlement Needs of Young Men in Prison.* London: Howard League for Penal Reform.

HM Prison Service (2004) *Addressing Alcohol Misuse: A Prison Service Alcohol Strategy for Prisoners.* London: HM Prison Service.

Prime Minister's Strategy Unit (2004) *Alcohol Harm Reduction Strategy for England.* London: Strategy Unit.

Singleton, N., Farrell, M. and Meltzer, H. (1999) *Substance Misuse among Prisoners in England and Wales.* London: ONS.

See also the 'Drugs and alcohol' section of the Ministry of Justice/National Offender Management Service website (**http://www.noms.homeoffice.gov.uk/managing-offenders/reducing-re-offending/drugs-alcohol/**). Drugs.gov supplies information on drugs interventions programmes, though not specific, alcohol-related information (**http://www.drugs. gov.uk/drug-interventions-programme/**). The Alcohol Concern website contains articles relating to alcohol misuse among prisoners (**http://www.alcoholconcern.org.uk/servlets/hom**).

## ALTERNATIVES TO IMPRISONMENT

As the prison population of England and Wales has risen above 80,000, the need to provide alternatives to custody grows more pressing. Alternatives to imprisonment currently used by sentencers include community payback, restorative justice, prolific offender schemes and specialized centres for women.

There is growing evidence to suggest that community sentences are more effective in cutting crime than imprisonment. Of all offenders commencing community penalties in the first quarter of 2002, 54 per cent were reconvicted within two years compared with 67 per cent who were imprisoned (Shepherd and Whiting 2006).

### Recent history

In the late 1960s, the only alternative to custody was the probation order. This was joined by the 'suspended sentence' and the community service order, and the late 1980s saw the introduction of 'punishment in the community' in the form of the combination order and the curfew order (more commonly known as 'tagging'). Following this, a new generation of orders has been implemented, including the drug treatment and testing order (DTTO).

The Criminal Justice Act 2003 replaced the various kinds of community order for adults (community punishment orders, community rehabilitation orders, combination orders and DTTOs), offering sentencers a 'menu' of possible requirements. Coming into force in April 2005, courts are now able to choose different elements to make up a bespoke community order that is relevant to the particular offender and the crime(s) he or she committed. It combines punishment with changing offenders' behaviour and making amends – sometimes directly to the victim of the crime. It can also encourage the offender to deal with any problems that might be a factor in his or her offending, such as drug use. The range of options available within a generic community order include compulsory (unpaid) work; home detention curfew (tagging); and mental health treatment, drug treatment and testing, and alcohol treatment (these last three can only be used with consent of the offender).

### Community order

Unpaid work – or community service as it is sometimes known – was introduced in 1972 and is one of the Probation Service's most successful interventions. Every year offenders are sentenced by the courts to perform up to 300 hours of unpaid work, and communities benefit from over 5 million hours of free labour. Charities, community organizations and local authorities provide work places and benefit from offenders' contributions. This is particularly appropriate for people whose crimes have harmed a community, such as being drunk and disorderly or committing anti-social behaviour or criminal damage. It may also be used for serious one-off offences, such as high-level drink driving or driving while disqualified. Unpaid work can also give offenders new skills and opportunities for practical learning in real situations which prepares them for employment or formal training. It can also help offenders who have dropped out of the educational system to read, write and develop numeracy skills, as well as requiring them to learn discipline by adhering to a timetable for appointments, etc. The latest incarnation of the community order is 'community payback', launched in July 2005. This is an initiative to involve the public in the selection of unpaid work projects. Projects are still determined and managed by local probation areas but there are opportunities, through local panels, for the public to have their say in the work they want done by offenders in their communities.

### Women

Given that the vast majority of women behind bars have been convicted for non-violent crimes, it follows that community-based alternatives to custody can be more appropriate for them. Scotland has taken a much more proactive approach than England and Wales in this regard. In 1998, following a series of suicides at Scotland's only women's prison, Corton Vale, the Social Work Services and Prisons Inspectorate for Scotland recommended the provision of community-based diversion and non-custodial disposals which specifically address the needs and circumstances of women offenders. This led to the establishment of the 218 Project in Glasgow, which opened its doors in January 2004. This project is funded by the Scottish Executive and enables women to address the root causes of their offending. It provides a detox facility, residential units and outreach to health and housing services.

In England, the only places which offer such a facility for women are the Asha Centre in

Worcester and the Calderdale Centre in Sheffield. The Fawcett Society (2004) has high-lighted the urgent need for the establishment nationally of non-custodial provision designed with women's needs in mind in a bid to reduce female rates of reoffending. In March 2005 the government allocated £9.15 million to two pilot community centres (the 'Together Women Programme') as alternatives to custody for women offenders. Baroness Scotland has also set up a 'Review of Vulnerable Women in the Criminal Justice System', chaired by the Labour peer, Baroness Jean Corston, which was due to report in early 2007.

## Restorative justice

Restorative justice (RJ) is a process whereby all the parties with a stake in a particular conflict or offence come together to resolve collectively how to deal with the aftermath of the conflict or offence and its implications for the future. Offenders have the opportunity to acknowledge the impact of what they have done and to make reparation, and victims have the opportunity to have their harm or loss acknowledged and amends made.

RJ is a relatively new idea in the UK but it has been practised across the world for many years. RJ's reputation in the UK has often suffered as it has not been attached to any robust research. However, in January 2007, the Smith Institute, in association with the Esmée Fairbairn Foundation, published a report which inde-pendently examined the evidence on RJ from Britain and around the world (Sherman and Strang 2007). The aims of the project were to bring together the results of RJ trials in order to set out a definitive statement of what constitutes good-quality RJ, as well as to draw conclusions as to its effectiveness (with particular reference to reoffending), and to predict the role that RJ might play in the future of Britain's youth and criminal justice systems. The research found that RJ substantially reduced recidivism more than prison (adults) or as effectively as prison (youths) and also reduced crime victims' post-traumatic stress symptoms and related costs.

## Prolific offender schemes

It is estimated that about 10 per cent of offenders are responsible for half of all crime nationally. Cracking down on this relatively small number of offenders is clearly crucial in reducing crime levels overall. To this end, the government announced the Prolific and Other Priority Offenders programme in 2004. The programme enables local areas to target their most troublesome offenders using a 'carrot and stick' approach. Participants are offered fast-track help with their problems, such as drug addiction, poor education and unem-ployment. At the same time they are warned that any breaches or non-compliance with the scheme will result in swift action by the police to bring them back to court. Early indications show that, overall, these projects have reduced crime by around 10 per cent, but a closer look at individual projects demonstrates that, when well managed and resourced, these schemes can have a dramatic effect on reducing re-offending. Among the more successful are the Thames Valley IRIS (Intensive Recidivist and Intervention Scheme), which has cut reoffend-ing by more than half, and the Tower Project in Blackpool.

## Public opinion and alternatives to custody

There is no doubt that the use of alternatives to custody could be significantly increased. However, alternatives to imprisonment have suffered from an image problem and have been frequently dismissed by the media and the gen-eral public as being weak and ineffective. In response to this perception, there has been a gradual introduction of tougher community penalties, alongside the more traditional alter-natives (such as fines and cautions), which are designed to show the public that alternatives to custody are not simply soft options. People may be sceptical about prisons but they are sceptical, too, about the alternatives. However, a recent joint survey carried out by the campaign group, SmartJustice, and Victim Support (2006) found that over two in three victims of crime believe that prison does not work and want to see more creative solutions to crime in the community.

This replicates earlier work carried out by the Joseph Rowntree Foundation (Millie *et al.* 2005) indicating that people wanted to see tougher community penalties and residential drug treatment instead of custody.

*Sinead Hanks*

### Related entries

*Abolitionism; Desistance; Intermittent custody; Probation Service; Public perceptions; Rehabilitation; Reoffending; Women in prison.*

**Key texts and sources**

Bottoms, A., Rex, S. and Robinson, G. (eds) (2004) *Alternatives to Prison: Options for an Insecure Society.* Collumpton: Willian.

Fawcett Society (2004) *Women and the Criminal Justice System.* London: Fawcett Society.

Millie, A., Jacobson, J., McDonald, E. and Hough, M. (2005) *Anti-social Behaviour Strategies: Finding a Balance.* Bristol: Policy Press/Joseph Rowntree Foundation.

Shepherd, A. and Whiting, E. (2006) *Re-offending of Adults: Results from the 2003 Cohort.* London: Home Office (available online at **http://www.homeoffice.gov.uk/rds/pdfs06/hosb2006.pdf**).

Sherman, L.W. and Strang, H. (2007) *Restorative Justice: The Evidence.* London: Smith Institute.

SmartJustice (2006) *Crime Victims Say Jail Doesn't Work* (available online at **http://www.smartjustice.org/**).

See also the following websites: the Scottish Parliament (**http://scottish.parliament.uk/business/commitees/historic/justice1/reports-02/j1r02-pats-01.htm**); Rethinking Crime and Punishment (**http://www.rethinking.org.uk/**); SmartJustice (**http://www.smartjustice.org/**); and the Prison Reform Trust (**http://www.prison reformtrust.org.uk/**).

## APPRECIATIVE INQUIRY (AI)

Appreciative inquiry is an approach to management science that learns from optimal performance rather than seeking to solve problems. It has been used in prisons since the late 1990s as both a research technique and as an approach to performance improvement.

Appreciative inquiry (AI) originated in the USA in the 1970s (for the background to AI, see Elliott 1999). The original research and writing were done at a time when three influences came together. First, traditional analytical management science, based on a 'clockwork' understanding of organizations (take them apart, fix whatever is malfunctioning and put them together again), was not having much success in mega-corporation America. Secondly, there was (associated with the rise of postmodernism), a resurgence of interest throughout the behavioural sciences in the role and function of language. Thirdly, social scientists were becoming aware of the implications of quantum physics for their discipline. For example, the notion of self-organizing as opposed to chaotic systems seemed replete with insights into the way human organizations may behave.

In the UK it was not until the late 1990s that AI was applied to prisons. The first application was at Wandsworth Prison following a hostile report from HM Inspectorate of Prisons. Senior managers did not believe that the prison was as bad as it was represented and commissioned a team from the Institute of Criminology at Cambridge University to look further. The team launched an AI involving staff and prisoners and produced a report which did not directly contradict the inspectorate but put the work and achievements of Wandsworth in a broader setting.

Thereafter AI was used extensively both in 'pure' prisons research and, increasingly, in performance-related work which resulted in the identification of no or low-cost ways in which performance could be enhanced (Elliott and Greaney 2004). It did this by identifying best practice and then looking for ways in which that could be made more common or universal. In performance enhancement, the usual approach is for a small team of consultants to train a cross-disciplinary, cross-hierarchy work group of about 12 in the art of appreciative interviewing. Essentially this involves challenging the interviewee to reflect on his or her experiences of the prison (or a unit of it) working most effectively and identifying the obstacles to making that effectiveness more general. The work group interviews 30–40 per cent of the staff (and, more recently, a small subset of prisoners) and analyses the data with the help of the consultants to identify easy wins and the longer-term strategic changes that may be necessary.

One of the challenges of AI in this application is that it raises consciousness and expectations among the staff. If the senior management team (SMT) fails to deliver at least some of the changes, this can have a negative impact on staff morale and trust. In contrast, where the SMT is seen as valuing the opinions of the staff and being ready to act upon them, the effect can be remarkable.

*Charles Elliott*

### Related entries

*Decency; Measuring the Quality of Prison Life (MQPL); New public management (NPM); Performance management; Research in prisons.*

#### Key texts and sources

Elliott, C. (1999) *Locating the Energy for Change: A Practitioner's Guide to Appreciative Inquiry.* Winnipeg: IISD.
Elliott, C. and Greaney, C. (2004) 'Improving performance through appreciative inquiry', *Prison Service Journal*, 156: 35–39.

## ARCHITECTURE

Prison architecture can be understood as a symbolic or allegorical statement of the establishment's internal regime and/or the prevailing penal philosophy. Among the issues that can be profoundly affected by prison architecture and design are levels of violence, bullying and drug use, and prisoner–staff relations.

Political judgements, policy priorities and public sentiments all play a role in the architectural design, construction and location of penal institutions. Moreover, the symbolic and ideological forms with which prison buildings are invested have a vital role to play in explaining the internal power relations of the regime. The architecture of incarceration over the last three centuries has reflected the penal philosophies of the period, which can broadly be characterized as a desire for reform at the end of the eighteenth century; a move to more repressive practices in the mid-nineteenth century; and a concern for prisoner rehabilitation in the twentieth century (Muncie 2001).

The first purpose-built prisons designed to punish and reform rather than simply to detain emerged in the late eighteenth century when, for the first time, architecture was explicitly used to convey penal philosophy: prisons were to suggest 'places of real terror' (Evans 1982: 169). The loss of America as a transportation colony in 1776 resulted in a 20-year period of rapid prison construction in England, which was heavily influenced by the reformer, John Howard (1726–90). In an attempt to improve living conditions, Howard decreed that prisons should be located in open country and close to running water, and prison architects were encouraged to incorporate as much ventilation as possible into their designs (Jewkes and Johnston 2007). While the explicit reason for the removal of the prison from towns and cities to more isolated rural areas was to prevent disease (specifically, to curtail 'gaol fever' which was reaching epidemic proportions), it was none the less a radical move that sequestered prisons from everyday life.

Howard's observations concerning ventilation, hygiene and segregation dovetailed with a growing desire to establish proportionality between offences and penalties. Consequently, the architecture of the classification system was based on preventing physical contagion and keeping different classes of prisoners apart. However, by the time the separate and silent systems came into being in the early nineteenth century, the architecture of incarceration was constructed around the prevention of *moral* contagion. Prison accommodation thus became increasingly enclosed and cellularized to keep inmates apart (Jewkes and Johnston 2007).

Ironically, as interior spaces became more enclosed and claustrophobic, prison façades became more expansive and grandiose, with designs that communicated to the public a clear message about punishment from the 'carefully scripted' construction of their exterior architecture (Pratt 2002: 39–40). Three competing architectural designs can be discerned during the nineteenth century: 'neoclassical' prisons, built on the model of the classical temple; 'gothic revivalist' prisons which incorporated turrets, towers, portcullises, battlements and gargoyles, and evoked images of medieval confinement; and prisons characterized by 'functional austerity' which were underpinned by a belief that prison design has a moral influence – both on inmates and on the community at large.

During the era of functional austerity, the degrees of bleakness or ugliness that were incorporated into prison design extended beyond the physical buildings into almost every aspect of life within. Punishment in the Victorian prison became a highly regulated and impersonal system designed to contain and control; a rationale that was reflected in the use of the crank to break the spirit and cause bodily suffering (Muncie 2001). Designed by Joshua Jebb and opened in 1842, Pentonville was the epitome of functional austerity, communicating a sense of loss and deprivation via its stark appearance. The only decorative features on its exterior were the gatehouse and clock tower (the latter intended to symbolize the regularity and order inside, and the deprivation of time rather than the infliction of physical punishment (Pratt 2002)). Inside, the building was designed broadly along the lines of Bentham's Panopticon, with four three-storey wings radiating from a central hall.

The penal philosophy of repression continued to be symbolically manifested in the functional austerity of design throughout the second half of the century, culminating in the last major prison of the 1800s, Wormwood Scrubs (opened in 1884). However, by the beginning of the twentieth century the prison authorities were striving to 'soften' the spartan exterior of prison buildings with landscaped gardens, fountains and flower beds, although there were limits to what could be done to beautify prisons in densely populated urban areas (Jewkes and Johnston 2007). During the first half of the twentieth century, a number of prison sites in cities were sold off and prisons were relocated, often to converted army camps, airfields and country houses. Not only did these developments represent a change in penal philosophy as a more therapeutic discourse emerged but they also paved the way for a concept that radically changed the face of the penal estate: the open prison (Dunbar and Fairweather 2000). The military origins of many of the buildings suited the purpose: there was no need for high perimeter walls, the expansive buildings allowed a relatively unrestricted degree of movement around the prison and the surrounding land could be used for farms and gardens. Thus, not only did the open establishment bring flexibility to a system previously concerned only with uniformity but it also facilitated links between prisons and the communities in which they were located (Dunbar and Fairweather 2000).

Between the end of the Second World War and the end of the century, the prison estate expanded from 39 prisons to 136. Mostly sporadic and unplanned, this expansion was in large part a response to the problems of overcrowding and the inexorably rising prison population. As attitudes to prisoners moved from detention and retribution towards training and rehabilitation, the Home Office was forced to consider seriously how prison design impacts upon the lives of its occupants. Some 22 new prisons were built between 1959 and 1969 and, following the 1966 Mountbatten Review, a plethora of new situational security measures were instituted, including more control gates, less prisoner association, the retreat of staff into offices and the zoning of the prison to prevent prisoners enjoying free access. Mountbatten also underlined the need for new prisons to be built for the purpose of decent and humane containment, a philosophy that emerged at the height of modernism. Consequently, like the civic and municipal buildings of this period that blight many towns and cities in the UK, prisons became functional, concrete and bland. This trend continued into the 1980s and 1990s and, while the new prisons of this period revealed in their design an increased attention to their location and surrounding landscape, this frequently resulted in penal institutions that looked like private hospitals, no-frills chain hotels or the kind of corporate HQ you might expect to find in a business park. There appeared to be little imagination in prison architecture, and aesthetic considerations remained submerged by the imperative to disguise penal institutions – they simply blended in with the environments, whether urban or rural.

In the new millennium the brief to prison architects has begun to direct more attention to the relationship between staff and inmates, thought to be fundamental to the smooth operation of a prison. Discourses of therapy and rehabilitation have given way to new ideas concerned with helping inmates to change and improve as a result of their own efforts – backed up by a system of incentives and earned privileges linked to behaviour. Spatial organization is instrumental in this respect. For example, Feltham Young Offender Institution (opened in 1983) accommodates relatively small groups of inmates (50–70) in discrete housing units staffed by officers who operate informally and interact with inmates in the living area while having a clear sight of all cell entrances. Removing the paraphernalia of security gates and grilles is intended to improve job satisfaction among officers, as it encourages the building of relationships and dispenses with the notion of prison officers as mere 'turnkeys', a philosophy that may become more widespread with the growth of the private sector (see Privatization).

None the less, it must be remembered that ancient prisons like Pentonville and Wormwood Scrubs are still in operation. Furthermore, the emergence of a new punitiveness has arguably resulted in a return to austerity in prisons, and political discussions are now taking place concerning the establishment of 'superprisons' that follow the model set by the architects of the supermax in the USA, with maximum attention to security and minimum respect for human rights and dignity. In addition, it should be noted that prisons which have relatively relaxed security arrangements and which seem, on the face of things, to offer a better quality of life for their inhabitants are frequently sites for greater social problems as complex inmate networks develop in the form of gangs and cliques. As a

result, many inmates express a preference to be locked up for 23 hours a day, and some prison officers are equally resistant to working in new generation prisons.

*Yvonne Jewkes*

### Related entries

*Farms and gardens; Howard, John; New generation prisons (NGPs); New punitiveness; Panopticon; Privatization; Separate and silent systems; Supermax prisons; Transportation; Victorian prisons.*

**Key texts and sources**

Dunbar, I. and Fairweather, L. (2000) 'English prison design', in L. Fairweather and S. McConville (eds) *Prison Architecture: Policy, Design and Experience.* Oxford: Architectural Press.

Evans, R. (1982) *The Fabrication of Virtue: English Prison Architecture, 1750–1840.* Cambridge: Cambridge University Press.

Jewkes, Y. and Johnston, H. (2007) 'The evolution of prison architecture' in Y. Jewkes (ed.) *Handbook on Prisons.* Cullompton: Willan Publishing.

Muncie, J. (2001) 'Prison histories: reform, repression and rehabilitation', in E. McLaughlin and J. Muncie (eds) *Controlling Crime.* London: Sage.

Pratt, J. (2002) *Punishment and Civilisation: Penal Tolerance and Intolerance in Modern Society.* London: Sage.

For a vision of future prison design – the Creative Prison project – see **www.rideout.org.uk/creative_prison.aspx**

## ARGOT (PRISON)

Prison argot is a form of slang, sometimes unique to the prison but normally borrowing from external cultures, which describes the world from the perspective of the prison.

Every culture contains specific ways of talking, so when convicted criminals are sent to prison to serve their sentences they inevitably learn new forms of language (Cardozo-Freeman 1984). Prison argot, originally defined as the language or jargon of thieves, is a particular form of slang (Einat 2005) – in some circumstances, a complete language – capable of describing the world from the perspective of the prison. It has been argued that prisoners live, think and function within the framework defined by the argot (Encinas 2001), whose vocabulary may supply alternative names for objects, psychological state of minds, personnel roles, situations and the activities of prison life. Experienced inmates use argot fluently and can switch between regular names and their argot counterparts, and the degree of familiarity with argot is an important symbol of group membership among prison inmates (Einat 2005).

Argot usually 'borrows' syntax, intonation rules and terminology from the source language – from criminal cultures outside the prison, general slang and the jargon of the streets – while also including terms that are rarely used (with the same meaning) outside the prison (Encinas 2001). Since argot reflects the way of life within a group, it is unsurprising that the prisoner language is, as Sykes puts it, 'pungent, vivid, racy and irreverent ... tinged with bitterness and marked with self-lacerating humour' (1958). Prison language is also strikingly clear and stripped of cliché, as befits the raw emotional context of incarceration.

Argot marks out the primary 'axes of life' in the prison – its main concerns and preoccupations – and harbours value judgements about appropriate behaviour that help guide prison conduct (Sykes 1958). Accordingly, much contemporary prison argot relates to drugs and the practices and status of drug users and dealers. Argot has other functions beyond classifying and mapping the prison social system. Through words whose meaning is known only to the initiated few, it expresses and reinforces group membership, shared identity and loyalty. Where argot is unknown even to prison staff, it also protects prisoners' privacy, even in the presence of intense surveillance, and may be a significant aid to resistance.

The degree to which prison argot represents a unique language varies greatly. The special language of 'wolves, punks, and fags' reported by Sykes (1958) to describe sexual acts within a maximum-security US prison portrayed a sexual culture that was more or less unique to prisons or, at least, was only encountered by most prisoners within the prison context. Israeli prisoners use a complex vocabulary for which outsiders require translation whereas, in the UK, there are few terms that are unique to the prisoner community. Such differences may relate to levels of social distance and hostility between prisoners and their custodians, cultural differences between prisoners (i.e. the need to construct a rich, common language) and the degree to which the prison experience is isolated and thus distinct from life in the community.

*Ben Crewe and Tomer Einat*

### Related entries

*Drugs; Identity and self; Importation model; Inmate code; Subcultures.*

**Key texts and sources**

Cardozo-Freeman, I. (1984) *The Joint: Language and Culture in a Maximum Security Prison.* Springfield, IL: Charles Thomas Publishing.

Einat, T. (2005) '"Soldiers", "sausages" and "deep sea diving": language, culture and coping in Israeli prisons"', in A. Liebling and S. Maruna (eds) *The Effects of Imprisonment.* Cullompton: Willan Publishing.

Encinas, G.L. (2001) *Prison Argot: A Sociolinguistic and Lexicographic Study.* Laham, NY, and Oxford: University Press of America.

Sykes, G.M. (1958) *The Society of Captives: A Study of a Maximum Security Prison.* Princeton, NJ: Princeton University Press.

# ASSAULTS

The term 'prison assault' refers to one individual initiating the use of violence against another.

There are three types of prison assault: prisoner-on-prisoner, prisoner-on-staff and staff-on-prisoner. Most is known about the occurrence of prisoner-on-prisoner assault. In 2005, there were over 18,000 adjudications for violent offences recorded in English and Welsh prisons. Yet this figure is thought to underestimate the true extent of prison assault due to a reluctance by prisoners to report incidents of assault to prison staff (Bottoms 1999). Self-report studies reveal that between 10 and 20 per cent of adult prisoners have been assaulted, while approximately 33 per cent have been threatened with violence (Edgar *et al.* 2003). Prison assault, therefore, is a widespread phenomenon representing a serious threat to the prisoners' personal safety, as well as impeding the ability of HM Prison Service to provide safe, secure, well ordered establishments in which prisoners are treated humanely, decently and lawfully. For this reason, a Violence Reduction Strategy was launched in May 2004, requiring each prison to implement changes aimed at reducing violence and the fear of violence.

Most incidents of prisoner-on-prisoner assault tend to occur out of the sight of prison staff and over issues such as drugs, debts, verbal insults, queue-jumping, issues arising while sharing a cell, cell theft and self-defence (Edgar *et al.* 2003). Prisoners tend to explain their use of violence as a means of demanding respect and defending their reputation. Some prisoners describe using violence as a means of gaining status in the prison due to prisoner norms emphasizing 'toughness'. Others engage in assault because prisoner norms lead them to believe that, by doing so, their chances of being victimized in the future are reduced (Edgar *et al.* 2003). Assaults may also occur as prisoners use violence to defend themselves and their property and as a form of physical retaliation for when they feel wronged.

While less is known about the occurrence of prisoner-on-staff assaults, it seems that the majority of these assaults occur in situations in which a prison officer attempts to assert power over a prisoner (Bottoms 1999) – for example, when an officer explicitly commands a prisoner to do something, when a prisoner feels he or she has been unjustly treated or when a prison officer conducts a search of a prisoner's body or cell. Assaults can also occur as prison officers intervene to stop prisoners fighting and as they attempt to move prisoners from one part of the prison to another. Accordingly, prisoner-on-staff assaults appear to be linked to wider issues, such as power, legitimacy, fairness and how prisoners expect to

be treated. However, little is known about the occurrence of staff-on-prisoner assaults.

Theoretical approaches to understanding prison assault have mainly focused on explaining the occurrence of prisoner-on-prisoner assaults. Sykes (1958) argues that there are five main deprivations or 'pains' of imprisonment. For Sykes, imprisonment represents a psychological threat to an individual's sense of self due to his symbolic rejection by society, the powerlessness of the prison regime and the prisoner's inability to demonstrate his masculinity through heterosexual relationships. By engaging in assaults, male prisoners are believed to be attempting to return a sense of power and respect to their masculine identity, as well as protecting themselves and their property and demonstrating their 'toughness'.

Edgar *et al.* (2003) build on this work to argue that prisoners use aggressive behaviour to make statements about their identity and self, social context, power and reputation. Based on their interviews, they conclude that prisoners use violence when they feel wronged, manipulated, disrespected, insulted or threatened. They suggest that prisoner-on-prisoner assaults tend to occur out of a concern for the prisoner's reputation, the failure of the prison to meet basic human needs and prisoner norms of 'toughness' and retaliation. They also focus on the importance of interpretation and social norms for influencing prisoners' involvement in prison violence. However, these approaches are limited in their ability to explain adequately why some prisoners engage in prison assault while others do not.

A review of the research literature suggests that some individuals are more inclined to engage in prison assault than others, particularly young men in prison (Bottoms 1999). In an attempt to understand why this is so, recent work has examined whether some prisoners are more prone to feel a psychological need to appear 'tough' and defend their identity than others (Butler forthcoming). This research suggests that how individuals construct their self-narrative can influence their involvement in prison assault. Prisoners who appear insecure in their identity seem to be more likely to engage in prisoner-on-prisoner assault due to their susceptibility to prisoner norms of 'toughness' and the use of violence as a means of ego defence.

Consequently, understanding how a prisoner's self-narrative can influence his involvement in prison assault may help us to understand why some prisoners are inclined to engage in confrontations over issues such as respect, status, power, legitimacy and fair treatment while others are not. However, further research is required to understand the occurrence of staff-on-prisoner assault.

*Michelle Butler*

### Related entries

*Adjudications; Deprivations/'pains of imprisonment'; Identity and self; Legitimacy; Masculinity; Order and control; Power; Violence; Violence reduction.*

**Key texts and sources**

Bottoms, A.E. (1999) 'Interpersonal violence and social order in prisons', in M. Tonry and J. Petersilia (eds) *Prisons.* Chicago, IL: University of Chicago Press.

Butler, M. (forthcoming) 'Prisoner confrontations: the role of shame, masculinity and respect.' Unpublished thesis, University of Cambridge.

Edgar, K., O'Donnell, I. and Martin, C. (2003) *Prison Violence: The Dynamics of Conflict, Fear and Power.* Cullompton: Willan Publishing.

Sykes, G. (1958) *The Society of Captives: A Study of a Maximum Security Prison.* Princeton, NJ: Princeton University Press.

# AUDIT

Audit was originally a financial and management tool for ensuring accounts were accurate and there was robust organizational governance. These methodologies have been developed in prisons as part of wider performance management. Initially this was a means of measuring compliance with security requirements but has subsequently been applied to a wide variety of areas. More recently, there has been an increasing focus on developing audit methodologies that better measure quality.

Audit is an approach that was originally developed in financial management as a means of ensuring the accuracy of financial accounts. However, recent years have seen the expansion of this method as a tool for managing wider aspects of performance, and audit can be seen as an integral part of the new public management approach (Pollitt *et al.* 2003). The traditional role of audit is one that is central to prison management. A Corporate Internal Audit Department is responsible for assessing the effectiveness of risk, control and governance arrangements, not only for financial management but also for wider organizational management.

The wider development of audit methodologies initially arose following dramatic escapes from high-security prisons in 1994 and 1995. It was recommended that the auditing of security procedures be improved and formalized which led to the setting up of a quasi-independent Standards Audit Unit, responsible for checking compliance with security requirements. This has expanded to cover 59 areas, including suicide prevention, activities and catering. However, audits have been criticized as focusing on process rather than quality or outcomes. For example, measuring whether support plans for prisoners at risk of self-harm are completed does not address how good or effective those reports are (Bennett 2007). In recent years, there has been a move to introduce more rounded audit. In particular, the development of a tool for Measuring the Quality of Prison Life (MQPL) has provided an important additional contribution.

The method of audit has also changed over time. When audits were initially introduced, they were exclusively conducted by the Standards Audit Unit. However, since that time self-audit has developed, and each prison must conduct an audit of every area at least every two years. The role of the Standards Audit Unit has become focused on quality checking self-audit, conducting MQPL and examining critical areas, such as security.

Overall, the audit function has grown in significance, emerging from its narrow financial position to become a major element of risk and performance management. While retaining a role as a process-based, compliance measure, it has become more focused on quality and out-comes and the effectiveness with which key risks are managed.

*Joyce Drummond Hill*

### Related entries

*Measuring the Quality of Prison Life (MQPL); New public management (NPM); Performance management; Risk; Security.*

**Key texts and sources**

Bennett, J. (2007) 'Measuring order and control in HM Prison Service', in Y. Jewkes (ed.) *Handbook on Prisons*. Cullompton: Willan Publishing.

Pollitt, C., Sirre, X., Lonsdale, J., Mul, R. and Summa, H. (2003) *Performance or Compliance? Performance Audit and Public Management in Five Countries.* Oxford: Oxford University Press.

# B

## BARLINNIE

> The Barlinnie Special Unit (BSU) in Glasgow opened in 1973 with the purpose of treating violent and long-term prisoners. Although generally considered to be a successful penal experiment, the unit was controversially closed down in 1995.

### Barlinnie Special Unit's origins

The Barlinnie Special Unit (BSU) was opened on 5 February 1973 in the old women's wing of Barlinnie Prison in Glasgow. The unit was instituted after a working party report (*Treatment of Certain Male Long Term Prisoners and Potentially Violent Prisoners*) was published by the Scottish Home and Health Department in 1971. This report suggested that a special unit should be established in the Scottish penal system 'for the treatment of known violent inmates, those considered potentially violent and selected long-term inmates' (cited in MacDonald and Sim 1978: 25).

The report was published after a number of violent confrontations between long-term prisoners and prison staff (as well as demonstrations by prisoners) had occurred in Scottish prisons in the late 1960s and which continued into the early 1970s. Similar confrontations and demonstrations had also taken place in England. Here the prison authorities planned two control units, one of which was established at HMP Wakefield. Prisoners were to spend six months in a regime which was 'intentionally austere' and 'explicitly punitive'. In March 1975, 'after public protests about the inhumane conditions in the ... units', the Home Secretary

announced their 'temporary closure', an announcement he had to repeat the following October when it was revealed that three prisoners had been sent to the Wakefield unit after the first announcement (Fitzgerald and Sim 1982: 111–2).

Initially, in Scotland, the state also responded punitively to the confrontations and demonstrations. Ideologically, it mobilized a positivist discourse which individualized and reduced the systemic problems in Scottish prisons to the activities of a small group of 'bad apples'. It then isolated these prisoners in the segregation unit in Peterhead Prison and in the notorious 'cages' at Inverness Prison, and engaged in physical brutality towards them. Jimmy Boyle described his time in the 'cages':

*The caged area is approximately 9 ft. by 6 ft. The only moveable objects besides the human body are a small plastic chamber pot – lidless, a woollen blanket and one book that is issued each week. Human contact is made three times a day when the 'screws' enter to search the body of the prisoner. His mouth, armpits, anus and the soles of his feet are searched each time even though he could not have left the cell between searches. This humiliation and degradation takes place daily. There is no communication between the 'screws' and the prisoners. He is alone and at the complete mercy of the 'screws' who take full advantage of his helplessness. Brutality and abuse of human rights is rife. If a prisoner is particularly awkward then punishment takes the form of leaving his food just outside of reach behind the cage bars until it is cold, or he receives it with spittle in it (1977 cited in MacDonald and Sim 1978: 23–4).*

### The evolution of a new kind of penal regime

Originally, the unit's regime was based on a traditional psychiatric orientation. It was seen very much as a last chance; if prisoners did not respond to the regime, the next step for them was Carstairs, the state mental hospital, without any possibility of a release date (Fitzgerald and Sim 1982). However, this psychiatric orientation, and the positivist discourse which underpinned it, did not come to dominate the unit's everyday life. Instead, the regime evolved into a system which was based on individual responsibility and accountability, and collective support and solidarity. Prisoners could follow their own daily routine, wear their own clothes, decorate their cells, cook their own food, receive uncensored mail and have unrestricted access to visitors. There was also a weekly community meeting:

> To discuss any issues that may have arisen. Any member of the community – either staff or prisoner – who 'lets the side down' by breaking the rules, can end up in the 'hot seat' where his actions are discussed, criticised and chastised by other members of the community, again whether staff or prisoner ... This, according to both the staff and the inmates, is a much more effective means of control than the measures used in the traditional system, measures which, in the majority of cases, serve only to make the prisoner more resentful and bitter
>
> (MacDonald and Sim 1978: 26–7).

Ken Murray, the unit's first principal nursing officer, described its philosophy in terms that were quite different from conventional prison officer work as it was practised in Peterhead and the 'cages':

> The methods that we introduced into the Unit ... are based on a very simple attitude, that being that we should speak to the prisoners and suggest to them that we should, together find ways and means best suited for the method where we could live tolerably with each other ... There's never been one single incident of a prison officer being attacked in the Special Unit by a prisoner (www.justiceaction.org.au/actNow/Briefs PDF/InsProp.pdf).

As early as July 1974, Alex Stephen, the chair of the original working party, argued that the unit had already had a 'significant depressurising effect' on the Scottish prison system. He noted that there appeared to 'be an astonishing degree of co-operation between staff and prisoners'. Stephen also made a further important and intriguing point: 'I do not think this Unit is going to give us all the answers to prison treatment but it might help to formulate the right questions. We tend to ask why is a prisoner violent. Should we not be looking for the situation that avoids violence altogether?' (cited in Carrell and Laing 1982: 7). A number of autobiographical accounts by prisoners have attested to the unit's positive philosophy and, crucially, to the role of this philosophy in radically changing their attitudes and behaviour. For Jimmy Boyle, 'what made the Unit unlike any other place was the way staff and prisoners were allowed and encouraged to sit down and talk together. This was the single most important factor in the Unit' (1984: 8). Johnny Steele (2002: 210) described how the unit encouraged him to examine his inner self, 'and there's nothing more hurtful than the truth'. Eventually, 'All the bitterness and hatred seemed to have abandoned me; the instinct for revenge, which so often flared up in me, had extinguished. This was all I needed to get out of life, this friendly, loving feeling, this human feeling that had been gone from my life for so long' (2002: 215).

### A political embarrassment

Between its opening in February 1973 and its eventual closure in January 1995, the unit achieved an international reputation for its positive and empathic philosophy towards long-term prisoners. However, it was also subjected to fierce media and political criticism and, during its existence, was never accorded more than the status of an 'experiment'. The key question is: why was this? To answer this question it is important to situate the unit, and its philosophy, alongside a number of other progressive policy developments in British prisons in the last four decades: Parkhurst C Wing, Glen Parva and Grendon Underwood therapeutic communities and Blantyre House resettlement prison. All these places have either been shut down, fundamentally changed or left on the margins of the penal system. Why? Arguably because these regimes, while not entirely unproblematic, none the less have challenged the retributive, punitive philosophy that historically (and contemporaneously) has underpinned and legitimated the broad direction of penal policy in the UK (Sim 2007). As Hugh Collins, another BSU ex-prisoner, notes:

> The Special Unit had become a political embarrassment over the years. For the main part, the Unit worked but what the authorities hated was that they had been proved wrong on the question of treatment. Prisoners like myself had shown that we were not animals: we had shown that if we were treated properly, then we in turn could respond, possibly even change
>
> (1997: 162).

The closure of the unit came from a report by a Scottish Office working party published in November 1994. The processes involved in the final production of this report – the limited time allowed to submit evidence, the announcement of the unit's closure on a Friday afternoon, the disparaging of the unit's defenders and the limited range of prison literature used by the report's writers – support Collins' argument that politicians and policymakers regarded 'experiments' like the unit as a 'political embarrassment'. The closure went ahead despite the positive evidence from the prisoners who were sent there, and the officers who worked there, that it was possible to rehabilitate those long-term prisoners who had been dismissed by the penal system, the mass media, the political establishment and wider society as incorrigible atavists who were incapable of redemption. In the intervening years, it is debatable if the prison authorities in Scotland (and in England) have learnt any fundamental lessons from units like Barlinnie with respect to responding empathically to such prisoners. Indeed, it could be argued that the intensification and consolidation of authoritarian law-and-order ideologies since the mid-1970s have further marginalized any idea that the supportive philosophy underpinning such units

should be central to the state's penal policies for both long *and* short-term prisoners.

*Joe Sim*

### Related entries

*Long-term prisoners; New generation prisons (NGPs); New punitiveness; Therapeutic communities; Violence.*

**Key texts and sources**

Boyle, J. (1977) *A Sense of Freedom.* London: Pan.
Boyle, J. (1984) *The Pain of Confinement.* Edinburgh: Canongate.
Carrell, C. and Laing, J. (1982) (eds) *The Special Unit: Barlinnie Prison – its Evolution through its Art.* Glasgow: Third Eye Centre.
Collins, H. (1997) *Autobiography of a Murderer.* London: Macmillan.
Fitzgerald, M. and Sim, J. (1982) *British Prisons* 2nd edn. Oxford: Blackwell.
MacDonald, D. and Sim, J. (1978) *Scottish Prisons and the Special Unit.* Glasgow: Scottish Council for Civil Liberties.
Sim, J. (2007) *The Carceral State: Power and Punishment in a Hard Land.* London: Sage.
Steele, J. (2002) *The Bird that Never Flew.* Edinburgh: Mainstream.
The Scottish Executive report (2007) on Barlinnie can be found at **http://www.scotland.gov.uk/ Publications/2007/02/01130102/0.**

## BIFURCATION

Coined by Anthony Bottoms in 1977, the term 'bifurcation' refers to the differentiation between penalties for serious and minor offences. While prison sentences for serious criminals lengthen, the range of non-custodial penalties for minor offenders grows. This allows governments to control prison populations, while still being seen to protect society from serious and persistent offenders.

Bifurcation is associated with what have been termed 'alternatives to imprisonment' or, more recently, 'community sentences'. In the 1950s and 1960s, it became clear that the range of alternatives to custodial sentences would need to be increased if expanding prisoner numbers were to be contained. For many commentators in the 1970s and 1980s, the emergence of a bifurcated sentencing policy appeared to herald the possible phasing out of the use of imprisonment for all but the most serious offenders. The government began to make a greater range of penalties available but, in accordance with the model of judicial independence to which the UK government then adhered, it issued no guidance to sentencers as to how the greater range of non-custodial sentences was to be used.

Sentencers' resistance to these moves and government's inability to shape sentencing policy directly meant that, by the mid-1980s, the use of imprisonment for adult offenders was still rising. The government's response to this was the radical shift in sentencing policy that culminated in the Criminal Justice Act 1991. The Act was an attempt to address the apparently conflicting pressures both to control the prison population and, at the same time, to appear tough on crime. It sought to establish the principle that punishment should be proportionate to the offence and to increase the rationality and consistency of sentencing by offering a structure to support sentencers' decision-making (Ashworth 2002). In addition to offering more non-custodial punishments, the Criminal Justice Act 1991 also allowed longer sentences for violent and sexual offences (Muncie and Wilson 2004).

Cavadino and Dignan (2007) argue that this change in policy was marked symbolically by a significant shift in language from 'alternatives to imprisonment' to 'punishment in the community'. In order to make non-custodial sentences credible to sentencers and to make it possible to divert less serious offenders from custody, this tougher language was matched with non-custodial sentences that restricted offenders' liberty more than ever before. Cavadino and Dignan (2007) suggest the term 'punitive bifurcation' to reflect the ironic situation that attempts to reduce the use of imprisonment for relatively minor offences in reality contributed to increasingly punitive sentences across the board.

Explicit attempts to divert offenders from prison came to an end with the outcry surrounding the murder of the toddler, James Bulger, by two 10-year-old boys in 1993, which broke the consensus that prison should be a sanction of last resort (Muncie and Wilson 2004). Michael Howard's term as Home Secretary in the 1990s placed law and order at the centre of political debate (crystallized in his infamous 'prison works' speech), and serious discussion of seeking alternatives to custody has since then been largely absent from political debate (Ashworth 2002).

*Abigail Rowe*

### Related entries

*Alternatives to imprisonment; 'Prison works'; Sentencing policy.*

**Key texts and sources**

Ashworth, A. (2002) 'Sentencing', in M. Maguire *et al.* (eds) *The Oxford Handbook of Criminology* (3rd edn). Oxford: Oxford University Press.
Bottoms, A.E. (1977) 'Reflections on the renaissance of dangerousness', *Howard Journal of Penology and Crime Prevention*, 16: 70–96.
Cavadino, M. and Dignan, J. (2007) *The Penal System: An Introduction* (4th edn). London: Sage.
Muncie, J. and Wilson, D. (eds) (2004) *Student Handbook of Criminal Justice and Criminology*. London: Cavendish.

# BLACK AND MINORITY ETHNIC (BME) PRISONERS

Black and minority ethnic (BME) prisoners are those prisoners from ethnic groups who do not self-classify as white British using the 2001 census codes. These codes include those of mixed, Asian/Asian British, black/black British and Chinese/other ethnic groups. Each category can be further broken down to reflect national, regional or continental origins (e.g. Asian/Asian British – Pakistani; black/black British – Caribbean).

Since the ethnic monitoring of prison populations began in 1985, it has been evident that some black and minority ethnic (BME) prisoners are disproportionately likely to be imprisoned in England and Wales, compared with their representation in the general population. In June 2005, the proportion of black prisoners relative to the population was 7.1 per 1,000, compared with 3.2 for mixed prisoners, 1.5 for Asian prisoners, 1.4 for white prisoners and 0.5 for prisoners from Chinese and other ethnic backgrounds (Home Office 2006). There are complex reasons for the higher rates of incarceration, particularly of black prisoners, which include them having elevated rates of offending linked to their disadvantaged position in society and experiencing racial bias that results in harsher sentencing. The lower levels of imprisonment among some Asian and Chinese groups have been less fully explicated but may be linked to socio-economic status and cultural factors, particularly for women (Phillips and Bowling 2007). Prisons in England and Wales are made even more ethnically diverse by their foreign national population which, in June 2005, stood at 12 per cent of the male prison population and 19 per cent of the female prison population. Prisons also exhibit some religious diversity and, while the most common faith practised in prison is Christianity, over two thirds of Asian prisoners are Muslim (Home Office 2006).

Within the tense environment of the prison, then, it seems likely that ethnic, religious, national and cultural diversity could create the conditions for conflict and disorder among prisoners. Marked by a lack of trust, fear, boredom, physical and emotional deprivation, overcrowding, and verbal and physical victimization, the prison setting presents particular obstacles to cohesive social relations. However, the 'indigenous model' of US prison culture and integration suggests that, because certain deprivations/'pains of imprisonment' (such as the deprivation of liberty, property, privacy, an authoritarian regime and so on) are universally experienced by prisoners, they possess a functional shared identity which disregards ethnicity, instead uniting prisoners in solidarity against prison officers (Sykes 1958). In sharp contrast, the importation model emphasized the influence of external statuses on prisoner subcultures, with racial and ethnic cleavages as the defining features of US prisons, structuring social hierarchies, the informal economy, religious activities and prisoner relations (Jacobs 1979). The UK evidence points to the need for an integrationist approach. Genders and Player's (1989) comprehensive study of race relations in five prisons in the mid-1980s revealed pervasive racial prejudice among prisoners, which largely resulted in an avoidance of contact and verbal aggression rather than physical conflict. Social groupings by ethnicity were noted by prisoners but were seen as reflecting commonalities of experience rather than being conflictual. Sometimes prisoner unity prevailed where prison staff were seen to restrict the activities of prisoners in some way. More recently, HM Inspectorate of Prisons' (2005) thematic inspection, *Parallel Worlds*, found that across all prison types (juvenile, young offender, women, adult men), Asian prisoners more frequently reported racist bullying than any other prisoners. Overall, however, the vast majority of prisoners (85 per cent+) in different establishments did not report racist victimization by other prisoners, which is undoubtedly a positive finding. This finding does not indicate any clear evidence of the importation model in the UK.

Politically, current concerns around race relations and racism in prison have been framed by the racist murder of Asian prisoner, Zahid Mubarek, in Feltham Young Offender Institution in March 2000. Following the conviction of his white cellmate, Robert Stewart, the Commission for Racial Equality (CRE) announced a formal investigation into HM Prison Service, amid broader complaints of racist bullying and discrimination in two other prisons (Parc and Brixton). The CRE (2003) investigation reported that there were failures of prison establishments to protect against the racist abuse and harassment of staff and prisoners; to remove racist graffiti; and to take disciplinary action against racist perpetrators.

Since the 1980s the Prison Service has also had to consider how the effects of ethnic, religious and national diversity among prisoners could impact on the relationships between prisoners and predominantly white British prison officers. In 1988, at the Court of Appeal, a black prisoner received £500 compensation (in the *Alexander* v. *Home Office* case) after being denied a kitchen job. It was shown that comments based on racial stereotypes in his assessment and induction reports at Parkhurst Prison had led to him being discriminated against. One section of the report read: '[h]e displays the usual traits associated with people of his ethnic background, being arrogant, suspicious of staff, anti-authority, devious and possessing a very large chip on his shoulder, which he will find very difficult to remove if he carries on the way he is doing.'

Subsequent academic and policy research has consistently documented patterns of direct racial and indirect racial discrimination against BME prisoners (Phillips and Bowling 2007), and the area of service provision was extensively examined in the CRE (2003) investigation. This report concluded that prisons were failing to provide equitable access to work because of the negative stereotyping of black prisoners. This also resulted in their being over-represented in formal disciplinary actions and mandatory drug testing, and under-represented in the enhanced level of incentives and earned privileges (IEP). The Prison Service was also castigated for not protecting BME prisoners from victimization when they made complaints of racism against prison officers. Poor efforts at providing a culturally sensitive service to BME prisoners in relation to food and diet and faith communities were also criticized.

More recently, research Measuring the Quality of Prison Life (MQPL) in 49 prisons found that minority ethnic membership (black, Asian and Chinese/other) was the most significant predictor of perceptions of poor race relations (Cheliotis and Liebling 2006). Some 9 per cent of white prisoners even felt that black and Asian prisoners were treated unfairly compared with them. This compared with 42 per cent for black prisoners, 41 per cent for Asian prisoners and 30 per cent for Chinese/other

prisoners. These negative beliefs were closely linked to views about prison officers' unfair exercise of their discretion in distributing privileges, controlling discipline, providing access to information and responding to requests and applications. BME prisoners' lower ratings on measures of dignity, trust, family contact and order raise significant implications for fairness, decency and race equality in the prison setting. In attempting to explain these negative perceptions, Edgar and Martin (2004) have suggested that processes of 'informal partiality' may operate in prison as BME prisoners believe they have been the victim of racial discrimination by prison officers, although this cannot usually be proven. Perceptions of negative stereotyping and being disadvantaged by prison officers' use of discretion in receiving benefits or being disciplined occur in the context of routine exchanges in prison. However, such interactions, which demonstrate the daily exercise of power by prison officers, lack oversight or monitoring and may, therefore, be open to abuse.

We are now 20 years on since the introduction of the first race relations policy in prisons, when racism among prisoners and between prisoners and staff was more prevalent. It is undoubtedly the case that relations between prisoners are now broadly more positive. However, there are some worrying continuities in the experiences of BME prisoners. Inequalities in treatment which operate to the disadvantage of BME prisoners present an ongoing threat to establishing penal legitimacy among these prisoners (Cheliotis and Liebling 2006).

*Coretta Phillips*

**Related entries**

*Deprivations/'pains of imprisonment'; Discretion; Faith communities; Food and diet; Importation model; Incentives and earned privileges (IEP); Mandatory drug testing; Measuring the Quality of Prison Life (MQPL); Mubarek Inquiry; Race relations.*

**Key texts and sources**

Cheliotis, L.K. and Liebling, A. (2006) 'Race matters in British prisons: towards a research agenda', *British Journal of Criminology*, 46: 286–317.

Commission for Racial Equality (2003) *A Formal Investigation by the Commission for Racial Equality into HM Prison Service of England and Wales. Part 2. Racial Equality in Prisons.* London: Commission for Racial Equality.

Edgar, K. and Martin, C. (2004) *Perceptions of Race and Conflict: Perspectives of Minority Ethnic Prisoners and of Prison Officers.* Home Office Online Report 11/04 (available online at **http://www.homeoffice.gov.uk/rds/pdfs2/rdsolr1104.pdf**).

Genders, E. and Player, E. (1989) *Race Relations in Prison.* Oxford: Clarendon Press.

HM Inspectorate of Prisons (2005) *Parallel Worlds: A Thematic Review of Race Relations in Prisons.* London: Home Office.

Home Office (2006) *Statistics on Race and the Criminal Justice System, 2005.* London: Home Office.

Jacobs, J.B. (1979) 'Race relations and the prisoner subculture', in N. Morris and M. Tonry (eds) *Crime and Justice.* Chicago, IL: University of Chicago Press.

Phillips, C. and Bowling, B. (2007) 'Ethnicities, racism, crime and criminal justice', in M. Maguire *et al.* (eds) *The Oxford Handbook of Criminology* (4th edn). Oxford: Oxford University Press.

Sykes, G.M. (1958) *The Society of Captives: A Study of a Maximum Security Prison.* Princeton, NJ: Princeton University Press.

See also the National Body of Black Prisoner Support Groups' website (**http://www.nbbpsg.co.uk/about.php**). The website of the IQRA Trust aims to provide a better understanding of the needs of Muslim prisoners (**http://www.iqraprisonerswelfare.org/**).

# BOOT CAMPS

> Boots camps are American shock incarceration regimes for adults and juveniles, which emphasize discipline and physical training in a military-style environment. They are generally restricted to non-violent or first-time offenders.

The origins of the boot camp lie in survival training for US military personnel during the Second World War. They were introduced in the USA from 1982 (first in Georgia and Oklahoma) in response to prison overcrowding and to a belief that short periods of retributive punishment would change or deter 'offending behaviour'. Originally aimed at adult offenders, the juvenile system did not immediately adopt boot camps because of questions about their appropriateness for young people. However, as the population of juveniles in prison increased sharply, correctional officials began to turn to boot camps as a way of delivering a 'short, sharp shock' to less serious, usually first-time, juvenile offenders and as providing an alternative to longer periods of penal confinement. By the mid-1990s the US federal government and about two thirds of the 50 states were operating some 120 boot camp programmes, run by a mixture of public and private bodies.

Sentences in boot camps generally range from 90 to 180 days. Typically, detainees face pre-dawn starts, enforced shaved heads, silent regimes, military discipline, no access to media and a rigorous and abusive atmosphere for 16 hours a day. These techniques are designed to promote fear, degradation, humiliation, discipline and 'respect for authority' in order to impose total compliance. Such regimes have consistently failed to live up to correctional expectations: the deterrent effect of military training has proved negligible. In fact, some researchers have found that boot camp 'graduates' are more likely to be rearrested more quickly than other offenders. The authoritarian atmosphere has denied access to effective 'treatment', and there have been occasional lawsuits from inmates claiming that elements of the programme are dangerous and life threatening. Significantly, they have had no impact on the prison population. Indeed, the enduring popularity of boot camps appears to rely more on an emotive nostalgia for some mythical orderly past rather than on any measure of effectiveness. Moreover, boot camps tend to be more labour intensive and more expensive to operate, particularly if used as an alternative to probation or a community-based programme. For black youths (who represent the vast majority of the juveniles sentenced to boot camps in

America) as well as for those with emotional, behavioural or learning problems, degrading tactics appear particularly inappropriate and damaging.

The boot camp, as described above, is quintessentially American. The idea of shock incarceration, though, has proved attractive to other jurisdictions. In the UK, for example, detention centre regimes, particularly in the early 1980s, were explicitly geared to delivering a 'short, sharp shock'. In the following decade the idea was revived when the UK's first 'boot camp' was opened in 1996 at Thorn Cross Young Offender Institution in Cheshire. But instead of a military-based regime it employed a 'high intensity' mixture of education, discipline and training. A second camp, opened at the Military Corrective Training Centre in Colchester in 1997, promised a more spartan American-style regime. However, the notion of handing 'offenders' over to a military authority provoked an avalanche of complaints from virtually all sides of the criminal justice process. Eventually, pressure from the Prison Service – on grounds of cost, if not effectiveness and/or human rights violations – was successful in shutting down the Colchester camp barely 12 months after its opening and when only 44 offenders had gone through its regime. The high-intensity training regime at Thorn Cross continues, though evaluations of its 'success' have been somewhat mixed. In general it appears to have had no effect on future rates of reconviction, although reoffenders are recorded as having committed fewer offences. The latter has been attributed to education and training, employment, mentoring, resettlement and throughcare programmes rather than Thorn Cross's military drill components.

By the start of the twenty-first century the heyday of boot camps appeared to be over. In the USA, North Dakota, Colorado, Georgia and Arizona all abandoned boot camps in the 1990s after mounting allegations of abuse and negligible effects on recidivism. In 2005, 14-year-old Martin Lee Anderson was killed by drill instructors at Bay County Boot Camp in Panama City, Florida. The subsequent outcry led to the closure of Florida's five state-run boot camp facilities for juvenile offenders. Nevertheless, the idea of 'military training' remains a popular political soundbite (as witnessed by the suggestion by the Scottish National Party in 2006 that it reopen the Airborne Initiative based at Braidwood House in Carluke, Lanarkshire, as an alternative to imprisonment for repeat offenders aged 18–25). In America, private operators continue to run punitive programmes for juveniles, often paid for by parents seduced by the promise of a 'quick-fix solution' and by the hope of 'scaring their kids straight'.

*Barry Goldson and John Muncie*

### Related entries

*Alternatives to imprisonment; Borstals; Education and training; Employment and industries; Prison population; Young offender institutions (YOIs).*

---

**Key texts and sources**

Farrington, D., Ditchfield, J., Hancock, G., Howard, P., Jolliffe, D., Livingston, M. and Painter, K. (2002) *Evaluation of Two Intensive Regimes for Young Offenders. Home Office Research Study 239.* London: Home Office.

National Institute of Justice (2003) *Correctional Boot Camps: Lessons from a Decade of Research.* Washington, DC: US Department of Justice.

Parent, D.G. (1995) 'Boot camps failing to achieve goals', in M. Tonry and K. Hamilton (eds) *Intermediate Sanctions in Over-crowded Times.* Boston, MA: Northeastern University Press.

Simon, J. (1995) 'They died with their boots on: the boot camp and the limits of modern penality', *Social Justice,* 22: 25–48.

---

## BORSTALS

Borstals are penal regimes for young people with an emphasis on physical labour, moral reformation and discipline backed by corporal punishment. An English invention, they existed in this name for 80 years. They were subsequently renamed 'youth custody centres', which in turn evolved into the contemporary young offender institutions.

The Gladstone Committee of 1895 first proposed the concept of a training prison for young people, in order to separate those aged 16–21 from adults. The prison commissioner, Sir Evelyn Ruggles-Brise (1857–1935), established the first institution at Borstal Prison in Borstal, near Rochester in Kent in 1902. Statutory recognition of this new form of penal 'treatment' was provided in the Prevention of Crime Act 1908. The second Borstal was opened at the site of a former reformatory at Feltham, Middlesex, in 1911. The first purpose-built Borstal, Lowdham Grange, opened in 1931.

The Borstal system was heralded as a major liberal breakthrough. The separation of young prisoners (under 21-year-olds) from adults in specially designated closed institutions was seen as a major step towards the retraining of the young offender. In the prevailing spirit of individual rehabilitation, Borstal 'trainees' could be held on a semi-indeterminate basis of between one and three years. Release was dependent on professional assessments of 'behavioural improvement'. The regime was based on strict discipline, hard work and drill, and on corporal punishment designed, in the words of Ruggles-Brise, to promote 'industrious labour' and 'respect for authority'. It was directed specifically at those considered as of 'criminal habits and tendencies' or those associating with 'persons of bad character' but who were believed to be redeemable. The 'incorrigible' were explicitly excluded from Borstal and sent to prison. On release, the offender was placed on a period of licensed supervision of at least six months.

From the outset, Borstals attracted criticism for instituting long periods of confinement of up to three years for offences that would not ordinarily attract more than six months' detention. However, it was also claimed that Borstals had a remarkable initial success in preventing reoffending. The first survey in 1915 reported reconviction rates as low as 27–35 per cent. In 1961, the Criminal Justice Act reduced the minimum age for Borstal training to 15, made it easier to transfer young people from approved schools and integrated Borstals into the prison system. This integration meant that the training component declined and their regimes became

yet more punitive. The role of Borstal as an alternative to imprisonment was undermined, and it was turned instead into a primary punitive institution that acted as a funnel into the prison system. As a result, younger children and young people with less serious offences were increasingly subject to 'tougher punishment' (as graphically represented in Roy Minton's 1979 film, *Scum*). The reconviction rate (which had stayed at 30 per cent throughout the 1930s) increased to 70 per cent in the 1970s, suggesting that Borstal accentuated forms of behaviour it was designed to suppress. In 1982, Borstals were renamed 'youth custody centres' and, in 1988, were included in a wider network of young offender institutions (YOIs).

*Barry Goldson and John Muncie*

### Related entries

*Alternatives to imprisonment; Boot camps; Discipline; Rehabilitation; Reoffending; Training prisons; Young offender institutions (YOIs).*

---

**Key texts and sources**

Behan, B. (1958) *Borstal Boy*. Berkeley, CA: Windhover.
Hood, R. (1965) *Borstal Re-assessed*. London: Heinemann.
Radzinowicz, L. and Hood, R. (1990) *The Emergence of Penal Policy*. Oxford: Clarendon Press.

---

# BULLYING

Bullying refers to the use of physical, psychological and verbal aggression to intimidate others to submit to the will of another and/or cause emotional upset.

There is debate surrounding the concept of bullying, particularly when it is applied to a prison population (Edgar *et al.* 2003; Ireland and Ireland 2003). According to Farrington (1993), bullying is generally unprovoked, repeated and based on a power imbalance, and it includes an intention to cause harm and involves some form of physical, psychological and/or verbal abuse. Yet there remains no universally agreed-upon definition of bullying. Edgar *et al.* (2003) investigated the occurrence of prison violence and suggest that there are four defining features of prison bullying. These include one individual establishing a position of dominance over another; the use of intimidation to create a position of dominance; the abuse of power to exploit another; and the persistence of exploitation over a period of time.

Ireland (2002) reviewed the occurrence of bullying in prison and suggests that bullying behaviour, particularly physical and verbal bullying, is more prevalent among younger prisoners than adult prisoners. Similarly, Ireland suggests that male and female prisoners engage in similar types of bullying behaviour but that this differs in the frequency within which it occurs. Based upon a review of the literature, Ireland proposes that physical bullying appears to be more prevalent among male prisoners, while psychological bullying seems to occur more frequently among female prisoners. However, Ireland concludes that more research needs to be conducted before any firm conclusions can be drawn.

There are also difficulties with the definition of bullying as not all prisoners believe that bullying involves an imbalance of power or persists over a period of time. Ireland and Ireland (2003) examined how male prisoners define and understand the concept of bullying in prison. They found that, for the majority of male prisoners, bullying is perceived as involving verbal and/or physical aggression, with bullies 'taking things' from others or forcing others to submit to their will. They also found that victims can sometimes provoke bullying behaviour through their actions and only sometimes consider bullies to be stronger and more powerful than their victims. Further, prisoners do not believe that bullying must persist over a period of time or involve a power imbalance. Rather, most of the men feel that a single act can be considered bullying and that bullying can sometimes occur accidentally.

This understanding of bullying differs from how bullying has been conceptualized in the literature.

Edgar *et al.* (2003) also highlight some of the ambiguities inherent in the definition of bullying. In particular, they focus on the imprecise nature of the concept of bullying because whether behaviour is defined as bullying or not depends upon whether the victim 'feels' intimated. As a result, there is little consensus regarding what behaviours constitute bullying or why individuals engage in bullying. Edgar *et al.* argue that the concept of bullying, as defined in the literature, is too narrow and subjective to be helpful in understanding the occurrence of prison violence. Consequently, a deeper understanding of the occurrence of bullying is required before some of the differences between how bullying is academically understood and experienced by prisoners can be reconciled.

*Michelle Butler*

### Related entries

*Masculinity; Power; Violence; Young offender institutions (YOIs).*

---

**Key texts and sources**

Edgar, K., O'Donnell, I. and Martin, C. (2003) *Prison Violence: The Dynamics of Conflict, Fear and Power.* Cullompton: Willan Publishing.

Farrington, D.P. (1993) 'Understanding and preventing bullying', in M. Tonry (ed.) *Crime and Justice: A Review of Research.* Chicago, IL: University of Chicago Press.

Ireland, J.L. (2002) *Bullying among Prisoners: Evidence, Research and Intervention Strategies.* Hove: Brunner-Routledge.

Ireland, J.L. and Ireland, C.A. (2003) 'How do offenders define bullying? A study of adult, young and juvenile male offenders', *Legal and Criminological Psychology*, 8: 159–73.

Inquest provides independent legal advice to the bereaved families of those killed in custody (http://www.inquest.org.uk/). See also http://www.hmprisonservice.gov.uk/adviceandsupport/prison_life/bullying/.

# THE BUTLER TRUST

The Butler Trust supports the most prestigious awards scheme for good practice in working with offenders in prisons and on probation.

The Butler Trust works to recognize, promote and celebrate good work carried out on behalf of the public by prison and probation staff in their work with offenders. It seeks to help the community learn about the hidden work carried out in corrections in their name (see www.thebutlertrust.org.uk). The trust was established in 1985 to promote and disseminate a scheme then known as the HM Prison Service Annual Award Scheme. In 2005, the trustees approved the extension of the Annual Award Scheme to include employees of the National Offender Management Service (NOMS) and probation staff working with offenders in the community in England and Wales. During 2005, criminal justice social work agencies in Scotland and the Probation Board of Northern Ireland agreed to join the scheme from 2006. HRH The Princess Royal has been the trust's royal patron since 1985. She undertakes 10–12 engagements a year for the trust and has presided at every annual award ceremony, usually at Buckingham Palace. This has proved to be very popular with award winners, their families and the staff involved in their nomination.

The trust started a development programme in 1998 in response to the needs of major award winners to take their work further. The trust has a thriving volunteer programme, consisting largely of retired prison staff, of whom there are currently ten. They visit Butler Trust local assessment panels to provide encouragement and advice. The trust has a local assessment panel in all UK prison establishments. Most establishments incorporate the Butler Trust panel into their performance recognition committee.

The chair is typically Head of Human Resources. A lack of formal recognition of sustained quality work and innovation was the primary reason for the creation of the trust. For some years the trust offered the only public recognition of 'ordinary work extraordinarily well done', but in the last seven to eight years there have been big changes in the three prison services. All now have recognition awards of their own which complement the trust's work, including Prison Officer of the Year Awards in which all governors in England and Wales participate.

The cultural shifts that have allowed recognition schemes to emerge balance the more hard-edged performance management measures introduced in recent years, including smarter financial management, performance management, more open criticism by HM Inspectorate of Prisons, accountability for performance and market testing for prisons assessed as poor performers. The trust still has an important role in recognizing quality performance because it does so from a fiercely independent position. Moreover, for the last ten years the trust has helped many award winners develop their work. Increasingly, the emphasis has been on spreading good practice, an aspect which has not been effective in UK prison services. This has been done, for example, through holding conferences where award-winning work is described and celebrated.

*Tim Newell*

## Related entries

*Decency; HM Prison Service; Key performance indicators (KPIs) and key performance targets (KPTs); National Offender Management Service (NOMS); Performance management.*

---

**Key texts and sources**

The Butler Trust's website is at http://www.thebutlertrust.org.uk/.

# C

## CARCERAL SOCIETY

'Carceral society' refers to the processes of surveillance and classification developed as punishment techniques in the modern prison and how these disseminate throughout society. Carceral societies are defined not only by the expansion of the prison but also by the proliferation of discipline beyond it in relation to the control and targeting of a range of human behaviours.

The term 'carceral society' has been used by critical criminologists to characterize the proliferation of social controls defined through a continuum of behavioural correction that extends beyond the walls of the prison. In this way, 'incarceration' has come to mean more than locking people up and points instead to an impetus for control and behavioural curtailment within a range of social settings. Thus punishment and control are associated with legal and extra-legal prohibition and mobilize a range of techniques – normative rules, spatial exclusion, self-surveillance and the application of knowledge – to the task of identifying and classifying 'problematic' behaviour.

### Foucault and 'panopticism'

Coined by Michel Foucault, the carceral society has its roots in the 'technologies' of 'disciplinary power' developed as rationalities for punishment in the modern prisons between 1760 and 1840. In this period shifts in punishment occurred from the public spectacles of torture and execution (monarchical punishment) to the techniques of 'soul training' geared towards the production of obedient and 'docile' individuals (carceral punishment). Disciplinary power (as developed in the new prisons) subjected human behaviour to spatial and temporal control via hierarchies of surveillance, classification and routinization. These practices were underpinned by the exercise of normalizing judgements orchestrated by professional groups armed with new scientific knowledges developed within the disciplines of psychology and criminology. This professional gaze emerged as a key component of disciplinary power under the principle of panopticism – where the few can observe the many (see Panopticon). Panopticism ensured a more intense, 'efficient' and automatic functioning of power built into the architecture of the prison as a 'political technology' that provided a laboratory to monitor, train and correct individual behaviour (Foucault 1977: 203–5). Here a regime of 'conscious and permanent visibility' encouraged prison inmates to regulate and discipline their own behaviour under conditions of constant, yet unverifiable, observation (Foucault 1997: 201).

Crucially for Foucault, disciplinary power has a tendency to become operative outside the prison walls as a new instrument of government – 'not to punish less, but to punish better' and 'to insert the power to punish more deeply into the social body' (1977: 82). The spread of disciplinary power brought with it the possibility of 'the utopia of the perfectly governed city' (1977: 198), where the surveillance of the norm proliferates and spreads throughout other total institutions (schools, hospitals, workplaces, army and asylums). This is the 'disciplinary society', born in the nineteenth century and developed into the twentieth century, where 'the judges of normality are present everywhere'; 'We are in the society of the teacher-judge, the doctor-judge, the educator-judge, the "social worker"-judge' (Foucault 1977: 113). The drive to 'normalize' people is exercised widely over individual bodies, gestures, behaviours, aptitudes and attainments. This idea of the carceral or disciplinary society undermines any formal dichotomy thought to exist between punitive and non-punitive institutions. The spread of disciplinary power invests itself deeper into social life creating, in Foucault's words, 'hundreds of tiny theatres of punishment' (1977: 113).

## Cohen and the 'carceral net'

Following Foucault, Stan Cohen urged criminologists to look to the density of urban life in which disciplinary social control is embedded. Thus 'community control' provides the seedbed for the carceral society whereby a range of institutions are encouraged to takes responsibility in controlling quasi-legal infringements. Intense interventions are, in Cohen's view, falsely depicted as 'alternatives to imprisonment' (such as tagging offenders, curfews, probation orders, anti-social behaviour orders). The dispersal of carceral control has many incarnations – community corrections, intermediate treatment, neighbourhood watch, private security and latterly the use of public surveillance cameras – of which Cohen provides a critical mapping. First, the move to informal, private and communal controls is 'widening the net' of the formal system and bringing about 'an increase in the total number of deviants getting into the system in the first place'. Secondly, a 'thinning of the mesh' is occurring, increasing 'the overall level of intervention, with old and new deviants being subject to levels of intervention (including traditional institutionalization) which they might not have previously received' (Cohen 1985: 44). Thirdly, the dispersal of social control blurs the 'old' boundaries between formal/informal and public/private forms of control resulting in 'more people [getting] involved in the "control problem" [and] more rather than less attention … given to the deviance question' (Cohen 1985: 231). Thus a more insatiable processing of deviant groups is taking place, albeit by 'new' experts in new locations. However, 'the most fundamental fact about what is going on in the new agencies is that it is much the same as what went on and is still going on in the old systems'

(1985: 79). Critical writers have challenged the 'newness' of social controls – whether relayed through the notion of 'risk' or the plurality agency responsibility – as they are overwhelmingly targeted at the usual troublemakers, the poor and public infringements on the streets (Cohen 1985: 358; Coleman 2004).

## A feminist critique

The concept of the carceral society raises questions about the nature of social controls – their authorization, rationale, targeting and their consequences for social justice. However, it would be a mistake to see the concept as homogeneous and applying uniformly to different social groupings. Instead, carceral techniques operate within an asymmetry of power relations and denote a relentless process of classification, control and exclusion aimed at groups delineated by age, sex, race, behaviour, moral status and mental state in a manner that reflects and reinforces material hierarchies of power.

Howe (1994: 40) argues that the literature on carceral practices is a 'more penile-than-penal discourse' and has failed to account for the differential forms of control directed towards women within the formal justice setting and beyond. Disciplinary practices developed in women's prisons are quite distinct from those found in men's prisons in respect of gendered norms underpinning surveillance regimes geared to 'training' for domesticity, motherhood and dependency. Moreover, outside the prison, women are controlled through discourses of femininity in a range of situations: the home, in public, at work and through social policy. In the public realm, for example, women have been subject to the regulation and supervision of their 'femininity' through the threat and implementation of male violence, the labelling of women's behaviour (via the importation of negative sexual stereotypes) and the continual reinforcement that a 'woman's place' is in the private sphere where violence will also be utilized to control 'deviant' behaviour. The social control of women has, therefore, been socially constructed through the lens of gender that has differentiated between the 'proper' roles of men and women, along with a prevalent ideology that has posited these differences as 'natural'. Feminists have drawn attention to the differential treatment of women in the criminal justice system and how regimes of control found here are gendered and are as much about the penalization of stepping outside ascribed 'feminine' boundaries as about the control of 'crime'. Foucauldian carceral theorists have downplayed the control of women in civil society but have also ignored how state control, far from being always negative can have progressive consequences for women when intervening around domestic violence (Howe 1994: 115). More broadly, feminist analysis has explored the carceral in more informal settings, outside criminal justice. Such analysis has drawn attention to how self-surveillance operates in everyday beauty and feminization practices where female self-surveillance and even self-harm occur as part of a relatively invisible carceral continuum that proscribes female body 'management' and subjectivity.

### The carceral state

Clearly the carceral society has significance beyond Foucault's initial deliberation. It indicates the expansion of the prison population in the USA and UK and how contemporary democratic societies are overshadowed by a hyperactive penal state. Here the criminalization of poverty sits alongside a militarized carceral urban landscape (Davis 1990). The racialized, gendered and class nature of expanding punishment and normative regulation remains an important issue in the excavation of the carceral society and indeed the 'carceral state'. The power of the latter remains 'focused on the visible, while the broader, often invisible harms done to the society – state violence, deaths at work, environmental degradation, income tax evasion, corporate criminality, domestic violence – still remain on the margins of the governing class's consciousness' (Sim 2007). The ideological and material power of the carceral state, together with the contradictions and unintended consequences found in state penal policy, remain an important object of critical scrutiny in discerning and challenging the formal and informal contours of the carceral society. As the writers mentioned here note, the agency and resistance of those under carceral supervision play a part in questioning the right and appropriateness of carceral punishment. Both daily acts of resistance and scholarly critical scrutiny call into question the reproduction of social divisions that carceralization engenders, while revitalizing the call for social justice in contradistinction to visions of a carceral society.

*Roy Coleman*

### Related entries

*Alternatives to imprisonment; Discipline; Panopticon; Power; Total institutions.*

**Key texts and sources**

Cohen, S. (1985) *Visions of Social Control.* Cambridge: Polity Press.
Coleman, R. (2004) *Reclaiming the Streets: Surveillance, Social Control and the City.* Cullompton: Willan Publishing.
Davis, M. (1990) *City of Quartz: Excavating the Future in Los Angeles.* London: Verso.
Foucault, M. (1977) *Discipline and Punish.* (trans. A. Sheridan) London: Allen Lane.
Howe, A. (1994) *Punish and Critique: Towards a Feminist Analysis of Penality.* London: Routledge.
Sim, J. (2007) *The Carceral State: Power and Punishment in a Hard Land.* London: Sage.

## CATEGORIZATION AND ALLOCATION

Categorization is the process by which individual prisoners are assessed based on their risk of escape and risk to others. The system is used to identify the appropriate level of security required to detain that individual safely. Allocation is the process by which prisoners are identified for prisons that meet the level of security they require. This process will take account of individual need and the availability of suitable services.

Security categorization was introduced after a series of high-profile escapes in the 1960s in order to ensure that the most stringent security conditions were applied to those who were identified as presenting the greatest danger (Mountbatten 1966). Today, categorization is still based on an objective assessment of the likelihood that a prisoner will attempt to escape and the risk he would present should he do so although, in exceptional circumstances a prisoner can be categorized at a higher level on the basis of the threat he presents to order and control. The four security categories for male adult offenders are as follows (HM Prison Service 2000):

- *Category A*: prisoners whose escape would be highly dangerous to the public or the police or the security of the state, no matter how unlikely that escape might be, and for whom the aim must be to make escape impossible.
- *Category B*: prisoners for whom the very highest conditions of security are not necessary, but for whom escape must be made very difficult.
- *Category C*: prisoners who cannot be trusted in open conditions, but who do not have the resources and will to make a determined escape attempt.
- *Category D*: prisoners who can be reasonably trusted in open conditions.

Prisoners should be placed in the lowest security category consistent with the needs of security and control.

Categorization will take place following sentence and then be reviewed when circumstances change for short-term prisoners (less than a 12-month sentence), every six months for medium-term prisoners (12 months to less than four years) and annually for long-term prisoners (four years and over). A separate categorization review system is in place for Category A and life-sentence prisoners. Remand prisoners are either treated as potential Category A or are uncategorized (Category U), which is treated as equivalent to Category B. Young offenders are categorized as suitable for 'open' or 'closed conditions', although they may be placed in Category A or restricted status. A similar system operates for women in prison, although they may, in addition, be allocated to 'semi-open conditions'.

Once prisoners have been categorized, they are allocated to a prison of that category. As there may be several prisons of that category, the allocation decision also takes account of the suitability of the prisoner for the type of accommodation available, the prisoner's individual needs, the availability of services to meet those needs and their closeness to the prisoner's home. While the aim of the categorization and allocation system is to ensure that prisoners are held in the most suitable prisons, the reality is that the pressures of the prison population reduce discretion and require that prisoners are simply placed in available spaces within their security category.

*Jamie Bennett*

### Related entries

*Category A prisoners; Escapes and absconds; Life-sentence prisoners; Overcrowding; Risk; Security.*

**Key texts and sources**

HM Prison Service (2000) *Categorisation and Allocation* (PSO 0900). London: HM Prison Service.

Mountbatten, Lord of Burma (1966) *Report of the Inquiry into Prison Escapes and Security*. London: HMSO.

See also the Prisoners' Families helpline Q&A section about categories (**http://www.prisonersfamilies helpline.org.uk/php/bin/readarticle.php? article code=9252**) and the 'Your rights as a prisoner' section of Liberty's website (**http://www. yourrights.org.uk/your-rights/chapters/the-rights-of-prisoners/classification-and-categorisation/ classification-categorisation-and-allocation.shtml**).

## CATEGORY A PRISONERS

Category A prisoners are those who present the greatest risk to the public and who are held in the highest conditions of security. It is a fundamental objective of the Prison Service to prevent escapes by these prisoners.

All prisoners are assessed under the categorization and allocation system and placed in one of four security categories. The highest security category is Category A. These are 'prisoners whose escape would be highly dangerous to the public or the police or the security of the state, no matter how unlikely that escape might be, and for whom the aim must be to make escape impossible' (HM Prison Service 2004). There are approximately 1,000 Category A prisoners in England and Wales, and HM Prison Service has a target to ensure that there are no escapes by Category A prisoners.

Within Category A, there are three different escape categorizations: standard, high and exceptional risk. Standard risk accounts for the majority of Category A prisoners. They are not considered to have the determination and skill to overcome the range of security measures which apply to them, have no history of escape planning and do not have access to outside resources to assist an escape. High escape-risk prisoners, on the other hand, have a history and background which suggest that they have the ability and determination to overcome the range of security measures which apply to them. In addition, there may be current information to suggest that they have associates or resources which could be used to plan and carry out an assisted escape attempt, or there may be information that the prisoners or associates have access to firearms or explosives and were willing to use them in committing crime or avoiding capture. In 2006, there were fewer than 100 high escape-risk prisoners. Exceptional escape-risk prisoners usually have the same features that apply to high escape-risk, but the nature and extent of the external resources which could be called upon to mount an escape attempt are such that they require additional measures. In 2006, there were no prisoners classified as exceptional escape risk.

Category A prisoners are held in high-security prisons. They have a range of security measures that apply to them, including searching, control of movement, closer observation, controls on communications, restrictions on visits and special measures during transfers outside the prison. More stringent measures apply to those in high escape risk than those in standard. Prisoners identified as presenting an exceptional escape risk are held separately in special security units.

Prisoners may be identified as being potential Category A prisoners while on remand. Once convicted, their category will be reviewed. If prisoners are placed in category A, they will be reviewed two years after conviction, and annually thereafter. The arrangements for Category A prisoners were clarified and strengthened following the escape of six category A prisoners from Whitemoor Prison in 1994 and three from Parkhurst Prison in 1995 (Learmont 1995). No Category A prisoners have escaped since that time.

*Jamie Bennett*

### Related entries

*Categorization and allocation; Escapes and absconds; High-security prisons; Searching; Security; Special security units.*

**Key texts and sources**

HM Prison Service (2004) *Category A Prisoners: Review of Security Category* (PSO 1010). London: HM Prison Service.
Learmont, J. (1995) *Review of Prison Service Security in England and Wales and the Escape from Parkhurst Prison on Tuesday 3rd January 1995* (Cm 3020). London: HMSO.

## CELEBRITY PRISONERS

Society's obsession with celebrity is most evident in the popular media, and a story about prisons may be more likely to make the news if it has a well-known name attached to it. Imprisoned offenders may become media 'celebrities' by virtue of the notoriety of their crimes. Equally, individuals who already have a high profile in public life may become even more newsworthy if convicted and imprisoned.

The notion of 'celebrity prisoners' may be unpalatable to many, but it appears to have been a growing phenomenon since the mid-1960s when the crimes of notorious offenders, such as Myra Hindley and Ian Brady, Ronnie and Reggie Kray, and George Blake and Ronnie Biggs (both of whom escaped from custody), fuelled speculation in the press that a new breed of 'super-criminal' had emerged who mocked a judicial system that no longer carried the death penalty. In the subsequent four decades the media industries have grown exponentially, and the news values that shape the selection and construction of media stories have evolved. In the twenty-first century, individuals whose crimes meet a certain threshold of horror, or whose offences are explained by reference to their sexuality or sexual deviance, and involve multiple victims and/or child victims, frequently achieve a macabre kind of celebrity that guarantees their newsworthiness throughout their – often very lengthy – prison sentences (Jewkes 2004).

Of particular note in this regard is Ian Huntley who, since the death of Myra Hindley in prison in 2002 and the release of Huntley's ex-partner, Maxine Carr, in 2004, has become Britain's most newsworthy inmate. Many stories concerning Huntley are vehicles for the press to criticize the Prison Service (e.g. when staff at Woodhill Prison failed to spot that an undercover journalist had gained a job as a prison officer and taken photographs of Huntley and his cell in April 2004). But Huntley also carries the dubious distinction of being a 'filler' for the tabloids on quiet news days, and a stock narrative concerns the friendships he has formed in prison with other tabloid folk devils (e.g. 'Baby killer makes friends with Ian Huntley', *News and Star* 3 November 2004; 'Huntley's new pal is serial slayer suspect', *People*, 7 November 2004).

Stories about prisoners tend to fall into one of five categories: celebrity inmates, pampered prisoners, sexual relations in prison, lax security (resulting in suicides or escapes) and abuses or assaults on inmates (Jewkes 2005). However, so salient is the news value 'celebrity' that, arguably, all stories concerning prisons and prisoners are more likely to be reported if they have an (in)famous name attached. For example, while stories characterizing prisons as holiday camps fuel the media's view of a criminal justice system that is soft on crime, they are frequently pegged on favourite figures of hate. Hence, the *Sunday Mirror* of 28 December 2003 reports that Maxine Carr enjoyed an 'extraordinary festive knees-up behind bars' in which she told jokes, played party games, 'enjoyed a hearty meal' and 'boasted' about how much she was looking forward to freedom. It is arguable that it was the press treatment and celebrity construction of Carr, rather than the crime for which she was convicted (conspiring to pervert the course of justice), that resulted in her needing to be given a new identity, protected by an indefinite High Court order, when she left prison in 2005. The theme of sexual relations in prisons is also rendered more titillating by the addition of a 'celebrity' slant. While Carr was subject to scrutiny in this respect (Jewkes 2005), the most infamous example of newspapers insinuating sexual relations between celebrity inmates was the photograph published in many newspapers in 1995 showing Myra Hindley and Rose West holding hands in the high-security wing of Durham Prison.

An acquaintance with the processes of news production also helps us understand why most deaths in custody are not considered newsworthy. Suicides and attempted suicides are most likely to reach the pages of the press if the story concerns a 'celebrity' inmate. In such cases, the story is likely to conform to other key news values: it is likely to meet the required 'threshold' for inclusion and is reduced ('simplified') to an event that was both 'predictable' and therefore preventable (Jewkes 2004). The suicides of Fred West and Harold Shipman are notable examples. The more general trend, however, is for prison suicides to go unreported. Similarly, escapes generally only feature in the national press if the inmate concerned is well known and/or is especially dangerous. The fifth theme underpinning media reports of prisoners – the abuses or assaults inflicted by staff or by other inmates – is all but invisible in the British media. The exception, as ever, are attacks on well-known inmates, which tend to be widely reported (e.g. the stabbing of Peter Sutcliffe in the eye by a fellow inmate in Broadmoor in 1997 or the many assaults on Ian Huntley since his conviction in 2003).

The conviction of an individual who is already a media celebrity and who takes personal and professional risks by engaging in criminal activity also constitutes a cardinal news story, especially when his or her public status is perceived to guarantee him or her special privileges while in prison. Most memorable in this respect is Jeffrey Archer (convicted of perjury and perverting the course of justice in 2001) who signed a multi-million-pound book deal and enjoyed working at the Theatre Royal in Lincoln while serving his prison sentence. Another celebrity widely regarded as benefiting from his media persona is pop star Pete Doherty (convicted of drugs offences and held on remand but never given a custodial sentence). However, not all convicted celebrities enjoy the benefits of fame or are successfully rehabilitated in the public imagination. Gary Glitter is unlikely to rebuild his career in the UK following his conviction for sexual offences against children in 2006, and arguably the most famous celebrity prisoner in British history remains Oscar Wilde (convicted of gross indecency in 1895), whose crime led to public disgrace and whose incarceration in Reading Gaol is widely believed to have precipitated his early death three years after release. Each of these cases illustrates the extent to which those who work in the news media are especially drawn to stories that unite celebrity with crime and deviance because they provide a titillating juxtaposition of high life and low life for an audience who, it is assumed, lead conventional and law-abiding 'mid lives' (Barak 1994).

*Yvonne Jewkes*

### Related entries

*Prisons in film; Prisons in news; Prisons on television; Public perceptions.*

**Key texts and sources**

Barak, G. (ed.) (1994) *Media, Process, and the Social Construction of Crime.* New York, NY: Garland.
Jewkes, Y. (2004) *Media and Crime.* London: Sage.
Jewkes, Y. (2005) 'Prisoners and the press', *Criminal Justice Matters*, 59: 26–9.

# CERTIFIED NORMAL ACCOMMODATION (CNA)

Certified normal accommodation (CNA) is the Prison Service's own measure of uncrowded accommodation.

Under Section 14 of the Prison Act 1952, accommodation can only be used for the purposes of imprisonment if it has been certified that its size, lighting, heating, ventilation and fittings are adequate for health and provided it allows the prisoner to communicate at any time with prisoner officers. The Woolf Report (published following widespread disorder in prisons in 1990 in part resulting from prison overcrowding), described the requirements of the Prison Act as providing inadequate protection against the use of overfull or unsuitable accommodation. In response, new measures were introduced for certifying cells and managing potential overcrowding.

The first part of this change was to identify the certified normal accommodation (CNA), which is HM Prison Service's own measure of uncrowded accommodation. CNA represents the good, decent standard of accommodation that the service aspires to provide all prisoners. Any prisoner places provided above CNA are referred to as overcrowding places. Baseline CNA is the sum total of all certified accommodation in an establishment, except cells in punishment or segregation units and healthcare cells or rooms. In-use CNA is baseline CNA less those places not available for immediate use – for example, damaged cells, cells affected by building works and cells taken out of use due to staff shortages. However, CNA does not provide a legally enforceable maximum population. It is recognized that prisons and individual cells can be overcrowded up to a specified maximum capacity.

Operational capacity is the total number of prisoners that an establishment can hold without serious risk to good order, security and the proper running of the planned regime. It is determined and approved by area managers using operational judgement. This will normally be equal to, or greater than, baseline CNA. It may be set greater than CNA, particularly at local prisons, to allow for an agreed, safe level of overcrowding. It cannot exceed the sum of the certified maximum capacities of all the accommodation in use.

These methods of measuring and managing accommodation capacity have introduced a degree of order. However, as long as the prison population continues to grow, prisons, particularly local prisons, are unlikely to be able to eliminate overcrowding, let alone move towards achieving the more ambitious aim of eliminating all enforced cell-sharing as recommended in the Woolf Report and the Mubarek Inquiry.

*Jamie Bennett*

### Related entries

*Local prisons; Mubarek Inquiry; Overcrowding; Prison Act; Prison population; Woolf Report.*

---

**Key texts and sources**

HM Prison Service (2001) *Certified Prisoner Accommodation* (PSO 1900). London: HM Prison Service.

---

## CHAPLAINCY

**The prison chaplain is one of the three statutory posts identified in the Prison Act 1952. Chaplains are responsible for the provision of facilities to practise religion in each prison.**

In England and Wales, the presence of chaplains in prisons has been officially recognized since the eighteenth century. In the last century, the Prison Act 1952 established the position of chaplains in the prison system, requiring that three officials be appointed to every prison of which the chaplain was one, along with the governor and medical officer. At that time the chaplain and any assistant chaplain had to be a clergyman of the Church of England appointed by the Secretary of State and officiating under

the authority of the bishop of the diocese in which the prison was situated. Where the number of prisoners of another denomination was sufficient to merit it, the Secretary of State appointed a minister of that denomination. If no minister had been appointed, non-conformist ministers were allowed to visit prisoners of their denomination.

The latter half of the last century saw an increase in the multi-faith population of England and Wales. In response to this change, reflected in the prison population, the Chaplaincy Department formed an advisory group representing the main faiths (i.e. Buddhism, Christianity, Hinduism, Islam, Judaism, Church of Jesus Christ of Latter Day Saints and Sikhism), and this group later became the Chaplaincy Council.

The number of full-time and part-time chaplains directly employed in the Prison Service (including prisons managed in the public and private sectors) at the time of writing are shown in Table 1. In addition there are many hundreds of sessional and volunteer chaplain.

Table 1 Full-time and part-time chaplains in the Prison Service

|  | Full time | Part time | Unknown work pattern |
|---|---|---|---|
| Christian | 188 | 111 | 15 |
| Jewish | 0 | 1 | 0 |
| Muslim | 34 | 33 | 3 |
| Hindu | 1 | 0 | 1 |
| Sikh | 1 | 1 | 0 |
| Other religions | 0 | 2 | 1 |
| Total | 224 | 148 | 20 |

Each prison has a chaplaincy team, which usually consists of paid staff and volunteers. The responsibilities and duties of the chaplains are set out in the *Religious Manual*, which provides information relating to the faith and practice of the main faith groups to be found in Britain. Chaplains provide for corporate and private worship, pastoral care and for the religious education of prisoners. They also liaise with the prison authorities to ensure that the prison's regime makes provision for the religious needs of the prisoner (e.g. dietary requirements and the need for time out of the working day to observe religious festivals). In addition, many chaplains carry out generic duties in the prison, contributing to the delivery of programmes which form part of the prisoners' rehabilitation during their time in prison.

An area co-ordinating chaplain offers specialist professional help and support to the chaplaincy teams in the 13 areas of the Prison Service in England and Wales, meeting together regularly with local chaplaincy team members at area chaplaincy meetings. The national Chaplaincy Council, which meets six times a year and is chaired by the Chaplain General, plays a key role in relation to Prison Service Chaplaincy Headquarters, providing a forum for consultation on a broad range of policy issues to be looked at from a faith perspective. Its membership comprises the Chaplaincy Headquarters team, faith advisers and an area chaplain.

*Peter Hammersley*

### Related entries

*Black and minority ethnic (BME) prisoners; Faith communities; Human rights; Religion and faith; Staff (prison).*

---

**Key texts and sources**

See HM Prison Service's 'Statement of purpose' links to religious groups involved in prisons (http://www.hmprisonservice.gov.uk/ adviceandsupport/prison_life/religion/).

---

# CHILD PROTECTION

Legislation requires prisons to protect children in custody or those who come into contact with prisons for other reasons, such as via family contact.

Child 'abuse' can mean physical attack, sexual interference or mental harm. It can also be caused by neglect, where people who are responsible for children fail to provide proper care. The best way to keep children safe is to be alert to signs of abuse. Victims can be any age and from any social background. The younger the child, the more vulnerable he or she is and the more serious the damage if it is not stopped. It is particularly important to be alert to injuries occurring in families, which may be occasioned by violence, crime or heavy drinking, or where there is mental illness, poor housing conditions or financial hardship.

The current child protection system is based on the Children Act 1989. However, there is no single piece of legislation that covers child protection but, rather, a number of laws and guidance that are continually changing. Legislation covering child protection can be divided into two main categories. First is civil law, which covers *public law* relating to systems and processes in place to minimize the risk of children coming to harm and the action that should be taken if children are at risk. This also covers *private law*, which deals with family proceedings, such as divorce and contact. Secondly, criminal law deals with people who have offended or are at risk of offending against children. In practice, some Acts may include provisions that relate to both civil and criminal law.

The Children Act 2004 was accompanied by a range of documents entitled *Every Child Matters: Change for Children* (2007). The government's aim is for every child, whatever his or her background or circumstances, to have the support he or she needs to be healthy, to stay safe, to enjoy and achieve, to make a positive contribution and to achieve economic well-being. This means that the organizations providing services to children will be sharing information and working together to protect children and young people from harm and to help them achieve what they want in life. In future, children and young people will have far more say about issues that affect them as individuals and collectively.

*Working Together to Safeguard Children*
(HM Government 2006) made a number of
recommendations with regard to child
protection responsibilities. Specifically,
Recommendations 2.108–2.113 set out the
roles and responsibilities of HM Prison
Service. Concerns can arise from all parts of
the service – from the visits service through to
mother and baby units in prison. All prisons
have local arrangements to safeguard children,
with a committee to advise both the governor
and the local safeguarding board on issues
relating to child protection. This will involve a
team whose head will be part of the senior
management team. It is the responsibility of
that team to ensure that staff receive basic
child-protection training; that there are designated child protection officers to ensure that
concerns are dealt with; and that a management structure is in place to ensure strategic
development that joins up with the main business of imprisonment.

*Glynis Williams*

### Related entries

*Children in custody; Girls in prison; Mother and
baby units (MBUs); Multi-agency public protection arrangements (MAPPAs); Young men in
prison; Young offender institutions (YOIs); Youth
Justice Board (YJB).*

#### Key texts and sources

HM Government (2006) *Working Together to
Safeguard Children: A Guide to Inter-agency
Working to Safeguard and Promote the Welfare of
Children.* London: HMSO.
The documents, *Every Child Matters: Change for
Children*, are available online at http://www.
everychildmatters.gov.uk/. The Howard League
for Penal Reform's website contains several articles
regarding the league's standpoint on the imprisonment of children (http://www.howardleague.
org/).

## CHILDREN IN CUSTODY

Children in custody refers to prisoners under
the age of 18, often referred to as 'juveniles'.
In the UK, 'custody' comprises a variety of
locked institutions: young offender institutions, secure training centres and secure
children's homes (in England and Wales);
young offender institutions and secure
accommodation (in Scotland); and young
offender centres and secure accommodation
(in Northern Ireland). The substantial majority of children in custody are held in
institutions managed by the respective prison
services within each jurisdiction.

The practice of detaining children in specialist
forms of custody in the UK can be traced back
to the establishment of the first penal institution exclusively for children at Parkhurst Prison,
for boys, in England in 1838. Since that time a
range of policy initiatives, statutory developments and carceral experiments have created
and sustained a panoply of custodial institutions, including reformatories, industrial
schools, Borstals, approved schools, remand
centres, detention centres, youth custody centres, young offender institutions, secure units
and secure training centres. Even if the stock
and flow of child imprisonment varies across
time and place – often contingent upon the
political vagaries of youth justice policy – ultimately, penal institutions retain a permanent
foothold within national and international
youth justice systems.

A range of international human rights standards, treaties, rules and conventions apply to
children in custody. The United Nations' Rules
for the Protection of Juveniles Deprived of their
Liberty (the JDL Rules) and the United Nations
Convention on the Rights of the Child
(UNCRC), both adopted by the United Nations
in 1990, are particularly important. The primary
purpose of such instruments is to mediate the
use of custodial institutions for children and,
when used, to safeguard the rights and needs of
child prisoners. Article 37(b) of the UNCRC, for

example, provides that the detention of children in custody should only be applied as 'a measure of last resort and for the shortest appropriate period of time'. Despite such rights-based protective provisions, however, some youth justice jurisdictions continue to place significant numbers of children in custody.

In the UK in recent years, youth justice law, policy and practice have taken a punitive turn, particularly in England and Wales. In 2006, for example, greater use of custody for children was made in England and Wales than in most other industrialized democratic countries in the world. Such penal practice has generated a consistent stream of critique from a wide range of authoritative sources, including international human rights bodies, parliamentary committees, independent inquiries, state inspectorates, academic research, penal reform organizations and children's human rights agencies. Despite the weight and authority of such critique, however, successive governments since 1993 – both Conservative and New Labour – have continued to pursue a 'tough' line with regard to youth justice policy.

Much of the concern that centres around children in custody derives from the particular vulnerabilities of child prisoners. Throughout the world, child prisoners are routinely drawn from some of the most disadvantaged, damaged and distressed families, neighbourhoods and communities. Poverty, family discord, public care, drug and alcohol misuse, mental distress, ill-health, emotional, physical and sexual abuse, self-harm, homelessness, isolation, loneliness, circumscribed educational and employment opportunities, and the most pressing sense of distress and alienation are defining characteristics of children in custody. In the UK, research has revealed that approximately half of children held in custody at any given time have been, or remain, involved with social services departments and other welfare agencies, and a significant proportion have biographies scarred by adult abuse and violation. In 2001, a major review of the educational needs of children in custody in England and Wales by HM Chief Inspectorate of Prisons and the Office for Standards in Education found that 84 per cent

of child prisoners had been excluded from school; 86 per cent had not regularly attended school; 52 per cent had left school aged 14 years or younger; 29 per cent had left school aged 13 years or younger; and 73 per cent described their educational achievement as 'nil'. In short, the combination of poverty and structural exclusion, neglect by welfare, education and health agencies, and a 'tough' policy climate renders such children profoundly vulnerable.

The vulnerabilities of children in custody are often compounded by the very experience of detention itself. Indeed, the conditions and treatment typically endured by child prisoners routinely violate their emotional, psychological and physical integrity. It is widely recognized that bullying is particularly problematic. The most obvious expression of bullying is physical assault. Child prisoners are also exposed to many other forms of 'bullying', however, including sexual abuse, verbal abuse, psychological abuse, extortion and theft. For example, lending and trading cultures – particularly in relation to tobacco – often involve exorbitant rates of interest that accumulate on a daily basis. Moreover, in 2006, a major independent inquiry led by Lord Carlile of Berriew exposed problematic yet routine practices in custodial facilities holding children in England and Wales, including the use of physical restraint, solitary confinement and strip searching. High rates of self-harm among child prisoners, together with the deaths of 29 children in penal institutions in England and Wales between 1990 and 2005, raise the most serious questions regarding children in custody.

The humanitarian critique of child imprisonment is compounded by the enormous fiscal expense incurred by placing children in custody and the spectacular failings of custodial institutions when measured in terms of crime reduction and community safety. In 2003–4, for example, child imprisonment in England and Wales cost £293.5 million and, in October 2004, a parliamentary select committee reported that reconviction rates stood at 80 per cent with regard to released child prisoners. The combination of the provisions of international human rights instruments, burgeoning human rights concerns, the damaging consequences of placing children in custody, the huge expense of child imprisonment and the minimal positive return in creating a safer society has led many leading criminological commentators to advocate the implementation of reductionist strategies and abolitionism.

*Barry Goldson and John Muncie*

### Related entries

*Abolitionism; Borstals; Bullying; HM Inspectorate of Prisons; Human rights; Secure training centres; Young offender institutions (YOIs).*

---

**Key texts and sources**

Goldson, B. (2002) *Vulnerable Inside: Children in Secure and Penal Settings.* London: Children's Society.

Goldson, B. and Coles, D. (2005) *In the Care of the State? Child Deaths in Penal Custody in England and Wales.* London: Inquest.

Miller, J. (1991) *Last One Over the Wall: The Massachusetts Experiment in Closing Reform Schools.* Columbus, OH: Ohio State University Press.

Muncie, J. and Goldson, B. (eds) (2006) *Comparative Youth Justice.* London: Sage.

The Howard League for Penal Reform's website contains several articles regarding the league's standpoint on the imprisonment of children (http://www.howardleague.org/).

---

# CITIZENSHIP

Citizenship is a term used to describe the relationship between an individual and the state.

The concept of citizenship is imprecise and contested. The dictionary definition is 'a native or inhabitant of a state', and the term is often used in a narrow sense related to immigration or nationality law. In classical times, the concept implied a privileged status above that of slaves or other inhabitants. In revolutionary France or the USA or among radicals, it was used to imply a sense of freedom, often in contrast to the situation of those who were still 'subjects' of a hereditary sovereign. It can thus be used 'exclu-sively' or 'inclusively', with very different implications and connotations.

In recent debates, citizenship has been used to counter the individualism that had become pervasive. It is associated with the ideas of public duty and social responsibility, and is used to emphasize shared interests, often among people from different ethnic backgrounds. For the Labour government since 1997, citizenship has been connected with duties and obligations, such as to obey the law; to be of good behaviour; to care for and control one's children; and to work and pay taxes (Faulkner 2006). Observing those duties has been seen as being in conflict with human rights legislation. In the programme for 'civil renewal', the government supported the concept of 'active citizenship', which suggested that people should give some of their time to voluntary work for the benefit of their community. Responsibility for the programme was transferred to the Department for Communities and Local Government in 2006, where it became part of a wider range of policies.

There has been less emphasis generally on offenders' own rights and responsibilities as citizens, and the notion of 'less eligibility' has had some influence. Community service has long provided opportunities for offenders to work for the benefit of local communities, but it has rarely been seen in this way and it has always been marginal to the main tasks of the prison and probation services. The concept of citizenship was implicit in Lord Wilberforce's judgment in *Raymond* v. *Honey* (1983 [1983] 1 AC 1) that 'in spite of his imprisonment, a convicted prisoner retains all civil rights that are not taken away expressly or by necessary implication', but that judgment has not had much practical effect. The concept is also implicit in restorative justice and in approaches to the treatment of offenders which emphasize prisoners rebuilding their lives. The issue of voting rights for prisoners is an important symbolic issue.

Some prisons have begun to consider the concept of citizenship (Pryor 2001). For example, therapeutic communities in prison provide an experience of full membership of a community which provides a living learning experience. Similarly, many aspects of resettlement can be seen as enabling offenders to take on the responsibilities of being a citizen. Approaches such as these are on the margins of penal policy. But they may have potential as a force for penal reform.

*Tim Newell*

### Related entries

*Civil renewal; Legitimacy; Less eligibility; Responsibility; Restorative justice (RJ); Therapeutic communities; Voting rights.*

---

**Key texts and sources**

Faulkner, D. (2006) *Crime, State and Citizen: A Field Full of Folk* (2nd edn). Winchester: Waterside Press.

Pryor, S. (2001) *The Responsible Prisoner: An Exploration of the Extent to which Imprisonment Removes Responsibility Unnecessarily and an Invitation to Change.* London: HM Prison Service.

The Prison Reform Trust's website discusses the idea of identity and citizenship among prisoners (http://www.prisonreformtrust.org.uk/subsection.asp?id=432).

---

## CIVIL RENEWAL

Civil renewal is a government policy designed to ensure that people and government work together for the benefit of the community. However, the idea of involving citizens in efforts to prevent crime, and of giving them some responsibility for this, has a history going back to the Middle Ages.

In the document *Together We Can* (2005), the government defined civil renewal as being:

*[A]bout people and government working together to make life better. It involves more people being able to influence decisions about their communities, and more people taking responsibility for tackling local problems, rather than expecting others to. The idea is that government can't solve everything by itself, and nor can the community: it's better when we work together.*

Civil renewal became a theme of the Labour government's policy when David Blunkett, then Home Secretary, introduced it, saying that 'civil renewal must ... play a crucial role in our reform of the criminal justice system ... the system must be accessible and accountable to local people first and foremost, which means it must be open, transparent and firmly rooted in the community' (2003).

A Civil Renewal Unit and an advisory Active Citizenship Centre were set up within the Home Office, and connections were made with other departments' work on subjects such as social exclusion, teaching citizenship, social cohesion, encouraging volunteers and community justice. Three key ingredients were active citizens, speaking for their communities; strengthened communities, with the capability and resources to work out shared solutions; and partnerships between public bodies and local people. Civil renewal was to be seen more as an ethos than a programme of work.

The government set out its intentions in detail in *Together We Can*, first published in 2005. This covered various subjects, such as citizenship, democracy, regeneration, cohesion and sustainability, and it included a number of practical examples which local authorities (which could become designated as 'civic pioneers') and the voluntary and community sector were encouraged to follow, with measures by which the government would judge their performance. The section concerned with reducing crime focused mainly on the familiar subjects of responsive policing, neighbourhood watch, antisocial behaviour, gun crime and drugs. Departmental responsibility for civil renewal was transferred from the Home Office to the newly constituted Department for Communities and Local Government in May 2006. With this move came a change of name, with the establishment of the Community Empowerment Division within the Local Democracy Unit.

A paper written in 2004 by Faulkner and Flaxington suggested a number of other ways in which civil renewal might influence criminal justice and the treatment of offenders, including the involvement of volunteers and the voluntary sector, typically in work with offenders or victims; issues regarding the rights and responsibilities of victims, including the opportunity to be involved in restorative justice; opportunities and encouragement for offenders themselves to become active and responsible citizens, including both work undertaken for communities and support to other offenders in turning away from crime; and the engagement of local citizens both in dialogue and consultation, and more actively in the governance of their local services and institutions.

The National Offender Management Service (NOMS) and the Youth Justice Board (YJB) have been active in pursuing the first of these, especially in encouraging volunteers to work as mentors or as members of referral panels in youth justice, and in engaging voluntary and community organizations to provide specified services for offenders in prisons or in the community. The rights and expectations of victims have been prominent in the government's action to 'rebalance the system in favour of the victim' and in restorative justice. The government has paid less attention to the possibilities of civil renewal for offenders themselves, except in the limited context of enabling local people to have a voice in deciding the type of unpaid work offenders could be required to undertake as part of community punishment. Any schemes for enabling offenders, and especially prisoners, to become active and responsible citizens – for example, the collaboration between Spring Hill Prison and Oxford Citizens' Advice – rely on the enthusiasm of individuals and are always vulnerable to operational pressures or political sensitivity. There is very little consultation and, apart from independent monitoring boards, no genuine involvement of local citizens or communities in the governance of prisons. The indications for the Probation Service are that such involvement as remains will be further diminished by the changes that are intended in the membership and status of probation boards.

There has been some ambiguity about the government's intentions in promoting civil renewal and its underlying social values. On one interpretation, the aim was to generate a stronger sense of local responsibility, discretion and empowerment, independent of government

and based on the values of tolerance, compassion and social inclusion and on a sense of common belonging. On another, it was to enlist citizens, communities and voluntary and community organizations in delivering the government's programmes and policies, and to engage them as agents of social control. However that may be, 'local empowerment' in some form is likely to be a continuing theme of government policy, whichever political party holds office. Whether and how far it will extend to the administration of justice or the treatment of offenders is harder to judge.

*David Faulkner*

### Related entries

*Citizenship; Independent monitoring boards; National Offender Management Service (NOMS); Responsibility; Youth Justice Board (YJB).*

**Key texts and sources**

Blunkett, D. (2003) *Civil Renewal: A New Agenda (the Edith Kahn Memorial Lecture).* London: Home Office.
Faulkner, D. and Flaxington, F. (2004) 'NOMS and civil renewal', *Vista*, 9: 90–9.
The Home Office document, *Together We Can* (2005), and subsequent reviews published by the Department for Communities and Local Government, can be found at **www.together wecan.info**.

## CLOSE SUPERVISION CENTRES

Close supervision centres are specialist units designed to manage, treat and reintegrate prisoners whose presence is disruptive and violent in prison.

### Introduction of close supervision centres

A system of close supervision centres (CSCs) was introduced in February 1998 to replace the previous network of units established after the Control Review Committee (CRC) report in

1985. The previous units operated relatively unstructured open regimes in small, secure, self-contained units at Parkhurst, Hull and Woodhill Prisons, but many disruptive prisoners were unable to cope with the open nature of these units and were held instead in long-term segregation on a continuous assessment scheme (CAS), whereby they were continually transferred between the segregation units of high-security prisons. Although, therefore, a proportion of difficult and disruptive prisoners experienced full and stimulating regimes, an approximately equal proportion were consigned to continuous segregation.

Following the Woodcock and Learmont Reports of 1994 and 1995, published following escapes from two high-security prisons, more closely managed regimes were introduced, and it was decided that the system for managing prisoners who presented very serious control problems should be reviewed. A project team, led by a prison governor, presented its report in February 1996, recommending that the previous CRC units be modified to provide more structure and be based on progression through a staged system where access to successive stages would be earned by co-operative behaviour. The declared purpose of the new CSC system was 'to secure the return of problematic or disruptive prisoners to a settled and acceptable pattern of institutional behaviour'. The model was accepted and a new system of CSCs opened in February 1998.

The Prison Rules were amended to introduce a new Rule 46 that allowed the Secretary of State to direct a prisoner's removal from association and his placement in a close supervision centre to maintain good order or discipline, or to ensure the safety of staff and/or other prisoners. Under this rule the authorities are obliged to review this decision every month, at which point the period can be extended, but there is no requirement for independent scrutiny of this power as there is with Prison Rule 45. A system of care and management planning ensures that each CSC prisoner is reviewed each month on the basis of reports submitted from unit staff to a central CSC selection committee (CSCSC).

Woodhill Prison was identified as the location for the staged units: a structured regime for new receptions, an intervention regime for those who showed signs of progress and a restricted regime for those who failed to conform. Later a segregation unit was added for those repeatedly challenging the regime at the lowest level. Two further units were designated in Hull and Durham, the former offering a full regime in preparation for a return to the mainstream and the latter operating a therapeutic regime for those whose behaviour was so disturbed that they were not considered suitable for the staged system at all. In May 1999, the Hull unit closed and moved to Durham G Wing. Despite being part of a national system, the management of these widely dispersed units was the responsibility of the governors of the establishments in which they were located.

### Inspection of CSCs

In August 1999, the CSCs were subject to inspection by HM Chief Inspector of Prisons (2000). By this time about a quarter of the 36 prisoners in the CSC system had progressed and three quarters had regressed. The latter were being held either in the restricted or segregation units in Woodhill or in the segregation units of high-security prisons, the latter recreating the previous 'continuous assessment scheme' the system was designed to replace. Those in the segregation unit were subject to continuous segregation in punishment conditions, were subject to a sub-basic regime, were unlocked by six staff in personal protective equipment and were allowed only closed visits. This invited severe censure from HM Chief Inspector of Prisons (HMCIP). Not only were CSC prisoners being held in punishment conditions without limit of time, but they were also being held outside the CSC system in high-security prison segregation units for open-ended periods and without any formal oversight from independent monitoring boards.

It was also pointed out that many CSC prisoners had a combination of challenges, both behavioural and emotional, that made it very difficult for them to sustain a pattern of settled behaviour that would allow them to progress towards a full regime, and that in the mean time their problems were exacerbated by isolation and a lack of mental stimulation. It was recommended that regime decisions should be based on individual need, including mental health need, and that prisoners should all be fully occupied either in their cells or in association, where risk assessment allowed.

HM Prison Service responded with Phase 2 of the CSC system. This aimed to meet the care and management needs of prisoners individually and to provide in-reach mental health support. The punishment regime was stopped and three regimes introduced at Woodhill providing progressively less control and segregation, and offering opportunities to progress. Other units offered pathways on from Woodhill, with Durham continuing to operate two units: the activity-based regime for those preparing to return to mainstream location and the unit for those with a history of highly disturbed behaviour. In April 2002, an exceptional risk unit opened at Wakefield for those who presented a chronic and long-term risk and, in October 2004, a unit at Whitemoor opened in the previous special secure unit to replace the Durham units.

These CSC units were drawn into a single system managed from Woodhill, with a dedicated governor chairing an operational management group that included the dispersed units and officially designated cells in high-security segregation units. The governing governor of Woodhill chaired the monthly CSCSC that considered new referrals and made operational decisions concerning the continued selection and location of each prisoner. The Director of High Security continued to chair a quarterly steering group, but he relinquished the chair of the advisory group to an independent member. This group was renamed the Advisory Group on Difficult Prisoners (AGDP) and its remit was extended in July 2004 to include strategic advice on the management of challenging prisoners in all parts of the prison system. The independent monitoring boards in each prison with CSC units or designated cells were given a specified role in overseeing the treatment and conditions for CSC prisoners.

The CSC system continued to evolve under the influence of mental health staff and prison-wide initiatives, such as the violence reduction strategy and treatment for prisoners identified as meeting the criteria for dangerous and severe personality disorder (DSPD). Between October 2004 and September 2005, a violence reduction programme was successfully piloted at Woodhill and, in late 2005, the CSC system entered Phase 3 and was recast as a violence reduction strategy for disruptive prisoners.

In August 2005, while the CSC system was on the cusp of this change, it was visited again by HMCIP (2006). Credit was given for a decrease in numbers of about 15 per cent, for the developing mental health provision, for the focus on violence reduction and for the exceptional risk unit that provided as full a regime as was compatible with segregation. However, the provision of in-cell activity for men who spent considerable periods in solitary confinement was considered to be inadequate, and greater use of occupational therapy was recommended to support mental health and to encourage behavioural change.

It was also considered necessary for there to be more effective individual clinical (as opposed to operational) management of CSC prisoners from the centre, provided by a responsible medical officer of consultant forensic psychiatric status, rather than a patchwork of poorly coordinated provision in different locations. The operational reviews required under Rule 46 and carried out centrally by the CSCSC fell short of a full clinical review of their care and management needs. Another concern was the continued use of designated cells in high-security segregation units to hold CSC 'lodgers' for indefinite periods for control purposes. Though their use for control purposes appeared to have diminished and they were also being used for accumulated visits, respite and testing prior to deselection, they were used for considerably longer periods when used for control purposes. In these circumstances, although there was operational management from the centre, the holding prison did not take responsibility for case management and planning during that time. A greater degree of clinical involvement in these decisions and local case management of prisoners held in these cells were recommended.

Finally, HMCIP continued to call for increased external monitoring of the system, involving independent monitoring boards in the CSC advisory group and strengthening their responsibilities in relation to prisoners within the CSC system (including those in designated cells). It stressed that, in this most hidden part of the prison system, robust external monitoring and scrutiny were essential to maintain public confidence and to protect both prisoners and staff.

*Monica Lloyd*

### Related entries

*Barlinnie; Dangerous and severe personality disorder (DSPD); Dangerousness; High-security prisons; HM Inspectorate of Prisons; Mental health; Segregation; Violence reduction.*

---

**Key texts and sources**

HM Chief Inspector of Prisons (2000) *Inspection of Close Supervision Centres.* London: HM Inspectorate of Prisons.

HM Chief Inspector of Prisons (2006) *Extreme Custody: A Thematic Inspection of Close Supervision Centres and High Security Segregation.* London: HM Inspectorate of Prisons.

King, R.D. (2007) 'Security, control and the problems of containment', in Y. Jewkes (ed.) *Handbook on Prisons.* Cullompton: Willan.

A full download of HM Inspectorate of Prisons' inspection of close supervision centres is available at http://inspectorates.homeoffice.gov.uk/hmiprisons/thematic-reports1/close-supervision.pdf.

---

# CLOTHING

Convicted prisoners have traditionally worn prison uniform. These requirements were relaxed in the 1990s, but clothing remains a controversial issue.

A classic image of prison life is Vincent van Gogh's painting, *La Ronde des Prisonniers* (1890) – a desolate crowd trudge round a yard in single file, shabbily dressed in ill-fitting striped uniforms. The prison uniform has become embedded in popular imagination, symbolizing prisons as controlling machinery, eliminating individuality. While this popular perception has persevered, the reality is that the uniform has diminished in prison life since the early 1990s. Unconvicted prisoners have traditionally been allowed to wear their own clothes, in recognition of the fact that they are presumed innocent and therefore are not subject to the full rigours of prison life. However, until the early 1990s, convicted prisoners were expected to wear a uniform, a requirement that has statutory effect (HM Prison Service 1999).

Following the riots throughout the prison system in 1990, the Woolf Report was published, providing a blueprint for a prison system that was more humane. In relation to clothing, the report recognized that the provision of prison clothing was inadequate, describing prisoners as being dressed in 'ill-fitting, dirty clothing' (Home Office 1991: 395). The report suggested that this had a detrimental impact on morale and on staff perceptions of prisoners. It was recommended that prisoners be allowed to wear their own clothing. This led to a wide expansion in the facility for prisoners to wear their own clothes, although the move required the availability of laundry facilities.

In the mid-1990s, the introduction of incentives and earned privileges (IEP) led to a link between permission to wear one's own clothing and good behaviour. It is now common for the privilege of wearing one's own clothing to be offered to those who are on the standard or enhanced levels, but not those on the basic level. One exception to these general rules is that prisoners who are identified as an escape risk or Category A prisoners may be required to wear distinctive, high-visibility clothing, either in the prison or when escorted outside. This clothing is intended to prevent or impede escapes.

More recently, prison uniform has made an ominous return as part of the drift towards a 'new punitiveness' in the UK and USA. In particular, this includes the reintroduction of traditional prison uniforms and humiliating clothing (such as pink underwear issued in prisons in Arizona) in order to make punishment more humiliating. The stigma of wearing certain kinds of clothing has also been a feature of attempts to make community penalties more punitive and to increase public confidence in the criminal justice system. For example, there has been some public discussion in the UK regarding the use of highly visible uniforms for those carrying out community work as part of their sentence (Hinsliff 2005).

Traditionally, the prison uniform has symbolized the machine-like nature of the penal system, and the introduction of choice and autonomy in clothing was an important part of the humanizing reform project. Although choice remains the common practice, the rise in public support for more punitive approaches has seen the return of the prison uniform as a means of making punishment a more unpleasant and painful experience for offenders.

*Jamie Bennett*

### Related entries

*Deprivations/'pains of imprisonment'; Identity and self; Incentives and earned privileges (IEP); Legitimacy; New punitiveness; Public perceptions; Woolf Report.*

#### Key texts and sources

Hinsliff, G. (2005) 'US-style uniforms for yobs in new disorder crackdown', *Observer*, 15 May (available online at **http://observer.guardian.co.uk/politics/story/0,6903,1484282,00.html**).
HM Prison Service (1999) *Prison Rules 1999: The Young Offender Institution (Amendment) (No. 2) Rules 1999* (PSO 0100). London: HM Prison Service.
Woolf, Lord Justice and Tumin, S. (1991) *Prison Disturbances April 1990.* (cm 1456) London: HMSO.

## COMMUNICATION

Communication refers to contact between prisoners and those outside prison, notably family and friends and legal representatives. The main methods of communication are correspondence and telephone calls, which can provide a lifeline to prisoners and families who wish to keep in touch.

Correspondence is the oldest and cheapest form of contact for both prisoners and families of prisoners. In England and Wales, prisoners are entitled to one or two free letters a week, but can send out as many as they wish at their own expense and there are no limits on the number they can receive. Telephones for prisoners' use were introduced into low-security prisons in 1988 and, after a recommendation in the Woolf Report, their provision was swiftly extended to all categories of prison. Originally, prisoners bought phonecards but these could be used as a form of currency and, following concerns that prisoners could contact witnesses and/or victims of their offence, they were replaced by PIN phones. A list of the telephone numbers prisoners wish to call is submitted for approval, and the cost of calls is deducted from credit in their PIN phone account.

Despite these provisions for communication, it has been estimated that over 40 per cent of prisoners lose contact with their families during their imprisonment (NACRO 2000). The exact reasons for this are unclear, but the challenges involved in maintaining contact through letters and telephone calls may well be a contributing factor. Telephone calls from prison are over five times more expensive than those from outside (Prison Reform Trust 2006), and access to telephones may be restricted, particularly if the time spent out of cell is limited. In some local prisons, where demand is high, calls may be automatically cut off after ten minutes. While this may stop the phones being dominated by individual prisoners, it can cause considerable distress if family or relationship problems are under discussion, and both parties may avoid awkward subjects that cannot be tackled in such a short space of time. Furthermore, both correspondence and telephone calls are subject to surveillance for security reasons. Telephone contact is randomly monitored and, although routine censorship is only carried out in Category A establishments, all post may be read (with the exception of correspondence to and from legal representatives) if ordered by the governor. The lack of privacy caused by such surveillance can constrain discussion of personal, sensitive issues (Richards *et al.* 1994), which may in turn contribute to relationship difficulties and, ultimately, family break-up. It is also worth noting that prisoners do not yet have access to more modern methods of communication, such as e-mail and text messaging, which might considerably facilitate contact with the outside world.

*Alice Mills*

### Related entries

*Families of prisoners; Security; Visits and visiting orders; Woolf Report.*

**Key texts and sources**

Nacro (2000) *The Forgotten Majority: The Resettlement of Short Term Prisoners*. London: Nacro.

Prison Reform Trust (2006) 'Inside criminal justice', *Prison Report*, 69: 4.

Richards, M., McWilliams, B., Allcock, L., Enterkin, J., Owens, P. and Woodrow, J. (1994) *The Family Ties of English Prisoners*. Cambridge: Cambridge Centre for Family Research.

## COPING

Coping refers to the successful adaptation, by the prisoner, to the stressful and austere environment of prison. It leads to improved self-esteem, autonomy and self-respect. When prisoners are not coping, a range of outcomes may result, such as depression, violence towards staff, bullying of other prisoners, self-harm or suicide.

Inmates react to prison in a range of different ways. Some find it a place of security and cope well, if passively, with the authoritarian environment, the inevitable loss of personal choice and the physical, sensory and social deprivations. This might be because they have been institutionalized by previous experience of confinement or because it fulfils their need for safe containment at that particular point in their lives. Others find prison a frightening, disorienting and dehumanizing place and struggle to cope, particularly on entry and in the early stages of their incarceration. Historically, remand prisoners have consistently shown particularly high levels of distress, perhaps because of the uncertainty about outcomes, and perhaps because they have been confined in local prisons that are characterized by high levels of overcrowding and dysfunction. This struggle to cope can manifest itself in a range of behaviours, such as bullying peers, intransigence towards prison officers, violence towards others or the self, and depression and withdrawal.

The most serious indication of a failure to cope is self-inflicted harm that, in its most extreme form, results in death. In 2002, the Social Exclusion Unit reported that 37 per cent of women prisoners and 20 per cent of male prisoners had previously attempted suicide. This cannot be unrelated to the fact that the prison population as a whole comprises the most vulnerable and marginalized groups in society, and prison does not deliver the complex interventions and consistent support that are needed.

Prisoners are 13 times more likely than the general population to have been in care as a child; 10 times as likely to have been a regular school truant; 13 times more likely to have been unemployed; 6 times more likely to have been an unusually young father; and 2.5 times more likely to have a family member already convicted of an offence. The majority of prisoners have the basic skills levels of an 11-year-old; their general health is on the whole poor, with high levels of hepatitis, TB, HIV, drug or alcohol addiction, and mental health problems (SEU 2002). These factors are evidence of the gaping abyss of need, in terms of helping inmates to cope with the extreme environment of prison.

The concept of 'poor copers' has been influential in research and practice since first articulated by Liebling (1991), when it attempted to explain the interaction between prisoners and the prison environment in relation to levels of suicide and self-harm. In her study of young prisoners, using a subject group with a recent history of intentional self-harm and a control group chosen at random, Liebling

(1992) used the concept of coping ability to explain a range of differences observed between the two groups. Other researchers (Towl and Forbes 2000: 99; Medlicott 2001: 25–6) have criticized the labelling process that is implicit in coping theory as inappropriate. All prisoners experience personal crises at some point and move in and out of coping modes. Staff can help by recognizing times of crisis, such as first entry into prison, and by providing appropriate support at the time it is needed. Stereotyping prisoners as 'poor copers', in the harsh and somewhat judgemental culture of prison life, can obscure this support process by defining individuals as inadequate and therefore less deserving. Peer acceptance is another important part of coping and adaptation, and labelling can jeopardize this.

Risk assessment has been a formalized attempt to label prisoners – by means of the F2052SH documentation and procedures – at particular risk of self-harm, but every year prisoners kill themselves who were not so identified. The issue is complicated by the fact that persistent but limited self-harm is sometimes self-disclosed by prisoners as the preferred form of adaptation to prison life (see, for example, Medlicott 2001: 25). The question arises as to whether such prisoners fit the crude classification of 'coping' or 'not coping'. The picture is further complicated when suicide sometimes unintentionally results from just such behaviour that 'went wrong'.

In her interviews with prisoners, identified by the staff as 'coping' or 'not coping', Medlicott (2001) found the distinction unworkable, since many prisoners identified as 'copers' (who had never been identified as being at risk) disclosed secret resolve and intention about suicide, highly developed over a long period of time, if certain personal circumstances were to prevail. She used the label of 'coping now' or 'not coping now' to indicate the state of mind as disclosed by the prisoner at the time of interview, a state of mind that is fluid and changeable over the duration of a prison sentence. But she pointed out that coping classifications use the language of a psychiatric or pathology model, and they can serve to neutralize the real problems that all

prisoners have in adapting to prison. They tend to locate the problem of adaptation firmly in the prisoner and obscure recognition of the fact that the prison environment is essentially problematic. When coping classifications are operationalized in practice, they legitimate awarding special attention to some prisoners and withholding it from others.

Prisoners' own narratives show that they discuss how to cope with their time (Medlicott 2001: 175), that they learn about coping from each other and that coping is an ongoing learning process. For example, 'Gerry' speaks of the cycle of stages and proposes that all prisoners go through the same stages but at different speeds and in different ways (2001: 175–6). Clearly, external events, such as bereavement and family breakdown, have the capacity to plunge prisoners back into extreme distress at any time.

*Diana Medlicott*

### Related entries

*Bullying; Deprivations/'pains of imprisonment'; Overcrowding; Risk; Self-harm; Solidarity; Suicide in prison; Violence.*

---

**Key texts and sources**

Liebling, A. (1992) *Suicides in prisons*. London: Routledge.

Medlicott, D. (2001) *Surviving the Prison Place: Narratives of Suicidal Prisoners*. Aldershot: Ashgate.

Social Exclusion Unit (2002) *Reducing Re-offending by Ex-prisoners*. London: Social Exclusion Unit.

Towl, G. and Forbes, D. (2000) 'Working with suicidal prisoners', in G. Towl *et al.* (eds) *Suicide in Prisons*. Leicester: British Psychological Society.

---

## COST OF PRISONS

Almost £2 billion is spent annually operating prisons. The costs of individual prisons are usually expressed in terms of cost per prison place or cost per prisoner. The costs vary significantly between types of prison.

HM Prison Service cost £1.83 billion in 2005–6 (HM Prison Service 2006). Approximately 81 per cent of this is accounted for by staff costs. In terms of individual prisons, this is usually expressed in terms of cost per prisoner place or cost per prisoner. Cost per place is calculated by dividing the net expenditure for a period by the average certified normal accommodation (CNA) across that period. Cost per prisoner is calculated by dividing the net expenditure for a period by the average population across that period. Establishments' performance is published in the annual report (HM Prison Service 2006).

In 2005–6, the average cost per place was £28,486, while the average cost per prisoner was £26,993. However, there are significant differences between different types of prison. The cheapest prisons are unsurprisingly those with the lowest level of security: open prisons. On average, an open prison place costs £20,183. However, on cost per prisoner, Category C prisoners are cheaper. This is a result of the under-occupancy in open prisons. The most expensive are male high-security prisons, which cost £43,904 per place and £50,491 per prisoner. Prison places for women, juveniles and young offenders are also more expensive than those for adult male offenders.

There are 14 contracted prisons, all of which have at some stage been subject to market testing; 3 are operated by the public sector and 11 are managed by private sector providers (NOMS 2006). In comparison with the public sector prisons, these contracted prisons are more expensive on a per prison place and per prisoner basis. The only exception are the high-security prison places provided by Manchester Prison, which are significantly less expensive than the closest comparator prisons (Woodhill and Belmarsh). However, caution needs to be exercised when drawing such simple comparisons, as each prison is expected to deliver a different set of services, which have different cost implications.

In order to meet government spending targets, prisons must annually identify efficiency savings, where plans are implemented to deliver the same service at reduced cost. This is usually achieved by reducing the number of staff required or lowering the grade of staff employed. Other sources of efficiencies include the contracting out of ancillary services (such as catering, the prison shop and prisoner transport services) to private sector providers. It has been argued that the introduction of commercial competition and benchmarking through the private prisons has been a spur to greater efficiency in the public sector.

*Jamie Bennett*

### Related entries

*Accountability; Certified normal accommodation (CNA); Key performance indicators (KPIs) and key performance targets (KPTs); Market testing; New public management (NPM); Performance management.*

**Key texts and sources**

HM Prison Service (2006) *Annual Report and Accounts, April 2005–March 2006.* London: HM Prison Service.

National Offender Management Service (2006, 2006a) *Office for Contracted Prisons: Statement of Performance and Financial Information: April 2005 to March 2006.* London: National Offender Management Service.

## CUSTODY PLUS AND CUSTODY MINUS

> Custody plus is an approach that allows sentencers to impose a penalty that combines a short period in prison with community penalties. Custody minus enables sentencers to impose a suspended prison sentence with condition that community penalties be carried out.

In 2001, the Home Office published a review of sentencing, known as the Halliday Report. Among the recommendations were significant changes to short-term prison sentences – primarily, two proposals known as custody plus and custody minus.

A short-term prison sentence (i.e. less than 12 months) was called 'plain custody'. This would normally result in prisoners' automatic release at the halfway point, and possibly earlier under home detention curfew. There would be no supervision requirements, although they would remain at risk of recall to custody. Custody plus was aimed at making short-term sentences more effective by enabling a short period of custody to be combined with conditions equivalent to community sentences, such as probation supervision, community work, curfews or drug testing. A custody-plus sentence would be between 28 and 51 weeks in total, combining between 2 weeks and 13 weeks in custody with at least 26 weeks on licence. This was enacted under the Criminal Justice Act 2003, but has not been implemented because of the significant resource implications, particularly as Halliday envisaged that there would be a presumption that sentences of less than 12 months contain a 'plus' element unless the court was satisfied that it was unnecessary in the interests of crime reduction.

Custody plus has been criticized on the basis that it will lead to the 'creative mixing' of punishments to produce sentences that are more severe than would previously have been awarded. It has also been argued that it will lead to 'net-widening' and more people going to prison, as sentencers will be attracted to the option of a 'short, sharp shock' of imprisonment (see Rex and Tonry 2002).

Custody minus was proposed to address the perceived inadequacies of suspended prison sentences. As these sentences effectively meant that, providing no further offence was committed, no punishment was imposed, they were perceived as inadequate. Custody minus was intended to allow a suspended sentence to be combined with community punishments. This was enacted in the Criminal Justice Act 2003 as the suspended sentence supervision order, which could include between 6 months and 2 years' supervision, and between 26 and 49 weeks' licence. In 2005, there were 481 suspended sentence orders made, compared with 5,848 suspended sentences, indicating that this new order has only limited application.

These new approaches have the potential to blur the lines between community and custodial penalties. It could be argued that such creative mixing may lead to sentences that can more effectively meet a range of aims. However, these new initiatives have been criticized for their potential to make sentences more onerous and for increasing the number of people sent to prison, either for short sentences or as a result of breach of conditions.

*Jamie Bennett*

### Related entries

*Alternatives to imprisonment; Bifurcation; New punitiveness; Politics of imprisonment; Probation Service; Sentencing policy.*

**Key texts and sources**

Home Office (2001) *Making Punishments Work: Report of a Review of the Sentencing Framework for England and Wales.* London: HMSO.

Rex, S. and Tonry, M. (eds) (2002) *Reform and Punishment: The Future of Sentencing.* Cullompton: Willan Publishing.

# D

## DANGEROUS AND SEVERE PERSONALITY DISORDER (DSPD)

Dangerous and severe personality disorder (DSPD) units provide services in prison or health settings for those who are dangerous to the public as a result of personality disorders.

The dangerous and severe personality disorder (DSPD) programme came about as a result of a commitment in the 2001 *Labour Manifesto* to set up a pilot service in response to acute public concern about the most serious violent and sexual crimes. The concern focused on dangerous people who were not diagnosed with a treatable mental illness and so could not be detained under the Mental Health Act.

The first DSPD unit was established at Whitemoor Prison in 2000. The governance of the national programme is now located in the Health Partnerships Directorate (jointly funded by the Home Office and Department of Health). Further high-secure units are now operational at Frankland Prison, Broadmoor Hospital and Rampton Hospital. Medium and low-secure units and community services are also up and running on a pilot basis within the NHS. There are further plans to establish services in lower-security prisons in order to provide progression pathways within the prison system for those who have completed treatment in high-secure units.

Service delivery is controlled by a national *Planning and Delivery Guide*, ensuring consistency across the services (DSPD Programme 2005). A rigorous assessment process determines whether referred offenders meet the criteria, which are threefold: there must be evidence of dangerousness in past offending behaviour; complex personality disorder (PD); and a functional link between the PD and the offending behaviour. Because there is no clear evidence base for what reduces the risk of offending in this group, each service develops its own treatment model, within the national parameters. The models vary between cognitive-behavioural approaches, using established manualized programmes, and more holistic strategies which incorporate attention to emotional factors and past experiences, especially trauma in early life.

At a time when the understanding of personality disorder itself is developing and involves controversy among experts, much emphasis is placed on evaluation and research. Because measuring reoffending will only be possible in the long term, an evaluation has been commissioned that will apply various measures of personal change and risk reduction. Another major part of the programme is to establish a common data set providing information about the offender group.

Policymakers stress that this is a pilot programme. However, because of the resources involved, it would take considerable political will to expand it to a mainstream service. It is estimated that 2,000–2,500 offenders currently in prison meet the criteria for admission, and current provision supports a maximum of 300 high-secure beds. The implementation of the service has still to reach that total, chiefly because of challenges in recruiting the right staff and of developing a safe environment for a population whose behaviours are unstable. For many people diagnosed with DSPD, their exclusion from services as 'untreatable' has often stood proxy for the perception that they are unmanageable.

*Martin Kettle*

## Related entries

*Dangerousness; Life-sentence prisoners; Mental health; Reoffending; Risk; Sentence planning; Sentencing policy.*

**Key texts and sources**

DSPD Programme (2005) *Dangerous and Severe Personality Disorder (DSPD) High Secure Services for Men: Planning and Delivery Guide.* London: Department of Health, Home Office and HM Prison Service.
Details of the DSPD Programme's current evaluation can be found at http://www.dspdprogramme.gov.uk/pages/research/research1.php. See also http://www.dspdprogramme.gov.uk/home_flashindex.php.

# DANGEROUSNESS

Dangerousness is a label given to certain violent and sexual offenders. If offenders are deemed 'dangerous', it can mean they are imprisoned for longer than is commensurate with their original offence.

## Defining 'dangerousness'

There is no crime of 'dangerousness' in England and Wales, yet offenders can be indirectly punished if they fall into this category. The law considers dangerousness to be a pathological attribute of character: 'a propensity to inflict harm on others in disregard or defiance of the usual social and legal constraints' (Floud and Young 1981: 20). Very few offenders, however, are dangerous all the time, and some may never be again, so it should not be considered a character trait. Although we have a commonsense understanding of dangerousness, professionals in the criminal justice and mental health systems are still yet to reach a consensus on a workable definition, which is a crucial issue to confront when sentencing. The practical and technical problems in predicting and deciding who is dangerous and who should go to prison are also of key concern, as is the role that politics plays in such a decision.

The concept of dangerousness, specifically in relation to dangerous offenders, is not anything new. Indeed, dangerousness was of concern to people in pre-modern society. Although the term 'dangerousness' has remained, what constitutes dangerousness and what is regarded as dangerous, shifted throughout the nineteenth and twentieth centuries. It is a relative concept, informed by public attitudes and values to crime and punishment, as well as being shaped by a series of laws introduced to govern the dangerous.

## The legislative framework

It is this so-called dangerousness legislation that gives the courts extended powers to deal with those deemed 'dangerous'. For example, protective sentences can be imposed under a number of provisions, which include s. 80(2)(b) of the Powers of Criminal Courts (Sentencing) Act 2000 (formerly s. 2(2)(b) of the Criminal Justice Act 1991) by which courts may extend the 'normal sentence' that may be appropriate for a serious 'violent' or 'sexual' offence if of the opinion that only such a sentence would be adequate to protect the public from 'serious harm' from the offender. The prospective harm must be of a grave nature, and s. 31(3) of the Criminal Justice Act 1991 further provides that 'serious harm' for the purposes of these sections means 'protecting members of the public from death or serious personal injury, whether physical or psychological, occasioned by further such offences committed by [the defendant]'. Section 109 of the Powers of Criminal Courts (Sentencing) Act 2000 also provides for automatic life sentences for offenders who commit a second 'serious offence'. 'Extended sentences' are further used under s. 85 of the Powers of Criminal Courts (Sentencing) Act 2000, as well as discretionary life sentences. The Criminal Justice Act 2003 has, however, recently repealed the provisions of the Powers of Criminal Courts (Sentencing) Act 2000. But because the new provisions only came into force on 4 April 2005, the old provisions still apply to relevant offences committed before that date. Routinely, dangerous people who have committed an offence have been dealt with in one of the aforementioned ways, while individuals in need of treatment have been processed through the mental health system. There is, however, one other category that has emerged – that of the dangerous person with a severe personality disorder (DSPD) who is untreatable and can also be subject to indeterminate sentencing (McAlinden 2001). The criteria laid out in the legislation still leave unanswered questions, such as how likely and how serious the predicted harm must be before it is justifiable to lengthen a prison sentence beyond its proportionate term, and how prospective psychological harm should be interpreted (Ashworth 2004).

### Predicting risk

The archetypal dangerous offender may be a violent and sexual one, but deciding who is 'dangerous' is far from straightforward. It is a judgement made by predictions of an offender's future dangerousness, based on probabilities by looking at his or her past behaviour, personal characteristics and social situation. The decision ultimately rests with the judiciary who are required to weigh (often) complex medical evidence regarding predicted behaviour with conventional legal factors. The accuracy of this prediction is key to consideration of the sentence the offender receives.

The prediction of human behaviour can never be 100 per cent accurate, but recent literature suggests that, in certain situations, clinicians *can* accurately predict dangerousness using both clinical and actuarial assessment. Clinical assessments are those that take place in a controlled setting. The clinician has full access to records of the individual's behaviour, and these can be assessed without any personal interaction between the clinician and the individual in question. Actuarial predictions are less subjective and are based on analyses of statistics, compiled from a series of previous offenders, to determine the actuarial or statistical class to which the offender in question belongs and, from this, to determine the offender's suitability for imprisonment or release.

The biggest concern of critics of dangerousness is what is called a 'false positive' – someone who, it is falsely predicted, will be violent if released when in fact he or she would not be.

Society's media-fuelled fear of 'false negatives', however, ensures public opinion is firmly in favour of imprisoning dangerous offenders for extended periods of time, in an effort to keep them off the streets. A 'false negative' is an offender who is released from prison and is falsely predicted will not be violent but goes on to commit further violent acts. Despite the media-orchestrated hype surrounding false negatives, it is likely that there are far more false positives who remain in custody and who simply do not enter into the public conscience. It is therefore understandable that clinicians and those on parole boards tend to err on the side of caution when assessing and predicting 'dangerousness', because the consequences of a false judgement have a differential impact – 'false negatives' may produce an inquiry, while 'false positives' may simply contribute to a bottleneck in the system with no individual blame attached.

As well as the problems that dangerousness presents legislators with on a practical level, it is an ethically provocative concept. It is not surprising that extended prison sentences are met with public approval, but it should be remembered that the principles of proportionality ('just deserts') and offender's civil liberties are being compromised in a populist punitive climate of punishment. This changing conception of punishment gives great weighting to public protection and victims' rights. This, combined with an increasing societal dissatisfaction with the perceived leniency of the punishment of 'dangerous' offenders, has seen an increase in the use of prisons, in spite of the availability of more non-custodial sentences. The direct sufferer is the offender, who may spend more time than is necessary in prison, but the indirect sufferer is the community, who have to spend more money than is necessary on imprisonment. It would seem that offenders are being punished for the risk they pose rather than simply matching the punishment to the crime, although it is an oversimplification to say that people are being punished for crimes they have not committed. This can be viewed as a responsible step for the criminal justice system to take: the fundamental justification for having such a system is, after all, to protect citizens from harm to their person and property inflicted unjustifiably by others. On the other hand, the preventative confinement of dangerous offenders is shown to have little impact on crime rates and is therefore only of marginal value as a protective device. The imprisonment of dangerous offenders is superficially attractive, and it is possible to say there is a distinct lack of interest in evidence that does not fit with the political mood.

### Public perceptions

The symbolic value of labelling offenders 'dangerous' should not, however, be underestimated. Courts rarely impose protective sentences: it is their mere existence that holds symbolic value. Singling out certain kinds of conduct as dangerous is essentially a political process. Being seen as tough on dangerous offenders is an electoral vote-winning strategy. There is little disputing the importance of public protection in cases of vivid danger, but it is perhaps an exaggerated demand from a misinformed and misdirected public.

There is no perfect balance with the punishment of dangerous offenders – imprisonment certainly raises more questions than it answers. It is an ethically ambiguous concept. Even if dangerousness could be easily defined and accurately predicted, is it justifiable to deny someone his or her freedom based on an assessment of his or her past behaviour to predict his or her future behaviour patterns? The use of extended and indeterminate sentencing for dangerous offenders has undoubtedly caused critics to highlight such concerns but, at the same time, increased punishment has attracted significantly more support from the media and the public as a result of their scaremongering.

*Sophie Holmes and Keith Soothill*

### Related entries

*Dangerous and severe personality disorder (DSPD); Just deserts; Public perceptions; Risk; Sentencing policy; Sex offenders.*

**Key texts and sources**

Ashworth, A. (2004) 'Criminal Justice Act 2003. Part 2. Criminal justice reform – principles, human rights and public protection', *Criminal Law Review*, July: 516–32.

Bottoms, A.E. (1977) 'Reflections on the renaissance of dangerousness', *Howard Journal of Penology and Crime Prevention*, 16: 70–96.

Brown, M. and Pratt, J. (eds) (2000) *Dangerous Offenders: Punishment and Social Order*. London: Routledge.

Floud, J. and Young, W. (1981) *Dangerousness and Criminal Justice*. London: Heinemann.

McAlinden, A. (2001) 'Indeterminate sentences for the severely personality disordered', *Criminal Law Review*, February: 108–23.

Walker, N. (1983) 'Protecting people', in J.W. Hinton (ed.) *Dangerousness: Problems of Assessment and Prediction*. London: George Allen & Unwin.

## DEATH PENALTY

Otherwise known as capital punishment, the death penalty was abolished in the UK in 1965 and replaced with the mandatory life sentence. Although still relatively common in some parts of the world, the only Western democracy to retain the death penalty is the USA.

### The USA's attachment to capital punishment

The USA is the capital of capital punishment in the Western world. The death penalty is common in some parts of the world and is particularly prevalent among non-democratic, totalitarian nations like China, where executions are often public and are counted in the thousands each year. In contrast, European countries, including England, France and Spain, abolished the death penalty in the middle of the last century. For the current generation of English and continental Europeans, the death penalty is but a distant memory.

Not so in the USA. Since 1977, with the well publicized execution by firing squad of Gary Gilmore, more than 1,000 prisoners have been executed. Another 3,300 prisoners sit on death rows awaiting execution in the 38 US states that have the death penalty. Executions occur with some regularity in the USA, but the number of executions and capital convictions has been dropping off in recent years. The major reason for these declines is thought to be a growing concern about wrongful convictions or miscarriages of justice and the possibility of executing an innocent man or woman. These concerns are quite plausible. Since 1973, more than 120 prisoners have had their death sentences vacated, primarily as a result of DNA testing. Examination of these cases suggests many faults and frailties in the justice system. For example, the limits of eye witness testimony have become apparent. Many of the exonerated were identified by eye witnesses who confidently testified against them in open court. Several condemned offenders made false confessions that were the product of the individual's mental disabilities or extreme duress. Prosecutorial or law enforcement misconduct, reliance on faulty science and informant or 'snitch' testimony were also prevalent sources of error in wrongful conviction cases. In the light of these systemic flaws, Americans have found it harder and harder to rally behind the ultimate sanction in recent years.

In addition to growing concerns over wrongful convictions and the possibility of executing an innocent person, a myriad of other concerns has influenced popular opinion about the death penalty. The race of the homicide victim has proven to be a potent predictor of capital punishment. Offenders who kill white victims – and especially black offenders who kill white victims – have a much greater likelihood of being charged, convicted and put to death for a capital murder. There is, as well, a growing concern about the quality of representation afforded to indigent individuals charged with capital crimes and the ways in which the quality of legal representation can affect the likelihood of wrongful or arbitrary convictions in capital cases. Recent Supreme Court rulings prohibiting the execution of vulnerable groups – persons with mental retardation and juveniles – have also given citizens pause. Surely offenders in these groups have been executed in the past? Will we one day discover new groups that should be, but have not been, spared the death penalty?

## Botched executions

In the last decade, the limits of execution technology have raised concerns about the humaneness of modern executions and this, too, may have affected the number of executions carried out across the country. Until the mid-1990s, most Americans believed that electrocutions were quick and painless and thus humane. Execution teams, as it happens, pride themselves on quick and painless killings, which they take to be the essence of humane executions. Several botched executions, including one in which a man's head appeared to be engulfed in flames (due to a defective sponge in the execution cap) and another in which a nosebleed of considerable proportions covered the man's chest in blood, have dampened public enthusiasm for electrocutions (Greer 2006). Inmates in states that used the electric chair filed appeals challenging the constitutionality of electrocution as a method of executions. Before the Supreme Court ruled on the issue, however, states shifted to lethal injection as their primary or secondary method of execution.

Lethal injection is the main method of execution in the USA. This method, unlike electrocutions, has the benefit of *looking* both tame and painless. Recent studies indicate that appearances might be deceiving, however, and that lethal injections may in fact be excruciatingly painful. The problem with lethal injection lies in the combination of drugs. At present, the 'drug cocktail' comprises a painkiller, a paralytic and a drug to stop the heart. If the mixture of drugs administered to the offender does not include a sufficient dose of the anaesthetic, the condemned man or woman will consciously choke to death but, as a result of the paralytic drug, will be unable to move or speak. A person dying in the throes of agony may seem to experience a peaceful and even serene death as the result of an ostensibly humane method of execution.

Concerns about the drug cocktail and the prospect of excruciating pain have resulted in delays of executions in several states, most recently in California, Florida and Maryland. In all likelihood, the courts will order the various states to fix this problem (the problem with lethal injection is seen as a technical problem, not a constitutional problem) and executions will resume. But it is unlikely that executions by lethal injection will ever again be seen as uniquely humane.

### Life without parole: still a death penalty?

Against this backdrop of concern about humane methods, it is important to note that life without parole has emerged in the USA as a viable alternative to the death penalty. Life without parole is sometimes called a 'true life sentence' because offenders are sentenced to spend the remainder of their natural lives in prison. A better term for this sentence might be 'death by incarceration', since these persons are, in effect, sentenced to die in prison. Life without the possibility of parole can thus be thought of as the USA's 'other death penalty'.

Public support for the death penalty drops dramatically when life without parole is offered as an alternative. In some polls, Americans actually prefer life without parole rather than the death penalty (in fact, the most recent study showed that Kentuckians preferred life without parole over the death penalty by a wide margin). Similarly, conviction rates in capital cases fall when life without parole is an option for the jury to consider. This suggests that, at bottom, support for the death penalty in the USA hinges on incapacitation. Americans want to be assured that the man or woman they are about to sentence for aggravated murder will never again set foot in the free world.

The growing appeal of life without parole may reflect that fact that this sanction is a species of death penalty. Unfortunately, death by incarceration is a sanction that is meted out to a wide range of offenders in the USA, not simply capital murderers. Some recidivists, especially under 'three-strikes' and other mandatory sentencing laws, and some drug offenders, are eligible for life without parole. Similarly, any homicide and many major felonies are eligible for this sanction. Even juveniles, no longer subject to the death penalty in the USA, can be sentenced to life without parole. At the time of writing, over 2,000 teenagers live in US prisons under the sentence of death by incarceration. Over 33,000 prison-

ers, overall, are serving life without parole in US prisons. The death penalty may one day be abolished in the USA or languish from lack of use, but harsh penal sanctions (such as life without parole) promise to be robust and enduring features of the US justice system.

*Robert Johnson and Jennifer DiCastro*

### Related entries

*Abolitionism; Dangerousness; Life-sentence prisoners; Miscarriages of justice; Parole; Security.*

---

**Key texts and sources**

Greer, C. (2006) 'Delivering death: capital punishment, botched executions and the American press', in P. Mason (ed.) *Captured by the Media: Prison Discourse in Popular Culture.* Cullompton: Willan Publishing.

Johnson, R. (1998) *Death Work: A Study of the Modern Execution Process.* New York, NY: Wadsworth.

Details of the Innocence Project's 'Causes and remedies of wrongful convictions' are available online at **http://www.innocenceproject.org/causes/index. php**. The Constitution Project's document, *Mandatory Justice Revisited*, is available online at **http://www.constitutionproject.org/pdf/ MandatoryJusticeRevisited.pdf**. The Death Penalty Information Center document, *Capital Punishment in Context: A Resource for College Courses*, can be found at **www.capitalpunishmentincontext.org**.

See also the following websites: Death Penalty Info (**http://www.deathpenaltyinfo.org/**); Amnesty International (death penalty) (**http://web.amnesty. org/pages/deathpenalty-index-eng**); and FCO (**http://www.fco.gov.uk/servlet/Front?pagename= OpenMarket/Xcelerate/ShowPage&c=Page&cid= 1065715424996**).

---

## DEATHS IN CUSTODY

In any given year, a number of prisoners will die while in custody. The cause of their death can range from suicide, old age and illness to murder.

While suicide in prison custody has long been the subject of academic and pressure group interest, both in the UK and abroad, there is a growing awareness that, especially as the prison population continues to rise, prisoners can die in a variety of circumstances while in custody. For example, as increasing numbers of elderly people are being incarcerated, the number of older prisoners who die while in custody has increased dramatically. Wilson (2005), for example, using materials provided in response to parliamentary questions from Sandra Gidley, the Liberal Democrat spokesperson for older people, was able to show that, between 1997 and 2003, 10 per cent of those who died in prison custody were aged 65 or over, and that, in 2001, 15 per cent of all those who died were aged 65 or over, despite the fact that this age group only made up 2 per cent of the prison population (see also Crawley 2007).

In trying to make sense of these figures it is important to remember that many elderly prisoners will have long-standing health issues. For example, a thematic review by HM Chief Inspectorate of Prisons in 2004 about the needs of elderly prisoners demonstrated that more than 80 per cent of older prisoners have a long-standing chronic illness or disability, and, of these, more than a third suffer from a cardiovascular disease and more than a fifth from respiratory disease. Overall, the inspectorate concluded that the health of older prisoners is worse than that of their peers in the community (HM Chief Inspector of Prisons 2004). As Wilson (2005: 109) points out, all this 'underscores the need for there to be good health care provision for this age group after they have been incarcerated'. None the less, Stuart Ware, the 67-year-old former prisoner who co-founded the self-help group for older prisoners called Pacer 50Plus, described healthcare provision for the elderly in prison as a 'lottery' (cited in Wilson 2005: 111).

The culture and organization of prisons do not make it easy to establish empirical data about the causes or the extent of deaths in prison custody. For example, in trying to uncover the circumstances of the death of their son, Christopher Edwards, at Chelmsford Prison in November 1994, Paul Edwards, Christopher's father, had to work in partnership with the campaigning organization *Liberty* to take matters to the European Court of Human Rights (ECtHR) to discover the truth. In a landmark judgment in July 2002, the ECtHR ruled that the UK had breached the European Convention on Human Rights on four counts relating to the death of Christopher. As Paul Edwards commented: 'the police and the prison were protecting themselves. You cannot imagine the litany of lies, misinformation and stonewalling' (cited in Wilson 2005: 73). Of note, the campaigning organization *Inquest* now compiles annual statistics about the range of deaths in custody, broken into categories such as 'self-inflicted deaths', 'non-self-inflicted deaths', 'homicide' and deaths 'awaiting classification'.

There has been relatively little academic or popular interest in the number of homicides in custody each year, although this has changed of late, especially in the light of the inquiry and publication of the final report of the Mubarek Inquiry into the racist murder of Zahid Mubarek at Feltham Young Offender Institution in March 2000 (Keith 2006). So, too, has there been growing Home Office interest in this subject (see, for example, Sattar 2001), and from academics (see, for example, Wilson 2005). Indeed, Wilson suggests that, when looking at figures from 1998, 'you were ten times more likely to be murdered in jail than in the community' (2005: 76).

While there is now growing policy, academic and pressure group interest in this area, there has as yet been little investigation into the causes of why so many people suddenly die after release from prison custody, often in 'approved probation hostels'. Yet figures released from the National Probation Service – prior to the development of the National Offender Management Service (NOMS) – showed that, between 1998 and 2002, 87 people died in probation hostels, often in the first few weeks after their release from prison (cited in Wilson 2005: 39).

*David Wilson*

### Related entries

*Ageing prisoners; Homicide in prison; Mubarek Inquiry; Self-harm; Suicide in prison.*

**Key texts and sources**

Crawley, E. (2007) 'Imprisonment in old age', in Y. Jewkes (ed.) *Handbook on Prisons*. Cullompton: Willan Publishing.

HM Chief Inspector of Prisons (2004) '*No Problems – Old and Quiet*': *Older Prisoners in England and Wales*. London: HM Inspectorate of Prisons.

Keith, Justice (2006) *The Report of the Zahid Mubarek Inquiry*. London: HMSO.

Sattar, G. (2001) *Rates and Causes of Death among Prisoners and Offenders under Community Supervision*. *Home Office Research Study* 231. London: Home Office.

Wilson, D. (2005) *Death at the Hands of the State*. London: Howard League for Penal Reform.

The UK Parliament's Joint Committee on Human Rights' third report (2004) (deaths in custody) can be found at http://www.publications.parliament.uk/pa/jt200405/jtselect/jtrights/15/1502.htm.

# DECENCY

The 'decency agenda' was launched by the Prison Service in 2002 and is the latest incarnation of the policy to humanize prisons. This particular incarnation is distinguished, however, by the development of a tool to provide quantitative measurement of decency in prisons.

At the 2002 Prison Service conference, then Deputy Director General, Phil Wheatley, set out the test for decency in prisons. In brief, this comprises no punishment outside the rules; standards delivered; clean and properly equipped facilities; prompt attention to concerns; protection from harm; actively filled time; and fair and consistent treatment (cited in Coyle 2003: 27–8). Wheatley went on to suggest that an overarching test of decency of a particular prison was whether or not the staff would be happy with their relatives being held there.

Of course, commitment to providing humane prison regimes has long been a feature of prison reform. The development of this particular aspect of morality became increasingly important following the publication of the Woolf Report after the widespread and serious prison riots of 1990. This report particularly emphasized the need for prisons to be humane and to ensure that justice was kept in balance with security and order, and control. The Woolf Report has often been credited with achieving significant progress in improving prison conditions and facilities for prisoners. The observance of prisoners' human rights and the improvement of prison conditions have also been an area where organizations such as HM Inspectorate of Prisons and the European Committee for the Prevention of Torture have a formal role, and the introduction of the Human Rights Act 1998 provides both legal remedy and a general duty for state institutions to observe individual rights.

However, the second half of the 1990s saw a reassertion of the primacy of security after the high-profile escapes from Whitemoor and Parkhurst Prisons. It was against this background that a series of scandals occurred, including the conviction of staff at Wormwood Scrubs Prison for the abuse of prisoners, highly critical inspectorate reports at Wandsworth Prison and Feltham Young Offender Institution, and the racist murder of Zahid Mubarek at Feltham. This led then Director General, Martin Narey, to state at the 2001 Prison Service conference that: 'I am not prepared to continue to apologise for failing prison after failing prison. I have had enough of trying to explain the very immorality of our treatment of some prisoners and the degradation of some establishments' (cited in Liebling assisted by Arnold 2004: inside cover).

These events marked the need for a rebalancing of priorities, and an increase in the attention given to the treatment of prisoners and respect for their individual rights. This was the aim of the decency agenda at its launch. The period following the Woolf Report had also seen the rise of the techniques of new public management, including a greater emphasis on performance measurement. It was perhaps not surprising that thoughts turned to how the concept of decency in prisons could be made measurable.

A tool for Measuring the Quality of Prison Life (MQPL) was introduced in 2001 and resulted in a measure of prisoners' experiences covering relationship dimensions (respect, humanity, relationships, trust, support) and regime dimensions (fairness, order, safety, well-being, personal development, family contact, decency) in order to provide a more holistic assessment of prison performance (Liebling assisted by Arnold 2004). By 2004, this had become a functioning tool, routinely being carried out in each prison once every two years as part of the Prison Service standards audit assessment. The attempt to merge humanity and performance management is perhaps one feature that distinguishes the decency agenda from other reform movements aimed at humanizing prisons, particularly as prisoners have such a direct role in assessing the prison's performance.

The decency agenda and MQPL have been criticized as legitimizing prisons (Wilson 2005), so misleading the public to consider them wrongly to be positive and constructive places and encouraging their greater use. However, there is a counter-argument that, on pragmatic grounds, prisons are not about to disappear, so there is a need to ameliorate their most damaging effects (Liebling and Maruna 2005).

Decency, therefore, is the latest incarnation of the policy of humanizing prisons. What perhaps marks this as different is the fact that it is being developed within the framework of new public management and it is, therefore, deploying quantitative measures, but is doing so in a way that directly involves prisoners.

*Jamie Bennett*

### Related entries

*Audit; Deprivations/'pains of imprisonment'; Fairness; HM Inspectorate of Prisons; Human rights; Legitimacy; Measuring the Quality of Prison Life (MQPL); Morality; Mubarek Inquiry; New public management (NPM); Woolf Report.*

**Key texts and sources**

Coyle, A. (2003) *Humanity in Prisons: Questions of Definition and Audit.* London: International Centre for Prison Studies.

Liebling, A., assisted by Arnold, H. (2004) *Prisons and their Moral Performance: A Study of Values, Quality and Prison Life.* Oxford: Oxford University Press.

Liebling, A. and Maruna, S. (2005) 'Introduction: the effects of imprisonment revisited', in A. Liebling and S. Maruna (eds) *The Effects of Imprisonment.* Cullompton: Willan Publishing.

Wilson, D. (2005) 'Book review: Alison Liebling, assisted by Helen Arnold (2004), *Prisons and their Moral Performance: A Study of Values, Quality, and Prison Life,* Oxford: Oxford University Press, Michael Tonry (ed) (2004), *The Future of Imprisonment,* Oxford: Oxford University Press', *Howard Journal,* 44: 229–31.

## DEPRIVATIONS/'PAINS OF IMPRISONMENT'

Sykes (1958) was the first to use the phrase 'pains of imprisonment' when he identified five areas in which prisoners experience distress as a result of their confinement: 1) the deprivation of liberty; 2) the deprivation of goods and services; 3) the deprivation of heterosexual relationships; 4) the deprivation of autonomy; and 5) the deprivation of security. The phrase has since been used extensively in theoretical and empirical studies of prison life.

The pains of imprisonment were first identified by Gresham Sykes (1958) in *The Society of Captives: A Study of a Maximum Security Prison.* Sykes argues that, although the modern pains of imprisonment might be a humane alternative to the physical torture and neglect which characterized pre-modern forms of punishment, they could be just as painful and as deeply felt as those which are directed at the body. Sykes identified five 'deprivations' of imprisonment, which he asserted were the most prevalent causes of distress and pain among prison inmates.

The 'deprivation of liberty', Sykes argues, exacts a two-fold punishment on inmates. First, prisoners are removed from free society and sent to carry out the term of their sentence in prison. As a result, prisoners lose both their physical freedom and their status as trusted members of society. Alongside this symbolic rejection, prisoners are confined and restricted by the rules, regulations and regime of prison life.

Whether or not the 'deprivation of goods and services' is seen as a deliberate aspect of the punishment associated with a prison sentence, the experience of losing access to goods and services is a painful one for the average inmate. Further, Sykes argues, the deprivation of material possessions affects an individual's self-image because in Western society (particularly) a man's self worth is often associated with his 'control and possession of the material environment' (1958: 69). The restriction or complete prohibition on possessions for prisoners, then, is painful both because prisoners have limited access to desired material goods and because they lose a certain pride of ownership that comes with acquiring personal possessions.

The 'deprivation of heterosexual relationships' is a pain of imprisonment acutely felt by prisoners, especially those serving lengthy sentences. As Sykes noted, many Westernized countries do not provide prisoners with the privilege of conjugal visits. There are both physiological and psychological problems and pains associated with the denial of intimate relationships between prisoners and their spouses or partners. Sykes also suggests that there are implications for a prisoner's self-confidence, gender identity (i.e. masculinity) and self-concept.

The 'deprivation of autonomy' relates to the loss prisoners experience as a result of the dependence created by the experience of imprisonment. Prisoners lose their ability to make their own decisions and choices and they must obey the rules and instructions of their warders. Prisoners, according to Sykes, feel frustrated by the reach of decisions made on their behalf by prison staff. That is, there are few areas of a prisoner's life over which prison staff do not have power and authority. In addition, the apparent arbitrariness of some of the decisions of staff or prison managers and the lack of justification for those decisions are sources of

aggravation for prisoners. Prisoners become dependent on staff and on the procedures and routines of prison life, and feel weak and helpless that they no longer have control over their lives. This, in turn, threatens the prisoner's self-image and feelings of self-efficacy.

Finally, Sykes argues that one of the primary pains of imprisonment is related to the 'deprivation of security'. Prisoners are subject to prolonged exposure to the company of men who may be violent, mentally ill or who, for a variety of reasons, might be threatening or aggressive. Prisoners cannot achieve a sense of security while living among men who, by the virtue of their circumstances, might be less likely than other men to obey the rules and conform to the norms of society. Further, Sykes suggests, the nature of inmate culture often requires men to 'prove themselves'. Prisoners, therefore, live in an unstable environment where they fear for their physical safety and harbour concerns about how they might be perceived if and when they are challenged by a fellow inmate.

Sykes argues that it is important to recognize the pains of imprisonment for what they are, but further states that they can be identified as the basis of a system of action among inmates. That is, prisoners develop particular cultural norms – the inmate code – that help to alleviate the pains and pressures caused by the deprivations of prison life. Sykes's description of the pains of imprisonment continues to be highly relevant to contemporary prisons. Not least, it emphasizes the profound deprivations beyond the loss of liberty that imprisonment entails. It is clear, however, that these pains and deprivations are not experienced homogeneously. Some prisons produce more pain than others, and incarceration is more painful for some prisoners than for others (Liebling assisted by Arnold 2004). The specific pains that prisoners experience depend not only on the intrinsic deprivations of prison life and the ways that particular institutions seek to address them, but also on the different needs and preoccupations that prisoners carry into the penal environment. Thus, there are significant differences between the primary pains experienced by male and female prisoners, with the latter finding their separation from children and intimate others, (and the possibility of being infertile by the time they are released) particularly painful aspects of imprisonment. Women in prison also exhibit greater concern than men about issues of privacy, personal health and bodily autonomy. These pains not only reflect the gendered concerns that they import into prison but also the nature of women's regimes, which are more petty and infantilizing than men's prisons.

Sykes's concern was to document the *intrinsic* pains of prison life – those that appeared to be the unavoidable outcomes of detaining people outside the normal bounds of society. Other pains may be the result of 'institutional thoughtlessness' (Crawley 2005). Thus, the elderly and disabled may experience imprisonment as particularly painful because the system is simply not geared up to recognize or cater for their specific needs. Elsewhere, pain may be inflicted on prisoners in more deliberate ways – either through regimes in which humiliation and material deprivation are integral parts of the sentence or through those illicit acts of brutality and indifference that appear endemic in many penal systems. Meanwhile, as the nature and mechanisms of imprisonment change, so too do the sources of pain and frustration. Thus, in the current UK prison system, prisoners frequently complain that they are expected to take responsibility for their own carceral management, and that everyday prison life has become psychologically oppressive and opaque.

The recognition that imprisonment (either intentionally or unintentionally) is a painful experience for prisoners has spurred numerous further considerations of this topic. These have looked at such areas as stress, coping and adaptation among prisoners (e.g. Zamble and Porporino 1988), specific difficulties of long-term imprisonment (e.g. Flanagan 1995) and the overall effects of imprisonment (e.g. Liebling and Maruna 2005).

*Deb Drake and Ben Crewe*

### Related entries

*Ageing prisoners; Disability; Homosexuality in prison; Identity and self; Inmate code; Masculinity; Solidarity; Subcultures; Women in prison.*

### Key texts and sources

Crawley, E. (2005) 'Institutional thoughtlessness in prisons and its impacts on the day-to-day prison', *Journal of Contemporary Criminal Justice*, 21: 350–63.

Flanagan, T.J. (ed.) (1995) *Long-term Imprisonment: Policy, Science, and Correctional Practice.* Thousand Oaks, CA: Sage.

Liebling, A., assisted by Arnold, H. (2004) *Prisons and their Moral Performance.* Oxford: Clarendon Press.

Liebling, A. and Maruna, S. (eds) (2005) *The Effects of Imprisonment.* Cullompton: Willan Publishing.

Sykes, G. (1958) *The Society of Captives: A Study of a Maximum Security Prison.* Princeton, NJ: Princeton University Press.

Zamble, E. and Porporino, F.J. (1988) *Coping, Behavior and Adaptation in Prison Inmates.* New York, NY: Springer.

## DESISTANCE

Desistance describes the avoidance of offending by those who have offended in the past. The study of desistance essentially asks why people stop offending.

To desist from something is to cease acting or behaving in a particular way or to refrain from continuing some particular action. As such, to desist from offending is defined as ceasing to offend. This pithy definition brings with it some not inconsiderable problems. These include: for how long does an individual have to have not offended in order for his or her desistance to be meaningful (one-off transgressors are of little interest to those studying desistance)?; and how long does an individual need to have not offended for before one can declare him or her to have desisted rather than just undergone a temporary lull? Are we expecting ex-offenders to become angels, or merely to reduce their offending to the same level as the rest of the population? How does one define desistance, given that it is the *repeated absence* of an event rather than the emergence of a more easily measured state (Farrall and Calverley 2006)?

Despite these terminological problems, the study of desistance has grown dramatically since the 1970s. The origins of desistance can be traced back to the 1930s, but the ball really got rolling in the 1970s with the initiation of a series of longitudinal studies of offending over the life course. From the 1980s, authors involved in these studies and other researchers studying desistance using qualitative data started to publish their findings. By the 1990s the publications were starting to become both more frequent and more developed (for example, see O'Brien 2001; Maruna and Immarigeon 2004).

Unlike, for example, the 'what works' movement, which starts with the research question 'what is the impact of what we do on rates of recidivism?', desistance research asks 'why do people stop offending?' This leads to a further question, namely, 'what can the criminal justice system do to assist (or at least not disrupt) these processes?' Studies of desistance score over the general 'what works' movement in a number of important ways. By exploring why people stop offending we are better able to understand the whole range of reasons why people cease committing crime, rather than being limited to focusing just on what officers of the criminal justice system can do. This more holistic approach helps to locate desistance as not just an individual decision but as a set of processes that are mediated by important social institutions (such as employment, educational institutions, the family, political engagement and peer relations) and also the role of these within the life course of individuals. A consideration of the role of social institutions and the individual offender's relationship with these at key points in his or her life also emphasizes to us the importance of understanding how these institutions operate and how they might be harnessed to assist desistance (McNeill 2006). That these institutions are also key elements of state-of-the-art explanations of patterns of offending over the life course suggests that the processes identified by those researching desistance are not at odds with more developed accounts of why people become engaged in crime over the life course.

The message from studies of desistance with regards to imprisonment is not a particularly optimistic one. Despite the view that prison offers people a chance to think about what they have done and to 'straighten out', prison appears to do more harm than good. Many studies have suggested that imprisonment achieves all the following for those men and women who are imprisoned, all of which are likely to reduce the chances of desistance, not increase them:

- A loss of custody or access to children, or at best having relationships severed or damaged.
- A loss of the 'web of connections' which reinforces non-criminal values and encourages the adoption of values and knowledge which make offending easier and more likely.
- The loss of accommodation.
- The loss of employment and therefore the income which may be used to support a partner and children.
- The acquiring of the stigma of 'ex-prisoner' and the attendant implications which this has for employment.

Regardless of whether one thinks that prisons ought to provide ex-inmates with greater resources or not, it is clear that the experience of imprisonment is far from being the Benthamite desire for reflection on one's sins and the acquiring of a determination to cease offending. Prison is not a sensible way of encouraging desistance. Imprisonment, even for quite short periods, has the potential to disrupt family relationships and employment patterns and opportunities, creates feelings of being 'held back' and can act as a breeding ground for future criminality. On release, many prisoners will experience a reduction in their resources and, depending on the length of time they have been incarcerated, they may have few memory traces of social rules and norms. In processes associated with the structuring of rules and resources, they may carry with them an 'inmate code' which makes adjustment to release outside even harder. The major impact, therefore, of imprisonment on the desistance process is, arguably, to disrupt the journey of 'going straight'. This is created via the removal of people from structures that favour 'maturation' (such as employment, family and the home). As such, imprisonment suspends the possibility of the benign reproductive processes whereby people's involvement in those structures listed above encourages actions that reduce offending and favour desistance and this, in turn, embeds them further into structures which assist desistance. This is not to suggest that prison ought never to be used but, rather, that our current use of it is far too common and that, in terms of encouraging people to cease offending, other sentence options look more effective in the long term. Unfortunately, since the death of the rehabilitative ideal, prison is increasingly seen as an effective way of managing those men and women who commit crimes in the UK.

*Stephen Farrall*

### Related entries

*Adjusting to release; Alternatives to imprisonment; Effects of imprisonment; Multi-agency public protection arrangements (MAPPAs); Prisonization; Rehabilitation; Reoffending.*

---

**Key texts and sources**

Farrall, S. and Calverley, A. (2006) *Understanding Desistance from Crime: Theoretical Directions in Resettlement and Rehabilitation.* Maidenhead: Open University Press.

Maruna, S. and Immarigeon, R. (eds) (2004) *After Crime and Punishment: Ex-offender Reintegration and Desistance from Crime.* Cullompton: Willan Publishing.

McNeill, F. (2006) 'A desistance paradigm for offender management', *Criminology and Criminal Justice*, 6: 37–60.

O'Brien, P. (2001) *Making It in the 'Free World'.* New York, NY: SUNY.

---

# DETERRENCE

Deterrence is a rationale for sentencing that asserts that punishment can prevent future offending. This may either be on an individual basis, where a tailored sentence leads an offender to calculate that crime does not pay, or a general basis, where severe penalties deter others from committing similar crimes.

Individual deterrence originally arose from the work of utilitarian philosophers such as Jeremy Bentham, who argued that penalties should be set at a level that ensures they outweigh the likely benefits of offending. However, such ideas are based on an assumption that potential offenders are responsible, rational and calculating – an assumption that has been called into question by numerous criminologists. In practical terms, such an approach supports the escalation of penalties for second and subsequent convictions, and also special penal regimes such as the unsuccessful 'short, sharp shock' detention centre experiment of the 1980s (Bottoms 2004).

The issue of general deterrence has been much more widely debated in academic literature due to the potential to support harsh penalties for a wide range of offenders, and also as it is a popular lay argument deployed particularly in relation to the death penalty. This literature largely presents the counter-argument that although there is an intuitive appeal to general deterrence, its effectiveness relies on a complex set of rationalizations. It has been suggested that, in order to be effective, five preconditions would have to be met: the offender would have to be aware that the average severity of punishment for the particular offence had been raised; he or she must take account of this at the time of the incident; he or she must believe there is a non-negligible likelihood of being caught; he or she must believe that the enhanced penalty will be applied to him or her; and he or she must be willing to refrain from the offence in the light of this enhanced penalty (Bottoms 2004).

Empirical evidence on general deterrence is limited, although there is no evidence that changes in the severity of penalties have a causal impact on offending. However, there is evidence to suggest that an increase in the likelihood of detection and conviction does have an impact in reducing crime (Von Hirsch *et al.* 1999). However, despite this evidence, the popular appeal of deterrence as a rationale of sentencing persists.

Deterrence has largely been discounted by academics as an effective approach to sentencing. However, it continues to resonate with politicians and the public as a 'commonsense' approach to sentencing. As a result, discourses of deterrence are likely to continue to be a feature of criminal justice politics.

*Jamie Bennett*

*Related entries*

*Death penalty; Just deserts; New punitiveness; Rehabilitation; Sentencing policy.*

---

**Key texts and sources**

Bottoms, A.E. (2004) 'Empirical research relevant to sentencing frameworks', in A. Bottoms *et al.* (eds) *Alternatives to Prison: Options for an Insecure Society.* Cullompton: Willan Publishing.
Von Hirsch, A., Bottoms, A., Burney, E. and Wikestrom, P.-O. (1999) *Criminal Deterrence and Sentencing Severity: An Analysis of Recent Research.* Oxford: Hart Publishing.

---

# DISABILITY

The Disability Discrimination Acts 1995 and 2005 place an obligation on prisons to ensure that all prisoners are able, with reasonable adjustment, to participate equally in all aspects of prison life.

Due to the rising prison population and the significant increase in older prisoners in custody, there is now believed to be a record number of disabled people in prison. The Disability Discrimination Act (DDA) 1995 defines a disabled person as: 'A person who has a physical, sensory or mental impairment which has a long term and substantial effect on their ability to carry out normal day to day activities.' Disability therefore covers physical, mental and sensory impairments and includes both visible and invisible impairments.

The DDA 1995 applies to HM Prison Service in relation to its work as a service provider (for example, in the provision of offending behaviour programmes, education and work). The Act requires reasonable adjustments to be made to ensure that a disabled prisoner has the same ability as a non-disabled prisoner to access services. The DDA 2005 goes significantly further than the 1995 Act and places specific duties on public bodies. These include ensuring that all policies take into account the needs of disabled prisoners, rather than simply responding reactively to individual prisoner's needs. It also places duties to eliminate harassment and discrimination, and to promote positive attitudes.

Despite a comprehensive legislative framework and set of prison policies, there remains a lack of knowledge about the needs of disabled people in prison and of the facilities that exist to help them. Although all prisons should have a disability liaison officer who acts as a point of contact, many prisoners and staff are unaware of the liaison officer's role and the support he or she can provide. Moreover, disabled prisoners frequently report that they are rarely given equal access to activities, and some complain of poor treatment. Such problems have included a wheelchair-bound prisoner being confined to his cell for 24 hours a day and being left sitting in his urine because of no facilities for him to bathe, and a deaf prisoner missing out on exercise and education due to not hearing shouted instructions. In addition, some disabled prisoners are inappropriately placed on healthcare units rather than on the main wings. Such placements can lead to reduced access to services and can be isolating. Disabled prisoners also report that they have to rely on other prisoners for help as this is not systematically provided by prison staff (Parry 2004).

To date, accurate information on the number of disabled prisoners and the types of needs they have has not been available. Under the DDA 2005 the Prison Service must collate and monitor statistical data. New monitoring systems have been introduced via computerized prisoner records. However, this information is reliant upon a newly arrived prisoner self-reporting disability. For a variety of reasons, a person may not disclose he or she has a disability. Nevertheless, these changes should mean that, in future, information about people with disabilities in prison will be increased.

*Finola Farrant*

*Related entries*

*Ageing prisoners; Education and training; Healthcare; Human rights; In-reach teams; Mental health.*

**Key texts and sources**

Parry, J. (2004) *Prisoners Information Book – for Disabled Prisoners*. London: Prison Reform Trust/Prison Service.
See also http://www.prisonreformtrust.org.uk/subsection.asp?id=249. The Disability Rights Commission website is at http://www.drc-gb.org/.

# DISCIPLINE

Discipline generally refers to control over body or mind, and to training with the aim of physical or mental improvement. Discipline, according to Foucault (1977), is a technology of power which incorporates surveillance and training in order to create law-abiding and conformist individuals.

Discipline generally refers to control over body or mind through external or self-imposed rules and regulations. It also refers to training with the aim of physical or mental improvement. In the prison setting, discipline is used 'to help maintain order, control, discipline and a safe environment' and 'to ensure that the use of authority in the establishment is lawful, reasonable and fair' (HM Prison Service 1995: 5).

In *Discipline and Punish* (1977), Foucault describes, through a historical analysis of penal change during the seventeenth, eighteenth and nineteenth centuries, how the object and exercise of punishment have shifted from the body through external control and force, to the body and 'soul' using both external and internal control to reform the individual. Punishment changed from a purely symbolic demonstration of power by an omnipotent sovereign to a reform process instigated by the state on behalf of its citizens aimed at normalizing an individual back into society. Discipline works through the rigorous control of time, behaviour and, ultimately, thought, and the disciplinary system

imposed in prison is compared with those which can be observed in factories, hospitals and the military (Foucault 1977: 149–62). According to Foucault, individuals were to undergo training to reform them back into 'normal', disciplined citizens. This new conception of discipline as a technology of power emphasized control over the individual who had 'done wrong' rather than control over specific 'risk' groups, such as the poor. The principal object of discipline was thus the 'control of individuals' in order to create conforming citizens (Smart 1983).

Bentham's Panopticon lies at the heart of the disciplinary society, and it has been argued that the spread of everyday surveillance throughout late modern societies – CCTV, credit checks, databases, etc. – supports Foucault's analysis and indicates the dispersal of discipline throughout the penal system, creating a carceral society. However, Foucault's account has been criticized for concentrating solely on imprisonment as a sanction and thus neglecting other important penal developments, such as the rise of the fine, community service and compensation orders, in analysing penal trends. It should be noted that Foucault was more concerned with the analysis of the exercise of power than with penal progress aimed at rehabilitation. Prison simply served as an example through which power could be analysed (Smart 1983: 79). Nevertheless, some penal trends, which clearly also represent the exercise of power by the state towards its citizens, raise further questions about how prevalent discipline as a technology of power is in contemporary society.

*Martina Feilzer*

*Related entries*

*Carceral society; Panopticon; Power; Risk.*

**Key texts and sources**

Foucault, M. (1977) *Discipline and Punish* (trans. A. Sheridan). London: Allen Lane.
HM Prison Service (1995) *Prison Discipline Manual*. London: HM Prison Service.
Smart, B. (1983) 'On discipline and social regulation: a review of Foucault's genealogical analysis', in D. Garland and P. Young (eds) *The Power to Punish*. London: Heinemann Educational.

# DISCRETION

Penal discretion refers to the decision-making processes of penal authorities regarding the privileging of one form of action (or inaction) above a number of other possible actions that could be taken in a particular set of circumstances. This process is structured, with the judgement reflecting the given *extra-legal* social and organizational rules adopted by the decision-maker.

The exercise of discretion in prison can take three different forms: *formal* discretion, when options available are explicit within a given prison rule, order, or other procedural guideline; *provisional* discretion, when decisions are more variable but subject to review and reversal by a more senior official or internal adjudication body; and *ultimate* discretion, which arises when the decision-making process is not subject to internal monitoring or has only restricted external review. Although prison staff normally exercise either formal or provisional discretion, given the inadequate nature of penal accountability, they may have opportunities to exercise ultimate discretion.

The use of discretion has been justified on the grounds that decision-making is always highly subjective: the law is often ambiguous, too rigid or unclear, and its use is inevitable. Liebling and Price (2001: 115) argue that the inevitability of discretion has three sources:

1. *The wording of rules themselves*: words are vague, have no settled meaning or can be reinterpreted in given circumstances.
2. *The situations to which the rules will apply*: no two situations are the same, so the application of the rules requires interpretation within a situational context.
3. *The organization's official purpose*: there may be conflict or confusion between organizational rules and aims, and so a balance must be reached to avoid any contradictions.

Penologists have also defended discretion on the grounds that any further efforts to introduce the rule of law into prison would not only fail to eliminate situational discretionary powers but could also make the life of prisoners even more oppressive than it currently is.

In principle, a number of positive outcomes could be achieved through the exercise of discretion. Discretion can be used as a means to tap into great wisdom or expertise, provide flexibility and facilitate individualized justice through allowing for equity, mercy and positive discrimination. This being said, the actual use of discretion is fraught with the danger of creating profound injustices. Through distancing itself from procedure, standards and specific lines of reasoning, the actual use of discretion may lead to decisions based on inappropriate considerations, carelessness or mistakes. There is nothing inherent within discretionary decision-making that ensures that like cases will be treated alike, or that outcomes will be equal or fair. Indeed, it may even militate against just outcomes. Discretion can also lead to unfavourable treatment of identifiable groups, as there are no checks on decisions being shaped by racial, sexual or other forms of discrimination.

The exercise of discretion has been heavily criticized by those looking to defend prisoners' human rights and legal accountability. For example, the American Friends Service Committee (1971: 129) argued that it is 'hypocritical and insidious to operate with a vague law and to use its vagueness as a screen to conceal the other motives and practices of a discretionary system'. They said that, if left unfettered, discretion can only blunt and twist any principles of justice, leading ultimately to arbitrariness. The merciful aspects of discretion would only be humane for those who 'gain the sympathy of the system or to those who have the power to merit special favour' (American Friends Service Committee 1971: 135). At its worst, penal discretion presents the beholder of office with a licence for abuse of power and corruption.

Discretion is not the unconstrained freedom to choose as advocates claim. Rather, it entails the structuring of decisions based on non-legal criteria, leading to patterned and predictable outcomes. Discretion is not an individual but a *collective* enterprise. The use of discretion will inevitably involve the application of rules, but the rules of discretion are structured through wider social and organizational discourses, with a patterned sequence of decisions, precedents and understandings shaping the 'natural' way of responding to certain situations or problems. The choice is between patterned outcomes based on legal rules and procedures, or other similarly predictable outcomes based on the interpretive frameworks of alternative social and organizational rules.

The nature of social rules may have an implicit or explicit discriminatory rationale, and one that is not open to public scrutiny or accountability. For Baumgartner (1992: 157), the customs, traditions, conventions and routine practices of criminal justice workers find their roots in discretionary practices based on specific categorizations and stereotypes. Social distance, constructions of respectability and social position have consistently informed assessments of the moral character of the offender. These factors provide the context of the social and organizational rules providing the interpretive framework which directs the exercise of penal power. The use of discretion is consequently based on the production and reproduction of these stereotypes, creating patterned discriminatory outcomes. Through this structuring of discretion, penal authorities develop their own informal or 'working' rules. These 'internal' organizational and occupational factors can become more important than legal rules in guiding their action and judgement.

While the elimination of *all* discretion is impossible and undesirable, it is clear that its regulation and control through the framework of the rule of law are essential for penal accountability. Rule-led decisions, if applied openly, consistently and dispassionately and rooted in principles of justice, equality and treating like cases alike, facilitate greater accountability as well as performing a normative function. Unnecessary penal discretion should be challenged and, where possible, replaced by more transparent and accountable forms of decision-making (Davis 1969).

*David Scott*

## Related entries

*Accountability; Fairness; Human rights; Legitimacy; Power; Prison officers.*

### Key texts and sources

American Friends Service Committee (1971) *Struggle for Justice: A Report on Crime and Punishment in America.* New York, NY: Hill & Wang.
Baumgartner, M.P. (1992) 'The myth of discretion', in K. Hawkins (ed.) *The Uses of Discretion.* Oxford: Oxford University Press.
Davis, K.C. (1969) *Discretionary Justice: A Preliminary Inquiry.* Chicago, IL: University of Illinois Press.
Liebling, A. and Price, D. (2001) *The Prison Officer.* Leyhill: Prison Service Journal.

## DRUGS

Over half of prisoners report that their offending is linked to drug misuse. The use of drugs in prison is also an issue that has a serious impact on prison culture and on order. Tackling drug misuse has therefore become a major strategy in the internal management of prisons and in attempts to reduce reoffending.

A drug is a chemical intoxicant that, when ingested, can lead to the modification of one or more body functions. Drugs are common – from caffeine in coffee and prescription medicines, to illicit drugs such as heroin. The use of a drug, in some form, is difficult to avoid. Some people choose to misuse drugs through experimentation – to experience new feelings – or recreationally, where a drug is used for a particular effect, often to enhance a situation. For a small but significant group, drug misuse becomes a habit where a dependency develops and, consequently, biophysical, psychological and social problems follow. It is often this group of people who resort to acquisitive crime to finance their addiction or who offend while under the influence of drugs.

Prisons accommodate a high percentage of offenders whose drug use has become problematic. Studies have reported that between 60 and 70 per cent of prisoners have misused drugs in the 12 months prior to imprisonment, with around 55 per cent reporting drug use linked to their offending and 53 per cent defining themselves as problematic users (see Wheatley 2007). In 2005, the Home Office estimated that approximately 136,000 offenders are imprisoned each year, and this is increasing. Using a crude estimate of problematic drug use (55 per cent), this suggests that 75,000 problematic drug misusers pass through the prison system annually – approximately 42,000 being present at any one time. Imprisonment can be an opportunity to engage people in the process of change and to address problematic drug use, which should reduce reoffending. The effective delivery of drug services has therefore become a strategic priority for the government and the Prison Service.

### Why use drugs in prison?

There are many different explanations for drug use in prison, and five fundamental explanatory models are worth noting (see Wheatley 2007). These models are not mutually exclusive and can complement each other – a drug can serve a variety of purposes for an individual:

1. *Self-medication model*: prison leads to a loss of privacy, isolation from family, loss of autonomy and boredom. Prison life can promote drug misuse in some individuals as a relief from the pains of imprisonment. Sleep deprivation, headaches, personality disorders, depression and anxiety are all problems frequently managed by drugs, the most popular substances being opiates and cannabis.

2. *Time-management model*: taking drugs can help pass time in prison by allowing the user to 'slip away' from the realities of his or her physical surroundings and from structural inequalities. Time is a basic structuring dimension of prison life and predominately externally controlled. However, prisoners sometimes manipulate how they experience time, often by sedation. Sedation promotes sleep and relaxation so that time appears to pass more quickly. Sedation is therefore used to limit the potentially damaging impact incarceration may have on someone.

3. *Social network model*: drug misuse in prison often enables individuals to connect socially to a wider group. Prisons can become less isolating when social relationships and networks are formed, and drugs may facilitate this. These social networks are often very fragile, unstable and volatile.

4. *Status model*: using and dealing in drugs can often promote status and satisfaction. The daily routine of drug acquisition and supply, where control, wealth, knowledge and power can be seen publicly, may promote drug activity. In prison, subcultures exist that respect anti-authoritarian, macho risk-taking and entrepreneurial activities, and in such circumstances drugs can provide many social pay-offs.

5. *Economic model*: in prison, using or supplying drugs fuels the prisoner economy. Supply, in particular, can elevate an individual in the prisoner hierarchy. This is often associated with the kudos that is awarded for the ability to organize the importation of drugs into prison. Drug importation can symbolize 'nerve', ambition, resistance to the system and 'connections', as well as enhancing financial reward. This is often referred to as 'powder power' (Crewe 2005).

In terms of getting 'high' and by, suspending time, gaining power and status, building social relations and exploiting economic opportunities, drug misuse in prison has multiple purposes (Crewe 2005). However, drug misuse in prison is not always self-promoting – it can be discouraging. Research shows that drug misuse can desist in prison. This may be because prisons are highly controlled and regulated environments where the availability of drugs is stifled in comparison with the community. In addition, drug use in prison can be stigmatizing, and the associated feelings of shame can discourage participation. Finally, many prisoners disclose being imprisoned for drug-related behaviours as a 'wake-up call', where change is promoted and abstinence achieved following 'hitting rock bottom' and realizing what can be done differently to achieve a life away from crime and drugs.

### What is the Prison Service doing about drugs?

The aim of the National Offender Management Service (NOMS) drug strategy is 'to address the needs of problematic drug users during their engagement with the correctional services … with a view to reducing their re-offending and the harm they cause to themselves and others' (Home Office 2005: 1–2). The strategy aims to reduce the demand and harm associated with problematic drug misuse through effective therapeutic interventions and by reducing supply into and around prisons. All prisons, especially local prisons and remand establishments, must deliver clinical services to manage the symptoms associated with withdrawal from drugs. These involve detoxification and maintenance-prescribing programmes as a lead-up to psychosocial interventions. Prison Service Order (PSO) 3550 informs this intervention (HM Prison Service 2002a).

The counselling, advice, referral, assessment and throughcare service (CARATS) is an easy-to-access intervention that provides a gateway, and it is available in all prisons. CARATS is informed by PSO 3630 (HM Prison Service 2002b). CARATS staff, who come from a variety of backgrounds, complete assessments of treatment need, create individual care plans and deliver individual and group support programmes. When more intensive interventions are required, CARATS refers to specific treatment programmes. CARATS staff are key workers in the offender management process and strengthen throughcare by being linked via a national Prison Service framework. CARATS links into the Drugs Intervention Programme (DIP), an aftercare service available nationally where support can be offered post-release. This can include housing support, family advocacy, education, training and employment opportunities, mental health treatment, and debts and benefit advice.

Eight established rehabilitation programmes are available in 115 prisons. Twenty-three of these programmes are delivered in dedicated accommodation. Drug rehabilitation programmes take four forms:

- *Cognitive-behavioural programmes* informed by social learning theory, where thinking skills are improved, emotional coping strengthened and new behaviours supported.
- *12-Step programmes*, based on the Minnesota recovery model, as adopted by Alcoholics and Narcotics Anonymous. Addiction is seen as a lifelong illness controlled by following the steps to recovery.
- *Therapeutic communities*, often hierarchical in orientation, that include incentives, structured activities, work allocation and peer support.
- *The Short Duration Programme*, a motivational enhancement and harm minimization groupwork course designed to encourage short-term prisoners to seek specific support within the community.

The Woolf Report advocated developing drug-free units or programmes to support prisoners. This emerged as voluntary drug testing (VDT) and is available in all prisons, informed by PSO 3620 (HM Prison Service 2000). When a prisoner agrees to VDT, he or she makes a commitment to remain drug-free and to become liable to a minimum of 18 urine tests per year to support this promise. When prisoners test positive, VDT staff refer to CARATS and other support services, who review current behaviour and assist with the re-establishing of new, more appropriate, behaviours.

Stopping drugs getting into prison is unlikely as so many different routes are used. As one route closes, another opens. Reducing the amount of illicit drugs reaching and being consumed by prisoners is a key strategic objective. This is known as supply reduction or interdiction. Three key principles inform supply reduction: detection, deterrence and disruption. Detection involves prison staff intercepting unauthorized items coming into the prison; prisoner, visitor and staff searching on entry and exit from the prison; surveillance; mobile phone detectors; mail searching; and drug dogs. Deterrence discourages drug-related activity and can include poster campaigns, awareness leaflets, low-level fixed furniture in visits halls and prison perimeter patrols by staff and dogs. Disruption techniques may involve prisoner transfers to other establishments or segregation units and using approved suppliers of prisoners' property. A Prison Service *Supply Reduction Good Practice Guide* exists to support interdiction and is available to all prison staff. Without supply reduction, treatment interventions and behaviour changes continue to be at risk, and relapse to unhealthy, inappropriate lifestyles becomes more probable.

*Michael Wheatley*

### Related entries

*Alcohol; Deprivations/'pains of imprisonment'; Desistance; Economy; Healthcare; HIV/AIDS; Mandatory drug testing; Offending behaviour programmes; Rehabilitation; Subcultures; Therapeutic communities; Time.*

**Key texts and sources**

Crewe, B. (2005) 'Prisoner society in the era of hard drugs', *Punishment and Society*, 7: 457–81.

HM Prison Service (2000) *Voluntary Drug Testing Units and the Framework for Voluntary Drug Testing* (PSO 3620). (available online at **http://pso.hmprisonservice.gov.uk/PSO_3620_voluntary_drug_testing.doc**).

HM Prison Service (2002a) *Clinical Services for Substance Misusers* (PSO 3550). (available online at **http://pso.hmprisonservice.gov.uk/PSO_3550_clinical_services.doc**).

HM Prison Service (2002b) *Counselling, Assessment, Referral, Advice and Throughcare Services* (PSO 3630). (available online at **http://pso.hmprisonservice.gov.uk/PSO_3630_carats.doc**).

Home Office (2005) *The National Offender Management Service (NOMS): Strategy for the Management and Treatment of Problematic Drug Users within the Correctional Services.* London: NOMS.

Ramsey, M. (2003) *Prisoners' Drug Use and Treatment: Seven Research Studies. Home Office Research Study* 267. London: Home Office.

Wheatley, M. (2007) 'Drug misuse in prison', in Y. Jewkes (ed.) *Handbook on Prisons.* Cullompton: Willan Publishing.

See also the Rehabilitation for Addicted Prisoners Trust's website (**http://www.rapt.org.uk/**).

# E

## EARLY-RELEASE SCHEMES

Early-release schemes enable prisoners to leave custody prior to their normal release date. The two main schemes in England and Wales, apart from parole, are home detention curfew (HDC), using electronic monitoring to enforce curfew restrictions, and the early removal scheme (ERS), aimed at foreign national prisoners. In some circumstances, prisoners may also be eligible for periods of release on temporary licence (ROTL).

The majority of prison sentences are served partly in custody and partly in the community, with the relative proportions prescribed by law. Under the provisions of the Criminal Justice Act 2003, those sentenced to less than four years are released halfway through their sentence – if the sentence was more than 12 months, they are eligible for automatic conditional release (ACR). Those serving a determinate sentence of four or more years are eligible for parole or discretionary conditional release (DCR) at the halfway stage. While parole has long been a feature of penal policy, two more recent forms of early release are the home detention curfew scheme and the early removal scheme for foreign national prisoners subject to deportation.

Home detention curfew (HDC) for prisoners was introduced in January 1999. The scheme requires prison governors to consider prisoners serving more than three months but less than four years for early release, on condition that they agree to electronic monitoring, otherwise known as 'tagging'. A specified curfew on their liberty typically requires them to be at their place of residence from early evening until early morning. The length of the sentence determines the period that must be served before a curfew can be granted. All eligible prisoners must first satisfy a risk assessment, carried out by prison and probation staff, of whether they are likely to comply and whether they have suitable accommodation. Numerous categories of prisoners are statutorily excluded from the scheme (unless there are exceptional circumstances): those subject to a hospital order; violent and sexual offenders serving extended sentences; those facing deportation; those who have previously breached an HDC or an early-release licence; and those sentenced for fine default and contempt of court. The exclusion criteria became even more stringent in July 2003, though the scheme was extended to include young offenders.

The early removal scheme (ERS) was introduced by the Criminal Justice Act 2003 allowing eligible foreign national prisoners to be 'removed' from prison up to 135 days earlier than their normal release date, the period being dependent on the length of prison sentence. Again, there are statutory exclusions from the scheme. The ERS led to a substantial increase in foreign national prisoners becoming known to the Immigration and Nationality Directorate (IND), requiring it to revise its systems. Following a furore in spring 2006 over large-scale failure to deport foreign prisoners, an Imminent Release Team was set up in the IND to work with the Prison Service in ensuring that appropriate prisoners are considered for deportation. Emergency measures to ease overcrowding, announced in October 2006, included grants up to a maximum value of £2,500 for resettlement purposes offered to foreign prisoners in exchange for early release – not to liberty but to serve the remainder of their sentences in jails in their home countries.

Release on temporary licence (ROTL) allows limited periods of early release for compassionate reasons (e.g. funerals, marriage) or to help the prisoner improve his or her chances of resettlement after release (e.g. work experience, training, family visits). Applicants for ROTL are risk assessed by authorized senior managers, with the period of release allowed and its purposes always precisely defined.

Each of these early-release schemes can be undermined by media scares that public safety is being put at risk. Studies suggest that reconviction rates during early-release periods are similar to those of comparison groups (e.g. Dodgson *et al.* 2001), but such findings are obscured by headlines regarding specific cases of failure. Public opinion regarding the early release of prisoners is, like public opinion to sentencing, likely to be more favourable when the specific circumstances are known, but hostile publicity can have the opposite effect. For example, prisoners being released on ROTL to carry out needed voluntary work may still become the source of bitter prejudice following biased newspaper coverage (e.g. Burnett and Maruna 2004).

Episodes of mismanagement, as well as high-profile instances of serious reoffending during the licence period, have brought some notoriety to HDC and the ERS. The onus of responsibility to release some prisoners early does not rest easy with all governors. A leaked memo in February 2002 to the Director of the Prison Service revealed that only 25 per cent of those eligible for HDC had been allowed home. Similarly, the ERS has been associated with both underuse (eligible prisoners not considered or left waiting) and careless application, 'losing' into the community some foreign prisoners earmarked for deportation. These omissions arguably reflect what HM Chief Inspectorate of Prisons has identified as an 'institutional blind spot' in recognizing the different needs of foreign national prisoners, as well as a lack of monitoring by the immigration service.

Early-release schemes are more concerned with prison management than with a compassion or justice to prisoners, or with a reduction in reoffending. The prospect of HDC, like parole, serves as an incentive for good behaviour. Dodgson *et al.* (2001) reported that 37 per cent of sampled prisoners prior to release said that the prospect of being granted HDC influenced their behaviour in prison. The schemes are cost effective: electronic monitoring costs around £70 less per day on average than keeping an offender in prison (Committee of Public Accounts 2006), although present sentencing trends mean that places retrieved are immediately filled by other prisoners.

Most significantly, HDC and the ERS provide a means to ameliorating the overcrowding problem. Such a policy was tried on a large scale, in Illinois, until more long-term solutions to overcrowding could be found: as a consequence of releasing 21,000 prisoners early, the projected prison population was reduced by approximately 10 per cent but without affecting reconviction rates (Austin 1986). Yet early-release schemes in the UK have not forestalled a bulging prison population, presently in excess of capacity. There is a paradoxical circularity in a system that imprisons too many people, resulting in the need to make space by releasing more of them earlier, resulting in recalls for breach and some shocking failures which fuel punitive populism and fear of crime, in turn propelling an increased use of custodial sentences.

*Ros Burnett*

### Related entries

*Alternatives to imprisonment; Electronic monitoring; Foreign national prisoners; Overcrowding; Parole.*

**Key texts and sources**

Austin, J. (1986) 'Using early release to relieve prison crowding: a dilemma in public policy', *Crime and Delinquency*, 32: 404–502.

Burnett, R. and Maruna, S. (2004) *Prisoners as Citizens' Advisers*. London: Esmée Fairbairn Foundation.

Committee of Public Accounts (2006) *The Electronic Monitoring of Adult Offenders. Sixty-second Report of Session 2005–6* (HC 997). London: HMSO (available online at **www.publications.parliament. uk/pa/cm200506/cmselect/cmpubacc/997/997.pdf**).

Dodgson, K., Goodwin, P., Howard, P., Llewellyn-Thomas, S., Mortimer, E., Russell, N. and Weiner, M. (2001) *Electronic Monitoring of Released Prisoners: An Evaluation of the Home Detention Curfew Scheme. Home Office Research Study* 222. London: Home Office.

See also the CAB advice guide (**http://www. adviceguide.org.uk/p_early_release_from_prison_-_serving_your_sentence_in_the_community.pdf**). Information on HM Prison Service's home detention curfew is available at **http://www. hmprisonservice.gov.uk/adviceandsupport/before afterrelease/homedetentioncurfew/**.

## ECONOMY

> Economic activity among prisoners includes gambling, money lending, trading in goods, drug importation, alcohol manufacture and other illicit trading. Some level of economic activity among prisoners is inevitable and not necessarily inherently problematic, but attendant issues of indebtedness and the risky nature of some illicit economic activities do present problems for prison managers.

The prison economy includes the trading of goods (such as tobacco) that have been acquired by prisoners legally and which are then redistributed informally, and also activities that are wholly prohibited, such as gambling, the manufacture of alcohol and the trafficking of drugs. This illicit economy allows prisoners to alleviate some of the deprivations/'pains of imprisonment': goods traded can offer recreation and comfort, and profit enables prisoners to gain possessions, status and influence in prison, or even to save cash for use after release (Sparks *et al*. 1996; Crewe 2005).

Both staff and prisoners tend to regard some level of economic activity as inevitable, and not necessarily always problematic. Indeed, in so far as the activities that comprise the prison economy provide harmless activity and comfort to prisoners, it can be argued that they assist the smooth running of the prison. Some prisoners even suggest that staff members accept the trade in hard drugs because it keeps prisoners quiet and because powerful dealers are capable of delivering order on prison wings (Crewe 2005). Although some practices do carry specific risks (such as needle sharing or the consumption of hallucinogens or hooch, which can be harmful), there is some agreement that the biggest problems associated with the prison economy are those arising from the ways in which commodities are generated and distributed within markets. Because goods in prison are scarce, prices are high, at least in relation to incomes, but in some cases also compared with normal market prices (for example, heroin in prison can cost several times its street value). Interest and exchange rates are also high, with a standard interest rate of 100 per cent (Crewe 2005). Debt is thus inevitable in prison markets (Sparks *et al*. 1996).

Indebtedness causes major problems as even small sums may be pursued aggressively, especially and ironically in prisons where the overall prison economy – and average debt – is smaller. In prisons where inmates are allowed cash, debts can reach hundreds of pounds (Sparks *et al*. 1996). At the same time, prisoners successfully trading in drugs for cash accrue substantial power and influence.

The nature of prison economies varies between institutions. In prisons where prisoners are not allowed to hold any cash, the size of the economy, prices, levels of debt and incentives for dealers to corner markets remain lower than where prisoners have legitimate access to cash (Sparks *et al*. 1996). In these prisons, such commodities as tobacco are likely to take on the characteristics of a currency (Morris and Morris 1963). Today, drug dealing in 'cash free' prisons is generally user dealing among friends rather than 'baroning' (Sparks *et al.* 1996; Crewe 2005; see also Morris and Morris 1963 for a description of tobacco baroning). A cash economy will tend to expand because there is no theoretical limit to how much anyone wants, and the amount in circulation can be increased by illicit inflows from the outside.

*Abigail Rowe*

### Related entries

*Alcohol; Deprivations/'pains of imprisonment'; Drugs; Subcultures.*

---

**Key texts and sources**

Crewe, B. (2005) 'Prisoner society in the era of hard drugs', *Punishment and Society*, 7: 457–81.

Morris, T. and Morris, P. (1963) *Pentonville: A Sociological Study of an English Prison.* London: Routledge & Kegan Paul.

Sparks, R., Bottoms, A.E. and Hay, W. (1996) *Prisons and the Problem of Order.* Oxford: Clarendon Press.

---

## EDUCATION AND TRAINING

Education in prisons comes under the remit of the government Department for Education and Skills (DfES). Prisons are among the largest providers of education for language, literacy and numeracy in the UK. However, opportunities for prisoners to pursue further and higher education courses are under increasing pressure as funding priorities are directed at basic skills in an effort to reduce reoffending.

Research indicates that, before they ever come into contact with the prison system, most prisoners have a history of social exclusion, which includes high levels of educational disadvantage. Some 80 per cent of prisoners have writing skills at or below the level of an 11-year-old child, while 50 per cent have reading skills at or below that level (Social Exclusion Unit 2002). This compares with a national figure of 13 per cent. Over half of all male prisoners have no qualifications at all. The failure of other agencies to deal with these aspects of social exclusion leaves the Prison Service and its partners with the task of 'putting right' a lifetime of service failure. Consequently, along with strategies to address offending behaviour and reconviction rates, the teaching of basic skills has become a priority in prisons, not least because the three are believed to be connected. However, the government's instrumentalist approach to prisoner education and the formal linking of basic skills to a reduction in recidivism in key performance indicators are of concern to many who believe that *lifelong* education slows the revolving door of incarceration and reincarceration (Hayward 2006). Furthermore, while the low levels of literacy and numeracy that blight the prison population are inarguably a source of shame to UK society, when broken down into different kinds of establishments, a more nuanced picture emerges. For example, according to Home Office evidence, 37 per cent of female prisoners have participated in further education, while research indicates that, at one Category D prison in England, 69 per cent of prisoners had achieved GCSE O-level grades or above prior to imprisonment; 29 per cent had A-levels and 31 per cent had a degree and/or postgraduate qualifications (Hayward 2006).

Prison education programmes are diverse in their purpose, delivery and intended outcomes. All prison establishments are required to deliver a core curriculum which includes basic and key skills; English for speakers of other languages; an accredited social and life skills programme; and a qualification in information and communication technology (ICT). In addition, the education offered to prisoners might include vocational training designed to provide skills that will improve their employment prospects on release; vocational training designed to give them skills they can utilize while serving their sentence (e.g. ICT skills which can secure employment within prison; see below); offending behaviour and cognitive skills programmes designed to change thinking and modify behaviour; and faith-based programmes which aim to help prisoners adhere to their religious values and beliefs. However, these courses are implemented (or not) at a local level, and there are wide variations in the academic and vocational education provision offered in each prison (see Leech 2005 for a breakdown by prison). Currently, only about a third of prisoners are offered access to education, and it is not compulsory for adult prisoners.

In addition to the learning and skills programmes of the kind already mentioned, prisons offer their occupants the opportunity to go further in their academic studies, and foremost in this respect has been the delivery, since the early 1970s, of Open University (OU) courses. All prisons are able to offer OU access to prisoners (although some courses are prohibited or restricted in prisons), and the OU typically recruits over 300 students annually. However, academic learning in prison is fraught with difficulty. In addition to all the practical problems of studying in an environment with high noise and disruption levels, prisoners may face sharing a cell with someone who is not sympathetic to their need for quiet study, and they might also have limited access to sometimes poorly resourced libraries. They may also face the possibility of being 'shipped out' to a different prison where there is no provision for studying the course they are part of the way through. On top of these obstacles, students in prison have to negotiate adverse financial considerations. First, prisoners who wish to study face the disincentive of significantly lower 'wages' than those who work. Secondly, although the OU and other educational institutions do, under certain conditions, offer fee waivers, there are limited external funds to help students in prison register for distance-learning programmes. While many hundreds of students have benefited from the financial support of the Prisoners' Education Trust (PET), the trust is a registered charity relying on external donations to supplement funds it receives through the Offenders' Learning and Skills Unit (OLSU). Where it is able to meet the costs of course fees, it does so on three conditions: that the application is supported by the prison's education department (the recommendation is based on the prisoner's educational ability and offence); that the prison's education department agrees to contribute 10 per cent of

the fees; and that they can reassure the trust that there is a reasonable chance of the student completing the course before release. Even if a student prisoner meets all these criteria there is no guarantee that PET will be able to fund his or her studies; currently, around two thirds of applicants are successful (Hayward 2006; http://www.prisonerseducation.org.uk/).

### Computer and Internet access in prisons

A new, emerging threat to education in prisons is the restricted access to computers and the Internet that prisoners have. In relation to education beyond basic skills, access to computer technologies is becoming vital as education providers such as the OU move further towards online provision. More broadly speaking, there is growing evidence that Internet access would provide prisons with a far wider range of resources for delivering effective courses, and would offer prisoners and staff opportunities for the acquisition of new skills. But notions of prisoner empowerment do not sit easily with modern political rhetoric, which is arguably still more concerned with public perception than with prisoners' rights. Fears persist in the public imagination and in politicians' nightmares that the Internet will be used by inmates to view pornography, contact victims, intimidate witnesses or plot escapes. Meanwhile, stories periodically appear that seem designed to fuel media and public hostility about prisoners being allowed to study. For example, it was revealed in 2001 that the boys convicted of killing James Bulger in 1993 had both attained A-levels and had received education and training opportunities that they would not have enjoyed had they not been detained in custody.

The All-party Parliamentary Group for Further Education and Lifelong Learning has argued that facilities for distance learning and e-learning should be enhanced in every prison, and supervised Internet access made available to prisoners doing courses that require it, but currently only seven prisons offer Internet access. However, in January 2007, the National Offender Management Service (NOMS) announced its intention to pilot a project in Wandsworth Prison which includes the installation of a secure managed network of computers with access to approved websites and e-mail addresses for prisoners. In addition, Learndirect has installed servers and networked PCs in many prisons and, for several years, has used them to deliver courses in literacy and numeracy and to impart skills for employment. Similarly, networking company Cisco has set up centres in prisons under a scheme called the Prisons ICT Academy, teaching basic computer skills and PC maintenance. Swaleside and Gartree Prisons have ICT suites, and Chelmsford Prison has pioneered a scheme whereby foreign national prisoners can study online in their own language on condition that they study English language classes as well. While these developments are encouraging, the problem, as ever, is that there is no uniformity across the prison estate and policy is a matter of local discretion.

In line with its more general education policy, the e-learning facilities and training that currently exist in prisons are primarily directed at the basic-level skills end of the spectrum. While these initiatives are very important given the social exclusion many prisoners face both before they enter custody and when they try to resettle in the community, they represent only part of the picture. There is still a challenge for those who believe that further and higher education is an important opportunity that can help to rehabilitate offenders and give them the kinds of life choices that may encourage them to desist from committing crime. Vocational training is clearly hugely important for the majority of prisoners who need all the help they can get to resettle on release. But at the other end of the education spectrum, learning (as opposed to training), particularly in relation to degree programmes, is at risk of being squeezed.

*Yvonne Jewkes*

### Related entries

*Communication; Desistance; Employment and industries; Rehabilitation.*

### Key texts and sources

Hayward, D. (2006) 'Higher barriers: ex-prisoners and university admissions', in S. Taylor (ed.) *Prison(er) Education* (2nd edn). London: Forum on Prisoner Education.
Leech, M. (2006) *The Prisons Handbook 2006* (9th edn). Manchester: MLA Press.
Social Exclusion Unit (2002) *Reducing Re-offending by Ex-prisoners*. London: Social Exclusion Unit.
See also http://www.prisonseducation.org.uk/ and http://www.dfes.gov.uk/offenderlearning.

## EFFECTS OF IMPRISONMENT

While psychological studies generally have found limited evidence of long-term, harmful effects of imprisonment, and claims about the reformative effects of prison gain ground, there is a burgeoning sociological literature that seeks to remind us of the post-Second World War consensus that prisons harm.

*In order to be sound and reasonable, the design and operation of prisons should be based not on any particular theory or ideology, but on some fundamental understanding of how imprisonment affects individuals (Zamble and Porporino 1988: 2).*

*My whole heart and soul ache with the pain of being here (Boyle 1984: 71).*

Opinion varies as to whether prisons harm, repair or constitute a 'neutral' deep-freeze experience. Advocates of prison treatment suggest that programmes delivered during a prison sentence can improve offenders' thinking and behaviour, and that opportunities are offered for prisoners to gain qualifications and experience. Critics, on the other hand, argue that the prison experience leads to long-term psychological and social damage and that attempts to mask the punitive aspects of imprisonment under the guise of 'treatment' are dangerous. Canadian psychologists, Zamble and Porporino (1988), found in a cohort study that increased anxiety and depression at the early stages of custody often declined over time, leading the authors to conclude that imprisonment acted as little more than a deep freeze. Other studies (for example, on suicides in prison) suggest that the prison experience can sometimes be unbearable and leave deep scars on those who survive it.

The effects of imprisonment debate has methodological and historical dimensions, with competing ideological perspectives gaining ground at various points in time, alongside the rise and fall of social science, medical and other disciplines (and according to the political climate). The 'effects literature' provides contradictory evidence, some studies arguing that prison does not damage and may even repair. Sociologists have tended to emphasize the prison's damaging effects. Psychologists have, on the whole, found little evidence of harm (but their operationalization of the concept of harm has invariably been poor). Sykes, for example, famously argued in his sociological study, *The Society of Captives* (1958), that there were five main deprivations/pains of imprisonment. They were the loss of liberty (confinement, removal from family and friends, rejection by the community and loss of citizenship, resulting in lost emotional relationships, loneliness and boredom); the deprivation of goods and services (choice, amenities and material possessions); the frustration of sexual desire (prisoners were figuratively castrated by involuntary celibacy); the deprivation of autonomy (regime routine, work, activities, trivial and apparently meaningless restrictions – for example, the delivery of letters, lack of explanations for decisions); and the deprivation of security (enforced association with other unpredictable prisoners, causing fear and anxiety – prisoners had to fight for the safety of their person and possessions). These deprivations threatened the prisoner's sense of worth and self-concept. They provided the energy for the society of captives to act collectively (in solidarity), in order to mitigate their effects. They caused prisoners to generate alternative methods of gaining self-esteem. The minutiae of life were regulated with a bureaucratic indifference to individual need

and worth. The focus of some early sociological studies on 'adaptation' implied that coping with prison was a relatively straightforward task. Other studies have linked the prison experience to suicide (Liebling 1999), psychological breakdown (Cohen and Taylor 1972) and post-traumatic stress disorder. According to these and other accounts, prisons are structurally organized in ways that brutalize: 'The brutality which is sometimes shown to the prisoner by the warder is often only a reproduction of the brutality which the governor exhibits to the warder; and the brutality of the governor is often the result of the brutality of the Commissioners to him' (Morrison cited in McConville 1998: 712).

Several classic psychological studies have found limited evidence of long-term psychological damage, but these studies have included very limited measures of deterioration (such as IQ, concepts of 'father', verbal fluency and so on). More recent psychological studies have found evidence of difficulties among some prisoners in coping with the prison experience, as well as major difficulties on release. Aspects of prison life which are found to be particularly painful are entry into custody, solitary confinement, fear, the loss of privacy, the problem of passing time (it transforms from a resource to a tormentor) and having to 'wear a mask'. Haney argues that 'prisoners who labour both at an emotional and a behavioural level to develop a prison mask that is unrevealing and impenetrable risk alienation, emotional flatness and distance, and withdrawal from social interactions' (1997: 537). There is considerable evidence that the early experience of custody is especially traumatic (see Liebling 1999) and that it often constitutes an almost overwhelming transition or dislocation. It is clear that the experience of imprisonment can be painful for many prisoners (and that it is unbearable for some), despite common public and, occasionally, prison staff perceptions that prison is 'too soft' or that 'it would deter if it were more punishing'. Vulnerabilities are exposed by the social, material and psychological conditions of imprisonment (for example, by prolonged isolation, by fear and tension or by the pressure to 'save face'). This confounding of the material with the psychological conditions of imprisonment permeates popular commentary on the prison. Levels of distress, anxiety and depression are extremely high among prisoners. The experience of unfairness, inhumanity and coercive power, more prominent in some prisons than others, is both distressing and potentially damaging. A feeling of lack of safety has also been shown to predict levels of distress among prisoners. Recent research has found that the experience of a miscarriage of justice or wrongful conviction often leads to post-traumatic stress disorder, including emotional disconnection, loss of trust and meaning, depression and social withdrawal (Grounds 2005). Sudden changes to penal policy and parole legislation, for example, or even to location, can mean that prisoners' future prospects are subject to sudden and dramatic transformation. The combination of routine, control and unpredictability in prison makes surviving the experience very psychologically challenging.

Commentators on the prison often note that they should not inflict 'unnecessary and wanton pain'. Recent analyses have found that some prison environments are 'healthier' than others (HMCIP 1999; see Measuring the Quality of Prison Life (MQPL). (The Inspectorate of Prisons in England and Wales has developed a 'healthy prison' notion that consists of safety, respect, meaningful contact with family and constructive activities.) This suggests that some prisons with the same function may harm more than others, according to their management, organization, social and moral climate, and the culture among staff. These findings on the heterogeneity of prisons and their effects cast doubt on the 'just deserts'/'proportionality' thesis, which assumes that length of sentence equals the sum of discomfort or punishment experienced.

Desistance and recidivism studies suggest that prison weakens already vulnerable social and relational bonds, making it very difficult to re-establish these important links, and thereby making an independent contribution to the chances of an offender reoffending on release. These effects are cumulative so that, the more time spent in prison, the more difficult it becomes to form prosocial ties in the community or to earn a living. Prisons can also have negative effects on communities, on families of prisoners (especially on the development of children) and on prison staff. The collateral effects include the diversion of resources from education and training and from other public services, the reduction of community cohesion, the acceptance of time spent in prison as a normal life experience and the prisonization of the streets. Prison staff can experience a reduction in sensitivity to violence, cynicism, burnout and isolation (see Liebling and Maruna 2005).

At a time of the increasing use and varieties of imprisonment in most jurisdictions, including new forms of 'deep end' confinement such as supermax, close supervision centres and units for the severely personality disordered, Zamble and Porporino's (1988) call for increased understanding of the effects of imprisonment is especially urgent. There is a need for detailed longitudinal outcome studies, taking into account what goes on in the prison, any possible positive as well as negative effects and, importantly, differences between prisons.

*Alison Liebling*

### Related entries

*Close supervision centres; Coping; Deprivations/'pains of imprisonment'; Education and training; Families of prisoners; Just deserts; Measuring the Quality of Prison Life (MQPL); Prisonization; Solidarity; Suicide in prison; Supermax prisons.*

**Key texts and sources**

Boyle, J. (1984) *The Pain of Confinement*. Edinburgh: Canongate.

Cohen, S. and Taylor, L. (1972) *Psychological Survival: The Experience of Long-term Imprisonment*. Harmondsworth: Penguin Books.

Grounds, A. (2005) 'Understanding the effects of wrongful imprisonment', in M. Tonry (ed.) *Crime and Justice: An Annual Review of Research. Vol. 32*. Chicago, IL: University of Chicago Press.

Haney, C. (1997) 'Psychology and the limits to prison pain: confronting the coming crisis in the eighth amendment law', *Psychology, Public Policy and Law*, 3: 499–588.

HMCIP (1999) *Suicide is Everyone's Concern: Report of a Thematic Inspection on Suicides in Prison*. London: HMSO.

Liebling, A. (1999) 'Prison suicide and prisoner coping', in M. Tonry and J. Petersilia (eds) *Prisons, Crime and Justice: An Annual Review of Research. Vol. 26*. Chicago, IL: University of Chicago Press.

Liebling, A. and Maruna, S. (eds) (2005) *The Effects of Imprisonment*. Cullompton: Willan Publishing.

Sykes, G.M. (1958) *The Society of Captives: A Study of a Maximum Security Prison*. Princeton, NJ: Princeton University Press.

Zamble, E. and Porporino, F.J. (1988) *Coping, Behaviour and Adaptation in Prison Inmates*. New York, NY: Springer-Verlag.

# ELECTRONIC MONITORING

Electronic monitoring refers to the use of various electronic surveillance technologies to monitor the location and/or movement of individual defendants and offenders.

## Origins of electronic monitoring in the USA

The term 'electronic monitoring' (EM) originally referred to a range of technologies which can be used to achieve remote oversight of the locations and schedules of offenders under supervision in the community. The concept, and basic patents for the technology, were developed by behavioural psychologist, Ralph Kirkland Schwitzgebel, at Harvard University in the 1960s. Although it entailed the monitoring of movement rather than specific locations (although this was also possible), it was envisaged in humanistic, rehabilitative terms. No immediate commercial or correctional applications were found. It was only after Judge Jack Love of Albuquerque, New Mexico, persuaded an electronics engineer to develop the technology in the late 1970s and early 1980s – by which time the components were smaller, lighter and cheaper – that the concept took off, in the form of electronic house arrest rather than the monitoring of movement. Love's original intention was to find ways of supervising prisoners on home leave from the local penitentiary, but EM gained more ground as an adjunct or alternative to probation. For political reasons it was quickly discontinued in Albuquerque. Florida became the main site of experimentation with the new technology and remains the locus of innovation today.

The term 'tagging' was not used in the USA – the preferred terms there were house arrest, home confinement and home incarceration. Colloquially, among offenders, the experience was described as being 'on the box' – the box being the transceiver installed in one's home which, so long as the offender is present, picks up signals from his or her ankle-bracelet and relays them, via landline telephone (more recently cellular telephone), to the computer in the monitoring centre.

## The UK experience

'Tagging' was coined in 1981 in England by Tom Stacey, a private individual (novelist, publisher and prison visitor) who founded the Offender's Tag Association to promote (in his view) a more effective means of supervising offenders in the community than probation and, *inter alia*, a way of dramatically reducing the use of imprisonment. Initially rejected by the Home Office, it was subsequently included in its 'punishment in the community' initiative in 1988, despite much opposition from the Probation Service and the penal reform lobby, who saw EM as an unwarranted, unethical form of surveillance (Roberts 2005).

The first pilots in 1989–90 – using EM as a bail condition to reduce remand in custody – were only a limited success, but an EM curfew order was included in the Criminal Justice Act 1991 and piloted from 1996. Research indicated that the technology was reliable, that compliance rates were high and that the measure was cost-effective, despite an acknowledged element of 'net widening' (National Audit Office 2006). In 1999, the New Labour government made EM curfew orders nationally available and introduced an EM early-release scheme (home detention curfew) specifically to cope with a crisis of rising prison numbers. Bail, sentence and post-release schemes were subsequently introduced, for juveniles as well as adults, as, in 2005, were EM-control orders for a handful of terrorist suspects. By the autumn of 2006, just under 300,000 people had experienced tagging. Scotland piloted tagging from 1998 and introduced it nationally in 2001, permitting both restrictions of liberty 'to a place' (curfews) and 'from a place' (exclusion zones), although the latter have been little used. The tagging of juveniles (very controversial in Scotland's welfare-oriented youth justice system) was only introduced in 2004, and used sparingly. EM early release from prison began in July 2006 and is being used to solve problems of prison overcrowding. Northern Ireland has considered EM but thus far has not introduced it.

Schwitzgebel's (and Stacey's) original vision of EM as the monitoring of movement rather than restriction to a location has now been realized. Drawing on Florida's extensive experience, New Labour piloted satellite tracking in Manchester, the West Midlands and Hampshire, using the Global Positioning System (GPS) to monitor an offender's compliance with specified exclusion zones (around a former victim's home or public spaces in which crime might reasonably occur). This can be done in either real time (which is expensive) or retrospectively (using computerized records). Satellite tracking's future in Britain is uncertain, but the Netherlands and France are also experimenting with it. Voice verification technology, using telephones and a computerized voice print rather than a tag to authenticate an offender's presence at an agreed location, is not yet widespread anywhere. Remote alcohol monitoring, which combines a breathalyser with tagging or tracking technology, can be used to ensure that offenders do not drink alcohol while under cur-

few. It is used in the USA and in some mainland European countries.

### Emerging and future trends in EM

Contemporary EM has to be understood as part of 'the commercial–corrections complex', a global network of increasingly large and influential private organizations that provide services – usually prisons and prisoner escort services – to state criminal justice systems (Lilly and Deflem 1996). In respect of EM, there are two types of organizations involved: *full service providers*, such as (in Britain) Group4Securicor (G4S) and Serco, which provide both the technology and the monitoring staff; and *independent technology providers*, such as the Israeli-based ElmoTech, which provides technology either direct to statutory agencies such as the Belgian and Swedish correctional services or to full service providers such as Reliance which, until 2006, had the contract to deliver EM in Scotland (when it was replaced by Serco). The topography of the commercial–corrections complex has been in constant flux, as newcomers enter the market and as larger organizations take over smaller ones. Neither Racall-Chubb nor Marconi, who were involved in the original English pilots in 1989–90, are involved now. Serco was once in partnership with Wackenhut, an American-based private prisons company, jointly trading (in Britain) under the name Premier to run prisons, immigration detention centres and EM schemes. Premier purchased Geographix, a small company specializing in marine and road haulage tagging and tracking technology, to give itself in-house expertise in EM, and this has remained part of Serco. G4S, itself formed from the merger of two major security companies, recently purchased OnGuard Plus – the second independent technology provider it has bought – for much the same reason. Even more complex accounts could be given about commercial developments in other countries but, at root, it is a story about the security and telecommunications industry diversifying into, or getting co-opted into, the emerging corrections market. All the companies involved trade internationally and facilitate processes of policy and practice transfer.

The term 'electronic monitoring' need no longer be restricted only to supervision in the community and alternatives to prison; it is now possible to speak of *electronically monitored prisons*. ElmoTech's TRaCE technology in effect turns a prison into a 'smart' building, instantly pinpointing the location and movement of every ankle-tagged inmate and wrist-tagged member of staff and visitor, via a network of sensors high on the building walls. All can be monitored on a single screen in a small room. TRaCE was pioneered in the USA but has not yet become widespread, possibly because it has implications for custodial staffing levels. The Netherlands pioneered it in Europe and now uses it in three prisons. Sweden – which, in the 1990s, had decided against opening a new prison because of the success of its EM scheme – did create a new open prison in October 2004, utilizing an abandoned former tuberculosis hospital at Kolmarden, in a popular tourist area. Local people protested but, in April 2005, were reassured by the promise of constant internal monitoring of its 128 male prisoners and the creation of an electronic perimeter. The original inmates – serving sentences of up to two years – disliked being tagged but were threatened with removal to another, higher-security prison if they did not comply. Removal remains the penalty for tampering with the tag. Kolmarden has 20,000 square metres of building space and 10,000 square metres of land. Some 112 internal sensors monitor movement in and around the buildings, while 14 ten-foot high poles topped with sensors constitute the perimeter. 'Online headcounts' are done twice daily. Inmates must remain indoors after 4.30 p.m., but guards no longer do night patrols. Without the TRaCE technology Kolmarden would need 60 guards; as it is, it has 40. Absconding has been negligible. This technology has been considered for use in England and Wales but so far rejected.

EM is firmly established in England, Wales and Scotland as a form of community supervision, although the media, recognizing that while EM is indeed a surveillant penalty it is not a fully incapacitative one, have become more critical than they were at the beginning (Nellis 2005). The government has encouraged an ideological and practical split between EM and probation,

and service delivery by commercial organizations has reinforced this. Integration is greater in Sweden and Belgium, where social workers support and assist all tagged individuals. Which way is preferable is moot but, if the best of past practice with supervised offenders is not to be lost, the future uses of EM must be shaped in dialogue with humanistic ideals rather than being allowed to evolve in accordance with purely commercial or technological imperatives.

*Mike Nellis*

### Related entries

*Alternatives to imprisonment; Carceral society; Early-release schemes; New punitiveness; Open prisons; Sentencing policy.*

### Key texts and sources

Lilly, J. and Deflem, M. (1996) 'Profit and penality: an analysis of the corrections–commercial complex', *Crime and Delinquency*, 34: 3–20.

National Audit Office (2006) *The Electronic Monitoring of Adult Offenders*. London: HMSO.

Nellis, M. (2005) 'Electronic monitoring, satellite tracking and the new punitiveness in England and Wales', in J. Pratt *et al.* (eds) *The New Punitiveness: Trends, Theories and Perspectives*. Cullompton: Willan Publishing.

Roberts, J. (2005) *The Virtual Prison: Community Control and the Evolution of Imprisonment*. Cambridge: Cambridge University Press.

The Home Office's paper on the electronic monitoring of prisoners is available at **http://www.homeoffice. gov.uk/rds/pdfs/hors222.pdf**.

## EMPLOYMENT AND INDUSTRIES

Prison industries provide employment for prisoners. A range of different employment is offered, reflecting the different aims and views of the purpose of imprisonment, including aiding resettlement, paying back to the community and structuring the prison day.

The history of prisoner employment and work within prisons reflects wider changes in views about the purpose of imprisonment. The movement from the non-productive use of prison labour (for example, prisoners being placed on treadmills) to more ambitious and productive work heralds the start of what can be recognized as prisoner employment within prisons (McConville 1981).

Three interlinked but distinct strands have emerged in relation to employment. The first is its role in resettlement – to give prisoners the skills, training, experience appropriate to the labour market and, where possible, creating direct links with employers (Social Exclusion Unit 2002). The second is an economic and restorative argument. Imprisonment is expensive, and making use of prisoner labour to help provide goods and services is a legitimate way of offsetting the cost of imprisoning people. By providing such goods and services prisoners are helping to pay back to society the costs of their delinquent behaviour. The third role of prison employment is the benefit for prisoners in helping structure daily routines as well as being an important source of purposeful activity. The predominant practice of prisoner employment and industries is that the three key purposes all have equal validity, although the balance between them may vary between prisons or for individual prisoners within the course of a sentence.

The source of prisoner work can be either public or private sector. First, goods and services are provided primarily for the internal Prison Service market. The goods produced include clothing, window frames, furniture and printing; the services include working in farms and gardens, catering and domestic tasks, such as cleaning. Secondly, manufacturing, assembly and services are provided to the private sector under contract. The role of the private sector has been controversial due to the fact that, with the exception of a few experimental schemes, prisoners are paid nominal wages. As a result, the use of prison labour for commercial contracts has been criticized as exploitation.

*Simon Boddis*

## Related entries

*Activities; Desistance; Education and training; Identity and self; Rehabilitation; Restorative justice (RJ).*

### Key texts and sources

McConville, S. (1981) *A History of English Prison Administration. Volume I: 1750–1877.* London: Routledge & Kegan Paul.
Social Exclusion Unit (2002) *Reducing Re-offending by Ex-prisoners.* London: Social Exclusion Unit.
See also HM Prisons' 'prison enterprises' (http://www.hmpenterprises.co.uk/).

# ESCAPES AND ABSCONDS

Preventing escapes from prison is widely considered to be the primary task of prisons. While escape is generally taken to refer to people who get out of closed prisons unlawfully, many prisoners are also unlawfully at large as a result of absconding from open prisons or failing to return from temporary release.

The first duty of prisons is to keep in custody those committed by the courts. The prevention of escapes is crucial in maintaining public confidence. For example, a series of high-profile escapes in the 1960s, including that of the spy, George Blake, led to the introduction of the categorization and allocation system, including Category A prisoners and the development of high-security prisons. In addition, the escape of six prisoners from Whitemoor Prison in 1995 and three from Parkhurst Prison in 1996, both high-security prisons, led to major changes in the management of prisons and resulted in the then Director General, Derek Lewis, being sacked. Escapes from prison have declined from 42 in 1996 to three in 2005 (Home Office 2006).

Escapes from prison are those where a prisoner unlawfully gets out of a closed prison (i.e. Category A, B or C). This is the classic image of the prison escape – tunnelling out, climbing walls or sneaking out in vehicles. Although the Prison Service has a key performance indicator (KPI) and targets to ensure that escapes are less than a target figure and that there are no Category A escapes, policy only relates specifically to escapes from closed prisons. In order to qualify as a KPI escape, the prisoner must not only breach the perimeter but must also be at large for at least 15 minutes. However, there are other ways in which prisoners can become unlawfully at large, including escapes from escorts, absconding from open prisons and failing to return from temporary release.

Escapes from escort are where prisoners are outside the prison (for example, in hospitals, courts or in vehicles). These escorts may be carried out by prison staff or private companies contracted to delver this work. Escapes from prison escorts have declined from 42 in 1996 to 8 in 2005 and, from contractors, there has been a decline from 68 to 17 in that same period (Home Office 2006). In cases where prisoners unlawfully leave open prisons, they do not count as escapes because open prisons do not have walls and gates, so there is no significant physical barrier to prisoners leaving. Instead, prisoners allocated to open prisons are assessed as being sufficiently trustworthy to be held there. In 2005, 730 prisoners absconded, a decline from 1,139 in 1996 (Home Office 2006). Where prisoners do not return from any period of temporary release, this is described as a temporary release failure. There were 339 such failures in 2005, a decline from 442 in 1996 (Home Office 2006).

The overall picture is one of a decline in the numbers of prisoners unlawfully returning to the community. However, this is such a crucial area of the Prison Service's responsibility that a single event can have dramatic consequences.

*Jamie Bennett*

### Related entries

*Categorization and allocation; Category A prisoners; High-security prisons; key performance indicators (KPI) and Key performance targets (KPT) Open prisons; Security; Temporary release.*

### Key texts and sources

Home Office (2006) *Offender Management Caseload Statistics.* Home Office Statistical Bulletin 18/06. London: Home Office. (available online at **http://www.homeoffice.gov.uk/rds/pdfs06/hosb 1806.pdf**).

## EUROPEAN COMMITTEE FOR THE PREVENTION OF TORTURE AND INHUMAN OR DEGRADING TREATMENT OR PUNISHMENT (ECPT)

The European Committee for the Prevention of Torture and Inhuman or Degrading Treatment or Punishment (ECPT) is a Council of Europe organization with the right to inspect places of detention in member states and to write reports and make recommendations on its findings. Its members are usually experts in the criminal justice field from member states.

In 1987, the Council of Europe published the European Convention for the Prevention of Torture and Inhuman or Degrading Treatment or Punishment. It came into force in 1989. In order to monitor observance of the convention, the European Committee for the Prevention of Torture and Inhuman or Degrading Treatment or Punishment (ECPT) was established. The convention can be ratified by both members and non-members of the European Union. To date there are 46 members.

Under Article 1 of the convention, the mandate of the ECPT reads: 'The Committee shall, by means of visits, examine the treatment of persons deprived of their liberty with a view to strengthening, if necessary, the protection of such persons from torture and from inhuman or degrading treatment or punishment.'

The ECPT aims to be a non-judicial preventative machine, in a similar way to HM Inspectorate of Prisons in the UK. The visits conducted by the ECPT include unlimited access to places of detention, including prisons and juvenile detention centres, police stations, holding centres for immigration detainees and psychiatric hospitals. These visits are carried out by a delegation of two or more members, although the member for the country being visited does not form part of the delegation. The visits are either periodic visits, which are carried out in all member countries on a planned basis, or *ad hoc* visits organized to respond to a specific issue or concern. Inspections are conducted using specified and published standards. Following visits, a report is produced detailing what has been observed and making recommendations for improvement, to which the member state makes a detailed response. These reports are confidential, although many countries consent to the reports being published, along with their response. The ECPT will only breach confidentiality through the means of a public statement if the member state has refused to co-operate or refused to act upon recommendations from previous visits. The ECPT's members are independent and impartial experts from a variety of backgrounds, such as lawyers, doctors and specialists in criminal justice. They are elected for a four-year term by the Committee of Ministers, the Council of Europe's decision-making body, and can be re-elected twice. One member is elected in respect of each member state.

Evaluation of the work of the committee has concluded that it is a well managed organization producing credible reports. Although there are too many imponderables to conclude definitively that the work of the committee has led to a reduction of incidents of torture or ill-treatment, its work has had a beneficial impact both through specific recommendations being addressed and through a more general reinforcement of moral standards (Morgan and Evans 2001).

*Jamie Bennett*

### Related entries

*Accountability; Decency; HM Inspectorate of Prisons; Human rights; Independent monitoring boards; Measuring the Quality of Prison Life (MQPL).*

---

**Key texts and sources**

Morgan, R. and Evans, M. (2001) *Combating Torture in Europe.* Strasbourg: Council of Europe Publishing.

The Committee for the Prevention of Torture and Inhuman or Degrading Treatment or Punishment's website is at **http://www.cpt.coe.int/en/about.htm**. See also the Council of Europe's website (**http://www.coe.int/t/e/human_rights/1en_cpt.asp**).

# F

## FAIRNESS

> Fairness refers to the equal treatment of prisoners through due process and the rule of law. This can be contrasted to the lawless nature of prisons and the enforcement of prison officer authority through discretion rather than the fair application of rules.

Fairness infers that prisoners must be treated in an impartial and equal manner free from discrimination. This places a responsibility on prison authorities to ensure that the Prison Service complies with its own rules, orders and operational standards. In short, fairness requires that prisons are governed by the rule of law and the principle of due process. Liberal proponents of fairness have often rooted this concept within the principles of legality, decency or 'just deserts'.

The most influential proponent of fairness in prison in recent years has been Lord Justice Woolf. The Woolf Report (1991) into prison disturbances in April 1990 held that prisoners should not leave prison embittered or disaffected as the result of an unjust or unfair experience. For Woolf (1991: para. 1.149), prison authorities were under the obligation to 'treat prisoners with humanity and fairness and to act in concert with its responsibilities as part of the criminal justice system'. For Woolf, a fair and just prison would encourage a prisoner's self-respect, personal responsibility and law-abiding behaviour.

Woolf recommended a number of reforms to improve fairness in prison. Yet he did not seek improvements 'for prisoners for their own sakes. To think that would be to fundamentally misconceive the argument' (1991: para. 14.5). Woolf predicated fairness upon the fostering of prisoner responsibilities as opposed to the recognition of their inalienable rights of citizenship. Responsible choices could only be made if the most unfair aspects of prison life were dramatically reduced or eradicated. It was believed that only when prisoners knew that decision-making processes were fair, just and balanced would they fulfil their responsibilities.

Woolf omitted to analyse how fairness is undermined by the daily workings of prison life and the exercise of penal power. Created through law, containing individuals for law-breaking and places where nearly every aspect of life can be regulated by rules, the prison in practice is paradoxically a lawless agency where the fair application of rule of law is largely absent. Deeply structured within the normal practices of prison authorities is the mediation of power relations through discretion. The exercise of discretion places the prison officer above the rule of law and his or her actions beyond procedural restraints or mechanisms of accountability (Fitzgerald and Sim 1982). Officers enforce their personal authority rather than the rule of law in their daily function of maintaining order. Consequently, the very place designed to uphold the rule of law becomes characterized by the negation of law: lawlessness. The fair, equal and impartial application of law in prison remains more of an aspiration than a reality.

*David Scott*

### Related entries

*Accountability; Decency; Discretion; Just deserts; Power; Woolf Report.*

---

**Key texts and sources**

Fitzgerald, M. and Sim, J. (1982) *British Prisons* (2nd edn). Oxford: Blackwell.
Woolf, Lord Justice and Tumin, S. (1991) *Prison Disturbances, April 1990: Report of an Inquiry.* London: HMSO.

# FAITH COMMUNITIES

Faith communities are residential units in prisons that allow the beliefs of a particular religious faith to inform the practice of punishment.

There are three faith communities in England and Wales (at Highpoint, Swaleside and The Verne Prisons). The USA has 11, and others have been set up in Australia, Germany and New Zealand. Faith communities allow prisoners greater freedom to explore religious beliefs (their own and those of others), usually with the support of volunteers from faith-based communities outside the prison, and often with more progressive programmes than those found in standard regimes (Burnside and Lee 1997).

Four approaches can be identified: first, the *single prison* model, where the faith community takes over the entire prison (e.g. Lawtey Correctional Institution, Florida). Secondly, the *community within a prison* model, which is restricted to a self-contained part of the institution. Thirdly, the *single faith* model, where the community is identified with a particular faith. Fourthly, the *multi-faith* model, where the community is based on a number of faiths, such as Judaism and Islam (e.g. some Horizon Communities in the USA), although such programmes are heavily dependent on Christian volunteers for their viability. Faith communities operated by the Prison Service are a combination of the second and third models.

Faith communities originated with the founding of the Association for the Protection and Assistance of the Convicted (APAC), a Christian approach to prison reform that began in Brazil in the 1970s. A key part is prisoner participation in *Cursillo* (Spanish for a 'little course' in Christianity). Word spread about its model prison, Humaitá, during the early 1990s, assisted by the documentary film, *Love Is Not a Luxury*.

The first faith community took root in England and Wales at The Verne Prison in 1997. It was the first faith community to be tried in a prison outside South America. Its introduction stemmed from the pressing need to try something new in a part of the prison that was prone to riots. Certain limited elements of the APAC regime were combined with the Kairos Weekend (an adaptation of *Cursillo* to prisons).

Faith communities were initially criticized on human rights and equal opportunities grounds, although a full evaluation, carried out on four faith communities in England in 2000, found that they seemed to adhere to the spirit and the letter of the legislation. Overall, the evaluation found that faith communities were a signpost to the Prison Service in terms of promoting standards of decency, humanity and order in prisons (cited in Burnside *et al.* 2005). Government policy favours establishing partnerships with faith-based groups, although developing and maintaining a strong, trained, volunteer base is perhaps the greatest of the challenges facing faith communities in prisons.

*Jonathan Burnside*

*Related entries*

*Desistance; Human rights; Rehabilitation; Religion and faith; Therapeutic communities.*

### Key texts and sources

Burnside, J., with Adler, J., Loucks, N. and Rose, G. (2005) *My Brother's Keeper: Faith-based Units in Prisons.* Cullompton: Willan Publishing.
Burnside, J. and Lee, P. (1997) 'Where love is not a luxury', *New Life*, 13: 36–54.

# FAMILIES OF PRISONERS

Prisoners' families have been described as serving a second sentence, often viewed as guilty by association, facing social stigmatization, disapproval and sometimes actual harassment and violence. Yet, paradoxically, families are often invisible in media, public and academic discussion of prisons and punishment.

Wherever there are prisoners there are usually families and friends who are left behind. Although offenders may appear alone in the dock when given a custodial sentence, most prisoners have diverse family, kin and friendship networks. Many prisoners are parents themselves: Home Office research has shown that two thirds of women prisoners are mothers, and around 17,700 children lose their mothers to imprisonment every year. Although there are no accurate figures available, the Prison Reform Trust, a prominent British pressure group, estimates that more than 150,000 children in the UK currently have an imprisoned parent (Prison Reform Trust 2006). The rising prison population in the UK and the 'mass imprisonment epidemic' in the USA have re-energized debate, discussion and research into the impact of imprisonment on prisoners' family members.

### A second sentence

A substantial body of research over the last 40 years has documented the many and varied impacts of imprisonment on prisoners' wives, partners, children and parents (see Murray 2005), and recent US literature has documented the experiences of prisoners' families and communities as elements of the 'collateral consequences' of imprisonment – that is, as part of the associated impact of imprisonment on offenders, their families and communities (Travis and Waul 2003). Much of this research has tended to focus on a stereotypical depiction of the young male prisoner with a young wife or partner and small children, although this stereotype has been challenged by research that has begun to explore and document the diversity of prisoners' family relationships. It is clear from the literature that many prisoners' families experience a range of negative outcomes as a consequence of imprisonment, including both practical and emotional difficulties. Lack of information and support is a constant complaint and, in response to these, Action for Prisoners' Families has launched a helpline. In addition, a number of self-help and support groups exist at both a national and local level, although funding is often a problem.

Partners and families of prisoners can feel they are also serving a sentence. Social stigmatization can go as far as harassment and violence and, where the offence is serious or controversial, family members may be forced to move house and change their names in order to avoid hostility. As has been pointed out in the research literature, the female partners of male inmates often take on the status of their imprisoned men and become the target for media and societal disapproval. Female partners may experience loneliness and have to cope with managing money and the home for the first time. Many also have to learn for the first time how to deal with official agencies themselves. One of the most immediate impacts is financial. If a man is imprisoned, many families not only lose the main family income but women also have to face the extra burdens of 'standing by their man' from the outside. For example, they may bear the costs of telephone calls, buy clothes, trainers and toiletries, and send in books and other goods. Qualitative research studies have found that it is not uncommon for women to deprive themselves of essentials in order to supply goods for their imprisoned male partners. The negative financial consequences may also lead to housing changes as the result of mortgage arrears and the non-payment of rent, and this can make family life for prisoners' children very unstable. Visits also entail extra expense: although assisted visits are available for those on low incomes, only the transport costs are covered and, because many prisoners are held a long way from their homes, family members also need to pay for food and drink during the journey, and for drinks and snacks during the visit. Many partners show high levels of determination and commitment to maintaining contact and go to great lengths to sustain the imprisoned partners' involvement in family life, involving them in decision-making and trying to maintain family rituals for such occasions as birthdays in the visits room context. The demands of prison security, however, and variations between establishments, can make visiting difficult or restricted, and it must be remembered that, in the UK at present, there are no conjugal or private visits as there are in many other jurisdictions. Of course, the continuation of the relationship cannot be taken for granted as many marriages do not survive, either as a consequence of the nature and circumstances of the offending or as a result of stresses arising from the sentence. It is important to recognize that the responsibility for supporting prisoners and caring for their families is gendered. Regardless of the gender of the inmate, it is women who visit, write letters and supply prisoners with both items they need and items to make their prison stay more bearable. It is also primarily women who support other prisoners' family members through a number of self-help and support groups.

## Involving families in the resettlement of prisoners

In penal policy terms, prisoners' families have undergone something of a rediscovery in recent years. This has been aided by the explicit recognition in a report by the Social Exclusion Unit (2002) that prisoners' family ties can play a key role in promoting desistance and in preventing reoffending on release. As a consequence, family support initiatives and family tie schemes are now being justified not purely on humanitarian or social work grounds in order to benefit prisoners and their partners and children, but also with reference to their potential role in promoting prisoner well-being and in encouraging non-recidivism. This has led to calls for the involvement of families to a greater extent in sentence and pre-release planning, and to the identification of families as potential 'agents of resettlement'. A number of innovative schemes have been developed, such as those involving extended family visits, 'Storybook Mom' and 'Storybook Dad' projects, play schemes and homework clubs. Other prisons run parenting courses. These initiatives not only encourage prisoners to maintain relationships with their families, especially children, but can also have important by-products, such as improved literacy. However, although identifying prisoners' families as playing a central and important role in resettlement may help to improve recognition of their needs and appropriate responses, there are also important philosophical arguments that prisoners' next-of-kin should be supported for their own sake as they are 'fragile families' coping with profoundly challenging circumstances (Mills and Codd 2007).

## The impact of imprisonment on prisoners' children

The impact of parental imprisonment on children is also a matter of current concern. It is difficult to identify how many children experience the imprisonment of a parent. Sometimes prisoners do not want the prison authorities to know about their children because they fear they may be taken into local authority care. Sometimes children themselves do not know that a parent is imprisoned, because it is common for children not to be told the truth about where the absent parent has gone. Although some children benefit from parental imprisonment, such as where the parent has a chaotic lifestyle, mental health issues or drug or alcohol dependency, many children experience arrest, the trial and the subsequent sentence as profoundly traumatic. This can be particularly acute for the children of women prisoners, of whom many are lone parents. As Renny Golden (2005) writes in her work on the children of imprisoned women in the USA, many of the children of the women she interviewed were already living in difficult circumstances and experiencing a range of forms of social exclusion and deprivation. Hence the imprisonment of the mother was the loss of their only social anchor. Research has shown that prisoners' children are likely to develop emotional and behavioural problems, and many have difficulties at school. Although it is often taken for granted that prisoners' children are more likely to go on to become offenders themselves, and to some extent the statistics support this, it is difficult to quantify the likelihood of this and impossible to separate out the impacts of imprisonment from other socio-economic risk factors for offending. In the current context of the inexorable rise in the prison population, there are likely to be more and more families affected by these issues over the next decade.

*Helen Codd*

## Related entries

*Communication; Prison Reform Trust; Reoffending; Visits and visiting orders; Women in prison.*

**Key texts and sources**

Golden, R. (2005) *Mothers in Prison and the Families they Leave behind.* New York, NY: Routledge.

Mills, A. and Codd, H. (2007) 'Prisoners' families', in Y. Jewkes (ed.) *Handbook on Prisons.* Cullompton: Willan Publishing.

Murray, J. (2005) 'The effects of imprisonment on families and children of prisoners', in A. Liebling and S. Maruna (eds) *The Effects of Imprisonment.* Cullompton: Willan Publishing.

Prison Reform Trust (2006) *Bromley Briefings: Prison Factfile.* London: Prison Reform Trust.

Social Exclusion Unit (2002) *Reducing Re-offending by Ex-prisoners.* London: Social Exclusion Unit.

Travis, J. and Waul, M. (2003) *Prisoners Once Removed: The Impact of Incarceration and Reentry on Children, Families and Communities.* Washington, DC: Urban Institute Press.

The national federation for services that support families of prisoners can be accessed at http://www.prisonersfamilies.org.uk/. The website of Prison Advice (for prisoners and their families) is at http://www.prisonadvice.org.uk/.

# FARMS AND GARDENS

Farming, horticulture, forestry and grounds maintenance have been associated with the penal system for many years, in part because the Prison Service recognizes the therapeutic value of prisoners working with animals and plants.

It has always been a requirement for prisoners to work while in prison. In the early days, little thought was given to the value of the work offered. Boring, repetitive tasks were often carried out to keep the prisoners occupied. Yet, increasingly, it is being recognized that prisoners who have a history of bad behaviour and are resentful of authority and rules frequently improve their behaviour and become more co-operative when offered horticultural or agricultural work. Further, the positive role that working outdoors can play in prisoners' rehabilitation is an important part of the Prison Service's strategy to reduce the number of prisoners reoffending after release. A job, a home and a good relationship are considered the three most important factors in resettling a prisoner back into the community.

During the Second World War and the years immediately following, the need for increased food added impetus to employment in agricultural work. This led to prison gardens taking part in the 'Dig for Victory' campaign to produce vegetables for the prison kitchens. In 1947 the Prison Service managed 5,000 acres. By 1959 this had increased to 10,000 acres, the produce being used within the service and the surplus being sold on the open market. However, nationally, employment opportunities in agriculture (that is, livestock and field-scale cereal cropping) are now diminishing, with a predicted growth in horticultural activities (commercial horticulture defined as the production of vegetables and salads, and amenity horticulture defined as hard and soft landscaping, ground maintenance, etc.). To be able to continue to help prisoners to gain employment on release, the Prison Service has moved away from large-scale farming and now only 700 ha (1,700 acres) remain. There are currently only two commercial dairy farms and one commercial sheep farm, although a few prisons still retain small numbers of livestock. Some establishments show stock at local and national shows, with prisoners doing all the preparations and actual showing. Around six establishments have commercial horticultural units (some with farm shops attached).

A major part of the funds raised from the sale of land, stock and machinery has been used to enhance horticultural activities, both commercial and amenity. We know that there are skill shortages nationally in these activities and – bearing in mind that most prisoners come from urban areas – skills in amenity work are particularly relevant.

Overall there are about 85 establishments with active gardens parties, the majority successfully offering accredited training and providing mainly practical, 'hands on' experience, rather than the kinds of skills that will result in jobs with management grades. Because of this and because of the relatively short time often available, most establishments concentrate on practical qualifications at Entry Level and Levels 1 and 2. Where appropriate, some establishments also offer National Vocational Qualifications (NVQs).

A considerable number of prisoners have literacy and numeracy weaknesses and are sometimes wary of being taught basic skills, especially in special remedial classes. Prisoners are, however, willing to be trained as they work – hence the success of many prison farms and gardens. The Windlesham Trophy, a Prison Service annual competition to find the best prison gardens, provides a stimulus for prisoners and staff to strive for high standards, especially as the Royal Horticultural Society provides the judges for the final round. At some establishments prisoners are able, on licence, to work away from the establishment with commercial companies to gain valuable work experience.

*Chris Hartley*

*Related entries*

*Activities; Desistance; Employment and industries; Open prisons; Rehabilitation; Staff (prison).*

# FIRST-NIGHT CENTRES

> First-night centres are specialist units located in some prisons in order to hold prisoners during the first night. The aim is to ensure that prisoners are safely inducted into prison.

Self-inflicted deaths in prison occur disproportionately during the early stages of custody (HMIP 1999). First-night centres were created as part of the Prison Service's Safer Locals programme with the aim of reducing distress in those newly arriving in prison and of enabling staff better to identify prisoners at risk of harming themselves and needing ongoing support. First-night centres are predominantly found in local prisons, where a high proportion of prisoners are received direct from court, many of whom have little or no prison experience and are anxious about their circumstances. Many are withdrawing from drugs or alcohol, and a high percentage have a mental health condition.

A first-night centre is an area in a prison where new arrivals will spend their first night in an environment designed to help them adjust to entry into prison. They provide welcoming and calming environments separate from the main prison where staff and prisoner peer supporters help to reassure and settle prisoners. New and returning prisoners, particularly women, are concerned about family and other domestic issues. At Holloway Prison, for example, there is a scheme where people close to the prisoner can visit to see the accommodation in which the prisoner will have spent her first night. Typically, prisoners receive an induction pack which includes information about the prison, and this supplements the information provided verbally by staff and peer support 'insiders' in reception. New prisoners are also helped to make telephone calls to their families or friends.

The accommodation used in first-night centres will usually be double occupancy so that the prisoner, subject to risk assessment, can share a cell with another prisoner (sometimes a Samaritan-trained listener) in order to feel less isolated. First-night centres will often have some 'safer' ligature-free cells, although support through personal interaction is considered more important. It is good practice for establishments to have first-night officers with extended shift times, which allows them time to interact fully with prisoners. This is particularly useful as it helps staff to create a positive impression of what prison will be like and so reduce anxiety, but it also assists staff in identifying prisoners' needs, including mental and general health.

The quality of the reception and first-night processes should generally reflect the wider health of the establishment and should create in the prisoner the feeling that the prison environment is responsive and safe, and that he or she will be assisted to cope. All information gathered during this initial stage of imprisonment is shared with staff in the next stage of the induction process. An evaluation of the Safer Locals programme by the Prison Research Centre at the University of Cambridge found that staff and prisoners in the six pilot sites of the programme praised the improvements to the early period in custody, which they believed reduced distress (see Liebling *et al.* 2005).

*Nigel Hancock and Laura Graham*

*Related entries*

*Listener schemes; Local prisons; Mental health; Reception and induction; Self-harm; Suicide in prison.*

**Key texts and sources**

HM Chief Inspector of Prisons (1999) *Suicide is Everyone's Concern: A Thematic Review by HM Chief Inspector of Prisons for England and Wales.* London: Home Office.

Liebling, A., Tait, S., Durie, L., Stiles, A. and Harvey, J. (2005) 'Safer Locals evaluation', *Prison Service Journal*, 162: 8–12.

See also http://www.prisonadvice.org.uk/?q= firstnight for information on the first-night centres programme.

# FOOD AND DIET

> Meals must be available to all prisoners, providing choice and meeting their health and cultural needs.

The importance of food in prisons is so high that one governor described it as 'one of the four things you must get right if you like having a roof on your prison' (National Audit Office 2006). In prisons, mealtimes are a well recognized potential flashpoint between prisoners and staff. Portion sizes that are felt to be too small, monotonous meals and poorly cooked food can all too easily lead to confrontation and aggressive behaviour. As well as providing a basic need, food is one of life's pleasures. Having both enough to eat and making sure that meals are enjoyable goes a long way to ensuring stability and good morale. A few 'special' foods (such as chocolate, sweets, cakes and fresh fruit) usually outweigh their cost by their positive effect on mood and behaviour.

The provision of food is also a key element in ensuring decency in prisons. In particular, providing choice is important, as the prisoner population is not homogeneous, and meeting the diverse cultural and religious needs adds an extra dimension. It is also important for health reasons as giving prisoners the opportunity to choose a healthy, nutritionally balanced diet and providing enough knowledge to enable informed choices are crucial in promoting healthy lifestyles, especially for long-term prisoners who are dependent upon prison food to meet their nutritional needs. It has also been noted that:

*A high proportion of prisoners are from socially excluded sections of the community with lifestyles more likely to put them at risk of ill health than the rest of the population. Many have, for example, never registered with a doctor or a dentist. Many have drug habits or mental illness and live chaotic lives without a stable home. Prison gives an opportunity to improve the health and lifestyle of prisoners to the benefit of all (National Audit Office 2006: 7).*

The implication is that prison can be a place where the wider social needs of prisoners can be addressed, including promoting healthy living.

In English and Welsh prisons, prison governors have the ultimate responsibility for prisoners' diet. This responsibility includes approving food budgets and ensuring adequate meals are served. Prison kitchens are run by catering managers, often but not always professional caterers who are responsible for the implementation of set national standards, training of staff and control over the food budget. This is a substantial undertaking – in 2006, for example, the public sector Prison Service provided some 75 million meals at an average food cost per prisoner per day of under £2. Performance standards and policy are set and monitored by a small central team who visit prisons frequently.

The vast majority of prison kitchens also employ prisoners to help with the cooking. This provides a high level of purposeful activity but, in addition, provides the opportunity to train offenders so that, in some cases, they receive qualifications that enable them to gain employment in the catering sector on release. In addition, prisons have a small shop or 'canteen' which allows prisoners to purchase items including food, toiletries and other possessions. Prison shops have, over recent years, been contracted out to private sector providers. In some prisons, kitchen facilities are provided on wings in order to allow prisoners to prepare their own meals in addition to or as an alternative to those provided.

*Alan Tuckwood*

### Related entries

*Activities; Black and minority ethnic (BME) prisoners; Decency; Employment and industries; Healthcare; Race relations; Religion and faith.*

---

**Key texts and sources**

National Audit Office (2006) *Serving Time: Prisoner Diet and Exercise.* London: HMSO.

See also **http://www.nao.org.uk/publications/nao_reports/05-06/0506939.pdf** for the National Audit Office's report on prisoners' diet.

---

## FOREIGN NATIONAL PRISONERS

Foreign national prisoners are those held in UK prisons who do not hold a UK passport. The total number of foreign national prisoners in England and Wales in 2006 was 10,289.

Foreign national prisoners became the subject of intense public and political scrutiny when, in the spring of 2006, it was discovered that many had been released into the community without first being considered for deportation. The accompanying moral panic was fuelled by media reports exaggerating the dangerousness of this group, although there was no evidence that they were any more likely to reoffend than British ex-prisoners. Ironically, they had previously been referred to as 'forgotten prisoners' because they found it harder to communicate their concerns and had been seen as an easy population to manage in the prison estate, attracting little policy or operational attention.

The total number of foreign national prisoners in England and Wales trebled between the early 1990s and 2006, increasing from 3,446 (7.8 per cent of the prison population) in 1993 to 10,289 (13 per cent) in April 2006. This includes 880 women (up from 283 in 1993), constituting 20 per cent of the female prison population. There are no reliable figures on the number of post-sentence Immigration Act 1971 detainees, but there are certainly many hundreds of them, and there has been much criticism of the contribution of inefficient Immigration and Nationality Directorate (IND) case-working to their prolonged detention.

One reason for the rise in numbers is the increased sentence lengths for drug importation offences and the disproportionate numbers of foreign nationals imprisoned for such offences: in April 2006, 25 per cent of all foreign national prisoners were convicted of drug-related offences, compared with 12 per cent of British prisoners. The number of foreign nationals imprisoned for fraud and forgery offences (typically possession of false documents) also rose dramatically between 1994 and 2005, from 229 to 1,995. In April 2006, foreign national prisoners came from 172 different countries. Jamaicans (1,516) and Nigerians (904) constituted the two largest single nationalities. In regional terms, the highest proportion was from Europe (30 per cent), with Irish nationals accounting for nearly a quarter of this number. The largest proportion of the female foreign national population was from Africa (38 per cent).

Although there has been more attention to this group in recent years (see Bhui 2004), there had been no large-scale or definitive research to establish the main needs and challenges presented by this population until a thematic review was conducted by HM Inspectorate of Prisons (HMIP 2006). The review was based on in-depth interviews with 176 foreign national prisoners and more than 80 members of prison staff, as well as national surveys of both groups. Lack of family contact and immigration and language problems emerged as the main difficulties. Although prison staff were sympathetic and aware of the frequency – if not always the seriousness – of these problems, they were frustrated by a lack of relevant knowledge, guidance and training. There were few effective strategies or procedures in place, beyond thorough guidance on the prison's responsibility for liaison with IND. There is still no national policy for the management and support of foreign national prisoners, no practice guidelines to establishments and no audit standards, service-level agreements or contractual requirements.

*Hindpal Singh Bhui*

### Related entries

*Black and minority ethnic (BME) prisoners; Decency; Immigration detention; Prison population; Race relations; World prison populations.*

**Key texts and sources**

Bhui, H.S. (2004) *Going the Distance: Developing Effective Policy and Practice with Foreign National Prisoners*. London: Prison Reform Trust.

HM Inspectorate of Prisons (2006) *Foreign National Prisoners – a Thematic Review*. London: Home Office.

See also the Prison Service's web page (with attachments) about foreign national prisoners: http://www.hmprisonservice.gov.uk/adviceandsupport/prison_life/foreignnationalprisoners/.

## FRESH START

A 'Fresh Start' was the given name of the policy initiative introduced into the Prison Service in 1987 in order to resolve some of the long-standing problems related to the structure and organization of the service, particularly those associated with pay and conditions of service for prison officers.

The aim of the Fresh Start strategy was to reorganize prison officers' working arrangements and to adopt a more flexible approach to working practices; to improve staff relations and create a more rational management structure; and to improve the conditions of service for staff, thereby increasing job satisfaction. The scheme reflected a determined effort emerging within the Prison Service at the time to introduce values of economy, efficiency, effectiveness and management accountability into prisons (Liebling assisted by Arnold 2004). It arose partly in response to a report commissioned by the Home Office in 1985 which concluded that officers were working excessive and unnecessary amounts of overtime as a result of the way in which esta- blishments were staffed and the organization of shift systems. The report suggested that, contingent upon a revision of these shift systems, prisons could be run safely and efficiently with officers working an average of eight hours less.

According to the Woolf Report (1991: 339), staff working arrangements prior to the implementation of Fresh Start 'were of labyrinthine complexity'. They were considered unsatisfactory and inefficient by both prison officers and management for two main reasons. First, in order to supplement their perceived low level of basic pay, officers regularly sought opportunities, often with the collusion of local management, to receive large overtime payments (Coyle 2005). Before the introduction of Fresh Start, overtime was endemic and, during the mid-1980s, almost one third of the Prison Service pay bill was spent on overtime. Although the basic working week was specified as 40 hours, prison officers were working an average of 56 hours and some regularly worked 70 hours (Woolf 1991: 339). Officers were discontent because they felt required to work such long hours in order to take home reasonable pay and, at the same time, managers 'were faced with an arcane set of working practices which guaranteed virtually unlimited overtime in some prisons and no flexibility in the allocation of staff' (Coyle 2005: 88). Secondly, there existed a gulf between the prison officer rank (headed by the chief officer), seen as responsible for maintaining security and order and control, and the governor grades accountable for regimes, conditions and resource management, which resulted in ineffective line management. Officers and governors were recruited separately and had distinct career patterns. There was little movement between the two groups, which led to 'fragmented areas of command' (Woolf 1991: 339). The objective of Fresh Start was to eliminate these problems.

The inception of Fresh Start involved the phased abolition of overtime payments, a compensatory increase in the basic pay for prison officers for a fixed salaried 39-hour week and the unification of the grading structures for prison governors and prison officers. In practice this meant the rationalization of line management and, hence, the abolition of the chief officer rank. Fresh Start also included the creation of 'functional blocks' or 'group working', whereby dedicated staff groups were responsible for certain clearly defined functional tasks within each prison (such as residential, visits, security and operations). Any additional hours worked (due to unavoidable or emergency attendance or having to ensure minimum staffing levels were maintained) were to be met by providing 'time off in lieu' (TOIL).

In April 1987 the Prison Service issued, among other publications, a 28-page bulletin setting out the details of Fresh Start. In union ballots the package was overwhelmingly accepted (with over 80 per cent of officers and 90 per cent of governors being in favour): staff unsurprisingly welcomed considerably improved pay for fewer hours' work.

Fresh Start had a significant impact on prisons and on the working lives of prison officers. The introduction of functional, or group, working resulted in many officers being detailed to specific residential areas or wings within the prison for sustained periods of time. Although this continuity of working was well received, Woolf's inquiry received complaints that it also resulted in a sense of isolation from other work groups and therefore a reduction in teamwork. Crawley (2004: 185) maintains that less contact with staff from other areas consequently led to pronounced inter-wing competitiveness; wing-based, rather than establishment-based, identities; and an increase in solidarity among group members but a decline within the prison as a whole since 'each group has a tendency to put its own interests above those of other uniformed groups'.

Woolf's inquiry contains a detailed description of the fundamental reorganization of prison officers' working arrangements and of management within establishments, including comments on the way in which it was implemented and its effects on regimes. It also offers an explanation of the targeted 15 and 24 per cent efficiency savings (agreed with the Treasury) that would have to be made in order to finance the enhanced remuneration Fresh Start specified and the associated substantial increase in efficiency

that would be required to compensate for the reduction in working hours, including the implications this had for prison staffing levels.

The conclusion of Woolf's inquiry suggested that, despite evident improvements in line management and accountability, staff felt disillusioned and mistrustful of the extensive organizational change presented. He stated that despite containing 'many needed reforms', tackling inefficiencies and providing 'an important platform for developments in the future' Fresh Start had 'failed to achieve its potential' and that this was 'in part due to the way in which it was introduced' (1991: 338). Its inauguration was described as expeditious, lacking preparation and insensitive, and the deficiency in information provided by the Prison Service regarding the reduction in the availability of staff needed to achieve the stated efficiencies was criticized. The anticipated improvements in regimes and conditions for prisoners were found not to have materialized, no increase in job satisfaction was identified and staff expressed considerable regret at the loss of the esteemed position of chief officer. However, staff and governors agreed that Fresh Start's 'conceptual framework' was 'sound' and offered 'a constructive way forward' for the Prison Service (1991: 348).

*Helen Arnold*

### Related entries

*Cost of prisons; Governors; Industrial relations; New public management (NPM); Prison officers; Staff (prison); Woolf Report.*

### Key texts and sources

Coyle, A. (2005) *Understanding Prison: Key Issues in Policy and Practice.* Maidenhead: Open University Press.

Crawley, E. (2004) *Doing Prison Work: The Public and Private Lives of Prison Officers.* Cullompton: Willan Publishing.

Liebling, A. assisted by Arnold, H. (2004) *Prisons and their Moral Performance: A Study of Values, Quality and Prison Life.* Oxford: Oxford University Press.

Woolf, Lord Justice and Tumin, S. (1991) *Prison Disturbances, April 1990* (Cm 1456). London: HMSO.

The Association of Ex-offenders' website is at **http://unlock.org.uk/main.aspx**.

# FRIENDSHIP

Friendship is a neglected topic in prison sociology. However, detailed discussions of prisoners' personal relationships do exist, and it is possible to identify some common notions of what features of penal institutions are important in shaping inmates' relationships and themes in prisoners' descriptions of their relationships with one another.

Friendship appears throughout the prisons literature but has only infrequently received any focused attention. The concept of friendship has tended to be subsumed under discussions of the inmate code and prisoner solidarity and, in the case of women prisoners, a preoccupation with dyadic sexual relationships and the formation of pseudo-families. However, although diffuse, discussions of prison friendships highlight a number of significant features of prison life that remain fairly constant across time and between institutions, to which individual prisoners inevitably respond very differently, but which nevertheless generate several interesting themes and a common range of experiences.

A number of features of prisons appear salient in shaping the formation and nature of friendships between prisoners or, conversely, in prompting prisoners to avoid close relationships with other inmates. These typically include low levels of trust among inmates (acknowledged even in discussions produced at the height of academic faith in the inmate code); a general scarcity of material resources; isolation from other friendships, associations and sexual relationships; the transitory nature of the prison; forced proximity to individuals not of one's own choosing; and the dislocation of individuals from the wider context that facilitates authentication of their self-presentation. Prisoners' attitudes to prison friendships range from those who argue that trust and friendship are impossible in prison and those who are more comfortable spending time with staff rather than other prisoners, to those whose closest friendships have been prison friendships and who report that people – especially addicts – are more 'themselves' inside prison than out.

Morris and Morris's (1963) discussion of prisoners' relationships remains one of the most systematic accounts and continues to resonate with contemporary research. They argue that, as suggested above, the institution significantly influences prisoners' relationships and is as important as personal choice in determining whom individuals will befriend. Inmates typically categorize others as *mates*, *friends* and *acquaintances*. A prisoner explains:

> *Mates you do anything for; you give them anything they want and if he is involved in a punch up you go in. Friends you lend to but you don't give. If he's in a punch up you think about what might be involved before you go in. Acquaintances you don't want to know, and you couldn't care less what happens in a punch up (cited in Morris and Morris 1963: 224).*

A consistent pattern of friendship among prisoners emerges in the study. Most report having one mate, three or four friends and dozens of acquaintances. Mates are generally of longstanding acquaintance, often having met during previous sentences or on the outside. The singularity of the relationship of mates and the small numbers of friends reported were dictated not just by the narrowness of the inmate social world but also by the risks inmates perceived in intimacy with anyone beyond a small trusted circle. Morris and Morris describe the relationship between mates in particular as being both 'defensive alliances' against violence, intimidation and exploitation, and 'reciprocal supports' against the privations of imprisonment.

Morris and Morris reflect both the tensions of prison and the possibility of relationships between prisoners founded in genuine trust, and even affection. This is clearly reflected in the prison writings of Erwin James (2003), who describes a cluster of affectionate, respectful and supportive friendships within a hostile wider environment. In contrast, Giallombardo's (1966) study of an American women's prison describes prisoners' 'self-orientation' and a near-universal lack of trust. Giallombardo's analysis is undoubtedly shaped by contemporary discourses around womens' friendships, which portrayed them as fraught with competition and inferior to mens'. The predominance of single-site ethnographies makes reliable comparison between institutions and authors almost impossible. What is significant is that, although she advances very negative views of prisoners' interpersonal relationships, Giallombardo nevertheless identifies two forms of friend-like relationships. *Rap buddies* become friends on the basis of liking and mutual assurances of confidentiality. *Homeys* are inmates from the same area, between whom there is unequivocal loyalty and reciprocity, although they may not have met before imprisonment (Giallombardo 1966). Strong local loyalties of this kind also exist in contemporary prisons in England and Wales. Giallombardo suggests that solidarity with homeys is a kind of insurance for the future, as inmates from one's own locale can disseminate negative reports beyond the prison. This is especially important for career criminals and prisoners involved in street culture. Prisoners can be more confident that an inmate from one's own area is who he or she claims to be and has not, for example, been convicted of a stigmatized offence.

Greer (2000), among others, notes an apparent decline in formalized pseudo-familial relationships between women in prison, and finds instead mixed views on prison friendship. Like Morris and Morris, Greer found prisoners distinguishing between *friends* and *associates*, a widespread distinction in inmates' descriptions of prison relationships (see also James 2003). Like much recent research, Greer emphasizes the *range* of prisoners' attitudes to, and experiences of, friendship in prison. The comments of her participants are typical. Many said they had no friends in prison. Some resisted forming friendships that might be terminated abruptly by transfer or release. Longer-serving prisoners became disenchanted as successive companions left prison swearing to keep in touch and never did, although some had friendships that lasted beyond release (James 2003 corresponds with a number of prisoners who have been moved to another prison or released). Although most women described other prisoners as manipulative and self-serving, most also said they had at least one friend, some arguing that their strongest friendships had been forged in prison.

Many disagreed with the popular wisdom that friendship in prison was impossible, regarding it as necessary and inevitable. Greer concludes that while prisoners' need for support and companionship, their often similar backgrounds and shared experience of imprisonment may lead one to expect inmates to form close relationships, the problems that originally brought individuals to prison can ultimately lead to very complex relationships that are difficult to sustain as healthy friendships, either during a prison sentence or after release.

*Abigail Rowe*

### Related entries

*Identity and self; Inmate code; Solidarity; Subcultures; Women in prison.*

**Key texts and sources**

Giallombardo, R. (1966) 'Social roles in a prison for women', *Social Problems*, 13: 268–88.

Greer, K.R. (2000) 'The changing nature of interpersonal relationships in a women's prison', *Prison Journal*, 80: 442–68.

James, E. (2003) *A Life Inside: A Prisoner's Notebook.* London: Atlantic Books.

Morris, T. and Morris, P. (1963) *Pentonville: A Sociological Study of an English Prison.* London: Routledge & Kegan Paul.

# FRY, ELIZABETH

Elizabeth Fry (1780–1845) was a notable prison reformer, particularly in respect of women in prison.

Born in Norwich into a Quaker banking family in 1780, Elizabeth Gurney married Joseph Fry, also a banker, in 1799, and by 1812 she had borne him 12 children. She first visited Newgate Gaol in 1813 and was appalled by the filthy conditions and the degrading conditions in which women in prison were held. However, her work as a prison reformer began in earnest in 1817 when – with some like-minded middle-class ladies – she set up the voluntary Association for the Improvement of the Female Prisoners in Newgate. Similar 'ladies committees' were later set up in provincial gaols.

Fry's association aimed to provide decent clothes, secular and religious instruction and suitable work for the women. She endeavoured, by advice and example, to change their personal and moral behaviour and attitude to work, and she persuaded them to adopt a set of rules on behaviour. Fry believed that reading Scripture could transform their lives both in prison and after release, when they would work honestly, instead of resorting to reoffending. She argued that women should be treated separately and differently in prison, and she encouraged the authorities to appoint a matron to superintend the Newgate women, and to convey them to the hulks in a more dignified fashion. In 1823 Home Secretary Peel confirmed in his Gaol Act that all female prisoners could only be supervised by female staff under a matron. Fry also believed passionately in the need to train and rehabilitate and not just to punish women in prison, seeing them essentially as the victims of society. She expressed her views to a number of parliamentary inquiries and in her *Observations on the Visiting, Superintendence and Government of Female Prisoners* (1827).

She was also concerned with prison reform more generally. In 1819 she and her brother, John Gurney, published *Notes of a Visit Made to some of the Prisons in Scotland and the North of England in Company with Elizabeth Fry*, which revealed that many prisons had not improved at all since John Howard's (1726–90) visits more than half a century earlier. However, her influence waned from the late 1820s, and her husband's bankruptcy in 1828 further affected her reputation. She disagreed with the new breed of prison reformers who advocated separate cells, solitary confinement and a more deterrent and retributive regime. She believed strongly in the socializing effect of appropriate daytime work in association and separation only at night, and she spoke out against the dangers of solitary confinement. The new reformers felt that Fry really only wanted to improve existing prison practice, whereas they wanted a radical restructuring. They also objected to the role of well meaning lady visitors and the influence they appeared to exercise over prison officials. Fry continued to campaign for her vision of prison reform, with decreasing success, until her death in 1845.

*Laurie Feehan*

### Related entries

*Howard, John; Rehabilitation; Reoffending; Women in prison.*

---

**Key texts and sources**

Kent, J. (1962) *Elizabeth Fry*. London: Batsford.
Rose, J. (1994) *Elizabeth Fry*. London: QHS.
See also the Howard League for Penal Reform's chapter on Elizabeth Fry (http://www.howardleague.org/index.php?id=elizabethfry). The Elizabeth Fry Approved Centres for Women website is at http://www.efap.co.uk/.

# G

## GIRLS IN PRISON

The Youth Justice Board manages females under 18 years of age held in custody. There are over 400 girls in custody, with 70 per cent being held in prisons. The population has increased by 400 per cent in a decade.

The Youth Justice Board (YJB) has responsibility for the placement of girls in custody and decides whether they are placed in prison, secure training centres or local authority secure accommodation. Around 70 per cent of the 17-year-old girls in custody are placed in prison. There has been a disproportionate rise of girls in prison. Between 1993 and 2004, the number of custodial sentences imposed annually on girls under 18 increased from 114 to 444, a rise of almost 400 per cent. Worrall (2001) argues that statistics do not show that girls are committing more offences or becoming more violent, despite media claims to the contrary. Carlen (2002) notes that, although there has been an increase in violent crimes committed by young people, the gender ratio has remained around one female to five males.

The majority of girls in prison are serving short sentences. Of the 43 girls received into immediate prison custody in the last quarter of 2005, 29 were serving sentences of 6 months or less, 4 were serving sentences of 6 months to a year and 10 were serving sentences of 1 to 4 years. Around a quarter of the 17-year-old girls in prison are on remand. On 28 July 2006 there were 62 girls in prison, one aged 16 and 61 aged 17. Of these, 38 were serving a detention and training order, 13 were on remand, 8 were sentenced under s. 90/91 of the Power of the Criminal Courts Act 2000 and 3 were serving an extended sentence. Five Prisons hold girls aged 17 and under, providing 91 places. The units are based at Cookham Wood Prison in Kent, Downview Prison in Surrey, Eastwood Park Prison in Gloucestershire, Newhall Prison in Wakefield and Foston Hall Prison in Derby.

Girls account for a small fraction of the total prison population. They make up 0.1 per cent of the total prison population and 1 per cent of the female population in prison. Girls in prison are currently held separately from adults in designated juvenile units. However, this has not always been the case. In January 1997, the Howard League for Penal Reform published *Lost Inside*, the results of a year-long inquiry chaired by Baroness Masham into the use of prison custody for girls aged under 18. It found that girls were being held alongside adult women in adult jails, in breach of the UN Convention of the Rights of the Child. Prison staff were largely untrained in dealing with such vulnerable and damaged young girls. Following the publication of this report, the case of *R* v. *Accrington Youth Court ex parte Flood* [1998] 1 WLR156 judicially reviewed the Home Office policy to hold juvenile girls with adults in prison. The judgement declared it was unlawful for the Secretary of State automatically to place a young offender in an adult prison. In order to comply with the Flood ruling, the Prison Service stated that girls aged under 18 should only be held in designated young offender institutions. The Prison Service issued new rules on regimes for young women under 18 years old (PSO 4950). Girls were placed in designated juvenile wings within young offender institutions. However, in some prisons, girls were still mixing with adults (for example, in healthcare).

In March 1999, the government made a commitment to remove girls from prison custody as it was deemed not in their best interests to hold them there. In addition to the broader government commitments, the YJB stated that it saw it as an absolute priority to place all young women outside adult prisons and was determined to place them in more appropriate accommodation by mid-2002. There had been a gradual removal of the younger girls from prison custody and, in February 2003, the YJB announced its intention to remove all under 17-year-old girls from Prison Service accommodation. Instead, by 2006 the number of 17-year-old girls in prison had increased by 26 per cent since 1996. There no longer appears to be a commitment to keep 16-year-old girls out of prison custody. The YJB annual report for 2005–6 states that the recently opened prison unit for girls in Foston Hall has places for 16 and 17-year-old girls who are sentenced to custody. In July 2006 there were two girls aged 16 in prison.

The vast majority of girls in prison are vulnerable and damaged individuals. Research by the Howard League for Penal Reform (2004) found that 50 per cent of girls had experienced family breakdown, 36 per cent had a drug or alcohol problem, 17 per cent had self-harmed and 8 per cent had been a victim of physical or sexual abuse in the past. HM Inspectorate of Prisons carried out an unannounced inspection of Eastwood Park in October 2001. Inspectors met all 12 girls under 18 years old and noted the extensive personality disturbance and mental health problems presented and criticized the inappropriateness of detention in prison. An inspection at Newhall Prison in November 2003 noted the disproportionately high levels of self-harm and the use of force involving girls in that prison.

As there are so few prisons holding girls, they are often placed a long way from home. Research by the Howard League for Penal Reform (2004) found that this had a detrimental effect on their emotional well-being and rehabilitation, and also created problems when attending court or arranging visits.

*Lorraine Atkinson*

## Related entries

*Child protection; Children in custody; HM Inspectorate of Prisons; Secure training centres; Women in prison; Young offender institutions (YOIs); Youth Justice Board (YJB).*

### Key texts and sources

Carlen, P. (ed.) (2002) *Women and Punishment: The Struggle for Justice.* Cullompton: Willan Publishing.

Howard League for Penal Reform (1997) *Lost Inside: The Imprisonment of Teenage Girls.* London: Howard League for Penal Reform.

Howard League for Penal Reform (2004) *Advice, Understanding and Underwear: Working with Girls in Prison.* London: Howard League for Penal Reform.

Worrall, A. (2001) 'Girls at risk? Reflections on changing attitudes to young women's offending', *Probation Journal*, 48: 86–92.

The report on training for girls in detention under the age of 18 is available online at **http://inspectorates.homeoffice.gov.uk/hmiprisons/thematic-reports1/girlsinprison.pdf?view=Binary**. See also the Youth Justice Board's website (**http://www.yjb.gov.uk/en-gb/**).

# GOVERNORS

Prison governors are a key occupational group within the criminal justice system. Governors enforce the state's most severe penalty by running the 137 penal establishments in England and Wales. Governors hold in custody convicted and unconvicted citizens, deprive them of their freedom and enforce the rules and regulations that dictate prisoners' daily lives.

Each prison has an in-charge governor. The Prison Act 1952 (as amended) vests governors with formal authority and status. Governors are appointed by the Secretary of State under s. 7 of the Act and are, therefore, holders of a statutory office. The exercise of the Home Secretary's power under the Act to appoint persons to the office of governor has to be done rationally. Those making the appointment, therefore, have to satisfy themselves that the person to be appointed is fit and proper to hold the post and has the requisite knowledge, skills and experience to perform in the position, to an adequate standard.

As holders of the office of governor, incumbents exercise powers delegated by the Home Secretary, as well as their own statutory powers. Governors exercise power delegated by the Home Secretary in various circumstances, such as transferring a prisoner or discharging a prisoner temporarily on grounds of ill-health. In some cases the governor will act for the Home Secretary (for example, in relation to home detention curfew and release on temporary licence). The Act also confers on governors some statutory powers (such as the power to conduct adjudications on prisoners) and the Prison Rules authorize governors to take certain actions (for example, to segregate prisoners) which contribute to their formal authority and status. Governors have the freedom to use their legitimate authority and statutory powers without being unlawfully constrained or fettered. Under s. 8 of the Act, governors, as officers of the prison, have the 'powers, authority, protection and privileges of a constable' (*R* v *Secretary of State for Home Office, ex parte Benwell* [1985] QB 554). This status is useful to governors in carrying out their duties and gives them a certain amount of protection while doing so.

Governors are civil servants. Their annual salary is between £58,000 and £70,000. There are no specified hours that governors have to work, as they are termed 'all hours worked grades'. Governors are on call 24 hours a day, seven days a week. They are routinely expected to work some evenings, to make visits to their prisons at night (between 2300 and 0600 hours) and to work some weekends. They are entitled to 30 days' annual leave. The retirement age for governors is currently 60. Most governors are represented by the Prison Governors Association (PGA), which has the status and immunities of a trade union. A pay review body was established in 2001 to make recommendations on governors' pay, allowances and associated terms and conditions of employment.

Unlike their colleagues in other jurisdictions, governors are not required to have a legal qualification or to be a lawyer, and are not appointed directly to the office of governor. Governors are appointed from within the ranks of existing Prison Service staff and there is no provision for someone to join the Prison Service and take up a governor's post immediately. People wanting to be governors join the service as operational managers and, after suitable training and experience, become deputy governors, before taking up a post as governor of a prison.

Governors are required to undertake the duties and tasks as set out in their job descriptions. In addition, they have to ensure that the requirements of Prison Rules, other statutory obligations and line management are met. With the permission of the Home Secretary (under Prison Rule 8), governors may delegate any powers or duties to another officer of the prison. The legislation says very little more about the work and powers of a governor.

The warrant of the court, on whose authority the prisoner is sent to custody, is addressed to the governor and requires the governor either to produce the remand prisoner back to court or to keep the convicted prisoner in custody for the time determined. The prisoner is in the legal custody of the governor, who is accountable to the court for that secure custody (Prison Act 1952, s. 13). However, it is the Secretary of State who has the responsibility for the administration of prisons under the Prison Act and it is the policies of the Secretary of State that determine how prisoners are dealt with. The governor's accountability, therefore, is both to the court and to the Secretary of State.

Governors must balance the four functions of penal confinement (Faugeron 1996): the custodial function (preventing escapes); the restorative function (providing opportunities for rehabilitation and reform); the controlling function (ensuring order, safety and justice); and the maintenance function (providing decent and humane conditions). In doing so, governors exercise considerable personal power within their institutions. Prisoners can be physically restrained, segregated, transferred, confined to their cells, strip searched, refused physical contact with their families and released temporarily – all on the instructions of the governor. It has been pointed out that 'The key managerial role in the Prison Service is that of Governor … a well run prison runs more than anything else on the skill and approach of the Governor' (HM Prison Service 1997: paras. 4 and 9.14). The nature of the work, and the environment in which it is undertaken, led to the role of the governor being described as unique or *sui generis*. However, in recent years the role has undergone something of a transformation and has become more managerial and, some believe, less distinct as a *sui generis* profession.

A number of aspects of the governor's work have remained remarkably constant over the years. Throughout history, governors have been required to maintain a personal presence by frequently visiting all parts of the establishment; to adjudicate on at least some disciplinary matters; to sample the prisoners' food on a daily basis; to monitor closely prisoners in segregation and hospital; to undertake a number of symbolic and ceremonial duties; to liaise with the local community; and to deal personally with major incidents. Some facets of a governor's role and duties, however, have changed considerably. The amount of devolution has increased, but this has been matched with more monitoring and greater personal accountability. The scope for individuality and discretion has been reduced and replaced with a stronger degree of uniformity and regulation. Most significantly, governors today perform generic managerial roles and duties that managers and leaders in all organizations undertake. These general management tasks relate to finances, planning, human resources, auditing and monitoring. Governors also provide leadership, which includes developing and maintaining the vision of the prison; the representational and figurehead elements of their work; and creating meaning out of the conflicting aims and goals set for custodial institutions. In addition, governors must be effective incident commanders (acting in a 'command role') during incidents such as fires, riots, demonstrations, escapes, hostage taking and rooftop protests.

However, despite the changes to their work, governors will always need to be more than just general managers. Governors point to a number of reasons why this is the case: the nature of the custodial institution itself; the historical vestiges in the role; the level of discretion that governors still exercise over individuals; and the need for someone to regulate the operation of a prison on a daily basis. The reality is that governors must have an appreciation of, and be able to manipulate, the 'softer' elements of a prison (such as culture, emotions, tensions, expectations) in order to regulate its daily operation. This aspect of a governor's role – known as 'jailcraft' – has remained ever-present over the years.

Contemporary prison governance is still about creating a safe and secure establishment which has a positive ethos, and in which staff and prisoners are able to make a contribution to the community. This involves the governor crafting prison culture (both prison staff and prisoner subcultures) and understanding how to blend the various approaches to maintaining order. It entails demonstrating clear values and beliefs in order to make clear what is, and is not, acceptable behaviour and setting appropriate boundaries. It is about guarding against abuse of power and ensuring that staff exercise their authority legitimately and fairly. It requires imparting respect for the rights of others among both staff and prisoners, as well as ensuring that the rules are applied in a fair and reasonable manner. It involves exercising power and decision-making based on a firm moral foundation. It necessitates effectively channelling the extreme emotions and feelings of prisoners and managing relational and discretionary elements of the prison environment. It is about providing a range of constructive activities and promoting participation in those activities. It involves representing the establishment outside the walls and managing the boundaries with external stakeholders. But above all it is about creating hope and providing the opportunity for personal growth among staff and prisoners in what is a potentially damaging environment.

*Shane Bryans*

## Related entries

*Audit; Discretion; Fairness; Legitimacy; Power; Prison officers; Staff (prison).*

**Key texts and sources**

Bryans, S. (2000) 'Governing prisons: an analysis of who is governing prisons and the competencies which they require to govern effectively', *Howard Journal*, 39: 14–29.

Bryans, S. (2007) P*rison Governors: Managing Prisons in a Time of Change.* Cullompton: Willan Publishing.

Bryans, S. and Jones, R. (eds) (2001) *Prisons and the Prisoner: An Introduction to the Work of Her Majesty's Prison Service.* London: HMSO.

Bryans, S. and Wilson, D. (2000) *The Prison Governor: Theory and Practice* (2nd edn). Leyhill: Prison Service Journal Publications.

Faugeron, C. (1996) 'The changing functions of imprisonment', in R. Matthews and P. Francis (eds) *Prisons 2000 – an International Perspective on the Current State and Future of Imprisonment.* London: Macmillan.

HM Prison Service (1997) *Prison Service Review.* London: Home Office.

# GRIEVANCES

> Grievance procedures provide a mechanism for prisoners to make complaints regarding aspects of their detention. They are an essential means of ensuring that authority is exercised reasonably and proportionately by prison staff.

The European Prison Rules lay down that 'Prisoners, individually or as a group, shall   have ample opportunity to make requests or complaints to the director of the prison or to any other competent authority'. They further establish that 'if a request is denied or a complaint is rejected, reasons shall be provided to the prisoner and the prisoner shall have the right to appeal to an independent authority' (Rules 70.1 and 70.3). The equivalent UK Prison Rule (11) is much shorter and less specific. Nevertheless, a well developed complaints system is in place, although not all prisoners have confidence in it.

PSO 2510 details the grievance system that has operated since 2002. The order notes that an effective system for dealing with complaints is necessary to deal fairly, openly and humanely with prisoners. It adds that a good complaints system is also necessary to maintain order and control. The order says that the procedures are based on ten principles: openness, simplicity, ease of access, timeliness, fairness, responding at an appropriate level, confidentiality, appropriate redress, freedom from penalty and the use of the system to provide management information.

Most complaints from prisoners (like most grievances in the world at large) are dealt with informally. If a problem arises it is generally resolved by front-line staff on the wing or the landing. Thousands of these resolutions must occur each day; they are rarely recorded or given much further thought. However, if the informal methods do not work, prisoners should have free access to official complaint forms. Reasonably tight time limits are imposed on the replies to these forms, and senior managers should be auditing both timeliness and the quality of the responses. Although some prisoners are fearful of repercussions (or of being labelled as a troublemaker), reports from HM Inspectorate of Prisons suggest that the system works well in most establishments.

Special arrangements are in place to guarantee 'confidential access' if the complaint is especially serious or sensitive. A separate system also applies if the complainant alleges that there is a racial element involved. Prisoners may also sidestep the official grievance procedure by drawing their problem to the attention of independent monitoring boards or by writing to an MP, lawyer or one of the penal pressure groups. Prisoners dissatisfied with the official grievance mechanisms may also try to bring their complaints or problems to court. Major reforms to disciplinary arrangements, categorization decisions and correspondence have resulted from decisions of the courts (Livingstone and Owen 2003).

The independent Prisons and Probation Ombudsman can take up complaints once the internal procedures have been completed. The ombudsman's annual report contains examples of complaints he has investigated, along with more general comments on the effectiveness of the grievance system.

*Stephen Shaw*

*Related entries*

*Decency; Fairness; HM Inspectorate of Prisons; Human rights; Independent monitoring boards; Legitimacy; Prison Rules; Prisons and Probation Ombudsman; Woolf Report.*

**Key texts and sources**

Home Office (2002) *Prisoners' Requests and Complaints Procedure* (PSO 2510). London: Home Office.

Livingstone, S. and Owen, T. (2003) *Prison Law* (3rd edn). Oxford: Oxford University Press.

# H

## HEALTHCARE

Since their inception, prison healthcare services have been criticized for a lack of quality, suitability, scope and accountability. Government policy now supports a partnership between the NHS and the Prison Service aimed at improving the standards of healthcare in prisons, based on the concept that services in prison should be equivalent to those provided for the wider population.

The healthcare needs of prisoners have been an important consideration since the early days of the penal system, but the development of health services within prisons has been punctuated by controversy and criticism. The culture of providing 'care' has often been viewed as being at odds with the basic function of imprisonment – namely, the punishment of offenders.

Legislation passed in 1774 obliged gaols to appoint a resident medical officer to oversee the health of prisoners and, in 1899, the rank of hospital officer was instigated, a role fulfilled by discipline officers who received brief general healthcare training. Early prison healthcare placed an emphasis on preserving the physical and mental health of prisoners through the maintenance of hygiene, cleanliness and moral standards. In the twentieth century the influence of prison medical officers grew as they started to influence courts' decisions through the provision of psychiatric reports commenting on defendants' mental states and making treatment or punishment recommendations.

In recent years, healthcare services for prisoners have been publicly criticized on a number of accounts: the numbers of suicides in prison; the alleged inappropriate use of psychotropic medication for disciplinary rather than clinical reasons; interference from prison governors in clinical decision-making; overall poor standards of care; a lack of appropriately qualified staff; and a lack of openness and accountability due to the separation of prison-based services from the wider NHS (e.g. Sim 1990; HMCIP 1996).

In 1999, the NHS and the Prison Service entered into a formal partnership to improve the delivery of healthcare to prisoners. Emphasis was placed on the need for prisoners to receive services equivalent in scope and quality to those provided to the wider community (HMPS/NHS Executive 1999). Over a period of several years, financial responsibility for prison healthcare has passed from the Prison Service to local primary care trusts (PCTs), who are charged with working collaboratively with prisons to commission appropriate services responsive to actual clinical need. The clinical improvement partnership between the Prison Service and the NHS recognizes that, rather than being a separate entity, prisoners are in fact a subset of the wider community, albeit with discrete health needs. Research evidence shows that prison populations differ from the general population in terms of the types and prevalence of illness they experience.

In terms of physical illness, evidence from the UK shows that prisoners commonly experience chronic illness, one study reporting that nearly half of male, sentenced prisoners had some sort of long-standing illness or disability (Bridgwood and Malbon 1995). Other studies have shown higher rates of respiratory disorders, heart and circulatory disease, hepatitis infection and sexually transmitted diseases compared with the general population. Substance abuse problems are routine, and prisons have, over time, developed comprehensive detoxification and throughcare services for drug and alcohol users, although some interventions common in the community (for example, the provision of clean injecting equipment for those who continue to use drugs in prison) have not been implemented.

It is widely known that mental health problems are common in prison, with high rates of mental illness and personality disorder creating significant needs for intervention from both primary care and specialist mental health services (Singleton *et al.* 1998). Rates of suicide and self-harm among prisoners are also higher than those found in the general population. Work has been undertaken to improve the multidisciplinary care for prisoners considered to be at risk, although there is no evidence to date that these interventions have impacted positively on rates of suicide (Shaw *et al.* 2003). Rates of both mental health problems and suicide and self-harm risk are higher in women in prison than their male counterparts, presenting unique challenges to the delivery of effective interventions to women.

Healthcare services in busy local prisons, which experience a high turnover of prisoners and accept prisoners directly from court, are generally available around the clock; other types of prisons, with more stable populations, operate more limited services. The majority of healthcare in prisons is delivered in-house by qualified and auxiliary nursing staff employed by PCTs and by healthcare officers employed by the Prison Service. Primary care services are routinely contracted out to local general practitioners. Additional clinics for specialist services (for example, genito-urinary medicine, chiropody and optical care) are provided on a sessional basis by visiting professionals. Prisoners may also need to access services provided by local hospitals or regional NHS centres when the care required is too complex or specialized for the prison to provide directly, or when care is required as an emergency. Accessing care in outside hospitals generally has security implications (for example, to prevent escape) and thus incurs extra cost and planning. Many prisons have in-patient units where prisoners deemed to require 24-hour care are treated. These areas commonly host a rather disparate clientele who may be experiencing physical or mental illness, be detoxing from drugs or alcohol, be acutely suicidal or may be experiencing social or custodial difficulties on normal location. In-patient areas have also been traditionally vulnerable to having to provide accommodation for healthy prisoners during times of acute overcrowding, thus compounding management difficulties. It seems likely that the number of in-patient beds will reduce in the near future as care, especially for those with mental health problems, is redesigned and more care is provided while prisoners remain on ordinary residential wings.

Healthcare services in prisons are currently undergoing an intense process of change. The NHS and Prison Service have, in partnership, embarked on a large developmental work programme to meet better the health needs of those in prison. Financial control for prison-based services has been passed over to PCTs. A continued close partnership with the Prison Service is vital if this work programme is to succeed. Furthermore, spending on the healthcare needs of prisoners must not be affected adversely by political and media pressure, that may influence the direction of ultimately finite NHS resources away from services to prisoners and towards those viewed by society as being more 'deserving'.

*Jane Senior*

## Related entries

*Disability; Drugs; Local prisons; Mental health; Overcrowding; Self-harm; Suicide in prison.*

### Key texts and sources

Bridgwood, A. and Malbon, G. (1995) *Survey of the Physical Health of Prisoners, 1994.* London: Office of Population Censuses and Surveys.

HM Chief Inspector of Prisons (1996) *Patient or Prisoner? A New Strategy for Health Care in Prisons.* London: Home Office.

HM Prison Service/NHS Executive (1999) *The Future Organisation of Prison Health Care.* London: Department of Health.

Senior, J. and Shaw, J. (2007) 'Prison healthcare' in Y. Jewkes (ed.) *Handbook on Prisons*. Cullompton: Willan Publishing.

Shaw, J., Appleby, L. and Baker, D. (2003) *Safer Prisons: A National Study of Prison Suicides 1999–2000 by the National Confidential Inquiry into Suicides and Homicides by People with Mental Illness*. London: Department of Health.

Sim, J. (1990) *Medical Power in Prisons: The Prison Medical Service in England 1774–1989*. Milton Keynes: Open University Press.

Singleton, N., Meltzer, H., Gatward, R., Coid, J. and Deasy, D. (1998) *Survey of Psychiatric Morbidity among Prisoners in England and Wales*. London: Department of Health.

The Department of Health's web page on prison health is at **http://www.dh.gov.uk/en/Policyand guidance/Healthandsocialcaretopics/Prisonhealth/ index.htm**. See also the Centre for the Development of Healthcare Policy and Practice web page on prison health (**http://www.cdhpp.leeds.ac.uk/ services/prison.php?PHPSESSID=8dfaedab98388c 43fbdddf114f6ee403**).

# HIGH-RELIABILITY ORGANIZATIONS (HROs)

High-reliability organizations (HROs) operate in high-risk fields but do so without error over long periods. Attempts have been made to apply this theory to high-security prisons.

A high-reliability organization (HRO) is one that, potentially, can do catastrophic harm to itself and the public but operates effectively error-free over a long period of time (Roberts 1993). Typical examples are nuclear power plants, nuclear submarines and aircraft carriers. Due to the potentially catastrophic results of escapes of Category A prisoners for the public, politicians and professionals, attempts have been made to apply this theory to the operation of high-security prisons (Bennett and Hartley 2006).

The approach of HROs includes sophisticated organizational learning and culture. For example, safety will be given a very high priority, meaning that everyone will focus on this as his or her most important task, the whole organization will constantly scan for new threats and extensive expenditure may be made to manage risk. Roles will be decentralized in order to allow a more rapid response to error, or contingencies and apparently redundant security measures will be built in so that safety checks will be duplicated and repeated. Extensive standard operating procedures are used to clarify and regularize operations. This layering of safety measures provides a source of reliability. In high-security prisons, these approaches have been used to inform reviews of perimeter security and to develop methods to test security systems.

However, the application of the HRO concept has been criticized on two grounds (Bennett and Hartley 2006). First, it has been argued that the HRO approach was developed for organizations that use complex technology in a way that prisons do not and has not been developed for human service organizations that primarily work with people. Secondly, and relatedly, it has been argued that the HRO approach encourages a focus on the technology of security (or situational methods) at the cost of social methods, such as encouraging responsibility, respect and reform. As a result, it is argued that the HRO approach may change the balance between the security, care and control aspects of imprisonment, and may therefore have unwanted and unforeseen effects on the prison community.

As an approach to managing potentially dangerous offenders, the HRO concept may have its value in encouraging prisons to seek ideas from a range of different organizations. However, an over-reliance on the HRO approach is likely to cause significant operational problems.

*Jamie Bennett*

### Related entries

*Category A prisoners; Escapes and absconds; High-security prisons; Legitimacy; Risk; Security.*

**Key texts and sources**

Bennett, J. and Hartley, A. (2006) 'High security prisons as high reliability organisations', *Prison Service Journal*, 166: 11–16.

Roberts, K. (ed.) (1993) *New Challenges to Understanding Organizations*. New York, NY: Macmillan.

# HIGH-SECURITY PRISONS

High-security prisons are those that hold Category A prisoners – those who present the greatest risk and for whom escape should be made impossible.

There are currently eight high-security prisons. Three of them (Belmarsh, Woodhill and Manchester) are local prisons that hold prisoners while on remand and shortly after sentence. The other five (Frankland, Wakefield, Full Sutton, Whitemoor and Long Lartin) hold prisoners who are sentenced.

High-security prisons were established following a report into a series of high-profile escapes in the 1960s, including that of the spy, George Blake (Mountbatten 1966). This recommended that all Category A prisoners be located in a single prison. This approach has been described as the 'concentration' approach. However, a further report was commissioned, known as the Radzinowicz Report (Advisory Council on the Penal System 1968), which presented an alternative view that Category A prisoners should be spread out through a number of high-security prisons that would also hold Category B prisoners. Radzinowicz called for these prisons to provide a liberal regime within a secure perimeter. This approach, often described as the 'dispersal' approach, was adopted, and thus high-security prisons are often described as 'dispersal' prisons.

High-security prisons are complex and multifunctional. For example, they also have units that form part of the close supervision centres system, and the dangerous and severe personality disorder system, and they have the capacity to house special security units. A number also include vulnerable prisoner units.

These prisons have higher levels of physical and procedural security and are more expensive to operate than other types of prison. The Prison Service *Annual Report* for 2005–6 shows that the average cost of prison places in a high-security prison was £43,904, compared with an average cost of £28,486. The recent history of high-security prisons has been turbulent (Liebling 2002). In the late 1980s and early 1990s, there were challenges to order and control, which resulted in a number of riots. The most serious incidents were the escapes of six prisoners from Whitemoor Prison in 1994 and three prisoners from Parkhurst Prison in 1995 (Parkhurst was subsequently removed from the high-security estate). These resulted in two critical official reports that reasserted security values, including the introduction of incentives and earned privileges, enhanced searching and control of property. The effectiveness of this was assessed through formalized audit. This achieved the aim of preventing escapes, but there was concern that insufficient attention was given to issues of decency and reducing reoffending. This led to a rebalancing of priorities or 'the pursuit of a reconfigured legitimacy' (Liebling 2002: 100), which placed greater emphasis on those dimensions. However, the continued concern about the risk of escape has led to a recent re-emphasis on security through the application of the theory of high-reliability organizations.

*Jamie Bennett*

### Related entries

*Categorization and allocation; Category A prisoners; Close supervision centres; Dangerous and severe personality disorder (DSPD); Dangerousness; Escapes and absconds; High-reliability organizations (HROs); Official reports; Security; Special security units.*

**Key texts and sources**

Advisory Council on the Penal System (1968) *The Regime for Long-term Prisoners in Conditions of Maximum Security*. London: HMSO.

Liebling, A. (2002) 'A "liberal regime within a secure perimeter"?', in A. Bottoms and M. Tonry (eds) *Ideology, Crime and Criminal Justice: A Symposium in Honour of Sir Leon Radzinowicz*. Cullompton: Willan Publishing.

Mountbatten, Lord of Burma (1966) *Report of the Inquiry into Prison Escapes and Security*. London: HMSO.

# HIV/AIDS

Human immunodeficiency virus (HIV) targets and infects the immune system's white blood cells, called CD4 cells. HIV is the virus that causes acquired immune deficiency syndrome (AIDS). AIDS is the most advanced stage of HIV infection: after depletion of CD4 cells, the immune system becomes compromised and susceptible to opportunistic infections. It is widely acknowledged that prisons are a key setting for the transmission of HIV.

Prisons are a key setting for the transmission of HIV and various other infections. These infections may be airborne (such as tuberculosis), sexually transmitted or due to intravenous drug use. The rate of HIV and hepatitis C is significantly higher in UK prisons than in the general population. The rate of HIV infection for male prisoners is 15 times higher than the 0.3 per cent rate for those in the community. The hepatitis C rate of infection for male prisoners is 9 per cent and 11 per cent for females – a rate 20 times higher than the 0.4 per cent for those in the community.

The risk of transmission of HIV and hepatitis C is more acute in the prison setting due to unprotected sexual contact and the practice of sharing needles. The prison population has a high proportion of prisoners with problematic drug use and, although the majority reduce or stop their drug use at admission, many continue using drugs while some start using drugs (and/or injecting drugs) on incarceration. It is difficult to give an exact figure of the drug use that occurs in prisons in England and Wales. Research has estimated that between 14 and 30 per cent of prisoners use opiates, while approximately 20 per cent of prisoners have reported the use of heroin during their stay in prison. Furthermore, in Scottish prisons, where 10 per cent of prisoners are tested each month, 80 per cent of those who admit injecting heroin said they shared needles (Prison Reform Trust and National AIDS Trust 2005).

Being identified as HIV positive still brings with it stigma and discrimination, and it can discourage prisoners from seeking HIV testing or healthcare that can impact on their health and the effectiveness of treatment. Ensuring confidentiality is of crucial importance to those prisoners seeking care and treatment as it can assist in protecting them from such stigma and discrimination.

The importance of education and harm reduction is crucial in tackling discrimination and in enabling prisoners to reduce transmission risks. Harm reduction techniques are based on an acceptance that a problem exists: they represent a move away from 'zero tolerance' mentalities that do not address the stigma surrounding drug misuse/HIV infection or the underlying causes.

Irrespective of the evidence supporting the efficacy of harm reduction measures, many prisons have failed to take decisive action to provide access to essential prevention, care and treatment. Some prisons have implemented condom and sterilizing-tablet distribution schemes and opioid substitution treatment, but needle-exchange programmes are not available in UK prisons (Jürgens 2005).

International human rights guidelines (see Lines *et al.* 2004) call for prisoners to receive healthcare that is at least equivalent to that available for the outside population, including health promotion and disease prevention and treatment. There is recognition that prison health services must replicate what is happening in the wider community. The *Dublin Declaration on HIV/AIDS in Prisons in Europe and Central Asia* (Lines *et al.* 2004) is a key document that stresses the need for a consistent strategy on HIV and AIDS in prisons. It clearly sets out a pubic health and human rights approach to HIV in prisons, which requires that the following be made available:

- Access to treatment.
- Voluntary confidential HIV testing.
- Pre- and post-test counselling.
- The right to live free from stigma, discrimination and violence.
- Access to harm reduction measures to protect against HIV infection.

The UN Office on Drugs and Crime *HIV/AIDS Prevention, Care, Treatment and Support in Prison Settings: A Framework for an Effective National Response* (2006) recommended action no. 41 states that voluntary HIV testing, with pre- and post-test counselling, should be made available to prisoners free of charge. Nationally agreed standards and guidelines (the British HIV Association and the Medical Foundation for AIDS and Sexual Health) currently exist for the testing and treatment of HIV and, for hepatitis C, the NHS's '*Hepatitis C: Essential Information for Professionals and Guidance on Testing*' is available to ensure equivalence of healthcare for prisoners.

The treatment and care of prisoners who are HIV positive include the provision of antiretroviral therapy (ART). Combination ART significantly decreased mortality due to HIV infection and AIDS. Prisoners respond well to ART:

> [and] in high income countries, the right to enjoyment of the highest attainable standard of physical and mental health, in concert with the principle of equivalence, dictates that prisoners should have access to a high standard of care, including specialist consultation, diagnostic testing (CD4, viral load, viral resistance) and the full range of ARVs [antiretro-virals] licensed for sale within a particular country (Jürgens 2005).

Although the Prison Service has introduced some measures (i.e. condoms and sterilizing tablets) in an attempt to minimize the risk of transmission of blood-borne viruses, access to these measures is often limited. In addition, conflict between the control and caring roles

and moral and value judgements about what prisoners are entitled to can inhibit the implementation of services equivalent to those available in the community.

In the context of HIV and AIDS, prisoners' human rights are very often neglected at several levels: 'prevention, especially in relation to access to condoms and safe injecting drug equipment, sexual violence, access to medical treatment, privacy and discrimination' (http://www.aidsrights project.org.uk/our_work/prison/).

Research carried out by the Prison Reform Trust and National AIDS Trust (2005) clearly demonstrates a lack of policies on HIV, hepatitis and sexual health in most prisons, with over one third of prisons without an HIV policy, over half with no sexual health policy and with one in five not having a strategy for tackling hepatitis.

*Morag MacDonald*

### Related entries

*Drugs; Healthcare; Human rights.*

**Key texts and sources**

Jürgens, R. (2005) *HIV/AIDS and HCV in Prisons: A Select Annotated Bibliography*. Ottawa: Health Canada (available online in English and French at http://www.hc-sc.gc.ca/ahc-asc/activit/strateg/intactivit/aids-sida/hivaids-vihsida-pubs_e.html).

Lines, R., Jürgens, R., Stöver, H., Kaliakbarova, G., Laticevschi, D., Nelles, J., MacDonald, M. and Curtis, M. (2004) *Dublin Declaration on HIV/AIDS in Prisons in Europe and Central Asia*. Dublin: Irish Penal Reform Trust.

Prison Reform Trust and National AIDS Trust (2005) *HIV and Hepatitis in UK Prisons: Addressing Prisoners' Healthcare Needs*. London: Prison Reform Trust (available online at http://www.nat.org.uk/HIV_Testing_&_Care/ Prisons_&_detention).

UN Office on Drugs and Crime (2006) *HIV/AIDS Prevention, Care, Treatment and Support in Prison Settings: A Framework for an Effective National Response*. New York, NY: United Nations, co-published with the World Health Organization and the Joint United Nations Programme on HIV/AIDS.

Wheatley, M. (2007) 'Drugs in prison', in Y. Jewkes (ed.) *Handbook on Prisons*. Cullompton: Willan Publishing.

See also the UK AIDS and Human Rights Project website (http://www.aidsrightsproject.org.uk/our_work/prison/).

# HM INSPECTORATE OF PRISONS

HM Inspectorate of Prisons for England and Wales is required by statute to provide independent inspection of, in particular, the treatment and conditions of those in custody.

Prisons inspection in England and Wales dates back to the early nineteenth century, but the function was gradually absorbed by the Prison Commissioners. By the 1970s, inspection reports were criticized for their lack of independence and for being little more than internal, confidential reports to the commissioners' successor, the Prison Department. The current prisons inspectorate was established by the Criminal Justice Act 1982, once criticism of this lack of independent scrutiny reached a crescendo in the May Report (1979).

The post of HM Chief Inspector of Prisons was created as a Crown appointment rather than as a civil servant appointment to emphasize independence from the Prison Department and its successor, the Prison Service agency. The post-holder was barred from having worked in that service. Despite these important elements of independence, the inspectorate remains funded by the Home Office and answerable to the Home Secretary. Its influence, credibility and visible independence were, therefore, much dependent on its public profile and on displays of robustly independent reporting by successive chief inspectors, notably His Honour Judge Stephen Tumin, General Sir David (now Lord) Ramsbotham and the current post-holder, Anne Owers, CBE.

The inspectorate's legislative remit requires it to report to the Home Secretary in particular on the treatment and conditions of prisoners rather than to audit service efficiency or review governance and management effectiveness. This has led it to adopt an approach and methodology that are rooted in practical issues of humanity and decency, exploring the actual, rather than intended, outcomes for those in custody. This approach has been strengthened by the development of increasingly robust international human rights and penal norms – for example, the requirement on the UK to have independent inspection of places of custody under the Optional Protocol to the United Nations Convention Against Torture, which came into force in June 2006.

In recent years, the inspectorate has seen its role extend well beyond the boundaries of prisons and young offender institutions in England and Wales. Under the Asylum and Immigration Act 1999, it was given statutory responsibility to inspect immigration removal centres across the UK and, in the Immigration, Asylum and Nationality Act 2006, this remit was extended to immigration short-term holding facilities at air and sea ports and immigration escorts.

As more emphasis is placed on joint criminal justice system inspection, the inspectorate has begun to inspect court cells and court escorts jointly with HM Inspectorate of Courts Administration, and police cells jointly with HM Inspectorate of Constabulary. Routine commissions are also received from the Ministry of Defence to inspect the Military Corrective Training Centre, Colchester, and the Sovereign Base Areas Prison, Cyprus. Similarly, a number of external jurisdictions commission the inspectorate to visit their custodial facilities. For example, in 2005–6 visits were made to prisons in Northern Ireland, the Channel Islands, the Isle of Man and two federal women's prisons in Canada.

Broadening the scope of inspection has required the recruitment of an increasingly diverse and specialist staff. Around half the complement of prisons inspectors are drawn from within the prison system to ensure familiarity and experience, while the other half are drawn from specialist research, medical, legal, probation, social work, drug treatment and diversity policy backgrounds. In addition, to avoid burdening establishments with multiple visits and to maximize available expertise, inspections are conducted jointly with Ofsted, the Royal Pharmaceutical Society of Great Britain, the Dental Practice Division of the NHS Business Services Agency, the Healthcare Commission and territorial equivalents, such as Estyn (Wales), the Healthcare Inspectorate Wales, the Employment and Training Inspectorate (Northern Ireland) and HM Inspectorate of Education (Scotland).

Just as individual specialists have been recruited, so the five inspection teams have been required to specialize to increase consistency and professionalism. Thus, while prisoner numbers dictate that all teams inspect some adult male establishments, specialist women's, young adults', juvenile and immigration detention teams have been established. Individual inspectors are also expected to develop a policy interest and to take part in thematic inspections on particular topics, as well as cross-cutting reviews with other inspectorates.

Inspection frequency is conditioned by resources, which have traditionally been sufficient only to enable a full inspection of each adult prison and young offender institution every five years, and each juvenile facility and immigration removal centre every three years. In order to assess progress, follow-up inspections are conducted in the interim. Full inspections are usually announced and follow-ups unannounced. Unannounced inspections are an essential tool in the effective scrutiny of closed, secretive institutions. They allow the inspectorate to pursue concerns without advance warning and – by the same token – to provide powerful evidence that can vindicate prisons should assertions about poor practice prove ill-founded.

However, custody is a risk-laden context, and it would be unnecessarily inflexible and a poor use of scarce resources to base all inspections on chronology. Instead, in line with the government's Office for Public Sector Reform's (OPSR 2003) principles for public service inspection, risk assessment is increasingly used to determine the timing, nature and scale of prison inspection and to target inspection resources where they are most needed. To support risk assessments, the inspectorate holds intelligence files on all establishments and welcomes intelligence from a wide array of sources so that an up-to-date balance of risk and chronology can inform inspection planning.

Also in line with OPSR principles, the inspectorate has developed an impartial, transparent and evidence-based methodology to guide its inspections. This aims to support the improvement of services by revealing the actual – not merely the intended – outcomes for service recipients. To this end a battery of inspection tools is deployed, including confidential detainee surveys; focus groups; interviews with detainees, staff and visitors; documentary analysis; and painstaking observation.

Assessments are made against published inspection criteria or *Expectations* (HM Inspectorate of Prisons 2005a, 2005b, 2006). *Expectations* are independent criteria set by the Chief Inspector. While they inevitably reflect agency standards in most respects, they also go beyond them, where necessary, to reflect appropriately the requirements of international human rights and penal norms, and best practice.

Good inspection distils huge quantities of evidence into clear, consistent judgements against transparent criteria that allow stakeholders to understand the evidence and the reasons behind any recommendations for change. Accordingly, prison inspection reports contain a 'healthy prison' summary divided into the inspectorate's four tests of a healthy prison: safety, respect, purposeful activity and resettlement (HM Inspectorate of Prisons 1999).

A formal, four-point assessment of outcomes against each healthy prison test – ranging from 'performing well' through to 'performing poorly' – is then applied. These assessments feed back into the risk assessment process and inform future programming. They may also feed into the inspected agencies' internal performance management and review systems. Recommendations are carefully prioritized – into 'main recommendations', 'recommendations' and 'housekeeping points' – in order to focus managers' attention on key issues.

An essential part of the inspectorate's purpose is to give public assurance about the quality of the conditions for and treatment of those in custody. Accordingly, all reports – both institutional and the less frequent thematic ones – are published. A rigorous and timely publication programme is agreed in advance with the agency concerned and, therefore, with their respective ministers, and this generally ensures publication within four months of an inspection. This maintains report relevance and prevents the inappropriate obstruction or delay of difficult reports. Publication is frequently attended by significant media coverage.

As with any organization committed to continuous improvement, processes are in place to solicit and act upon feedback and complaints. Rigorous independent inspection can be bruising, and inspected bodies and other stakeholders must be able to challenge (or commend!) how they have been inspected. In-house researchers also routinely assess inspectorate impact by measuring acceptance of, and progress against, recommendations. Analysis for 2005–6 revealed that 97 per cent of recommendations were accepted and 72 per cent of recommendations had been implemented, wholly or in part, by the time of a follow-up inspection visit (HM Inspectorate of Prisons 2007). These are impressive indicators of impact.

As part of its programme of public service reform, the government recently sought to legislate to amalgamate all aspects of criminal justice inspection into a single inspectorate and, thus, to do away with a separate Inspectorate of Prisons. In the event, the proposal was defeated in the House of Lords, and the government, which had all along made clear its desire to retain robustly independent inspection of custody, withdrew the proposal. Instead, the five chief inspectors of criminal justice, including the Chief Inspector of Prisons, agreed to focus more closely on inspecting the effectiveness of the criminal justice system, while otherwise retaining their separate identities and responsibilities. This will, for example, cement work already underway between the Inspectorates of Prisons and Probation to inspect jointly offender management within the new National Offender Management Service.

In the light of this agreement between ministers and the chief inspectors of criminal justice, the Police and Justice Act 2006 requires the chief inspectors to work together to produce a joint inspection framework and annual programme of criminal justice inspections from 2008 to 2009. It also makes the Inspectorate of Prisons the formal 'gatekeeper' for all inspection activity in prisons, young offender institutions and immigration detention facilities.

The retention of the independent inspection of places of custody by a dedicated Inspectorate of Prisons has now been confirmed by the government. The scope, nature and sophistication of custodial inspection and its specific methodology will therefore continue to evolve. This surely is opportune, as events around the world continue to illustrate just how quickly places of custody can drift away from decency and humanity. Similarly, with the prison population in England and Wales reaching record levels, the importance of independent scrutiny to the maintenance of basic human rights in custody has, arguably, never been clearer.

*Nigel Newcomen*

## Related entries

*Accountability; Decency; European Committee for the Prevention of Torture and Inhuman or Degrading Treatment or Punishment (ECPT); Human rights; Independent monitoring boards; Measuring the Quality of Prison Life (MQPL); Performance management.*

### Key texts and sources

Committee of Inquiry into the UK Prison Services (1979) *Report* (the May Report) (Cmnd 763). London: HMSO.

Harding, R. (2007) 'Inspecting prisons', in Y. Jewkes (ed.) *Handbook on Prisons*. Cullompton: Willan Publishing.

HM Chief Inspector of Prisons (1999) *Suicide is Everyone's Concern*. London: Home Office.

HM Inspectorate of Prisons (2005a) *IRC Expectations: Criteria for Assessing the Conditions for and Treatment of Immigration Detainees*. London: Home Office.

HM Inspectorate of Prisons (2005b) *Juvenile Expectations: Criteria for Assessing the Conditions for and Treatment of Children and Young People in Custody*. London: Home Office.

HM Inspectorate of Prisons (2006) *Expectations: Criteria for Assessing the Conditions in Prisons and the Treatment of Prisoners*. London: Home Office.

HM Inspectorate of Prisons (2007) *Annual Report 2005–6*. London: Home Office.

Office for Public Sector Reform (2003) *The Government's Policy on Inspection of Public Services*. London: Office for Public Sector Reform.

Owers, A. (2007) 'Imprisonment in the twenty-first century: a view from the inspectorate', in Y. Jewkes (ed.) *Handbook on Prisons*. Cullompton: Willan Publishing.

## HM PRISON SERVICE

HM Prison Service is the organization charged with managing public sector prisons and young offender institutions in England and Wales.

### History and origins of HM Prison Service

The foundations of HM Prison Service (HMPS) were laid down at the end of the nineteenth century. Until 1877 there were broadly two systems of imprisonment in England and Wales. The majority of prisons were 'local prisons' (before 1865 known as gaols or houses of correction/bridewells). These were administered by magistrates through the quarter sessions for each county, and thus prison officers were employed by the county or borough usually authorized by local magistrates. Officers were also employed by the government in convict prisons, and beforehand in the national penitentiaries: Millbank and Pentonville, and at Parkhurst, established in 1838 for juvenile offenders. The convict service was established in 1850 and employees were engaged as either civil guard or officers within these establishments. The government had previously employed officers and guards to work at the hulks (prison ships), where prisoners were awaiting transportation – in the earlier period to America and later to Australia.

In 1877 the local prisons were centralized and thus administrative control was transferred to the government. This move brought the two systems together under the control of the Prison Commission appointed by and responsible to the Home Secretary. The Prison Commission was made up of three commissioners and their Chairman, Lieutenant-Colonel (later Sir) Edmund Du Cane (previously Du Cane had been Chairman of the Board of Directors of Convict Prisons). It was at this time that the paramilitary structure of the prison service was first implemented. The 'pyramidal' structure placed prison governors at the top, followed by (moving downwards in the hierarchy) the chief warder, principal warders, warders and then assistant warders (Thomas 1972). Even within the first few years of centralization there were signs of dysfunction within the organization: tensions arose between prisons and central management, complaints were made that civil servants were bypassing the commissioners, and governors seemed to have little influence on conditions of employment for staff (Coyle 2005).

The Prison Commission remained until 1963 when it was replaced by a new Prisons Department within the Home Office. Coyle (2005) argues that many critics predicted that moving prisons into the Home Office would have a detrimental effect on the ways that prisons were

managed, and on the relationship between staff and central headquarters. However, many issues (including low staff morale and structural problems) were clearly identifiable under the Prison Commission and had their roots in its formation in the late nineteenth century. But, throughout this time, there was little change in the way in which prisons were managed, provided they observed the Prison Rules and standing orders. Governors managed as they saw fit; it has only been since the 1990s that this has begun to alter (Coyle 2005).

### Recent developments

In 1988 HMPS adopted a *Statement of Purpose* – now displayed in the reception area of every prison – which states that: 'Her Majesty's Prison Service serves the public by keeping in custody those committed by the courts. Our duty is to look after them with humanity and to help them to lead law-abiding and useful lives in custody and after release' (Flynn 1998: 131). Since 1993, HMPS has had executive agency status which provides a degree of operating independence and accountability. The 1990s also saw the public sector lose its monopoly as a result of the introduction of competition. Initially, private prisons were accountable to HMPS for their performance. The *Statement of Purpose*, noted above, is now supplemented with a vision, six goals and five core values, and agency status has also seen the introduction of corporate and business plans showing clear targets and the use of key performance indicators and targets (such as number of escapes, number of assaults, number of positive drug tests, number of hours per week prisoners spend at purposeful activity) against which the performance is measured (Flynn 1998).

### The role of HMPS within the National Offender Management Service

Since June 2004, HMPS has been part of the National Offender Management Service (NOMS). This led to the transfer of significant amounts of policy work out of HMPS. NOMS is a large enterprise spanning several organizations, including prisons and probation. HMPS accounts for almost 70 per cent of the 70,000 NOMS staff. One of the roles of NOMS is to commission services and encourage competition, or 'contestability'. As part of this move, privately operated prisons are now accountable to NOMS. There are also a number of other organizations that commission services, including the Learning and Skills Council (which commissions education and skills training provision for prisoners), primary care trusts (which commissions healthcare services) and the Youth Justice Board (which commissions services for juvenile offenders under 18 years of age). HMPS also provides services for the Immigration and Nationality Directorate, which commissions immigration detention services at Dover, Haslar and Lindholme. HMPS now receives funding from a number of different sources and manages a range of services for different strategic partners. The service is led by a Director General and a management board that includes directors of operations, high security, security, health, finance and human resources. The prisons are organized in 13 areas, 12 of which are geographical, each led by an area manager. The other area is for high-security prisons, headed by a director. The area manager or director of high-security prisons manages the prison governors in his or her respective area.

HMPS has become more business-like over recent years. For example, it has developed a corporate structure and degree of independence and accountability that mirror private sector practice. In addition, it is increasingly having to compete for the delivery of work and is having to work with a more diverse range of commissioners and providers in order to be successful.

*Helen Johnston and Jamie Bennett*

### Related entries

*Accountability; Governors; Home Office; Ministry of Justice; National Offender Management Service (NOMS); Performance management; Prison Act; Prison officers; Prison population; Prison Rules; Staff (prison).*

### Key texts and sources

Coyle, A. (2005) *Understanding Prison: Key Issues in Policy and Practice.* Maidenhead: Open University Press.

Flynn, N. (1998) *Introduction to Prisons and Imprisonment.* Winchester: Waterside Press.

Thomas, J.E. (1972) *The English Prison Officer since 1850.* London: Routledge & Kegan Paul.

HM Prison Service's website is at **http://www. hmprisonservice.gov.uk/**.

## HOMELESSNESS

Homelessness is commonly perceived as describing a situation where a person is living on the streets. However, it also describes a situation where a person is in temporary accommodation. This is closely linked with both imprisonment and wider social exclusion.

Homelessness is diversely explained as a situation characterized by poverty, social exclusion, disengagement and isolation. It may be 'visible' in the form of individuals living in public places, or 'concealed' in cases where individuals stay temporarily with family and friends because no other housing alternative exists or is accessible to them. The problem of defining homelessness is further compounded by the manner in which the concept is interpreted. Carlen's (1996) research on young homeless people reported a tendency to interpret 'homelessness' as 'rooflessness'; therefore some of those residing in a hostel or other temporary accommodation, or engaged in employment or education, did not consider themselves homeless. Such differences in the interpretation of the concept indicate that the term 'homelessness' is 'encrusted with layers of other significations relating to (lack of) social ties and (lack of) social respectability' (Carlen 1996: 104). For many, homelessness is not a static situation but, rather, a process whereby individuals move within and between different housing circumstances, including periods of being homeless, being housed and/or being institutionalized (e.g. imprisonment).

The problem of defining and interpreting the concept of homelessness leads to difficulties in quantifying the extent of homelessness in the prison system. Prisoners may be reluctant to report being homeless due to concerns about stigmatization and discrimination; conversely, the Social Exclusion Unit (2002) reports a suspicion that prisoners classify themselves as homeless to obtain a higher rate of discharge grant. Notwithstanding these methodological and contextual struggles, homelessness is problematic for many prisoners. Estimates suggest that in the region of one third of individuals are not living in permanent housing prior to imprisonment (Social Exclusion Unit 2002), and a similar proportion of homeless individuals (shelter dwellers) are reported to have been returned to prison within two years of release (Metraux and Culhane 2004).

The causes of homelessness are complex and involve a multiplicity of individual, social and economic factors. Family conflict, whereby individuals are excluded from or voluntarily leave the family home, acts as a trigger for initial homelessness and also a risk factor for future and long-term homelessness. Individuals with a previous history of state care as children are over-represented in homeless populations, and a high prevalence of physical and/or sexual abuse among homeless individuals is also reported in existing studies. Data on the relationship between alcohol use, drug use, mental ill-health and homelessness suggest that these are contributory factors to homelessness but they may also occur as a consequence of adapting to the conditions of homelessness. Many of the factors associated with homelessness are also commonly reported among the general prison population. However, these factors are likely to be exacerbated by the homeless existence; for example, higher rates of arrest and incarceration are reported for homeless mentally ill persons than for 'comparison groups consisting of both other homeless persons and mentally ill persons who are stably housed' (see Metraux and Culhane 2004: 141).

In general terms, it can be said that two broad, but potentially overlapping, explanations exist to describe the relationship between homelessness and imprisonment. The first emanates from the body of literature that suggests homeless individuals are more likely to commit crime and be arrested due to the criminalization of street life, the stigmatization of homeless individuals and their use of criminal behaviour as an adaptive and survivalist strategy on the street (Snow *et al.* 1989). As a result, homeless individuals are likely to have higher reconviction rates and are at increased risk of custody. The second explanation is that the circumstances of being removed from the community due to imprisonment increase the risk of homelessness. In this configuration, homelessness results from the loss of public or private rented accommodation while in custody, through the accumulation of rent arrears or the confiscation of the property, through job loss and/or through a breakdown in family and social relationships. These problems are compounded by often limited pre-release housing advice to prisoners and a lack of co-ordinated support for prisoners on release to negotiate the homeless and housing networks, including assistance with accommodation and access to benefits or employment opportunities, where applicable. The accommodation needs of homeless prisoners span the full spectrum from fully supported accommodation to semi-independent and independent living housing. However, the cost of private rented accommodation and the often limited availability of local authority housing are likely to impact directly on the likelihood of remaining homeless. This, coupled with the potential use of strategies by public and private landlords to exclude homeless ex-prisoners because of concerns about offending and/or anti-social behaviour, is likely further to negate efforts to access accommodation.

Homelessness is a particular challenge to successful prisoner reintegration. While a substantial proportion of prisoners face housing problems on release, unsurprisingly, those at greatest risk of both homelessness and future imprisonment are those with a history of 'residential instability' prior to imprisonment (Metraux and Culhane 2004: 151). This suggests that, the more entrenched individuals become in the homeless and prison circuit, the more difficult it is to become detached from it. It also highlights the need for effective intervention to break the cycle of crime, homelessness and imprisonment for those newly homeless as a result of imprisonment, as well as for those with a history of homelessness. Regardless of whether homelessness precipitates imprisonment or vice versa, the concern is that 'the crossing over' between both situations 'threatens to transform spells of incarceration or homelessness into more long-term patterns of social exclusion' (see Metraux and Culhane 2004: 141–2).

*Mairead Seymour*

## Related entries

*Alcohol; Desistance; Education and training; Employment and industries; Mental health; Rehabilitation.*

---

**Key texts and sources**

Carlen, P. (1996) *Jigsaw: A Political Criminology of Youth Homelessness.* Buckingham: Open University Press.

Metraux, S. and Culhane, D.P. (2004) 'Homeless shelter use and reincarceration following prison release', *Criminology and Public Policy*, 3: 139–60.

Snow, D., Baker, S. and Anderson, L. (1989) 'Criminality and homeless men: an empirical assessment', *Social Problems*, 36: 532–49.

Social Exclusion Unit (2002) *Reducing Re-offending by Ex-prisoners*. London: HMSO.

For information on resettlement, see **http://www.resettlement.info/**. See also **http://www.hmprisonservice.gov.uk/adviceandsupport/beforeafterrelease/resettlement/**.

---

# HOME OFFICE

The Home Office historically is one of the three great departments of state. Its current responsibilities, which have been considerably reduced in the last 50 years, are based on its original purpose of 'maintaining the Queen's Peace'. Since the Home Office was split in 2007 (to accomodate a new Ministry of Justice) its focus has been policing, counterterrorism, crime, drugs, immigration, asylum and national identity.

The Home Office came into being on 27 March 1782 when responsibility for what were essentially home affairs was separated from responsibility for foreign affairs. Because the minister appointed to the former was a peer and the person appointed to the latter was a commoner, the Home Secretary took, and continues to take, precedence over all other secretaries of state. The subsequent development of the Home Office – or Home Department as it is properly called – has seen its role change a great deal. Its responsibilities formerly included matters as diverse as factories, fire services, workshops, magistrates' courts, quarries, gambling, public censorship, children, broadcasting and constitutional issues. Its main responsibilities in the twenty-first century stem from its original and continuing purpose to 'maintain the Queen's Peace' (Newsam 1954).

Today, the Home Office describes its purpose as being 'to build a safe, just and tolerant society, by putting protection of the public at the heart of everything it does' (http://www.homeoffice.gov.uk). The Home Office has responsibility throughout the UK for immigration and counterterrorism (including the Security Service, or MI5 as it is commonly referred to). Policing, probation, prisons and youth justice now come under the authority of the Ministry of Justice.

The Home Office employed just 16 staff in 1785 but now employs over 9,000 as part of its headquarters operation – but with plans to reduce this to 5,700 by 2010. In addition, over 20,000 staff work for the 42 probation boards in England and Wales; over 17,000 work for the Immigration and Nationality Directorate (IND); and over 45,000 work either in or in support of the 140 prisons in England and Wales. The annual Home Office budget is over £13 billion. The budget is managed using targets, which are directly related to its six objectives, which form part of its 'public service agreement' (PSA) with the Treasury.

Traditionally, the Home Office structure was based on it departments (such as the Prison Department) and administrative 'divisions' which it directly controlled. Today, several of its functions are performed by agencies or services semi-independently. The reform of public services, which began in the 1980s, has seen an essentially 'administrative' culture replaced by one which is more 'managerial' and business-like, reflecting new public management approaches. This change is also reflected in three recent structural alterations within the Home Office and in the development of 'agencies' and 'non-departmental government bodies' (NDPBs), which are part of wider reform of the organization of Whitehall.

The first structural change was prompted by the need to co-ordinate the work of the courts, the Crown Prosecution Service and the other criminal justice agencies. In 2002 the Home Office, the Department for Constitutional Affairs and the Attorney General's office jointly established the OCJR. Among other things, the OCJR oversees the 42 local criminal justice boards of England and Wales. The second structural alteration saw the establishment in 2004 of NOMS. The purpose of NOMS is to strengthen the management of offenders so as to reduce reoffending, by co-ordinating the work of the Prison and Probation Services and by separating the function of 'commissioning' from the function of providing or delivering those services. The third structural change was the establishment in 2007 of the Ministry of Justice, which took over the responsibility for prisons, probation, youth justice and sentencing (see 'Ministry of Justice').

Agencies and NDPBs were introduced so that certain operational and service delivery functions of public services can be performed at arm's length from ministers and their 'parent' departments of state, and on a more business-like footing. Agencies, which are administrative not statutory bodies, were first established in the late 1980s. The Prison Service became an agency in 1992, and the Home Office currently has responsibility for three agencies: the Forensic Science Service, the Criminal Records Bureau and the Identity and Passport Service. From April 2007, the Home Office also has responsibility for the National Policing Improvement Agency, and the IND was also due to become an agency by then.

The development of agencies and NDPBs has helped clarify the distinctions between 'pol-

icy' and 'operations', and most operational matters and casework can be dealt with at arm's length from ministers. However, the Home Office is traditionally a difficult political command, and the management of its business far from straightforward. The comparative frequency with which crises in some aspect of Home Office business occur illustrates this. The crisis which arose about how the cases of foreign national prisoners were handled resulted in the publication in July 2006 of a plan to reform the Home Office which ultimately led to the establishment of the Ministry of Justice.

*William Payne*

## Related entries

*HM Inspectorate of Prisons; HM Prison Service; Independent monitoring boards; Ministry of Justice; National Offender Management Service (NOMS); New public management (NPM); Politics of imprisonment; Prisons and Probation Ombudsman; Sentencing policy.*

### Key texts and sources

Hennessy, P. (1991) *Whitehall*. London: Pimlico.
Home Office (2006) *From Improvement to Transformation*. London: Home Office.
Newsam, F. (1954) *The Home Office*. London: George Allen & Unwin.
See also the Home Office's website (http://www.homeoffice.gov.uk).

## HOMICIDE IN PRISON

**The murder or manslaughter of a prisoner by another prisoner while in custody.**

Prisoners can die in a variety of circumstances while serving their sentence. However, while academic and policy attention has often been focused on suicide in prison, there has been relatively little interest in the numbers of prisoners who are murdered each year. Of late this has begun to change, especially with the Mubarek Inquiry related to the racist murder of

Zahid Mubarek by his cellmate at Feltham Young Offender Instituion in March 2000. So too there has been growing academic interest in the phenomenon of murder inside (Wilson 2005), policy interest relating to the introduction of a violence reduction strategy and more general interest in issues of order and control (Sattar 2001).

It is difficult to determine exactly how many murders take place in prison each year, as the closed and secret nature of prison ensures that almost everything that happens behind the prison's walls – even murder – remains difficult to uncover and even more difficult to measure with any certainty. However, by using available materials, Wilson (2005) found that there were, on average, two murders recorded in prison each year from 1993 to 2003. This would equate to a rate of three murders per 100,000, and is thus three times greater than the murder rate in the community. Indeed, in 1998 you were ten times more likely to be murdered in prison than in the community (Wilson 2005). However, Home Office officials have been at pains to point out that 'homicide is a relatively rare event in the general community and in prison' (Sattar 2001: 1).

These official qualifications notwithstanding, the phenomenon of prisoner-on-prisoner murder poses serious questions for the Prison Service in relation to how to maintain order. Indeed, Sattar's evidence that over half of those prisoners who were murdered were murdered by their cellmate in or near their cell (including Zahid Mubarek) suggests that the policy of cell-sharing, even at a time of growing prison numbers, has to be reconsidered. Quite apart from Zahid Mubarek, there are also Christopher Edwards, Anthony Hesketh, Shahid Aziz and Karelius Smith, all of whom were murdered by their cellmates. Indeed, Smith was murdered by Glenn Wright, who attempted to murder at least two more of his cellmates. It is very difficult to determine the motives behind prisoner-on-prisoner murder, although these can range from racism, as in the case of Robert Stewart's murder of Zahid Mubarek, to simple altercations or issues

related to the prisoner's mental health and the Prison Service's failure to act on these issues.

*David Wilson*

### Related entries

*Assaults; Bullying; Close supervision centres; Deaths in custody; Mental health; Mubarek Inquiry; Violence; Violence reduction.*

---

**Key texts and sources**

Sattar, G. (2001) *Rates and Causes of Death among Prisoners and Offenders under Community Supervision. Home Office Research Study 231.* London: Home Office.

Wilson, D. (2005) *Death at the Hands of the State.* London: Howard League for Penal Reform.

---

## HOMOSEXUALITY IN PRISON

By design, most prisons are single-sex institutions. The deprivation of heterosexual relationships constitutes one of the most significant 'pains of imprisonment', and the replacement of heterosexual relations (at least temporarily) with same-sex sexual ones is not uncommon in prison.

The deprivation of heterosexual relationships constitutes one of the most significant 'pains of imprisonment', and the replacement of heterosexual relations (at least temporarily) with same-sex sexual ones, as well as the permanent psychological impact of same-sex sexual relations on prisoners, has been widely documented (Struckman-Johnson *et al.* 1996). To date, the majority of the criminology-penology literature varies considerably in the definition of same-sex sexual relationships in prison (genital fondling; failed attempts at intercourse; verbal harassment; sexual extortion; kissing; implicit references to fellatio and/or anal sex; intercourse), and it refers to two main categories: consensual relations and same-sex sexual rape (Struckman-Johnson *et al.* 1996).

## Consensual homosexuality among inmates

Traditionally, inmates engaging in consensual same-sex sexual relations in prison have been categorized into two dichotomous groups: 'true homosexuals' and 'situational homosexuals'. The first group is composed of men who had a homosexual orientation prior to incarceration – men who 'imported' their behaviour from the streets to prison (Eigenberg 2000). These individuals engaged in same-sex sexual activity because 'they were born that way... and adopted the same role in prison as they would have in the free community' (Koscheski et al. 2002: 16). Prisoners generally refer to them in negative terms, such as 'exceptional characters', 'fish', 'fags', 'queens', 'woman-like' and 'fuck-boys'.

In comparison, 'situational homosexuals' are heterosexual men who demonstrate same-sex sexual conduct due to the social structure of prison and because lack of opportunity for relations with women produces and promotes homosexual conduct within its walls. Here, the individual's sexual conduct contrasts with his sexual identity: 'the fact that an individual engages in sexual relations with a person of one gender or the other does not make that individual heterosexual or homosexual' (Koscheski et al. 2002: 112). Consequently, many researchers believe that most situational homosexual men will return to heterosexual sexual conduct once they return to the community.

'Situational homosexuals' are often categorized into various subgroups according to different criteria. For example:

- *The dominance/submissiveness of the sexual partners*: 'inserter' and 'insertee', 'bitches', 'sissies', 'queens' and 'broads' (Koscheski et al. 2002).
- *The subjective perception of sexual identity*: 'aggressive wolfs' – inmates who entered prison with a heterosexual orientation, keep their heterosexual identity in prison and maintain their masculinity by sexually assaulting younger, weaker inmates; 'non-aggressive wolfs'/'teddy bears' – prisoners who entered prison with a heterosexual identity, maintain their masculine self-image by taking active roles during sex, but perceive themselves as bisexual (Hensley 2001).
- *The motivation for engaging in same-sex sexual activity*: 'fags' – prisoners who engage in same-sex sexual activity because that is their sexual preference; 'punks' – inmates who choose to engage in same-sex sexual conduct in self-defence or in return for goods and services (Hensley 2001).

## Same-sex sexual rapes in prison

The bulk of criminological-sociological studies regarding same-sex rape, in general, and same-sex rape in prison, in particular, perceives rape as an act of power, violence and politics. According to this perspective, prison rape is a sexual manifestation of aggression rather than an aggressive demonstration of sexuality. It serves, practically as well as symbolically, as a statement of one's masculinity and strength, and it occurs for the same reasons it takes place in the community: to hurt, humiliate, dominate, control and degrade; to strip the victim of his status as a 'man' and force him to assume the role of a 'woman' and become a slave in the fullest meaning of the word (O'Donnell 2004).

The majority of male rape victims in prison suffer from an acute disruption of physiological, psychological, social and sexual life. Some victims experience difficulty in telling family and friends about the rape, others encounter disruption in male–female relationships, and several turn to suicide in prison (or on release) to escape the trauma and fear of rape. An increased understanding of the nature of prison sex may assist in comprehending the dynamics of male prison subcultures.

*Tomer Einat*

## Related entries

*Deprivations/'pains of imprisonment'; Masculinity; Subcultures; Suicide in prison.*

**Key texts and sources**

Eigenberg, H.M. (2000) 'Correctional officers and their perceptions of homosexuality, rape, and prostitution in male prisons', *Prison Journal*, 80: 415–33.

Hensley, C. (2001) 'Consensual homosexual activity in male prisons', *Corrections Compendium*, 26: 1–4.

Koscheski, M., Hensley, C., Wright, J. and Tewksbery, R. (2002) 'Consensual sexual behavior', in C. Hensley (ed.) *Prison Sex: Practice and Policy*. London: Lynne Rienner.

O'Donnell, I. (2004) 'Prison rape in context', *British Journal of Criminology*, 44: 241–55.

Struckman-Johnson, C., Struckman-Johnson, D., Rucker, L., Bumby, K. and Donaldson, S. (1996) 'Sexual coercion reported by men and women in prison', *Journal of Sex Research*, 33: 67–76.

# HOWARD, JOHN

John Howard (1726–90) was a notable English prison reformer of the eighteenth century.

The pioneering penal reformer, John Howard, visited almost every county gaol in the UK and many penal institutions and fever hospitals across Europe, and he lobbied for healthcare and regime reform in prisons. He conducted the first comprehensive survey of penal establishments.

Born probably in 1726 and brought up in Bedfordshire, he inherited a fortune. After his first wife died, he set off on European travels, but his ship was captured by privateers and he was held in a dungeon experiencing the hardship that inspired his life's work. His health was always fragile but he managed to run his estate and improve the conditions of his tenants while continuing to travel extensively.

On being appointed High Sheriff of Bedfordshire – unusually for a religious dissenter (he was a Congregationalist) – he took the responsibility of overseeing the county gaol seriously. He found that debtors were not released until they had paid for their keep and he unsuccessfully tried to change the system so that gaolers were paid a salary. His visits to neighbouring gaols drew his attention to the prevalence of gaol fever and smallpox that was killing prisoners and infecting staff and the wider community.

Howard spent 17 years visiting prisons, local gaols, bridewells, hospitals and houses of correction in Britain and on the continent. He undertook some 350 visits to 230 different institutions, which included gaols in Switzerland, Germany, Bohemia, Italy, the Netherlands, Spain, Russia and France. He travelled by public carriage or on horseback accompanied only by his groom, taking meticulous notes. By 1783 he estimated that he had travelled 42,033 miles. He was persistent, using financial inducements and sometimes disguises and subterfuge to gain entry. In 1777 he financed the publication of *The State of the Prisons in England and Wales, with Preliminary Observations*, and an *Account of some Foreign Prisons,* which included detailed descriptions and drawings of almost every county gaol, much of which would be familiar today.

He recommended purpose-built gaols that would have natural light and ventilation and where prisoners would sleep separately instead of the mixing of adult men, women and children. He wanted to see honest labour and voluntary work. He gave evidence to parliamentary committees and worked with other leading social reformers to urge reform of the financial corruption of incarceration and improvements to the care and treatment of prisoners.

He was well known and respected during his lifetime but his puritanical religiosity impelled him to refuse honours and led him to become increasingly frugal in his lifestyle. He died in 1790 of fever contracted when visiting a hospital in Kherson, Russia, and he is buried there. His second wife pre-deceased him, and his son died insane. The first statue erected in St Paul's Cathedral was that of John Howard, wearing a toga, paid for by public subscription. His greatest memorial is the sturdy tradition of penal reform in Britain and the Howard League for Penal Reform, established in his name to continue his work.

*Frances Crook*

*Related entries*

*Fry, Elizabeth; Howard League for Penal Reform; Nacro; Prison Reform Trust; Voluntary sector.*

---

**Key texts and sources**

Howard, J. (1777a/1973) *The State of the Prisons in England and Wales.* London: Patterson Smith.

Howard, J. (1777b/1973) *Prisons and Lazarettos: An Account of the Principal Lazarettos in Europe.* London: Patterson Smith.

McConville, S. (1981) *A History of English Prison Administration 1750–1877.* London: Routledge & Kegan Paul.

See also http://www.howardleague.org/index.php?id=johnhoward.

---

# HOWARD LEAGUE FOR PENAL REFORM

**The Howard League for Penal Reform is a leading UK prison reform organization.**

The first organization ever to be founded to work for penal reform, the Howard League for Penal Reform, was established in 1866, the year that the first royal commission on capital punishment abolished public executions. The then Howard Association concentrated on improving prison conditions, notably work inside prisons, and campaigned against the death penalty worldwide. It joined with the Penal Reform League in 1921. The early work supported the establishment of probation, the ending of physical punishments inside prisons and the founding of a fund for victims. It set up the Magistrates' Association by hosting the first meeting and acting as a secretariat, in an attempt to introduce consistency and to reduce overly punitive sentencing. The Howard League for Penal Reform's mission is to help to create a safer society where fewer people are victims of crime. It works on the principle that community sentences make a person take responsibility and live a law-abiding life in the community, and that offenders should make amends for what they have done.

During the twentieth century the organization carried out original research into such issues as suicide prevention, the treatment of mothers in prison, sex offenders, children in custody and the confiscation of the proceeds of crime. It utilized classic voluntary sector tactics to investigate, educate and persuade the general public and those in positions of authority. The charity made the transition from being close to, and identified with, the Home Office and penal authorities during the first half-century, to become increasingly more independent and challenging in the latter half of the twentieth century.

In 2000 the Howard League successfully took the Home Secretary to judicial review on his refusal to apply the protections of the Children Act 1989 to prisons. It subsequently established a law department to help individual children in custody challenge the conditions of their incarceration and to pursue test cases to establish change across the system.

The charity conducts inquiries and monitors prisons and community sentences. It runs demonstration projects including, in 2005, establishing the world's first social enterprise employing prisoners on a fair wage – a graphic design studio. It also lobbies government and provides educational materials to national and international bodies, having consultative status with both the United Nations and the Council of Europe.

While the bulk of its work is concentrated on prisons and community sentences, it has always had a much wider remit that includes public education on such issues as crime prevention. For a decade from 1995 it ran a schools-based education programme dealing with citizenship and crime prevention that was delivered to more than 20,000 children across the country and that involved 3,000 adult volunteers. In 2005 it started to support the founding of student societies in universities to foster and train the penal reformers of the future.

With a turnover of around £1 million and 19 staff (including six prisoners), it is a medium-sized charity, managed by a board of trustees and accountable to a membership of some 4,000 individuals and affiliates.

*Frances Crook*

*Related entries*

*Howard, John; Nacro; Prison Reform Trust; Voluntary sector.*

---

**Key texts and sources**

See http://www.howardleague.org/.

---

## HUMAN RIGHTS

> The concept of human rights rests on the notion that people have universal rights which cannot be removed or interfered with by the state or other bodies. Although the view that certain rights are inalienable has existed for many centuries, most people now perceive human rights to be those contained in the European Convention on Human Rights.

Ever since the enactment of the Human Rights Act (HRA) 1998 in October 2000, the term 'human rights' has been used to cover a wide area of state procedures, policies and law which would previously have been referred to as 'civil liberties'. Strictly speaking, the notion of human rights encompasses those inalienable rights which are considered to exist independently of the political process, whereas civil liberties refers to the limits on government power to protect individual freedoms.

In modern times, the view that certain rights needed to be protected on a universal level arose out the experiences of the Second World War and resulted in the United Nations Universal Declaration of Human Rights in 1948 and the European Convention on Human Rights (the ECHR, also referred to as the Convention for the Protection of Human Rights and Fundamental Freedoms) in 1950. The UK played a key role in the drafting of the ECHR and was the first state to ratify it in 1951. The ECHR also established a court – the European Court of Human Rights (ECtHR) – to enforce the human rights obligations of its signatory states.

While the UK has been a signatory to the ECHR from its inception, it did not become part of domestic law until 2000 because the widespread view was that the rights and freedoms guaranteed by the convention could be delivered under common law. However, UK citizens retained the right to petition the ECtHR, and research has indicated that, in the years before the HRA came into force, UK prisoners made more applications to the ECtHR than any other single group in Europe. It has been argued that the lack of a written constitution in the UK meant that the common law was unable to protect human rights adequately.

The rights protected by the ECHR are intended to be the fundamental rights which should apply to all citizens in all democracies. They include rights ranging from the right to life, through the right not to be enslaved, to the right to respect for one's property. They have been loosely divided into three categories. The first are the absolute rights, including the prohibition on inhuman or degrading treatment or punishment. It is not possible for the state to place restrictions on these rights.

The second are known as limited rights, relating to fair trial procedures and the right to liberty. These are qualified as, although, for example, the right to liberty is protected, the state is allowed to qualify this right by passing laws to allow for detention on remand or after conviction, for immigration purposes or for mental health reasons. Surprisingly, the right to life is a limited right in that the article recognizes that the state may have to take life in extreme circumstances.

The third set of rights are the qualified rights as, although they are protected by the ECHR, the state can impose restrictions on the rights where it is necessary for the wider public good. The qualified rights include the right to a private and family life, freedom of expression and freedom of assembly. It is these rights that are often the most problematic to define because they are dependent upon a balancing act being performed between the individual and wider society. The problem is particularly acute in the prisons context because the simple fact of imprisonment means that there will be an inevitable interference with these rights on a daily basis. Searching, visits and interpersonal communication all fall within the ambit of the right to a private and family life, but the requirements of prison security mean that there will inevitably be restrictions on these rights in the prison context. It is the question of whether those restrictions are necessary which brings into play the difficult HRA issues.

When assessing whether there is an infringement of a convention right, the ECtHR has introduced into UK law the concept of *proportionality*. Traditionally, English law asked whether the actions of the state were reasonable and would only interfere if they were not. In contrast, the ECtHR will assess whether the interference with the human right is proportionate and whether it is the minimum interference necessary. In the context of searches of prisoners' legal correspondence (which was considered to be an interference with the right to access the courts), the House of Lords held that where human rights are in issue, the domestic courts must apply the same proportionality test that is utilized by the ECtHR (*R (Daly)* v. *Home Secretary* [2001] UKHL 26). The ECtHR requires that any laws (including rules, regulations and simple policy) which seek to restrict rights must be published and accessible. The reasoning behind this approach is to ensure that people are made aware of the reasons for restrictions being in place and the extent of those restrictions.

The ECHR requires the state to guarantee the rights and freedoms in the convention, not just to refrain from interfering with them. This requirement imposes *positive obligations* on the state to ensure that ECHR rights are properly observed by other citizens and by the state itself. Governments must ensure that demonstrators can express their opinions free from interference from others and, in the prisons context, it has been held that prison staff have to ensure cell-mates are not exposed to unacceptable risks from each other (*R (Amin)* v. *Home Secretary* [2003] UKHL 51). The duty to take steps to protect human rights is even more pronounced when it comes to the actions of the state itself. Prisoners are particularly vulnerable

as they are dependent upon the state, and many of the cases where positive obligations have been placed on the state have arisen in this context. This has included requiring prison staff to take appropriate steps to protect prisoners from their own actions (*Keenan* v. *UK* (2001) 31 EHRR 38), as well as the duty to investigate events properly when people die while in custody (*R (Middleton)* v. *Home Secretary* [2004] UKHL 10).

As the duty to protect human rights falls upon the state, this can involve limiting or infringing the rights of others to achieve the appropriate balance. There has been some debate as to whether some rights and freedoms are more important than others. The traditional view is that there is no hierarchy of rights. However, on occasion the courts have suggested that it will usually be more important to protect the right to life in preference to the qualified rights, such as freedom of expression (*Venables & Thompson* v. *NGN Ltd & others* 08/01/01).

Although the HRA makes ECHR rights directly enforceable, it does not prevent UK citizens from taking cases to the ECtHR. The requirement is that all domestic legal remedies are first exhausted, and so if litigation in this country does not succeed, an application can still be made to the ECtHR. This occurred in the case of adjudications conducted in prisons. The Court of Appeal held that these did not involve a loss of liberty and so they were not criminal charges. The ECtHR disagreed, finding that, as they could result in additional days being awarded to prisoners, they amounted to criminal charges and so should be conducted by judicial figures, not prison governors (*Ezeh & Connors* v. *UK* (2004) 39 EHRR 1).

One of the reasons why the HRA has been so contentious is because it was seen as a direct challenge to parliamentary supremacy. Historically, the separation of powers has meant that, while the courts can interpret Acts of Parliament, they cannot strike them down. The HRA, however, allows the courts to make minor amendments to laws if they consider it necessary – to write in extra words to comply with ECHR rights or to issue a declaration that the law is incompatible with human rights. The

House of Lords has held that the laws which allowed the Home Secretary to set lifers tariffs and the power to detain foreign nationals without trial were in breach of ECHR rights (*R (Anderson)* v. *Home Secretary* [2003] 1 AC 837; *A & others* v. *Home Secretary* [2004] UKHL 56). Some commentators have seen this as a direct attack on the long-standing principle that Parliament is supreme and argue that it gives too much power to judges to change the laws.

*Simon Creighton*

### Related entries

*Communication; Remand; Searching; Security; Visits and visiting orders.*

**Key texts and sources**

Lazarus, L. (2006) 'Conceptions of liberty deprivation', *Modern Law Review*, 69: 738.

Starmer, K. (1999) *European Human Rights Law.* London: LAG.

Wilson, C. (2006) 'The ECHR: bringing rights home', in M. Leech (ed.) *The Prisons Handbook 2006.* Manchester: MLA Press.

The European Court of Human Rights' website is at **http://www.echr.coe.int/ECHR/**. Liberty's web page on human rights is at **http://www.liberty-human-rights.org.uk/index.shtml**. See also **http://www.yourrights.org.uk/your-rights/chapters/the-rights-of-prisoners/parole/life-sentence-prisoners.shtml**.

# IDENTITY AND SELF

> The psychological survival of a prison sentence may rely on prisoners' potential to nurture a private sense of self that preexists and is entirely divorced from the socially sanctioned identity of 'prisoner', and also to construct a public identity that enables them to 'fit in' with the social environment of the prison.

Although individual identities and social identities are often regarded separately, each is routinely related to, and entangled with, the other. In the context of prisoners' identities, a necessary precursor for the creation and maintenance of a convincing public persona is the construction of a healthy, private, interior sense of self, and vice versa. Indeed, without a stable sense of self *and* the necessary 'macho' credentials to fit in with the prevailing culture of masculinity, many men in prison find incarceration intolerable (Jewkes 2002).

One distinction that can be made between self and identity is that the former emphasizes difference while the latter stresses similarity. On entering prison, the individual is – to the outside world – labelled a 'prisoner' (along with other labels, such as 'criminal' or 'deviant'). The negative connotations of such labelling may have become even more significant since the resurgence of expressive correctional initiatives designed publicly to stigmatize and shame the offender (collectively known as the new punitiveness). Prisoners' ability to resist such negative identifications, rather than internalizing them, may be critical in determining how successfully they adapt to imprisonment. Put simply, public image may become self-image.

For some, this is not necessarily problematic; indeed, the strategy of prisonization is a device that provides the acclimatized inmate with the status and power necessary to absorb any sense of social rejection implicit in the label 'prisoner'. Many prisoners, however, may fear that the ascription 'prisoner' diminishes or even subsumes all other aspects of their identities. Consequently, while it may be possible to assume certain outward characteristics in order to fit in with the prison culture, such traits are likely to be little more than a façade, constructed to mask the 'real self' beneath (Jewkes 2002).

The self, then, might best be conceptualized as the emotional 'core' which people carry with them from context to context. It represents a place of retreat: when the public work of identity management becomes too arduous, it is important to have a private place where the public façade can be put aside and one can 'be oneself'. This distinction is usually conceptualized as 'backstage' and 'frontstage' (Goffman 1959). Imprisonment may involve disruption of the equilibrium between the two spheres: if forced to share a cell with one or more other inmates, prisoners may be continually in an enforced state of 'frontstage' with little opportunity to restore their sense of self. If locked up on their own for prolonged periods, however, prisoners may suffer equally in their inability to draw on the strategies, resources and prior experiences necessary to construct and present an acceptable identity frontstage.

*Yvonne Jewkes*

### Related entries

*Masculinity; New punitiveness; Prisonization; Structure/agency ('resistance').*

**Key texts and sources**

Goffman, E. (1959) *The Presentation of Self in Everyday Life*. New York, NY: Anchor.

Jewkes, Y. (2002) *Captive Audience: Media, Masculinity and Power in Prisons*. Cullompton: Willan Publishing.

# IMMIGRATION DETENTION

There are ten immigration detention centres in the UK, holding 2,700 people. These facilities are designed to prevent detainees from disappearing into the community. Controversially, they hold children as well as adults.

There are currently just over 2,700 detention places in ten immigration detention centres, nine of which are in England and one – Dungavel – in Scotland. The detention centres hold adult men, women and, most controversially, children. Three centres are currently designated to hold children – Dungavel, Tinsley House near Gatwick Airport and Yarl's Wood in Bedfordshire. The first two are intended for short durations only, but Yarl's Wood holds children for longer periods. All have at various times been found to be deficient in their capacity to provide for the emotional and educational needs of children (e.g. HM Inspectorate of Prisons 2005).

Immigration detention centres are formally known as immigration 'removal centres', though this is something of a misnomer given that some detainees win their asylum cases and are not therefore removed from the country. They hold foreign nationals awaiting decisions on their asylum claims or for deportation following a failed application. They are run on behalf of the Immigration and Nationality Directorate (IND) by private contractors and, in the case of three centres, by the Prison Service. One centre, Oakington in Cambridgeshire, is known as a 'reception' centre because its primary purpose is to hold newly arrived asylum seekers whose claims are considered by the IND to be suitable for 'fast-track' processing. However, for some

years it has also held a large number of detainees whose cases were deemed to be unfounded and who could therefore theoretically be removed from the country relatively quickly. In addition to the detention centres, there are over 30 smaller short-term holding facilities, most of which are non-residential holding rooms located at airports and other ports of entry. A considerable number of people are also held for immigration-related matters in police cells for up to seven days before being transferred to the detention estate or remanded to prison, but no figures for these people are available. A number of foreign nationals who have served a sentence for a criminal offence are also detained in prisons after the end of their sentences. However, it is hard to get an accurate estimate of the number of detainees being held in prisons, mainly as a result of poor identification and recording practices. There has also been much criticism of inefficient IND caseworking, which has led to poor decisions and prolonged detention.

The power to detain foreign nationals was first established by the Immigration Act 1971 and the decision to detain is essentially an administrative one, exercised by IND staff. Although such decisions result in the extreme measure of deprivation of liberty, they are not subject to the level of scrutiny and critical assessment of evidence which accompany decisions to imprison people who have committed criminal offences. Detention is indefinite, but detainees can apply for bail or judicial review at any stage. However, the quantity and quality of legal advice have reduced as a result of recent restrictions on Legal Aid, and this means that detainees can find it very difficult to challenge IND decisions. Most detainees are held for only a few days, but an increasing number are in detention for prolonged periods. In June 2006, 705 (28 per cent) were detained for up to 14 days, 160 (6 per cent) for 6 months to a year and 75 (3 per cent) were detained for a year or more (Home Office 2006).

Detention is nominally aimed at stopping foreign nationals from 'disappearing' into the community while their claim is being processed or removal arrangements are made, and is intended only for those people who are not considered to be reliable enough to report to the authorities. However, it is questionable if it remains a last resort, given that the number of detention spaces has expanded more than tenfold since 1993 when there were only about 250 places. Detention of foreign nationals now appears to have become an integral and increasing part of government policy. It is unclear whether it is considered as merely an administrative response to the need to keep track of people or if it is also seen as a deterrent to illegal immigration and false asylum claims. In any event, there is currently no evidence that detention has any effect on the levels of illegal entries or asylum claims.

In order to bring some element of independent scrutiny to the immigration detention estate, HM Inspectorate of Prisons was charged under the Asylum and Immigration Act 1999 with the duty to inspect all immigration removal centres in the UK. In 2002, the inspectorate received specific funding to carry out regular inspections of immigration removal centres and short-term holding facilities and has thrown light on this previously closed world. Important findings have been the lack of effective basic policies and structures for the management of self-harm, bullying, race relations and grievances, though all have started to improve. A common finding has been that, while centre staff make considerable efforts to care for detainees sensitively and decently, they can do little to mitigate the feelings of insecurity and despondency created by immigration detention. Although many detainees have lived in the country for several years, they often have no opportunity to close their affairs or to collect property prior to detention, and children have sometimes been detained while sitting or preparing for exams. Inspection has also highlighted the frequent and generally inexplicable movement of detainees around different detention centres, which is also a source of much frustration for detainees (see HM Inspectorate of Prisons 2006, 2007).

*Hindpal Singh Bhui*

*Related entries*

*Black and minority ethnic (BME) prisoners; Foreign national prisoners; HM Inspectorate of Prisons; HM Prison Service; Home Office; Human rights; Race relations.*

**Key texts and sources**

HM Inspectorate of Prisons (2005) *Report of a Full Announced Inspection of Yarl's Wood Immigration Removal Centre.* London: Home Office.
HM Inspectorate of Prisons (2006) *Annual Report.* London: Home Office.
HM Inspectorate of Prisons (2007) *Annual Report.* London: Home Office.
Home Office (2006) *RDS Asylum Statistics, 2nd Quarter, April–June 2006.* London: Home Office.

## IMPORTATION MODEL

Unlike earlier theories of 'prisonization', the importation model argues that an inmate's mode of adaptation to prison is influenced by factors external to the immediate context of the prison, as well as by the immediate conditions of imprisonment.

The importation model of prisonization was postulated in challenge to the deprivation model (also called the 'indigenous' or 'functional' model). This earlier model argues that the ways in which prisoners adapt to the privations and pressures of the prison generate its particular social system and subcultures. The degree to which an inmate becomes 'prisonized' – that is, socialized into the inmate subculture – is related to the degree of pressure exerted by the experience of imprisonment. The deprivation model thus conceives of the prison as an essentially closed social system.

This thinking remained largely unchallenged until the 1960s, when the notion of importation was introduced by Irwin and Cressey (1962). Their argument drew on the theory of latent social roles, which points out that members of a group may draw on cultures other than the immediate one to inform their understandings (Becker and Greer 1960). Irwin and Cressey accepted that prisoner subcultures arose in response to the particular problems presented by living in prison, but argued that it was likely that prisoners would look to their prior experiences (their latent social roles/culture) outside the prison for solutions to the problem of coping with imprisonment.

In short, although a prison subculture might arise because of the conditions of imprisonment, the particular form that subculture takes may not in itself be the logical outcome of the specific conditions of the prison (Thomas and Foster 1972). Furthermore, one of the key points in Irwin and Cressy's argument was to highlight the similarities between prisoner subculture and other criminal subcultures – it is clear that there is an inevitable degree of cross-fertilization between the two. Irwin and Cressey suggest that, rather than one coherent inmate subculture, there are several, and that the orientation of a prisoner towards a particular subculture was likely to be influenced by his or her personal history and prior socialization, the type and quality of contact with individuals and the world outside during imprisonment, and the inmate's perceptions of the prospects for his or her future beyond release. Thus, as Thomas and Foster (1972) point out, the importation model is not necessarily in conflict with the deprivation model of prisonization. It is perhaps for this reason that it has more often been drawn on in relation to other substantive issues than debated in isolation, suggesting a high degree of acceptance among prison sociologists.

Since the 1960s, the importation model has been discussed in relation to a broad range of issues. These include the use of drugs in prison, homosexuality, adaptation to prison, suicides, violence, race and diversity, religion and faith, criminal activity inside prisons and others. This substantial body of work collectively offers strong support for importation theory by showing often measurable correlations between a prisoner's background, continuing relationships, future plans and how he or she responds to imprisonment.

*Abigail Rowe*

*Related entries*

*Drugs; Homosexuality in prison; Prisonization; Religion and faith; Subcultures; Violence.*

**Key texts and sources**

Becker, H.S. and Greer, B. (1960) 'Latent culture: a note on the theory of latent social roles', *Administrative Science Quarterly*, 5: 304–13.

Irwin, J. and Cressey, D.R. (1962) 'Thieves, convicts and the inmate culture', *Social Problems*, 10: 142–55.

Thomas, C.W. and Foster, S.C. (1972) 'Prisonization in the inmate contraculture', *Social Problems*, 20: 229–39.

# INCAPACITATION

Incapacitation is a theory of punishment which proposes that sentencing can contribute towards reducing crime by removing potential offenders from the community, so eliminating their capacity to commit offences.

There are two broad approaches to incapacitation, or the removal of offenders from the community: collective and selective incapacitation. Collective incapacitation involves sentencing, perhaps applying extended sentencing to groups such as serious sexual or violent offenders without any attempt to measure individual risk. The theory holds that, during the period of the sentence, these individuals cannot commit further offences. Selective incapacitation proposes that high-risk individuals are identified and detained for extended periods of time or until their risk is reduced and, as a result, they cannot commit further offences during this period of detention. These approaches have found some support in recent sentencing policy developments. For example, mandatory minimum sentencing and indeterminate and extended public protection sentencing introduced under the Criminal Justice Act 2003 are examples of this approach. Another illustration is the growing focus on persistent offenders, with the belief that a relatively small number of offenders commit a disproportionately high level of crime and, as a result, identifying and targeting these individuals would have a disproportionately beneficial impact on reducing offending.

There have been a number of criticisms of the incapacitation approach. The two major criticisms relate to the question of accuracy and the question of principle (Mathiesen 2006). In relation to accuracy, it is generally recognized that predicting future risk for low-level routine offending such as burglary is relatively straightforward, but predicting more serious offending, such as violent and sexual offending, is notoriously unreliable. As a result, it is argued that incapacitative strategies directed at these groups are likely to result in a high number of false positives and to be inefficient in directing resources towards people who do not actually present the level of risk assumed. The second criticism is that, on ethical grounds, the punishment of potential *future* conduct violates the fundamental principle that people should be punished for their past behaviour only. It is further argued that it is likely to result in particularly unfair treatment towards individuals who are falsely identified as presenting a future risk. Finally, in relation to the moral dimensions of punishment, incapacitation makes no claims to rehabilitate offenders.

Incapacitation is therefore a particularly controversial approach because it is premised on a prediction of future conduct rather than being rooted in past actions and is not concerned with changing behaviour. However, with the growth in actuarial risk assessment techniques and the desire to manage crime more effectively, these approaches have grown in influence. While there is some potential benefit in targeting persistent low-level offenders where prediction is reliable, the real desire is to identify and predict future serious offending, but this has a low level of reliability and carries significant risks for both effectiveness and human rights.

*Jamie Bennett*

### Related entries

*Desistance; Deterrence; Just deserts; 'Prison works'; Rehabilitation; Reoffending; Risk; Sentencing policy; Sex offenders.*

**Key texts and sources**

Mathiesen, T. (2006) *Prison on Trial* (3rd edn). Winchester: Waterside Press.

## IN-CELL TELEVISION

As the name suggests, in-cell television refers to TV sets that are rented by prisoners for their own personal use in their cells. Part of the incentives and earned privileges (IEP) initiative, in-cell television is designated an earnable privilege and can be removed from prisoners as a punishment.

In the UK, in-cell television was first given formal recognition in 1991 in the Woolf Report following disturbances at Strangeways, although other European countries (e.g. France) had already implemented it as early as 1985. Prior to in-cell television, prisoners had been allowed to watch television only in association rooms. Although some prisons were able to provide more than one television (tuned to different channels in an attempt to prevent disagreements over what was watched), association rooms were regarded as one of the major 'flashpoints' in prisons and it was common for seating to be bolted to the floor to minimize the potential for violence.

In-cell television was initially introduced as a trial experiment in 1992 at Stocken and Garth Prisons. Although acknowledged a success by prisoners, staff and governors in those prisons, its history was dogged by prevarication and persistent rumour that it would be withdrawn. In 1995 Home Secretary Michael Howard rejected the advice of Sir John Learmont who, following the escape of three high-security inmates from Parkhurst Prison, recommended extending in-cell television across all prisons as a measure to enhance prisoner–staff relations and improve security. Somewhat contrarily, Howard announced instead that the 20 prisons which had the facility would be required to remove televisions from cells almost immediately.

However, soon afterwards there was a change of government and, despite a continuation of the 'get tough' political rhetoric of the Conservative era, New Labour's electoral victory in 1997 heralded the expansion of in-cell television across the prison estate.

Discussions of in-cell television have been dominated by the question of whether television is 'good' for prisoners. This debate seems as pointless and patronizing as wider discussions of whether television is 'good' for children, adolescents, the poorly educated and socially excluded. Ideas about the individuals most likely to be adversely affected by media content are underpinned by positivist notions of 'otherness' that dovetail with concerns about television constituting 'bad' culture and eroding traditional values and cultural ties. The linking of television and prison inmates thus conveniently brings together two scapegoats in the frequent, if methodologically unsound, attempts to link media images with rising crime.

It is unsurprising, then, that in-cell television has been the subject of heated debate over the last three decades, a controversy that lies, in part, in the fact that incentives and earned privileges were designed to meet public expectations about what kind of place prison should be. For the public – informed by a popular media who persist in presenting prison as a 'kind of country club for the lower classes' (Johnson 2005: 256) – television might seem a 'luxury' that criminals do not deserve. The principle of less eligibility is unconvincing in this context as 99 per cent of British households have at least one television set. Yet, despite this penetration, prisoners' access to television remains a contentious subject. The very attributes that are viewed positively by in-cell television's supporters – that it normalizes the prison regime, links inmates to the outside world, minimizes contact time between inmates and officers (thus reducing staff costs) and makes earlier lock-up times acceptable to prisoners – are equally viewed as potentially negative qualities by its detractors.

In addition to historic notions of less eligibility and contemporary ideas about prisoners being an 'undeserving' underclass, one of the latent concerns that may have impeded its progress is the belief that electronic media are eroding the 'totality' of total institutions and allowing prisoners to participate in wider debates about their treatment and rights. Meyrowitz (1985) argues that the impact of electronic media on prisons, and the resulting inclusion of prisoners in the public sphere, is the latest development in a gradual democratization via the mass media, whereby previously marginalized or formally isolated groups – women, children, the poor, the disabled, ethnic minorities and homosexuals – have had access to, and been included in, all spheres of public participation. The introduction of in-cell television has thus led to a redefinition of the nature of 'imprisonment' and to a *de facto* revision of the prison classification system. In addition to the physical variables of 'high security' and 'low security', we must now add the communication variables of 'high information' prisons versus 'low information' prisons (Meyrowitz 1985: 117–18).

However, this argument, while theoretically plausible, does not stand up to empirical analysis. Research findings contradict the idea that in-cell television normalizes prison or even offers the same kinds of communications experiences that most of us in the broader community enjoy (Lindlof 1987; Jewkes 2002). Even relatively 'media-rich' institutions still feel profoundly isolated from the larger society, and a limited and regulated level of exposure to the outside world via television paradoxically can serve to intensify feelings of being removed from normal life. Research shows that many prisoners report watching little television simply because it is too painful to be reminded of a world that they are no longer part of. Similarly, prisoners cannot enjoy the same sense of participation in mediated events that free citizens do because, in prison, communication almost always flows in one direction. Consequently there is a palpable sense of frustration that the outside world impacts on them, but that they can do little to impact on it (Jewkes 2002).

A further impediment to the participation of prisoners in the public sphere is temporal. While the pace of life and progress of technology in the outside world have quickened dramatically, the mobility rate at which prisoners move through space and time is limited by their spatial horizons, their access to goods and services and their restricted means of mobility. Television can help prisoners 'escape' their confinement to a limited extent but it is still structured by institutional restrictions on space and time. In addition, at the same time as computers, the Internet, satellite and digital television, mobile phones, MP3 players, personal digital assistants and a myriad of other new technologies have expanded the social worlds of free citizens almost to the four corners of the globe, they have created a new level of disconnection between prison and society. Prison inmates are limited to the most modern technology readily at their disposal, terrestrial television, which renders them – especially those on basic privileges – 'cavemen in an era of speed-of-light technology' (Johnson 2005: 263; cf. Jewkes 2007).

Perversely, then, despite public unease about prisoners 'living it up' behind bars, in-cell television may actually reproduce disadvantage and deprivation. Prison officers appear to be almost universally in favour of it because it is regarded as having a 'calming' effect on prisoners (although before in-cell television was introduced, staff expressed a great deal of resistance along the lines of the sentiments expressed by the public and popular media). However, its role as an 'electronic babysitter' has to be seen alongside its potential drawbacks. Because of its status as an earnable privilege and incentive to good behaviour, its potential as a relatively easy means of punishment has made many prisoners ambivalent, recognizing that technology in prisons tends to be used for purposes of control and punishment, rather than reform or rehabilitation (Jewkes 2002; Johnson 2005). As earlier lock-up times are introduced, opportunities for inmates to interact with others are reduced, education and training are cut back and some inmates are effectively coerced into having, and paying rental on, televisions if they are to enjoy other privileges associated with 'enhanced' status, it might be suggested that in-cell television is being used as a 'sweetener' to mask, or compensate for, the situational control measures that are creeping back into the logic of imprisonment (Jewkes 2002). Johnson (2005) reports a similar

story in the USA, where prison visits, telephone calls, work release programmes, compassionate leaves, permission to decorate cells and keep pets, facilities to cook one's own food and permission to receive personal property and wear civilian clothing have all been eroded in prisons where the one 'perk' allowed is in-cell television.

*Yvonne Jewkes*

### Related entries

*Communication; Incentives and earned privileges (IEP); Less eligibility; Rehabilitation; Security; Time; Woolf Report.*

**Key texts and sources**

Jewkes, Y. (2002) *Captive Audience: Media, Masculinity and Power in Prisons.* Cullompton: Willan Publishing.

Jewkes, Y. (2007) 'Prisons and the media: the shaping of public opinion and penal policy in a mediated society', in Y. Jewkes (ed.) *Handbook on Prisons.* Cullompton: Willan Publishing.

Johnson, R. (2005) 'Brave new prisons: the growing social isolation of modern penal institutions', in A. Liebling and S. Maruna (eds) *The Effects of Imprisonment.* Cullompton: Willan Publishing.

Lindlof, T. (1987) 'Ideology and pragmatics of media access in prison', in T. Lindlof (ed.) *Natural Audiences: Qualitative Research of Media Uses and Effects.* Norwood, NJ: Ablex.

Meyrowitz, J. (1985) *No Sense of Place: The Impact of Electronic Media on Social Behaviour.* Oxford: Oxford University Press.

## INCENTIVES AND EARNED PRIVILEGES (IEP)

In 1995, largely as a result of increasing assault rates and levels of drug use in prisons (which in turn were linked to increased hours spent out of cells), the Prison Service introduced a new policy of incentives and earned privileges (IEP) for prisoners. This policy linked prisoner behaviour, as assessed by prison officers, to different levels of material privileges.

*IEP is part of what's helped to sort this prison out. The concept is simple – prisoner behaves, prisoner gets extra phone card. It's the subtleties behind it we need to think about. It feeds into so many things. There are some dangers in it, too. We probably need to think about it a bit harder, understand it better. There are some big issues hidden in it (senior manager, Prison Service).*

The policy for incentives and earned privileges (IEP) was introduced in 32 first-phase prisons in July 1995 and to all prisons by July 1996. The policy sought 'to ensure that prisoners earn privileges by responsible behaviour and participation in hard work and other constructive activity' (*Instruction to Governors 74/1995: Incentives and Earned Privileges*). Within this overall purpose, five main aims were identified. To:

1. provide that privileges generally are earned by prisoners through good behaviour and performance and are removable if prisoners fail to maintain acceptable standards;
2. encourage responsible behaviour by prisoners;
3. encourage hard work and other constructive activity by prisoners;
4. encourage sentenced prisoners' progress through the prison system; and
5. create a more disciplined, better controlled and safer environment for prisoners and staff.

The IEP policy effectively gave increased power and discretion to prison staff to determine newly differentiated privilege entitlement. Several similar schemes had been implemented during earlier periods of history (for example, the Borstal system for young offenders was effectively an earned release scheme; see Liebling and Bosworth 1994). Prison officers were required to form judgements about a prisoner's behaviour, which would in turn form the basis of a decision taken (technically at a higher level by a senior rank or a review board; but see Liebling *et al.* 1999) about his or her level of privilege entitlement. Prisoners could be allocated to 'Basic', 'Standard' or 'Enhanced' levels of privileges.

The IEP scheme is based on a rational choice model of human (in this case, prisoner) behaviour and on a set of assumptions about the subjective value of specific material privileges.

For example, good behaviour could result in higher levels of pay, longer and more frequent visits, more access to temporary release and accommodation in better areas of a prison. The policy tries to distinguish between facilities prisoners need to enhance their opportunities for the future (which should be available to all) and material privileges which make life in prison easier but which are not related to reoffending. In practice, this distinction is difficult to make (for example, in the case of access to longer family visits).

In a national evaluation of the operation and effects of the policy, major and important differences appeared between prisons in their use of IEP. For example, the five prisons studied varied widely in their use of the Basic regime (the lowest level of privileges, regarded as a punishment by prisoners) in terms of numbers, criteria and precise details of the regime and material provision. These differences were linked to other systematic differences between establishments (including, for example, not only the perceived aims of the IEP policy but also the nature and extent of control problems in each establishment, the quality of staff–prisoner relationships and the perceived compliance of the prisoner population). The research found that wings in some establishments developed significantly different practices, with distinct outcomes for prisoners, and that these practices reflected identifiable differences in broader aspects of each wing's style and operation. These different wing styles were not explained by population differences alone but reflected qualitative diversity in staff approaches towards prisoners. Some staff resorted to formal means of control more readily than others. The relatively high use of privilege removal (punishment) was often associated with distant and poor staff–prisoner relationships. On one wing of a pilot prison where high numbers of prisoners were placed on the Basic regime, staff were 'retreating into their offices' rather than mixing with prisoners. Very few prisoners reported having been warned about their behaviour, despite the relatively high use of Basic (and the due-process requirement that staff warn prisoners before formally placing them on a Basic level of privilege entitlement). Conversely, where staff–prisoner relationships were close and highly rated, resort was less frequently made to privilege removal as a means of control. Staff used their verbal skills, their 'tactics of talk', to cajole prisoners into compliance. There seemed to be a link between the quality of staff–prisoner relationships and the use of *formal* rather than *informal* sanctions. On the wing with poor staff–prisoner relationships and a high resort to formal sanctions such as the use of Basic, a major disturbance followed. This was an empirical illustration of the maxim that 'staff–prisoner relationships matter' and of the findings of several other studies that the way staff use their authority is inextricably linked to the nature and quality of their relationships with prisoners (see further Liebling and Price 2001). Other risks inherent in the policy include 'double jeopardy': the tendency to adjudicate formally on prisoners at the same time as a decision was taken to reduce their privilege level. The policy requires judgements to be made on the basis of a pattern of prisoner behaviour over time but, in practice, single incidents often lead to reduced entitlement.

Some version of the policy is currently used in most prisons. Some prisons (for example, young offender institutions) use formal points schemes. The policy was revised in 1999 following disappointing results from the national evaluation, which suggested that, if not very carefully implemented, the policy could backfire, creating resentment and hostility particularly among older and longer-term prisoners. Some justice safeguards were introduced – for example, emphasizing the requirement for decisions to be taken by a review board rather than by an individual (see IG 90/1999).

*Alison Liebling*

### Related entries

*Borstals; Discretion; Fairness; In-cell television; Power; Young offender institutions (YOIs).*

### Key texts and sources

Bottoms, A.E. (2003) 'Theoretical reflections on the evaluations of a penal policy initiative', in L. Zedner and A. Ashworth (eds) *The Criminological Foundations of Penal Policy: Essays in Honour of Roger Hood.* Oxford: Oxford University Press.
Liebling, A. and Bosworth, M. (1994) 'Incentives in prison regimes', *Prison Service Journal*, 98: 57–64.
Liebling, A., Muir, G., Rose, G. and Bottoms, A.E. (1999) *Incentives and Earned Privileges in Prison. Research Findings* 87. London: Home Office Research, Development and Statistics Directorate.
See also **http://www.pso.hmprisonservice.gov.uk/ PSO_4000_incentives_and_earned_privileges.doc**.

## INDEPENDENT MONITORING BOARDS

Independent monitoring boards are groups of lay people appointed by the Home Secretary with the statutory role of monitoring the fairness and decency of the treatment of prisoners.

By law, every prison in England and Wales must have an independent monitoring board (IMB). These generally comprise between 12 and 20 unpaid lay people appointed by the Home Secretary from the local community. Individual members are appointed to a specific prison for three years and, subject to review, may be reappointed for further terms of three years. In appointing individual members of boards, the minister seeks to ensure that each board is diverse and representative both of the wider community and of the community in prison. There is currently a statutory requirement, dating from the Prison Act 1952 which prescribes many of the current functions of boards, that each board should have two magistrates among its members. A recommendation for the requirement to be removed has yet to be implemented (Home Office 2001).

The role of each board is primarily to monitor the day-to-day life of a particular prison. They are required to meet once a month and, between meetings, at least one member of the board should carry out an inspection visit to the prison. In practice, boards generally carry out these visits by rota at least once a week. Board members have unrestricted access to the prison subject only to appropriate security considerations. In addition to their monitoring visits they also deal with requests from individual prisoners and must be notified promptly by the governor of any serious incident so that they may attend to monitor the situation. Boards are required to submit an annual report to the Secretary of State. These are generally published on the IMB website and, in many cases, through the local and national press.

The work of IMBs is complementary to that of two other statutory agencies, HM Inspectorate of Prisons and the Prisons and Probation Ombudsman. Although the current name has only been in existence since 2003, the organization has a long history, first as 'visiting committees of justices' and more recently as 'boards of visitors'. The change of name in 2003, to independent monitoring boards, followed the recommendations of the Lloyd Review (Home Office 2001). It was intended to define more clearly boards' current non-executive monitoring role and to avoid confusion with prison visitors.

IMBs in England and Wales trace their origin back to the visiting committees of justices established in the reign of Queen Elizabeth I (Board of Visitors 1988). The justices were given significant powers to regulate and control gaols, as well as carrying out an inspectorial role. Responsibility for appointing these committees lay with the justices. That situation continued largely unchanged until the Prison Act 1877 which centralized control of local prisons, thereby removing the managerial role of the visiting committees although they retained their disciplinary function. The Act defined more formally the role of the committees, bringing them under the control of the Secretary of State and guaranteeing them free access to every part of the prison and to the prisoners. The duties of the committees were also more clearly defined and included an obligation to meet at the prison once a month and for one or more of their number to visit the prison each week.

The nineteenth century saw the development of convict prisons, which had a system of professional inspection but remained outside the scope of independent monitors until the Prisons Act 1898. The current system of monitoring prisons, in England and Wales is generally traced to the establishment by that Act of boards of visitors for each of the convict prisons. The Act further defined the role of visiting committees, which continued to operate in local prisons until 1971. The boards of visitors established by the Prison Act 1898 were to be appointed by the Secretary of State and at least two of their members had to be magistrates. They were required to meet at least eight times a year and to arrange for a member of the board to visit the prison at least once between meetings. A contemporary account, published in the *Economic Journal* of December 1898, described their establishment as 'a salutary innovation'.

Boards of visitors were extended to all prisons following the Courts Act 1971, which abolished the quarter sessions and, with them, the visiting committees, which had continued to operate in local prisons. Over the next 20 years there was a growing scrutiny of boards' continuing responsibility for adjudications under the prison discipline system, which was increasingly seen as being at odds with their watchdog role. A Home Office report of 1984 raised a number of issues with regard to the perception of boards' independence and effectiveness, finding that those in prison often associated them with management and that their effectiveness was impaired by their close relationship with the governor (Maguire and Vagg 1984). A number of cases before the Court of Appeal and the European Court of Human Rights also focused attention on the disciplinary role of boards, which was finally removed in the Criminal Justice Act 1991. Thereafter boards continued to exercise an executive role solely with regard to the authorization of the continuing segregation of prisoners for purposes of good order or their own protection.

The most recent review of the effectiveness of boards (Home Office 2001) led to the removal of those remaining executive powers, and boards now have a purely monitoring role with some safeguards to ensure that their comments, particularly with regard to segregation units, are addressed. That review has also brought about a number of other changes, including a more formal role for the National Council of Independent Monitoring Boards. IMBs also now operate in immigration detention centres, with similar functions to those in prisons.

*Jim Haines*

### Related entries

*Accountability; Grievances; HM Inspectorate of Prisons; Home Office; Human rights; Immigration detention; Prison Act; Prisons and Probation Ombudsman; Segregation.*

**Key texts and sources**

Boards of Visitors (1998) *A Brief History of the Boards of Visitors, 1898–1998*. London: HMSO.
Home Office (2001) *Review of the Boards of Visitors: A Report of the Working Group Chaired by Rt Hon Sir Peter Lloyd MP*. London: Home Office.
Maguire, M. and Vagg, J. (1984) *The Watchdog Role of Boards of Visitors*. London: Home Office.
Wright, M. (1982) *Making Good: Prisons, Punishment and Beyond*. London: Burnett Books.
See also www.imb.gov.uk.

# INDUSTRIAL RELATIONS

Industrial relations refer to the relationship between managers and unions. In prisons, this has been dominated by relations with the Prison Officers' Association (POA), which represents virtually all the prison officer grades in England and Wales.

Although there are a number of unions that represent different grades and professions in prisons, industrial relations (IR) are dominated by the Prison Officers' Association (POA). The POA represents 96 per cent of all prison officer grades in England, Wales and Northern Ireland, with over 26,000 members, and it has been widely portrayed as a narrow, outdated and militant relic, while managers are seen as either colluding with this or ineffective in tackling the issues (Black 1995).

From the early 1900s, prison staff sought the right to unionize but, in 1911, the Home Secretary, Winston Churchill, made a definitive statement that prison officers were like policeman, soldiers and sailors and it was therefore inappropriate for them to form unions (Thomas 1972). Despite this statement, underground action continued, particularly through the publication of the *Prison Officers' Magazine* and through the unofficial National Union of Police and Prison Officers (NUPPO). In the face of ongoing industrial unrest, the government formed the Prison Officers' Representative Board (PORB), made up of officials and officer representatives, meeting twice a year in order to provide a forum for officers to make suggestions, air concerns or share complaints. This board was widely derided for its lack of rigour and independence, and, as a result, the underground action continued. It was not until 1939 that the Prison Commissioners finally agreed to recognize the POA.

Following the Second World War, there was a period of social reform, most notably characterized by the creation of the welfare state. In prisons, reform focused on developing rehabilitative ideals. The POA resisted this liberalization, particularly criticizing what it considered to be a consequence of this liberalization – a loss of order and an increase in violence. The POA published its progressive document, *The Role of the Modern Prison Officer*, in 1963, which argued that prison officers should take on welfare and rehabilitation roles. This was widely seen as being motivated by self-interest, preventing the erosion or marginalization of prison officer jobs as the function of prisons changed (Thomas 1972).

From the 1960s onwards, the POA became increasingly militant. Industrial action was identified as a contributory factor in prison disorder during the 1970s, particularly after 1975 when the POA National Executive Committee recognized the right of branches at individual prisons to decide for themselves what action they should take over local disputes, leading to a dramatic increase in the frequency, range and extent of industrial disputes. In 1986 industrial action directly led to widespread riots affecting 40 prisons, causing damage totalling £5.5 million. This catastrophe marked the high-water mark of union power and a low point in IR.

A more positive signal arose from the Fresh Start package introduced in 1987. This abolished paid overtime, which at that stage accounted for one third of the pay budget, abolished the chief officer grade, introduced a unified structure running from officer to prison governor, increased pay and reduced working hours. The loss of overtime and the failure of the POA to move effectively into representing governor grades after the abolition of the chief officer started to erode its power. However, the Woolf Report published following the Strangeways Prison riot of 1990 stated that Fresh Start had failed to redress the IR malaise.

The 1990s saw the adoption of a more robust managerial approach. In 1993, following a ballot on industrial action in opposition to the introduction of privatization, the Prison Service took legal action, exploiting the legal anomaly that, as prison officers had the powers of a constable, they did not have the full legal protection of a trade union and could be sued for damages arising from industrial action (Lewis 1997). This case effectively undermined the power of the POA, making industrial action unlawful, a situation that was confirmed by legislation under s. 127 of the Criminal Justice and Public Order Act 1994. The POA was in disarray and, throughout the 1990s, significant changes were implemented, including the opening of private prisons, the extensive regrading of prison officer posts and efficiency saving measures (such as reduced staffing levels in prisons). This period therefore marked the eclipse of the POA as a national force. However, local branches continued to play an important role in individual prisons. While many individual branches and unions were able to exert a positive influence on prisons and their members, the late 1990s were a period when the spotlight was directed towards branch officials, who were exerting a malign influence on individual prisons (in particular, Wormwood Scrubs and Feltham, from where a

branch official was compulsorily transferred in July 2001 due to his militancy).

When the New Labour government came to power in 1997, there was some hope that its election would signal a new approach to prison IR, including the removal of s. 127 and the realization of the party's commitment to bring private prisons back into the public sector. Although this did not happen, the public sector was allowed to compete for private prison contracts when they came for renewal and, in 1998, the Home Secretary signalled his willingness to replace s. 127 with a voluntary 'no strike' agreement and to introduce an independent pay review body. However, negotiations were protracted, and it was not until 2001 that they were implemented.

This voluntary agreement marked a significant modernization in IR procedures. In particular, disputes would ultimately be resolved by independent arbitration through the Arbitration, Conciliation and Advisory Service, where previously they had been settled by the Deputy Director General of the Prison Service. In 2004, the voluntary agreement was superseded by a Joint Industrial Relations Procedural Agreement, and s. 127 was finally removed in 2005. The POA also has a Facilities Agreement with the Prison Service, which commits the service to provide time for national and local POA officials to carry out their role. The POA also has access to promote its service to all newly recruited prison officers. Taken together, the contemporary approach to IR could be described as 'sophisticated modern', characterized by IR now having a strategic purpose: unions are recognized as having a legitimate and defined role and are used as a means of negotiation, consultation and representation. Membership will therefore be encouraged and procedures formalized (Fox 1974).

The changing nature of IR is particularly apparent in the co-operation in performance testing of prisons – a process by which poorly performing prisons have an opportunity to develop an improvement plan which, if not adequate, may result in them being offered to the private sector. In addition, there is evidence that, in individual prisons, governors and local branches are working successfully in a spirit of partnership, including delivering difficult work, such as efficiency savings (Bennett 2004). This suggests there is a 'new paradigm of co-operation' emerging and that the 'logic of enterprise' is being accepted, where the interests of the organization and employees are shared. However, the extent of this change should not be overestimated. The majority of people remain neutral, joining the union largely for individualized protection, while a small but significant minority of disaffected and change-resistant individuals seek a home in the POA and can exert significant influence (Elliott 2006). The power of this group means that even officials who do not hold hostile views occasionally have to display such attitudes in order to play to their electorate (Bennett 2004).

IR in prisons has been characterized as outdated and anachronistic and, although there are members of the POA who hold hostile views, significant change has occurred in recent years, marking the emergence of a more co-operative partnership.

*Jamie Bennett*

### Related entries

*Fresh Start; Market testing; Performance management; Prison officers; Privatization.*

---

**Key texts and sources**

Bennett, J. (2004) 'Jurassic Park revisited: the changing nature of prison industrial relations', *Prison Service Journal*, 156: 40–5.

Black, J. (1995) 'Industrial relations in the UK Prison Service: the "Jurassic Park" of public sector industrial relations', *Employee Relations*, 17: 64–88.

Elliott, C. (2006) 'Speaking of performance improvement', *Prison Service Journal*, 163: 30–4.

Fox, A. (1974) *Beyond Contract: Work, Power and Trust Relations.* London: Faber & Faber.

Lewis, D. (1997) *Hidden Agendas: Politics, Law and Disorder.* London: Hamish Hamilton.

Thomas, J. (1972) *The English Prison Officer since 1850: A Study in Conflict.* London: Routledge & Kegan Paul.

See also the Prison Officers' Association website (http://www.poauk.org.uk/index.htm).

---

# INMATE CODE

The 'inmate code' is the set of values, norms and maxims that prisoners promote as a guide to appropriate conduct within their community.

The 'inmate code' represents one of the key empirical and theoretical areas of prison sociology. It can be defined as the set of values, norms and maxims that prisoners publicly express as a guide to appropriate conduct, or the idealized template of prison behaviour. As summarized by Sykes and Messinger (1960: 8), this value system has five main tenets: don't interfere with other inmates' interests, or 'never rat [grass] on a con'; don't lose your head, or 'play it cool and do your own time': don't exploit or steal from other prisoners; don't be weak, or 'be tough – be a man'; and 'be sharp' – don't ever side with or show respect for prison officers and representatives.

This normative system was described in 1940 by Donald Clemmer (1940/1958). However, Sykes and Messinger sought to theorize both its sources and the functions it served in the prison. Noting that it could be found across a diverse range of prison regimes, they inferred that its origins lay in the intrinsic properties of imprisonment. The code was thus seen as a means of collectively alleviating, albeit never completely, the pains, losses and threats to morale and personal identity that imprisonment entailed. By being loyal, generous and respectful towards their peers, by not exploiting others or interfering with their interests, by dealing with their predicament with fortitude, by resisting the expectations, judgements and company of staff and, in these ways, by developing a shared, positive identity, prisoners could mitigate the practical and psychological problems of incarceration.

The code is an ideal that all prisoners have reason to promote and which most vehemently assert, but which few actually adhere to. Most prisoners deviate in one form or another from its tenets, and are labelled and judged accordingly in prison argot. None the less, the code set the parameters for inmate conduct and remains a powerful agent of socialization. Much research has focused on the dynamics of this process of assimilation into prison culture and values. Wheeler (1961) found that prisoner attitudes conformed most closely to the code when they were furthest from the outside world – that is, when the pains of imprisonment were most acute and prisoners were most reliant on the prisoner community for social and psychological support.

Such findings support Sykes and Messinger's theorization that the inmate code is a 'problem-solving mechanism' and that its origins lay in the terms and experience of imprisonment itself. But this notion that the code is distinctive to, and is forged within, the penal environment has been challenged by a number of studies that highlight the porousness of the prison walls and the similarities between prisoner norms and those in the outside world. Irwin and Cressey (1962) illustrate the ways that prisoners 'import' into the prison values, behaviour patterns and expectations from the external community and adapt to imprisonment in ways that are often consistent with these existing identities. The inmate code is thus an adapted version of criminal, street and mainstream values 'within the official administrative system of deprivation and control' (Irwin and Cressey 1962: 153). Jacobs (1977) describes a prisoner community that had been fragmented by ethnic and racial conflict and in which there is no single or solidarity code of behaviour to which prisoners pledge allegiance. Codes of loyalty apply only to in-group members, while prisoners who are unaffiliated with gangs – and whose code is 'trust no one' – are considered legitimate targets of exploitation. Moreover, it is not the inmate code that cushions prisoners from the pains and deprivations of imprisonment but the gang system, imported from the city streets, which provides social and economic support and a source of group identity. More recently, it has not only been argued that street values are imported into, and reconstituted by, the prison but also that the values of the prison are then re-exported into the outside community.

The 'importation–deprivation' debate still provides the main framework for discussions of the inmate code. It is generally accepted that the code represents a distorted and adapted version of norms taken from the outside community, and that it is determined by a combination of institutional and external variables. Thus, for example, custody-oriented prisons tend to generate more oppositional values than those that are more therapeutically focused, where systematic attempts are made to discourage conventional norms about not informing on other prisoners and not disclosing to staff. As is broadly consistent with deprivation theories, in the UK, the code appears more binding in higher-security prisons than those where prisoners are closer to release. However, it is clear that external, imported variables play a major part in determining the norms of the prisoner community. Mathiesen's (1965) account of a Norwegian treatment-oriented establishment describes a prisoner community where contact with staff is acceptable and where there is no 'honourable' prisoner identity – as reflected in the country's less developed criminal culture. Likewise, women's prisons have traditionally exhibited less powerful prohibitions on grassing, expressing emotion and fraternizing with staff than men's prisons – features that are said to reflect differences in gender norms between men and women in general. Indeed, many commentators have recently drawn attention to the manner in which the inmate code in men's prisons is deeply inscribed by ideals of masculinity, which celebrate physical toughness, emotional fortitude, autonomy and in-group loyalty, and which are placed under direct threat by the nature of incarceration.

The inmate code is more complex, ambiguous and negotiable than basic maxims suggest. There may be no strong consensus on its terms or interpretation – no simple, single code that all prisoners recognize. Although prisoners tend to agree that informing is wrong, some may consider it justified in certain situations (for example, when life may be at risk). While some young offenders use norms against weakness to justify persecuting the vulnerable, in adult prisons such behaviour contravenes norms proscribing exploitation. Likewise, some prisoners consider the charging of interest for loans as 'shrewd business', while others regard it as an abuse of solidarity (Crewe 2005). Motivations for espousing the code also vary greatly, with some prisoners being normatively committed to its terms and others merely pragmatic in its assertion. Clemmer (1940/1958) argues that code violations are most likely to occur among prisoners with loyalties to people both within and outside the institution (i.e. where allegiances were stretched). Violations may also be strategic: intelligent prisoners may use the code as a *means* of exploitation – for example, by discouraging others from informing on their activities. Indeed, while early theorists argued that, in the absence of the inmate code, prison life would be all the more alienating, insecure and conflictual (and that, despite its anti-institutional nature, the code contributed to institutional order by curbing the more disruptive elements within the prisoner community), Jacobs's work illustrates how ideals of toughness and machismo had become the *basis* for interpersonal aggression and victimization. It should also be noted that conforming to the code may cause rather than alleviate some frustrations. For example, some prisoners find the need to suppress their emotions a significant source of pain.

Recent research has confirmed the way that the code has evolved to fit the imperatives of contemporary imprisonment. In the USA, white-collar criminals and white prisoners who are unattached to white supremacist gangs have developed a highly defensive code: 'don't gamble, don't mess with drugs, don't mess with homosexuals, don't steal, don't borrow or lend' (Hassine 1999: 42). The exhortation to avoid drug use is also found in the UK, as are a number of other guidelines for conduct: be clean and hygienic, look after your physical health; be sincere – don't try to be something you're not; and treat teaching staff with respect.

*Ben Crewe*

### Related entries

*Adjusting to release; Argot (prison); Deprivations/'pains of imprisonment'; Economy; Importation model; Masculinity; Prisonization; Solidarity; Structure/agency ('resistance'); Subcultures.*

### Key texts and sources

Clemmer, D. (1940; 2nd edn 1958) *The Prison Community*. New York, NY: Holt, Rinehart & Winston.

Crewe, B. (2005) 'Codes and conventions: the terms and conditions of contemporary inmate values', in A. Liebling and S. Maruna (eds) *The Effects of Imprisonment*. Cullompton: Willan Publishing.

Hassine, V. (1999) *Life without Parole: Living in Prison Today* (2nd edn). Los Angeles, CA: Roxbury.

Irwin, J. and Cressey, D. (1962) 'Thieves, convicts and the inmate culture', *Social Problems*, 10: 142–55.

Jacobs, J. (1977) *Stateville: The Penitentiary in Mass Society*. Chicago, IL: University of Chicago Press.

Mathiesen, T. (1965) *The Defences of the Weak: A Sociological Study of a Norwegian Correctional Institution*. London: Tavistock.

Sykes, G. and Messinger, S. (1960) 'The inmate social system', in R.A. Cloward *et al.* (eds) *Theoretical Studies in the Social Organization of the Prison*. New York, NY: Social Science Research Council.

Wheeler, S. (1961) 'Socialization in correctional communities', *American Sociological Review*, 26: 697–712.

## IN-REACH TEAMS

In-reach teams in prison are multidisciplinary teams commissioned by local mental health NHS trusts. These teams differ from prison to prison and comprise a variety of members of staff (e.g. mental health nurses, psychiatrists, social workers, clinical psychologists and occupational therapists). They aim to provide to prisoners specialist mental health care similar to that which they could receive in the general community.

In-reach teams were introduced in England and Wales in three waves: the first teams were set up in 2001–2 and the final ones in April 2006. The document, *Changing the Outlook: A Strategy for Developing and Modernising Mental Health Services in Prisons* (HMPS and DH 2001), set out the plan to develop in-reach teams. This document more widely set out an approach shared by the Department of Health and the Prison Service to modernize mental health services in prisons. In-reach teams were thought to form an integral part of achieving this aim.

There is debate concerning what the mental in-reach teams are supposed to do. In-reach teams were initially set up to provide a service to those with severe and enduring mental health problems. In reality, in-reach teams also receive as referrals prisoners who do not have a diagnosable mental illness. The Sainsbury Centre for Mental Health (SCMH 2006) found that in-reach team members differed in their views of whether they should see someone who does not have a diagnosed mental illness. Although many individuals in prison do suffer from mental health problems (see Singleton *et al.* 1998), others do not, but these people may still have difficulties adapting to life in prison and may suffer from high levels of psychological distress (see Harvey 2007). These people, although not being labelled with a specific diagnosis, are also in need of the help that can be provided by mental health professionals.

Researchers have begun to examine the role of in-reach teams in prisons. Most notably, the SCMH (2006) has examined the role of in-reach teams in London. In its report, the SCMH recognized that the creation of in-reach teams marks the most significant development in mental health provision to date, but it also stated that the teams had been set up without guidance. Alison Liebling and her colleagues considered the role of in-reach teams as part of the *Safer Locals Evaluation* (2005), and Harvey (2007) has examined how willing young men are to seek support from an in-reach team compared with other sources of support. Finally, Jenny Shaw and her colleagues are conducting a three-year evaluation of in-reach teams, which is due to be completed by 2007.

Mental health in-reach teams mark an important step towards providing prisoners with a service that is comparable with what they would receive in the community. More work is needed to ensure that these teams are tailored to the individual needs of the prisoners and prison and to ensure that there is continuity of service so that people who have received input continue to receive support when they return to the general community.

*Joel Harvey*

*Related entries*

*Healthcare; Mental health.*

**Key texts and sources**

Harvey, J. (2007) *Young Men in Prison: Surviving and Adapting to Life Inside.* Cullompton: Willan Publishing.

HM Prison Service and Department of Health (2001) *Changing the Outlook: A Strategy for Developing and Modernising Mental Health Services in Prisons.* London: Department of Health.

Liebling, A., Tait, S., Durie, L. and Stiles, A. (2005) *The Safer Locals Evaluation.* London: Home Office.

Sainsbury Centre for Mental Health (2006) *London's Prison Mental Health Services: A Review. Policy Paper* 5. London: SCMH (available online at **http://www.markwalton.net/04/mdo/archives/London_prison_mental_health_services.pdf**).

Singleton, N., Meltzer, H., Gatward, R., Coid, J. and Deasy, D. (1998) *Psychiatric Morbidity among Prisoners in England and Wales.* London: ONS.

# INTERMITTENT CUSTODY

Intermittent custody, sometimes described as part-time imprisonment, is a sentence in which the time served is shared between the community and the prison.

Intermittent custody, often referred to as part-time prison, was introduced by the Criminal Justice Act 2003 as part of a package of measures to deal with offenders who would normally have received short custodial sentences. It is now no longer used.

Beginning as a pilot project in two prisons (Kirkham for male and Morton Hall for female offenders) in January 2004, it had similarities with part-time prison schemes in the Netherlands and Belgium (Jennings 1996). Its aim was to divert from full-time custody low-risk offenders whose offences justified prison but who would have suffered some of the disproportionate outcomes of a short-term sentence.

The sentence was designed to prevent loss of employment and accommodation and family break-up while, at the same time, retaining a punitive element. In the case of women, a further aim was to reduce the incidence of children being taken into care as a result of the mother receiving a full-time custodial sentence (Armour 2005). The sentence involved spending part of the week in prison and part in the community under probation supervision. The overall sentence was expressed in terms of weeks, within which the custody period was expressed in terms of days. There was no remission as in an ordinary full-time sentence, although home detention curfew could be granted. Either the offender served the custodial element during the week or at the weekend. Where offenders were employed, and because of the difficulties of arranging child-care cover with family members during the week, weekend custody was usually more appropriate and therefore more frequently imposed.

For intermittent custody to be used, the custody threshold had to have been passed, meaning that the offence would have been serious enough to justify a custodial sentence: intermittent custody was not a substitute for a community punishment. The offender had to agree to the sentence and to the conditions therein – due mainly to the degree of trust and responsibility it entailed. (For this reason the sentence was unsuitable for offenders with drug problems that were not under control.) If the offender did not agree to those conditions, then full-time custody was imposed. If the offender subsequently failed to comply with the terms, an application for a variation order to full-time custody was made to the sentencing court. The rate of compliance with the sentence was high, probably due to the considerable benefits it held compared with full-time prison sentences.

Although the costs of intermittent custody were lower than for ordinary sentences, in October 2006 the National Offender Management Service decided to discontinue the pilots, largely because of the cost of expanding the sentence into other prisons at a time when prison places (and, therefore, resources) were at full stretch. Also, an intermittent custody place, used only for part of the week, effectively ties up a place that could otherwise be used full time.

If intermittent custody is ever reintroduced, then centres would ideally be situated in urban areas. The number of eligible offenders would probably remain fairly small, but wherever jobs, accommodation and family units are maintained, then the chances of further offending are reduced.

*Damian Evans*

### Related entries

*Alternatives to imprisonment; Families of prisoners; Responsibility.*

**Key texts and sources**

Armour, W. (2005) 'Weekend prison', *The Magistrate*, 61: 272–4.
Jennings, A. (1996) 'A case for part-time imprisonment', *Prison Service Journal*, 108: 12–14.

# J

## JUST DESERTS

'Just deserts' (or proportionality) is a rationale for sentencing that is based on the premise that the amount of punishment should be in proportion to the degree of wrongdoing.

Just deserts (or proportionality) is a retributive rationale of punishment. The basis of this approach is that punishment is justified as a morally appropriate response to crime and that the amount of punishment should be in proportion to the degree of wrongdoing. These arguments have their origin in the works of such philosophers as Kant and Hegel. The approach is retributive in as much as it is backward-looking, focusing on the offence rather than any potential question of the future conduct of the offender, as with rehabilitation or deterrence. This approach is also based on a political outlook that everyone is entitled to equal treatment and that offenders have a right to be treated fairly and proportionally.

The two main elements of the just deserts approach are described as 'cardinal' and 'ordinal' proportionality (Von Hirsch 1993). Cardinal proportionality is concerned with the quantum of punishment, which should be in proportion to the crime committed. For example, a six-month prison sentence for dropping a chewing gum wrapper would be considered to be disproportionate. The appropriate scale of punishment is described as an 'anchoring point' and would be determined by the history and culture of the jurisdiction. The second element, ordinal proportionality, is concerned with how different offences are related to one another.

Proportionality was the basis of sentencing reforms under the Criminal Justice Act 1991, which states that the sentence awarded should be 'commensurate with the seriousness of the offence'. The Act includes controversial clauses that apply to sentencing for multiple offences and guidance on taking into account previous convictions. In relation to sentencing for multiple offences, the Act states that, in deciding the type of penalty to be imposed, the court can only take account of the combined seriousness of two of the offences. In relation to previous convictions, the Act essentially restates the principle that a good previous record could mitigate a punishment, but previous convictions cannot justify imposing a punishment that is not proportionate with the offence.

The Act proved to be unpopular with the public, politicians and the judiciary. The sections relating to previous convictions and multiple offences were quickly changed and, within two years, the Lord Chief Justice found in the case of *Cunningham* ((1993) 96 Cr. App. R. 422) that the phrase 'commensurate' should be interpreted to mean 'commensurate with the punishment and deterrence that the offence requires'. Subsequently, just deserts has been ignored in reforms such as the introduction of automatic life sentences, and the Criminal Justice Act 2003 identifies a range of different sentencing objectives, of which proportionality is just one. Moreover, the 2003 Act explicitly states that persistent offenders merit more severe penalties (see Rex and Tonry 2002).

*Jamie Bennett*

### Related entries

*Deterrence; Politics of imprisonment; Rehabilitation; Sentencing policy.*

### Key texts and sources

Rex, S. and Tonry, M. (2002) *Reform and Punishment: The Future of Sentencing.* Cullompton: Willan Publishing.
Von Hirsch, A. (1993) *Censure and Sanctions.* Oxford: Oxford University Press.

# K

## KEY PERFORMANCE INDICATORS (KPIs) AND KEY PERFORMANCE TARGETS (KPTs)

> Key performance indicators and targets are quantitative performance measures used to measure, respectively, the Prison Service as a whole and individual prisons.

Key performance indicators and targets (KPIs and KPTs) are quantitative performance measures. KPIs measure the performance of the Prison Service as a whole, whereas KPTs are used to measure individual prisons. The use of these measures emerged in the early 1990s as part of the new public management agenda, which saw the incorporation of private sector practices into the public sector. In 2006–7, there were 11 KPIs and 47 KPTs (HM Prison Service 2006), which fall into five broad categories. 'Decency' covers areas such as suicide, responses to complaints and overcrowding. 'Organizational efficiency and effectiveness' covers areas such as cost per prisoner place, staff sickness and training. 'Reducing reoffending' includes purposeful activity, offending behaviour programmes and education accreditations. 'Order and control' considers issues such as serious assaults and accidents. 'Public protection' focuses on areas such as escapes, absconds and security audit scores.

Producing such a large number of measures has its problems. First, it is difficult to take in all the information and to get an overall picture of performance. Secondly, it difficult to analyse performance changes over time or to compare prisons. Thirdly, it does not differentiate the more important from the less important targets. In order to address these issues, an analytical tool has been developed known as the 'weighted scorecard'. This gives the prison an overall score which is calculated by taking account of its performance on all KPTs – a system often described as a 'league table'.

The development of performance measures has been contested in prisons and in the wider public sector. Some arguments relate to the impact on management, suggesting that KPIs and KPTs make managers more bureaucratic and less sensitive to the human dimensions of their work. A second strand of criticism relates to the appropriateness of output measurement in prisons. For example, it has been argued that the measures are opportunistic and cannot capture prison life accurately or comprehensively. However, it is now generally accepted that such measures can be useful in monitoring and structuring management action, although care needs to be taken in the design of the measures in order to reflect the nature of prison work, and there should not be an over-reliance on these to the exclusion of other indicators (Coyle 2002). An example of this is the development of a tool for Measuring the Quality of Prison Life (MQPL), an attempt to design measures that can be used for both performance management and research that are specifically tailored for prisons.

Quantitative performance measurement is now an integral feature of prison management and, while the extent to which it is used remains contested, there is broad agreement that some degree of measurement is appropriate for both monitoring and directing organizational performance.

*Jamie Bennett*

### Related entries

*HM Prison Service; New public management (NPM); Performance management.*

**Key texts and sources**

Coyle, A. (2002) *A Human Rights Approach to Prison Management: Handbook for Prison Staff*. London: International Centre for Prison Studies.

HM Prison Service (2006) *Key Performance Indicators, Key Performance Targets and Additional Measures: Sources and Calculations Guidance Notes, 2006–2007*. London: HM Prison Service.

For information on KPTs (with an attached targets document), see http://www.hmprisonservice.gov.uk/news/latestnews/index.asp?id=2627,38,6,38,0,0.

## KOESTLER AWARDS

The Koestler Awards scheme is an annual nationwide competition in which offenders submit creative work which is judged by experts in the arts. The artists receive feedback about their work from expert judges and some receive a cash prize.

The Koestler Awards are organized by the Koestler Trust, which is chaired by Sir David Ramsbotham, former Chief Inspector of Prisons. The trust is a charity funded by private donations, although it receives some support from the Government. The Koestler Awards aim to offer offenders a goal to work towards and, in the process, to support their rehabilitation. The Koestler Trust views the arts as a positive way in which offenders can engage in the education process when they might otherwise find it difficult. Many prisoners have low self-esteem, a fear of failure and destructive emotions and, for many of the awards' recipients, it is the first time they have received any positive recognition for work they have done. The competition categories are wide ranging, including traditional arts and crafts (such as sculpture), ceramics and woodcraft, as well as more modern modes of expression (such as video and film making, website design and desktop publishing). There are also categories for written work (such as prose and poetry) along with music composition and performance of the spoken word. The numerous and diverse categories attract many entrants – over 4,000 in 2005. Entrants come through heads of learning and skills, prison education co-ordinators and education managers, supported by other senior staff, who act as local agents for the prize. Anyone in a UK prison, young offender institution, high-security psychiatric hospital or secure unit is eligible to enter, as well as those referred by the Probation Service.

In addition to the recreational and rehabilitative benefits an offender gains from his or her involvement in the arts, there are cash prizes awarded to approximately a quarter of those who enter. Prizes range in value from £20 to £60, and there are special awards of £100 given for outstanding work. There is also the opportunity for works in the visual arts categories to be displayed at an exhibition each September. Works can be sold at the exhibition, allowing the offender the chance to give money back to his or her family or to save for his or her release.

The Koestler Trust was founded in 1962 by the writer and journalist, Arthur Koestler. Koestler was born in Budapest and lived and worked in a variety of countries before being imprisoned for three months in 1936 by the Fascists while he was reporting the Spanish Civil War. On the outbreak of the Second World War he was imprisoned in France. He escaped in 1940 and made his way to England, where he was imprisoned in Pentonville Prison for entering the country without a permit. These experiences of imprisonment gave him a personal understanding of the dehumanizing nature of incarceration and motivated him to start the trust with the intention of supporting prisoners in making constructive use of their time in creative endeavour.

*James Mehigan*

### Related entries

*Education and training; Rehabilitation.*

**Key texts and sources**

The Koestler Trust's website is at http://www.koestler trust.org.uk.

# L

## LEGAL SERVICES

Legal services refers to the provision of legal advice and representation which, for those who require publicly funded services (commonly referred to as legal aid), is largely provided by organizations contracted to the Legal Services Commission.

Legal services are provided by solicitors in private practice, law centres or specialist voluntary sector advice agencies, such as the Prisoners' Advice Service and the Citizens Advice Bureau (CAB). CAB operates a few advice centres in prisons. In theory, prisoners have precisely the same entitlement to access legal services as those at liberty.

For people on benefits or low incomes, there is an entitlement to receive publicly funded legal advice and representation, or legal aid. This is administered by the Legal Services Commission, which awards and administers contracts in specialist (or contract) areas. The Legal Services Commission is divided into two sections, the Community Legal Service, which pays for the delivery of advice on civil law matters, and the Criminal Defence Service, which provides services in respect of criminal proceedings. Civil law includes areas such as family law, housing, immigration and claims for compensation.

Prison law is a subsidiary of the criminal contract, and publicly funded work in this area can only be delivered by firms or organizations holding a criminal contract. Legal aid for prison law operates at several levels: advice and assistance work allows for advice and written representations to be made; advocacy assistance allows for representation at specialist panels, such as Parole Board hearings and adjudica-tions; and certificated work permits representation in litigation before the courts.

The legal aid system has been under constant reform and is currently moving to a system where all work is paid for by fixed fees. Most criminal defence work is already under a fixed-fee regime. The report on the provision of legal aid prepared by Lord Carter in 2006 envisages that this will be extended to prison work as well as criminal defence work. These reforms have led to concerns that there will be insufficient providers of legal services to meet demand. This has already occurred in the field of immigration law.

Both the domestic and international courts have strongly defended the rights of citizens to have free access to the courts. This encompasses the right to obtain independent legal advice as well as actually commencing or defending court proceedings. The right to legal advice and access to the courts has always been an area of tension in prisons, with the requirements of prison security coming into conflict with the right of prisoners to access and retain confidential legal material. Many of the early cases from the European Court of Human Rights involving the UK were concerned with protecting this right (the case of *Silver* v. *UK* (1983) 5 EHRR 347 confirmed that prisoners do not have to air their grievances within the prison system before seeking legal advice). The right to confidential legal advice is enshrined in the Prison Rules 1999 (Rule 39). It continues to be staunchly upheld in domestic law (*R* v. *Home Secretary ex parte Leech* [1994] QB 198; *R (Daly)* v. *Home Secretary* [2001] UKHL 26), even to the extent where it protects the right of prisoners to receive visits from journalists investigating miscarriages of justice (*R* v. *Home Secretary ex parte Simms* [2000] 2 AC 115).

*Simon Creighton*

*Related entries*

*Adjudications; Grievances; Human rights; Parole.*

**Key texts and sources**

Creighton, S., King, V. and Arnott, H. (2005) *Prisoners and the Law*. Haywards Heath: Tottel.

*Legal Action*, the monthly bulletin of the Legal Action Group, is available online at http://www.lag.org.uk/. The Legal Services Commission's website is at http://www.legalservices.gov.uk/. Lord Carter's *Review of Legal Aid Procurement* (2006) is available online at http://www.legalaidprocurementreview.gov.uk/publications.htm. The Criminal Information Agency's website is at http://www.criminal-information-agency.com/. See also CAB's website (http://www.citizensadvice.org.uk/).

# LEGITIMACY

In general terms, the concept of legitimacy refers to the claim by people exercising powers, and especially powers of decision over other people, to hold and use their power in a justified way. It also concerns the question of whether less powerful people acknowledge those justifications and how they respond to the decisions made about them or to the conditions imposed upon them. A number of authors have argued that this is of central relevance to the ways in which power is deployed, and order maintained or disrupted, in prisons.

Thinking about the legitimate and non-legitimate use of power has a very long history, not only in social and political theory but also in the practical design and management of institutions. Whether legitimacy is claimed on grounds of divine appointment, legal form, personal charisma, democratic election or whatever, examples of settled organizations or communities where it is entirely irrelevant may be few and far between, perhaps especially in the modern era (see further Beetham 1991). While this holds implicitly for criminal justice practices, including imprisonment, it is only

relatively recently that the legitimation of power in prisons has arisen as an explicit issue.

At bottom the notion of legitimacy draws attention to the distinction between the simple *power* of a social actor and his or her *authority*. Authority is, roughly speaking, taken here to mean that the actor and his or her actions enjoy sufficient acceptance in relevant ways among the members of a given population that they feel a greater readiness, even an obligation, to comply with his or her laws, instructions and requests. It is probably safe to say that, traditionally, the term is most often applied to the actions of states and their agents and employees (soldiers, police officers, judges, tax and customs officers, prison officers and the like) in their dealings with citizens. However this is not the only feasible application, and the picture is complicated by recent developments, such as the privatization of public services.

It should be obvious from this account that a power holder's ability to enforce his or her wishes will be greater if the subjects believe his or her power to be held legitimately, for then subjects will have some *moral* reasons to obey. That is to say, their compliance will not simply be the product of coercive force or threat, nor just of an instrumental calculation of costs and benefits, or only a matter of habituation. There will instead (or additionally) be a perception that one *ought* to comply because this distribution of power is sufficiently well grounded in some combination of law, tradition, personal credibility, general utility, democratic deliberation (or whatever) as to command moral assent. It is more or less a matter of definition that legitimate uses of power are more stable and less costly than non-legitimate ones, and that 'rulers' (for which read all manner of officials and office-bearers in a multitude of different institutional and cultural settings, and not just kings, generals or dictators) have a profound interest in sustaining their legitimacy as far as they can. At the same time this constrains their actions in a host of sometimes surprising ways since they need to show that what they do is to some extent consistent with the principles on which they claim legitimacy. Thus even in situations where power seems formally to lie overwhelmingly on one side, as in a military installation or a prison, arbitrary, contemptuous or grossly inconsistent uses of power can have drastic consequences for institutional legitimacy. The conditions under which the powerful can safely disregard considerations of legitimacy entirely in the long run will be rare indeed. Those who apply this kind of thinking to imprisonment (for example, Sparks and Bottoms 1995; Sparks et al. 1996) claim that such conditions do not obtain in the prisons of Western liberal democratic countries today.

This is not to say that prisons usually enjoy a high degree of legitimacy in the eyes of the people who are confined in them. However, it is to claim that legitimacy is a relevant evaluative principle in respect of issues such as legality, compliance with international standards or indeed more everyday matters, such as fairness in the application of procedures and in the manner of prisoners' treatment at the hands of prison staff. Moreover, if legitimacy is a variable issue – something that can be present or absent in differing degrees in different times and places – then this may be crucial to understanding the diverse institutional climates of prisons, their stabilities and instabilities and, on occasion, their capacity for riots and other major breakdowns of order. In these respects legitimacy is something that can be studied and assessed and may be a property of social relations that can be cultivated in practice, at least to some material extent.

Those who argue that legitimacy is an important concept, perhaps indeed a key concept, in understanding prison life, claim a number of analytic advantages for it. For example, Sparks and Bottoms (1995) suggest that Lord Woolf's Report (1991) into the disorders that rocked the English prisons in 1990, which focuses in part on the existence of a sense of injustice and resentment on the part of prisoners who took part in or supported the disturbances, can be read as implicitly foregrounding the problem of legitimation. Legitimacy, thus considered, refers not only to the material conditions of confinement (important as these are), nor even to the propriety of formal procedures, but also to the manner of people's handling in everyday exchanges. This, such observers suggest, returns attention to the

connection between the larger-scale institutional properties of prison systems and the routines, transactions and kinds of conduct that constitute them (see, further, Sparks et al. 1996). This is relevant, they argue, to comparing, contrasting and evaluating different institutions, regimes and environments.

Moreover, there may be special reasons for thinking carefully about how institutions respond to troublesome incidents and people on the grounds that arbitrary, inconsistent or disproportionate interventions in critical situations invite negative evaluations of legitimacy both by protagonists and by onlookers. In this regard it appears to be precisely in moments where the legitimacy of systems and decisions is placed most acutely in question that being seen to act legitimately is most salient. A further irony of incarceration is that it brings together numbers of people who lack motives to acknowledge institutional legitimacy and whose self-presentation may be consciously tough and confrontational, yet who are placed in a position of utter dependency. In both these respects prisons pose the problem of legitimacy in a special way – at its boundaries, where it appears least feasible. Yet, to attempt to operate a prison system without regard to the challenge of legitimation is at best to provoke instability and, at worst, to produce a condition of violent tyranny and unconstrained abuse of power.

At the same time, because legitimacy is a concept with very widespread application, this also draws attention to the points of similarity and connection between prisons and other kinds of institutions (schools, military installations and so on) and practices (policing, teaching, nursing, even catering). Prisons are special, on this view, but not so unique as to defy all comparison. The tightest connections tend to be drawn with studies of policing, on which a rich literature exists (see, for example, Tyler and Huo 2002).

Not everyone accepts these arguments, of course. Carrabine (2004) has suggested that, from the point of view of many prisoners, power in prisons represents an inevitable 'external fact', something to be undergone and endured with little or no reference to its legitimacy.

Liebling assisted by Arnold (2004) problematizes the idea in a rather different way. She suggests that legitimacy, while a key issue, ought not to be regarded as a master category. Thus, she notes, prisons not only raise questions of 'order, fairness and authority' but also of 'trust, respect and well-being' (2004: xviii). Among Liebling's point here is that there are very important aspects of the emotional texture of prison life, of people's emotional well-being and interpersonal behaviour that are not well encapsulated by the notion of legitimacy alone. This seems an important corrective. Nevertheless, many observers of imprisonment today (including Liebling) continue to find the concept of legitimacy analytically useful. Conversely, it has not yet been convincingly shown that it can safely be disregarded, either in scientific discourse or indeed in practice.

*Richard Sparks*

## Related entries

*Measuring the Quality of Prison Life (MQPL); Morality; Penal Crisis; Politics of Imprisonment; Power; Riots (prison)*

**Key texts and sources**

Beetham, D. (1991) *The Legitimation of Power*. London: Macmillan.

Carrabine, E. (2004) *Power, Discourse and Resistance: A Genealogy of the Strangeways Prison Riot*. Aldershot: Ashgate.

Liebling, A., assisted by Arnold, H. (2004) *Prisons and their Moral Performance*. Oxford: Clarendon Press.

Sparks, R. and Bottoms, A.E. (1995) 'Legitimacy and order in prisons', *British Journal of Sociology*, 46: 45–62.

Sparks, R., Bottoms, A.E. and Hay, W. (1996) *Prisons and the Problem of Order*. Oxford: Oxford University Press.

Tyler, T.R. and Huo, Y.J. (2002) *Trust in the Law: Encouraging Public Cooperation with the Police and Courts*. New York, NY: Russell-Sage Foundation.

Woolf, Lord Justice and Tumin, S. (1991) *Prison Disturbances, April 1990*. London: HMSO.

# LESS ELIGIBILITY

The principle of less eligibility is based on the notion that those in prisons (or workhouses, historically) should endure material living conditions that compare unfavourably with those of similarly disadvantaged people outside these institutions.

The principle of less eligibility became prominent in the 1830s and 1840s, after the introduction of the New Poor Law in England and Wales in 1834. The New Poor Law tried to reduce the number of able-bodied, poor people receiving relief from the state in their homes (outdoor relief) and provided stricter regulations which entailed the greater use of indoor relief – being sent to the workhouse in order to receive shelter and food and to be put to work. Less eligibility thus applied to workhouses and prisons and was based on the idea that conditions within these institutions needed to be worse than the living conditions for poor honest free people on the outside. This would discourage the poor from going to the state for maintenance and would deter individuals from committing crime.

However, this ideology also caused friction between workhouses and prisons. Many commentators claimed that the poor committed petty criminal offences in order to be sent to prison, where they would receive better food or medical care, for example. It was also argued by many poor law-guardians and overseers that the 'prison held no terrors for workhouse inmates' (McConville 1981: 239) and that the conditions, particularly the food and diet, were better in prison. There is evidence to support the idea that the inmates of workhouses would smash the windows or burn their clothes, particularly during the winter months, in order to get sent to the local prison, where, they believed, the diet would be better. The government argued that this problem could be overcome by ensuring uniformity in prison regimes across the country, a significant feature of Victorian prison policy. Yet the government was constrained by health concerns when it came to the issuing of prison diets, so many prison authorities relied on the use of the treadwheel as a means of enforcing the required degree of less eligibility (McConville 1981).

Although we do not necessarily talk in these terms in the twenty-first century, there remain many examples when discussing penal policy in general, and prison conditions in particular, that reflect the principle of less eligibility. These examples are often used in the media to promote the notion that prisons are 'soft' or resemble 'holiday camps'. The introduction of in-cell television, the yearly newspaper reports on the cost of Christmas dinner for prisoners and the frequent comparisons between the cost of school dinners for children and the cost of meals for prisoners all reflect a steadfast adherence to the virtue of less eligibility (Jewkes 2007). All these examples are underpinned by ideas, historically and contemporarily, about those who are 'deserving' and 'undeserving' in society (Sparks 1996).

*Helen Johnston*

### Related entries

*Food and diet; In-cell television; Incentives and earned privileges (IEP); Politics of imprisonment.*

---

**Key texts and sources**

Jewkes, Y. (2007) 'Prisons, public interest and the popular media', in Y. Jewkes (ed.) *Handbook on Prisons*. Cullompton: Willan Publishing.

McConville, S. (1981) *A History of English Prison Administration. Volume One: 1750–1877*. London: Routledge & Kegan Paul.

Sparks, R. (1996) 'Penal "austerity": the doctrine of less eligibility reborn?', in R. Matthews and P. Francis (eds) *Prisons 2000: An International Perspective on the Current State and Future of Imprisonment*. Basingstoke: Macmillan.

---

# LIBRARIES

---

Access to library services is an important aspect of the activities in prison, and the prison library has come to play as important a role in the prison community as that of a library in a local neighbourhood.

---

Once the preserve of the prison chaplain and a repository of 'improving' works, the prison library has come to play an equal role in the prison community to that of a library in a local neighbourhood. This change was rooted in the early 1980s when a move began to put professional librarians into prisons to develop services. The publication by the Prison Libraries Group of the Library Association of *Guidelines for Prison Libraries* in 1981 set new standards and encouraged local authorities to develop their prison libraries. In 1992, a major report, *Prison Libraries, Roles and Responsibilities,* recognized the need to formalize the provision of prison library services by way of service-level agreements between individual governors and the local library authority. A revised edition of *Guidelines for Prison Libraries* (published in 1997) recognized the changes in both the Prison Service and in public libraries and provided a more aspirational vision of the future of library services in prisons (Collis and Boden 1997). In 2003, a multidisciplinary group with representatives from the Prison Libraries Group of the Chartered Institute of Library and Information Professionals, the Society of Chief Librarians and the Social Inclusion and Offenders Unit of the Department of Education and Skills was formed to develop a new specification for prison libraries. A major survey was commissioned to establish existing levels of provision. This determined the direction of the group and the specification was published in 2006 (Social Inclusion and Offenders Unit 2006).

The prison library should provide and actively support offenders in accessing books, in reading, in learning, in obtaining information and in taking part in digital citizenship. This is not a passive role but requires the involvement of the prison library service in a wide range of activities (such as reader development, family reading, partnership activities and the imaginative provision of information) that directly relate to the needs of individuals in the prison community.

Reading for pleasure is a key element of provision. It is becoming generally accepted that reading for pleasure is often the trigger for the development of lifelong learning, which can contribute to rehabilitation and can reduce the risk of reoffending. Libraries can also enable prisoners to develop the necessary information retrieval and literacy skills to enable them to lead a full and law-abiding life after release. Prison libraries offer essential support to prisoners undertaking formal learning by stocking a range of materials to support the education curriculum. Libraries play an important role in the development of independent learners, offering opportunities and support for informal learning. Prison librarians also work with their colleagues in public libraries and prison resettlement departments to encourage and enable prison library users to become public library users after release.

*Sue Wilkinson*

### Related entries

*Activities; Education and training; Rehabilitation.*

---

**Key texts and sources**

Collis, R. and Boden, L. (1997) *Guidelines for Prison Libraries* (2nd edn). London: Library Association Publishing.

Social Inclusion and Offenders Unit (2006) *The Offender Library, Learning and Information Specification*. London Social Inclusion and Offenders Unit.

See also the Department for Education and Skills' libraries web page (with attachments): **http://www.dfes.gov.uk/offenderlearning/index. cfm?fuseaction=content.view&CategoryID=3& ContentID=9**. The Prison Libraries Group website is at **http://www.cilip.org.uk/specialinterestgroups /bysubject/prison**.

---

# LIFE-SENTENCE PRISONERS

Life-sentence prisoners are those sentenced indeterminately. They include those who have received mandatory, discretionary and automatic life sentences, and those who are detained under indeterminate public protection sentences.

Life sentences are, since the abolition of the death penalty in England and Wales, the most severe custodial penalty that can be imposed on an individual. There are four types of life sentence: mandatory, discretionary, automatic and indeterminate public protection. Mandatory life sentences are imposed for murder, and their introduction is often regarded as the tacit agreement made between politicians and the public in order to secure the abolition of the death penalty. Discretionary life sentences may be imposed following conviction for one of around 70 offences, depending upon the seriousness of the offence. Automatic life sentences were introduced under the Crime (Sentences) Act 1997. This provided for a life sentence to be imposed automatically following conviction for a second time of a serious sexual or violent offence. Automatic sentences were repealed and replaced under the Criminal Justice Act 2003, which provided that a person convicted of one of 65 violent offences or 88 sexual offences could be detained indefinitely for reasons of public protection. These last two measures, in particular, have fuelled a growth in the life-sentence population.

A life sentence does not usually mean that a prisoner spends his or her whole life in prison. However, it does mean that after release and for the rest of their life, individuals may be recalled to prison if their behaviour is considered to present a risk to the public. All life sentences are split into two parts. The first part is the period served for the purposes of retribution and deterrence and must be served in custody. This is known as the tariff. Although previously this had been set by the Home Secretary, it is now set by judges. Once this period has been served, the life-sentence prisoner would only be released if it is so directed by the Parole Board (or a lifer review panel). This is based on an assessment of the risk the individual presents to the public. On average, a mandatory life-sentence prisoner spends 14 years in prison, a non-mandatory lifer six years and an indeterminate public protection detainee has an average tariff of only 30 months (Home Office 2006a).

England and Wales have more life-sentenced prisoners than any other country in the Council of Europe (Aebi 2005). At the end of June 2006, there were 7,274 prisoners serving indeterminate sentences (NOMS 2006). The country with the next highest number is Turkey, which, in

2004, had just under 1,900. This means that England and Wales have over three times more people in custody serving life sentences than any other European country. This has increased and continues to increase at a remarkable rate. Since 1995 when it stood at 3,289, it has grown by 121 per cent (Home Office 2006a). So what accounts for this growth, and why do England and Wales top the European league?

There is no doubt that the sentencing framework has become much tougher in recent years. The Criminal Justice Act 2003 introduced harsher life sentences for the offence of murder, substantially raising the tariffs. Under the new legislation, a whole life tariff should be applied to adults over the age of 21 who commit multiple murders; a terrorist murder; a murder of a child following abduction or involving sexual conduct; and a murder where the offender has been previously convicted of murder. A minimum of 30 years is to be served for a range of cases, including the murder of police or prison officers; murder involving a firearm; and killing done for gain, including burglary and robbery. Any other murder has a 15-year starting point. These tariffs are higher than the average amount of time a mandatory life-sentence prisoner spends in custody and are therefore likely to have an inflationary impact.

As well as this growth in the length of custody, there is also an increasing diversity of offences that are being punished with life sentences. This has particularly resulted from first automatic life sentences and subsequently indeterminate public protection sentences. For example, life sentences have become more common for rape and robbery (Hough et al. 2003). Indeterminate public protection sentences have been used widely for robbery and assault with intent to rob (40 per cent) and wounding with intent to cause grievous bodily harm (21 per cent), and have been generally awarded to younger people rather than life sentences (Home Office 2006a).

These changes in the 'front-door' of entry into imprisonment show a pattern where longer sentences are being applied to a wider range of offences. These changes are a feature of new punitiveness – the trend to make punishment more severe in response to popular sentiment.

As well as direct policy changes, sentencers themselves admit that political and media pressure has had an impact on how they exercise their discretion in sentencing, moving them in a direction that is more severe (Hough et al. 2003).

Popular punitiveness also has an impact at the 'back-door' of imprisonment, when prisoners are released, supervised in the community and subject to recall. For example, it could be suggested that the Parole Board has been more cautious in its decisions regarding the release of life-sentence prisoners. For example, despite the rise in the population, releases fell from 223 in 2003 to 200 in 2005 (Home Office 2006a). Supervision, it has been argued, has also become more rigorous, with demands placed on probation and multi-agency public protection panels (MAPPAs) to manage risk robustly. This has led to a dramatic jump from 44 recalls of prisoners on life licence in 2003 to 111 in 2005 (Home Office 2006a). These changes are therefore silting up the flow of life-sentence prisoners going out of the prison system, so contributing to the population increase.

In other Western European nations, offences that can attract life sentences in England and Wales do not do so, and mandatory life sentencing is unusual or restricted to cases involving genocide and other crimes against humanity. In other countries, the exercise of discretion by judges ameliorates the potential use of life sentences. For example, Germany has mandatory life sentences for murder, but has just under 1,800 lifers. In England and Wales the essential mental element (*mens rea*) to establish guilt is premeditation ('malice aforethought'), while in Germany there has to be in addition one of seven specific motives. Research has found that the need to ascribe specific types of motive in Germany significantly reduces the proportion of homicides designated as murder, compared with England and Wales, despite there being similar homicide rates (McGeorge and Weber 2001).

So what does the future hold? Are England and Wales likely to remain the life-sentence capitals of Europe? The introduction of indeterminate public protection sentencing is certainly fuelling a dramatic rise in the number of life-sentence prisoners entering prisons. In addition, a number of high-profile cases in early 2006 focused attention on the parole process and led the Home Office to set out reforms intended to enhance public protection and enforcement. These reforms include that, in future, a victim's voice is to be introduced in the most serious cases heard by the Parole Board and a decision to release an offender must be made unanimously. There are also plans for a national enforcement agency with targets for the time by which an offender who breaches his or her licence conditions is returned to custody (Home Office 2006b). In combination, these reforms are likely to lead to more life-sentenced prisoners staying in custody beyond their release date and being recalled to custody after release. It seems, therefore, that prisons in England and Wales will continue to hold more life-sentence prisoners than any European country for the foreseeable future.

*Enver Solomon*

### Related entries

*Dangerousness; Death penalty; Deterrence; Long-term prisoners; New punitiveness; Parole; Rehabilitation; Risk.*

#### Key texts and sources

Aebi, M. (2005) *Council of Europe Annual Penal Statistics SPACE I: 2004 Survey on Prison Populations.* Strasbourg: Council of Europe.
Home Office (2006a) *Offender Management Caseload Statistics 2005: England and Wales.* London: Home Office.
Home Office (2006b) *Rebalancing the Criminal Justice System in Favour of the Law-abiding Majority: Cutting Crime, Reducing Reoffending and Protecting the Public.* London: Home Office.
Hough, M., Jacobson, J. and Millie, A. (2003) *The Decision to Imprison.* London: Prison Reform Trust.
McGeorge, M. and Weber, H. (2001) 'Imprisonment for homicide: European perspectives concerning human rights', in D. Farrington *et al.* (eds) *Sex and Violence.* London: Routledge.
National Offender Management Service (2006) *Population in Custody Monthly Tables: June 2006, England and Wales* (available online at http://www. homeoffice.gov.uk/rds/pdfs06/prisjun06.pdf).
For information and attachments, see http://www. hmprisonservice.gov.uk/adviceandsupport/prison_ life/lifesentencedprisoners/. See also Liberty's web page 'Your rights' (http://www.yourrights.org.uk/ your-rights/chapters/the-rights-of-prisoners/ parole/life-sentence-prisoners.shtml).

# LISTENER SCHEMES

> Listeners are prisoners selected and trained by the Samaritans in order to provide support to other prisoners.

Listeners are selected prisoners who are trained and supported by the Samaritans. Using Samaritans guidelines, they provide a confidential, sympathetic ear to fellow prisoners who may feel suicidal or otherwise in crisis. Listener schemes assist in preventing suicide and reducing self-harm, and generally help alleviate the feelings of prisoners in distress. Listeners' support can help to reduce the isolation which may lead to acts of self-harm or suicide. Training to become a listener takes about 12 hours (six two-hour sessions). At the end of their training, listeners are provided with a certificate which acknowledges they have successfully completed the course.

The listener scheme has North American origins. In 1979 the Samaritans of Boston, Massachusetts, trained selected prisoners to become 'Samaritans in residence'. In 1991 the first team of listeners was introduced in the UK, at Swansea Prison, since when the numbers and the extent of schemes have grown hugely. There are currently 118 listener schemes in prisons in England and Wales. Samaritans have a long history of working in partnership with the Prison Service, and their 2001 'Risk 1' strategy for developing listener schemes, particularly in about 40 high-risk establishments across the UK, was a key plank of the Prison Service's wider suicide prevention strategy (Samaritans 2001). Some 2,656 new listeners were recruited and trained between 1 October 2001 and 31 March 2004, and a further 900 listeners in the first six months of 2006. Between January and June 2006, there were approximately 46,600 listener contacts.

The opportunity to become a listener is open to anyone who has the necessary listening and befriending skills, irrespective of their offence, legal status or their willingness to engage in offending behaviour programmes. Similarly, prisoners should have equal access to listeners across the entire prison, irrespective of their offence or status. Awareness that a listener scheme is available in an establishment is created through such means as the use of posters, leaflets, badges, T-shirts, referrals by 'insiders' (other prisoners who help new prisoners settle during reception) and induction sessions.

Listeners typically see individual prisoners in the latter's cells, but in many prisons also in care suites and in 'time-out rooms'. These aid listeners in their task by providing a 'space' that is less institutionalized and more normalizing. Care suites are rooms where, if necessary, two listeners can spend the whole night, or one listener can spend a short period, with a prisoner who has been identified as being at risk. They can be rooms where two listeners live and work. Typically, there is room for two listeners and an 'at risk' prisoner to remain overnight with the environment split into two areas – a listener sleeping/personal area and a peer-support area for consultation and fitted out to create a less institutional environment. This can be achieved with the use of soft seating sited around a low table in the peer-support area.

On release from prison, some listeners are keen to continue their befriending work. The Samaritans advise that listeners should be released for 12 months before officially applying to become a Samaritan, but they are able straightaway to join in some branch activities, such as support and training sessions for Samaritan volunteers working in prisons.

*Nigel Hancock and Laura Graham*

### Related entries

*Local prisons; Responsibility; Self-harm; Suicide in prison; Voluntary sector.*

#### Key texts and sources

Samaritans (2001) *Risk 1 Project – a Strategy for Higher Risk Prisoners.* Summary available http://www.hmprisonservice.gov.uk/assets/documents/100004C3peer-support.pdf

See the Samaritans' website (**http://www.samaritans.org/know/prisons/listener.html**) and the Prison Service's website (**http://www.hmprisonservice.gov.uk/adviceandsupport/prison_life/peersupport/**).

## LOCAL PRISONS

Local prisons constitute one of the largest sectors of the prison estate, currently numbering 44 in England and Wales. Their main function is to serve the courts by holding those remanded in custody awaiting or during trial. However, they also hold sentenced prisoners, some of whom end up serving their entire sentence in a 'local'.

Often thought of as little more than transit camps because of the constant movement of prisoners to and from court, local prisons ('locals') do more than house prisoners during their trial. Indeed, it is estimated that around 75 per cent of the local prison population comprises those already sentenced to short, medium, long and even life terms (HMCIP 1999 cited in Cavadino and Dignan 2007). There are currently 33 male locals and six female locals within the public sector (plus seven prisons serving the Scottish courts and one in Northern Ireland). A further five locals are privately run. Some prisons have multiple functions. For example, Elmley Prison in Kent is a male local, a Category C training prison, a vulnerable prisoner unit and a young offender institution. All local prisons are 'closed' – that is, inmates are held in secure conditions, usually commensurate with a Category B classification.

Locals are generally thought of as the prison institutions least fit for their purpose. Presenting some of the 'most acute penological problems of the English prison system' (Sparks 1971: 7), they are frequently old and shabby, chronically overcrowded, poorly resourced and with higher suicide rates than any other type of prison. Many belie their origins as Victorian prisons when the Prisons Act 1865 re-designated gaols and houses of correction as 'local prisons' to distinguish them from government-run convict prisons. The term 'local' has been retained because most were built in local communities and take prisoners predominantly from the immediate environs, thus enabling inmates to retain ties with family and locality. However, as the inmate population increases and the prison estate is squeezed further, particularly at the point of entry, there is no longer any guarantee that inmates will be accommodated close to home. Given that local prisons are the first experience of custody for all adult offenders (and some young offenders), this only compounds their other negative aspects and helps to explain why entry into prison for the first time is such a traumatic experience for many inmates.

While it is difficult to generalize, the regimes of locals suffer by comparison with other types of prison. Work, education and training, and other constructive activities tend to be more limited (or non-existent), visits, communication and recreation may be restricted, and hours spent out of cell can be minimal (in many locals, just one hour per day). All these restrictions can be explained by the twin problems of overcrowding and the fact that the first responsibility of any local prison is to escort inmates to court, thus placing heavy demands on staff (Sparks 1971). It is ironic, then, that these are the institutions that house the majority of prisoners on remand; logically, those still presumed innocent might expect better treatment than those proved guilty (Cavadino and Dignan 2007).

*Yvonne Jewkes*

### Related entries

*Activities; Communication; Education and training; Overcrowding; Prison population; Remand; Training prisons; Victorian prisons; Visits and visiting orders; Young offender institutions (YOIs).*

---

**Key texts and sources**

Cavadino, M. and Dignan, J. (2007) *The Penal System: An Introduction* (4th edn). London: Sage.
Sparks, R.F. (1971) *Local Prisons: The Crisis in the English Prison System.* London: Heinemann.

---

# LONG-TERM PRISONERS

The definition of long-term prisoner has varied over the years and, currently in England and Wales, applies to persons serving four years or more.

The definition of what constitutes a long-term prisoner in the UK has for many years been based on pragmatic considerations. Before the creation of the national Prison Commission in 1878 it would have applied to those serving sentences in convict prisons as opposed to those in local prisons. In more recent times it has been linked to parole eligibility. When conditional release on parole was first introduced as a result of the Criminal Justice Act 1967, the threshold for consideration was a sentence of more than 18 months. The Criminal Justice Act 1991 increased the threshhold for parole to sentences of four years or more.

Decisions about whether to release a prisoner under parole conditions have always been based on a consideration of a wide variety of reports. When the parole system was first introduced, a high priority was given to reports prepared by the prison authorities, many of which referred to the prisoner's behaviour in prison and commented on whether he or she had demonstrated any sign of personal reform, particularly through learning new skills or undertaking education. It took time for staff to get to know the prisoner in question and to collate the information needed for these reports. This was one of the main reasons why the parole threshhold was initially set where it was, since it meant that the prisoner had to be in prison for at least 12 months.

While awaiting trial, most prisoners, then as now, were held in local prisons. Prisoners who received sentences that would make them eligible for release on parole were transferred to the new style of prisons built during the 1960s and 1970s. These were described as 'training prisons' and, as their name implied, were intended to provide those serving longer sentences with opportunities for education and vocational and industrial work. Examples are Gartree (1965), Albany (1967), Coldingley (1969) and Long Lartin (1971) and, in Scotland, the original Shotts Prison (1978). The philosophy underlying these prisons was that those held there would be given as much internal freedom of movement as was compatible with the deprivation of liberty. Architecturally, this concept was evidenced by the hotel-like corridors in the accommodation wings (Bottoms and Light 1987).

The watershed year of the Prison Service in the twentieth century was 1966. The escape of George Blake led to the Mountbatten Report and the introduction of security Categories A, B, C and D. Physical security arrangements, both around the perimeter and internally, at training prisons such as Gartree, Albany and Long Lartin, were upgraded so that they could accommodate the newly designated Category A prisoners and the internal regimes became much more regimented. Henceforth, each convicted prisoner was assigned to one of the four security categories; the longer the sentence, the greater likelihood of a higher security category.

As the number of prisoners began to rise in the later years of the twentieth century, it was decided that the prisons holding long-term prisoners should be protected from overcrowding. Prisoners in the 'training prisons' each had their own cell and had regular access to education, training, work and other facilities.

In the decade between 1992 and 2002, the average length of sentence being imposed by the court increased. In 1992, 42 per cent of prisoners were serving four years or more and, by 2002, this had risen to 48 per cent. In 1992, 42 per cent of prisoners were serving between 12 months and four years. By 2002 that proportion had gone down to 38 per cent. The proportion serving less than 12 months also decreased slightly. These statistics indicate that the rise in the prison population in England and Wales has been caused not only by the fact that more people are being sent to prison but also because people are being sent there for longer periods.

This increase in the proportion of prisoners who are serving long sentences, as defined by eligibility for parole, together with the overall increase in the prison population, has meant that, in terms of how a period of imprisonment is served, the distinction between those serving long sentences and those serving shorter sentences has become blurred. Many long-sentence prisoners are now subject to uncertainties about where they will serve their sentences and to a lack of access to activities, as has always been the case with those serving shorter sentences.

There has been concern at an international level about the situation of the increasing number of prisoners being given long sentences and how best to manage them. European ministers of justice considered this matter in 2001 and expressed concern about 'the increase, in many countries, in the number and length of long-term sentences, which contribute to prison overcrowding and impair the effective and humane management of prisoners in full conformity with international human rights standards'. They established a committee to consider the management of these prisoners. The report of this committee was subsequently adopted by the Committee of Ministers (2003). The recommendation defined a long-term prisoner as 'one serving a prison sentence or sentences totalling five years or more'. It described the aims of the management of life-sentence and other long-term prisoners as being:

*to ensure that prisons are safe and secure places for these prisoners and for all those who work with or visit them; to counteract the damaging effects of life and long-term imprisonment; to increase and improve the possibilities for these prisoners to be successfully resettled in society and to lead a law-abiding life following their release.*

*Andrew Coyle*

### Related entries

*Life-sentence prisoners; Local prisons; Parole; Short-term prisoners; Training prisons.*

**Key texts and sources**

Bottoms, A.E. and Light, R. (1987) *Problems of Long-term Imprisonment.* Aldershot: Gower.
Committee of Ministers (2003) *Recommendation of the Committee of Ministers to Member States on the Management by Prison Administrations of Life Sentence and other Long-term Prisoners (Adopted by the Committee of Ministers on 9 October 2003 at the 855th meeting of the Ministers' Deputies)* (Rec. (2003) 23E). Strasbourg: Council of Europe.

# M

## MANDATORY DRUG TESTING

> Mandatory drug testing involves prisoners being legally compelled to comply with urine testing for the presence of controlled drugs under the Criminal Justice and Public Order Act 1994.

Problematic drug use is linked to offending for a high percentage of prisoners currently serving sentences in prisons in England and Wales. Studies report between 60 and 70 per cent of prisoners having misused drugs in the 12 months prior to imprisonment, with around 55 per cent reporting drug use linked to their offending (Wheatley 2007). A Home Office-commissioned study conducted in 2005 revealed that about 2 in every 5 prisoners (39 per cent) had used some illicit drug at some time in their current prison, 1 in 4 (25 per cent) said they had used drugs in the past month and 1 in 6 (16 per cent) in the past week (Singleton *et al.* 2005). In prison, illicit drug use is prohibited: a prisoner is guilty of an offence against the prison discipline if he or she administers a controlled drug to him or herself or fails to prevent the administration of a controlled drug upon him or herself by another person, and the prisoner may be punished at an adjudication (Prison Rule 51:9). Tackling problematic drug use while in prison has become a key strategic objective.

The Prison Service first set out measures to combat problematic drug use in prison in 1995 when it introduced mandatory drug testing (MDT) using urine samples. This was given legislative effect by the Criminal Justice and Public Order Act 1994, and testing has been operational in all prisons in England and Wales since March 1996. The MDT programme has three main objectives: to deter prisoners from misusing drugs and to discourage initiation through fear of being caught and punished; to gather information and to measure patterns of drug misuse in prison; and to identify individuals in need of treatment and to direct them to helping agencies.

There are five elements to the MDT programme, commonly separated and referred to as two categories of testing – random and non-random. Random testing is where prisoners are identified for testing on a random basis from a computer-generated list, which is refreshed monthly. All prisons are required to test a fixed proportion (between 5 and 10 per cent) of their prisoner population every month.

There are four different types of non-random tests. 'Suspicion testing' is when staff or others working with a prisoner make a referral for testing because they have reason to believe the prisoner has misused drugs. Reasonable suspicion of drug use may include behaviour out of character, or drugs or drug-taking paraphernalia found in possession. The 'frequent test' programme is a programme of tests recommended for prisoners with a previous history of misusing drugs (Class A mainly), over a set period – usually six tests conducted over a three-month period. The appropriateness of the prisoner's continued participation on the programme is reviewed monthly. 'Reception testing' is when a prisoner is tested on reception into a prison. Reception testing helps to identify treatment need, builds a picture of the individual's drug use and provides a message to those entering the prison that drug use will not be tolerated. 'Risk assessment' is where a test(s) is conducted to assist with the decision-making process when a prisoner is being considered for a privilege or a job, or where a high level of trust is to be granted.

PSO 3601 (HM Prison Service 2004) sets out the framework within which MDT should be conducted in prisons, including sample collection, chain of custody procedures, response when prisoners test positive, health and safety, healthcare matters and independent analysis procedures. This also sets out that establishments with an average population in the previous 12 months of 400 or more must random test at least 5 per cent of their population each month. Establishments with an average population of less than 400 must test at least 10 per cent of their population each month. No more than 15 per cent of the population per month may be random tested. Target levels of testing must be achieved every month, not just over a period of 12 months. At least 14 per cent of random tests must be conducted at weekends. Weekend testing must not take place less frequently than once in every three weekends. All prisoners appearing on the main randomly generated list must be tested, except those declared by healthcare to be unfit for testing and those already discharged. A reserve list may be used when the main list is exhausted, but names from this list must be tested in strict order of appearance on the list. Governors and area managers must agree the target level for random MDT positives, taking into account the national target. The national target in 2006–7 was to achieve less than a 10 per cent positive rate of drug misuse as measured by random MDT, and this was one of the key performance indicators and targets for prisons.

The Prison Service estimated that, between 1997 and 2004, the positive rate for all drug types combined fell from 24.4 to 12.5 per cent with detected opiate use decreasing to its lowest ever rate. That trend, in addition to indicating that MDT is a deterrent, may also indicate the creative ways prisoners are able to avoid detection. Methods include contaminating urine samples with soap hidden under nails, to timing drug use or changing drug types to fit in with estimated testing times. Concern has been expressed that MDT causes prisoners to switch from cannabis to heroin in order to reduce the chance of detection, since cannabis may be detected for longer in the urine. A pattern of urinalysis results does not unambiguously support this conclusion (Edgar and O'Donnell 1998).

*Simon Matthews*

### Related entries

*Adjudications; Deterrence; Drugs; Key performance indicators (KPIs) and key performance targets (KPTs); Rehabilitation; Security.*

**Key texts and sources**

Edgar, K. and O'Donnell, I. (1998) *Mandatory Drug Testing in Prisons: The Relationship between MDT and the Level and Nature of Drug Misuse.* London: Home Office.

HM Prison Service (2004) *Mandatory Drug Testing (PSO 3601)* (available online at **http://pso. hmprisonservice.gov.uk/PSO_3601_mandatory_ drugs_testing.doc**).

Singleton, N., Pendry, E., Simpson, T., Goddard, E., Farrell, M., Marsden, J. and Taylor, C. (2005) *The Impact of Mandatory Drug Testing in Prisons.* London: Home Office.

Wheatley, M. (2007) 'Drugs in prison', in Y. Jewkes (ed.) *Handbook on Prisons.* Cullompton: Willan Publishing.

The Home Office's reports on the impact of drug testing are available online at **http://www. homeoffice.gov.uk/rds/pdfs05/rdsolr0305.pdf** and **http://www.homeoffice.gov.uk/rds/pdfs05/r223.pdf**.

## MARKET TESTING

Market testing describes a commercial competition for the delivery of services where the current provider is invited to compete along with other potential suppliers.

Prisons have been at the forefront of privatization in the UK since The Wolds Prison opened as the first privately managed jail in 1992. Faced with a rising prisoner population, the Conservative government had turned to the private sector to provide extra accommodation through the private finance initiative (PFI) (see the *Citizen's Charter* 1992). The public sector was excluded from the early competitions, which saw a succession of new prisons built with public funds but managed and operated by the private sector.

The public and private sectors first competed openly in a market test for Manchester Prison in 1994. This was the first competition to involve an existing public sector establishment, and the in-house bid was selected ahead of private sector competitors. Subsequently, the public sector also succeeded in winning back Buckley Hall in 2000 and Blackenhurst in 2001 through retests after the initial private sector contracts expired, while private operators retained contracts for The Wolds and Doncaster.

The Prison Service adopted market testing as part of its internal efficiency strategy and invited private sector operators to bid for the delivery of discrete functions within establishments. The largest of these 'make-or-buy' reviews led to the transport and escorting of prisoners between courts and prison establishments being contracted to a range of commercial providers. The move was seen as generating improvements in cost and effectiveness and providing evidence that some custodial services could be delivered more effectively by the private sector.

There is little information to show how the operational performance of PFI and market-tested prisons compares with others. A report by the Comptroller and Auditor General concluded that, although the performance of PFI prisons had been mixed, competition had brought wider benefits to the Prison Service (NAO 2003). In particular, increased competition gave force to the decency agenda in the public sector, which was an area where private sector providers were seen to do better (for example, through the use of first names and effective mentoring schemes for prisoners).

The market-testing approach has been adapted by the public Prison Service with its performance-testing programme, which challenges underperforming establishments to deliver an in-house bid for improving across the range of services or face contracting out. The perceived threat of privatization engaged staff

and trade unions with the change process, and the process has been successful in turning around problematic establishments. However, unions maintain a principled objection to market testing.

Despite the union position and arguments from critics who maintain that privatization has no place in the delivery of key public services, market testing remains a key part of the reforms planned by the National Offender Management Service (NOMS). Contestability is central to NOMS plans to improve offender management by securing a mixed economy of providers from the public, private and voluntary sectors (Carter 2003).

*Steve Gillespie*

### Related entries

*Industrial relations; National Offender Management Service (NOMS); New public management (NPM); Performance management; Privatization; Voluntary sector.*

**Key texts and sources**

Carter, P. (2003) *Managing Offenders, Reducing Crime: A New Approach.* London: Strategy Unit.
National Audit Office (2003) *The Operational Performance of PFI Prisons.* London: NAO.

## MASCULINITY

Prisoners are overwhelmingly young, male, unemployed and drawn from the lower socio-economic groups. It is unsurprising, then, that in men's prisons, masculinity is 'apt to move to an extreme position' (Sykes 1958: 98).

Much of the so-called prison importation literature suggests that criminal perspectives learnt on the outside give rise to an enhanced or exaggerated form of masculine identity and self within prison. Indeed, the desire to prove one's masculine credentials, which frequently leads to criminal behaviour, conviction and imprisonment in the first place, may itself be a prerequisite to a successful adaptation to life inside. Once in prison, the intensity of the desirable male image is magnified: 'the harsher the environment and the scarcer the resources, the more manhood is stressed as inspiration and goal' (Gilmore 1990: 224 cited in Jewkes 2002: 55). Equally, research on the deprivations associated with imprisonment emphasizes that prisoners frequently develop a reputation for aggressiveness and physical strength as a mode of coping and adaptation. A common pastime in prison is bodybuilding, and the serious pursuit of an excessively muscular physique is significant in terms of the presentation of self as a powerful and self-controlled individual.

In short, a 'hyper-masculinity' is cultivated whereby the 'normal' values and behavioural patterns of powerful men take on an extreme form. As in any organization, a climate of fear is bound to lead to the exploitation of weaker individuals by more powerful ones and, in prison, the illusion of power seems, on the surface at least, to resemble traditional patterns of patriarchy, with vulnerable prisoners such as paedophiles and sex offenders being routinely objectified, intimidated and subjected to violence. Homosexuality in prisons frequently takes the form of aggressive advances made by dominant individuals towards younger and/or weaker prisoners. Hegemonic masculinity in prisons, then, is clearly as bound up with aggression and violence as it is on the outside. That is not to say that the most violent men (in respect to their crimes or to their behaviour in prison) are the most powerful inside; indeed, the volatile offender is more likely to be marginalized than respected. Nevertheless, a certain degree of controlled aggression is required in order to survive the psychological and physical rigours of imprisonment. Ascendancy achieved by means of threats, bullying and predatory aggressiveness is *not* hegemony, but the necessity of establishing a no-nonsense, tough reputation on reception into a new institution is well documented in personal accounts of life inside.

However, as Crewe (2007) observes, these dynamics are complex and, in the UK at least, prisons do not exhibit a homogeneous culture of ruthless and uncompromising machismo.

Further, we must recognize that the culture of masculinity varies between (and even within) prisons. As Sim (1994) observes, the hegemonic masculinity and controlled use of violence and aggression that prevail in open prisons – which traditionally have a high percentage of older and middle-class offenders (including convicted police officers) and contain many prisoners nearing the end of their sentence – are markedly different from the hegemonic masculinity of young offender institutions which may be relatively uncontrolled and normalized. Moreover, while Sykes suggests that prisoners who conform to the inmate code are 'real men', we should be alert to the danger that, by focusing on the 'hyper-masculinity' of men's prisons, we portray the prisoner world as a lawless and amoral jungle (Crewe 2007). Even in young offender institutions, violence and intimidation may be bound by norms and rules that are understood by victims as well as perpetrators, and can thus be characterized not as a pathological manifestation of abnormal otherness but as part of a normal pattern of behaviour which is sustained and legitimated by a wider culture that values expressive manifestations of aggression, power and group loyalty (Sim 1994).

The masculine hegemony that typifies adult male prisons has been challenged in so-called 'experimental' or 'progressive' prisons such as the (now closed down) Barlinnie Special Unit and the therapeutic communities (for example, Grendon Underwood Prison). These prisons are widely regarded as having successfully challenged the violent, brutalizing, hyper-masculine culture of conventional regimes and offer an alternative model of imprisonment based on therapeutic discourses and creative pursuits. While prisoners who have spent significant time in the traditional, mainstream prison system frequently find it immensely difficult to adjust to a regime that encourages staff, fellow prisoners and, indeed, themselves to see beyond their identities as violent hard men, most commentators believe that the prevailing culture of conventional prisons only perpetuates a spiral of potential offending. As Sim (1994) suggests, incapacitating rapists in prisons where there is frequently a status hierarchy that positions all sex offenders at or near the lowest level not only confronts them with a culture of masculinity that does nothing to change their attitudes or behaviour, but may also eventually return them to society more damaged and brutalized than previously.

*Yvonne Jewkes*

### Related entries

*Barlinnie; Coping; Deprivations/'pains of imprisonment'; Homosexuality in prison; Identity and self; Importation model; Inmate code; Therapeutic communities; Young offender institutions (YOIs).*

---

**Key texts and sources**

Crewe, B. (2007) 'The sociology of imprisonment', in Y. Jewkes (ed.) *Handbook on Prisons*. Cullompton: Willan Publishing.

Jewkes, Y. (2002) *Captive Audience: Media, Masculinity and Power in Prisons*. Cullompton: Willan Publishing.

Sim, J. (1994) 'Tougher than the rest? Men in prison', in T. Newburn and E. Stanko (eds) *Just Boys Doing Business*. London: Routledge.

Sykes, G. (1958) *The Society of Captives: A Study of a Maximum Security Prison*. Princeton, NJ: Princeton University Press.

---

# MEASURING THE QUALITY OF PRISON LIFE (MQPL)

The Measuring the Quality of Prison Life (MQPL) survey was designed by Alison Liebling and Helen Arnold as part of a Home Office Innovative Research Challenge Award in 2001. It consists of a series of questionnaire items organized statistically into dimensions intended to reflect 'what matters' most to prisoners. The survey has been routinely used in several research studies and by the Prison Service in all prison establishments in England and Wales since 2002.

Sociological interest in the effects and qualities of correctional institutions used to be much greater than it is today. Research studies on differences between coercive and treatment environments, and between different kinds of treatment environments (sometimes, but not always, including specific programmes), were linked to an interest in explanations for success or failure on release. This kind of research was needed, according to many, until correctional programmes become so overwhelmingly curative that no measures are necessary. Research of this nature more or less ceased with the demise of the rehabilitative ideal, following disappointing research results, scepticism as to the positive effects of institutions and changing penal ideologies away from intervention and discretion towards 'just deserts' and retributive penal strategies. Sociological research in prisons switched its focus from 'treatment effects' to adaptation strategies, or prisoner social life, and then, according to Simon (2000), ceased altogether (particularly in the USA) as managers found ways of governing prisons 'without the social'.

Unusually, the Prison Service in England and Wales continued to be selectively fairly supportive of sociological research over the 1980s onwards, so there exist considerable empirical data on, for example, problems of order and control, legitimacy, race and diversity, staff–prisoner relationships, violence, suicides in prison and the use of discretion by prison officers. This research has argued that prisons are complex and deeply relational environments, where how people treat each other, and feel treated, really matters. There are psychological, relational and emotional dimensions to prison life, which are at least as important in shaping the prison experience as material variables, such as the architecture and design of the prison or the number of hours out of cell.

There has, however, been considerable dissatisfaction with the current state of understanding of prisons expressed by practitioners, scholars and critics over recent years. This is because it is widely recognized that standard or official measures of prison performance do not fully capture the real, but difficult to measure, aspects of prison life mentioned above. There are limitations inherent in key performance indicators and targets (KPIs and KPTs) and in audit ratings which cannot always reflect the quality of a prison accurately enough. This has important implications, as it can lead to feelings of unfairness, disillusion with the techniques (and therefore with those responsible for conducting and using them) and failings in accountability. It is a serious matter if a prison is meeting all its KPIs yet is found to have a hostile staff culture in its segregation unit, for example. So measuring prison quality is a complex and evolving craft, for which different kinds of tools are needed to capture the whole picture.

The MQPL survey was devised with the above considerations in mind following carefully organized, appreciative exercises and individual interviews conducted with staff and prisoners over a five-week period in each of five prisons. The methods used were deliberative, time-consuming and based on the identification of the values underlying all that was said. There emerged from these exercises considerable agreement over what the most important areas of prison life were. These areas mattered most, and varied most between prisons of the same type. They were respect, staff–prisoner relationships, trust, humanity, support, safety, fairness, order, well-being, family contact and personal development. Using these deliberative methods, the research team, alongside staff and prisoners, crafted a series of items or statements thought to reflect each dimension. The draft survey was then piloted with 100 randomly selected prisoners in each of five prisons. Once the results were analysed, the questionnaire was revised, the dimensions refined and comparisons were made between prisons. The survey has been used to measure differences in the 'moral performance' of establishments and the consequences of these differences for prisoners (Liebling assisted by Arnold 2004; see also Liebling and Arnold 2002).

Ongoing research using versions of the MQPL survey has demonstrated significant variations in the quality of prison life, some departures from official measures of the prison and links between MQPL scores and, for example, levels of prisoner distress. It has also been possible, using the large data set available from the Prison Service, to investigate variations in

perceptions of prison quality by ethnic group (Cheliotis and Liebling 2005), by gender and by public or private sector management.

There has been a 'quality revolution' in the prisons domain, but this revolution has brought with it several untested assumptions about the *concept* of quality. Staff working in prisons, as well as critics of the prison, have expressed considerable discomfort about the impoverished version of prison performance imposed by modern managerialist techniques. The MQPL survey represents an attempt to develop a more satisfactory theoretical and conceptual approach to the question of prison climate or quality, without the inevitable distortions of managerialism driving the quest. It is hoped that this analysis (and extended use of the survey) will generate further reflection and research on the role and nature of the prison, and will provide a challenge to simplistic political messages about the prison's effectiveness.

*Alison Liebling*

## Related entries

*Accountability; Architecture; Audit; Discretion; Just deserts; Key performance indicators (KPIs) and key performance targets (KPTs); Legitimacy; Order and control; Prison officers; Race relations; Suicide in prison; Violence.*

### Key texts and sources

Cheliotis, L. and Liebling, A. (2006) 'Race matters in British prisons: towards a research agenda', *British Journal of Criminology*, 45: 1–32.

Liebling, A. and Arnold, H. (2002) *Measuring the Quality of Prison Life. Research Findings* 174. London: Home Office Research, Development and Statistics Directorate.

Liebling, A., assisted by Arnold, H. (2004) *Prisons and their Moral Performance: A Study of Values, Quality and Prison Life*. Oxford: Clarendon Press.

Simon, J. (2000) 'The "Society of Captives" in the era of hyper incarceration', *Theoretical Criminology*, 4: 285–308.

See also http://www.homeoffice.gov.uk/about-us/freedom-of-information/released-information/foi-archive-offender-management/3013-quality-prison-life-reports?view=Html.

# MENTAL HEALTH

The prevalence of mental disorder is much higher among the prison population than in the general population and, as imprisonment is likely to have a negative effect on mental health, it is often argued that mentally disordered offenders should not be sent to prison at all but should be cared for by community health and social services.

It is widely recognized that a high proportion of prisoners suffer from mental health problems. Research carried out in 1997 suggested that over 90 per cent had one or more of the five psychiatric disorders studied (personality disorder, psychosis, neurosis, hazardous drinking and drug dependence), and between 42 and 61 per cent suffered from three or more (Singleton *et al.* 1998). Prisoners also have considerably higher rates of serious mental illness in comparison with the general population, with functional psychosis being approximately ten times more common among prisoners. There are essentially two explanations for these high levels of mental disorder. First, a large number of people sent to prison have pre-existing mental health problems, and this is thought to have increased since the introduction of community care policies and the closure of many large psychiatric hospitals. Secondly, imprisonment can itself create or exacerbate mental health problems. Aspects of the prison regime and environment (such as a lack of constructive activity, fear of other prisoners, isolation from sources of support such as family and friends, being locked in a cell for long periods of time, and overcrowded and dirty conditions) can all have a debilitating effect on mental health and therefore also contribute to the increased risk of suicide and self-harm in prison.

Under the Mental Health Act 1983, prisoners with serious mental illnesses can be transferred out of prison to secure psychiatric care. However, this process can take a considerable amount of time due to a shortage of appropriate beds in psychiatric facilities, and disputes over funding and the 'treatability' of the offender. Only a very small proportion of prisoners with mental health problems are ever transferred, so provision therefore needs to be made for the majority who do not fall under the Mental Health Act 1983. Healthcare in prisons, including mental healthcare, has traditionally been subject to considerable criticism. Until 1992, it was provided by the Prison Medical Service, which was seen as substandard in comparison with the NHS and more concerned with control and custody than care, and accusations were made that psychotropic drugs were administered for control purposes rather than therapy (Sim 1990). Even after 1992, when specialist services began to be contracted into prisons, mental health provision was lacking in many establishments and, where it did exist, it was highly dependent on localized arrangements with mental healthcare providers. Many commentators, including HM Chief Inspectorate of Prisons, have long argued that, in order to improve prison healthcare and ensure equivalence of provision with that of the general population, responsibility for prison healthcare services should be transferred to the NHS.

In 2001 the prison mental health strategy, *Changing the Outlook*, proposed the development of improved mental health services for prisoners in line with the NHS policies, to ensure that prisoners have access to the same range and quality of services as the general population (Department of Health *et al.* 2001). To realize this, multidisciplinary mental health in-reach teams funded by local primary care trusts have been established to provide specialized services to prisoners in the same way as community mental health teams do to patients in the community. Since their introduction, access to mental healthcare in prisons and continuity of care for those already known to outside mental health agencies have undoubtedly improved. However, several factors, including the 'formal and informal networks of penal power' (Sim 2002: 300), may conspire to restrict their impact in prison and make the goal of offering care equivalent to that in the community largely unachievable. The treatment provided by in-reach staff tends to rely heavily on medication. Few prisons have the facilities to offer therapeutic activities such as day care, and the effectiveness of any mental health promotional work is also likely to be limited if prisoners are locked in their cells for most of the day with little or no opportunity to undertake constructive activity. Furthermore, the key tasks of the prison to punish and to maintain order and control continue to conflict with notions of care and treatment, and mental health workers have experienced hostility when they are seen to 'care' for prisoners (Sim 2002) or have challenged prison practices that are detrimental to good mental health. As a result, some in-reach teams have already faced considerable staff retention and recruitment difficulties, and some staff may even end up taking on the values of the custodial culture in order to fit in. Finally, due to high demand and the current emphasis on risk assessment and management, in-reach services are likely to concentrate on those with severe mental disorders whose behaviour is problematic to the prison, meaning that prisoners with more moderate problems will not necessarily benefit from such measures.

Mental healthcare provision has nevertheless improved in recent years, and significant hopes are pinned on in-reach teams to tackle the high level of mental health need in the prison population and consequently to help to reduce the number of suicides in prison. However, in the eyes of many observers, while punishment continues to be the primary purpose of prison, it remains an unsuitable place for treatment.

*Alice Mills*

### Related entries

*Healthcare; HM Inspectorate of Prisons; In-reach teams; Self-harm; Suicide in prison.*

#### Key texts and sources

Department of Health, HM Prison Service and National Assembly for Wales (2001) *Changing the Outlook: A Strategy for Developing and Modernising Mental Health Services in Prisons.* London: Department of Health.

Sim, J. (1990) *Medical Power in Prisons: The Prison Medical Service in England, 1774–1989.* Milton Keynes: Open University Press.

Sim, J. (2002) 'The future of prison health care: a critical analysis', *Critical Social Policy*, 22: 300–23.

Singleton, N., Meltzer, H., Gatward, R., Coid, J. and Deasy, D. (1998) *Psychiatric Morbidity among Prisoners in England and Wales.* London: Office for National Statistics.

The Mental Health Organization's website is at http://www.mind.org.uk/. The website of Revolving Doors (a charity concerned with mental health and the criminal justice system) is at http://www.revolving-doors.co.uk/. See also the Mental Health Primary Care in Prison's website (http://www.prisonmentalhealth.org/).

## MINISTRY OF JUSTICE

The new Ministry of Justice brings together the functions of the Department for Constitutional Affairs with responsibilities hitherto held by the Home Office, including the National Offender Management Service and Youth Justice. The ministry is to have lead responsibility for criminal law and sentencing.

In March 2007, the Prime Minister announced that, from May 2007, a new Ministry of Justice was to take over the staff and responsibilities of the Department for Constitutional Affairs (formerly the Lord Chancellor's Department) and many of the functions hitherto managed by the Home Office – the National Offender Management Service, including the Prison and Probation Services, Youth Justice and the Office of Criminal Justice Reform. The ministry will have lead responsibility for criminal law and sentencing, while the Home Office retains responsibility for security, as well as for the police, crime reduction, drugs, immigration and asylum, identity and passports.

Hitherto, the government department with responsibility for prisons had always been the Home Office. When John Reid became Home Secretary in May 2006, he described his department as 'not fit for purpose'. The proposed remedy was to separate the functions of security and policing, which remain with the Home Office, from the responsibilities for courts, criminal justice and the implementation of sentencing. The distinguished former Lord Chief

Justice Woolf expressed misgivings about the pace of the reform, saying that any rearrangement of the 'checks and balances' of the Constitution should be considered very carefully and not rushed through (BBC 2007). In particular, he reflected that the Lord Chancellor has traditionally enjoyed a close relationship with the judiciary and was anxious that this might be jeopardized when the new minister's portfolio was extended.

While the changes seem precipitate to some, the idea of a Ministry of Justice is scarcely new. The Liberal Democratic Party *Election Manifesto* of 1992, for example, included the idea. A number of reform groups have campaigned for this too, with the Legal Action Group insisting that it would improve the transparency and independence of appointments to the judiciary. It should also be noted that all European jurisdictions (except Spain) have a Ministry of Justice and, as a matter of constitutional principle, it is distinct from the Ministry of Internal Affairs/Interior. In France, the Ministère de l'Intérieur et de l'Aménagement du territoire is responsible for policing, while the Ministère de la Justice is in charge of judicial administration and the implementation of punishment. Similarly, in the German federal government, the Bundesministerium des Innern is quite distinct from the Bundesministerium der Justiz. When new member states join the Council of Europe, this separation is among the first principles on which the council insists: a formal separation of powers between the agencies of security and justice, including the implementation of punishment, is held to be an important human rights safeguard. It was more than a little ironic that the UK, one of the council's founder members, had almost alone retained a Home Office that held responsibility for penal affairs (Coyle 2007).

The introduction of change received some criticism for the speed at which it was carried out and for some matters of detail, in particular that certain policy areas critical to crime and punishment, such as anti-social behaviour and drugs, remain within the Home Office.

However, the policy received a generally warm reception from pressure groups not only because of the practicalities but also from the values implied in the notion of a Ministry of *Justice*. The use of this term suggests a balance that is different from that espoused by the Home Office, a department essentially concerned with *order* and *security*. Many commentators have a hope and expectation that this organizational change will herald a corresponding change in values. This may take its most crucial practical form through exposing and putting to test issues of constitutional principle. In particular, while some hold that judges should take account of pressures on the prison population, others have argued that 'judicial independence' requires that the judiciary retains the power to sentence as they think right while the government should provide the required resources. These arguments will take on a new character when the same minister is responsible both for sentencing policy and for prisons. Whether this will be a good thing is a matter for debate and it is much too early to appraise the significance of the change; how the arrangements will develop over time is at this point a matter for speculation.

*Rob Canton and Jamie Bennett*

### Related entries

*Home Office; Human rights; National Offender Management Service (NOMS); Sentencing policy.*

---

**Key texts and sources**

BBC News (2007) 'Woolf fears Home Office reforms' (available online at http://news.bbc.co.uk/1/hi/uk_politics/6586437.stm).

Coyle, A. (2007) *Prisons and the Ministry of Justice* (available online at http://www.kcl.ac.uk/depsta/rel/icps/new.html).

The Ministry of Justice website is http://www.justice.gov.uk/index.htm.

# MISCARRIAGES OF JUSTICE

> A miscarriage of justice is a criminal conviction which an appeal court later finds to have been unsafe, especially if it had previously been tested, but left unchanged, by the ordinary appeal mechanism.

Trials cannot be about truth, philosophers will tell us. They are about evidence. Evidence is tested by asking witnesses questions about it. All witnesses are inaccurate because the process of describing something in words can never convey exactly the same impression as the one experienced. Some witnesses are sincere and as accurate as they can be within the limitations of language. Some witnesses are sincere but mistaken, or bad at explaining themselves, or simply deluded. Some witnesses are evasive or tell downright lies. Over the centuries, the criminal trial evolved as the UK's best effort at testing evidence to the point where it is capable of proving the legal elements of an offence. Like everything else humans do, it falls short of perfection. Sometimes guilty people 'get away with it', and sometimes innocent people are convicted.

It is impossible to know how frequently miscarriages of justice happen. No one can tell whether a miscarriage has taken place unless he or she knows the truth about the crime. The only people who could know the truth from their own observation are going to be there in the courtroom as defendants or witnesses, or else keeping out of sight and hoping never to go to court. Any statistics, however well informed, can never be anything but guesswork and speculation (Nobles and Schiff 2000).

The first thing to do if someone feels he or she has been wrongly convicted is to appeal. This usually requires expensive legal advice, but it is still possible to appeal even if the appellant is not represented. The courts have to receive a notice of appeal within 28 days of the conviction, although it is possible for an extension to be granted. For an appeal from the magistrates' court no special form is required; this simply requires a note or letter giving the basic details of the conviction and stating an intention to appeal (at this stage it is not necessary to say why). This will be followed by a whole new trial at the Crown court, not before a jury, but a judge and two different magistrates. About half the people whose appeals go ahead at the Crown court win their cases. The balancing risk is that the appellant might have to pay a big bill for the costs of the appeal if they lose, and could even have the sentence increased (although this is quite rare).

From a Crown court conviction, there is a form called 'Form NG' (Notice and Grounds). This is available from the appeals officer at a prison, from any Crown court office or the Courts Service website. It is sent to the Crown court were the original trial took place. They will put together a small file containing, for example, the judge's summing-up and forward it to the Criminal Appeal Office at the Royal Courts of Justice in the Strand. It is considered first of all by a 'single judge': one of the regular Court of Appeal judges sitting at a desk with a pile of similar files, trying to spot the ones that have a chance of success. About three quarters of all the files are rejected at this stage. If the single judge thinks there is an arguable case to make, 'leave to appeal' will be granted and the file will go forward for a full hearing in a courtroom in front of three different judges. The Criminal Appeal Office will grant a new representation order (if the appellant qualifies financially) for a barrister (and perhaps a solicitor) to represent the appellant.

If the single judge cannot see any arguable basis for a successful appeal, he will write a short explanation for his view which will be returned to the appellant. On the back is a place where the appellant can sign to say that they disagree with that view and want a 'full court' (a panel of three judges) to think again about giving permission to appeal. Again this is subject to a quick turnaround as it must get back to the Criminal Appeal Office within 14 days. About a quarter of the people who renew their applications for leave to appeal in this way find that the full court see the case differently from the single judge.

A turndown from the Court of Appeal (or the Crown court, if it was a magistrates' court conviction) is not the end of the road. The Criminal Cases Review Commission (CCRC) can still 'refer' a case back to an appeal court, whereupon it skips the 'leave' stage and goes straight for a full hearing in court. There is a lesser kind of legal aid funding available through any solicitor with a Legal Services Commission criminal contract, but most people are not represented by a lawyer when they first apply to the CCRC. There is an application form (not compulsory) on the CCRC website, or available in prisons or from the CCRC office in Birmingham.

The CCRC cannot refer the case just because the evidence was weak and it thinks the jury might have made a mistake. There has to be some new evidence or some new legal argument that was not raised at the trial or in subsequent attempts to win an appeal. This does not need to be ready for the CCRC, but the applicant must say what kind of new evidence there might be, where it might look for it and why it would win an appeal if it was found. This is a detailed and sometimes slow process. Fewer than 5 per cent of applications make it to an appeal but, once they are in court, they stand about three chances in four of succeeding if the CCRC has referred the case.

*John Wagstaffe*

### Related entries

*Effects of imprisonment; Human rights; Legal services; Long-term prisoners; Mental health.*

#### Key texts and sources

Nobles, R. and Schiff, D. (2000) *Understanding Miscarriages of Justice*. Oxford: Oxford University Press.

The Criminal Cases Review Commission's website is at http://www.ccrc.gov.uk. The website of Innocent (an organization that supports and campaigns for innocent people in prison) is at http://www.innocent.org.uk/. The Innocence Network's website (an organization aimed at turning over wrongful convictions) is at http://www.innocencenetwork.org.uk/index.htm.

## MORALITY

Morality (or moral performance) refers to the fair and reasonable treatment of prisoners in custody, and the internal penal practices, values and sensibilities within a prison.

General definitions of morality are multifarious but frequently refer to the practice of good moral conduct or adherence to a system of moral principles. Both concern aspects of thoughts and behaviour that relate to commonly accepted notions of right and wrong (a wrong act being one that 'manifestly harms others or their interests, or violates their rights or causes injustice'; (Holloway 1999)). The *Stanford, Encyclopedia of Philosophy* defines morality as 'an informal public system applying to all rational persons, governing behaviour that affects others, and has the lessening of evil or harm as its goal'. Essentially, morality is about human ethics and codes of conduct.

It has been argued that prisons constitute special moral places (Goffman 1987: 80) where relationships and the treatment of one party by another really matter. Prisons and imprisonment raise questions of fairness, order, authority, respect and legitimacy in 'an exceptionally palpable way' (Liebling 2004: xviii). The concept of morality and of the existence of a moral obligation on prisons in their treatment of prisoners is encapsulated in the second part of the Prison Service's *Statement of Purpose*, which declares a duty to 'look after' those committed to custody by the courts 'with humanity and help them lead law-abiding and useful lives in custody and after release'. In addition, the service claims it will adhere to a number of values, including 'Care for prisoners', where prisoners 'will be treated with fairness, justice and respect as individuals'. The recognition of the relevance of penal values such as these, particularly within/at the staff–prisoner interface, was most notably achieved in the work of Liebling (2004) and her notion of the 'moral performance' of prisons (see Measuring the Quality of Prison Life (MQPL)).

Since the Prison Service was granted executive agency status in 1993 it has developed many of the characteristics of what is now widely known as 'managerialism' or new public management, where central management sets clear objectives for the 'delivery' of a certain level of 'services', and where monitoring systems to measure these and facilitate their implementation were established. With the aim of ensuring the general rising of standards of economy, efficiency and effectiveness, an increasing number of managerialist initiatives were adopted, and which thereby defined the prevailing approach to prison management. Progress towards the obtainment of the Prison Service purpose, vision, goals and values, and, hence, the performance of individual prison establishments, was gauged using a number of quantifiable and comparable measures, or key performance indicators and targets. These cover such aspects of imprisonment as escapes, assaults, overcrowding, sanitation, purposeful activity, time out of cell, visits and costs. It was from the more established, customary and conventional modes of performance measurement (including the practice of standards auditing) that the concept of the moral performance of a prison evolved, and was in part a response to the received criticisms and limitations of 'traditional' methods of assessment and measurement to depict accurately the degree to which a prison was successful in operating in accordance with standards and principles or adequately to portray the quality of prison life experienced by those working or living within the walls. Contemplation of a wider moral dimension to a prison's performance represents an alternative or supplementary means of evaluating the effectiveness of a prison, and in many ways constitutes an extension of the Prison Service 'decency agenda' (which denotes one central value).

The term 'moral performance', as described by Liebling (2004) in her theoretical account and empirical study of prisons and their moral practices, arose out of extensive discussions with staff and prisoners about 'what matters' in prison, and her analysis of recent prison history which suggested that the role of values in prison life had changed considerably during a period of rapid modernization during the 1990s. In exploring in prisons 'the existence of values, the use of power, the experience of justice and injustice, the role of trust, and, through these notions the complexity of the prison world' and in the attempt to conceptualize, describe and evaluate establishments in these moral terms, Liebling argues 'for the instatement of an explicitly moral agenda' (2004: xvii). The pursuit of a moral agenda in prisons recognizes the importance of the individual and human interactions and relationships in the quality of life experienced, and values inherent within them.

The moral performance of a prison is concerned with the moral treatment of prisoners. It offers both a conceptual framework for thinking about a prison's performance and a model and methodology for the evaluation and Measuring the Quality of Prison Life (MQPL). Liebling's research included the development of a highly structured and standardized self-completion questionnaire as a tool to measure some of the fundamental features of prison life. The questionnaire integrates both relationship dimensions and regime, or legitimacy, dimensions that 'constitute ... an approximate operationalisation of the broad "decency" concept currently in use by the Prison Service ... Decency in this sense has a broad meaning incorporating reasonable and fair treatment' (Liebling and Arnold 2002: 6).

In contrast to traditional performance measurement processes, the focus of moral performance is on the qualitative and less tangible aspects of prison life, of the harder to define and measure internal penal practices and sensibilities such as the nature of relationships, respect, fairness, trust, safety (both psychological and physical), support, well-being, humanity, personal development and decency, as well as those associated with security and order. Liebling maintains that many of these values resemble those of any civil society. Her research findings suggest that 'prisons differ to a significant extent on these dimensions ... prisons differ, in ways that can be identified, in their culture or "moral performance"' (2002: 5).

*Helen Arnold*

*Related entries*

*Decency; Fairness; Legitimacy; Measuring the Quality of Prison Life (MQPL).*

---

**Key texts and sources**

Goffman, E. (1961) *Asylums: Essays on the Social Situation of Mental Patients and Other Inmates.* London: Penguin Books.

Holloway, R. (1999) *Godless Morality: Keeping Religion out of Ethics.* Edinburgh: Canongate.

Liebling, A. (2004) *Prisons and their Moral Performance: A Study of Values, Quality and Prison Life.* Oxford: Clarendon Press.

Liebling, A. and Arnold, H. (2002) 'Evaluating prisons: the decency agenda', *Prison Service Journal*, 141: 5–9.

---

# MOTHER AND BABY UNITS (MBUs)

Mother and baby units (MBUs) are designated separate living accommodation within women's prisons which enables mothers to have their children with them while in prison up to the age of 18 months.

Children have lived with their mothers in prison in some form for over one hundred years. Mother and baby units (MBUs), as we know them today, have developed since the 1960s, and there are now seven units nationally with 77 places. They are dispersed across the country to assist in resettlement, closeness to home and maintaining family contact. Two units take babies up to 9 months of age and the others take babies up to 18 months of age, although there is some flexibility in the upper age limit in individual cases, dependent upon circumstances. All units can accommodate one set of twins.

Every woman prisoner who is pregnant or who has a child of comparable age in the community to those in the units may apply for admittance to an MBU of her choice. Over 100 women give birth while in prison custody every year. Once a woman applies to be allocated to a unit, a dossier of information will be compiled

and an admissions board will be held, chaired by an independent chair who is not a prison employee but has a background in social or legal work. The board recommends a decision to the governor, who then makes the final decision on admission. There have been questions raised about whether this process inadvertently discriminates against women with treatable mental disorders (Birmingham *et al.* 2006).

Once on a unit, the mother must abide by a behavioural compact and remain free from illegal drugs. Women on maintenance programmes can be admitted to MBUs. Nursery provision exists on all the units so that the mother can attend work or offending behaviour programmes if medically fit to do so. Healthcare equivalent to that in the community is available to the mothers and their babies. Mothers retain parental responsibility for their child on the unit and have a great deal of trust placed in them. For example, they are not locked in their rooms because the babies are not prisoners.

However, these units can inevitably be difficult places for children to be brought up. While there is limited information on the health and development of children in these units, there is some recent research on the mothers themselves. This has shown that, while most mothers are in better condition than most female prisoners and the screening has proved effective in sifting out those with severe mental health problems, there is a high level of undiagnosed and untreated depression among mothers in these units (Birmingham *et al.* 2006). This can have longer-term consequences for the development of the children.

For women serving long sentences, where separation from her chid is inevitable, expert advice is that separation is better done earlier in a child's life in order to minimize trauma. Ideally, this should be at six months of age and certainly no later than nine months. There have been a number of legal challenges in recent years, either about refusal to admit to a unit or when to separate a mother from her child. The most important of these decisions has been *R (F)* v. *Secretary of State for the Home Department (2004) unreported*, which demonstrated that the courts are prepared to accept Prison Service policy that a planned separation before 18 months can be in the child's best interest where the mother is not due for release until after the child is 18 months old.

*Jenny Adams Young*

*Related entries*
*Child protection; Families of prisoners; Healthcare; Mental health; Women in prison.*

---

**Key texts and sources**

Birmingham, L., Coulson, D., Mullee, M., Kamal, M. and Gregorie, A. (2006) 'The mental health of women in prison mother and baby units', *Journal of Forensic Psychiatry and Psychology*, 17: 393–404.

HM Prison Service (2005) *Mother and Baby Units* (PSO 4801). London: Home Office.

See also the website of Women in Prison (**womeninprison.org.uk**).

---

# MUBAREK INQUIRY

The Mubarek Inquiry investigated the events surrounding the death of 19-year-old Zahid Mubarek in Feltham Young Offender Institution (YOI) in 2000. The two-volume Keith Report into the inquiry was published on 29 June 2006.

Zahid Mubarek was a young Asian man from East London. He had left school at 15 and was convicted, for the first time, on a number of charges relating to theft from a motor vehicle in January 2000. He was sent to Feltham YOI which, at the time, had a history of overcrowding and was described in the official report into the case as 'a gigantic transit camp' (Keith 2006: 618). Mubarek was murdered by his cellmate, Robert Stewart, on 21 March 2000 at 3 a.m., the morning he was due to be released. Stewart had a history of mental health problems and violence as well as having shown many signs of racism. The murder weapon was a table leg that he had broken away from furniture in the cell.

After his death, Mubarek's family asked the Home Office to hold an inquiry but this was

declined, the Home Office stating that its own internal inquiries were sufficient. The family appealed to the High Court who found the refusal to be in breach of their rights under the European Convention on Human Rights. This was overturned by the Court of Appeal and the family appealed to the House of Lords. In 2003, the House of Lords ordered the Home Secretary, David Blunkett, to initiate an inquiry into Mubarek's death as the state had an obligation not only to ensure that the right to life is protected but also to investigate publicly the death of a prisoner due to failures of the prison system.

The inquiry was chaired by Mr Justice Keith, a High Court Judge. Of the 183 statements gathered, 62 witnesses were called upon to give oral evidence to the inquiry. Sixty-seven days of hearings took place between May 2004 and April 2005. The inquiry also took into consideration the findings from earlier inquiries undertaken by the Prison Service and the Commission for Racial Equality. The final report was published on 29 June 2006 and it paints a bleak picture of the state of Feltham YOI at the time of the murder. Feltham had low staff morale, high staff turnover and insufficient resources to cope with the large number of young people it was expected to accommodate. The report states: 'There are many lessons to be learned from Feltham's decline, but the most important is that population pressures and under-staffing can combine to undermine the decency agenda and compromise the Prison Service's ability to run prisons efficiently' (Keith 2006: 650).

Described by his personal officer as a 'very strange young man', the Keith Report details Robert Stewart's life and his experience in the prison system. Before entering the prison system at Hindley YOI in September 1997, there was evidence of prolific offending, a history of self-harm, a fascination with fires, a lack of care for his personal safety and early diagnosis of a potential personality disorder. The materials documenting these aspects of Stewart's childhood were not given to the Prison Service when he arrived at Hindley, and this was 'the first of many missed opportunities to address how he should have been managed while in custody' (Keith 2006: 573).

In the subsequent years, Stewart passed much time in different YOIs before arriving at Feltham. The report of the inquiry documents many failings on the part of the various institutions and individuals in recording, assessing and treating Stewart while he was in custody. It details the systemic failings of the Prison Service, individual institutions, HM Chief Inspectorate of Prisons, the Independent Monitoring Board and the Probation Service. Over 20 staff were criticized for shortcomings that precipitated the murder. Despite the Prison Service having evidence of Stewart's personality disorders and racist tendencies, information was not properly shared, and this led to Stewart being treated incorrectly by the Prison Service. For example, he never underwent a medical examination at Feltham, which may have picked up his personality disorder.

The inquiry – often described as the Prison Service's 'Stephen Lawrence Inquiry' – found a casual disregard for racist language and abuse among the staff at Feltham. While acknowledging that institutional racism was an established fact within the Prison Service and at Feltham, the report recommends that the Home Office considers recognizing the concept of 'institutional religious intolerance' (Keith 2006: 546). However, one of the most sensational suggestions – that Mubarek and Stewart were put in the same cell deliberately to spark a fight and to allow prison officers to bet on the outcome – was dismissed by the inquiry.

The report made 88 recommendations in total, the most significant of which was that the elimination of enforced cell-sharing should be a priority. Other recommendations were made about issues such as weapons searches, information handling, assessment of prisoners, race and diversity training, and enhancing the pastoral role of imams in prisons. On the whole, however, the inquiry was more neutral in tone and more supportive of the Prison Service than many commentators had hoped.

*James Mehigan*

## Related entries

*Decency; HM Inspectorate of Prisons; Independent monitoring boards; Mental health; Official reports; Overcrowding; Probation Service; Race relations; Violence; Young offender institutions (YOIs).*

### Key texts and sources

Keith, (2006) Justice *The Report of the Zahid Mubarek Inquiry*. London: HMSO.
See also **http://www.zahidmubarekinquiry.org.uk/**. The Home Office's response to the Mubarek Inquiry's report is available online at **http://www.homeoffice.gov.uk/about-us/news/ mubarek-report**.

# MULTI-AGENCY PUBLIC PROTECTION ARRANGEMENTS (MAPPAs)

Multi-agency public protection arrangements (MAPPAs) are the means by which the police, probation and prison services (working together as the 'responsible authority') carry out their statutory responsibilities to assess and manage the risk of harm posed by sexual and violent offenders.

Multi-agency public protection arrangements (MAPPAs) grew out of the closer working relationship the police and probation services developed in the late 1990s to manage high-risk offenders. The Criminal Justice and Court Services Act 2000 first put these arrangements on a statutory footing. That Act required the police and probation services, acting jointly as the 'responsible authority' in each of the 42 areas of England and Wales, to set up arrangements to assess and manage the risk of harm posed by sexual and violent offenders specified in the legislation. Each responsible authority was also required to review its arrangements and to publish an annual report, including the number of MAPPA offenders in the area. The legislation also enabled the Home Secretary to issue guidance to the responsible authorities on the discharge of their duties, helping to maintain consistency (*MAPPA Guidance* 2006).

Sections 325–327 of the Criminal Justice Act 2003 developed the 2000 Act's provisions in three important respects. First, the Prison Service was made part of the responsible authority. Secondly, in recognition of the important part other agencies can play in assessing and managing these offenders, a duty to co-operate with the responsible authority was imposed on every youth offending team (YOT); the health bodies; local education and local housing authorities and registered social landlords; Job Centres Plus; and providers of electronic monitoring services. Thirdly, the 2003 Act requires the Home Secretary to appoint two 'lay advisers' to each responsible authority to assist in carrying out its review of the MAPPA.

Most MAPPA offenders do not pose a high risk of harm. In 2004–5 out of the total of 45,000 MAPPA offenders, about 30 per cent were considered a high or very high risk, which required them to be managed at either of the two higher of the three levels of MAPPA operation – Level 2 or Level 3 (Level 3 is sometimes referred to as the multi-agency public protection panel, or MAPPP). The remaining 70 per cent of MAPPA offenders were assessed as being suitable for supervision principally by one agency alone.

MAPPAs are not infallible, however, as a number of inspection reports and the reviews of cases in which MAPPA offenders seriously reoffended have indicated (HM Inspectorate of Probation 2006). Apart from the shortcomings that may be identified in the way that certain cases are managed, those closely involved in MAPPAs have always warned that assessing risk is not a science and managing it is often complex. A MAPPA provides not only a means of co-ordinating multi-agency work in the management of sexual and violent offenders but also potentially a means of explaining to the public the nature of this diverse and difficult task.

*William Payne*

### Related entries

*Desistance; Electronic monitoring; HM Prison Service; New punitiveness; Probation Service; Rehabilitation; Responsibility; Risk; Sex offenders; Violence.*

### Key texts and sources

HM Inspectorate of Probation (2006) *An Independent Review of a Serious Further Offence Case: Damien Hanson and Elliot White.* London: Home Office.

The *MAPPA Guidance* (2006) is available online at **www.probation.homeoffice.gov.uk/files/pdf/ MAPPA**. See also the Home Office's website (with reports attached): **http://www.noms.homeoffice. gov.uk/protecting-the-public/Supervision/mappa/.**

# N

## NACRO

Nacro is the largest voluntary agency working in the fields of crime reduction and offender resettlement in the UK. It is engaged in a wide range of activities, including supporting ex-offenders directly, working with organizations that are involved with ex-offenders and conducting lobbying work.

Nacro (formerly the National Association for the Care and Resettlement of Offenders) is a registered charity which resettles offenders and carries out preventive work with disadvantaged 'at risk' young people. Established in 1966, Nacro was formed as a successor to the former National Association of Discharged Prisoners' Aid Societies. Its initial purpose was to act as a national umbrella body providing support, advice, training and representation for voluntary organizations involved in the resettlement of prisoners. However, from the early 1970s Nacro also began to establish and manage direct services for offenders and people at risk of offending.

Nacro is now the largest voluntary agency in the field of crime reduction and offenders' resettlement. It is governed by a council of 15 trustees. In 2005–6 Nacro had a turnover of £63 million, employed 1,750 full and part-time staff and provided direct services to around 60,000 people (offenders and people at risk). During that year it carried out work including accommodating over 3,000 people in its supported housing projects; training 10,000 people in its employment and education centres in 47 towns and cities; working in the process with over 600 local and national employers; advising 10,000 prisoners through its prison-based resettlement workers; working with 14,000 young people in its preventive youth activity programmes; and advising over 20,000 people through its Resettlement Plus Helpline. In addition, Nacro provides consultancy, training, resettlement and evaluation services in relation to prisoners' resettlement, race equality and criminal justice, mentally disordered offenders and youth crime.

Nacro also campaigns and lobbies for reform of the criminal justice and penal system, particularly in four main priority areas – the resettlement of prisoners, the reduced use of imprisonment, socially inclusive crime prevention and equality in the criminal justice process. Currently, 49 per cent of Nacro's work concerns the resettlement of offenders, 43 per cent prevention of crime and 7 per cent work for reform of the criminal justice system.

*Paul Cavadino*

### Related entries

*Rehabilitation; Voluntary sector.*

---

**Key texts and sources**

Nacro's website is at **www.nacro.org.uk**

---

## THE NATIONAL OFFENDER MANAGEMENT SERVICE (NOMS)

The National Offender Management Service (NOMS) is an organization responsible for delivering government targets to reduce re-offending. It aims to improve end-to-end sentence management, enhancing joint working between the prison and probation services, informed by research on effective interventions. It also has a brief to improve efficiency and effectiveness through competition for both the delivery of core services and the provision of ancillary services, including services to reduce reoffending.

The National Offender Management Service (NOMS) was established in 2004 and marked a major step in New Labour plans to reform prisons as public services. The genesis of NOMS was the Carter Report (2003), which provided the blueprint for these reforms. In particular, the report identified two elements to the new approach required: first, the need for prisons and probation to be focused on the management of offenders throughout the whole of their sentence, informed by research on what works to reduce reoffending; secondly, that effectiveness and value for money could be further improved through greater use of competition from private and voluntary providers. Although the government immediately accepted the recommendations (Blunkett 2004), there was scepticism from many professionals and commentators, particularly regarding the plans for increased competition.

The establishment of NOMS led to some quick changes in the organization of prisons and probation. For example, many policy responsibilities moved from Prison Service headquarters, and private prisons were removed from Prison Service managerial responsibility and, instead, managed through a new office within NOMS. The Chief Executive of NOMS took on a line management responsibility for the director generals of prisons and probation. Ten regional offender managers were appointed in order to take forward the work on a regional basis.

NOMS was given national responsibility for delivering government targets to reduce reoffending. This meant that a high profile was given to the delivery of services to encourage desistance and rehabilitation. Seven pathways were identified to reducing reoffending: accommodation; education, training and employment; health; drugs and alcohol; finance, benefit and debt; children and families; and attitudes, thinking and behaviour. This strategy was informed by research evidence and provided a comprehensive framework for effective rehabilitative services. The pathways initiative was generally viewed positively, as were the plans to improve collaborative working between prisons and probation. Such joint working had been developing through initiatives such as the shared risk assessment tool (OASys) and through collaboration in sentence planning and risk management (e.g. multi-agency public protection arrangements). The centerpiece of the new initiative was the development of a new offender management model based on the idea of end-to-end sentence management. This has been piloted in the north west and is now being developed nationally (Adams 2007).

In terms of improved competition, NOMS was to become a commissioning body, purchasing services from providers from the public, private and voluntary sectors. This would include not only purchasing prison places but also support services, such as offending behaviour programmes. The proposal envisaged that all prisons, including those in the public sector, would be subjected to routine market testing, irrespective of their performance. This would operate in a similar way to how contracts for private prisons work. Contracts are awarded for a defined period, at the end of which there is an open competition for the contract with the final decision being 'based only on their cost effectiveness in reducing re-offending' (Blunkett 2004: 14). This contrasts with the previous approach where the private sector was allowed to bid for new or poorly performing prisons and for a limited range of ancillary services, such as catering, prison shop and escort services.

The first competition under this new policy was announced in March 2005. This involved a cluster of three prisons on the Isle of Sheppey in Kent, all of which were performing well. However, following professional and union opposition, there was ministerial intervention, and the competition was suspended. Instead, the prisons were provided with a time-bounded opportunity to present a plan to develop their performance, and there was agreement to develop a wider reform package with the main union, the Prison Officers' Association. Although the national reform package was not realized, the prisons did successfully complete their development plan. This intervention effectively meant that the introduction of increased competition in prisons would not be as quick or as extensive as first conceived.

By 2006, plans for improved competition were revived, although this time in relation to probation services. Here it was proposed that competition from the private sector should be introduced for the first time. At the time of writing, the new legislation was still progressing through Parliament and was proving to be as controversial as the introduction of private prisons in the early 1990s.

The development of NOMS is an important element in the New Labour plans for reform of the criminal justice system specifically and public services more generally. However, it has proven to be a divisive and contested development. Resistance and rethinks have meant that progress has not been as rapid or comprehensive as may once have been hoped. Nevertheless, NOMS is an organization that continues to retain an important and growing place in the criminal justice field.

*Jamie Bennett*

### Related entries

*Desistance; Market testing; Multi-agency public protection arrangements (MAPPAs); New public management (NPM); Offender Assessment System (OASys); Offending behaviour programmes; Privatization; Rehabilitation; Reoffending; Sentence planning.*

#### Key texts and sources

Adams, M. (2007) 'Integrated offender management: aspiration or reality for the North West Pathfinder?', *Prison Service Journal*, 169: 42–9.
Blunkett, D. (2004) *Reducing Crime – Changing Lives: The Government's Plans for Transforming the Management of Offenders.* London: Home Office.
Carter, P. (2003) *Managing Offenders, Reducing Crime: A New Approach.* London: Strategy Unit.
See also the Home Office's website (http://www.noms.homeoffice.gov.uk/).

## NEW GENERATION PRISONS (NGPs)

The term 'new generation prison' (NGP) describes prisons designed and planned along the lines of the campus model pioneered in the USA in the 1960s and 1970s. The aim is to create a more positive penal environment to assist the rehabilitation of offenders and to reduce reoffending rates.

The 'new generation' of prisons consists of discrete housing units built on a campus-style model with central areas for association. Each area is staffed by prison officers who operate informally and interact with inmates in the living area while having a clear sight of all cell entrances. This model of informal supervision is aimed not simply at aiding surveillance and control but also at facilitating communication so that the role of officers is no longer to watch and respond to inmate problems, but to predict and prevent them (Bottoms 1999). Feltham YOI, opened in 1983, was the first NGP to be built in the UK following the Home Office's Prison Design Briefing System (PDBS) (1989) and the Woolf Report (1991), both of which advocated the housing of relatively small groups of inmates (50–70) in wings resembling houses. The plan was also put into practice at Woodhill, Doncaster and Lancaster Farms. By contrast, NGPs have existed in the USA since the early 1970s when three 'metropolitan correctional centers' were opened in New York, Chicago and San Diego with the specific aim of downgrading the punitive aspects of incarceration (Tartaro 2006).

The success of NGPs and their attempts to combine situational crime prevention strategies with 'direct supervision' have been mixed, demonstrating that prison architecture must be viewed alongside a multitude of local factors. Evaluations of the three American pioneer institutions produced broadly favourable findings, with violent incidents dropping significantly (Tartaro 2006). In the UK, the two young offender institutions mentioned – Feltham and Lancaster Farms – are perceived rather differently with regard to their success on issues such as bullying, violence and suicide. While

Lancaster Farms has received positive reports for its regime and staff–prisoner relations, Feltham is still struggling to shake off a poor reputation acquired over 20 years of damning inspectors' reports and the murder of a young man by his cellmate in March 2000.

### Blueprints for the future

The new generation philosophy received a fillip in 2005 when the Design Museum's Designer of the Year Award was won by Hilary Cottam for her design of the twenty-first century 'learning prison' (Jewkes and Johnston 2007). The key feature of the design is that movement within the prison is minimized by the creation of a series of autonomous physical units or 'houses' – simple spaces in which groups of prisoners live, work and learn. Rather than moving prisoners around the prison to collect food, attend workshops and classes, go the gym, visit the doctor and so on, these houses are semi-autonomous, and specialists are entrusted to come to teach, treat and perform administrative tasks *in situ*. The houses are constructed as if on a chequerboard – i.e. discrete units with exterior communal spaces between each one to which inmates have relatively free access, thus reducing the cost associated with allowing inmates supervised time in the open air. Despite incorporating a shop, a health centre, a sports hall, a five-a-side football pitch, an indoor swimming pool, a multi-faith centre, an administration block, a visiting area and a central library stack containing up to 20,000 books (which are distributed to the houses in a mobile unit), the entire development has a considerably smaller footprint than the 'typical' traditional prison, thus keeping costs of land (and, subsequently, staffing in a smaller total space) to a minimum.

The cells are designed with learning and purposeful activity in mind. The bed is fixed high on the wall and is visible from the door, mitigating the risk of hanging. At a desk in front of the window a networked computer provides the tools for study and communication via an intranet/prison cable TV network. Each cell is paired with a neighbouring one: a buddying cell linked by sliding doors controlled by the indi-vidual prisoners, but overridden by staff in case of an emergency such as self-harm or suicide. It is claimed that the architecture of this NGP fulfils both a social and psychological role, enhancing inmates' quality of life in an environment where prisoners are judged not by their conformity but by their varied activity and achievement (Henley 2003). However, the design team are at pains to emphasize that, while the prison appears to be liberal, the arrangement of space is designed with discipline and order in mind. Nevertheless, the new prison environment is non-institutional and normalized, and is consequently not mentally and emotionally repressive (Henley 2003).

A similar blueprint for an NGP has been developed by the team behind the Creative Prison, which includes architect Will Alsop, staff and prisoners at Gartree Prison, and Rideout (see **www.rideout.org.uk**). Their view is that, although considerable progress has been made in recent years in *some* prisons, due largely to the desire among individual governors and staff to create more humanitarian, learning-centred regimes, these endeavours are frequently compromised not just by unworkable criminal justice policies but by the legacy of old, Victorian buildings (Rideout 2006: 4):

> If prisoners are to leave prison and not return, their time inside must be spent in activities that are conducive to good mental health as well as to learning and rehabilitation. These issues are crucially informed by considerations such as light, views, space and appropriateness of architectural design to facilitate good staff–prisoner relationships.

The Creative Prison – named Paterson Prison – is envisaged as a 'super-enhanced' prison for adult males who are designated Category 'C': low-risk prisoners who have been on 'enhanced' status for a minimum of one year (see Incentives and earned privileges (IEP)). Attendance at Paterson would be for two years minimum, three years maximum and, should a prisoner fail to comply with the rules or withdraw from education, he would be moved back to the mainstream prison system in much the same way as therapeutic communities currently operate.

For staff, too, the new generation design promises to alter radically their primary duties and purpose. Instead of spending their time shuttling prisoners to and from workshops, education, visiting areas, association spaces, etc., with all the attendant security measures that accompany such movement, staff have a more positive role in the education and rehabilitation of prisoners, for which they are paid higher wages than they currently receive. It is thought that a more highly motivated group of officers and governors will be the result.

### Pros and cons

This Utopian vision of penal space is attractive to those who believe that traditional prison design fails prisoners in its purpose, as set out in the Prison Rules to encourage them to 'lead a good and useful life'. However, the twenty-first century prison's attempts to harmonize design and purpose have been questioned by some prison architects who claim that the design could be claustrophobic and could make it difficult to control violence and bullying. This concern is supported by findings from some UK prison research, which shows that freedom of movement can be abused by prisoners, who use it as an opportunity to trade drugs, 'settle scores' or physically assault fellow inmates in spaces hidden from the gaze of staff. However, advocates of the new generation philosophy maintain that violence and fear of violence are diminished in NGPs because the presence of staff in living areas ensures that a power vacuum is not created and conflicts do not easily arise. Furthermore, inmates have much to lose by being removed and placed back in the traditional prison system (Tartaro 2006). The perceived success of NGPs in the USA may be evidenced by the fact that they doubled in number between 1995 and 2000 (from 147 to 300), although it must also be noted that partial implementation of the new generation philosophy (e.g. building a cutting-edge prison with a normalized regime but not giving its staff adequate communication skills training) has

diluted its positive impact in many institutions (Tartaro 2006).

The 'Learning Prison' and the 'Creative Prison' have yet to be tested in practice, and the strong support they have received from ministers has to be viewed alongside concomitant discussions of the establishment of 'superprisons' in the UK, following the model set by the US supermax. Arguably, their realization will depend, not on political backing, but on the support of private prison providers whose mission to make money and satisfy their shareholders may make them averse to the NGP. Perhaps the biggest barrier is public perceptions of what a prison *should* look like: a normalized physical environment (which might include carpets, soft furnishings, coffee machines, telephones and televisions) may prove controversial among those who believe that these are indicators of a prison management that is soft on crime.

*Yvonne Jewkes*

### Related entries

*Architecture; Bullying; Education and training; Incentives and earned privileges (IEP); Mental health; Public perceptions; Suicide in prison; Supermax prisons; Therapeutic communities; Victorian prisons; Violence.*

**Key texts and sources**

Bottoms, A.E. (1999) 'Interpersonal violence and social order in prisons', in M. Tonry and J. Petersilia (eds) *Prisons.* Chicago, IL: University of Chicago Press.

Fairweather, L. and McConville, S. (2000) *Prison Architecture: Policy, Design and Experience.* Oxford: Architectural Press.

Henley, S. (2003) *The 21st Century Model Prison* (available online at http://www.spacesyntax.net/symposia/SSS4/fullpapers/03Henleypaper.pdf).

Jewkes, Y. and Johnston, H. (2007) 'The evolution of prison architecture', in Y. Jewkes (ed.) *Handbook on Prisons.* Cullompton: Willan Publishing.

Rideout (2006) *The Creative Prison: Creative Thinking within the Prison Estate.* Stoke-on-Trent: Rideout/Creative Arts for Rehabilitation (available online at www.rideout.org.uk).

Tartaro, C. (2006) 'Watered down: partial implementation of the new generation jail philosophy', *Prison Journal,* 86: 284.

# NEW PUBLIC MANAGEMENT (NPM)

New public management (NPM) describes the trend in public service which emerged in the 1980s to introduce managerial practices from the private sector and to improve performance through commercial competition.

'New public management' (NPM) emerged from the new-right ideology of the 1980s, which promoted the private sector, market discipline and small government (Hood 1991). This movement sought to improve the public sector by a combination of competition (including privatization and contracting-out) and managerialism, which promotes the centrality of managers and the adoption of scientific approaches to management. Scientific approaches include explicit performance measures; breaking monolithic bureaucracies into smaller units; using private sector practice in human resource issues, such as recruitment and pay; and a stress on greater discipline in resource use by cutting costs and raising labour and union discipline.

There is not a single, unified approach to NPM; instead, four broad models have been identified (Ferlie *et al.* 1996). First, the *efficiency drive* emphasizes private sector practices, making the public sector more 'business-like'. Secondly, *downsizing and decentralization* focuses on breaking large bureaucracies into smaller, more flexible units. Thirdly, *in search of excellence*, based on the human relations school, emphasizes organizational culture. Fourthly, *public service orientation* is a fusion of public and private sector ideas with a distinct public service mission.

In prisons, NPM took root during the early 1990s and initially reflected the *efficiency drive* model. Reforms included the Prison Service becoming an agency, providing operational independence from the Home Office. In addition, a Director General with no previous public sector experience, Derek Lewis, was recruited from the commercial sector. He introduced more business-like management, including explicit goals and quantifiable measures known as key performance indicators and targets. The

reforms also included two controversial measures: the opening of the first private prison in 1991 and the outlawing of industrial action by prison officers under s. 127 of the Criminal Justice and Public Order Act 1994.

Some prison managers criticized NPM for increasing administrative burdens so that managers could not be people-centred leaders, for ignoring the moral dimension of prisons and for being too concerned with quantity and efficiency rather than quality and effectiveness. These mirror criticisms made regarding similar reforms in other parts of the criminal justice system, including courts, police and probation. However, over time, within prisons there has grown a belief that NPM practices have contributed towards improvements. In the criminal justice system generally, it has been observed that NPM is no longer 'new' but has become routine and institutionalized (McLaughlin *et al.* 2001).

Since the election of the New Labour government in 1997, prisons have seen an evolution in NPM. Developments reflecting the *efficiency drive* model have continued. For example, quantitative performance measures have been developed, including more sophisticated forms of analysing performance management information. The 'Benchmarking Programme' includes a four-point performance ratings system, which triggers specific, targeted management action to reward good practice or develop performance, including, in the most extreme cases, offering poorly performing prisons to private sector providers. In 2004, the National Offender Management Service (NOMS) was created, a commissioning body for correctional services including prisons and probation. The new organization emphasized the importance of 'contestability' in achieving reductions in reoffending and created wider opportunities for contracting out ancillary services and introducing routine market testing for prisons, irrespective of their performance.

Alongside these developments, since 1997 there has also been an introduction of reforms that re-engage with values. Examples include the launch of the 'Decency' agenda in 2002 to encourage the delivery of services sensitive to prisoners as citizens. Decency has been further scrutinized via the development of a tool for Measuring the Quality of Prison Life (MQPL), which gives prisoners a stake in performance management and attempts to make the moral dimension of prison performance measurable. Community involvement has been improved, both by reinvigorating independent monitoring boards and by encouraging voluntary sector partnerships. Section 127 was revoked in 2005 and replaced with a 'no strike' agreement, marking a move to more co-operative industrial relations. In addition, the prominence being placed on reducing reoffending by NOMS acts to support rehabilitative work. These reforms reflect the *public service orientation* model of NPM (Bennett 2007), and this re-engagement with values has also been noted in other criminal justice agencies (McLaughlin *et al.* 2001).

These approaches suggest there is tension in prisons as to the shape of managerial reform. This became particularly acute in March 2005, with the announcement of the market testing of three prisons on the Isle of Sheppey in Kent. This was a 'test case' of 'contestability' as the prisons were not underperforming. However, following ministerial intervention, the competition was suspended and, instead, the prisons were provided with a time-bounded opportunity to develop their performance, tied to a wider national reform package agreed with the Prison Officers' Association. Although the reform package floundered, the public sector plan was accepted. The case showed that the pace and extent of 'contestability' may not be as extensive as originally conceived. The case also represents a model of reform based on a *public service orientation* rather than *efficiency drive*.

In prisons, as with the criminal justice system generally, there is a need to balance the demands for efficiency with those of community values. Although NPM has been accepted and institutionalized, there are ongoing concerns that efficiency has taken precedence over values. Achieving the balance between these competing demands is the central challenge of NPM in prisons.

*Jamie Bennett*

## Related entries

*Audit; Decency; Industrial relations; Key performance indicators (KPIs) and key performance targets (KPTs); Market testing; National Offender Management Service (NOMS); Performance management; Privatization.*

### Key texts and sources

Bennett, J. (2007) 'Measuring order and control in HM Prison Service', in Y. Jewkes (ed.) *Handbook on Prisons*. Cullompton: Willan Publishing.

Ferlie, E., Ashburner, L., Fitzgerald, L. and Pettigrew, A. (1996) *The New Public Management in Action*. Oxford: Oxford University Press.

Hood, C. (1991) 'A public management for all seasons', *Public Administration*, 69: 3–19.

McLaughlin, E., Muncie, J. and Hughes, G. (2001) 'The permanent revolution: New Labour, new public management and the modernization of criminal justice', *Criminal Justice*, 1: 301–18.

## NEW PUNITIVENESS

'New punitiveness' refers to the growth in imprisonment and the resurgence of other expressive and symbolic penalties in many Western countries at a time when crime has been in decline.

### What is 'new punitiveness' (and what is 'new' about it)?

One of the first identifications of this emerging trend in Western penality was made by David Garland (1996), although at that time he referred to it as a 'revived punitiveness' (1996: 463) and as 'the emergence of a more divisive, exclusionary project of punishment' (1996: 466). It has also been referred to as the 'punitive turn', although 'new punitiveness' has probably become the most common shorthand response to describe the formal responses to crime which it has inspired since the early 1990s. What is it, though, that is 'new' about new punitiveness, and to what extent is policy more punitive than before as a result?

First, it departs radically from the understandings that regulated the levels and intensity of penal sanctions for most of the post-war period. These ensured that penal policy was developed 'behind the scenes' by civil servants, in conjunction with their governments, who would also draw on advice from academics and other elite groups. Meanwhile, the general public was almost completely excluded from any involvement in such matters. The emotion and commonsense values they brought to penal affairs were kept at bay, while policy was developed along a usually rational, humanitarian and cost-effective path (which in reality could often turn out to be far removed from any of these intents). Furthermore, while it was expected that levels of imprisonment would reflect crime patterns, from the 1970s it was increasingly thought that this sanction should be used only as a 'last resort'. Those societies that imprisoned the least and that also had the most humane penal institutions – particularly the Netherlands and the Scandinavian countries – were looked upon as setting the standard for the rest of the civilized world to follow.

However, the new punitiveness represents an almost complete reversal of these identifying characteristics and expectations. Even though crime in general terms has been falling, increases in imprisonment need no longer represent shame but instead can become emblems of political virility and public security: 'prison works', the British Home Secretary, Michael Howard, famously declared in 1993. It worked not in terms of reconviction rates, of course, which is how it had previously been judged, but in terms of incapacitating growing numbers of the criminal population. At the same time, the influence on policy of the general public – or those who claim to speak on its behalf, such as law-and-order lobby groups, the tabloid press, talkback radio hosts and so on – has significantly increased, while that of the criminal justice establishment has diminished. These new influences speak a penal language – 'three strikes', 'zero tolerance' and so on – that emanates from the USA, the Western country which punishes the most and the most inhumanely, with a penal agenda that many other countries at the beginning of the twenty-first century have begun to follow. Governments from both the left and right of the political spectrum have aligned themselves more closely with such representations of the public mood and have sought to disparage or distance themselves from the values of those establishment elites who had previously been in control of penal debate and knowledge (Loader 2006). In such ways the emotive, *ad hoc* and volatile forces of populism have been able to leave their imprint on policy development. New punitiveness tries to position crime victims at the centre of the criminal justice process, the issue then being the extent to which offenders have to be punished and have to pay the victims back in some way for the harm done to them, rather than any needs or deficiencies of the offenders' own that their crimes have brought to light. At the same time, long-standing criminal justice rights and processes that are thought to favour criminals at the expense of the law-abiding community may be curtailed or annulled. The rights of the community increasingly supersede the rights of individual criminals.

Secondly, as a consequence, levels of imprisonment have significantly increased across many modern societies. Leaving aside the exceptionalism of prison rates in the USA which began their rise to the current level of 737 per 100,000 of population in the 1980s, since 1995 imprisonment rates in England have increased from 99 per 100,000 of population to 145 in 2005. A similar rate of increase has taken place in New Zealand – from 128 to 187 over the same period. Even more spectacularly, the rate in the former icon of liberalism, the Netherlands, has increased from 66 to 127; while there have been increases in the Scandinavian countries as well, even if at a significantly lower rate (in Sweden, for example, from 65 to 78). However, while new punitiveness has been most closely associated with rising imprisonment, it also seeks to turn the punishment of offenders into a symbolic spectacle of reassurance for the onlooking public, and into one of humiliation and debasement for its recipients. Hence the development of naming and shaming penalties, in various mechanisms, in the USA, Britain and New Zealand. Furthermore, it is associated with an intolerance of all kinds of unwanted intrusions into everyday life that has led to the prosecution of quality-of-life offending (public drunkenness, begging, etc.) and the British anti-social behaviour legislation.

In addition, the new punitiveness has been directly and indirectly associated with deteriorating prison conditions. In some jurisdictions, particularly in the USA, new levels of austerity have been introduced – shaved heads, stigmatic uniforms, parades and so on – amid rhetoric about containment and control rather than rehabilitation, replicating the 'tough on crime' approach beyond the prison. More generally, though, because of overcrowding the growth in prison numbers has caused (notwithstanding a simultaneous expansion of the prison estate) many of the important reforms carried out in the 1990s which liberalized and humanized prisons in England to be undermined, if not abandoned altogether.

## The political, social and cultural contexts of new punitiveness

What is it, then, that has brought about new punitiveness? The decline in social cohesion and solidity in Western society from the 1970s seems to lie at its heart. This can be seen in a number of important areas of public and private life. There has been the decline of deference to elites and establishment figures and the hitherto unquestioned acceptance of the values they represent. Instead, ordinary people demand more of a say in governance matters, including crime and punishment. At the same time, there is less trust in politicians and existing political processes: globalization has weakened the authority of sovereign states, making their rulers appear vulnerable to external forces and organizations which they have little control over. This again encourages the general public to put their trust in extra-parliamentary pressure groups or populist politicians who seem to offer magical, commonsense solutions to problems such as crime. There has been the collapse of employment security; family life has been shattered by divorce, and marriage has given way to more transient cohabiting practices; and there have been declines in church attendance, trade union membership and various other forms of community involvement. At the same time personal security is put in jeopardy by what seems to be an inexorable rise in crime. Precisely because of the above changes, most people gain their understanding of this matter from the media – which are likely to distort and exaggerate its reality (Jewkes 2004). As such, rising crime, irrespective of more accurate statistical gauges to the contrary, becomes one of the most obvious emblems of the decline in social cohesion. The more this seems to be unravelling, the more strident will be the calls for more expressive, symbolic punishment, which the new configuration of penal power is now placed to put into practice. Tyler and Boeckmann (1997) thus argue that people in the USA generally support that country's three-strikes laws – not because of their fears of crime but because of their perceptions that social cohesion is deteriorating. Tougher sanctions are seen as a way of restoring the authority of the criminal law and reaffirming social solidity.

However, not all Western countries are following this pattern. In Canada, France and Germany, prison populations have stabilized or declined over the same period. In these and other countries, immunity to new punitiveness has been provided by such matters as a continued commitment to welfarism, trust in expertise rather than suspicion of it, a strong central state authority which remains firmly in control of penal debate, and media that help to provide a public education service rather than one which sensationalizes and alarms. In general, an inclusive model of governance can act as a shock absorber in times of dramatic social change. Finland, for example, suffered a deep recession in the early 1990s. Unemployment reached 20 per cent, but this made no impact on levels of crime, disorder or imprisonment, which continued their downward path for another decade (Pratt 2006). We thus need to recognize that, while the new punitiveness has had a dramatic effect in some societies, it has made no headway at all in others and is not inevitable.

*John Pratt*

### Related entries

*Overcrowding; Prison population; 'Prison works'; Security; Welfarism.*

**Key texts and sources**

Garland, D. (1996) 'The limits of the sovereign state: strategies of crime control in contemporary society', *British Journal of Criminology*, 36: 445–71.

Jewkes, Y. (2004) *Media and Crime*. London: Sage.

Loader, I. (2006) 'Fall of the Platonic guardians: liberalism, criminology and political responses to crime in England and Wales', *British Journal of Criminology*, 46: 561–86.

Pratt, J. (2006) *Penal Populism*. London: Routledge.

Pratt, J., Brown, D., Brown, M., Hallsworth, S. and Morrison, W. (eds) (2005) *The New Punitiveness: Trends, Theories, Perspectives*. Cullompton: Willan Publishing.

Tyler, T. and Boeckmann, R. (1997) 'Three strikes and you are out, but why? The psychology of public support for punishing rule breakers', *Law and Society Review*, 31: 237–65.

# 'NOTHING WORKS'

'Nothing works' describes an academic analysis of a body of research on interventions in prison settings undertaken between 1945 and 1967. It reflected the finding at that time that most of these interventions were poorly developed and implemented, and that few could be shown to have any positive impact in reducing criminal recidivism.

The term 'nothing works' derives from a paper by Martinson (1974) which summarized a more detailed report undertaken with two colleagues. This reported the results of an analysis of 231 evaluations of interventions with offenders, undertaken between 1945 and 1967. Based on this, he concluded that '[w]ith few and isolated exceptions the rehabilitative efforts that have been reported so far have had no appreciable effect on recidivism' (Martinson 1974: 25). This report was widely interpreted as demonstrating that 'nothing works' in the rehabilitation of offenders. A National Academy of Science panel concurred with this belief when it reviewed the area (Sechrest *et al.* 1979), although by this time Martinson had tempered some of his earlier views. The term 'nothing works' was current at a time when public policy and opinion were moving the public away from rehabilitation and towards retribution or deterrence as justifications for the punishment of offenders.

Martinson's conclusions were not universally accepted and it was suggested that the initial research was seriously flawed. First, it was argued that the methodology used was inadequate, with poor-quality data included in the analysis. Additionally, many of the interventions included in the analysis were very poorly implemented. Despite such concerns, the phrase 'nothing works' gained a wide currency in professional circles and among policymakers. This was followed by a reaction against this analysis, with the development of a similarly clichéd and over simplistic 'what works?' literature.

Both terms represent a parochial view of intervention work with offenders focused on a narrow part of the available evidence base on psychological therapies (Crighton 2006). The notion of evidence-based practice (EBP) effectively subsumes both narrow conceptions by addressing a range of interventions which may be effective in reducing levels of criminal behaviour, either individually or as part of a number of separate interventions co-ordinated into an integrated 'programme' of assessment and interventions.

*David Crighton*

### Related entries

*Desistance; Offending behaviour programmes; Psychology in prisons; Rehabilitation.*

**Key texts and sources**

Crighton, D. (2006) 'Methodological issues in psychological research in prisons', in G. Towl (ed.) *Psychological Research in Prisons*. Oxford: Blackwell.

Martinson, R. (1974) 'What works? Questions and answers about prison reform', *The Public Interest*, 35: 22–45.

Sechrest, L., White, S. and Brown, E. (1979) *The Rehabilitation of Criminal Offenders*. Washington, DC: National Academy of Sciences.

# O

## OFFENDER ASSESSMENT SYSTEM (OASys)

The Offender Assessment System (OASys) is a standardized risk assessment tool used by both prisons and probation in England and Wales.

As a tool for the assessment of risk, and for informing and planning the management of risk, the Offender Assessment System (OASys) is a key instrument in the project of establishing an end-to-end offender management system in the criminal justice system. The risk assessment is carried out initially by the Probation Service at the pre-sentence stage, and is reviewed and updated regularly (at intervals which vary with the length of the sentence) to ensure that at every decision stage – sentencing, intervention planning, setting licence conditions, parole reviews, early-release decisions, multi-agency public protection arrangements, reviews, etc. – reliable risk information is available without duplication of work. In the early stages, all OASys assessments on prisoners were carried out by staff in prisons. The new offender management process being developed by the National Offender Management Service (NOMS) is intended to keep OASys throughout the sentence (whether a custodial or community sentence) in the hands of the Probation Service in the offender's home area.

OASys treats risk under two headings: 'risk of reoffending', and 'risk of harm'. The risk of reoffending section combines actuarial information about the individual's history, especially offending history, with a dynamic assessment of risk factors and protective factors (i.e. those which are positively likely to reduce risk). The chief sections in this part are offending history and offence analysis, accommodation, education and employment, financial management, relationships, lifestyle and associates, drug misuse, alcohol misuse, emotional well-being, thinking and behaviour, attitudes, and health. The risk of harm section covers risk to other adults, to children and to the offender him or herself, and other risks, such as breach of trust. A scoring system is incorporated that produces a 'risk of reoffending score' from 0 to 168, with bands defined to attribute low, medium and high risk. The scoring system, and the weightings within it, are calculated (and regularly reviewed) on the basis of research by the central OASys Data, Evaluation and Assessment Team in NOMS. A final section in OASys covers sentence planning: on the basis of the assessment made, the assessor (in consultation with the offender, who is engaged throughout the process, and normally in consultation with a wide range of others involved in the management of this offender) records recommended objectives and interventions.

OASys was originally developed as a paper-based system because the Home Office took the view that there was no existing tool that met all the needs for offender management. However, it is founded on evidence-based predecessor tools and, indeed, incorporates one in its entirety. The assessment of risk among offenders is a developing and controversial area among criminologists and related academic disciplines, and there is by no means a unanimous acceptance that it is credible in all respects. There will continue to be a necessary tension between keeping it unchanged – so that performance and outcomes can be consistently measured over time – and adapting it in response to new research findings in the field (Moore *et al.* 2006).

*Martin Kettle*

## Related entries

*Multi-agency public protection arrangements (MAPPAs); National Offender Management Service (NOMS); Parole; Risk; Sentence planning.*

---

**Key texts and sources**

Moore, R., Howard, P. and Burns, M. (2006) 'The further development of OASys: realising the potential of the Offender Assessment System', *Prison Service Journal*, 167: 36–42.

See also the Home Office's probation website (http://www.probation.homeoffice.gov.uk/files/pdf/Info%20for%20sentencers%203.pdf).

---

# OFFENDING BEHAVIOUR PROGRAMMES

Offending behaviour programmes are psychological interventions accredited as contributing to reducing reoffending among those who complete them.

## Offending behaviour programmes: what are they?

Offending behaviour programmes (OBPs) are psychological interventions with the primary aim of reducing reoffending by directly targeting psychological factors related to the commission of crime. The programmes have to be accredited by the independent Correctional Services Accreditation Panel (CSAP), which confirms that the programmes does, or is likely to, reduce recidivism. In 2006, 14 OBPs had been accredited for use in the Prison Service for England and Wales:

- Three cognitive skills programmes: Enhanced Thinking Skills (ETS), Cognitive Skills Booster and Reasoning and Rehabilitation (R & R, now discontinued within the Prison Service).
- Six sex offender treatment programmes (SOTPs): Core SOTP, Extended SOTP, Rolling SOTP, Adapted SOTP, the Better Lives Booster Programme and the Healthy Sexual Functioning Programme.

- Three programmes for violent offenders: the Healthy Relationships Programme (HRP) for domestic violence offenders, the Cognitive Self Change Programme for persistently violent individuals and the Chromis Programme, for violent offenders with psychopathic personality disorder.
- An anger management programme: CALM (Controlling Anger and Learning to Manage it).
- A resettlement programme: FOR (Focus on Resettlement).

## What do they involve?

OBPs are all based on cognitive-behavioural principles (see McGuire 2002). That is, they offer participants the chance to try out new ways of thinking (e.g. taking the perspectives of others) and new ways of behaving (e.g. responding to conflict). OBPs use a variety of methods, such as group discussion, role play, games and individual presentations to the group. All bar one of the accredited OBPs are mainly delivered in a group format, usually involving eight to ten prisoners in a group (the Healthy Sexual Functioning Programme is a one-to-one programme, where one therapist works with one prisoner; the HRP and Chromis programme involve some one-to-one sessions alongside group work). OBPs are structured or semi-structured programmes, with some being more psycho-educational in nature and others containing considerable flexibility to adjust to individual need. Programme length varies according to the number and complexity of the needs being addressed. Prison-based OBPs follow the risk–need–responsivity principles of offender rehabilitation. That is, higher-risk offenders receive longer treatment, all offenders are assessed before entering an OBP to ensure they have the needs that the programme is designed to address and the programmes use methods to which offenders are known to respond. Some OBPs also follow the principles of the Good Lives Model of offender rehabilitation. This approach aims to build the skills necessary to achieve life contentment, with the expectation that doing so will reduce the desire to offend. All OBPs place respect for other people at the heart of what they do, so that programmes staff communicate respect for their group members who, in turn, are encouraged to develop and display respect for each other and for society at large. OBPs are also an important part of the public protection agenda, and feed into risk assessment and risk management activities.

## How are they managed?

A central unit in the Prison Service – the Offending Behaviour Programmes Unit (OBPU) – is responsible for programme design, implementation support, staff training, integrity monitoring and evaluation of all accredited OBPs. In prisons, OBPs are managed by a tripartite team comprising a treatment manager (responsible for treatment integrity, staff supervision and clinical decisions), a programme manager (responsible for integration into the prison regime and wider institutional support) and a resettlement manager (responsible for the interface with the Probation Service and facilitating proper follow-up after release). It is anticipated that the role of the resettlement manager will change with the implementation of offender management. Programmes are facilitated by multidisciplinary teams, usually including prison officers and psychology staff, but with many other grades and disciplines of staff involved as well. All staff delivering OBPs are specially trained for the task and receive ongoing supervision and support.

## How are they monitored?

Programme integrity is an important matter for OBPs. This refers to the need for OBPs to be delivered in the way that was intended when they were designed. If a programme is not monitored, it may drift over time into a different type of intervention altogether. Such treatment drift is known to be a major threat to the effectiveness of OBPs. Hence, OBPs have detailed monitoring procedures associated with them. All sites delivering programmes have an annual audit, which involves a site inspection from a central audit team, as well as (for some programmes) a 'clini-cal audit' of material produced by the offenders in the programme to check that they understood the programme. Furthermore, all group sessions are videotaped, and the group supervisor observes a proportion of sessions on-site. A further proportion is watched by monitors at OBPU, who report on the integrity of each group and on the skills of the facilitators.

## Do they work?

The evidence suggests that OBPs *can* work, but they do not *always* work. That is, repeated evaluations of the same programme show that in some contexts the programme reduces offending, but not all. The design of the programme is not the only factor that has to be right for a programme to work. OBPs also have to be properly implemented, supported by prison management, delivered in a motivational style, carefully supervised and externally monitored (see Bernfeld *et al.* 2001). Even more importantly, post-programme work (such as community supervision) should operate consistently with the values and principles of the programmes. The level of oversight needed to achieve these demands can be hard to achieve with large-scale programmes. It is also hard to design a research study that reliably isolates the impact of the OBP from the many other services offenders receive. Randomized controlled trials are viewed by many as the gold standard for programme evaluation but, in practice, these are extremely difficult, if not impossible, to conduct, particularly on a large scale (Hollin and Palmer 2006). When cost-benefits analyses of programmes have been conducted, they usually indicate that OBPs are value for money. However, OBPs should not be expected to work if they are provided in isolation from the other services an offender receives.

*Ruth Mann*

## Related entries

*Activities; 'Nothing works'; Psychology in prisons; Rehabilitation; Risk; Sentence planning; Sex offenders; Therapeutic communities.*

**Key texts and sources**

Bernfeld, G., Farrington, D. and Leschied, A. (eds) (2001) *Offender Rehabilitation in Practice: Implementing and Evaluating Effective Programmes.* Chichester: Wiley.

Hollin, C. and Bilby, C. (2007) 'Addressing offending behaviour: "what works" and beyond', in Y. Jewkes (ed.) *Handbook on Prisons.* Cullompton: Willan Publishing.

Hollin, C. and Palmer, E. (2006) *Offending Behaviour Programmes: Issues and Controversies.* Chichester: Wiley.

McGuire, J. (ed.) (2002) *Offender Rehabilitation and Treatment: Effective Programmes and Policies to Reduce Re-offending.* Chichester: Wiley.

See also the Prison Service's offender behaviour programmes web page (http://www.hmprisonservice. gov.uk/adviceandsupport/beforeafterrelease/offend erbehaviourprogrammes/). The Crime Reduction website is at http://www.crimereduction.gov. uk/workingoffenders/workingoffenders3.htm.

# OFFICIAL REPORTS

Official reports are publications from government bodies such as the Home Office, the National Offender Management Service (NOMS) and the Prison Service. They are the official source of knowledge on how prisons operate and include the publication of annual reports and accounts, corporate plans and framework documents. An official report may also be the outcome of a specially commissioned inquiry into a problem acknowledged by the government as requiring high-profile investigation, such as the Keith Report (2006).

Major prison reports often arise through politically embarrassing scandals. Recent inquiries have included the Woolf Report (1991) on prison riots and the Learmont Report (1995) on escapes and absconds by Category A prisoners. In addition, under the terms of Prison Service Order 1300, there have been a number of small-scale prison inquiries examining controversies such as assaults on prisoners by staff, prisoner-on-prisoner violence and allegations of racism. Since 2001 the Prison Service Investigations Unit has been responsible for internal reports. Prisoner complaints, suicides and other deaths in custody are reported on by the Prisons and Probation Ombudsman as and when required, while independent monitoring boards produce regular reports on the prison under their jurisdiction. Additionally, HM Chief Inspectorate of Prisons reports on regular prison inspections as well as providing influential thematic studies.

### Official reports as 'regimes of truth'

The authors of these official reports act as 'authorities of delimitation' (Foucault 1972: 41), sanctioning a particular knowledge as the 'true' version of events. The key to understanding their role is through grasping the complex relationship between power, knowledge and the production of 'truths'. Knowledge is not objectively nor impartially fashioned. Rather, knowledge is created or produced through the exercise of power; what Foucault described as the power/knowledge axis. Established in each society is a 'regime of truth' (Foucault 1980: 133) – that is, the political, economic and institutional mechanisms and procedures that originate, regulate, circulate and distribute statements pertaining to provide accurate descriptions of reality. It is through such a regime that distinctions between true and false statements are made.

The regime of truth is exclusionary in that it places narrow confines on what can be deemed as worthy of attention. Only certain ways of thinking are considered appropriate, and the discursive structure both *rules in* and *rules out* certain ways of interpreting events What becomes constructed as the legitimate interpretation is linked with hierarchies of credibility and power. For knowledge to be utilized the 'knower' must establish a right to speak, as the authority of a statement is linked to the status of the speaker. Not all voices will be heard, and not all speakers are viewed with the same standing or subsequently invested with the ability to provide a 'truthful' account of events and circumstances. It is not just what is said but also who says it. Each statement maps out its present usage and, as each statement leads on to further statements, lays the parameters of what can be said in the future. The statements of official reports are both instrumental in the *production* and *reproduction* of power relations. In other words, they perform a central role in how 'penal truth' (Sim 1994) is institutionalized.

Although official inquiries present themselves as open and 'entirely independent of government' (Keith 2006: 9) and claim to provide a thorough, comprehensive and impartial account, they are not written in a power vacuum. They constitute, and are constituted by, official penal discourse. Official reports are a 'view from above', disseminating authorized knowledge and defining and setting the parameters or scope of a problem and possible means of resolution. As a result, certain ways of conceiving imprisonment are presented as legitimate while others are de-legitimated and effectively defined out or marginalized as 'irrational' social policy options.

For Burton and Carlen (1979: 13, 48), the function of official inquiries is 'primarily to allay, suspend and close off popular doubt' through representing 'failure as temporary, or no failure at all, and to re-establish the image of administrative and legal coherence and rationality'. Through remedying 'legitimacy deficits' (1979: 95), official reports renew or guarantee the authority of the institutions of the capitalist state, performing closure to debate and erasing contesting or critical approaches. They may limit damage by pointing out that, after all, the crises which led to the deployment of the inquiry were not as serious as first thought, or that the failures uncovered are temporary blips that can be easily rectified though new procedural reforms or closer adherence to existing policies.

Yet official reports do not normally provide a whitewash. More likely, they incorporate and rearticulate criticism within official discourses. In this way certain problems and social harms are recontextualized so that their potential to undermine the legitimacy of official penal reality is dramatically curtailed. This being said, official reports cannot address the deeply ingrained crises of moral and political penal illegitimacy. They sidestep such issues by predicating their analysis on individual pathologies or, more progressively, by focusing on institutional cultures rather than locating the prison within its broader socio-economic, political or structural contexts.

In order to analyse official inquiries effectively it is necessary, then, to have an appreciation of how they are influenced by other recent government publications. More specifically, questions should be asked regarding the circumstances in which the report was commissioned: who were the authors and advisers, and what was their depth of expertise? What timescale restraints were imposed? What were the administrative support and legal powers of the inquiry? What were the terms of reference and their interpretation? What was the methodology adopted? What range of people submitted evidence? Which voices were privileged or denied legitimacy? What were the recommendations, and how did they conform or deviate from existing knowledges? What was the response of government?

### The Keith Report

A recent official inquiry that illustrates these themes is the Keith Report, published on 29 June 2006 following the Mubarek Inquiry. This investigated Robert Stewart's violent attack on his 'pad mate', Zahid Mubarek, the night before Zahid was due to be released from Feltham Young Offender Institution. Zahid died eight days later on 28 March 2000. A public inquiry into the events which led up to the murder, and how similar events could be prevented, followed a protracted legal struggle brought by Zahid's uncle, Imtiaz Amin. Though the chairman of the inquiry, Mr Justice Keith, adopted an open methodology, holding public hearings, seminars and focus groups, and undertaking an extensive documentary review, he interpreted the terms of reference in a restrictive way. In a bulky report (volume one was to total 552 pages), Keith maintained that he was not required to 'provide a comprehensive account of all the reasons for any systemic shortcomings which may have contributed to what happened to Zahid' (2006: 32).

Although some prisoner evidence was accepted as reliable, its credibility was generally cast in a negative light. For example, Keith

(2006: 500) stated that, with regards to prisoners detailing previous offences and racist beliefs, '[i]nvariablly what the prisoner says is not reliable … There is no reason to suppose that prisoners always tell the truth'. Some 25 of the 63 chapters in volume one focus on the catalogue of failures to identify or address Stewart's problems. Yet here Keith simply reproduced dominant official discourses, constructing Stewart's racism and violence within medical knowledges and individual pathologies on dangerous and severe personality disorder (DSPD).

The inquiry operated within the official definition of 'institutional racism' adopted by Lord Macpherson in his report on the death of Stephen Lawrence in 1999. Feltham was 'infected' (Keith 2006: 31) with institutional racism, and Keith provided a damning account of the systemic failings of prison staff to adhere to procedural guidelines (when they existed), and the dominance of a culture rooted in indifference and insensitivity to racial and religious differences. Keith recommended expanding the current definition of institutional racism to include 'institutional religious intolerance', though had to confess that this was 'not a topic which the inquiry has investigated' (2006: 546).

The 88 recommendations of the report largely proposed amendments or greater adherence to Prison Service policies, sending a reassuring message that 'much of what would have been recommended is now in place' and that 'many of the systematic shortcomings this report has laid bare have been eliminated' (2006: 443). Keith questioned the evidence of some prison officers, naming and shaming those who he deemed culpable, but was largely supportive of a Prison Service that was doing 'the best it can with the resources its has' (2006: 552). The report created closure, but failed to consider the legitimacy of imprisonment within the exclusionary policies of state racism.

Official reports, then, operate within given regimes of truth, clawing back credibility and legitimacy. Certain explanations, solutions and subjugated knowledges are denied space, while the location of the prison in wider structural fault lines is excluded from analysis, leading to the production of sanctioned knowledges and circumventing acknowledgement of the crises of penal legitimacy.

*David Scott*

### Related entries

*Assaults; Dangerous and severe personality disorder (DSPD); Deaths in custody; Escapes and absconds; HM Inspectorate of Prisons; Independent monitoring boards; Legitimacy; Mubarek Inquiry; Prisons and Probation Ombudsman; Riots (prison); Suicide in prison; Violence; Woolf Report.*

**Key texts and sources**

Burton, F. and Carlen, P. (1979) *Official Discourse: On Discourse Analysis, Government Publications, Ideology and the State.* London: Routledge & Kegan Paul.

Foucault, M. (1972) *The Archaeology of Knowledge.* London: Routledge.

Foucault, M. (1980) 'Truth and power', in C. Gordon (ed.) *Power/Knowledge: Selected Interviews and other Writings, 1972–1977 by Michel Foucault.* London: Longman.

Gilligan, G. and Pratt, J. (eds) (2004) *Crime, Truth and Justice: Official Inquiry, Discourse, Knowledge.* Cullompton: Willan Publishing.

Keith, Justice. (2006) *The Zahid Mubarek Inquiry.* London: HMSO.

Sim, J. (1994) 'Reforming the penal wasteland? A critical review of the Woolf Report', in E. Player and M. Jenkins (eds) *Prisons after Woolf: Reform through Riot.* London: Routledge.

## OPEN PRISONS

Open prisons hold Category D prisoners in conditions of minimal security.

The first British open prison was established at New Hall Camp in 1933. There are currently 19 open prisons in England and Wales, of which four are women's prisons and, in total, 6 per cent of the prison population (4,500) is held in open conditions. The rationale of the open prison regime lay in the belief that, by allowing prisoners more interaction with the community, open prisons would provide the opportunity of 'returning offenders to their families and communities as productive citizens' (Morris and Rotham 1998: 196). Sir Alexander Paterson (a member of the Prison Commission from 1922 to 1947) encapsulates this sentiment in his famous aphorism: 'You cannot train a man for freedom under conditions of captivity' (Morris and Rotham 1998: 332).

In 1966 Lord Mountbatten recommended that every prisoner should be placed in one of four security categories. Category D is those prisoners who could be trusted in open conditions. Thus open prisons are suitable only for those who present minimum security risk and are unlikely to abuse by misbehaviour the degree of freedom available there. For example, Ford Prison has become renowned for accommodating 'celebrity prisoners' and white-collar criminals, including George Best (who served three months for a drink-driving offence), Jeffery Archer and the Guinness trio of Gerald Ronson, Ernest Saunders and Anthony Parnes.

The precise reasons for establishing open prisons remain a topic of debate, and their role is subject to regular scrutiny. In 1979 and then again in 1996, the open prison estate was subject to review relating to their role, purpose and function. The first recommendation in the 1996 review was to provide a definitive statement of the purpose of open prisons: 'Providing the opportunity to deal with less serious offenders in conditions that are less damaging to the prisoner and at the least cost to the public purse' (Newell 1996: 16). Open prison regimes developed on the basis of individual governors and their view about what was appropriate. This has produced institutions that are diverse in approach and in the range of facilities on offer (Newell 1996: 13).

Controversially, due to the increasing prison population and overcrowding in the prison estate, open prison are receiving more prisoners in the middle stages of sentences. This threatens the type of prisoners traditionally received and challenges the role of the open prison.

*Azrini Wahidin and David Wilson*

*Related entries*

*Categorization and allocation; Celebrity prisoners; Escapes and absconds; Overcrowding.*

### Key texts and sources

Morris, N. and Rotham, D. (1998) *The Oxford History of the Prison.* Oxford: Oxford University Press.
Newell, M. (1996) *The Open Prison Review.* London: HMSO.

## ORDER AND CONTROL

Order and control are both relative concepts. In this context, order refers to a relatively stable set of relationships which most participants find acceptable and worth maintaining. Control refers to measures available, usually to staff, to help maintain or restore order, some of which form the parameters of the daily routine, but others may be introduced as circumstances dictate (i.e. when a control problem has arisen).

The problem of order and control is closely related to, and has often been conflated with, the problem of security. In much of the early literature on prisons and in many official reports on these problems, it was considered that the 'causes' of the problems of security and control were essentially the same – that certain prisoners, especially dangerous and long-term prisoners, would not only be the most likely to attempt to escape and abscond but also the most difficult to control (the 'rotten apple' theory). Indeed, the dispersal policy, implemented following the recommendations of the Radzinowicz Report in 1968, was predicated upon such a belief, dispersing high-risk prisoners among several prisons rather than concentrating them in a single institution, in the expectation that this would 'dilute' the control problem. It did not do so and many of the dispersal prisons quickly became the locations of major riots and disturbances which continued through the 1970s and 1980s.

In reality, although the issues of security and control sometimes empirically coincide, more frequently they do not. Thus, empirically, there are *some* prisoners who constitute both security and control problems but there are also many potentially dangerous prisoners, whom one would not wish to escape, who present no control problems at all. Equally, there are large numbers – often young men in prison serving short sentences in conditions of low security – who may in some circumstances create control problems but who might never think of trying to escape. The problems are analytically separable and, depending on the way the problems are analysed, may lead to different policy solutions.

In the USA control problems have typically been regarded as a matter of individual responsibility on the part of prisoners and used to be dealt with by transfers around the mainstream prison system ('smelling diesel'). Now, however, those whom wardens regard as the 'worst of the worst' are more often transferred to lockdown control units or, more recently, to highly restrictive supermax prisons where, allegedly, 'bad behaviour gets you in and good behaviour gets you out' – policies that raise significant questions about human rights and the mental health of those incarcerated. In England and Wales control problems were similarly traditionally regarded as matters of individual and local responsibility: those regarded as unmanageable were transferred from segregation unit to segregation unit on what was known officially as the Continuous Assessment Scheme (but to staff and prisoners as the 'magic roundabout' or 'merry-go-round'). In 1974, in response to disturbances in the dispersal prisons, there was a brief flirtation with American-style control units, which were established at Wormwood Scrubs and Wakefield Prisons, but one was hardly used and the other quickly abandoned after concerns about possible sensory deprivation.

Since 1984, with the *Report of the Control Review Committee* (Home Office 1984) established in the wake of further riots in dispersal prisons, it has been increasingly recognized that control problems are a product of several variables, including the individual characteristics of prisoners, the circumstances in which they are held and the way they are managed by staff. It has also been recognized that a significant number of prisoners who are difficult to manage suffer from what is now called dangerous and severe personality disorders (DSPD). A system of Control Review Committee (CRC) small units attempted to provide different regimes for different types of prisoners: one was an avowedly 'structured' regime based on 'carrot-and-stick' principles, but others offered psychiatric and psychological support. A proposed unit which might have followed a model analogous to that pioneered at Barlinnie in Scotland, involving degrees of self-governance, was never established. The CRC units constituted an interesting experiment but were seen as remote and had little impact on the wider system. The small unit concept, however, was not abandoned, and the CRC units evolved into what are now called close supervision centres (CSCs), which were reorganized on a more systematic basis with the intention that prisoners would progress from more restricted to less restricted regimes before a return to the mainstream. This was linked in part to the philosophy of incentives and earned privileges and indicated a partial return to the individual responsibility model but without losing sight of the need to develop positive programmes. The CSC system has gone through several stages of development and, following criticism from HM Chief Inspectorate of Prisons highlighting the need for better and earlier diagnosis of mental health problems, now operates on the basis of individual sentence plans, which in theory at least provide different regimes tailored to individual needs. As currently constituted, the CSC system comprises three units at Woodhill Prison operating restricted, structured and programmed regimes; one at Wakefield Prison where exceptional risk prisoners are segregated; and one at Whitemoor Prison offering a more open regime, with an assessment centre at Long Lartin Prison. The programmed unit at Woodhill piloted a violence reduction programme now operated from Whitemoor and, at the time of writing, the CSC system is being recast as part of a broader violence reduction strategy which also takes account of prisoners who are diagnosed with DSPD.

Conceptually, our understanding of the nature of order and control has advanced in recent years. In the two decades following the Second World War it was assumed that staff and prisoners reached some kind of 'accommodation' which enabled them to live together more or less peaceably. As we have seen, in the 1960s Radzinowicz conflated the issues of security and control, and his policy of dispersing security risks in order to dilute potential control problems foundered, intellectually if not quite literally, as riots and disturbances spread and persisted in most, but not all, of the dispersals. The CRC became the first official body to begin to separate the issues of security and control, to recognize that prisoners who were control problems in some situations were not in others and to advocate an alternative to dispersal policy. But the CRC also marked a watershed because it opened up the system to outside opinion and research through the establishment of a research and advisory group. One of the most important products of that initiative was the conceptually sophisticated study by Sparks et al. (1996) of Albany, one of the most riot and disturbance prone of the dispersal prisons, and Long Lartin, one of the very few which had not achieved notoriety in that regard. However, their study did not uphold the easy conclusion which the CRC might have expected: that somehow Long Lartin, having been free of riots throughout its history, would have some replicable formula for success and be regarded as 'good' by staff and prisoners, whereas Albany, with its history of repeated riots, would possess identifiable features to avoid that would be regarded as 'bad' by staff and prisoners. It was not like that. Whereas by the time of their research Albany had adopted a fairly rigid 'situational' approach to maintain order, essentially by reducing opportunities for disorder, Long Lartin adopted a more 'social' approach, developing a relatively relaxed climate based on interpersonal relationships.

Although Long Lartin was popular with prisoners and Albany was unpopular, in fact there were hidden benefits at Albany and problems just below the surface at Long Lartin. Despite their very different approaches, *both* prisons now maintained a kind of order. If situational and social control seem to define the ends of a continuum of possible styles in England and Wales, however, it should be noted that there are many other possibilities to be found in other, less developed societies.

Any residual power in the 'rotten apple' theory was dispelled when riots and disturbances occurred in low-security prisons, local prisons and remand centres during the late 1980s, culminating in the riot at Strangeways Prison in Manchester in 1990. The Woolf Report (Home Office 1991) concluded that the key requirement for stability and order in prisons was that security, control and justice should be held in a proper balance. Research by King and McDermott had already demonstrated the deterioration of regimes across all types of prison since 1970, and the study by Sparks et al. not yet fully published, found that issues of fairness and consistency (akin to Woolf's notion of justice) were central to whether prisoners regarded regimes as legitimate. Taking the concept of legitimacy beyond the traditional Weberian understanding based simply on *belief in the appropriate authority*, Sparks et al. (1996) insisted that, for regimes to be regarded as legitimate, they must also be *morally justifiable*. In this sense, they argued that neither Albany nor Long Lartin was fully successful in establishing the legitimacy of its regime, even though both provided a kind of order.

*Roy D. King*

### Related entries

*Barlinnie; Close supervision centres; Dangerous and severe personality disorder (DSPD); Escapes and absconds; Fairness; HM Inspectorate of Prisons; Human rights; Incentives and earned privileges (IEP); Legitimacy; Long-term prisoners; Mental health; Official reports; Riots (prison); Security; Supermax prisons; Violence reduction; Woolf Report; Young men in prison.*

**Key texts and sources**

HMCIP (2006) *Extreme Custody: A Thematic Inspection of Close Supervision Centres and High Security Segregation.* London: HMSO.

Home Office (1984) *Managing the Long-term Prison System: The Report of the Control Review Committee.* London: HMSO.

Woolf, Lord Justice and Tumin, S. (1991) *Prison Disturbances, April 1990* (cm 1456). London: HMSO.

King, R.D. (2007) 'Security, control and the problems of containment', in Y. Jewkes (ed.) *Handbook on Prisons.* Cullompton: Willan Publishing.

King, R.D. and Morgan, R. (1980) *The Future of the Prison System.* Farnborough: Gower.

Sparks, R., Bottoms, A.E. and Hay, W. (1996) *Prisons and the Problem of Order.* Oxford: Clarendon Press.

# OVERCROWDING

Overcrowding occurs where prisons hold more prisoners than they are designed to accommodate.

What constitutes overcrowding in the prison context varies dramatically from country to country. In some countries in Eastern Europe and Central Asia it may mean up to one hundred prisoners spending most of their days and nights in rooms that might comfortably hold 30 or so prisoners. There will be one bed for every three prisoners, each taking a turn of eight hours to sleep, with the strongest sleeping during the night and the weakest required to sleep in the daytime and then standing or sitting as best he can during the rest of the day and night. Prisoners in one country in sub-Saharan Africa have described how they sleep in up to five batches: while one batch sleeps for four hours on the floor, the others stand around the walls of the cell waiting for their turn.

In prisons in England and Wales, the vast majority of sleeping accommodation for prisoners is intended for single occupancy. However, for many years the rising number of prisoners has meant that two and sometimes three prisoners have had to live in cells intended for one person. The Prison Service annual report, 2005–6, indicated that 23.7 per cent of prisoners

were held in accommodation intended for fewer prisoners. In local prisons for adult males, that proportion rose to 49 per cent.

Even when two prisoners are sharing a cell designed to hold one person, this is not always described as overcrowding. There are no specific criteria about what should be the minimum amount of cell space for one person. The Prison Act 1952 requires that 'no cell shall be used for the confinement of a prisoner unless it is certified by an inspector that its size, lighting, heating, ventilation and fittings are adequate for health'. In practice this certification is provided by the Prison Service area manager, who reaches an agreement with prison governors about what is known as the level of 'certified normal accommodation' (CNA). This figure is reached by a process of negotiation, based on the number of single or multiple-occupation cells. The CNA was used to define the number of prisoners to be held in a prison. When the current pressure on prison places began in the early 1990s, the Prison Service initially coped with it by redefining capacity. Overnight, cells which had been built to hold one prisoner were said to be capable of holding two persons. A new classification of 'operational capacity' was introduced. This was 'a safe level of overcrowding', and the Prison Service only accepts that a prison is beyond its capacity when the number of prisoners goes above the operational capacity.

In the report following its visit to the UK in 2003, the European Committee for the Prevention of Torture expressed concern at the way the Prison Service defined its capacity:

*A new Prison Service order sets out the cell occupancy levels which can be certified for operational capacity. In the CPT's opinion, the cell capacities approved by the Prison Service are too high; in particular, placing two persons in cells measuring as little as 6.5 m², including the sanitary facilities, cannot be considered acceptable. European Committee for the Prevention of Torture, Inhuman or degrading Treatment or Punishment (2005) Report to the Government of the United Kingdom of the Visit to the United Kingdom and the Isle of Man carried out by the European Committee for the Prevention of Torture, Inhuman or Degrading Treatment or Punishment from 12–23 May 2003 Strasbourg: CPT: 18*

Furthermore, the Prison Rules make clear that cells were intended primarily as 'sleeping accommodation' (Rule 26). The expectation was that prisoners would spend the bulk of each day out of their cells, involved in work, education or training. The current reality, as recorded regularly in the reports of HM Inspectorate of Prisons, is that the bulk of prisoners spend the vast majority of each 24-hour period locked in their cells. A former director general of the Prison Service has described graphically what this means in practice:

*The conditions in which prisoners have to live in overcrowded cells, cells in which they have to eat together and in which they have to defecate in front of one another are we know deeply inadequate ... but where we unnecessarily allow prisoners to languish in doubled up cells nearly all day and every day, the inadequate becomes the unacceptable (Martin Narey, Prison Service conference, February 2003).*

The consequences of overcrowding do not only affect living accommodation. If a prison is holding more than 75 or 80 per cent people than it was designed for, as some of the most overcrowded prisons are, there will be tremendous pressure on basic facilities, such as the kitchen, the laundry, utilities and sewage systems (Coyle 2005). Prisoners' access to constructive activities, such as education, work and training, will be severely limited, partly because of lack of facilities and partly because staffing levels are likely to be based on the design capacity of the prison rather than the actual number. The consequences will also be felt by the families of prisoners since access to visits will be reduced, both in terms of quantity and quality.

There are two obvious methods of dealing with prison overcrowding: to provide more prison spaces or to reduce the number of prisoners (International Centre for Prison Studies 2004). No jurisdiction in the world has ever built its way out of prison overcrowding. Sir Alexander Paterson recognized this in the early years of the twentieth century when he wrote: 'Wherever prisons are built, Courts will make use of them. If no prison is handy, some other way of dealing with the offender will possibly be discovered'. The increase in prison numbers has happened in an era during which, by any measurement, overall crime has been falling. This makes no sense. What a previous Lord Chief Justice described as 'the cancer of overcrowding' also prevents the Prison Service from fulfilling its stated objective of providing 'safe and well-ordered establishments' in which prisoners are treated 'humanely, decently and lawfully'.

*Vivien Stern*

### Related entries

*Certified normal accommodation (CNA); European Committee for the Prevention of Torture and Inhuman or Degrading Treatment or Punishment (ECPT); HM Inspectorate of Prisons; Local prisons; Prison Act; Prison population; Prison Rules.*

### Key texts and sources

Committee for the Prevention of Torture (2000) *11th General Report on the CPT's Activities.* Strasbourg: Council of Europe.

Council of Europe (1999) *Recommendation No. R (99) 22 of the Committee of Ministers to Member States Concerning Prison Overcrowding and Prison Population Inflation.* Strasbourg: Council of Europe.

Coyle, A. (2005) *Understanding Prisons: Key Issues in Policy and Practice.* Milton Keynes: Open University Press.

International Centre for Prison Studies (2004) *Guidance Note 4 on Prison Reform: Dealing with Prison Overcrowding.* London: International Centre for Prison Studies.

Ruck, S.K. (1951) *Paterson on Prisons: Being the Collected Papers of Sir Alexander Paterson.* London: Frederick Muller.

See also the Prison Reform Trust's website (**http://www.prisonreformtrust.org.uk/**).

# P

## PANOPTICON

The Panopticon was an architectural concept proposed by Jeremy Bentham in the late eighteenth century. It was subsequently used by Michel Foucault as illustrative of the movement of the target of modern punishment from the body of the offender to his or her 'soul'.

### Panopticon as architectural concept

The idea for the Panopticon arose from Bentham's 1787 trip to St Petersburg. He was there to visit his brother, Sir Samuel Bentham, who was working for Prince Potemkin. Samuel had designed a textile mill for the prince's estate. It was a two-storey, circular building. The centre was occupied by an inspector's lodge. Workstations radiated out from this central point and could be partitioned off from one another. Workers would sit with their backs to the centre and the centre itself was obscured from view. Peepholes allowed whoever stood in the inspector's lodge to observe the workers, but the observers could not themselves be seen. Jeremy Bentham saw the utility in this 'Inspection House' or 'Elabatory' for a range of institutions: hospitals, schools and, of course, the prison.

Bentham first developed a Panopticon prison design for a competition in the *St James Chronicle* for a new prison to be located in Middlesex. The plans on which he collaborated with the architect, William Reveley, were published as *Panopticon; or The Inspection House* in 1791. The proposed building consisted of six storeys with a span of between 100 and 180 feet. The lodge at the centre was replaced with an observation tower. An arrangement of galleries would allow guards to look into the cells that were positioned on the building's circumference, unobserved. In turn, the head-keeper could watch the guards through peepholes from the central tower. In these designs, it was proposed that there be up to four prisoners in each cell.

The Panopticon was premised on the duality of the seen and 'not seen'. The prisoner would be perpetually on display, the guard perpetually obscured. The individual in the cell would come to take on the dual role of prisoner and guard. Never knowing if they were *actually* being observed, the prisoners would internalize the surveillant gaze of the guard and modify their behaviour accordingly. The Panopticon design, Bentham believed, would thus have profound effects: 'Morals reformed – health preserved – industry invigorated – instruction diffused'. In contrast, Henry Bougham, a Whig MP, referred to it as 'a scheme absolutely and perfectly vicious in principle'.

Following the recommendation of prison reformers of the period, such as John Howard, Bentham suggested that members of the public be allowed to view the workings of the prison. The 1791 drawings depict a public gallery located above the central office thereby adding a further layer of surveillance. It was Bentham himself who would act as contractor *and* operator. However, it was not to be. After initial interest in the construction of a Panopticon in Paris in 1791, Bentham encouraged the British Home Secretary, Henry Dundas, to approve its construction. In 1784 an Act was passed which allowed for the purchase of a site and for a contract to run the prison, but it would take until 1799 for the land to be acquired and, in 1811, the project was officially abandoned. A governmental committee was concerned that the system by which the Panopticon's operators profited from prisoners' labour could be abused. Such abuse of 'farming' had plagued previous generations of prisons. The site was subsequently used for the construction of the equally ill-starred Millbank Penitentiary. The 'simple idea in architecture' that Bentham had trumpeted had proved markedly more complicated in practice.

While no buildings have been built that were precisely mimetic to Bentham and Riveley's plans, we see conceptual echoes of the Panopticon in a number of prison designs. The Isle of Pines Prison in Cuba and the Illinois State Penitentiary, otherwise known as Stateville, both possess distinctive circular buildings. The Panopticon's influence came instead through its potency as a metaphor.

### Panopticon as metaphor

In *Discipline and Punish*, Foucault (1977) uses the Panopticon to explore the coming together of power, knowledge and the body. The opening of the book juxtaposes the grisly details of a regicide's execution in 1757 with the precise timetable of a prison in Paris some 80 years later. The two passages graphically illustrate the contrast in forms of punishment between the early modern and modern periods. It is not intended to indicate a sense of progression or improvement; rather, that the techniques of power had shifted. The modern prison then was not a site of spectacular vengeance but of transformation, of discipline. Indeed, the Panopticon was a 'compact model of the disciplinary mechanism' (Foucault 1977: 197). Through a 'certain concerted distribution of bodies, surfaces, lights [and] gazes' power flows through the architectural machinery of the Panopticon (1977: 202). The Panopticon afforded individualized treatment, containment and observation. As such, the architectural configuration of the Panopticon entailed that the 'power relations involved [were], in a sense, automated and objective' (Garland 1990: 146).

The notion of 'panopticism' extends beyond the walls of the Panopticon itself. The surveillance and disciplinary techniques described by Foucault could be found in buildings that had little resemblance to the Panopticon. These networks of power – frequently characterized as constituting a *carceral society* – did not need a Panopticon to operate. Contemporary writers have subsequently questioned the applicability of the Panopticon metaphor and instead highlight the dichotomy of the Panopticon and Synopticon. Mathiesen (1997) used the terms 'synopticon' and 'synopticism' to describe a 'viewer society'. It is no longer simply the few that watch the many but also the many that watch the few. However, if, as Jay (1992) suggests, modernity itself was characterized by scopophilia, the desire to *see*, then the Panopticon would have been a perfect exemplar of the modern prison.

*Michael Fiddler*

### Related entries

*Carceral society; Discipline; Howard, John; Power.*

**Key texts and sources**

Foucault, M. (1977) *Discipline and Punish*. London: Allen Lane.
Garland, D. (1990) *Punishment and Modern Society*. Oxford: Clarendon Press.
Jay, M. (1992) 'Scopic regimes of modernity', in S. Lash and J. Friedman (eds) *Modernity and Identity*. Oxford: Blackwell.
Mathiesen, T. (1997) 'The viewer society: Michel Foucault's "Panopticon" revisited', *Theoretical Criminology*, 1: 215–34.

## PARAMILITARY PRISONERS

Paramilitary prisoners are members of paramilitary organizations who have been incarcerated for actions in pursuit of their organization's goals and objectives. The term is used to describe members of a wide variety of armed or military-like groups, including FARC and ELN in Colombia; EZLN in Mexico; Hamas, Hezbollah and Fatah in the Middle East; ETA in Spain; and the IRA and Loyalist factions in Northern Ireland.

The term 'paramilitary prisoners' traditionally refers to those prisoners who are members of revolutionary or guerrilla organizations formed in order to fight the current government of a country or region or other paramilitary groups. Often these prisoners are categorized as terrorists by those who oppose their political ideology and methods and by the state which imprisons them. Definitions tend to be ideological and pejorative: few more so than 'terrorism'. The task of distinguishing between 'terrorism', 'guerrilla warfare', 'political violence' and other related behaviours is problematic for reasons other than conceptual and technical difficulties. Each of these descriptive terms makes evaluative judgements about the actors' motivations, their relationship with the wider society and the legitimacy of their actions.

After conducting international research on paramilitary prisoners, Gormally and McEvoy (1995) adopted the more neutral term of 'politically motivated prisoners'. In many cases paramilitary prisoners claiming allegiance to paramilitary groupings consider themselves political prisoners, but this categorization has been a major source of conflict itself. For example, in Northern Ireland prisoners incarcerated in relation to the conflict and referred to as paramilitary prisoners constantly fought for political recognition. Moreover, there were periods throughout the conflict when the political nature of paramilitary prisoners received informal recognition. The most explicit recognition came with the 'special category status' granted to prisoners convicted of terrorist crimes between 1972 and 1975. These prisoners were held in segregated accommodation away from 'ordinary' prisoners and prisoners of opposing paramilitary groups. Essentially, the prisoners put in place military-style command structures and were granted free association, were permitted to wear their own clothes and were allowed to hold educational lectures. In 1976, the British government 'phased out' special category status, introducing a policy of 'criminalization' recommending that no prisoner convicted of 'terrorist' type offences should be entitled to special category status. This policy led to confrontation by way of 'blanket protests', 'dirty protests' and the hunger strikes of 1980 and 1981, which culminated in the deaths of ten prisoners. Although the British government never formally granted paramilitary prisoners in Northern Ireland political status, it is argued that they received *de facto* political status (McEvoy 2001; McEvoy *et al.* 2007). Following the hunger strikes in 1980–1, special category privileges were restored, which was followed by the segregation of prisoners according to political affiliation in 1992 and, finally, the early-release provisions for 'qualifying' prisoners under the terms of the Good Friday Agreement 1998 (Dwyer 2004).

*Clare Dwyer*

### Related entries

*Legitimacy; Political prisoners; 'War on terror'.*

**Key texts and sources**

Dwyer, C. (2004) 'The complexity of imprisonment: the Northern Ireland experience', *Cambrian Law Review*, 35: 97–114.

Gormally, B. and McEvoy, K. (1995) *Release and Reintegration of Politically Motivated Prisoners in Northern Ireland: A Comparative Study of South Africa, Israel/Palestine, Italy, Spain, the Republic of Ireland and Northern Ireland*. Belfast: NIACRO.

McEvoy, K. (2001) *Paramilitary Imprisonment in Northern Ireland: Resistance, Management and Release*. Oxford: Oxford University Press.

McEvoy, K., McConnachie, K. and Jamieson, R. (2007) 'Political imprisonment and the "War on terror"', in Y. Jewkes (ed.) *Handbook on Prisons*. Cullompton: Willan Publishing.

The report into the separation of paramilitary prisoners at Maghaberry Prison is available online at http://www.parliament.the-stationery-office.co.uk/pa/cm200304/cmselect/cmniaf/302/302.pdf. See also the Northern Ireland Prison Service's website (http://www.niprisonservice.gov.uk/).

# PAROLE

Parole is a system for the early release of prisoners serving medium or long-term sentences on a risk-assessed and supervised basis, with the threat of recall to prison.

Parole, a system for the early release of medium and long-term prisoners, was first introduced in the Criminal Justice Act 1967. While prisoners had usually been released on remission without serving the whole of their sentence in custody, parole formalized the arrangement and allowed release at an earlier stage, as well as including arrangements for supervision in the community up to the normal point at which the prisoner would have been released on remission. Parole had two main aims: first, to relieve the pressure of the growing prison population; and, secondly, to maximize the potential for offender rehabilitation (Coyle 2005).

Prisoners were eligible for parole after serving one third of their sentence or 12 months, whichever was longer. This meant, in effect, that prisoners serving 18 months or more would be eligible for parole. There was a three-tier process. The initial recommendation would be made at a prison by a local review committee. This would then be considered by the national Probation Board, who would make a recommendation regarding suitability for release. The final decision would then be taken by the Home Secretary although, in routine cases, this decision was made by an official acting on his behalf. The process was relatively restrictive and, in the early years, only a quarter of eligible prisoners were released (Cavadino and Dignan 2007). During the 1970s, Home Secretary Roy Jenkins encouraged greater use of parole, particularly for less serious offenders, and consequently early release grew.

In 1983 and 1984, three major changes in practice were introduced. First, those serving over five years for sexual, drug or violence offences or arson would only be released in exceptional circumstances. Secondly, certain life-sentence prisoners would only be released after serving 20 years in custody. Thirdly, eligibility for parole was reduced to six months in custody. These changes reflected the emerging practice of bifurcation, where less serious offenders are managed in less restrictive ways while more serious offenders are dealt with more punitively. However, this policy was also pragmatic, encouraging the release of less serious offenders in order to relieve the pressure of growing prison

numbers. During the 1980s, approximately 60 per cent of those eligible were released on parole (Cavadino and Dignan 2007).

Continued concern about the system led to the establishment of a widespread review led by Lord Carlisle, the major recommendations of which were implemented in the Criminal Justice Act 1991. This introduced the main elements of the new early-release schemes. Under the proposals, prisoners serving less than four years in custody would be automatically released early. Discretionary release would be available to those serving four years or more in custody. They would be eligible for parole between the halfway and two-third point of their sentence, at which stage they would be automatically released. These reforms changed parole in three further important respects. First, the process was streamlined by removing the local review committee and giving the Home Secretary power to approve – or veto – parole decisions for those serving long prison sentences. Secondly, the criteria for release were clearly established, and the Home Secretary was given delegated authority to set appropriate conditions. Thirdly, prisoners were given rights to make representations regarding parole decisions, thus providing some degree of procedural fairness and transparency.

The rate of release has fluctuated over the last decade from 36 per cent at its lowest point in 1996–7, to 53 per cent in 2002–3 and 2003–4 (Parole Board 2006). However, the parole system can be vulnerable to political, media and public pressure. For example, the system came in for considerable criticism following two high-profile murders committed by parolees in 2006, which resulted in a dramatic drop in the granting of parole (Anon 2006). The reduction in releases along with increasing use of recalls can form a back door to imprisonment, contributing to the high, and increasing, prison population.

Parole continues to be an important part of the prison system, both in terms of improving effectiveness and more pragmatically in helping to manage the prison population. However, it has consistently been dogged by criticism, both on the basis of individual high-profile cases and a more general criticism that early-release schemes mean that the public are misled or short-changed regarding prison sentences.

*Jamie Bennett*

### Related entries

*Bifurcation; Desistance; Early-release schemes; Probation Service; Recall; Rehabilitation.*

---

**Key texts and sources**

Anon (2006) 'Fewer life prisoners released on parole', *Guardian*, 6 November (available online at **http://www.guardian.co.uk/crime/article/ 0,,1940808,00.html**).

Cavadino, M. and Dignan, J. (2007) *The Penal Crisis: An Introduction* (4th edn). London: Sage.

Coyle, A. (2005) *Understanding Prisons: Key Issues in Policy and Practice*. Maidenhead: Open University Press.

Parole Board (2006) *Annual Report and Accounts of the Parole Board for England and Wales, 2005–6*. London: HMSO.

See also the Parole Board's website (**http://www. paroleboard.gov.uk/**).

---

# PENAL CRISIS

The 'penal crisis' is a shorthand phrase used to refer to the parlous state of the penal system, encapsulating a combination of severe problems (or 'crises'), including high and rising numbers of prisoners; overcrowding and squalid conditions in prisons; unrest among prison staff and inmates; escapes, riots and disorder; an overworked and demoralized Probation Service; a lack of strategic direction; and general 'crises' of penal resources and 'legitimacy'.

### Penal crisis or a series of penal crises?

Should the term 'penal crisis' be applied to penal systems such as that of England and Wales? One view is that, in the words of former Director General of the Prison Service, Richard Tilt, there is no crisis 'but there are some very serious problems which may well get worse'

(1998: 13). But why not describe such a state of affairs as a 'crisis'? Is it just a matter of semantics (or terminological fetishism)?

It can be argued that it is (paradoxically) the very enduring and chronic nature of the penal system's problems that makes the word 'crisis' inappropriate. We think of a crisis as something that comes to a head, followed alternatively by disaster, defusal or subsidence, not as something that rumbles on for decades. Yet there has been persistent discussion of a crisis, at least since 1970 (see Fitzgerald and Sim 1982: ch. 1). Fitzgerald and Sim (1982: 3) even claim that 'the prison system in Britain has been in a perpetual state of crisis since the Gladstone Committee report of 1895'. If to be in crisis means that the whole system is on the brink of total collapse or explosion, then there is probably no crisis. But there may be a crisis in two senses identified by Morris (1989: 125). First, we have 'a state of affairs that is so acute as to constitute a danger' and, secondly, the penal system may be at a *critical juncture*, much as a seriously ill person may reach a 'turning point at which the patient either begins to improve or sinks into a fatal decline'. Such a 'state of affairs' could be a relatively long-lasting phenomenon.

Alternatively, we can think of the penal system as not in a constant state of crisis but with a permanent tendency to throw up *recurring* crises, typically and repeatedly followed by inadequate official attempts to diagnose and cure the problems. Fitzgerald and Sim (1982: 3) refer to a 'pattern of crisis–partial inquiry–crisis–partial inquiry'. Ultimately, it may be a matter of choice and preference whether to use the 'C' word. Using it carries overtones of drama and urgency surrounding the state of the penal system; those who are concerned to avoid alarmism prefer to use other language.

### Competing accounts

Whether or not we call it a 'crisis', there exist different 'accounts' of its nature and causes, variants of which underlie much discourse about penal matters. The *orthodox account* is presupposed by much media reportage and, at least until the Woolf Report (Woolf and Tumin 1991), versions of it were also regularly found in official reports on prison riots and disturbances. This account locates the crisis specifically within the prison system rather than in the whole penal system or any wider context. The high prison population, overcrowding, bad prison conditions, understaffing, unrest among prison staff and poor security are seen as interacting with a 'toxic mix' of different types of difficult prisoners, leading to riots and other break-downs of order and control in prisons.

Cavadino and Dignan (2007: ch. 1) criticize the orthodox account for ignoring the wider contexts of the crisis, for not fitting the facts (for example, when and where prison riots occur), for its 'positivistic' nature and for omit-ting vital factors: most importantly, the realm of *ideology*, which encompasses the beliefs and moral reactions of human actors (including prisoners and other 'penal subjects'). Notably, the orthodox account ignores the sense of injus-tice among prisoners which Woolf saw as fundamental to an understanding of prison riots. Cavadino and Dignan – drawing on the work of Bottoms (1980), Hall (1980), Fitzgerald and Sim (1982) and Woolf and Tumin (1991) – proffer an alternative 'radical pluralist' account, in which material and ideological factors are seen as interacting to create a crisis (or a set of interlocking 'crises'). On the material side, there is a general *crisis of penal resources*, largely gen-erated by the high prison population. On the ideological side, the penal system suffers from a generalized *crisis of legitimacy*. Legitimacy is power that is perceived as being morally justi-fied, and the penal system is lacking in such justification in the eyes of many, including pris-oners, prison staff, politicians and members of the public. On the one hand, some feel that the system is inhumane and unfair to penal sub-jects; on the other, many feel (or are led to believe) that it is, on the contrary, over-lenient, lax and insecure. On both sides the system may be seen as inefficient and hopelessly ineffective at controlling crime and protecting the public. This 'crisis of legitimacy' is seen as the source of the visible problems of the penal system, includ-ing riots, political and industrial relations problems and a crisis in the Probation Service.

In turn, the most important factor in fuelling the penal crisis is sentencing policy, which Cavadino and Dignan describe as 'the crux of the crisis' (2007: ch. 4). Excessive, inconsistent and increasingly harsh sentencing is seen as the main cause both of the high and rising prison popula-tion (and therefore of the crisis of resources) and of the sense of injustice felt by penal subjects (and therefore of the crisis of legitimacy), and also of many additional crises that afflict the penal system. All these crises are exacerbated by an absence of strategic planning and direction on the part of both the government and the penal services. This is reflected in an ongoing failure to address the various crises and an excessive preoc-cupation instead with a host of short-term micro-managerial concerns relating to the setting of standards and measuring performance outputs while ignoring the many negative outcomes asso-ciated with current penal policies.

### International comparisons

Penal crises were studied in an international and comparative context by Cavadino and Dignan (2006), who examined the penal systems of 12 different countries for signs of 'crisis'. They found that the kind of penal crisis that has become familiar in England and Wales in recent decades was far from universal. It was generally associated, not surprisingly, with high and rap-idly rising levels of imprisonment. These in turn were most likely to be found in countries with *neoliberal* political economies, which include the USA, Britain, Australia, New Zealand and South Africa – countries where an individualistic cul-ture went along with a punitive mentality and a resulting tendency to penal crisis. Less prone to such crises were the *conservative corporatist* countries (such as Germany), where a more communitarian culture fostered a belief in the re-socialization of offenders and a more lenient penality. Lower again on the scale were the Nordic *social democracies* such as Sweden and Finland, where communitarianism and egalitar-ianism combined to promote a lower prison population and less tendency to crisis. Japan (described as *oriental corporatist*, the most com-munitarian society studied) had the lowest imprisonment rate and lacked many facets associated with the penal crisis experienced in other countries, though it is not entirely crisis-free by any means. However, there has been a very general international tendency (linked with 'globalization') for societies of all kinds to move in the general direction of neoliberalism – with its associated harsh penality – in recent decades, leading to some signs of penal crisis arising even in countries like Sweden (see New punitiveness). If such trends continue, the outlook for penal systems throughout the world could be bleak.

*Michael Cavadino and James Dignan*

### Related entries

*Industrial relations; Legitimacy; New punitiveness; Official reports; Order and control; Overcrowding; Power; Prison population; Probation Service; Riots (prison); Security; Sentencing policy; Woolf Report.*

#### Key texts and sources

Bottoms, A.E. (1980) 'An introduction to "the coming crisis"', in A.E. Bottoms and R.H. Preston (eds) *The Coming Penal Crisis: A Criminological and Theological Exploration.* Edinburgh: Scottish Academic Press.
Cavadino, M. and Dignan, J. (2006) *Penal Systems: A Comparative Approach.* London: Sage.
Cavadino, M. and Dignan, J. (2007) *The Penal System: An Introduction* (4th edn). London: Sage.
Fitzgerald, M. and Sim, J. (1982) *British Prisons* (2nd edn). Oxford: Blackwell.
Hall, S. (1980) *Drifting into a Law and Order Society.* London: Cobden Trust.
Morris, T. (1989) *Crime and Criminal Justice since 1945.* Oxford: Blackwell.
Tilt, R. (1998) *Howard League Magazine*, November: 13.
Woolf, Lord Justice and Tumin, S. (1991) *Prison Disturbances, April 1990* (Cm 1456). London: HMSO.

## PERFORMANCE MANAGEMENT

Performance management describes the system for setting targets and measuring delivery in an integrated way, from the whole organization, to business units and, ultimately, to individuals.

Performance management describes an integrated system that creates a circular flow of target setting and feedback on delivery from the organization to individual employees. Prisons, in common with other organizations, have formalized business planning and individual appraisal systems that, in theory, are linked. However, what is distinct about prisons is the model used to manage the performance of individual establishments (Laming 2000). This model describes performance in three areas: output, process and quality. 'Output' is concerned with quantitative performance measures, known as key performance indicators and key performance targets (KPIs and KPTs). 'Process' describes performance against audit standards across a range of areas. 'Quality' describes more qualitative assessments, including independent monitoring boards, HM Inspectorate of Prisons reports and the results of prisoner surveys, known as Measuring the Quality of Prison Life (MQPL). The performance of a prison can only be captured if the full range of measures is taken into account.

Subsequently, this information has been used to assess prison performance. On the basis of this, each prison, both public and privately operated, is awarded a performance rating, which could be described as a 'star rating' system. The four ratings are as follows:

- *Level 4*: exceptionally high performing, consistently meeting or exceeding targets, no significant operating problems, achieving significantly more than similar establishments with similar resources. At the end of 2006, there were 27 prisons at Level 4, one of which was privately operated. Six of these prisons are also identified as 'high-performing prisons'.
- *Level 3*: meeting the majority of targets, experiencing no significant problems in doing so, delivering a reasonable and decent regime. At the end of 2006, there were 93 prisons at this level, including seven private prisons.
- *Level 2*: basically stable, secure and providing a limited but decent regime; experiencing significant problems in meeting targets and/or experiencing major operational problems. At the end of 2006, there were 18 prisons at this level, including three private prisons.

- *Level 1*: failing to provide secure, ordered or decent regimes and/or has significant short-falls against the majority of key targets. At the end of 2006, there were no prisons at this level.

Those prisons that fall into Level 1, or underperform consistently, may be subject to a performance test: a time-bounded opportunity to deliver an improvement plan which, if not acceptable, may result in the prison being offered to the private sector without an opportunity for the public sector to bid. Those that are not in Level 4 will complete a performance improvement plan, which is a time- bounded and supported opportunity to develop the establishment.

The move to more comprehensive performance assessment, simplified overall measurement with comparative 'league tables' and the use of consequences arising from performance in prisons has been mirrored in the public sector more generally (Bennett 2007).

*Jamie Bennett*

### Related entries

*Accountability; Audit; HM Inspectorate of Prisons; Independent monitoring boards; Key performance indicators (KPIs) and key performance targets (KPTs); Market testing; Measuring the Quality of Prison Life (MQPL); Privatization.*

### Key texts and sources

Bennett, J. (2007) 'Measuring order and control', in Y. Jewkes (ed.) *Handbook on Prisons*. Cullompton: Willan Publishing.

Laming, Lord of Tewin (2000) *Modernising the Management of the Prison Service: An Independent Report by the Targeted Performance Initiative Working Group*. London: Prison Service.

## PHYSICAL EDUCATION (PE)

Physical education (PE) relates to prisoner access to gymnasium and other exercise and sports facilities. The provision of PE is popular in prisons, and the use of gym facilities and exercise equipment is very high.

The historical image of physical education (PE) in prison includes regimented strolling around a prison yard in ever-decreasing circles, or the pointless grind of the treadmill. Such images conjure up a picture of PE as being about monotonous routinization and control. However, in contemporary prisons, PE has come to cover a range of aims, including the provision of purposeful activity; providing accreditations and assisting prisoners with numeracy and literacy; improving prisoners' skills relevant to employment; and improving prisoners' self-esteem and motivation. PE also plays a crucial part in maintaining order and control, both by providing an opportunity to learn to deal with aggressive and negative thoughts in an appropriate manner, and building relationships between staff and prisoners.

The provision of PE is popular in prisons, and the use of gym facilities and engagement in exercise are higher for prisoners than the national average. There is also evidence that prisoners are less likely to be overweight compared with the general population and have lower blood pressure. However, there are significant numbers of prisoners, both male and female, who are in poor physical shape, often due to substance misuse.

As PE is popular among prisoners, it is often used as a route to addressing a wider range of offending behaviour needs, including numeracy, communication and literacy. It can also be used more directly to address offence-related needs, including tackling substance misuse and improving stress, behaviour or anger management (for example, see Oddie 2004).

In England and Wales, prison PE facilities are generally a sports hall complemented by designated cardiovascular and weights areas. Some sites are fortunate in that they also have a sports field which permits some outside activities. The Prison Service has a long-established tradition of training prison officers as PE instructors. In this way, skills in managing prisoners are allied to specialist training. Prison governors set the balance of PE delivery, within nationally agreed performanace standards, to meet the needs of the establishment and individual prisoners.

In some countries, the provision of PE has become controversial and has been criticized as an example of luxurious living in prisons or, alternatively, as a source of support for anti-social behaviour as men bulk up on weights making them more capable of using violence. As a result, some prison systems have limited access to weights equipment and have even gone as far as reintroducing pointless exercise in the form of enforced marches as a form of degrading punitiveness (Pratt *et al.* 2005). However, such developments have so far been avoided in the UK, where PE continues to play an important role in all aspects of prisons, from decency to order and control, to reducing reoffending.

*Alan Tuckwood and Simon Boddis*

## Related entries

*Activities; Education and training; Healthcare; New punitiveness; Prison officers.*

---

**Key texts and sources**

Oddie, S. (2004) 'Exercise and drug detoxification', *Prison Service Journal*, 156: 21–4.

Pratt, J., Brown, D., Brown, M., Hallsworth, S. and Morrison, W. (2005) 'Introduction', in J. Pratt *et al.* (eds) *The New Punitiveness: Trends, Theories, Perspectives.* Cullompton: Willan Publishing.

See also the National Audit Office's website (http://www.nao.org.uk/publications/nao_reports /05-06/0506939.pdf).

---

# POLITICAL PRISONERS

---

There is no universal definition of the term 'political prisoner'. It has been argued that the term can include all prisoners, prisoners of war, prisoners of conscience and radicalized 'ordinary' prisoners.

---

The determination of whether an individual fits within the definition of 'political prisoner' depends on how that term is defined and who is doing the defining. The term has various, if not wholly different, interpretations among scholars, governments, international organizations and individuals. Some critical criminologists have argued that *all* prisoners can be described as political. In the late 1960s and early 1970s, the radical claim was that, since violations are against criminal codes defined by the politically powerful, all offences are political and all those who are serving prison sentences are 'political prisoners' (Schishor 1980). Similarly, Schafer (1974: 19) suggests:

> *In the broadest sense it may be argued that all crimes are political crimes in as much as all prohibitions with penal sanctions represent the defence of a given value system or morality which the prevailing social Powers believes...[M]aking acts criminal offences is a protection of the interests, values and beliefs of the law-making Power, actually the political social system which regards certain things as right and worthy of safeguarding with the threat of penal consequences.*

Schafer (1974: 145) also defines 'convictional criminals' – i.e. those who are convinced of the truth and justification of their own beliefs and who will carry out 'ordinary crimes' (e.g. murder, kidnapping, robbery, etc.) as a means to a higher political and ideological end.

## Categories of political prisoner

International organizations for human rights have different approaches to defining the term 'political prisoner', reflecting the political affiliations and perspective of the organization concerned. For example, the official position of the International Committee of the Red Cross simply states that a 'political prisoner is a political prisoner' thereby maintaining no formal definition of the term. The reasoning behind its refusal to define the term explicitly may be based on the organization's goal of being granted access to individuals who have been detained regardless of their categorization (see **www.redcross.org**).

Amnesty International defines a 'political prisoner' as a person who has committed criminal offences for political motives. Amnesty's interpretation is deliberately broad, treating as a 'political prisoner' anyone who is imprisoned, or on conviction risks being imprisoned, where there is a significant political element in the motivation of the authorities, in the acts or motivation of the prisoner or in the immediate context in which the trial or the alleged crime took place. Political prisoners may be people imprisoned for membership of an armed opposition group or for committing ordinary crimes, such as assault or murder, in support of a political group or objective. The political element may also reside in the context of the crime – for example, for crimes committed in a highly charged political atmosphere: 'Any prisoner in whose case a strong political element is present – such as the motives behind the prisoner's actions, the actions themselves or the reasons for his or her arrest by the authorities – can be identified as a political prisoner' (Amnesty International 2006). When Amnesty International began to campaign for the release of political detainees it originally limited its mandate to 'prisoners of conscience' (POCs); in other words, people detained solely because of their beliefs or because of their ethnic origin, sex, colour, language, national or social origin, economic status, birth or other status, who have not used or advocated violence. POCs are distinguished from others who had used or advocated violence. For example, former president of South Africa, Nelson Mandela, was adopted as a POC by Amnesty International in 1962. However, he was removed from this categorization in 1964 after he was convicted on a sabotage charge because of his use of violence.

A further category of political prisoner is 'prisoner of war' (POW). Ordinarily, opposing soldiers captured during international armed conflict must be treated as POWs, in accordance with the third 1949 Geneva Convention Relative to the Treatment of Prisoners of War. Under the Geneva Convention, a POW is defined as any 'member of the armed forces of a Party to the conflict' who has 'fallen into the Power of the enemy'. To be recognized as having POW status, a captured person has to fit within one of the six categories in Article 4 of Geneva Convention III (see **http://www.unhchr.ch/html/menu3/ b/91.htm**). Designating detainees as POWs is an important factor in determining the treatment they should receive at the hands of a detaining power. The Geneva Convention Relative to the Treatment of Prisoners of War, 12 August 1949, 75 UNTS 135 (GC III) accords certain fundamental protections for those individuals who are entitled to POW status. Notably, POWs are bound to give their name, rank, date of birth and identification number, and may not be compelled by coercive means to give any further information (Article 17); and POWs are to be repatriated 'without delay after cessation of active hostilities' (Article 118).

One final category of 'political prisoner' to be discussed here has been described as the 'radicalized 'ordinary' prisoner' (McEvoy *et al*. 2007). Essentially, this category refers to prisoners serving a sentence for 'ordinary' crime who, while incarcerated, become radicalized. McEvoy *et al*. provide examples of the transformation of 'ordinary' black prisoners in the USA, including high-profile activists such as Malcolm X and George Jackson, whose politicization was heavily influenced by readings on colonial conscientiousness and revolution. A further example is the Islamic radicalization that is rumoured to be taking place in prisons in the UK. It is claimed in a Home Office report that the prison has become one of the key sites of radicalization for young Muslims: 'some are drawn to mosques where they may be targeted by extremist preachers; others are radicalised or converted whilst in prison' (Leapman 2005 cited in McEvoy *et al*. 2007).

It is apparent that the term 'political prisoner' is both a highly controversial and, in some instances, a highly contested term. It is difficult to provide an absolute definition, and any attempt to postulate a universal definition should be approached cautiously.

*Claire Dwyer*

### Related entries

*Human rights; Paramilitary prisoners; 'War on terror'.*

## Key texts and sources

Amnesty International (2006) *Amnesty International Handbook* (available online at **http://www.amnesty-volunteer.org/aihandbook/ index.html**).

McEvoy, K. (2001) *Paramilitary Imprisonment in Northern Ireland: Resistance, Management and Release*. Oxford: Oxford University Press.

McEvoy, K., McConnachie, K. and Jamieson, R. (2007) 'Political imprisonment and the "War on terror"', in Y. Jewkes (ed.) *Handbook on Prisons*. Cullompton: Willan Publishing.

Schafer, S. (1974) *The Political Criminal: The Problem of Morality and Crime*. New York, NY: Free Press/Macmillan.

Schishor, D. (1980) 'The new criminology: some critical issues', *British Journal of Criminology*, 20: 1–19.

# POLITICS OF IMPRISONMENT

Crime and punishment are major concerns in any community and are matters that are ongoing subjects of political debate.

When then Labour Home Secretary, David Blunkett, told a gathering of journalists in January 2004 that he had felt like celebrating on hearing of the suicide in prison of the notorious serial murderer, Dr Harold Shipman, his remarks struck many as symptomatic of a political populism all too characteristic of the politics of imprisonment under New Labour.

Blunkett's oafish comments certainly appear a world away from the observations of another former Home Secretary who, in 1910, argued that the 'mood and temper of the public in regard to the treatment of crime and criminals is one of the most unfailing tests of the civilisation of any country'. Winston Churchill, the former Home Secretary in question, was hardly a soft-hearted do-gooder. In the same year that he spoke of civilization's 'unfailing tests' he sent in the police and army against the striking miners of Tonypandy in south Wales. Yet the contrast between Churchill's lofty pieties and Blunkett's barroom banter offers a reminder of the way in which the political context of policy and debate about law and order, prison and prisoners, has changed.

## Terminology

Before going further, a few words on concepts and terminology are necessary. The 'politics of imprisonment' might be understood in a variety of ways. Debates and disputes about aspects of imprisonment among the main political parties is one example. The lobbying activity of penal reformers is another. The way in which these various groupings relate to the media or members of the public is an added dimension of the politics of imprisonment.

The 'politics of imprisonment' further relates to the political choices involved in the decision to use imprisonment as a response to crime. There is also the political context within which imprisonment comes to be prioritized, or deprioritized, in relation to other policy options. The connotations of 'the politics of imprisonment', in other words, are various. This dictionary entry cannot do justice to all these various meanings, but it is important to bear them in mind in any extended examination of the issue.

## Changes in the politics of imprisonment since the end of the Second World War

The evolution of penal policy since 1945, and the shifting politics associated with this evolution, has been the subject of much detailed study. Any attempt to summarize such a complex set of historical processes is bound to be unsatisfactory in one way or another. But in broad outline three overlapping and interrelated phases can be distinguished: the 'penal welfarism' period up until the late 1960s; the emergence of 'authoritarian populism' from the early 1970s; and the development of a 'new consensus' on penal politics from the early 1990s to the present day.

In the years immediately following the Second World War, a political consensus about the overarching principles of governmental policy – full male employment, the welfare state, a mixed economy of state and private activity – provided the context for a related political consensus on prisons policy, often referred to as 'penal welfarism' (Garland 2001). The expressed purpose of policy was the rehabilitation of prisoners and their reintegration back into society.

Responsibility for policy formation tended to rest with a relatively small network of politicians, civil servants, penal reformers and criminologists (Ryan 2003; Loader 2006). In party-political terms, law and order was largely absent as a site of contestation. It hardly figured at all in the election manifestos of the main political parties during the 1940s and 1950s.

The wider political context in which penal welfarism flourished – a low official crime rate and a generalized commitment to the welfare state and low unemployment – was none the less significant. Penal policy does not develop or operate in isolation from other areas of governmental policy. There is a strong correlation, for instance, between a country's welfare state arrangements and the severity of its penal sanctions (Cavadino and Dignan 2006; Downes and Hansen 2006). The more expansive the welfare state provision, the less severe the penal sanctions, and vice versa. The post-war political consensus around the importance of the welfare state did not *determine* the consensus on penal welfarism. Indeed, in historical terms, penal welfarism predates the establishment of the welfare state. But the welfare state did provide an important context, in both material and ideological terms, for penal welfarism's continued expression.

From the late 1960s, the post-war welfare consensus started to disintegrate. The underlying cause was a series of social and economic dislocations that placed the British state under significant pressure. What emerged was a new form of politics, dubbed 'authoritarian populism' by one influential thinker (Hall 1980). The grounding assumptions of the welfare state came under sustained critique as influential voices associated with the emerging Thatcherite agenda sought radically to reset the terms of the political debate. Far from being a hand-up to the enterprising poor, they argued, the welfare state had fostered a layer of scroungers living off the hard work of others. The answer to the problems of crime and disorder lay in the disciplinary activities of the police and judiciary, backed up by strong laws and unflinching political will. The political programme implemented in the wake of the Conservative Party's election

victory in 1979, among other things, unpicked key elements of the post-war settlement and implemented a far more 'assertive' approach to law and order.

With the advantage of historical distance, the impact of these political upheavals on the longer-term politics of imprisonment was momentous, though at the time this was far from clear. Between the early 1970s and the early 1990s, for instance, the prison population in England and Wales grew only slowly. Indeed, it declined in the late 1980s and early 1990s. Most of the Home Secretaries of the Conservative era are considered to have been more liberal on prison matters than their New Labour successors.

Yet to focus narrowly on the politics of imprisonment is to ignore the wider import of the politics of law and order during this period. One of the lasting political achievements of the Conservative governments of the 1980s and 1990s was to reshape public and political understanding of the nature of the problems of crime and insecurity, persuading us to think of them as problems of control rather than welfare (Garland 2001).

### Expansion of imprisonment and the 'new consensus'

So it is that the new consensus on penal policy that emerged during the 1990s has manifested a starkly different politics of imprisonment than did the earlier, post-war consensus. Since 1993 the prison population in England and Wales has nearly doubled. In place of a concern to limit the use of imprisonment comes an ostentatious celebration of its virtues. 'Prison works', Michael Howard told the 1993 Conservative Party conference. In its 2005 election manifesto, Labour proudly drew attention to the thousands of new prison places built since 1997. Offender rehabilitation and reintegration are still part of the expressed purpose of penal policy. But this commitment is located much more overtly within a punitive and coercive policy framework.

Party-political concerns have no doubt played a role in shaping the politics of this new consensus. Spouting the nostrums of a penal reformist agenda might earn an MP or minister

Brownie points in the editorial pages of the *Guardian* newspaper. The mass circulation tabloids, and the readership they deliver, will generally be less appreciative. When toughness is the watchword of penal policy, no one wants to be portrayed as being 'soft on crime'.

Yet the salience of such party-political considerations is itself a function of the underlying political choices made about prison and about a broader set of social and economic policy options. Prison occupies no 'natural' place in modern society. The prison population has no 'natural' size. Both are, at heart, the result of political decisions (Sparks 2007).

The questions raised by the fact of imprisonment are, therefore, ultimately political ones. At a time when an expansive welfare state and greater economic equality are marginal to the main trajectory of political debate and policy, we should not be surprised that crime, prison and punishment are ever-present features.

*Richard Garside*

### Related entries

*Legitimacy; New punitiveness; 'Prison works'; Public perceptions; Rehabilitation; Welfarism.*

### Key texts and sources

Cavadino, M. and Dignan, J. (2006) *Penal Systems: A Comparative Approach.* London: Sage.

Downes, D. and Hansen, K. (2006) *Welfare and Punishment: The Relationship between Welfare Spending and Imprisonment.* London: Crime and Society Foundation.

Garland, D. (2001) *The Culture of Control: Crime and Social Order in Contemporary Society.* Oxford: Oxford University Press.

Hall, S. (1980) *Drifting into a Law and Order Society.* London: Cobden Trust.

Loader, I. (2006) 'Fall of the "Platonic guardians": liberalism, criminology and political responses to crime in England and Wales', *British Journal of Criminology*, 46: 561–86.

Ryan, M. (2003) *Penal Policy and Political Culture in England and Wales.* Winchester: Waterside Press.

Sparks, R. (2007) 'The politics of imprisonment', in Y. Jewkes (ed.) *Handbook on Prisons.* Cullompton: Willan Publishing.

# POWER

In the social sciences, power is a concept that refers to relations between social actors. Punishment and, particularly, imprisonment are often used as an exemplar of how extreme power is exercised by the state.

Political philosophers and sociologists have long aimed to explain the emergence, expressions and consequences of power in any given society. The concept of power refers to relations between all social actors, but it has been analysed most often through its exercise by the state towards citizens. A number of writers have used the most extreme and intrusive form of power exertion by the state towards its citizens (namely, the power to punish) as an exemplar of how power relations are constructed, legitimized and can work in practice.

In *Discipline and Punish*, Foucault (1977) outlines the shift from mainly corporal punishment through torture and execution to carceral punishment during the seventeenth, eighteenth and nineteenth centuries. He tracks historical changes in the penal system in order to draw conclusions about the meaning of these changes for our understanding of power. Following this historical analysis, he discards the juridical understanding of the power to punish – i.e. that power is directly linked to the law or the sovereign/state. Instead, he conceptualizes the interdependence between knowledge and power – i.e. that power is only possible through knowledge, and vice versa.

Foucault argues that the aims of punishment have changed because the technologies of power have evolved and, with these new technologies, new forms of knowledge – the human sciences – have emerged. The object of the power to punish has moved from being purely corporal (the body) to both corporal and mental (body and soul). In modern societies power over the body is exerted through control over the mind (Foucault 1977: 149–62). The idea of the new technologies of power, surveillance and the training of individuals is to create citizens who strive through internal and external means of control to be law-abiding, to be normal and to conform not only with criminal law but also with society's existing structures and inequalities (Hudson 2002).

In the context of prisons, however, the concept of power relations has a pragmatic meaning beyond the philosophical considerations outlined above. The question of the legitimacy of punishment has a clear influence on power relations in prison. In addition, the way power is exercised in prison by governors and prison officers, not only in applying a punishment imposed by the judiciary (on behalf of the state) but also punishment for breaches of prison rules, has implications for the level of perceived legitimacy of the prison system and thus the smooth running of a particular prison.

*Martina Feilzer*

### Related entries

*Governors; Legitimacy; Prison officers; Prison Rules.*

---

**Key texts and sources**

Foucault, M. (1977) *Discipline and Punish* (trans. A. Sheridan). London: Allen Lane.
Hudson, B. (2002) 'Punishment and control', in M. Maguire *et al.* (eds) *The Oxford Handbook of Criminology*. Oxford: Oxford University Press.

---

## PRISON ACT

The Prison Act 1952 is the chief piece of legislation in England and Wales affecting prisons.

The Prison Act 1952 is the main piece of legislation which principally concerns prisons in England and Wales. Technically, it is a 'consolidation Act' – a piece of legislation that brings together the various responsibilities and powers conferred by previous Acts on the Home Secretary for the provision, maintenance and operation of prisons (Coyle 1996). Naturally, other pieces of legislation also affect prisons (see Creighton and King 2000; Leech 2005). These include the various Acts which deal with prison sentences; those which regulate health and safety and race equality; and the Human Rights Act 1998. Since 1952, the Prison Act has been amended, most notably by the Criminal Justice Act 1961 (which abolished the Prison Commission and replaced it with the Prison Department of the Home Office, from which the Prison Service developed as an agency in 1992) and by the Criminal Justice Acts of 1982 and 1988, which respectively abolished Borstals and introduced young offender institutions (YOIs). The provisions of two other Acts are also of note: the Criminal Justice Act 1991, which empowered the Home Secretary to contract out the building and running of prisons; and the Criminal Justice and Public Order Act 1994, which expanded the 1991 Act's contracting-out provisions and imposed a statutory prohibition on prison officers from taking industrial action.

The Prison Act defines in some detail the Home Secretary's comprehensive responsibilities for prisons:

1. To create new prisons; to rebuild, enlarge and refurbish existing prisons; to designate buildings or parts of buildings as prisons; to acquire and own land and property for those purposes; and to close prisons (ss. 33 and 35–37).
2. The 'general superintendence of prisons' and, either directly or by contract, to provide for the maintenance of prisons and prisoners (s. 4); and to report on every prison annually and to lay that report before Parliament (s. 5).
3. To appoint officers and staff to run prisons (s. 3) and members of each prison's independent monitoring board (s. 6).
4. To direct in which prisons prisoners shall be held – and to transfer prisoners from one prison to another (s. 12) – and temporarily and conditionally to discharge prisoners due to ill-health (s. 28).
5. To provide special cells for the temporary confinement of violent or refractory prisoners and to satisfy himself that each prison has sufficient accommodation for prisoners and for the certification of that accommodation (s. 14).
6. To make rules for the management of prisons and for the classification, treatment, employment, training, discipline, control and temporary release of prisoners (s. 47).

The last provision is probably the one that impacts most directly on prison life on a daily basis. The Prison Rules and YOI Rules, made under s. 47 of the Prison Act, are 'secondary legislation' and provide the framework within which all prisons operate. The Act also empowers the Home Secretary to refer to HM Inspectorate of Prisons matters on which it shall report (s. 5A); to appoint non-Church of England ministers (s. 10); to make payments to prisoners on discharge (s. 30); to make rules for the photographing and measuring of prisoners (s. 16); and to direct whether time 'unlawfully at large' shall be ignored (s. 49).

Therefore, the Act makes clear that it is the Home Secretary who is responsible for prisons, even though the day-to-day running of prisons and most operational matters are in the hands of the Prison Service. However, the Act does not create 'HM Prison Service', which remains an administrative body staffed by civil servants who are formally part of the Home Office. The Prison Service's status as an 'agency' sponsored by the Home Office is defined by its *Framework Document* (HM Prison Service 1999). While this gives the Prison Service a distinct operating identity and a certain independence from the Home Office, it is an administrative not a legislative arrangement, and the Secretary of State is the person named in litigation as the Prison Service has no legal persona. Essentially, the Prison Service is line managed by the Home Office.

Certain provisions of the Prison Act distinguish prison officers and prison governors from other civil servants. Section 7 requires every prison to have a governor, a chaplain and a medical officer and such other officers as are required. Section 8 gives prison officers the powers of a constable when on duty, thereby enabling them to search prisoners and visitors to prisons and, where necessary, to use force. Section 8A empowers governors to authorize staff who are not prison officers to conduct rub-down searches of prisoners. Sections 16A and 16B authorize prison officers to test prisoners for drugs and alcohol. Section 13 declares that every prisoner shall be deemed to be in the legal custody of the governor of the prison.

The provisions of the Prison Act apply to all prisons, and most of them to contracted-out prisons, which are also the responsibility of the Home Secretary. However, the staff of contracted-out prisons are not civil servants and, as such, cannot be given the powers of a constable that s. 8 gives to prison officers. The Criminal Justice Act 1991, which empowered the Home Secretary to contract out prisons, therefore made separate legislative provision for the contracted-out prisons' equivalent of prison officers (prisoner custody officers) to search and use force. Similarly, contracted-out prisons also require a civil servant (called the 'controller') to perform adjudications and to authorize segregation and temporary release.

*William Payne*

### Related entries

*Accountability; Adjudications; HM Inspectorate of Prisons; Independent monitoring boards; Industrial relations; Prison Rules.*

**Key texts and sources**

Coyle, A. (1996) *The Prisons We Deserve*. London: HarperCollins.
Creighton, S. and King, V. (2000) *Prisoners and the Law*. London: Butterworths.
HM Prison Service (1999) *Framework Document*. London: HMSO.
Leech, M. (ed.) (2005) *The Prisons Handbook* (9th edn). Manchester: MLA Press.

## PRISONIZATION

'Prisonization' is a term popularized by Donald Clemmer in 1940 to indicate the process of socialization or assimilation that takes place when a prisoner enters prison.

Although often characterized as a destructive process, prisonization is not simply a form of institutionalization as described by some (Zamble and Porporino 1988). Like institutionalization, prisonization may involve the acceptance of inferior roles and a large degree of passivity in relation to the formal structures of the institution. But it also indicates a positive willingness to accept the norms and values of the prison community and is a rather more proactive survival strategy by which inmates learn how to 'play the system' and to use the underground prison economy and the existence of subcultures and hierarchies to their advantage. These illegitimate activities, far from grinding down the inmate, actually provide him or her with the status and power necessary to ameliorate the sense of social rejection and loss of status inherent in the label 'prisoner'. For example, those who are involved in contraband economies are arguably deflecting official attempts to socialize them through formal channels and, instead, constructing their identities around notions of resistance and counterculture, demonstrating that there may be an inverse correlation between prisonization and socialization.

The argument that the more prisonized an inmate becomes, the less conventionally socialized he or she will be supports the argument that socialization takes the form of a U-shaped curve (Wheeler 1961). Put simply, the inmate enters prison with an outsider's perception of what it will be like. By the middle of his or her sentence, he or she comes to adopt an insider's perspective on the prison world and is, at this stage, most 'prisonized'. The inmate reverts to an outsider's view in the final months of his or her sentence in preparation for release.

Many inmates, however, refuse to accept the idea that they will become aculturized to the prison world and fear that being 'a prisoner' diminishes or even subsumes all other aspects of their identity and self. Consequently they resist prisonization and spend much of their prison sentences trying to hold on to their pre-prison selves, through contact with friends and families, continuation of occupations or hobbies, or through the consumption of popular cultural artefacts that were important to them on the outside.

*Yvonne Jewkes*

## Related entries

*Economy; Identity and self; Structure/agency ('resistance'); Subcultures.*

### Key texts and sources

Clemmer, D. (1940/1958) *The Prison Community.* New York, NY: Holt, Rinehart & Winston.

Zamble, E. and Porporino, F.J. (1988) *Coping, Behaviour and Adaptation in Prison Inmates.* New York, NY: Springer-Verlag.

# PRISON OFFICERS

Prison officers are by far the largest group of staff employed in the Prison Service of England and Wales. Although the chief pressure on prison officers is to prevent escape (the maintenance of security is their primary task), they must also ensure good order in prisons and provide prisoners with a proper degree of care.

## Occupational culture

The prevention of escape and the maintenance of order and control remain the primary tasks of the prison officer. However, prison officers are also expected to carry out the task of providing care and are increasingly required to engage in activities concerned with 'treatment' and rehabilitation. Indeed, the modern prison officer's role encompasses a relatively high level of rehabilitative work with prisoners and the delivery (and in some cases development) of courses oriented towards issues as diverse as sex offending, drug awareness and good parenting.

Despite the complexity of their task, prison officers see themselves as part of an unvalued, unappreciated occupational group. This perception is long-standing and is, in part, a result of the relative invisibility of their work. Prison officers' understanding is that they are regarded by the public (who do not see what they actually do) as unintelligent, insensitive and brutal – individuals who routinely assault prisoners and are capable of little more than locking and unlocking cell doors. Moreover, and perhaps more importantly, they feel unvalued by their own managers. Indeed, for much of the past hundred years the Prison Service of England and Wales has simmered with staff discontent because managers are seen as failing to attach real value to prison officers' 'sharp end' knowledge of prisoners and prisons. As a result, prison officers generally feel a strong sense of social isolation both from their own managers and from society at large.

In contrast to the police, prison officers – their lives and working practices in the prison, their feelings about the work they do and their relationships with prisoners and their fellow officers – have been poorly documented and, hence, poorly appreciated and understood. It is only through relatively recent work (see especially Kauffman 1988; Liebling and Price 2001; Crawley 2002, 2004) that we have begun to understand the impact of the prison as a place of work and the psychological and emotional adjustments that ordinary men and women must make in order to become prison officers.

Historically, prison officers were ex-military (male) personnel and, like prisoners, were physically segregated from the wider community by being required to live in Prison Service 'quarters' located in the prison grounds. This arrangement – which no longer exists – prevented social interaction between prison officers and their families and the local community. As a result, prison officers became isolated from wider (non-prison-based) customs, values and norms. For prison officers, the occupational culture – and the social interactions generated by it – is a significant component of the job itself. In the prison, *how* things are done can be as important as *what* is done, and occupational (that is, informal) rules and norms underpin how officers relate to their inmates, to each other and to their superiors. Occupational norms determine how officers respond (i.e. positively, negatively or with indifference) to institutional changes, how experienced officers accommodate the gaucheries of new recruits and how male officers accept (or not) the growing numbers of women and ethnic minority recruits now entering a traditionally white, male, working-class sphere.

## The role of the prison officer

Of the 48,000 members of staff working in the Prison Service of England and Wales, the largest group by far is made up of prison officers. In September 2000, there were 19,118 officers, and a further 5,048 senior and principal officers (Liebling and Price 2001). Recruitment into the Prison Service is carried out locally rather than nationally. Since devolution of the recruitment process, each prison is responsible for recruiting the officers it requires. Jobs are advertised in local Job Centres, and those wishing to apply must contact the prisons directly. Candidates must be aged between 18 years and 62 years at the time of appointment. Candidates must also be fully physically fit (the recruitment process involves a medical and fitness test); however, the Prison Service operates a guaranteed interview scheme for disabled people (as defined in the Disability Discrimination Act 1995) who meet the minimum published criteria for appointment. Roughly 17 per cent of prison officers are female. At the end of 2005, 5.7 per cent of staff were from ethnic minority groups. Entry-level training takes place over an eight-week period. After basic training, new recruits are given a brief induction course into the routines and working practices of the prison in which they are to work. They are then supervised by more experienced officers as the realities of prison work emerge (see Arnold *et al.* 2007 for an overview of prison officers' recruitment and training).

One of the key lessons taught to new recruits is that they must develop a suspicious mindset when dealing with prisoners. Like police officers, prison officers are specifically trained to be constantly on the lookout for potential, as well as actual, 'trouble'. For prison officers, the ability to 'read' people and situations is seen as crucial for the maintenance of order and, indeed, for their own safety. In addition, once they start work 'on the landings', new officers will find that, like nurses, they are expected to remain emotionally detached (Crawley 2004). They are warned, during basic training, not to get too friendly nor too relaxed with prisoners, on the grounds that this may lead to 'conditioning' and hence to compromises of security (see Home Office 1994). 'Detachment' is a strategy commonly employed by prison officers to avoid being manipulated by prisoners. Indeed, the fear of being seen as a 'soft touch' colours all aspects of officers' interactions with prisoners, even with regard to easily granted requests such as an extra telephone call. But maintaining emotional detachment is not easy. Occasionally, unanticipated emotions overwhelm prison officers, and this can be a significant threat to work identity and to a carefully constructed professional self (Crawley 2004).

Of key relevance here is the fact that the social world of the prison officer is relatively small, intimate and domestic in character – certainly compared with the world in which the police officer moves. While police officers have high visibility and a wide network of social contacts (they deal with law-abiding members of the general public as well as offenders), prison officers largely deal with people convicted of, or awaiting trial for, a criminal offence. Moreover, the degree of intimacy involved in working with prisoners is great compared with that experienced in police work. While a police officer will not have to spend time with an individual he or she has treated roughly or unfairly, a prison officer may well have to spend months or even years with that individual – both in the context of everyday living routines and when the prisoner is ill or distressed. For these reasons, prison officers become acutely aware of the value of building positive relationships with those in prison. Close proximity to prisoners in the context of a relatively intimate environment makes it extremely difficult for staff to maintain – at least for any length of time – the notion of 'them and us', and many *do* develop close bonds with certain prisoners. It is for this reason that officers must engage in 'emotional labour' if they are to maintain credibility in the eyes of fellow staff. This means that they must learn to 'manage their feelings in order to create facial and bodily displays appropriate to, or consistent with a situation, role or an expected job function, and with socially accepted norms' (Hochschild 1983 cited in Crawley 2004). Prison officers pride themselves on being able convincingly to hide their feelings over time and under pressure, but emotional labour can take its toll. Indeed, the lack of affect produced by the need routinely to mask feelings can, over time, become the standard emotional response to events outside the prison setting, and this can put great strains on family life. Put simply, the prison officer role – the attitudes and demeanours it generates – is extremely difficult to leave at the prison gate. This 'spillover' of prison work derives from four key issues: danger, routinization, desensitization and contamination (Crawley 2002, 2004). This combination ensures that the potential for role engulfment is high, and officers' ability to come 'out of role' low. Indeed, as officers and their families willingly testify, a striking aspect of prison work is the strain of living in, and moving between, two worlds – only one of which is contained within high walls.

*Elaine Crawley*

### Related entries

*Assaults; Discipline; Order and control; Power; Rehabilitation; Security; Staff (prison).*

**Key texts and sources**

Arnold, H., Liebling, A. and Tait, S. (2007) 'Prison officers and prison culture', in Y. Jewkes (ed.) *Handbook on Prisons*. Cullompton: Willan Publishing.

Crawley, E. (2002) 'Bringing it all back home? The impact of prison officers' work on their families', *Probation Journal*, 49 (4).

Crawley, E. (2004) *Doing Prison Work: The Public and Private Lives of Prison Officers*. Cullompton: Willan Publishing.

Home Office (1994) *Report of the Enquiry into the Escape of Six Prisoners from the Special Security Unit at Whitemoor Prison, Cambridgeshire on Friday 9th September 1994* (the Woodcock Report). London: HMSO.

Kauffman, K. (1988) *Prison Officers and their World*. Cambridge, MA: Harvard University Press.

Liebling, A. and Price, D. (2001) *The Prison Officer*. Leyhill: Prison Service Journal.

See also the Prison Officers' Association website (**http://www.poauk.org.uk/**).

# PRISON POPULATION

'Prison population' refers to the total number of individuals detained in a prison system.

In England and Wales the prison population has grown from just under 10,000 prisoners in 1940 to approximately 80,000 prisoners at the end of 2006 (Home Office 2006). The last 13 years, in particular, has seen the number of prisoners in English and Welsh prisons almost double in size, rising from just over 40,000 prisoners in 1993. The prison population in Scotland has also risen from just over 1,300 prisoners in 1940 to over 8,600 prisoners in 2006 (Scottish Executive 2006). Prison numbers in Scotland, however, have not risen as dramatically as in England and Wales. For example, the population of Scottish prisons rose from approximately 5,200 prisoners in 1993 to 8,600 prisoners in 2006. This represents an increase of 30 per cent compared with an almost 100 per cent increase in the number of prisoners in England and Wales during the same period.

The use of imprisonment in England and Wales represents one of the highest in Western Europe, with over 140 individuals per 100,000 being detained in the Prison Service (see World prison populations). The reasons for this high rate of imprisonment are thought to include a change in the way crime is perceived; more punitive and less tolerant approaches to dealing with crime; longer sentences; a lack of confidence in effective community rehabilitation programmes; increased reliance on the use of imprisonment as a sanction against criminal behaviour; and a belief that 'prison works'.

Despite this increase in the use of imprisonment, the characteristics of English and Welsh prisoners appear to have remained somewhat stable, with the majority of prisoners tending to be males from disadvantaged communities. In October 2006, there were over 75,300 males and 4,400 females imprisoned in English and Welsh prisons. Of these, over 68,000 were adults, 9,228 were young adults and 2,518 were between the ages of 15 and 17 years (Home Office 2006). The bulk of these prisoners were serving sentences for offences involving violence against the person, drugs, robbery and burglary. Other offences include sexual offences, theft, fraud and motoring offences.

Figures from the Social Exclusion Unit (2002) indicate that English and Welsh prisoners are more likely to have lower levels of education, fewer qualifications and to have previously been excluded from essential services. Prisoners appear to be 20 times more likely to be excluded from school than the general population. Fifty per cent of prisoners are believed to have no general practitioner before entering the Prison Service, while 80 per cent of those with a drug-misuse problem have never been referred to a drug treatment service. The basic reading, writing and numeracy skills of most prisoners are also very poor. Eighty per cent of prisoners have the writing skills of an 11-year-old child, while over 50 per cent have numeracy and reading abilities at or below the level of an 11-year-old. In addition, over 50 per cent of prisoners have no formal qualifications, while only 15 per cent of individuals in the community appear to have no formal qualifications (see Education and training).

Prisoners also report higher rates of drug and alcohol addiction, unemployment and problematic upbringing than are evident in the general population (Social Exclusion Unit 2002). Two thirds of male prisoners and over half of female prisoners report using drugs in the previous year compared with 13 per cent of men and 8 per cent of women in the community. Similarly, over 60 per cent of male prisoners and 35 per cent of female prisoners have engaged in hazardous drinking, compared with 38 per cent of men and 15 per cent of women in the general population. Almost 50 per cent of prisoners report running away from home as a child while 27 per cent were taken into care. In contrast, only 11 per cent of the public report running away from home as a child and 2 per cent recall being taken into care.

The prison population also appears to suffer from more mental health disorders, psychotic disorders and homelessness than would normally be expected. The findings from the Social Exclusion Unit (2002) reveal that approximately

70 per cent of prisoners suffer from two or more mental disorders compared with 5 per cent of men and 2 per cent of women in the community. Similarly, 7 per cent of male prisoners and 14 per cent of female prisoners suffer from a psychotic disorder compared with roughly 0.5 per cent of the public. Homelessness is also higher among prisoners, with almost a third of prisoners experiencing homeless in comparison with 0.9 per cent of the general population.

In addition, black and minority ethnic groups tend to be over-represented in the prison population. During 2005, one in four English and Welsh prisoners was from a minority ethnic group, compared with one in eleven in the general population (Home Office 2006). Black prisoners are the largest ethnic minority group, and between 1999 and 2002 the number of black prisoners increased by 51 per cent compared with an overall increase of 12 per cent in the total prison population (HM Prison Service and Commission for Racial Equality 2003).

Further, just over 50 per cent of ethnic minority prisoners are foreign nationals. The vast majority of foreign national prisoners tend to be serving sentences for drug-related offences and originate from countries such as Jamaica, Ireland, Nigeria, Pakistan, Turkey and India (Prison Reform Trust 2004). In the last ten years, the number of foreign national prisoners in England and Wales has increased by 152 per cent, compared with a 55 per cent increase in the number of British nationals detained during the same time period.

In conclusion, the prison population in England and Wales appears to consist of a high number of disadvantaged individuals, many of whom have a history of unemployment, homelessness, drug and alcohol addiction, poor skills and mental health problems. This raises questions about why the prison population consists of such high numbers of disadvantaged prisoners and whether there are sufficient services in place to help prevent such individuals entering the prison system.

*Michelle Butler*

## Related entries

*Alcohol; Black and minority ethnic (BME) prisoners; Drugs; Education and training; Foreign national prisoners; Mental health; 'Prison works'; Rehabilitation; World prison populations.*

### Key texts and sources

HM Prison Service and Commission for Racial Equality (2003) *Implementing Racial Equality in Prisons: A Shared Agenda for Change.* London: Home Office.

Home Office (2006) *Population in Custody* (available online at **http://www.homeoffice.gov.uk/rds/**).

Prison Reform Trust (2004) *Forgotten Prisoners: The Plight of Foreign National Prisoners.* London: Prison Reform Trust.

Scottish Executive (2006) *Prison Statistics* (available online at **http://www.scotland.gov.uk/Publications**).

Social Exclusion Unit (2002) *Reducing Re-offending by Ex-prisoners.* London: Social Exclusion Unit.

The *World Prison Population List* is available online at the Home Office's website (**http://www.homeoffice.gov.uk/rds/pdfs2/r188.pdf**). The Prison Service's Population Bulletins are available online at **http://www.hmprisonservice.gov.uk/resourcecentre/publicationsdocuments/index.asp?cat=85**. For prison population statistics by ethnic group, see **http://www.statistics.gov.uk/STATBASE/ssdata set. asp?vlnk=7363**.

## PRISON REFORM TRUST

The Prison Reform Trust was founded in 1981 with the aim of creating a just, humane and effective penal system. The trust does this by inquiring into the system; by informing prisoners, staff and the wider public; and by influencing Parliament, government and officials towards reform. It is constituted to provide information, research and education.

The Prison Reform Trust's objectives are to improve treatment and conditions; to promote citizenship and human rights; to respect diversity and the needs of minority groups; to support prisoners and their families; and to promote community solutions to crime.

The principles the trust advocates are as follows:

- Prison should be reserved for those whose offending is so serious that they cannot serve their sentence in the community.
- Prisoners and their families should be treated with humanity and respect and have access to clear information and the opportunity to represent themselves and have their views taken into account.
- The Prison Service should provide constructive regimes in decent, safe conditions that ensure the well-being of prisoners and prepare them for resettlement in the community.
- The general public, Parliament and those responsible for incarcerating offenders should be fully informed about the state and effectiveness of the UK's criminal justice system.
- As the most severe punishment in the UK, imprisonment should remain the ultimate responsibility of the state, in order to safeguard prisoners' human rights.

For a small, independent charity, the Prison Reform Trust (PRT) has a high national profile and an extensive reach. Independent press monitors show average monthly printed press coverage of 11.5 million people. Since 2002, the PRT has provided the secretariat to the All Party Parliamentary Penal Affairs Group. Hansard monitoring indicates the way in which the PRT informs parliamentary debate. The PRT stays aware of current concerns and keeps its feet on the ground through the 5,000 prisoners and their families in contact each year with its advice and information service and through regular prison visits.

It is not always easy to measure success in a charity which, of necessity, works with and through others to effect reform. Early achievements include the PRT's contribution to the development of sex offender treatment programmes, the ending of slopping out in prisons, the establishment of the office of the Prisons and Probation Ombudsman and the publication of prisoners' information booklets translated into 22 languages. More recently, the PRT has informed reforms in prison health, in particular mental health, HIV/AIDS and hepatitis, education and family support. Its applied research has led to an increase in the number of prisoner councils, and its provision of expert evidence for the European Court of Human Rights and the Grand Chamber helped to overturn the blanket ban on prisoners' voting.

The PRT produced the first information for disabled prisoners, initiated a major programme of work on learning disability and is monitoring the implementation of the Disability Discrimination Act 1995. In 2006 it made a significant contribution to maintaining the independence of the prisons inspectorate, conducted a review of RESPECT's work to support black and minority ethnic prison staff, and succeeded in calling a halt to the transportation of pregnant women in prison vans or 'sweatboxes'. Its campaign, SmartJustice, has succeeded in gathering massive public support for a reduction in the use of prison for vulnerable women and children. While the PRT is not abolitionist and understands the need for an effective, humane penal system, its dearest wish is to end chronic overcrowding and any needless use of imprisonment, and to drive prison numbers back down to what Lord Woolf, when Lord Chief Justice, referred to as an 'unavoidable minimum'. The way to achieve this is through the integration of social and criminal justice policy.

*Juliet Lyon*

### Related entries

*Disability; Voting rights; Women in prison; Woolf Report.*

**Key texts and sources**

Woolf, Lord Justice (2001) *The Woolf Report: A Decade of Change?* London: Prison Reform Trust.
The Prison Reform Trust's website is at http://www.prisonreformtrust.org.uk/. For the Youth Justice Board's response to the recent Prison Reform Trust's report, see http://www.yjb.gov.uk/en-gb/News/YJBrespondstoPrisonReformTrustreport.htm. For the Prison Reform Trust's recent campaign 'Innocent until proven guilty', see http://www.innocentuntilprovenguilty.com/.

# PRISON RULES

> The Prison Rules are statutory instruments issued by the Home Secretary under the authority of the Prison Act 1952 in order to direct the day-to-day administration of prisons.

The Prison Act 1952 is the main law relevant to prisons, and the Prison Rules are made under the authority of this Act. Separate rules have been made for young offender institutions, although they are very similar to the main Prison Rules. The Prison Rules leave a great deal of discretion to the prison authorities, so the Prison Service issues guidance through other documents, including prison service orders (PSOs), prison service instructions (PSIs) and other documents. PSOs are permanent directions that replace the mixture of standing orders, circular instructions, instructions to governors and so on that are issued to clarify and update existing rules and requirements. PSIs are short-term directions that include a mandatory element. Until PSOs replace them, standing orders indicated how prison authorities are to exercise their discretion, with a view to promoting consistency, while circular instructions amend the standing orders and provide further detail. A *National Security Framework* also informs prison governors about how to interpret the Prison Rules, though this document is not generally available to the public.

The Prison Rules were not designed to be legally enforceable. The fact that the rules are a statutory instrument therefore makes their precise legal status confusing, as this status implies that they have statutory force (Prisons Ombudsman 1998). Indeed, the *Prison Officers' Training Manual* states that the rules are statutory 'and accordingly have the force of law' (cited in Loucks 2000: 8). PSO 0001 further confuses the issue, stating that the word 'mandatory' in PSOs and instructions 'implies that some legal liability, disciplinary punishment or managerial disapproval may follow if the order is not carried out', evident from the use of terms such as 'must', 'will' and 'are required to' (Loucks 2000).

Courts in England and Wales have consistently refused to recognize the Prison Rules as legally enforceable, and their exact legal status remains unresolved. The most effective means of challenging the Prison Rules in England and Wales thus far has been through judicial review. The Prison Rules may not be a legally binding document, but they constitute a 'doctrine of legitimate expectation' by which prisoners (and indeed staff) should be able to expect the authorities to follow in their exercise of power and discretion over others. The Human Rights Act 1998 has extended this legal protection, prohibiting public authorities to act in ways that are incompatible with the European convention, unless the domestic primary legislation is in itself incompatible (Loucks 2000). Criminal law applies equally in prisons, so proceedings may be brought against both prisoners and staff. Some remedies against breaches of the Prison Rules are possible under civil law, such as negligence, trespass against the person or false imprisonment, and misfeasance in public office, but such cases are very difficult to prove in the prison context.

The Prison Rules in England and Wales cover a wide range of issues, including female prisoners; religion; medical care; physical welfare and work; education and libraries; communications; property and searching; special control, supervision, use of force and mandatory drug testing; disciplinary offences and punishments; officers and others with access to prisons; and independent monitoring boards. The rules nevertheless contain a number of significant gaps. The key performance indicators and targets, and audit standards for the Prison Service, for example, refer to the amount of purposeful activity that should be available and the amount of time prisoners should spend out of their cells. The rules, however, do not mention these issues, nor do they address discharge or discharge grants, sentence planning, personal officer schemes or the impact of custody on voting rights and marriage. Sentence calculation and parole are also absent from the rules, although they have been included in the past.

Prisoners are entitled to receive written information about rules and regulations upon admission. In practice this consists of the *Prisoners' Information Book*, a summary guidebook published jointly by the Prison Service and the Prison Reform Trust and available in a wide range of languages (HM Prison Service and Prison Reform Trust 2002). Access to the full rules and regulations other than those that risk breaching prison security is otherwise possible through prison libraries.

Guidance is available in Europe and internationally to inform the content and application of domestic Prison Rules. The European Prison Rules, based on the United Nations Standard Minimum Rules for the Treatment of Prisoners, were revised in January 2006 (Council of Europe 2006). These rules do not constitute a convention: they are not binding in international or domestic law but, rather, are intended as guidelines for domestic administrations and for the European and domestic courts. The Prison Rules in England and Wales often fail to meet the minimum standards outlined in the European Rules (Loucks 2000). The tendency instead is to treat the European guidance as aspirational rather than as basic standards of decency for prisons.

*Nancy Loucks*

## Related entries

*Accountability; Prison Act; Prisons and Probation Ombudsman.*

### Key texts and sources

Council of Europe (2006) *European Prison Rules Rec.* (2006) 2. Strasbourg: Council of Europe.

HM Prison Service and Prison Reform Trust (2002) *Prisoners' Information Book*. London: HM Prison Service and Prison Reform Trust.

Loucks, N. (2000) *Prison Rules: A Working Guide*. London: Prison Reform Trust.

Prisons Ombudsman (1998) *Annual Report, 1997* (Cm 3984). London: Home Office.

For Liberty's document, *Your Rights, Prison Rules*, see **http://www.yourrights.org.uk/your-rights/chapters/the-rights-of-prisoners/prison-rules/ index.shtml**.

# PRISONS AND PROBATION OMBUDSMAN

The Prisons and Probation Ombudsman heads an independent office with two main functions. The ombudsman investigates complaints from prisoners and those on probation supervision. He also investigates all deaths of prisoners, of those held in immigration detention and of the residents of probation approved premises.

The setting up of the office of the Prisons and Probation Ombudsman for England and Wales can be traced directly to the prison riots in Strangeways and elsewhere in 1990 and the subsequent Woolf Report. Woolf said that one of the central causes of the disturbances was the belief of prisoners that their grievances were not properly investigated. The first Prisons Ombudsman began work in 1994, and the office was rebadged as Prisons and Probation Ombudsman when the remit was extended to those subject to probation supervision in 2001. The role was further extended to the investigation of deaths in custody in 2004.

The word 'ombudsman' is Swedish (it means agent or representative of the people), and the first ombudsman's office was established in Sweden in 1809. The idea of independent complaints handling on the part of the citizen did not spread to the UK until the late 1960s, with the appointment of the Parliamentary Commissioner for Administration. Thereafter, a long list of specialized ombudsmen has developed in both the public and private sectors.

At the beginning of the 1980s, there was lobbying for a separate ombudsman for prisoners from the lawyers' organization, Justice, and from the Prison Reform Trust. However, this had little or no impact until Lord Woolf's inquiry into the 1990 disturbances. Woolf recorded that a theme of prisoners' evidence was that their actions were a response to the manner in which they were treated by the prison system. He went on to argue that there had been an absence of 'justice' in the management of prisons and that recourse to an independent element was a necessary part of the process.

This recommendation was accepted in principle by the government in its white paper, *Custody, Care and Justice* (Home Office 1991). The white paper argued that 'There should be an independent avenue of appeal against a disciplinary finding once avenues within the Prison Service have been exhausted … Appeals against decisions made in response to complaints should also be considered by the same independent body' (1991: para. 8.8). Following a consultation period, the first Prisons Ombudsman, Sir Peter Woodhead, was appointed in May 1994 and began receiving complaints in the final weeks of October that year. He was supported by a small staff team.

The ombudsman operates at the apex of the prison grievances system, so complainants must first have exhausted the internal remedies (this is a feature common to almost all ombudsmen). The principal subjects of complaint have changed little over the years: prison disciplinary decisions, lost or damaged property, categorization and allocation decisions, visits, early or temporary release, the content of reports to the Parole Board. However, the number of complaints received has grown substantially, more than doubling in the five years after 1999–2000 to just short of 4,500.

Wherever possible, the ombudsman expects his investigators to try to resolve complaints informally. Only one in ten investigations results in a formal report. Instead, the aim is to negotiate, conciliate or mediate a settlement between the parties. The current ombudsman, Stephen Shaw (in post since 1999), has said he believes this restorative approach to problem-solving is particularly well suited to complaints in a prison context (Shaw 2006). When the ombudsman does decide to issue a formal report, he can only make recommendations, not binding decisions. However, it is extremely rare for such recommendations to be rejected – at most, one or two each year. In contrast, when the office was first set up in the 1990s, as many as one in five recommendations was rejected by the Prison Service.

The Prisons and Probation Ombudsman's terms of reference cover policy issues as well as how they are implemented in practice. This gives the postholder greater freedom compared with those ombudsmen who are constrained to judging whether there has been 'maladministration'. But the hierarchical nature of the complaints system (and the delays that inevitably result) means that some prisoners are more likely to use the ombudsman's service than others. Adult long-term prisoners are over-represented in the ombudsman's caseload. Those serving short-term sentences or held on remand are significantly under-represented. Women in prison are slightly under-represented, but the major correlation is not with sentence length or gender but with age. Those held in young offender institutions, especially juveniles, refer few complaints to the ombudsman.

The extension of remit to probation in 2001 made only a marginal impact – with the complaints received numbering only in the hundreds. The major change in the reach, visibility and authority of the ombudsman came in April 2004 when the office became responsible for the investigation of deaths in custody. This role encompasses all deaths (self-inflicted, accidental, natural causes and homicide) of prisoners, the residents of probation hostels (approved premises) and those held in immigration detention. Around 225 such investigations are mounted each year, and the ombudsman's office has more than doubled in size, including the appointment of two Deputy ombudsmen. The ombudsman's reports are published (post-inquest and in anonymized form) on his website (**www.ppo.gov.uk**). Although only a limited number of reports are yet available, this will build into a uniquely valuable archive.

There are other specialist ombudsmen arrangements for prisoners in Canada, Argentina, parts of the USA, and in Scotland and Northern Ireland (and many generalist ombudsmen take up a lot of prisoner complaints). But none has quite the same mix of responsibilities or authority as the Prisons and Probation Ombudsman for England and Wales. Together with HM Inspectorate of Prisons and the local independent monitoring boards, the Ombudsman plays a major role in ensuring the accountability of the penal system.

*Stephen Shaw*

### Related entries

*Accountability; Deaths in custody; Grievances; HM Inspectorate of Prisons; Independent monitoring boards; Woolf Report.*

---

**Key texts and sources**

Home Office (1991) *Custody, Care and Justice.* London: HMSO.

Prisons and Probation Ombudsman (2006) *Annual Report* (Cm 6873). London: HMSO.

Shaw, S. (2007) 'A specialist ombudsman for prisoners', in *International Ombudsman' Institute* and Linda C. Reif (ed) *The Inernational Ombudsman Yearbook. Vol 8.* Boston MA: Brill.

The Prisons and Probation Ombudsman's website is at http://www.ppo.gov.uk/.

---

## PRISONS IN FILM

Dominated in the public imagination by *The Shawshank Redemption*, prison films remain difficult to define. Largely, cinematic representations of prison rely on generic characters and a limited number of narratives. However, some films offer thoughtful treatments of prison which challenge the use of incarceration and its mechanisms for pain delivery.

Most people are capable of listing quite a few films concerning prison. This list usually begins with *The Shawshank Redemption* (director Frank Darabont 1994) and is likely to include *The Birdman of Alcatraz* (John Frankenheimer 1962), *Cool Hand Luke* (Stuart Rosenberg 1967), *Papillon* (Franklin J. Schaffner 1973), *Midnight Express* (Alan Parker 1978), *Brubaker* (Stuart Rosenberg 1980), *Mc Vicar* (Tom Clegg 1980), *Scum* (Alan Clarke 1983) and *The Green Mile* (Frank Darabont 1999). Everybody knows a prison film when he or she sees one – every-

one, that is, apart from those who attempt to write about them. Defining a prison film has proved contentious. Films about incarceration fit into a number of sub-genres, most notably death-row films such as *Dead Man Walking* (Tim Robbins 1996) and *The Life of David Gale* (Alan Parker 2003); and prisoner-of-war films like *Stalag 17* (Billy Wilder 1957) and *The Great Escape* (John Sturges 1963). There have also been comedies, musicals, science fiction and films about sport all set in and around prison. Additionally, there are a number of films which could be considered to be about prison but which have very few scenes situated in one, the clearest example being Spike Lee's *25th Hour* (2002) concerned with the last 24 hours of freedom of a man about to begin a seven-year sentence for drug dealing. Conversely, there have been films set in prison which provide very little engagement with their surroundings at all, the jail merely a backdrop to the narrative – e.g. Laurel and Hardy's *The Hoose Gow* (James Parrott 1929) or Elvis Presley's *Jailhouse Rock* (Richard Thorpe 1957), for example.

Defining what constitutes a prison film is certainly awkward around the edges of the genre, with overlap in crime films, social problem films and teen pics. However it is a question perhaps better left to cinema genre writers than to criminologists, for it is the contribution of prison films to public knowledge about incarceration that is more pertinent. The manner in which prison and the prisoner is constructed in media culture offers an important intervention into wider debates about the aim and role of prison, sentencing and so on. This is more likely in films about prison than in films concerning other elements of the criminal justice system, such as the police or courts. Given its relative invisibility and the public's limited penal knowledge or personal experience, for many people prison means *Bad Girls*, newspaper headlines and *The Shawshank Redemption*.

As one such cultural construction of incarceration, the prison film is problematic in a number of respects. While there have been over 350 films about prison released in the UK since the silent melodrama *Prison Bars* in 1901, the vast majority have escaped public attention, as a result of a limited cinematic release, their availability or their confinement to the straight-to-video/DVD market. Consequently, engagement with prison in cinema is often restricted to the most well-known examples of the genre, which are not necessarily representative of the larger corpus. The 1930s, for example, produced easily the largest number of films of any decade, accounting for nearly a quarter of all prison films made (88). In the decade of economic depression in the USA, the prison offered film-makers an allegory for the disempowerment, injustice and isolation felt by the masses. While some of these films received Oscar nominations and awards, such as *I am a fugitive from a Chain Gang* (Mervyn LeRoy 1932), *The Criminal Code* (Howard Hawks 1931) and *The Big House* (George W. Hill 1930), the great majority remain unseen and/or ignored. Yet some subsequent legends of Hollywood appeared in many prison films of that decade, such as James Cagney in *The Mayor of Hell* (Archie Mayo 1933) and *Each Dawn I Die* (William Keighley 1939); Edward G. Robinson in *Two Seconds* (Mervyn LeRoy 1932) and *The Last Gangster* (Edward Ludwig 1937); and George Raft also in *Each Dawn I Die* and *Invisible Stripes* (Lloyd Bacon 1940). For every *Shawshank Redemption* or *Scum*, there is an *Animal Factory* (Steve Buscemi 2000) or a *Pot Carriers* (Peter Graham Scott 1962).

One of the reasons for the audience's perceived familiarity with the genre is the prison film's limited narrative arc. One of the challenges for film-makers is how to build a story around what is a highly structured, repetitive and restrictive institution. In truth, most scripts and direction do not rise to the challenge, and thus plots almost always centre around one or several themes: the wrongfully convicted heroic protagonist; escape; riot; brutality and violence; the demise from individuality to collective, anonymous ignominy; or death in prison. The consistency and durability of these representational tropes have as much to do with money as they do with the desire to communicate penal authenticity. The commodification of entertainment in post-war Western cinema has ensured mainstream film-making minimizes commercial risk through repetition. Frequently this means films about prison are reduced to the lowest common denominator – usually violence, and sex. The latter is particularly

prevalent in an exploitative sub-genre of women-in-prison films, the most well known of which are the *Women's Penitentiary* series in the 1970s, but which persist in contemporary cinema: *Chained Heat 2001* (Lloyd A. Simandl 2000) and, of course, *Werewolf in a Women's Prison* (Jeff LeRoy 2006).

Sexual assault is also a common occurrence in the prison film and one component of the discourse of prison violence which permeates most cinematic constructions of incarceration. Prison is frequently depicted as a brutal institution that punishes, degrades and humiliates. For those concerned with prison reform and abolitionism, such a construction presents opportunities for an exploration of the futility and inhumanity of incarceration, and to raise the profile in public debate and to mobilize opinion towards reform and abolition of the prison industrial complex. However, a closer reading of most prison films reveals not only a reluctance to challenge the existing penal system but also a scopophilic treatment of interpersonal violence: a quasi-celebration in which prison films revel in the stabbings, rapes and beatings between, and of, prisoners. This construction relies on the portrayal of the prison population as inhuman 'other', generating fear in the public who perceive the need to keep such dangerous prisoners locked up. In the vast majority of cases, prisoners are represented as shorn of any humanity and, consequently, deserving the harsh and brutal punishment meted out to them. Where there is sympathetic portrayal of a prisoner – usually the protagonist – this, too, is achieved by representing the rest of the prison population as dehumanized monsters and animals. While the prison hero or heroine is afforded character, emotional development and agency, the rest of the jail is mere cardboard cut-out and cliché. Consequently, prison is constructed as necessary – to keep such psychotic deviants caged and incapacitated, and the public safe. In simple cinema economics, violence sells; stories exploring the socio-economic factors that underpin the inherent injustice in the penal industrial complex do not.

There are, of course, exceptions to the generic dross churned out by film studios in the search for a quick profit. Such films attempt to challenge the use of prison as punishment and to explore its extensive deployment as an institutional mechanism for pain delivery. Critically acclaimed films such as *I am a Fugitive from a Chain Gang*, *Caged* (John Cromwell 1950), *Birdman of Alcatraz* and *Brubaker* (Stuart Rosenberg 1980) have all sought, in different ways, to confront their audiences with the harsh realities of prison life. But other less well-known examples like *Riot in Cell Block 11* (Don Siegel 1954), *Fortune and Men's Eyes* (Harvey Hart 1971), *Silent Scream* (David Hayman 1991) and *Prison Song* (Darnell Martin 2001) have offered thoughtful treatments of prison issues overlooked by their more mainstream generic counterparts: mental health, masculinity, homosexuality and prison privatization. There are also several film-makers who have contributed important work to the prison film canon, such as Argentinean director, Hector Bebenco (*Caradiru* 2003 and *Kiss of the Spider Woman* 1995), and actor, writer and director, Yilmaz Gurney, himself a former political prisoner in Turkey (*Duvar* (*The Wall*) 1983 and *Yol* (*The Way*) 1982).

*Paul Mason*

### Related entries

*Prisons in news; Prisons on television; Public perceptions.*

---

**Key texts and sources**

Ek, A. (2005) *Race and Masculinity in Contemporary American Prison Narratives.* London: Routledge.

Jarvis, B. (2004) *Cruel and Unusual: Punishment and US Culture.* London: Pluto Press.

Mason, P. (2006) 'Hollywood's prison film: towards a discursive regime of imprisonment', in T. Serassis *et al.* (eds) *Images of Crime III. Representations of Crime in Politics, Society, Science, the Arts and the Media.* Freiburg: Max Planck Institute.

Mason, P. (2007) 'Prison decayed: cinematic penal discourse and populism, 1995–2005', *Social Semiotics* 16(4): 607–620.

Nellis, M. (2006) 'Future punishment in American science fiction movies', in P. Mason (ed.) *Captured by the Media: Prison Discourse and Popular Culture.* Cullompton: Willan Publishing.

Schauer, T. (2004) 'Masculinity incarcerated: insurrectionary speech and masculinity', *Journal for Crime, Conflict and Media Culture*, 1: 28–42.

For details of the Prison Film Project, see http://www.theprisonfilmproject.com/index.html.

---

## PRISONS IN NEWS

More prevalent than many people think, the majority of prison stories in British newspapers offer a partial and misleading representation of incarceration. Some broadsheet coverage aside, prison stories are framed within a discourse of risk and fear bolstered by a reliance on elite pro-prison sources. Prisoners' rights are largely represented as 'political correctness gone mad' at the expense of the taxpayer. Questions of race and deaths in custody receive little attention in comparison.

News is constructed. It does not simply exist independently of the will of news organizations, their owners, editors and journalists. The process by which crime and those who perpetrate it becomes newsworthy has become of increasing interest to writers and commentators since the important work of Steve Chibnall, Stan Cohen, Stuart Hall and Jock Young on constructions of crime news and deviancy amplification in the 1970s. Concerns have been expressed over the accuracy and quality of crime reporting, the need for its prevalence and also its potential to shape public opinion. This last contention is argued on two fronts. First, that the persistent over-representation of violent and sexual crime increases public fear and anxiety about the levels of crime, regardless of actual crime statistics. This has been dubbed 'the law of opposites' by Ray Surette, in which the characteristics of crime, criminals and victims represented in the media are the reverse of those reported in crime surveys. Secondly, that such reporting generates support for more draconian criminal justice measures and, in particular, the increased use of prison. Thomas Mathiesen, a leading prison abolitionist, has suggested that the magnification of violent and serious crime in the print media generates support for prison, which is seen by a fearful public as the only viable means of social control in late modernity.

The construction of prisons in the print media has an important contribution to make to the debates around what has been called 'penal populism' or 'populist punitiveness'. These contested terms offer accounts of the qualitative shift in punitive responses to crime by Western governments, in which harsher sentence provision is said to reflect the real or perceived public desire for such measures. Crueller and more emotive sentences are accompanied in media-friendly packages and sound bites. The manner in which prison and prisoners are constructed by the British press also serves to shape and inform public perceptions of prisons and punishment and, consequently, affects government policy. Recent British Crime Surveys have revealed that the public are unacquainted with numerous aspects of the criminal justice system and rely on the media for their information. Importantly, the survey has reported that just 6 per cent of the public consider their principal source of information to be inaccurate. This is particularly pertinent to prisons, where punishment remains hidden from public view and scrutiny. In this space between the reality of prison and public ignorance about it lie journalists and the media. Press discourses of prison, therefore, become a potent opinion-shaper for the public.

It has been argued by some that penal populism is a myth, based on the assumption of a punitive public. Public opinion research has suggested that the British public are not in fact supporters of harsh and/or lengthy prison sentences. Others have suggested that, even if the public are not themselves in favour of longer and harsher sentences, they are invoked in political rhetoric as a device for penal policy. It is more likely, however, that press coverage has a central part to play in this process, and that public opinion may well be irrelevant in this apparent triangulation between press, public and state. While in a liberal democracy the state must be *seen* to reflect public opinion in its criminal justice policy, in reality that opinion is largely one constructed by, and represented in, the printed press and other media. Recent research has suggested that 95 per cent of the claims about citizens or public opinion contain no supporting evidence, and that engagement with citizens by the news media remains superficial. Consequently, government policy on

prisons may reflect the values of newspapers more than it does public opinion. This would explain the apparent inconsistency referred to in accounts of penal populism which argue that the public do not hold deep-seated punitive views.

Contrary to what has often been written about penal newspaper coverage, prisons appear regularly in British news reports. Daily analysis carried out by the Prison Media Monitoring Unit in 2006 suggests, on average, there are around 100 stories about the UK's prisons and prisoners per month. However, the coverage is limited to several particular discourses. The first relates to Mathiesen's notion of news media creating conditions for the increased use of prison. Prisoners are largely represented through the language of dangerousness, fear and risk. This is constructed in several ways: lax regimes and security lapses; an emphasis on violence in prison; and a concentration on sex offenders and prisoners serving sentences for (often multiple) murder.

The last are mostly concentrated around a handful of prisoners, such as Ian Huntley, Rosemary West, Ian Brady, Denis Nielsen and Peter Sutcliffe. Sex offenders are invariably described as 'paedos', 'fiends' and 'beasts'. Often speculative rather than factual, such representations of prisoners are often contrasted with the apparent lax regimes that they are subjected to, and/or escapes. Such news reports feed into wider narratives and panics about the early release of prisoners, their continuing threat and the inadequate sentences originally handed down from the courts. This kind of reporting perpetuates the myths and the notoriety, which the media themselves have originally created, around such prisoners. The stories move from individual prisoners to generalize about the prison population as a whole. They frame prisoners across the penal estate within the discourse of dangerousness such that, to the readers of such reports, to be a prisoner *means* being a highly dangerous threat to society. Consequently, prison and, indeed, its increased use, is constructed as the only viable solution to crime control.

Also prevalent in news reporting of prison is the notion of undeserving prisoners with too many rights and privileges, often contrasted with the rights of the victim and his or her family. The 'unreasonable' demands made of the system by prisoners are constructed by newspaper reports in a prison-as-soft-touch discourse. Frequently, the rights claimed or awarded to prisoners are juxtaposed by sections of the print media with either the crimes committed by a minority of the prison population or the lack of facilities and/or rights of groups outside prison. Consequently, prison refurbishments are reported as the provision of luxury prison conditions for the most notorious and violent prisoners; compensation payments become the squandering of taxpayers' money; and rights laid down in the Prison Rules are represented as 'political correctness gone mad'. Prison inspectorate reports are often misrepresented with single paragraphs highlighted, while the other 60-odd pages, often critical of prison conditions, are ignored.

The notion of political correctness is an example of several narratives common to much tabloid reporting in Britain. The panics around immigration, 'soft-touch Britain' and the 'War on terror', for example, also find their way into prison stories, be it reports on the Islamification of Britain's jails, Abu Hamza demanding an i-pod to listen to recordings of the Koran or Muslim prisoners demanding their own halal sandwich toasters.

These discourses of prison constructed by the print media are supported by the 'expert' legitimating function of dominant pro-prison voices, used to represent public opinion. Whether constructed as the 'commonsense' view or 'political correctness gone mad', these preferred voices – the Conservative MP, the Prison Officers' Association, the pub landlord, the victim support group spokesperson – primarily define public opinion on prison. Further, as moral entrepreneurs they legitimize the process employed by many newspapers in mis-informing, mythologizing and distorting the aim and role of the UK prison system.

Not all of Britain's newspapers mislead and distort prisons and prisoners. The broadsheet press, and the *Guardian* in particular, are much more critical of prison and the treatment of prisoners, and bring to the attention of their readers stories about deaths in custody, for example, that are often ignored by the rest of the press. It is more probable also that the broadsheets will quote from a wider range of sources – prisoners and their families and prison pressure groups are more likely to be heard in the pages of the *Guardian* and the *Independent* than in the *Daily Mail*. In general, however, the reliance on government, criminal justice and punitive-minded sources by the British press serves to reinforce a partial, and often misleading, representation of what prison is and who prisoners are.

*Paul Mason*

### Related entries

*Dangerousness; Deaths in custody; Escapes and absconds; Prison population; Prisons on television; Public perceptions; Risk; Security; Sex offenders; Violence.*

**Key texts and sources**

Mason, P. (forthcoming) 'Misinformation, myth and distortion: how the press construct imprisonment in Britain', *Journalism Studies*, 8.

Mathiesen, T. (1995) 'Driving forces behind prison growth: the mass media.' Paper presented at the International Conference on Prison Growth, Oslo, Norway, April (available online at http://www.fecl.org/circular/4110.htm).

Ryan, M. (2006) 'Red Tops, populists and the irresistible rise of the public voice', in P. Mason (ed.) *Captured by the Media: Prison Discourse in Popular Culture*. Cullompton: Willan Publishing.

Solomon, E. (2006) 'Crime sound bites: a view from both sides of the microphone', in P. Mason (ed.) *Captured by the Media: Prison Discourse in Popular Culture*. Cullompton: Willan Publishing.

The bulletins of the Prison Media Monitoring Unit, Cardiff University, are available online at http://www.jc2m.co.uk/pmmu.htm.

# PRISONS ON TELEVISION

Television explores prison through a number of formats, including documentary, drama, comedy and reality TV. Most popular has been the comedy *Porridge*, the dramas *Bad Girls* and US imports *Oz* and *Prison Break*. These programmes, to varying degrees, lay claim to authenticity and to providing a platform for contemporary penal debate. Yet it is the less popular prison documentary that offers the greatest possibility for communicating and engaging with prison issues, largely unfettered by the demands of prime-time, mainstream broadcasting.

Television forms an important element of media representations of prison but, unlike film and news reporting, it is more disparate in its form, focus and appeal. It includes documentary, drama, made-for-TV film, reality TV, prison scenes in soap operas and so on. Consequently it is difficult to categorize or define a television prison canon in the same way one can do with cinema. One thing television does have in common with film and news, however, is the potential to shape public opinion, to influence the news agenda and to mould, in some way, contemporary debates about prison, prisoners and punishment. This may occur deliberately in documentaries that set out overtly to present an argument, or it may occur by chance: prison entering the discursive economy through unlikely sources, such as the imprisonment of a soap opera character, which sparks national press coverage and is mentioned by the Prime Minister in the British Houses of Parliament (*Coronation Street*'s Deidre Rachid jailed for credit-card fraud in a storyline from 1998).

Similar to film, televisual constructions of prison have the potential to reveal and open up the previously shrouded penal environment to the public gaze. Or, perhaps more precisely, television presents another construction of prison that may or may not challenge existing notions of punishment held by the public and/or depicted in other media. All this depends, of course, on television audiences: whether they watch such programmes and what messages, if any, viewers take away from them. A well crafted, scrupulously researched and excellently acted prison drama, for instance, may well provide a platform for debate on the failure of the prison system, but what if no one watches it or if the reformist message does not reach the sofa?

Take *Buried*, for example. If we exclude weekly drama series such as *Bad Girls* or *Within these Walls*, historically it has been rare for a British prison drama to extend beyond a single episode (the Channel 4 drama *Underbelly* was an exception at four one-hour episodes). *Buried* ran for eight weeks on Channel 4 and was described by then Chief Executive of the channel, Mark Thompson, as having the power to open eyes and to change minds about life inside Britain's jails in a way that could not be done in a news or current affairs programme. The series was critically acclaimed for its brave and brutal representation of the fictional Mandrake Hill Prison through the eyes and demise of new prisoner, Lee Kingley (Lennie James). Despite all this, Channel 4 took the title a little too literally and did, indeed, bury the series in late-night scheduling, leading to poor viewing figures and no recommissioning of a second series.

In contrast, the BBC sitcom *Porridge* has been an almost constant presence on British television screens. It would be no exaggeration to suggest *Porridge* had dominated, in sheer screen time at least, television depictions of prison. In the last ten years, *Porridge* has been shown 86 times on terrestrial television alone. This is particularly staggering given only 22 episodes of the series were ever made. Whether the programme communicates anything meaningful about prison, however, is open to question. Arguably, *Porridge*'s longevity owes more to the cast's excellent performances and the quality of the writing than to the prison setting, which is mere backdrop. Others, however, have suggested that the use of real prisoners as extras and the depth of research by scriptwriters Dick Clement and Ian La Frenais meant *Porridge* captured the penal Zeitgeist of the late 1970s. In the contrasting approaches of prison officers MacKay and Barrowclough was personified the welfare and justice models of 1970s UK penal policy (Jewkes 2006).

Somewhere between the under-consumed prison critique of *Buried* and the popular prison sitcom of *Porridge* lies *Bad Girls*. First shown in 1999, the ITV series about women in the fictional Larkhall Prison ran for eight series. Following on from previous women-in-prison television drams such as *Within these Walls* (1974–8) and *Prisoner Cell Block H* (1987–94), the series, in its early form at least, attempted to balance prime-time entertainment with the serious treatment of very real prison issues: isolation from family, suicide, drugs use, sex, violence, depression and so on. This is evidenced by the accompanying fact sheets on these issues available on the *Bad Girls* website and sourced from the Centre for Crime and Justice Studies at King's College London. Like *Porridge*, how much the series has impacted on public knowledge and understanding about prison is questionable. While *Bad Girls* aired a number of fundamental problems in incarcerating women, these remained framed within a mainstream ITV drama, where grim penal realities were largely subsumed by the glossy and the trashy: 'eight years of thrills, spills, blood, fights, snogs, escapes . . . and murder' gushes the website. A cursory glance at documentaries such as *Women on the Edge: The Truth about Styal Prison*, shown in February 2006 and detailing the six suicides in 12 months at the prison, puts *Bad Girls*' claims to verisimilitude into bleak context.

Undoubtedly, prison documentaries such as *Women on the Edge* do not attract the audience that dramas such as *Bad Girls* or *Porridge* have done, and audiences have different expectations of a drama than they do of a documentary. It is something of an irony, then, that the programmes most likely to address directly the flaw of prison are likely to be watched by the least number of people. That is not to diminish the power of documentary film. Rex Bloomstein, for example, has spent 30 years documenting life in prison for the disenfranchised. His work has made a significant contribution to criminological debates about social control and imprisonment (Bennett 2006). He is best known for the eight-part series about Manchester Prison, *Strangeways*, first broadcast in 1980 and repeated in 1990 after the riots at Strangeways in March 1990. The series' communicative design – fly-on-the-wall camera work and lengthy tracking shots of the prison's interior – still resonates in media representations of prison today. As a Channel 4 documentary noted in 1983, 'to the public eye, prison means Strangeways'.

Worthy of mention are several series imported from Australia and the USA. *Prisoner Cell Block H – Bad Girls* for the B-movie generation – was an Australian drama series which first appeared in 1987 on ITV and attempted to deal with some of the issues later explored by *Bad Girls* – violence, rape, death and drug use. Despite, or perhaps because of, its clunky acting and low production values, it assumed cult status and, at its height, was watched by over 10 million British viewers. More recently, and clearly with a much bigger budget, the US HBO prison drama, *Oz*, was broadcast over six series between 1997 and 2003 on UK screens. Like *Bad Girls*, the series claimed to offer an authentic and uncompromising treatment of life inside an experimental unit, Emerald City, in the fictional Oswald State Penitentiary. As with many contemporary prison films, however, the desire to appear authentic led to a narrative reduced to brutality and violence along racial lines. While clearly an element of prison life, the opportunity to explore and inform the public about prison was rather lost in the incessant and exploitative violence of the series (Jarvis 2006).

The most recent, improbable, yet extremely popular prison drama has been *Prison Break* (2006– ): the Fox Network drama about one man's desperate attempt to rescue his wrongfully convicted brother from death row. Luckily, our hero is not only an engineer with access to the prison's architectural plans but also knows a rather good tattoo artist who draws the prison's blueprints on his upper body. Thus he is able to plan the, er, 'prison break'. A true story, apparently...

*Paul Mason*

### Related entries

*In-cell television; Prisons in film; Prisons in news; Public perceptions.*

## Key texts and sources

Bennett, J. (2006) 'Undermining the simplicities: the films of Rex Bloomstein', in P. Mason (ed.) *Captured by the Media: Prison Discourse in Popular Culture*. Cullompton: Willan Publishing.

Herman, D. (2003) '"*Bad Girls* changed my life": homonormativity in a women's prison drama', *Critical Studies in Media Communication*, 20: 141–59.

Jarvis, B. (2006) 'The violence of images: inside the prison TV drama *Oz*', in P. Mason (ed.) *Captured by the Media: Prison Discourse in Popular Culture*. Cullompton: Willan Publishing.

Jewkes, Y. (2006) 'Creating a stir? Prisons, popular media and the power to reform', in P. Mason (ed.) *Captured by the Media: Prison Discourse in Popular Culture*. Cullompton: Willan Publishing.

Mason, P. (2000) 'Watching the invisible: televisual portrayal of the British prison, 1980–1991', *International Journal of the Sociology of Law*, 28: 33–44.

Mathiesen, T. (2001) 'Television, public space and prison population: a commentary on Mauer and Simon', *Punishment and Society*, 3: 35–42.

## 'PRISON WORKS'

The 'prison works' speech was first delivered by the new Home Secretary, Michael Howard, at the Conservative Party conference in 1993. The speech represented a near complete reversal of previous Tory Home Secretaries' views on criminal justice and opened the door to penal populism in the UK that has remained dominant for over a decade.

The so-called 'Thatcher era' in the UK is known for being somewhat extreme in numerous aspects. In terms of penal policy, however, the various Home Secretaries serving in the Thatcher and Major governments were, for the most part, moderate, balanced and cautious in their approach to the penal estate. A Tory white paper issued in 1990 famously declared that prisons were 'an expensive way of making bad people worse', and this was no mere rhetoric – under Home Secretary Douglas Hurd (1985–9), the prison population shrank by nearly 5,000. The Criminal Justice Act 1991 and the Woolf Report on prison conditions that same year signalled a new era of progressive sentencing reform.

In 1993, all this would change. On 12 February, a 2-year-old toddler named James Patrick Bulger was abducted, and two 10-year-olds were charged with his murder. A week later in Wellingborough, Northamptonshire, a young Tony Blair, then the shadow Home Affairs Spokesman, gave the first of many speeches signalling a new direction in Labour's approaches to dealing with crime. He called on British citizens 'to wake up and look unflinchingly at what we see'.

The Tory government went further. In a near complete turnaround in Conservative thinking on imprisonment, a 'strangely giggly' (Cohen 2002) Home Secretary, Michael Howard, boldly proclaimed that 'prison works' at the October 1993 Tory Party conference in Blackpool. The seductive sound bite would later be quoted either approvingly or disapprovingly thousands of times in public discourse. Howard's argument was not complicated, nor could there be any confusion in what he was advocating. He stated:

*Prison works. It ensures that we are protected from murderers, muggers and rapists – and it makes many who are tempted to commit crime think twice … This may mean that more people will go to prison. I do not flinch from that. We shall no longer judge the success of our system by a fall in our prison population* (Guardian 13 October 1993: 2).

He further argued that the UK should take 'the handcuffs off the police and put them back on the criminals where they belong' (*Guardian* 13 October 1993: 2).

The Tory government – and, later, more impressively, the New Labour government of Tony Blair – succeeded in doing exactly that. Between 1993 and 2007, the prison population nearly doubled from around 41,000 prisoners to around 80,000. The 'prison works' speech triggered a back-and-forth battle between Labour and Conservatives to see which party could be 'tougher' on crime, disorder and anti-social behaviour. Beginning with the Criminal Justice Act 1994, Home Secretaries since Howard have engaged in a seemingly endless effort to crack down on crime, almost always relying on the prison as the primary mechanism for doing so.

The 'prison works' speech cannot be blamed for all this. Indeed, Howard's speech should rightly be understood as both a reaction to New Labour's stance in the wake of the Bulger killing and as an echo of 'tough on crime' rhetoric from across the water in the USA. None the less, the 'citation trail' of the speech (and, more accurately, the two-word phrase 'prison works') is remarkable. A Google search on 'prison works' and 'Howard' turns up 13,000 hits. In just one of dozens of examples, at the Conservative Party spring conference of 2004, David Davis stated:

> Michael Howard and I agree on most things. But on this we agree most of all. Prison Works … Let us be clear: some criminals are incapable of reform … Prison serves a purpose – it keeps criminals locked up, so they can't hurt the community (http://www.conservatives. com/tile.do?def=news.story.page&obj_id= 91736&speeches=1).

Howard's 'prison works' speech has also been cited over 200 times in the academic, criminological literature, although almost always from a critical perspective. Howard's claims have almost no support from the criminological community, largely because Howard ignored several decades of criminological research on the effects of imprisonment, the deterrent value of incarceration and pathways to desistance from crime (see Liebling and Maruna 2005 for a review). At the same time, he did make selective use of some criminological research. Interestingly, one of the very few academic references Howard cited by name was the 'Oxford study of the dynamics of recidivism – a longitudinal study of property offenders released from prison (see Burnett 1992). Howard (1996) wrote: 'Prison – and the threat of prison – can also act as a deterrent to criminals. Ros Burnett of Oxford University – in a study based on interviews with prisoners – found that "for the whole sample, avoidance of imprisonment was the most frequently mentioned reason for not wanting to reoffend".' Howard interpreted this finding to demonstrate that imprisonment is an 'extremely effective deterrent'. In a follow-up to the Oxford Study, it was found that more than 80 per cent of the sample had been reconvicted of a serious crime (see Burnett and Maruna 2004). Although a lucky few ex-prisoners in the sample were able to break free of the cycle of crime and imprisonment, Burnett's research (like almost all other reconviction studies of released prisoners) suggests the exact opposite of the claim that 'prison works'.

*Shadd Maruna*

### Related entries

*Desistance; Effects of imprisonment; New punitiveness; Prison population; Woolf Report.*

---

**Key texts and sources**

Burnett, R. (1992) *The Dynamics of Recidivism.* Oxford: Centre for Criminological Research.

Burnett, R. and Maruna, S. (2004) 'So "prison works", does it? The criminal careers of 130 men released from prison under Home Secretary Michael Howard', *Howard Journal of Criminal Justice*, 43: 390–404.

Cohen, N. (2002) 'How Blair put 30,000 more in jail', *New Statesman*, 16 December (available online at http://www.newstatesman.com/200212160011).

Howard, M. (1996) 'Protecting the public', *Criminal Justice Matters*, 26: 4–5.

Liebling, A. and Maruna, S. (eds) (2005) *The Effects of Imprisonment.* Cullompton: Willan Publishing.

---

## PRIVATIZATION

Privatization – or 'contracting out' – refers to a process whereby the state hands over, under contract, the delivery of new or existing penal services to private operators. Sometimes private operators are global, profit-making organizations, sometimes local, non-profit making bodies, often registered as charities.

### The political genealogy of privatization

The state has rarely operated a complete monopoly in the delivery of penal services in modern Western democracies, and private providers have therefore never been wholly excluded from the business of inflicting punishment. To acknowledge this, however, is not to deny there has been a renewed interest in encouraging private operators to deliver more penal services in North America, Europe and Australia since the late 1980s. This new interest was partly driven by the rise of the new Right which sought to reduce the role of government across a whole range of activities, encouraging private companies rather than the state to finance, build and manage not only new prisons but also new hospitals and new schools.

The argument was that private involvement would enable governments to reduce the overall burden of public taxation, leaving it to the private sector to provide these key services, preferably in direct competition with public service providers, which would further help to reduce costs. The fact that some private operators would make a profit from their operations was not considered to be a problem. Indeed, the 'profit motive' was thought to provide the necessary incentive to secure high-quality services.

### Forms of privatization

There is no single model of privatization. In some countries (e.g. France and, on a smaller scale, Germany), the state still finances, builds and owns prisons but has handed out the management of some facilities to the private sector. In Britain, the USA and in some Australian states, on the other hand, private operators have in some cases taken over the whole burden of financing as well as building and managing new prisons. The advantage this has for the state is that, during the current period of tight fiscal discipline, it can keep the immediate capital cost of building new prisons off its balance sheet. This cost is initially borne by the private contractor, who then claws it back by entering into a long-term contract, lasting for up to 25 years, with the state which guarantees to send its prisoners there at a negotiated *per diem* cost.

The operation of such contracts is monitored, and companies have been fined for not meeting their contractual conditions (e.g. for not providing adequate educational provision for inmates). Private contractors have some-

times lost entire contracts, and several private institutions have been returned to the public sector. In most cases, on-site government monitors are responsible for overseeing the contracts, offering the state another lever of accountability. Attempts to compare the overall performance of these private prisons with state-run prisons – which still constitute the vast majority of prisons in all the countries mentioned – are as frequent as they are contentious.

Ancillary services, such as prisoner escort services, have also been put out to private tender. In the UK, for example, the transfer of all prisoners between prisons, and between prisons and the courts, is undertaken by private companies. Other UK companies have contracted to provide prison food; still others are responsible for the electronic monitoring of offenders released from prison into the community.

At the shallow end of the penal system, the government has also encouraged the involvement of private, non-governmental agencies in helping to provide community supervisions. Guidelines governing how these services are to be competitively tendered, to ensure 'value is added', have been drawn up by government for use in the newly formed National Offender Management Service (NOMS). While efficiency gains are paramount, the encouragement of non-governmental agencies at this end of the system is also driven by the acknowledgement by governments that managing offenders in the community cannot just be left to state but is the responsibility of all civic groups.

### Critics of privatization

There has been some criticism of private sector involvement at the shallow end of the system. It is argued, for example, that through new public management techniques the state now exerts more control over the emerging disaggregated, semi-private (or mixed) penal system than ever before; that both hard-working voluntary and for-profit organizations are being constrained by rigid national standards and over-optimistic performance targets.

However, it has been the decision to hand over prisons for profit to private companies in North America, Europe and Australia that has prompted the most controversy. Some critics of private prisons argue that they are morally repugnant. The argument is that, while all societies have rules, and those who break those rules must be punished, it is morally wrong to make those who deliver this pain on our behalf ever richer according to the quantum of pain they deliver. A contingent moral argument is that private operators will lobby for more prisons, thus delivering more pain by promoting the expansion of the deep end of the penal system.

On a more practical level, critics claim that the idea of private prisons was sold by the new right on the untested assertion that they would reform offenders more effectively than state-run prisons, where recidivist rates have historically been notoriously high. On the matter of costs, the arguments are more complicated. For example, critics argue that, where operating costs appear to make savings for government, it is almost entirely down to reducing staff costs. The claim is that, routinely, fewer guards are employed in private prisons and that those who are employed have poor conditions of employment and less job security. For these reasons there is much trade union opposition to private prisons. Claims of financial manipulation have also been levelled at one private sector company in the UK that successfully renegotiated its insurance liabilities on one of its prison operations without passing these savings to government.

### Advocates of privatization

Proponents of private prisons rebut most of these arguments. They claim that some of the objections are ideologically motivated, emanating from left-wing critics who remain committed to an over-centralized, high-spending nanny state. They claim that private contractors have always been involved in delivering punishment as builders of prisons, and that during periods of prison expansion they have increased their profits. What is new in principle, or morally questionable, about contracting out? As for the claim that, if they were to manage prisons, private contractors would inevitably put their legal duty to maximize profits before the interests of prisoners by cutting corners, this is surely something that would

quickly be spotted by external audit, or by on-site monitors? Indeed, rather than cutting corners, efficient, cost-conscious private operators argue that their practices will force up management standards in the public sector.

As to the fear that private operators might drive up the prison population by demanding longer prison sentences, they ask for the evidence, pointing out that the factors involved in rising prison rates are very complex, often reflecting wider social and political insecurities over which they have little control. True, private companies make no secret of the fact they have lobbied for the chance to finance, build and manage the new prisons that both politicians and public are demanding. But supporters would say: what is wrong with that, not least if it helps to reduce evident and widespread overcrowding that prison reformers take such exception to?

### Where we are now

While the introduction of private prisons has been a striking innovation, their spread has been less spectacular than their advocates anticipated. For example, the private sector's forecast in 1996 that it was on course to be managing 25 per cent of all UK prisons looks optimistic. Furthermore, although privatization has gathered momentum in individual American states, the dramatic rise in the prison population has meant that the overall proportion of American offenders held in privately owned or managed facilities is still very modest.

Critics of privatization find no difficulty in explaining this limited progress. They argue that private prisons have yet to demonstrate that they can either discipline or reform prisoners any more effectively than state-run prisons and that, relatedly, there is no reliable evidence that their competitive challenge has forced the public sector prisons significantly to raise their performance. Critics further argue that short-term operational cost savings, even where they can be demonstrated, need to be set against the fact that using such mechanisms as the Public Sector Finance Initiative (PFI), which enables the private sector to pick up the initial capital cost of building new prisons, only encourages governments to build more, which in the end the government still has to pay for through taxation.

The privatization of penal services mirrors a major reconfiguration of other branches of the criminal justice system – for example, policing, where a whole range of duties once regarded as traditional policing functions are now being 'hived off' to the private sector. However, this process has met resistance from professionals and others who argue that, in sensitive areas of social regulation such as policing and punishment where the state sanctions the use of 'legitimate force' the use of private operators, if not objectionable in principle, at least requires robust scrutiny.

*Mick Ryan*

*Related entries*

*Accountability; Audit; Electronic monitoring; National Offender Management Service (NOMS); New public management (NPM).*

**Key texts and sources**

Coyle, A., Campbell, A., Neufeld, R. and Rodley, N. (2006) *Capitalist Punishment: Prison Privatization and Human Rights.* London: Zed Books.
Harding, R. (1997) *Private Prisons and Public Accountability.* Buckingham: Open University Press.
James, A., Bottomley, A.K., Liebling, A. and Clare, A. (1997) *Privatizing Prisons: Rhetoric and Reality.* London: Sage.
Logan, C. (1990) *Private Prisons: Pros and Cons.* New York, NY: Oxford University Press.
Mehigan, J. and Rowe, A. (2007) 'Problematizing prison privatization: an overview of the debate', in Y. Jewkes (eds) *Handbook on Prisons.* Cullompton: Willan Publishing.
Price, B. (2006) *Merchandizing Prisoners: Who Really Pays for Prison Privatisation?* Westpoint, CT: Praeger.
Ryan, M. and Ward, A. (1989) *Privatization and the Penal System: The American Experience and the Debate in Britain.* Milton Keynes: Open University Press.
For the *Prison Privatisation Report International*, see http://www.psiru.org/ppri.asp.

# PROBATION SERVICE

The (National) Probation Service is the organization within the criminal justice system that has responsibility for those offenders serving sentences in the community rather than in custody.

The (National) Probation Service is headed by the National Probation Directorate, which manages the 42 probation areas across 10 regions in England and Wales. Currently employing in the region of 19,000 staff, the Probation Service now sits alongside the Prison Service in the newly established National Offender Management Service (NOMS), which is responsible for co-ordinating all the different organizations that work to reduce reoffending and to promote the rehabilitation of offenders.

Unlike its police and prison cousins, the Probation Service is a much less visible organization. It has no uniform, no imposing buildings (generally) and the only contemporary television or film work about it is a Steve Coogan comedy called *The Parole Officer* (for the American market!). As a result, the Probation Service has tended to take something of a backseat in the collective consciousness (Teague 2002). Whereas the police can be crudely stereotyped as 'catching criminals' and the Prison Service as 'locking them up', it is much harder to identify exactly what the Probation Service is for. Images of middle-aged, middle-class, university-educated and well-meaning do-gooders making hot cups of milky tea for criminals before letting them get off scot-free or taking them on scuba-diving holidays have plagued the Probation Service. As a result, it has been subject to a variety of shifts in focus that have tried to lead it away from its charitable origins and towards a more politically viable enforcement agency. The birth of NOMS in 2004, alongside the legislative diarrhoea of New Labour, leaves the current National Probation Service reborn yet again, with a new structure, sentencing framework and motto (and only narrowly escaping an entirely new name).

At the end of 2005 there were nearly 225,000 people under supervision by the Probation Service (Home Office 2006). Since the Criminal Justice Act 2003, the range of sentences the Probation Service has been responsible for has been brought together into one generic sentence called the community order, under which the court decides the specific conditions of the sentence. The exact blend of requirements attached to a community order is often informed by a pre-sentence report, which is prepared by the Probation Service at the request of the court to provide background information about the circumstances of the offence and the level of risk the offender poses to the public. A community order can be made up of a wide range of requirements, which include unpaid work (previously called community service) where the offender undertakes a set number of hours work for the benefit of the community (see Alternatives to imprisonment). A comparatively new, yet increasingly influential option is to put offenders on a programme where they attend classes designed to unpick and correct the psychological shortcomings that have led them into offending behaviour. Offenders can still be sentenced to one-to-one supervision with a probation officer but they can also be instructed to undertake drug or alcohol treatment; they can have restrictions imposed on their movement (e.g. curfews or bans from certain public places or activities); or they can be instructed to undertake education or basic skills training. The exact amount and type of activity will be decided by a range of factors taken into account by the court but will typically include type of offence, severity of offence, offending history and risk posed to the public.

While it would not be an over-exaggeration to say that this work comprises the vast majority of work in the Probation Service, it also engages with some other important activity. Some probation staff work in prisons to help develop sentence plans for offenders and to manage their release back into the community. Offenders who are sentenced to a year or longer are released on licence, which means they continue to be supervised by the Probation Service after leaving prison and that their release may also be subject to certain conditions. For some of those offenders released from custody, accommodation will be found in one of a hundred probation hostels dotted around England and Wales. These hostels are managed by the Probation Service and provide secure accommodation for higher-risk offenders deemed to pose an ongoing risk to the public. Hostels require residents to adhere to a regime designed to curb their freedom (a night-time cur-

few) and to continue to address their offending behaviour. High-risk offenders such as these are often monitored by multi-agency public protection arrangements (MAPPAs) which require the Probation Service to work with the police and Prison Service to maintain high levels of supervision for the most dangerous offenders. Outside its work with adult offenders, the Probation Service also has a responsibility to keep the victims of serious sexual and violent crimes informed about the progress of their offenders' sentence. Probation officers are also frequently seconded to youth offending teams and work with a range of voluntary and private sector partnerships that help to provide many of the essential services intended to reduce reoffending.

The Probation Service celebrates its centenary in 2007 and has undergone several major transformations during its one-hundred-year life. Originally legislated into existence in the Probation of Offenders Act 1907, the Probation Service has its roots earlier than this in the Church of England Temperance Society, which began sending missionaries to the police courts in 1876. There are several excellent histories of the Probation Service, most of which start in the late nineteenth century, two of the most recent being Vanstone (2004) and Whitehead and Statham (2006). Rather than become embroiled in the intricacies of how the Probation Service emerged, it is perhaps more useful in this short space to point to some of the most significant changes that have taken place throughout its history. In contemporary parlance, the motto of the Probation Service is 'enforcement, rehabilitation and public protection'. Yet it was not always so. Up until the Criminal Justice Act 1991, the motto had been 'advise, assist and befriend'. No clearer articulation of the change in culture and purpose within the Probation Service can be uttered (though the shift from calling people serving a community penalty 'offenders' rather than 'clients' is also very indicative). Yet the one-hundred-year process that has seen this change come about has witnessed the fortunes of different governing ideologies wax and wane within the Probation Service. From its evangelical and philanthropic origins, the Probation Service began to develop a strong professional identity and, in 1912, the National Association of Probation Officers was established to look after the interests of probation officers. Between about 1930 and the early 1970s, the Probation Service developed a treatment-based, rehabilitative ethos and gradually moved away from its religious origins towards more social work values. The training of probation officers eventually found itself in social work in the mid-1950s where it remained until 1997 when it was replaced by a separate Diploma in Probation Studies. During the mid-1970s the Probation Service suffered a profound crisis of confidence, as the research of Martinson (1974) suggested that 'nothing works' when trying to rehabilitate offenders. From this point onwards the rehabilitative ideal found itself under attack and in decline. The 1980s witnessed an increased use of community penalties as an alternative to custody (partly prompted by prison overcrowding), and the first real attempts by the Home Office to begin to govern the direction and activity of the Probation Service started in 1984 with the *Statement of National Objectives and Priorities.* By the late 1980s, a green paper on *Punishment, Custody and the Community* (1988) marked a watershed after which all governments have seemed intent on competing over how tough they can appear on crime, leading to a succession of attempts to strengthen the punitive aspects of community sentences.

In today's Probation Service the language of rehabilitation and treatment still remains, but is increasingly thought of alongside new terms such as risk assessment and offender management. The new penology (Feeley and Simon 1992) of assessing the risk posed by an individual provides a conceptual framework in which decisions are made about what is to be done with offenders. Recent high-profile cases such as the murder of John Monckton by two offenders under supervision have renewed politically charged and emotive criticism of the Probation Service as being unable to protect the public from dangerous offenders. It therefore appears that both the public and political perceptions of the Probation Service remain as perceptions where, unless offenders are safely under lock and key, they have been treated with a kindness and softness undeserved. As NOMS continues to flex its muscles; as parts of the Probation Service's duties are put out to commercial tender; as new occupational standards for the Probation Service are published; and as the future training of probation officers remains undecided, the current climate is one of uncertainty for the Probation Service. The only thing that seems assured is that the Probation Service will have to continue to adapt to the constantly shifting terrain on which it stands. It has survived turbulent times before, though not without cost to its values and image. What remains to be seen is in what form it will emerge from the controversies and vagaries that currently surround it.

*Simon Green*

### Related entries

*Alternatives to imprisonment; Ministry of Justice; Multi-agency public protection arrangements (MAPPAs); National Offender Management Service (NOMS); 'Nothing works'; Overcrowding; Rehabilitation; Reoffending; Risk.*

### Key texts and sources

Feeley, M. and Simon, J. (1992) 'The new penology: notes on the emerging strategy of corrections and its implications', *Criminology*, 30: 449–74.
Home Office (2006) *Offender Management Caseload Statistics. Home Office Statistical Bulletin* 18/06. London: Home Office.
Martinson, R. (1974) 'What works? Questions and answers about prison reform', *The Public Interest,* 35: 22–54.
Teague, M. (2002) 'Public perceptions of probation', *Criminal Justice Matters,* 49: 34–5.
Vanstone, M. (2004) *Supervising Offenders in the Community: A History of Probation Theory and Practice.* Aldershot: Ashgate.
Whitehead, P. and Statham, R. (2006) *The History of Probation: Politics, Power and Cultural Change,* 1876–2005. Crayford: Shaw & Sons.
See also the websites of the Probation Service (http://www.probation.homeoffice.gov.uk/output/Page1.asp), London Probation (http://www.probation-london.org.uk/) and the Ministry of Justice (http://www.justice.gov.uk/).

# PROPERTY

> Prisoners may have items of personal property while in prison, although possession may be restricted for security and other reasons.

Prisoners may retain personal property with them while in custody, although restrictions are placed upon the type and amount of property they are allowed to keep (HM Prison Service 2004). These restrictions meet a number of aims, including maintaining order and control and security; helping prisons to make best use of the limited space available; facilitating searching; and supporting the operation of incentive and earned privileges (IEP) schemes.

Prisoners are specifically allowed to have in possession, or to have access to, artefacts and texts required by their religion. The possession of other items is at the governor's discretion and in accordance with local published rules, often called the 'facilities' or 'privilege' list, and dependent on the prisoner's level under the IEP scheme. Common items include clothing, a stereo, games, books, jewellery, toiletries, smoking requisites, writing materials, photographs and medication.

The amount of property that prisoners may retain is limited by the policy on 'volumetric control'. This aims to ensure that cells do not become so cluttered that effective searching is difficult and that the quantity of property which accompanies prisoners on transfer, or is held in storage, is manageable. The amount of property allowed must fit into two standard-size volumetric control boxes, although some items are permitted in addition to this allowance, including a stereo, religious artefacts and legal papers. Excess property can be stored but this is, in principle, an exceptional or temporary measure, although in practice there is no power to require prisoners to dispose of property which has been accepted, nor to dispose of it without their consent. All property is recorded on manual records in order to maintain control of what is in the establishment and to provide documentary evidence in the event of compensation claims.

Prisoners may get access to property through a number of routes. They may have been received into prison with the property in question, although this is usually limited to clothing and small items of property. Items may be 'handed in', meaning brought in by visitors or posted in. Apart from the right to have religious items handed in – or, for unconvicted prisoners, to have clothing handed in – since the introduction of the IEP scheme, many establishments have limited the range of items that can be handed in or even disallowed any handing in at all. This is done to encourage prisoners' participation in IEP, to reduce the potential security risk associated with handed-in items and to make better use of scarce staff resources (i.e. saving time in searching items). Prisoners may also order items through mail-order catalogues, if they have space and money available. Again, local limitations may be set. The variation of rules between prisons is a source of frustration for prisoners and staff, as often prisoners will be allowed one item at one prison but not be allowed it in another.

*Jamie Bennett*

## Related entries

*Grievances; Incentives and earned privileges (IEP); Prisons and Probation Ombudsman; Searching; Security.*

### Key texts and sources

HM Prison Service (2004) *Prisoners' Property* (PSO 1250). London: Home Office.

For advice on what to do with property while in prison, see the Citizens' Advice Bureau's website (http://www.adviceguide.org.uk/p_prisoners_-_problems_with_property.pdf). See also the Prisoners Families website (http://www.prisonersfamilieshelpline.org.uk/php/bin/readarticle.php?articlecode=9262).

# PSYCHOLOGY IN PRISONS

> Psychology professionals are employed in prisons. While they are largely forensic specialists, a broader range of experts is now being recruited.

Over the past decade there has been a huge growth in the numbers of psychologists working in prisons. Never before has there been such financial investment in psychological services in prisons in England and Wales. To illustrate this growth, in 2000 just under £10 million was being spent annually on psychological services (after a period of still significant growth); by 2006, nearly £30 million was being spent annually. These figures represent a fraction of the full set of such significant injections of public money into psychological services for prisoners. This is because the figures refer exclusively to psychological staff directly employed by the Prison Service in England and Wales and do not include psychological services provided through the National Health Service, education authorities, private sector prisons and staff other than psychologists delivering psychological therapies. Also, the figures are derived from salary costs, and, in practice, there will be additional costs associated with the delivery of psychological services. In short, the psychological field is booming (Towl 2004a).

## The professionalization of psychological services in prisons in the twenty-first century

There have arguably been two key areas of change in the development and delivery of psychological services in prisons since about the start of the twenty-first century. First, from 1999 onwards the changing, by a vote of the membership, of the name of the specialist Division of the British Psychological Society (BPS) to the Division of Forensic Psychology has arguably had a significant impact on the professionalization of psychologists working in prisons. Secondly, the implementation of a series of organizational changes characterized by a strategic approach to service developments has had a major impact on the professionalization of psychological services.

Historically, psychologists working in prisons were referred to as 'prison psychologists'. This reflected their professional isolation and low status in comparison with other, more developed areas of applied psychological practice. The change of name of the professional BPS division, in combination with the earlier introduction of BPS chartership of qualified psychologists, gave a legitimacy to chartered psychologists employed by the Prison Service being able routinely to refer to themselves as 'forensic psychologists' or 'chartered forensic psychologists'. Forensic psychologists are also employed directly with health service providers. So this element of the professionalization of psychologists who work in prisons has served markedly to reduce professional isolation and to enhance the esteem staff were held in by their peers from other specialisms (Towl 2004a).

Some key organizational changes occurred during the period from 2000 to 2005. The most fundamental changes included the structural organization of psychological services to reflect the management structures already embedded in the Prison Service, which was organized around 12 geographical areas and two 'functional' estates – high-security prisons and women's prisons. By 2001 each had an area psychologist appointed and functioning to ensure the more professional organization and delivery of services in their areas, within central frameworks and standards devised by the national head of psychological services. Salaries for qualified staff increased markedly, and a promotion route was opened up for psychological assistants to trainee grades. Trainees experienced a number of improvements. For example, a system by which all were assigned supervisors was introduced, and all were given full support on their route to chartership.

The impact of such professionalization was felt in terms of greatly increased staff retention levels and the virtual disappearance of recruitment difficulties (where there had previously been some difficulties) for qualified staff. Over at least the past decade, there has never been a problem with the recruitment of trainees, with many applicants for each post. Subsequently, isolated reported difficulties in recruiting qualified staff can, in very large part, be accounted for in terms of an unwillingness to recruit applied psychologists from specialisms other than the forensic (Towl 2004a).

### Areas of activity

To a large degree, the areas of activity of psychologists in prisons depend on their employer and, to a lesser degree, their area of applied specialism. Psychologists across a range of applied specialisms will be involved, in one way or another, with risk assessment work. In forensic contexts such as prisons, 'risk assessment' can be used to refer to the risk of reoffending or, for example, the risk of suicide. Both are important. Many psychological staff employed directly by public sector prisons have traditionally been very involved in the delivery of structured offending behaviour programmes based on cognitive-behavioural principles. The purpose of such groupwork is to reduce the risk of the participants reoffending. Unfortunately the UK evidence for the efficacy of such interventions has often been disappointing, but this is a developing research base. Another area of risk assessment work is with life-sentence prisoners; again, this involves making an assessment of their risk of reoffending. But there is much else that goes on in terms of addressing other prisoner needs. Health service providers tend, unsurprisingly, to focus on prisoner mental heath needs. There are areas of commonality of interest between prison and health providers, such as in the area of drug-misuse work. Some psychologists provide individual interventions for prisoners who have experienced abuse or who suffer from low self-esteem. Roles for psychologists can vary a great deal: some will have very varied professional posts; others may do little else other than structured groupwork interventions. Psychologists also contribute in terms of work with staff (e.g. hostage-negotiation training) and work with HQ (for example, in the design of assessment centres for staff recruitment or promotion), and they are often part of individual prison senior management teams. They can also play a significant role in the vetting of research in prisons.

### Changes and future directions

One of the most striking developments in contemporary psychological practice in prisons has been the advent of a range of providers of such services. Primary care trusts and mental health trusts are increasingly providing a range of psychological services in prisons. On a much smaller scale, the same is true with education authorities, particularly in terms of providing services for children and young people in prison. Public sector prisons are increasingly seeing the benefits from employing a greater range of applied psychologists, including health, clinical, counselling and occupational psychologists. One broader development in professional psychology has been the growing recognition that each of these 'specialisms' has about 80 per cent in common in terms of their core competencies (Towl 2004b). Some forensic psychologists remain deeply protective of what they would see as their professional domain – i.e. prisons. Interestingly, in terms of organizational dynamics, this is also seen when clinical psychologists express similar concerns about 'their' health domain in the NHS. Putting aside such intra-professional rivalries, prisoners are set to benefit from greater access to a range of psychological services available through diverse employers. But such changes need to go further, with a greater emphasis placed on psychological therapies that would generally not be delivered by psychologists. This is an important distinction because, too often, discussion about 'psychology in prisons' has actually been about 'psychologists in prisons'. This debate needs to be broadened to embrace the contributions of others in delivering effective psychological therapies.

*Graham Towl*

### Related entries

*Life-sentence prisoners; 'Nothing works'; Offending behaviour programmes; Research in prisons; Risk; Suicide in prison.*

**Key texts and sources**

Towl, G. (2004a) 'Applied psychological services in HM Prison Service and the national Probation Service', in A. Needs and G. Towl (eds) *Applying Psychology to Forensic Practice*. Oxford: Blackwell.

Towl, G. (2004b) 'Applied psychological services in prisons and probation', in J. Adler (ed.) *Forensic Psychology: Concepts, Debates and Practice*. Cullompton: Willan Publishing.

Towl, G. (2006) 'Introduction', in G. Towl (ed.) *Psychological Research in Prisons*. Oxford: Blackwell.

# PUBLIC PERCEPTIONS

'Crime and punishment' is the frequent subject of public comment. The perception of prisons held by the public is more complex and contradictory than often assumed.

In terms of how much prison is used, 'tough talk does not necessarily mean a more punitive attitude to sentencing' (Home Office 2001: 118). Most people who support increasing the use of prison considerably underestimate its existing use. When confronted with real cases, most of the public find current sentencing levels about right or even too harsh. There is considerable scepticism about the value of increasing imprisonment as a policy option. In order to tackle overcrowding, twice as many people prefer tough community punishments or more residential drug treatment to constructing more prisons. Early-release schemes from prison are not very popular with the public, however. Only a quarter of the public prefer that measure as a way of dealing with overcrowding, although giving people information about the rationale for parole increases public support for it.

When the public were asked in 2003 about the purposes of prison which they rate as absolutely essential, keeping offenders securely and preventing escapes scored highest (73 per cent), followed by treating prisoners fairly regardless of race (68 per cent), helping prisoners to lead law-abiding lives on release (60 per cent) and treating prisoners humanely (49 per cent). When asked how confident they are that prisons were achieving these purposes, only a quarter felt very confident that they were keeping offenders securely, and only 10 per cent that they were treating prisoners fairly. Some 39 per cent were very confident in the preparation for release, but the highest vote of confidence was in the humane treatment of prisoners (62 per cent) (MORI 2003).

This may reflect the fact that, as far as the practice of imprisonment is concerned, most people think conditions in prison are too easy. Yet the public do not seem to support specific measures to make prisons more austere, such as removing in-cell television. They do think that prisoners should work, which may be regarded as part of the widespread support for the rehabilitative role they want the prison to play in providing opportunities for offenders to change their ways. The public are not convinced that prisons are successful in doing this. About half of the public agree that prisoners 'come out worse than they go in', but only 16 per cent disagree, with a large minority uncertain (Rethinking Crime and Punishment 2004).

Public perceptions of prison are rarely based on personal experience. Surveys suggest that only about one in five of the population say they have been inside a prison in any capacity – 8 per cent visiting a prisoner, 5 per cent as a part of their work, 1 per cent as a prisoner and 1 per cent as a volunteer, with 6 per cent giving 'another reason'. For most people, perceptions are more likely to be based on media representations.

There is, of course, a wide range of attitudes among members of the public. Most, but not all, studies suggest that older people tend to be more punitive than younger people. Evidence from the British Social Attitudes Survey shows that people in social classes A and B are less punitive than Cs and Ds. Salaried Liberal Democrat voters are the least in favour of harsher sentences (59 per cent); working-class Conservatives the most (90 per cent). Poorly educated tabloid readers are the least well informed (Jowell *et al.* 1997). While more people are likely to see reducing prison numbers as a 'bad' rather than a 'good' idea' in overall terms, the reverse is true among those in social classes A and B and those who read broadsheet newspapers (MORI 2001).

Psychological research suggests that, at an individual level, attitudes to punishment are mediated by psychosocial factors: emotional orientation, prejudice and fear of crime may be particularly important in this respect. We also know something about the factors that seem to concern people most about offending. Not surprisingly, the vulnerability of the victim and the persistence of the offending seem particularly significant. Research is consistent in finding that repeat offenders elicit little sympathy.

The International Crime Victims' Survey shows that, in comparison with other countries, the British tend to favour the use of prison more readily (Van Kesteren *et al.* 2000). Using a burglary case study to elicit sentencing preferences, the survey found UK countries consistently near the top of the table in terms of choosing prison. On average, 34 per cent of respondents from 16 countries preferred prison, with a range of 56 per cent in the USA to 7 per cent in Catalonia. Just over half the British sample opted for prison. Interestingly, most of the countries with above-average support for prison have cultural origins in Britain: the USA, Canada and Australia. The exceptions are Japan and the Netherlands, both of which have seen sharp increases in popular support for prison in recent years. On the whole, the countries in the least punitive half of the table share a mainland European or Scandinavian heritage. In all these countries, community service is more popular than prison.

These geographical and cultural differences suggest that attitudes are not unchangeable. Efforts to influence public attitudes have largely focused on the provision of information about the reality of imprisonment and prisons. While these have shown some impact, attitudes are based on emotions as well as reasoning, and strategies need to reflect this. It is also important that they reflect the florid reporting of issues in the press and broadcast media, which can exercise a disproportionate effect on the way people think and feel about crime and criminal justice.

*Rob Allen*

### Related entries

*Early-release schemes; In-cell television; New punitiveness; Parole; Politics of imprisonment; Prisons in film; Prisons in news; Prisons on television.*

---

**Key texts and sources**

Home Office (2001) *Making Punishments Work: Report of a Review of the Sentencing Framework for England and Wales.* London: Home Office.

Jowell, R., Curtice, J., Park, A., Brook, C., Thomson, K. and Brough, C. (eds) (1997) *British Social Attitudes: The 4th Report.* Aldershot: Ashgate.

MORI (2001) *Public Attitudes towards Prisons: Report to Esmee Fairbairn Foundation.* London: Esmee Fairbairn Foundation.

MORI (2003) *Crime and Prisons Omnibus Survey.* London: MORI.

Rethinking Crime and Punishment (2004) *The Report.* London: Esmee Fairbairn Foundation.

Van Kesteren, J., Mayhew, P. and Nieuwbeerta, P. (2000) *Criminal Victimisation in Seventeen Industrialised Countries.* The Hague, the Netherlands: Dutch Ministry of Justice. **http://www.wodc.nl/ Onderzoeken/Onderzoek_WOO187asp**

# R

## RACE RELATIONS

The Prison Service has a legal responsibility to eliminate discrimination and to promote good relations between different racial groups. Significant progress has been made developing and improving the management of this area. However, there have been high-profile failures, and it is widely recognized that there is an ongoing problem in making a difference to the real-life experience of black and minority ethnic staff and prisoners.

Managing race relations is particularly important in prisons, partly because of the responsibilities placed on public bodies in this area, but also due to the fact that black and minority ethnic (BME) people are over-represented in the criminal justice system, giving the issue a heightened sensitivity and significance.

The legal basis of the Prison Service's responsibilities is the Race Relations Act 1976, which outlawed discrimination on racial grounds in employment, training, housing, education and the provision of goods, facilities and services. The first comprehensive national race relations policy was introduced into prisons in England and Wales in 1991. Although initially welcomed as an example of good practice by the Commission for Racial Equality, implementation was inconsistent and, as a result, the aim systematically to tackle discrimination and to promote equality of opportunity was not realized (Commission for Racial Equality 2003). Subsequently, Prison Service Order 2800 (*Race Relations*) was introduced, and revised in 2000. This placed responsibilities on prisons to establish a race relations management team, to appoint a race relations liaison officer and to monitor key aspects of prison life, such as the use of force, adjudications, access to work or education, accommodation, the use of complaints and adjudications.

In 1999, the public inquiry into the Metropolitan Police's response to the racist murder of Stephen Lawrence heralded important changes in the police and all public services. This included the enactment of the Race Relations (Amendment) Act 2000, which placed on all public sector organizations a general duty to pay due regard to the need to eliminate unlawful racial discrimination; to promote equality of opportunity; and to foster good relations between persons of different racial groups. This was the first time that a positive legal obligation was placed on public bodies to promote good relations rather than simply avoid discrimination. The Prison Service introduced the RESPOND programme, which included the appointment of a specialist national race adviser, the setting of targets to improve the number of black and minority ethnic staff employed in prisons and the establishment of a national staff support group called RESPECT.

In 2000, the racist murder of Zahid Mubarek at Feltham Young Offender Institution highlighted the fact that there remained major problems with race relations in prison. As this case was subsequently investigated by the Commission for Racial Equality (2003) and was the subject of a public inquiry (Keith 2006), it remained in the news, and its impact on prisons has been compared with that of the Stephen Lawrence case on the police. These inquiries not only highlighted the existence of overt racism but also exposed institutional racism and the clear gap between the intention of policies and the realities of the service provided to black and minority ethnic prisoners and staff. A thematic review on race relations completed by HM Inspectorate of Prisons also highlighted the gap between the management view – based on audits and key performance targets – and the real, lived experience of black and minority ethnic staff and prisoners (HM Inspectorate of Prisons 2005).

As a result of the Mubarek Inquiry's findings, the Prison Service introduced a revised Prison Service Order 2800 (*Race Equality*) (HM Prison Service 2006). This attempted to create a more action-centred approach. Each establishment must now have a race equality action team, which is a subgroup of the senior management team and is chaired by the prison governor. This team is responsible not only for monitoring but also for drawing up and delivering a race equality action plan and is supported by a full-time race equality officer. Access to religion, the use of force and adjudications are among those areas now subject to race equality impact assessments which aim to ensure equality in service delivery. A range of measures is also used to monitor continually race equality in prisons. These include measuring representation in key areas of prison life, auditing processes, surveying visitors and surveying prisoners as part of measuring the quality of prison life (MQPL). This holistic approach ensures a mixture of objective management information and data on the lived experience of visitors and prisoners.

Significant progress has been made in the last 15 years in improving services for black and minority ethnic staff and prisoners. However, there have also been serious, high-profile failures, and it is widely acknowledged that ongoing problems are hindering significant improvements in the real-life experience of staff and prisoners.

*Jamie Bennett*

### Related entries

*Audit; Black and minority ethnic (BME) prisoners; Foreign national prisoners; HM Inspectorate of Prisons; Key performance indicators (KPIs) and key performance targets (KPTs); Measuring the Quality of Prison Life (MQPL); Mubarek Inquiry.*

### Key texts and sources

Commission for Racial Equality (2003) *Race Equality in Prisons: A Formal Investigation by the Commission for Racial Equality into HM Prison Service of England and Wales. Part 2*. London: Commission for Racial Equality.

HM Inspectorate of Prisons (2005) *Parallel Worlds: A Thematic Review of Race Relations in Prisons*. London: Home Office.

HM Prison Service (2006) *Race Equality* (PSO 2800). London: Home Office.

Keith, Justice (2006) *The Report of the Zahid Mubarek Inquiry*. London: HMSO.

See also the 'Race and diversity' page of the Prison Service's website (http://www.hmprisonservice.gov.uk/abouttheservice/racediversity/).

## RECALL

Once a prisoner has completed the custodial element of a prison sentence, he or she serves the remainder in the community. While in the community, prisoners can be recalled to prison to serve the rest of their sentence in custody if they reoffend, breach licence conditions or if it is considered in the public interest to return them to prison.

When a prison sentence is imposed on an offender, the expectation is that he or she will only spend part of that sentence in custody. Most offenders will access early-release schemes, such as home detention curfew or parole, or they will be released into the community under supervision at a designated point in their sentence. For example, those serving less than four years will be released at the halfway point of their sentence if they have not been released earlier under home detention curfew, while those serving four years or over will be released at the two-thirds point, unless they have been released earlier on parole.

While prisoners are in the community serving the remainder of their sentence, they may be subject to a period of supervision by the Probation Service. This will be based on the length of their sentence and the risk they are assessed as presenting. During this time they are liable to be recalled to prison on the grounds that they have committed a further offence, but also as a result of breaches of licence conditions or where recall is deemed to be in the public interest. Legislative changes over the last decade have allowed sentencers to increase the period of supervision in the community and to impose conditions on licences. The Criminal Justice Act 2003 continues this trend but also increases the scope for the Prison and Probation Services to make decisions on recalls rather than the Parole Board (Padfield and Maruna 2006).

The number of recalls has increased significantly over recent years. For example, recalls from home detention curfew have increased by 390 per cent since 2001 to 2,627 in 2005; the number of prisoners serving over one year who have been recalled has increased by 280 per cent since 2000–1 to 8,678 in 2005–6; and the number of life-sentence prisoners recalled has increased by 370 per cent since 2001 to 111 in 2005 (Home Office 2006). It has been argued that this increase in recalls is not as a result of changes in the behaviour of offenders but changes in administrative practice (Padfield and Maruna 2006). In particular, it has been suggested that probation services have been moved away from their client-centred welfare model to an approach based on risk management and punitiveness. As a result, licences have become more burdensome and supervision has become more assertive. This 'back door' into imprisonment has been criticized for its violation of individual rights, its discriminatory impact, its high cost and, ultimate, its ineffectiveness (Padfield and Maruna 2006).

*Jamie Bennett*

### Related entries

*Alternatives to imprisonment; Desistance; Early-release schemes; Electronic monitoring; Multi-agency public protection arrangements (MAPPAs); New punitiveness; Parole; Probation Service; Risk; Welfarism.*

**Key texts and sources**

Home Office (2006) *Offender Management Caseload Statistics, 2005: England and Wales* (available online at **http://www.homeoffice.gov.uk/rds/pdfs06/hosb1806.pdf**).

Padfield, N. and Maruna, S. (2006) 'The revolving door at the prison gate: examining the dramatic increase in recalls to prison', *Criminology and Criminal Justice*, 6: 329–52.

For an article about prison recalls, see **http://www.critest.com/recall.htm**.

## RECEPTION AND INDUCTION

Reception is the first place a prisoner goes on being received into custody. Induction takes place over the first few days of custody and provides orientation to newly received prisoners.

Reception describes the process that prisoners go through when they arrive at a prison, either from court or another prison. The Prison Service states that this process should be carried out with decency and regard for each prisoner's well-being. However, it may also be viewed as the start of the transformation of an individual in the community into a prisoner who is part of an institution (Goffman 1961) with a prison number allocated, the issue of prison clothing and rules and regulations that dictate almost every aspect of his or her daily life.

Prisoners will be taken directly from a prison escort vehicle into a holding area. Each prisoner will then be seen in turn by various designated prison and healthcare staff, almost as if on a conveyor belt, to ensure that the required information is gleaned and assessments made. The prison must confirm each prisoner's identity and the legality of detention, as well as personal information (Prison Service Order 0500). All prisoners will be first subject to a rub-down search and then a strip search. They will also be assessed to see if they are suitable to share a cell.

Prison staff collect all the prisoner's property he or she is not allowed to keep in his or her cell, including money. The range of things allowed in each prison varies. The confiscated property is then stored in sealed bags until the prisoner leaves the prison. All prisoners must undergo a healthcare assessment by trained healthcare staff before they leave the reception process. The healthcare assessment embraces immediate physical and mental health needs, issues relating to drug and alcohol abuse and the risk of suicide and self-harm. Prisoners are allowed to make telephone calls to allay family fears and to sort out home situations, which may be particularly necessary if custody is unexpected. New prisoners will also be allowed a visit within 72 hours. In the reception area, prisoners will receive information about prison life. This is usually in the form of written information but, sometimes, there is video or audio information available. Prisoners will also be given clothes, toiletries and first-night or comfort packs (including, for example, sweets, tea, tobacco, magazines).

Depending on the assessments made, prisoners will go on to the induction unit/wing, to healthcare, to the detoxification unit or to a first night in custody centre (see Howard League for Penal Reform 2006). Induction immediately follows reception. This is the way the prison integrates prisoners into daily life at that prison, its regime and any rules specific to that prison. There is also an emphasis on prisoners' responsibilities during their imprisonment. Induction must be an inclusive process which ensures that those with literacy or language barriers or other issues, such as disability, which affect their participation in a standard induction process, are addressed (see Prison Service Order 0550 for details). The length of induction should be dependent on individual prisoner's needs.

During the induction process, prison staff will try to help with emotional concerns and issues relating to the prisoner's life outside (for example, housing or children). They will outline prison procedures for everything, from laundry to help with substance misuse, to sorting out visits from family and legal representatives, to prison library times. The process will also identify the various people and groups that work in the prison, including staff responsibilities, voluntary groups, religious representatives and

prisoner support (listeners). This is also the point at which the Prison Service suggests it begins to prepare prisoners for release and resettlement in the community. The induction process aims to identify, describe and explain all the processes, routines and people involved in the prison environment. Strong links have been made between the quality of the processes that people go through during reception and induction and their vulnerability, feelings of safety and, ultimately, their likelihood to self-harm or feel suicidal (Liebling *et al.* 2005).

HM Inspectorate of Prisons outlines the expectations for the treatment of prisoners against which prisons are judged during inspections. There are specific expectations laid down for prisoners' first days in custody. The key concerns outlined relate to safety, the identification of individual prisoner's needs and an emphasis on communicating to prisoners the routine of prison and how to cope with imprisonment. None the less, the inspectorate's reports on the reception process can be mixed, as this extract from a report on one large local prison (HMCIP 2006: 24–7) illustrates:

> *Reception was clean but basic and unwelcoming. There were over 40,000 movements through reception each year ... Prisoners were often kept waiting in escort vans ... waiting up to 40 minutes ... Reception procedures were process-driven. Staff were relaxed and polite but addressed prisoners by surname alone and did not engage with them once the initial booking was completed ... The first night procedure appeared to be little more than a tick-box process ... procedures for the first 24 hours were not explained ... Contrary to the prison's local operating practice for prisoners' induction, not all new prisoners received a shower or telephone call and no activity packs or radios were provided ... Prisoners were given an information booklet but not asked if they could read.*

> *Anita Dockley*

### Related entries

*Alcohol; Clothing; Decency; Drugs; Healthcare; Mental health; Property; Self-harm; Suicide in prison.*

**Key texts and sources**

Goffman, E. (1961) *Asylums: Essays on the Social Situation of Mental Patients and Other Inmates.* New York, NY: Doubleday Anchor).

HM Chief Inspector of Prisons (2006) *Report of an Unannounced Full Follow-up Inspection of HMP Pentonville, 7–16 June 2006.* London: Home Office.

Howard League for Penal Reform (2006) *Care, Concern and Carpets: How Women's Prisons can use First Night in Custody Centres to Reduce Stress.* London: Howard League for Penal Reform.

Liebling, A., Tait, S., Durie, L., Stiles, A. and Harvey, J. (2005) 'Safer Locals evaluation', *Prison Service Journal*, 162: 8–12.

See **http://www.prisons.org.uk/ebk-s2-sample.pdf** for information on reception and induction, and also the Criminal Information Agency's website (**http://www.criminal-information-agency.com/ prison.php?subfile=prison_first_day**).

# REHABILITATION

In criminal justice, rehabilitation is a process, intervention or programme to enable individuals to overcome previous difficulties linked to their offending so that they can become law-abiding and useful members of the wider community.

Understanding of crime in the mid-nineteenth century was influenced by studies showing a statistical association between crime and social variables, such as class, environment and mental illness. As a result, earlier schools of thought attributing crime to choice and freewill were weakened by new perspectives of crime as socially determined and comparable with disease. The implication of this repositioning of offenders as the victims of circumstances was that they should be rehabilitated rather than punished. While this medical model helped to discredit harsh punishment, it also served to justify long periods of detention unrelated to the seriousness of the offence.

Belief in the 'rehabilitative ideal' that law-breaking tendencies could be changed by criminal justice interventions peaked in the 1960s but declined in the 1970s and 1980s when rumours that 'nothing works' became the prevailing orthodoxy. Another factor in a backlash against the rehabilitative enterprise were human rights objections to variations in sentences imposed for the same crime. 'Just deserts' became the primary rationale for sentencing, with an emphasis on *alternatives* to custody and to long periods of supervision rationalized on welfare grounds. Faith in rehabilitation was gradually revived from the late 1980s following new evidence that some interventions can be effective if appropriately implemented. By the last decade of the twentieth century, rehabilitation had renewed credibility. This 'new rehabilitationism', though, is more focused on offending behaviour than on the whole person, and the objective is to prevent reoffending with a view to increasing community security, rather than to rehabilitate an individual as an end in itself (Raynor and Robinson 2005).

While there is now a consensus that some interventions are effective sometimes, a prior favourable condition is that they are applied *within the community*. Although some prisoners might benefit from such provision as substance detoxification and basic skills training in custody, virtually no research supports the notion that imprisonment *per se* can be rehabilitative, and this is borne out by the high reconviction rates of ex-prisoners. Indeed, many experts regard prisons as antithetical to rehabilitation. Furthermore, overcrowded conditions, frequent failures to meet standards and contamination effects make prisons ideal circumstances for 'making bad people worse'. Indeed, for many, it is the damaging effects of imprisonment more than prior problems that create the need for rehabilitation.

It seems paradoxical, therefore, that the concept of rehabilitation has been regularly evoked in describing prison objectives. The birth of the modern prison service was influenced by Christian reformers who applied the rehabilitative ideal as a rationale for incarceration. More secular versions of rehabilitation developed in the twentieth century, influenced particularly by the growth of the 'psy' disciplines (psychology, psychiatry, psychoanalysis). With the resurgence of rehabilitation in recent years, the provision of offending behaviour programmes in prisons has become standard. Furthermore, although the dominant legal functions of imprisonment are punishment and custodial, the Prison Service includes in its *Statement of Purpose* its duty to 'help [prisoners] lead law-abiding and useful lives in custody and after release'.

Reconviction figures following custodial sentences make plain that these rehabilitative elements of imprisonment are too infrequently achieved. The report of the Social Exclusion Unit (SEU) in 2002 on reoffending by ex-prisoners was particularly influential in identifying the lack of a unified rehabilitation strategy, particularly in addressing issues relevant to certain groups: women, young adults, black and minority ethnic prisoners, and remand prisoners. It recommended that there should be a long-term, wide-ranging 'National rehabilitation strategy' involving a cross-government approach, including improved access to housing, healthcare, benefits, employment, education and training.

A Home Affairs Committee (2005) inquiry into prisoner rehabilitation endorsed the SEU findings and focused particularly on provision to help released prisoners access accommodation and employment as the best way of ensuring their rehabilitation. Criticisms included too much time in cells and too much non-purposeful activity; an inconsistency of provision across the prison estate; and inadequate provision for those with mental illness, for unconvicted prisoners and for 18–21-year-olds. For resettlement, it recommended a greater use of day-release schemes for gaining work experience and the identification of labour shortages and skills gaps in the external labour market that could be matched with vocational training and work programmes in prisons. For prison regimes, it recommended greater use of therapeutic communities and a community approach (developing close ties with local services) to complement 'normalization' of the prison experience (following a model operated in Sweden) whereby, instead of setting up specialist provision otherwise unavailable to inmates, the task of the Prison and Probation Services should be to facilitate offenders' access to existing services available more generally.

In response to these reports, the National Offender Management Service (NOMS) has produced a national action plan to reduce reoffending, including seven 'pathways' to meet the needs of prisoners and aims to integrate the work of the Prison and Probation Services. Successful implementation remains to be seen. It may be that control-orientated models will always be somewhat counterproductive to achieving the goal of rehabilitation because, for example, security regulations may compromise therapeutic practices. In recent years the Prison Service has been successful in preventing escapes but, as noted by Morgan (2002: 1159), 'the balance currently struck between security and rehabilitative and resettlement considerations, in the wake of the security scandals of the mid-1990s has been skewed unduly towards security'. Also counterproductive is prison overcrowding, resulting in more transfers between prisons, disrupted progress on rehabilitation programmes, stretched resources and more time spent in cells. Related to this, the most anti-rehabilitative flaw identified by the Home Affairs Committee (2005) is perhaps a repeated failure to meet the Prison Service target of providing an average of 24 hours' worth of purposeful activity for each prisoner per week, followed by the abandonment of this as a key performance indicator, presumably to avoid a future exposé of continuing failure.

*Ros Burnett*

### Related entries

*Alternatives to imprisonment; Desistance; Just deserts; National Offender Management Service (NOMS); 'Nothing works'; Offending behaviour programmes; Reoffending.*

**Key texts and sources**

Home Affairs Committee (2005) *Rehabilitation of Prisoners. First Report of Session, 2004–5. Volume I.* London: HMSO.

Morgan, R. (2002) 'Imprisonment', in M. Maguire *et al.* (eds) *The Oxford Handbook of Criminology* (3rd edn). Oxford: Oxford University Press.

Raynor, P. and Robinson, G. (2005) *Rehabilitation, Crime and Justice.* Basingstoke: Palgrave.

Social Exclusion Unit (2002) *Reducing Re-offending by Ex-prisoners.* London: SEU.

See also the website of Reform, an independent, non-party think-tank aimed at setting out an improved means of delivering public services (**http://www.reform.co.uk/website/crime/abetterway/rehabilitation.aspx**).

## RELIGION AND FAITH

Religion is that part of culture which is actively concerned with the patterns of belief and values which relate human experience and behaviour to an invisible order of things. The right of each individual to practise his or her religious faith is enshrined in the Prison Rules.

The word *religion* has been traced to Latin words meaning 'to be bound' and 'to be gathered together' (Ferm 1945). Religion lies at the heart of individual and social behaviour and is closely linked with morality, which facilitates constructive behaviour in society and provides the individual with the guidance to promote self-control (Geyes and Baumester 2005). It has been seen as contributing to the fundamental unity of the human race, traced through its spiritual history in which – in every culture, at every historical period – common religious ideas, themes and quests for meaning are in evidence (Campbell 2000). Faith entails both an assent to intellectual tenets of belief about the transcendent order of things and a personal commitment formed on the basis of those beliefs, which enables people to explore the meaning of their experience: 'A man's religious faith means for me essentially his faith in the existence of an unseen order of some kind in which the riddles of the natural order may be found explained' (James 1897). Hence, the influence which religion may exercise in prison consists of the help it gives to the individual to be in touch with the divine (however he or she conceives the divine) and with those dimensions to human life that are expressed in religious themes, such as love, forgiveness, loss, guilt, hope and inspiration.

Religion helps a person to be in touch with him or herself. It resonates with the experience of feelings as well as ideas and, to those whose life experience has starved their emotional development, religion may offer enrichment. The practice of religion may help the individual to get in touch with the social and corporate experiences of human life and the sense of belonging which can result from this. For this reason the Prison Service Chaplaincy, in its *Statement of Purpose*, states its commitment to serving the needs of prisoners, staff and religious traditions by engaging all human experience, and it affirms that faith and the search for meaning direct and inspire life (Chaplaincy Council 2003).

The contribution of religion has been seen by some as functioning as an impulse control system, leading to the expectation that religious people are less deviant and are given to breaking the law less frequently. The reason for this, it is suggested, is that religion recommends respect for social norms and forms of 'good behaviour'. Studies in a number of countries have tried to demonstrate that religiosity reduces criminal behaviour, addiction and substance abuse: religion appears to be more effective in reducing drug and alcohol abuse than other forms of deviance (Beit-Hallahmi and Argyle 1997). However, recent studies have proved less conclusive in demonstrating that religious faith is effective in significantly reducing rates of recidivism (Burnside *et al.* 2005).

It has been suggested that the concept of prisons in the form in which we know them was derived from the writing of a seventeenth-century Benedictine monk, in which he recommends that wrongdoers should experience a spell of monastic life in order to bring about their reformation. Being deprived of human companionship was intended to encourage communion with God. In the eighteenth century, the reformer, John Howard, after visiting prisons in Holland where services were held in a prison chapel, insisted that English prisons should make similar provision. Throughout the eighteenth and nineteenth centuries, religion played a central role in the life of prisons – it was given physical expression by the placing of the chapel at the centre of the building and spiritual expression by the insistence on each prisoner attending a religious service and by the prominent role of the chaplain in ministering to prisoners.

From the early days of the development of the prison system in the UK, religion has contributed to prisoner formation through the influence of Christian prison reformers and through chaplains providing pastoral care. It has been enshrined in legislation that defines the provision to be made for prisoners to practise their faith. In his prologue to the book *My Brother's Keeper: Faith-based Units in Prisons* (2005), Jonathan Burnside suggests five concerns lie at the heart of Christian belief and form the basis of involvement for work in prisons. These are concerns for prisoners as modelled by Jesus Christ during his lifetime; for human decency; for justice; for relationships; and for spiritual transformation. Many of these concerns are rooted in the Christian faith and are shared with members of other world faiths now represented in British society.

Concern for prisoners' religious lives motivated much of the prison reform movement of the nineteenth century, which was instigated by men and women of Christian faith as a result of their concern for those marginalized by society. Religion continues to be at the heart of reformists' involvement in the criminal justice system at various levels. Religious faith motivates many to be concerned for restorative justice and for the need for the rehabilitation of prisoners, both within society at large and within the criminal justice system. The number of religious charities which promote work with prisoners in custody and after release is evidence of the practical working out of these humanitarian concerns. In addition to the overtly religious organizations working with prisoners, religious faith provides the motivation for some of those who work as volunteers in the secular structures of the criminal justice system.

The last two decades have seen the development of multi-faith provision in prisons, reflecting the recognition of the development of a pluralistic society. The Prison Service provides for an individual to practise his or her faith and to receive the support of a minister belonging to his or her faith group or denomination. This response is embodied in the formation of multi-faith chaplaincy teams, its members belonging to the major faith groups to be found in the community at large, which in turn adds to the cultural diversity to be found in the practical expressions of religious faith and behaviour.

Prison chapels and world faith centres provide the sacred space where prisoners can share the important social experience of worship with fellow believers; a point of contact with the reality of this aspect of life outside the prison by meeting religious representatives from the community outside; and a place to reflect on one's own life experience and meaning. Within the institutional life of the prison (and the institutionalizing effects of confinement), experiences of worship and religious devotion may provide a restorative effect to counter the debilitating effects of prison life. Themes of justice and mercy, repentance and forgiveness, transformation and hope, expressed in the language and symbols of religious faith, may challenge the offender to re-evaluate his or her life and to reflect on the changes he or she needs to make.

The contribution religion and religious faith offers to those in prison is summed up in the Prison Service Chaplaincy handbook: 'By celebrating the goodness of life and exploring the human condition we aim to cultivate in each individual a responsibility for contributing to the common good'(Chaplaincy Council 2003).

*Peter Hammersley*

### Related entries

*Faith communities; Howard, John; Identity and self; Rehabilitation; Restorative justice (RJ); Staff (prison).*

**Key texts and sources**

Beit-Hallahmi, B. and Argyle, M. (1997) *The Psychology of Religious Behaviour, Belief and Experience.* London: Routledge.

Burnside, J., Loucks, N., Adler, J. and Rose, G. (2005) *My Brother's Keeper: Faith-based Units in Prisons.* Cullompton: Willan Publishing.

Campbell, J. (2000) *The Masks of God. Vol. 1. Primitive Mythology.* London: Souvenir Press.

Chaplaincy Council (2003) *Prison Service Chaplaincy Handbook.* London: Prison Service.

Geyes, A. and Baumester, R. (2005) 'Religion, morality and self-control', in R. Paloutzian and C. Park (eds) *Handbook of the Psychology of Religion and Spirituality.* New York, NY: Guilford Press.

James, W. (1897/1956) *The Will to Believe.* New York, NY: Dover.

See also the websites of Prison Fellowship (http://www.prisonfellowship.org.uk/?page= contactus) and IRQA Prison Welfare (http:// www.iqraprisonerswelfare.org/).

# REMAND

> Remand prisoners are those who are detained in prison during criminal proceedings. They may be held when unconvicted, before and during their trial, or when convicted but not sentenced. There is a presumption that those who are unconvicted or unsentenced should remain in the community on bail unless there are substantial grounds for believing that they would fail to appear at court, commit further offences or obstruct the course of justice.

In 2005, there were 84,846 prisoners received on remand and, at any one time, they comprised 17 per cent of the prison population. This is a decline from 1996, when remand prisoners made up 26 per cent of the population at any one time (Home Office 2006). There were 55,455 prisoners received untried in 2005, and 49,104 unsentenced (the difference between these figures and the overall figure is accounted for by those who were held on remand both untried and then unsentenced). The number of remand prisoners received was 8 per cent lower than 2002, but 28 per cent higher than 1995. Female remand receptions have grown more dramatically, increasing 105 per cent between 1995 and 2005. The remand population in 2005 comprised 74 per cent white people, 15 per cent black, 7 per cent Asian and 3 per cent mixed race. The main offences for men were violence against the person (25 per cent), other offences (largely breach of court orders; 18 per cent), theft and handling (15 per cent) and burglary (12 per cent), while for female offenders, 26 per cent were held on remand for theft and handling offences, and 15 per cent for violence. Adult men spend an average of 46 days on remand before conviction and 36 days after conviction awaiting sentence; for women, the average is 35 and 30 days – although such figures mask the wide variety of time people are held on remand, including a small minority held for over a year, and wide variations in regional practices in the use of remand (HMCIP 2000). At the conclusion of their trial or sentencing, less than half of remand prisoners receive a prison sentence (HMCIP 2000).

While on remand, prisoners are held in local prisons, close to the court at which their case is being heard. The Prison Rules state that unconvicted prisoners should be held in separate accommodation and should not be required to share a cell with convicted prisoners. However, the reality is that the pressure of overcrowding means that this is difficult to achieve in practice. As unconvicted prisoners are afforded the presumption of innocence, the Prison Rules accord them additional rights, including wearing their own clothing, and receiving additional visits, letters, money, books and writing materials. They are not obliged to work but may choose to do so. However, because local prisons are overcrowded and often have poor facilities, there is inconsistency in access to services for remand prisoners and there is difficulty in meeting their needs, including resettlement.

*Jamie Bennett*

*Related entries*

*Clothing; Local prisons; Overcrowding; Prison population; Prison Rules; World prison populations.*

**Key texts and sources**

HM Chief Inspector of Prisons (2000) *Unjust Deserts: A Thematic Review by HM Chief Inspector of Prisons of the Treatment and Conditions for Unsentenced Prisoners in England and Wales.* London: Home Office.

Home Office (2006) *Offender Management Caseload Statistics, 2005: England and Wales.* London: Home Office.

See also the Prisoners Families' website (**http://www.prisonersfamilieshelpline.org.uk/php/bin/readarticle.php?articlecode=9279**).

# REOFFENDING

Reoffending is defined in several ways, but most often as a proven further offence or officially recorded sanction for another offence committed during a specified follow-up period.

Reoffending is usually measured at specific points in the criminal justice system process (rearrest, reconviction or type of disposal), although self-report surveys of crimes committed are sometimes conducted. Each of these approaches has strengths and weaknesses, but the results of reoffending analyses are greatly influenced by the choice of measure employed. For example, rearrest rates among released prisoners are likely to be higher than reconvictions because not every arrest leads to a conviction.

However, reoffending measures derived from reconviction data have the important advantage of being readily accessible: reconviction data in England and Wales are systematically recorded through the Offenders Index (OI) and the Home Office Police National Computer (HOPNC). As a measure of 'proven' reoffending, reconviction data have been used for a number of purposes: to evaluate sentencing policy, i.e. to assess the relative merits of custodial sentences over community-based disposals (Lloyd *et al.* 1994); to provide a baseline against which to assess different management and treatment regimes for offenders; and to assess the probable impact of changes in criminal policy.

Until recently, the Home Office used the OI as the main source of conviction data. However, calculations based on OI data are susceptible to variations in the speed of the criminal justice system in securing convictions. For example, an offender may commit an offence during the two years after release from custody, but the conviction may only be secured some time beyond this period. The HOPNC has the advantage of containing the date of offence for each conviction. This improves the accuracy of the reconviction rate because offences committed during the follow-up period can be counted even if conviction is secured beyond this time. It also means that problems associated with pseudo-reconviction (offences committed before imprisonment, which do not reach sentence until during or after custody) are avoided. Another benefit of the HOPNC is that it includes all offences processed by the police, whereas the OI includes standard-list offences only. A two-year follow-up period has been used for the majority of reoffending studies, but having the date of the offence on the HOPNC means that one-year rates are now feasible and are likely to be more commonly used in future as they provide more timely results.

The Home Office has a public service agreement target to reduce the reoffending of both adults and juveniles by 5 per cent from a 2000 baseline against 'predicted' rates by 2006. These official figures specify the reoffending target in terms of a reduction in the HOPNC-derived reoffending rate, which is intended to measure the 'added value' of the correctional services over time. This is achieved by calculating a predicted reoffending rate that estimates the percentage of offenders who reoffend after controlling statistically for any changes over time in the characteristics of convicted offenders. The predicted rate is then compared with actual reconviction rates. Any change in reoffending is expressed as the percentage difference between the actual and predicted reoffending rate (Cuppleditch and Evans 2005).

There are, however, a number of well documented limitations to reconviction rates as a measure of reoffending (Lloyd *et al.* 1994). First, reconviction is an underestimate of actual reoffending because it only measures offences committed that result in a conviction – as few as 2 per cent of all crimes committed result in a criminal conviction (Lloyd *et al.* 1994). Secondly, as a simple 'all or nothing' measure, it does not reflect the frequency and severity of reoffending. An offender may have been reconvicted following release from custody but for an offence that was less serious than the original. Alternatively, the rate of offending may be much lower after release than during the equivalent period prior to sentence. Thirdly, the conventional two-year follow-up period means that reconviction data are not immediately available, potentially limiting the value in evaluating performance. Finally, there is also the possibility that evaluations of custodial interventions fail to measure the possible short-term impacts on reoffending. For example, an evaluation of a prison regime for young offenders showed a significant reduction in one-year reconviction rates (Farrington *et al.* 2000), but this had disappeared by the two-year follow-up point (Farrington *et al.* 2002).

Arrest data are used more frequently in the USA than in the UK to measure the effectiveness of sentencing and correctional interventions. Like reconvictions, arrest rates underestimate the extent of crime as they rely on offences being reported to the police. However, as a measure of reoffending, arrests do not offer the same degree of reliability as reconviction. This is because arrests do not necessarily result in conviction and are vulnerable to variations in policing practice. For example, a US Department of Justice comparison of prisoners released in 1983 and 1994 found a 5 per cent increase in rearrest rates but no change in the rate of reconvictions (Langan and Levin 2002). In the UK, the HOPNC includes arrest data but it is not always possible to differentiate arrests from other forms of contact with the police (e.g. summons).

Offenders' own accounts of their offending behaviour are a much closer measure of actual reoffending, without the distortions of the criminal justice system processes found in arrest or reconviction data. Self-report surveys also provide an opportunity to analyse factors known to be associated with offending behaviour (e.g. drug misuse) which are not captured by official data sources. However, there are a number of difficulties associated with obtaining these kinds of data. Self-report surveys are costly to conduct and released prisoners are a particularly difficult group to reach: the best results to date suggest response rates in the region of 60–70 per cent might be achieved. Self-report surveys also rely on offenders' ability to provide honest and accurate responses to questions about their offending behaviour. While there is evidence to support the reliability of self-reported offending data, survey estimates of offending behaviour should not be regarded as exact.

The HOPNC-derived reoffending rate will remain the primary measure of reoffending in England and Wales, but that should not preclude the use of alternatives that could usefully supplement this measure.

*Duncan Stewart*

### Related entries

*Desistance; National Offender Management Service (NOMS); Rehabilitation; Sentencing policy.*

**Key texts and sources**

Cuppleditch, L. and Evans, W. (2005) *Re-offending of Adults: Results from the 2002 Cohort. Home Office Statistical Bulletin* 25/05. London: Home Office. Available at **www.homeoffice.gov.uk/rds**

Farrington, D.P., Ditchfield, J., Howard, P. and Jolliffe, D. (2002) *Two Intensive Regimes for Young Offenders: A Follow-up Evaluation. Home Office Research Findings* 163. London: Home Office.

Farrington, D.P., Hancock, G., Livingston, M.S., Painter, K.A. and Towl, G. (2000) *Evaluation of Intensive Regimes for Young Offenders. Home Office Research Findings* 121. London: Home Office.

Langan, P.A. and Levin, D.J. (2002) *Recidivism of Prisoners Released in 1994. Bureau of Justice Studies Special Report.* Washington, DC: US Department of Justice.

Lloyd, C., Mair, G. and Hough, M. (1994) *Explaining Reconviction Rates: A Critical Analysis. Home Office Research Study* 136. London: Home Office.

# RESEARCH IN PRISONS

> Academic and evaluative research has been regularly conducted in prisons. Most prison research has focused on the views, conditions and experiences of prisoners, but increasing attention has been devoted to prison staff in recent years.

Prison research varies from administrative studies, such as programme and policy evaluations, to considerations of more theoretical questions about power and order. Researchers may be interested in the prison both as a unique social environment and as a domain in which phenomena, such as domination and psychological survival, can be observed with particular clarity. Certainly, in prison one sees extremes in the human condition and social arrangements (Liebling 1999).

Although research in prisons has been conducted since the nineteenth century, its formative period is generally considered to be the middle of the twentieth century, when there emerged a number of semi-ethnographic studies that charted the prison's social terms and functions. At this time, both in the USA and Europe, imprisonment was undergoing significant change as rehabilitative ideals took sway and the prison system took on a less authoritarian and more bureaucratic character. Much research focused on broad social concerns, such as order and inmate values, while linking these issues to changing penal ideologies and practices. In the USA, prison sociologists were considered a central part of the ambition to forge a more humane and successful prison system (Simon 2000). Researchers and practitioners operated in close alliance, and knowledge about the prison's inner world was seen as crucial for the rational governance of prisons.

Several scholars have noted the subsequent decoupling of prison research and prison management, and the general decline in empirically grounded studies of prison life, particularly in the USA. From the 1970s, as the rehabilitative doctrine was subjected to increasing criticism, it became less common for prison researchers to seek or be granted access to the prison's interior. The shift towards 'warehousing' prisoners meant that practitioners had less to gain from comprehending prisoners' values and adaptations, and more to lose from allowing researchers inside their establishments. Meanwhile, the interests of many researchers shifted to the sentencing policies behind the rapid increases in the prison population. Research declined for a number of other reasons: low levels of government funding; the difficulties of combining tenured academic positions with the commitments required to do sustained research; and the stringency of university ethics committees – originally designed to protect prisoners but, in practice, allowing a dangerous ignorance about their predicament. As Wacquant (2002: 385) has summarized, the result in the USA is that, at a time when the prison population has been exploding, prison ethnography has become 'not merely an endangered species but a virtually extinct one'. In recent years, many of the best accounts of prison life in the USA have been written by serving prisoners and journalists rather than academics.

The situation is less grave in the UK, where prison research has undergone something of a revival and where links between policymakers and some academics are strong. None the less, access is tightly controlled and is sanctioned by prison psychologists whose priorities and terms of reference are not always compatible with more sociological, critical and theoretical research. Studies commissioned by the Home Office do not face difficulties in terms of access, but problems can arise at the stage of publication if results are deemed politically sensitive or unpleasing. Clearly, then, there are dangers that prison research can become hostage to political fortune; that gatekeepers can restrict access to those who support their ends; that only a narrow research agenda may be pursued; and that findings may be harnessed for political and managerial purposes that might differ from the ends of researchers and research subjects. Prisoners understand all too well the relationship between knowledge and power, and often point out that, however well meaning, work does not always serve their interests. Despite such risks and the charge from some quarters that even reformist research may serve to legitimate the increasing use of the prison, it would be churlish to suggest that researchers should withdraw their interest in the prison's inner world and experience.

Few accounts of doing prison research give a convincing sense of its practical and personal realities. However, most suggest that prison research is intense, unpredictable and emotionally taxing, and that it may engender considerable feelings of uncertainty and trepidation. Yet prison research is rarely dangerous, and prisoners and staff are not only generally welcoming but are also often extremely candid about personal and political issues, and about activities deemed illicit by the institution. Here, researchers benefit from being among the very few people in the institution who do not directly exercise power over prisoners and to whom disclosure poses little risk. Prisoners also talk to researchers for more prosaic reasons: to get a break from the everyday routine or to discuss their lives with someone reasonably sympathetic. Co-operation may be less likely in higher-security establishments, where prisoners are more suspicious of the motives and potential uses of research. Disclosure is encouraged when researchers have a sustained presence in the research field that allows them to establish trust and credibility. Most prison researchers emphasize this need to 'put the time in' as the key to a successful project (King 2000).

Ethnographic and qualitative research methods tend to be favoured by prison researchers for a number of further reasons: they suit the humanistic perspective from which the majority of researchers operate; their relatively flexible nature is useful in an environment where the research process is unlikely to be smooth; and they are compatible with the position of relative ignorance with which most researchers enter the field (both because of the sparseness of the literature and because most researchers lack prior experience of the penal environment). Of course, it is very rare that prison research is fully ethnographic. Most studies are closer to something like 'reserved' or 'partial' participation, where the researcher

shares time with prisoners in their cells, workplaces and living units, but is unlikely to share their emotional world. It should also be noted that there is no intrinsic reason why prison research needs to be qualitative and that some of the most important texts in the field have used quantitative techniques.

Prison research involves a number of practical considerations and dilemmas. Some researchers choose not to carry keys, as a way of reducing the power differential between themselves and prisoners, while others feel that prisoners appreciate the advantages to the researcher in having free access throughout the institution. Some researchers have carried out small favours for prisoners – advocating or passing messages on their behalf – while others fear that getting involved in prisoners' lives can easily backfire. There is general agreement that good researchers need to be sensitive to their surroundings; to be clear and open about their research role; to be aware that their research can inconvenience staff and prisoners; to be emotionally as well as physically present; and to be capable of remaining, to some degree, neutral (King 2000).

However, questions of sympathy and partiality are complex and depend very much on context. Jacobs (1977) noted that, in *Stateville's* polarized environment, maintaining neutrality was almost impossible. Contact with staff was perceived by prisoners as being allied with the enemy, while factionalism among prisoners was such that getting closer to one group meant alienating others. In the UK, some research has been produced without any pretence of detached neutrality, while other studies have employed 'appreciative' approaches. Certainly, the prison is a world in which the production of an 'objective' account, on which all parties agree, is unlikely. Researchers often find themselves thrown from one 'reality' to another, depending on which institutional actors they question. As Liebling (2001) notes, though, it remains possible to appreciate all sides of a story. Maintaining an explicit commitment to the research itself may be a useful way of ensuring access to a variety of viewpoints.

A number of ethical issues are also pressing. With such a high number of prisoners having mental health problems, issues of informed consent are thorny. As in ethnographic research in general, it is hard for full consent to be established when observing or participating in public spaces. Unlike most environments, the prison is a place where research subjects are unable to abandon the research zone if they are reluctant to participate. In interview situations, most researchers inform prisoners that their terms of confidentiality do not hold in situations where there is a risk of serious injury to self or others, or in relation to serious breaches of security (such as an escape attempt). However, in the course of their fieldwork, researchers are likely to come across breaches of rules that place them in more ambiguous positions in terms of their loyalties to their gatekeepers and their primary research participants.

*Ben Crewe*

### Related entries

*Home Office; Prison population; Security; Staff (prison).*

---

**Key texts and sources**

Jacobs, J. (1977) *Stateville: The Penitentiary in Mass Society*. Chicago, IL: University of Chicago Press.

King, R. (2000) 'Doing research in prisons', in R. King and E. Wincup (eds) *Doing Research on Crime and Justice*. Oxford: Oxford University Press.

Liebling, A. (1999) 'Doing research in prison: breaking the silence', *Theoretical Criminology*, 3: 147–73.

Liebling, A. (2001) 'Whose side are we on: theory, practice and allegiances in prisons research', *British Journal of Criminology*, 41: 472–84.

Piacentini, L. (2007) 'Researching Russian prisons: a consideration of new and established methodologies in prison research', in Y. Jewkes (ed.) *Handbook on Prisons*. Cullompton: Willan Publishing.

Simon, J. (2000) 'The "Society of Captives" in the era of hyper-incarceration', *Theoretical Criminology*, 4: 285–308.

Wacquant, L. (2002) 'The curious eclipse of prison ethnography in the age of mass incarceration', *Ethnography*, 3: 371–98.

See also the websites of the Home Office (http://www.homeoffice.gov.uk/rds/prisons1.html) and of the International Centre for Prison Studies, King's College London (http://www.kcl.ac.uk/depsta/rel/icps/home.html).

## RESPONSIBILITY

Attempts have been made to offer prisoners opportunities to exercise some responsibility while in prison, although this can have the paradoxical effect of increasing control.

Since the introduction of the prison sentence, there have been attempts to offer incentives for prisoners to behave in prison and to reform in the longer term. Many of these attempts involve offering responsibility to prisoners. Incentives have included lowering the degree of constraint (for example, by lowering the prisoner's security category) and offering temporary-release or early-release schemes, including parole. These measures are based on a risk-assessed decision that prisoners can be trusted in lower-security conditions or in the community.

Measures are also taken in prisons to encourage responsibility through, for example, peer support schemes such as listeners, or restorative justice schemes that pay back to the community. Social approaches to maintaining order and control are also based on the belief that prisoners will respond positively to trust being placed in them. These exercises in responsibility are encouraged and reinforced through the incentives and earned privileges (IEP) scheme, which rewards responsible behaviour. It can also be argued that opportunities for rehabilitation, such as education and offending behaviour programmes, place responsibility with offenders for their own future conduct, and that they enable them to carry this responsibility more effectively.

Given these potential benefits, it has been suggested that prisons should maximize opportunities for prisoners to exercise responsibility (Pryor 2001). This can also be seen as a reflection of the policy to improve decency in prisons. However, it has also been argued that these strategies of 'responsibilization', where prisoners have responsibility for their own self-management and change, have a more subtle and contradictory effect (Hannah-Moffat 2000). In particular, opportunities for responsibility are accompanied by ever-more comprehensive surveillance and monitoring, such as mandatory drug testing and electronic monitoring. When offenders fail to comply with conditions, their resistance is used to trigger the use of traditional, punitive forms of punishment. This strategy therefore offers, on the face of it, a challenge to traditional notions of punishment but actually acts to re-legitimize and reinforce their use, as can be seen in increasingly stringent community supervision arrangements and the increase in recall to prison.

*Stephen Pryor and Jamie Bennett*

### Related entries

*Citizenship; Civil renewal; Decency; Incentives and earned privileges (IEP); Listener schemes; Rehabilitation; Restorative justice (RJ).*

### Key texts and sources

Hannah-Moffatt, K. (2000) 'Prisons that empower: neo-liberal governance in Canadian women's prisons', *British Journal of Criminology*, 40: 510–31.
Pryor, S. (2001) *The Responsible Prisoner: An Exploration of the Extent to which Imprisonment Removes Responsibility Unnecessarily and an Invitation to Change.* London: Home Office.

## RESTORATIVE JUSTICE (RJ)

Restorative justice (RJ) is an approach to criminal justice that promotes victims, offenders and the community working together to respond to crime and to prevent its recurrence. RJ is about building communities of care around individuals while not condoning harmful behaviour, and holding individuals accountable for their actions within systems of support.

Restorative justice (RJ) is driven by an engagement of all people affected by crime. These are most often identified as the victim, the offender, his or her individual support people (family, friends, others) and the community (Zehr 1990). This requires elevating the roles of those traditionally excluded from the process, particu-

larly the victim and the community (Umbreit 1996). Government, criminal justice professionals and society in general also need to be included in appropriate ways in these processes, although this may not involve providing solutions but taking an enabling role (Van Ness and Heetderks 2001). Inclusion involves the important elements of giving voice, accessibility and ownership of the process, and support.

Restorative approaches promote four goals: to enable the victim, offender and community to work together to understand what happened in the crime/conflict; to realize who has been affected by the events and how; to decide together what should happen in order to repair the harm; and to consider what can be arranged to help prevent the repetition of the harm. Restorative projects have been shown to bring benefits in meeting the needs of victims, in encouraging offenders to take responsibility for their actions and in helping communities of care to become part of the process of reconciliation and support. Thus RJ is about building communities of care around individuals while not condoning harmful behaviour, and holding individuals accountable for their actions within systems of support.

Restorative principles and practice can be operated in prisons as individual projects in their own right or in a more general way, influencing the administration of the prison. There are six different models of involvement with RJ, on a continuum from a discrete project to a whole-prison approach, and all have been implemented or attempted in different institutions. These approaches include individuals conducting conferences or victim–offender mediation with serving prisoners; a partnership between a prison and an outside organization to carry out mediation; projects led by an outside organization working with a number of prisons; a package of restorative approaches, developed jointly with prison management in a number of prisons; initiatives owned and driven by prison staff to influence the running of the prison; and a whole-prison commitment to incorporate RJ into its mission, so that the whole institution becomes a restorative prison.

The most straightforward way prisons can become involved in RJ is to facilitate mediation between the victims of crime and prisoners. This is not to be entered into without some thought and a careful consideration of the dynamics involved for all the parties, including the prison. There are other opportunities for prisons in which RJ could play a part, and these are set out below (Edgar and Newell 2006).

Through peer tuition, *induction programmes for prisoners* develop the expectation that the offender will take responsibility for the harm he or she has caused during the sentence. At the start of a sentence prisoners are often at their most sensitive and receptive. Induction programmes set the tone for an offender's time in prison and can be used to demonstrate restorative values of respect for all prisoners (irrespective of the nature of their offences), an open ear to their expression of need and inclusiveness – welcoming them as members of the prison community.

Through *detailed planning of how to use their time constructively*, prisoners are engaged as primary stakeholders in the development of plans for their sentence. The basis of these plans is to hold prisoners to account for their behaviour. Sentence plans encourage offenders to consider the effects of their behaviour on their victims and empower them to do something to make amends. This approach also helps staff to see the offence within the wider context of the community and the victim's needs.

Handling issues about *equality, diversity and race relations* through open ways of mutual respect can establish that such matters are taken seriously. Staff and prisoners' concerns will be handled fairly and openly whenever possible, recognizing the perceived victim's feelings and willingness for such a process. RJ suggests that *complaints and requests* are best dealt with in a person-to-person format, where each person is expected to explain his or her thinking.

Most prison systems have a structure for *enforcing the rules* and *maintaining order and control*. Adjudications, a key function in the enforcement of rules, set the tone for staff attitudes and prisoner compliance. RJ can introduce a dramatically different way of strengthening social order. Using a restorative approach, the prison would respond to an incident that broke the social order by asking what happened and what the individual was thinking at the time – asking him or her to reflect on the impact and on what he or she might do to put things right.

Restorative approaches counter the power imbalances that drive *bullying*, providing support for the victim, identifying the exploitation as unfair and hurtful, and drawing the offender to a commitment not to continue. From the perspective of conventional prison social order, imposed by the authority of the state, violence is against the rules. Through RJ, assaults and fights can be understood as the end result of disputes between prisoners. The *strategy for reducing violence* begins by training staff and prisoners in conflict-resolution awareness and mediation skills, perhaps through such a programme as the AVP (Alternatives to Violence Project) or through NVC (non-violent communication). Establishing peer mediators plays to the strengths of many prisoners in managing difficult settings and in being able to support each other.

In order to integrate restorative practices, principles and processes into the prison's life, it is important that *prison staff* feel they are treated with respect and consideration. Dispute and conflict resolution procedures and protocols can be developed to offer mediation and conferencing for staff with trained facilitators. The personal and professional management of staff should operate with the same principles of concern for the individual and respect for their personal development within the professional setting.

When sentence planning is done in partnership with prisoners, many possibilities for restorative approaches arise when preparing for release: to accept responsibility for the crime; to be accountable to the victims, both primary and secondary; and to make a commitment to the community to which the prisoners will return. The resources of the prison – work, education, leisure, offending behaviour programmes – can be channelled to this effect.

Preparation for *reintegration* should start early in the sentence and should engage the agencies that are likely to be affected by the prisoner's release, such as housing, health and employment, as well as the criminal justice agencies of police and probation. A conference with the family and community agencies while the prisoner is on home leave or temporary release from prison – with the prison providing some feedback about the course of the sentence and about future expectations – should make the process more purposeful. The family and victims could be involved in this process, which is focused on the issues of returning to the community.

There are many other examples of work with RJ in prisons. It is a strength of RJ that it is open to being tailored to the particular culture in which it is developed.

*Tim Newell*

### Related entries

*Adjudications; Citizenship; Education and training; Offending behaviour programmes; Responsibility; Violence reduction.*

### Key texts and sources

Edgar, K. and Newell, T. (2006) *Restorative Justice in Prisons: Making it Happen.* Winchester: Waterside Press.
Umbreit, M. (1996) *Responding to Important Questions Related to Restorative Justice.* St Paul, MN: Center for Restorative Justice and Peacemaking, School of Social Work, University of Social Work.
Van Ness, D. and Heetderks, K. (2001) *Restoring Justice* (2nd edn). Cincinnati, OH: Anderson Publishing.
Zehr, H. (1990) *Changing Lenses: A New Focus for Crime and Justice.* Scottdale, PA: Herald Press.
The Restorative Justice Consortium's website is at http://www.restorativejustice.org.uk/. For prison projects based on RJ principles, see http://www.inside-out.org.uk/. For a Home Office overview of RJ, see http://www.homeoffice.gov.uk/rds/pdfs/occ-resjus.pdf.

# RIOTS (PRISON)

The American Correctional Association (1996) defines three categories of collective violence in prison: 1) an incident, 2) a disturbance and 3) a riot. A riot is said to occur when significant numbers of prisoners control a major portion of the institution for a considerable period of time. A disturbance is a step down from a riot: there are fewer prisoners involved, and the administrators do not lose control of any part of the institution. In turn, an incident is less severe than a disturbance, with only a few prisoners involved and no occupation of any part of the prison.

This above official definition of collective unrest from the USA defines prison riots as the most dramatic form of confrontation between state authorities and prisoners, while suggesting that the problem of order is an endemic feature of institutional life. The level of victimization in prisons certainly indicates that intimidation, assaults and abuse routinely shape life for prisoners, whereas riots and disturbances are much rarer events in an institution's history and pose special problems as the prison itself is effectively lost to prisoners. It is important to emphasize that the term 'riot' is a pejorative one, and historians have shown how the label has been used by authorities to discredit collective protest throughout American and European history. Nevertheless, prisons will always contain antagonisms that make them susceptible to collapse.

Ever since the birth of the modern prison, prisoners have been involved in riots. Four distinctive phases of unrest have been identified (Adams 1992). 'Traditional riots' of the nineteenth and early twentieth century were mainly impromptu mutinies by fugitive prisoners trying to escape the harsh conditions of their confinement. An important exception in the UK was a major riot at Chatham Convict Prison in 1861, which involved over 800 prisoners and ushered in a change in penal philosophy towards even harsher deterrence. A later event –

the Dartmoor Prison mutiny of 1932 – attracted more attention than any other event in British penal history up to the 1960s.

The ascendancy of the rehabilitative ideal from the turn of the twentieth century up to the early 1960s provides a rather different context in which prison unrest occurred. 'Riots against conditions' were largely spontaneous demonstrations, as seen in a wave of riots in more than half-a-dozen English prisons during 1961. In contrast, riots from the mid-1960s up to the mid-1970s have been termed 'consciousness-raising riots', as they possessed clearly defined political agendas and prisoners could rely on hitherto unknown levels of support beyond the walls from the civil rights movement and rising expectations of social entitlements. For instance, in the USA, the Attica Prison riot in 1971 at the remote upstate New York maximum-security prison produced the slogan 'The solution is unity'. Yet during the 15 minutes it took state police to retake the prison, 39 people were killed, including ten hostages slain by the assault force in an indiscriminate hail of gunfire. Meanwhile in Britain, the early 1970s were noteworthy for the birth of a radical prisoners' movement that successfully organized large-scale protests in prisons around the country.

The collapse of the rehabilitative ideal in the last quarter of the twentieth century saw a shift in collective activity to 'post-rehabilitation riots' based on self-interest and predatory individualism. Although this characterization is open to dispute, the paradox is nevertheless illustrated by the two most infamous prison riots in US history. The riot at Attica in 1971 was widely regarded as a political struggle against oppression, racism and injustice, whereas the riot at the Penitentiary of New Mexico in 1980 is an example of the 'Balkanization' of prisoner society (the spatial segmentation of prisoners by race and ethnic background), during which 33 prisoners were murdered and a further 200 were mutilated, burnt and raped by other prisoners.

In the British context there is nothing approximating the level of bloodletting witnessed at these events. Nevertheless, the riot at Strangeways in 1990 sparked a period of unprecedented unrest. During a four-week period the state lost control of over 20 institutions, and the term 'crisis', which all too frequently has been employed to describe the condition of the prison system over the last three decades, became both highly visible and genuinely acute.

Clearly, prison riots are disturbing, complex and diverse events that raise profound questions over human action, social structure, historical context and political reasoning. Useem and Kimball's (1989) examination of prison riots provides a fresh understanding of prison disorder by introducing the issue of legitimacy as crucial to structuring institutional stability. Their argument is that well managed prisons generate conformity, whereas breakdowns in administrative control render imprisonment illegitimate in the eyes of the confined.

This study anticipates the Woolf Report's conclusion that the 25-day occupation of Strangeways Prison in Manchester was due to widely shared feelings of injustice and to the variable conditions under which the confined accept or reject custodial authority (Woolf and Tumin 1991). It is difficult to underestimate the significance of Lord Woolf's Report as it not only marks a decisive break with previous government understandings of prison unrest but is also universally regarded as the most important examination of the prison system in the last 100 years, while the recipe of reform he advocated is widely understood as one that will take the prison system out of the nineteenth century and into the twenty first. The concept of legitimacy locates the study of prison riots in the broader problem of order and control and establishes that there are no simple answers to the question of why prisoners rebel in the ways they do.

*Eamonn Carrabine*

### Related entries

*Assaults; Legitimacy; Order and control; Woolf Report.*

**Key texts and sources**

Adams, R. (1992) *Prison Riots in Britain and the USA*. London: Macmillan.

American Correctional Association (1996) *Preventing and Managing Riots and Disturbances*. Lanham, MD: American Correctional Association.

Useem, B. and Kimball, P. (1989) *States of Siege: US Prison Riots, 1971–1986*. Oxford: Oxford University Press.

Woolf, Lord Justice and Tumin, S. (1991) *Prison Disturbances, April 1990* (Cm 1456). London: HMSO.

# RISK

The concept of 'risk' has become a significant organizing principle for penal rationalities and strategies in late modernity.

The transition from modernity to late modernity involved social and economic changes that fostered public anxiety, uncertainty and a concern over 'risks'. Whereas the modernist notion of risk was used to refer to the potential for either positive or negative results, in late modernity, risk is understood as the probability that a dangerous, harmful or undesirable event will occur. The public's decreasing sense of security is especially evident in a fear of crime and the development of a 'crime consciousness' (Garland 2001). Bolstered by media and cultural representations, public alarm over risk, and in particular a violent offender's risk to reoffend, has transformed approaches to crime control. The response by government to the limitations of the modern criminal justice apparatus to provide protection to citizens has taken various, and often contradictory, forms which reflect new-right politics and a neoliberal agenda (Stenson and Sullivan 2001).

In conjunction with punitive modalities that govern the penal system, the creation of risk profiles on offenders signals the use of actuarial technologies in prisons. While the old penology was concerned with reforming the individual offender, in the new penology 'actuarial justice' is based on statistical techniques for identifying, classifying and managing groups by the levels of risk they pose (Feeley and Simon 1994).

Prediction tables and other aggregate classification systems are used to provide the basis for surveillance and confinement. At every level of the justice system, risk rationality is employed to determine the 'riskiness' of offenders when considering, for example, where they should be sentenced and when they should be released.

Risk assessment tools are often used to predict and manage offending behaviour, both inside and outside the prison. The development of these tools flourished in the 1990s and they include, for example, the Level of Service Inventory developed in Canada and the Offender Group Reconviction Score, which was initially implemented to predict parole recidivism following the Criminal Justice Act 1991 in the UK (see Kemshall 2003 for a discussion of the various strategies). The newest tools focus on the relationship between offenders' risk factors and criminogenic need factors. Whereas offenders are unable to change risk or static factors, such as past criminal convictions, the penal experts argue that criminogenic needs or dynamic factors, such as pro-criminal attitude, can be altered through rehabilitation or treatment programmes. This risk/need score in the prison therefore provides an indication of the level of security and supervision an inmate requires, as well as his or her treatment needs. Rather than offenders participating in generic rehabilitative programmes, the penal experts argue that this system allows for resources to be targeted to specific needs.

Risk assessment tools were developed in conjunction with a reconceptualization of rehabilitation, which is now understood within a framework of risk. Rehabilitative techniques in prison under the old penology were focused on individual welfare but are currently concerned with risk prevention and crime control. For example, cognitive skills training is a penal strategy that aims to restructure modes of thought and to teach, young offenders in particular, self-control or situational crime prevention tactics as a means of rehabilitation. In order to address substance abuse as a risk area, the young person is taught to recognize his or her 'triggers,' such as being with friends who use drugs, and to think about how he or she can avoid the situation and therefore manage this risk factor. The offender is 'treated' to the extent that the measures put in place reduce his or her risk to reoffend. Whereas the old penology was dominated in the 1960s by psychologists and psychiatrists and a focus on addressing the underlying causes of offending behaviour, rehabilitation strategies in prison are now the task of crime prevention advisers and risk managers (Garland 2001).

The argument by prison officials is that risk assessment techniques will prevent recidivism and subsequent custodial sentences, and will therefore strengthen the economy and effectiveness of the penal system. As Garland (2001) explains, the new 'culture of control' includes a scientific and economic style of intervention. However, penal systems are increasingly relying on risk rationality, with little consideration of the limitations. In particular, the officials' 'realist' conceptualization of risk is criticized from a 'constructionist' understanding for ignoring how risk is a sociocultural phenomenon that serves political and cultural functions. Definitions and interpretations of what constitutes 'risk' pivot on specific cultural and moral evaluations of behaviour which, several theorists argue, results in a bifurcation of control. Because actuarial prediction is calculated on a group basis, these methods tend to subject the socially included members of society to reintegrative sanctions for deviance and crime but reinforce the marginalized position of those groups located outside economic power through exclusionary sanctions, such as prison. Since the 1980s in the USA and the UK, the increasing use of prisons for warehousing 'high risk' populations has resulted in permanent offender populations. A related concern is that

risk prevention replaces individual rights as a principle of sentencing (Kemshall 2003), exemplified in the extreme by preventative detention measures for the mentally ill and suspected terrorists. Thus, risk is not concerned with justice (Hudson cited in Stenson and Sullivan 2001) but with minimizing *potential* harm.

In sum, 'risk' plays a significant role in the governing strategies of penal institutions in late modernity. Risk rationality, and the tools it produces, serves a political and economic function by reducing a reliance on imprisonment for those deemed low risk and by reserving prison for those, such as violent offenders and sex offenders, who are assessed to pose the greatest danger to society. However, as historians of penal policy have demonstrated, despite good intentions, no technique of control is without negative possibilities.

*Christie Barron*

### Related entries

*Bifurcation; Dangerous and severe personality disorder (DSPD); Rehabilitation; Security; Sentencing policy; Sex offenders; Violence.*

### Key texts and sources

Feeley, M. and Simon, J. (1994) 'Actuarial justice: the emerging new criminal law', in D. Nelken (ed.) *The Futures of Criminology*. London: Sage.

Garland, D. (2001) *The Culture of Control: Crime and Social Order in Contemporary Society*. Oxford: Oxford University Press.

Kemshall, H. (2003) *Understanding Risk in Criminal Justice*. Maidenhead: Open University Press.

Stenson, K. and Sullivan, R. (eds) (2001) *Crime, Risk and Justice: The Politics of Crime Control in Liberal Democracies*. Cullompton: Willan Publishing.

# S

## SANITATION

Sanitation refers to prisoners' access to toilet facilities and running water.

Until the mid-1990s, it was common for prisoners to have no access to a toilet in their cells and to be required to use a plastic chamber pot. Every morning, the pots would be emptied into sluice sinks in a communal toilet area. This ritual, known as 'slopping out', was one which disgusted both staff and prisoners.

The Woolf Report identified slopping out as a symbol of the inhumanity which existed in prisons, describing it as 'a blot on our prison system' (Woolf and Tumin 1991: 278). The report recommended that the Prison Service should ensure that all prisoners had continuous access to proper sanitation, a recommendation the Home Secretary accepted. The best long-term solution would have been taking three cells and converting the middle one into a toilet and shower area, which could be accessed by the adjoining cells. This, however, would have reduced capacity significantly. The preferred option was simply to install toilets in existing cells.

By the mid-1990s the Prison Service was able to announce proudly that slopping out had ended. While there could be little argument that using a flushing toilet rather than a chamber pot was an improvement, the improvement was relative. On average, prison cells are between six and eight square metres in area, and the installation of a toilet and wash basin in such a confined space makes it even more claustrophobic. The situation was bad enough when there was one prisoner in a cell but, in many cases, there are two or even three prisoners, sleeping in bunk beds. In many instances the toilet is not screened and therefore a person lying on the bottom bunk would be within a few inches of another person using the toilet. The comment is frequently heard that it is hard to decide whether the cell has become a bedroom with a toilet in it or a lavatory with a bed. Having spent a great deal of money at speed to install toilets in cells, it is unlikely that the Prison Service will have funding to provide more decent arrangements for many years to come.

As the number of prisoners has increased in recent years, every available bed space has been pressed into use, including cells which had previously been taken out of commission and had no toilets. In a number of instances (for example, at Portland Young Offender Institution in 2004), HM Chief Inspector of Prisons has found that prisoners did not have continuous access to toilet facilities. In Scotland in 2005 a significant proportion of prisoners still had to slop out. A remand prisoner, Robert Napier, sought a judicial review in 2001, claiming that these conditions amounted to 'inhuman and degrading' conditions in contravention of Article 3 of the European Convention on Human Rights. In 2004 the Court of Session in Edinburgh found that these conditions did indeed amount to degrading treatment (Coyle 2005).

While population pressures continue to place a limit on further developments in improving physical conditions, and even threaten progress made, legal intervention has consolidated the advances of the last 15 years.

*Andrew Coyle*

### Related entries

*Decency; Human rights; Woolf Report.*

**Key texts and sources**

Coyle, A. (2005) *Understanding Prisons: Key Issues in Policy and Practice.* Milton Keynes: Open University Press.

Woolf, Lord Justice and Tumin, S. (1991) *Report of an Inquiry into Prison Disturbances, April 1990.* London: HMSO.

# SEARCHING

Searching is an important tool of security in prisons. Searches may take the form of personal searches (usually rub-downs and strip searches) or accommodation (e.g. cell or workshop) searches.

Searching is among the most important tools for detecting and deterring threats to security and control in prisons (Learmont 1995). The Prison Rules authorize the searching of prisoners, staff and visitors. Searches may also be carried out on accommodation, correspondence and property. It is a fundamental principle that searching should be carried out in as seemly a manner as is consistent with discovering anything concealed.

Each prison must have a searching strategy agreed between the governor and the area manager. This will set out the main elements of how and why searching is carried out in the particular prison, including specifying the frequency of routine searching. The most frequent searches carried out are the use of hand-held metal detectors and rub-down searching. These searches do not involve the removal of significant items of clothing and can be carried out quickly. A rub-down search involves a searcher emptying the pockets of the person being searched and conducting a search by systematically running the flats of his or her hands over the person being searched. This is similar to searches carried out in airports. A metal detector may be used in addition to this or independently as a search for metal objects. A male member of staff cannot search females, but a female may search males, with their consent.

A full search involves a person removing his or her clothing in order that a visual check can be conducted and his or her clothing physically searched by hand. The person being searched will always have one half of his or her body covered at any time, and the search will only be carried out by persons of the same gender. The visual checking of intimate parts of the body or requesting that a prisoner 'squat' can only be carried out if authorized on the basis of a reasonable cause to believe that an item is concealed. Intimate searches that involve physical intrusion into a bodily orifice can only be carried out by a doctor with the consent of the prisoner. Such searches can only be carried out on staff or visitors by the police.

Searches of accommodation should be carried out as specified in the searching strategy. Cell searches involve both a full search of the prisoner and a search of the cell and all the property contained within it. A cell fabric check is carried out on a daily basis and is a visual and physical check of the fabric of the cell in order to ensure that there is no damage or evidence of escape. Other areas will also be searched on a regular basis, such as kitchens, gymnasium and workshops.

There are a number of aids that are used to assist searching. The most obvious examples include metal detectors and X-ray machines. However, another important aid is search dogs. These can be proactive dogs that search for drugs, ammunition or explosives in property or accommodation, or passive dogs that are used to detect and deter drug trafficking. High-security prisons also have dedicated search teams, consisting of specially trained officers to carry out more thorough, targeted searching using specialist technical equipment.

When prisoners do not comply with searching, a disciplinary offence may be committed, resulting in an adjudication. Moreover, compliance may be ensured through the use of force. The searching of visitors and staff without their consent is more limited and is usually only allowed where it is reasonably suspected that they have a firearm or drugs concealed, or if they have been arrested and it is reasonably suspected that they have items that relate to the offence, could aid an escape or may be used to harm themselves or others.

High levels of searching can cause resistance from prisoners, particularly where it is seen as excessive or punitive (Sparks *et al.* 1996). It is therefore important to ensure that searches are carried out in a way that is respectful and decent. For example, special advice is provided to prison staff concerning religion and culture in searching, and in managing sensitive issues, such as disability and gender dysphoria.

*Jamie Bennett*

### Related entries

*Disability; High-security prisons; Prison Rules; Religion and faith; Security; Use of force (control and restraint).*

---

**Key texts and sources**

Learmont, J. (1995) *Review of Prison Service Security in England and Wales and the Escape from Parkhurst Prison, Tuesday 3rd January 1995* (Cm 3020). London: HMSO.
Sparks, R., Bottoms, A. and Hay, W. (1996) *Prisons and the Problem of Order.* Oxford: Clarendon Press.

---

## SECURE TRAINING CENTRES

Secure training centres form one part of the juvenile secure estate (alongside young offender institutions and local authority secure children's homes) in England and Wales. They aim to provide education, vocational training and correction in secure accommodation for 12–17-year-olds. Such centres currently only exist in England and are unique in Western Europe.

Secure training centres (STCs) are purpose-built centres for child offenders – male and female – up to the age of 17. In 2006 there were four centres, all in England, and each run by private operators working under a private finance initiative with the Youth Justice Board for England and Wales and the Home Office. The four centres are Oakhill in Milton Keynes (opened 2004); Hassockfield in County Durham (opened 1999); Rainsbrook in Rugby (opened 1999); and Medway in Kent (opened 1998). Medway and Rainsbrook are run by Rebound, a subsidiary of Group 4; Oakhill is run by Securicor; and Hassockfield by Premier Custodial Group Ltd. Planning permission to build a fifth centre in Glynneath, Wales, was granted in 2003, whereas plans for a sixth at Brentwood, Essex, were abandoned in 2004.

STCs differ from young offender institutions (YOIs) in that they have a higher staff-to-young-offender ratio (a minimum of three staff members to eight 'trainees'), are smaller in size and admit children as young as 12 years old. The regimes in STCs, it is claimed, are more constructive and education focused. 'Trainees' are supposedly provided with formal education 25 hours a week, 50 weeks of the year.

STCs were originally formally proposed in 1993, just days after the murder of James Bulger. The plan then was to build five centres for 12–14-year-olds to tackle an assumed 'epidemic' of persistent offending. A secure training order for 12–14-year-olds was first introduced by the Criminal Justice and Public Order Act 1994. The contract for the first centre at Medway, however, was not signed until 1997, and the centre did not open until well into the first year of the Labour administration in April 1998. It then had places for 40 children. A further two centres of similar size at Rainsbrook and Hassockfield opened in 1999. In 2002 capacity at Medway and Rainsbrook was increased to 76 beds and at Hassockfield to 42. The fourth centre, Oakhill, opened in August 2004 with places for 80 children. In all, the four centres can now accommodate up to 274 children. In July 2006 their population was 234, at a cost of some £164,000 per place a year. The existence of STCs is widely assumed to be the root cause of an 800 per cent rise in the number of under 15-year-olds sent to custody in England and Wales between 1992 and 2001.

The detention and training order replaced the secure training order in 2000 and, as it was available for young offenders up to the age of 17, the STCs then began taking a wider age range. As well as detention and training order 'trainees', it also included young people serving longer terms of detention under ss. 90 and 91 of the Powers of Criminal Courts (Sentencing) Act 2000. The Criminal Justice and Police Act 2001 also enabled young people who had been remanded to the care of a local authority with a security requirement to be placed in an STC with the consent of the Secretary of State. Previously, it had not been possible for the unconvicted to be detained in an STC. In 2002, almost one third of 'trainees' were being held on remand; by 2003 that figure had risen to almost a half.

STCs have proved to be consistently controversial, in particular attracting criticism from the United Nations Committee on the Rights of the Child for enabling the incarceration of children at such a young age. An emphasis on security, and the fact that the children are referred to as 'trainees', defines the ethos. A third of all children in STCs are located over 50 miles away from their homes, and visiting hours are not open. An evaluation of the first two years of Medway found a reoffending rate of 67 per cent. Institutional support following release was notably lacking. The turnover rate of staff in STCs is also extremely high. The adequacy of their training has also been consistently questioned in Commission for Social Care Inspection reports. At Medway, 101 of 256 staff left in 2003.

Mounting concern about the suitability of such regimes for particularly young and vulnerable offenders has grown since two child deaths occurred at Rainsbrook and Hassockfield in 2004. The Carlile Inquiry was established after 15-year-old Gareth Myatt died after being restrained by staff at Rainsbrook STC. He was five feet tall, weighed less than eight stone and was just three days into a 12-month sentence. Lord Carlile's terms of reference were to investigate the use of physical restraint, solitary confinement and forcible strip searching of children in prisons, STCs and local authority secure children's homes and to make recommendations. A system of physical interventions, known as physical control in care, was developed in the late 1990s for use in STCs. In 2002, restraint was used on 2,461 occasions; in 2003 it was used on 3,289 occasions. It has been estimated that in each STC restraint is used about twice a day,

every day of the year. At Medway, 1,818 injuries to children as a result of restraint were reported between January 2004 and June 2005; at Rainsbrook there were 118, Hassockfield reported 177 and Oakhill listed 48 from its opening in August 2004 to August 2005. This suggests the routine use of physical control, not a technique of last resort. Lord Carlile's report in 2006 indeed recognized that such treatment would be considered abusive in other settings.

Further, in August 2004, 14-year-old Adam Rickwood became the youngest person to die in custody in the UK when he committed suicide at Hassockfield STC. Labour Peer Lord Judd said at the time: 'There should be no children in prison at all. It is simply not acceptable for a nation of our wealth to say that we cannot make special provision of secure care under local authority administration for youngsters, instead of putting them into the soul-destroying situation of prison' (House of Lords Debates 9 June 2005).

*John Muncie and Barry Goldson*

### Related entries

*Reoffending; Security; Young offender institutions (YOIs); Youth Justice Board (YJB).*

---

**Key texts and sources**

Carlile, Lord A. (2006) *An Independent Inquiry into the Use of Physical Restraint, Solitary Confinement and Forcible Strip Searching of Children in Prisons, Secure Training Centres and Local Authority Secure Children's Homes.* London: Howard League for Penal Reform.

Goldson, B. (2002) *Vulnerable Inside: Children in Secure and Penal Settings.* London: Children's Society.

Hagell, A., Hazel, N. and Shaw, C. (2000) *Evaluation of Medway Secure Training Centre.* London: Home Office Research, Development and Statistics Directorate.

See also the Youth Justice Board's website (http://www.yjb.gov.uk/en-gb/) and the website of the Commission for Social Care Inspection (http://www.csci.org.uk/find_a_report/secure_training_centre_inspect.aspx).

# SECURITY

'Security' in prisons has a variety of meanings, but is generally taken to describe the physical, procedural and dynamic elements that are used to prevent escape and to maintain control.

Maintaining security and preventing escapes can be described as the most fundamental purpose of prisons. Security has been a high-profile issue professionally and politically, especially since the escape of the spy, George Blake, in the 1960s, which led to a major review of prison security. This event led to the creation of high-security – or 'dispersal' – prisons and the implementation of the categorization and allocation process, which seeks to place prisoners in prisons appropriate to their risk of escape and offending.

Following high-profile escape attempts from two maximum-security prisons (Whitemoor and Parkhurst) in the mid-1990s, security in prisons was, again, reconsidered. The report of the Learmont Inquiry (1995) undertook a review of security in the Prison Service of England and Wales. In this report a number of 'basic' requirements of security in prisons were identified and clarified. For security in prisons to be upheld, the Learmont Report argued that proper attention needed to be given both to physical security and to security procedures. Physical security refers to the buildings and structures of prison establishments, the use of electronic security (such as CCTV, electronic movement detectors and electronic locks) and security audits (to ensure physical and electronic security measures are appropriately implemented in prison establishments). Security procedures refer to effective systems, co-ordinated nationally and locally, to ensure there is appropriate application of security measures (such as the security policies for prisoners' visits, searching and prisoner escorts).

Another way in which the term 'security' is used in the prisons context is in the phrase 'dynamic security', which was first introduced into the Prison Service lexicon by Ian Dunbar (1985). Dynamic security is an approach to establishment safety based on the relationship between staff and prisoners. In part, it means that everyone who works in a prison has a responsibility for security and control (Dunbar 1985: 43). In practice, however, 'dynamic security' means that staff should mix with prisoners and talk and listen to them while remaining alert to the atmosphere and the potential for incidents. Intelligence gathering is an aspect of dynamic security, but its overall purpose should be for the positive effect of reducing the coerciveness of prison environments.

*Deb Drake*

## Related entries

*Audit; Categorization and allocation; Category A prisoners; Escapes and absconds; High-reliability organizations (HROs); High-security prisons; Official reports; Risk; Searching.*

### Key texts and sources

Dunbar, I. (1985) *A Sense of Direction.* London: Home Office.

Learmont, J. (1995) *Review of Prison Service Security in England and Wales and the Escape from Parkhurst Prison, Tuesday 3rd January 1995* (Cm 3020). London: HMSO.

For details of the Prison Security Act 1992, see http://www.opsi.gov.uk/acts/acts1992/Ukpga_19920025_en_1.htm.

# SEGREGATION

Segregation units are discrete units in prisons used in order to remove prisoners from association with others.

Segregation is the shorthand word for what is referred to in the Prison Rules as 'removal from association'. Prison Rule 45 allows prison governors to remove a prisoner from associating with other prisoners to maintain good order or discipline, or for the prisoner's own protection. Such a decision must be reviewed by the Secretary of State or independent monitoring board (IMB) within three days, and should not exceed a period of one month for adults or 14 days for a prisoner under the age of 21 years.

Most prisons have segregation units where prisoners are held separately and association is not allowed, though this does not apply to open prisons where prisoners are only selected if they are considered safe and reliable with staff and prisoners. Many prisons have renamed their segregation units 'care and separation units', particularly in the women and juvenile estate, reflecting an increased understanding that prisoners unable to manage themselves in association often have considerable personal challenges.

Prisoners who are charged with an offence against discipline may also be kept apart from other prisoners pending the governor's first inquiry and, if found guilty of an offence on adjudications, may be confined to a cell for a period not exceeding 14 days for adults and 7 days for young prisoners. Violent or refractory prisoners may also be temporarily confined to a special cell and may also be restrained if they are in danger of hurting themselves or others, are damaging prison property or creating a disturbance. In these circumstances the use of force should be minimal, and the period of confinement should last only until the prisoner has settled. Special cells are always located within segregation units.

The balance of functions performed by segregation units has resulted in them becoming associated with punishment and control rather than care and management and, in many places, they have developed an austere and forbidding atmosphere. Some have been the location of staff brutality, and 20 per cent of all self-inflicted deaths between April 2004 and March 2006 occurred in segregation units. Coroners' inquests recommended regime and procedural improvements. At the same time, inspections of high-security prisons (where, in 2003, all the self-inflicted deaths were in segregation units) identified deficiencies in management scrutiny, safety, and support and regime quality, and criticized the practice of 'management by transfers' (the so-called 'merry-go-round') by which difficult prisoners were moved from one segregation unit to another. Findings from research into the effects of solitary confinement have underlined its particularly detrimental impact on fragile personalities, and the European Court of Human Rights *Keenan* judgment in 2001 highlighted the inappropriateness of cellular confinement for those with a diagnosed mental illness.

This prompted a review of Prison Service Order (PSO) 1700 (*Segregation Units*) that was published in November 2003 (HM Prison Service 2003). The healthcare centre is now informed within 30 minutes of the segregation of a prisoner, and a safety algorithm completed by a registered nurse within two hours to confirm whether there are any physical or mental health reasons why the prisoner should not be segregated. In these circumstances the prisoner is admitted to the healthcare centre rather than placed in segregation. Subsequently, a prisoner in segregation should be visited daily by a healthcare professional.

The IMB is also notified within 24 hours of the segregation of any prisoner and is expected to review the documentation and to speak to the manager authorizing its use to satisfy itself that the decision is justified. The IMB is also required to satisfy itself that any use of force, of special cells or restraints is justified and to sign to that effect, or to challenge the decision through a laid-down procedure. A multidisciplinary segregation management and review group (SMARG) is also now required to monitor the use of segregation in each prison, and individual reviews of segregated prisoners are required after the first 72 hours and every two weeks thereafter. These are chaired by a manager and are attended by a member of the healthcare centre and an IMB member. They may also be attended by psychologists, chaplains and mental health nurses in addition to segregation staff.

The PSO further specifies that regime restrictions for those segregated for management reasons should be limited to those activities that involve associating with mainstream prisoners. Access to such activities as domestic or legal visits, the use of the telephone, canteen, exercise and showers should be the same as for mainstream prisoners, and other regime elements, such as TV, radio/CD players, association within the unit and physical education access, can be used as incentives for those complying with targets set by segregation review boards.

Another challenge to the culture of austerity in segregation units has come from developments in the management of disruptive prisoners in close supervision centres in the high-security estate, where the input of mental health staff has been delivering holistic care and management to reduce violence and to support positive change in conditions that equate to segregation. Consequently, in November 2004 the Deputy Director General of the Prison Service announced a review of the role of segregation in the high-security estate to ensure a constructive, dynamic and caring environment that actively engages with prisoners; to ensure segregated prisoners are treated with decency and dignity; to prioritize safety and the prevention of suicide and self-harm; to address prisoners' individual needs, including mental health and sentence planning needs; to minimize the period of time that prisoners spend in segregation; to provide multidisciplinary case management through regular reviews by fully trained professional staff; to operate effective monitoring with regular internal and external scrutiny; and to ensure that each segregation unit has a development plan that is reviewed annually.

This strategy went live in April 2005, and HM Inspectorate of Prisons (HMIP) visited all the high-security prison segregation units over the next seven months to conduct a thematic inspection (HMIP 2006). This exercise confirmed that there had been an overall drop of around 7 per cent in the rate of use of segregation within six months of the new strategy being introduced, though this was not the case in all units. The reduction reflected a drop in the number of those segregated for less than 60 days, but no reduction in the number segregated for longer periods. The overall length of stay had in fact increased by 10 per cent, with particularly noticeable rises in two prisons. This may have reflected the fact that prisoners were held for longer in one unit rather than being moved around the system. A spot check carried out after a further six months confirmed that the numbers in segregation had not returned to their previous levels. This thematic inspection exposed the existence of a core of longer-stay segregated prisoners with complex needs, who could not be safely managed elsewhere. Though there was more psychiatric and therapeutic support in the units, it was not enough, and many prisoners were deteriorating further in lengthy solitary confinement. At the very least they needed individual, multidisciplinary and properly resourced care plans. HMIP stressed the need for more creativity in providing prisoners with activities to keep them occupied in their cells, and in creating opportunities for them to partake in activities out of cell and in association where individual risk assessment allowed.

Other concerns were significant differences in the physical environments and regimes of the different units, variation in the levels of staff used to unlock prisoners, wide variation in the use of unfurnished accommodation and some worrying gaps in its documentation. Independent oversight and monitoring needed strengthening, with a clearer role for IMBs and more opportunities for prisoners to speak confidentially to managers and specialists involved in their case management. Some disproportionate use of segregation and unfurnished cells for black and minority ethnic prisoners was not being picked up in monitoring and required action. HMIP acknowledged the positive progress that had taken place in the culture and management of segregation units in the high-security estate. It welcomed the introduction of multidisciplinary review and more mental health support. It stressed that, in the most extreme and hidden custodial contexts, robust management and vigorous independent scrutiny remained necessary to detect and prevent abuses of power and to maintain the momentum of change. It also acknowledged that there were equally needy prisoners held in segregation units outside the high-security estate who, now that they were not moved into high-security segregation, were held in units with fewer resources and less support. Ongoing attention was necessary to ensure that segregation was used as sparingly as possible and that the Prison Service met its duty of care to those for whom segregation units remained their only possible location.

*Monica Lloyd*

## Related entries

*Adjudications; Black and minority ethnic (BME) prisoners; Close supervision centres; Discipline; Governors; HM Inspectorate of Prisons; Human rights; Independent monitoring boards; Mental health; Prison Rules; Use of force (control and restraint).*

---

**Key texts and sources**

HM Chief Inspector of Prisons (2006) *Extreme Custody: A Thematic Inspection of Close Supervision Centres and High Security Segregation.* London: Home Office.

HM Prison Service (2003) *Segregation Units* (PSO 1700). London: Home Office.

For the management of segregation units, see the Prison Service's website (**http://pso. hmprisonservice.gov.uk/pso1700/man_seg.htm**).

---

## SELF-HARM

Self-harm is where a person deliberately inflicts harm upon him or herself. Research indicates that prisoners are particularly vulnerable to self-harm and suicide.

Research over the last decade has indicated that the prison population is particularly vulnerable to both suicide and self-harm (Liebling 1992; Hawton *et al.* 1997; Snow 2002; Borrill *et al.* 2005). The definition of self-harm as used in prison is any act where a prisoner deliberately harms him or herself irrespective of method, intent or severity of any injury. This can include a range of behaviours which involve inflicting pain, injury or damage to one's own body – for example, cutting, scratching or tying ligatures. The most common method of self-harm in prison is cutting. Some acts of self-harm result in mild damage to the body, requiring little or no medical treatment. Others may leave permanent physical scars or are life-threatening. People may injure themselves only once in response to an event or experience, or they may do so repetitively.

While not all people who self-harm have a mental disorder, self-harm is often associated with various mental health problems (such as personality disorders and psychosis) which are more commonly found in prisons than in the community. Self-harm is particularly common among women prisoners and young offenders, although male prisoners do harm themselves. Prisoners as a whole have a high incidence of previous suicidal behaviour and high rates of associated risk factors, such as mental illness, substance misuse, previous abuse, violent behaviour and victimization, and a lack of supportive social networks (Snow 2002).

In December 2002, the Prison Service introduced a revised system for self-harm data collection that requires prison staff to complete a form for every incident of self-harm known to occur within a prison establishment, the majority of which are minor. The introduction of such procedures has improved the validity and accuracy of the self-harm data collected. The form records details of method used, together with information about location, medical treatment, risk status and prisoner details. Self-harm is a high-volume incident and is subject to technical and recording problems. Nevertheless, the system provides a sensible indication of the scale of self-harm, but the numbers cannot be taken as absolute. The recorded information is subsequently entered on to the Prison Service's central Incident Reporting System database where it is regularly downloaded for analysis. Self-harm recording in prisons refers to the number of incidents of self-harm and not the number of prisoners who self-harm. Analysis of these numbers shows that a significant proportion of prisoners self-harm on more than one occasion and account for a disproportionate number of incidents. For example, in 2006, 1 per cent of the individuals who self-harmed accounted for about 25 per cent of all self-harm incidents. The presence of a single serial self-harming prisoner in any given period can materially affect the total number of incidents.

As a result of analysis of recorded self-harm incidents, support for staff working with prisoners who self-harm has been developed. This includes a 'Self-harm toolkit' which was developed in order to provide information and guidance for prison staff. Additionally, a 'Self-harm network' has been established and is a useful forum for people working with prisoners who self-harm to share good practice and to discuss issues in relation to self-harm, including interventions and strategies for managing self-harm.

Prisons are encouraged to develop local strategies to provide support to people who self-harm. As well as staff training, these can include targeted interventions for prisoners who self-harm (including support groups and structured programmes). It is known that repeated self-harm is a risk factor for suicide, but not all those who self-harm are suicidal. For many prisoners, self-harm is a way of managing distress, of blocking out painful and traumatic memories or of dealing with anger. Self-harm may be used as a coping strategy when common means of managing distress (e.g. use of drugs or alcohol, support from family) are not available. The purpose of any treatments is therefore to offer people a way of coping with distress that will be a viable alternative to self-harm.

The Prison Service's Safer Custody Group have devised ACCT (Assessment, Care in Custody and Teamwork), which is a multidisciplinary prisoner-centred care plan for prisoners who are identified as being at risk of self-harm. ACCT involves assessing the prisoner's needs, the delivery of planned care (which is regularly reviewed) and information sharing among prison staff about individual prisoners so that appropriate support can be provided. Additional support is offered to prisoners via the listener scheme, which is a system whereby selected prisoners are trained and supported by Samaritans, using Samaritans' guidelines, to listen in complete confidence to their fellow prisoners who may be in crisis, feel suicidal or who need a confidential sympathetic ear. The objectives of such a scheme are to assist in preventing suicide, in reducing self-harm and generally to help alleviate the feelings of those in distress.

*Nigel Hancock and Laura Graham*

## Related entries

*Coping; First-night centres; Listener schemes; Mental health; Suicide in prison; Women in prison; Young offender institutions (YOIs).*

**Key texts and sources**

Borrill, J., Snow, L., Medlicott, D., Teers, R. and Paton, J. (2005) 'Learning from "near misses": interviews with women who survived an incident of severe self-harm in prison', *Howard Journal of Criminal Justice*, 44: 57–69.

Hawton, K., Fagg, J., Simkin, S., Bale, E. and Bond, A. (1997) 'Trends in deliberate self-harm in Oxford, 1985–1995, and their implications for clinical services and the prevention of suicide', *British Journal of Psychiatry*, 171: 556–60.

Liebling, A. (1992) *Suicides in Prison*. London: Routledge.

Snow, L. (2002) 'Prisoners' motives for self-injury and attempted suicide', *British Journal of Forensic Practice*, 4: 18–29.

See also the Prison Service's web page on self-harm, with attached documents (**http://www.hmprisonservice.gov.uk/adviceandsupport/prison_life/selfharm/**). For the Howard League's 'Prison overcrowding and suicide' briefing paper, see **http://www.howardleague.org/index.php?id =suicides**.

## SENTENCE PLANNING

Sentence planning is the method for planning and managing the activities that prisoners do in custody and after release. The aim is to make the sentence as productive and effective as possible.

The Woolf Report, which examined the causes of the widespread prison riots of April 1990, took a broad view about the work required in order to improve prison conditions. One of the recommendations was that sentence plans be introduced (Woolf and Tumin 1991), the aim of which was to clarify what work and other activities prisoners should do during their sentence in order to maximize effectiveness and encourage rehabilitation. The intention was to identify and direct prisoners towards such activities as education and offending behaviour programmes. The report also traced some of the broader, long-term issues in sentence planning, including the need to consider not only what happened in prison but also after release. The first version of sentence planning was introduced in 1991, although it did not address work after release and was only used for those serving longer sentences. It was therefore replaced with a revised version that covered all prisoners and was jointly used by prisons and probation.

It was widely recognized that the sentence-planning process was not fully meeting its potential. One important measure introduced to help it achieve maximum effectiveness was a structured risk assessment tool used by prison and probation, known as the Offender Assessment System (OASys). This not only provided a more systematic and shared risk assessment but also provided an organizational needs assessment so that services could be developed to match identified need.

The introduction of the National Offender Management Service (NOMS) in 2004, with its focus on reducing reoffending, heralded a major revision of sentence-planning arrangements, with the development of an offender management model (Adams 2007). This model aimed to create 'end-to-end' sentence management, with each case being under the direction of an offender manager throughout the whole of the sentence from court, through prison and after release. While much of the direct work with the individual would be completed by offender supervisors or key workers, the introduction of the overall offender manager was aimed at creating greater consistency and commitment across different organizations. The process would utilize existing services, including OASys, education and offending behaviour programmes. However, the process would also be used to inform organizational developments and would be designed to ensure that the level of input to an individual was seen in context to the level of risk he or she presented. While this process is new and is still under development, it represents an important new initiative in sentence planning for offenders.

*Jamie Bennett*

### Related entries

*Desistance; Education and training; National Offender Management Service (NOMS); Offender Assessment System (OASys); Offending behaviour programmes; Probation Service; Rehabilitation; Woolf Report.*

#### Key texts and sources

Adams, M. (2007) 'Integrated offender management: aspiration or reality for the North West Pathfinder?', *Prison Service Journal*, 169: 42–9.
Woolf, Lord Justice and Tumin, S. (1991) *Report of an Inquiry into Prison Disturbances, April 1990.* London: HMSO.

## SENTENCING POLICY

Sentencing policy is the government's expressed position on what should happen to convicted offenders.

Sentencing policy is the expression of the government's views as to what should happen to convicted criminals. It is an area that is always in the public eye: the media can have a significant impact on it, and there is a welter of interest groups, many of which have entrenched views.

For centuries, sentencing policy has operated along two main continua: how harsh should punishment be? And how much can the state change offenders through rehabilitation? So, for example, on the first dimension, whipping and transportation have faded into history, but the prison population is comfortably the highest per captia in Western Europe. On the second, the debate about whether offending behaviour programmes reduce reoffending is a modern-day equivalent of the early twentieth-century separation of felons. Those thought capable of reform were sent to Maidstone, and those perceived as hardened criminals were sent to do hard labour at Dartmoor.

In more recent times, there has been a significant swing of the pendulum towards a belief that targeting the right interventions for particular offenders will make a difference. Opinions have gone full circle over 20 years since the 1980s, when the view that 'nothing works' prevailed. That is to say, whatever the state did to, or with, offenders, they would be as likely to reoffend. This led to the sentencing framework in the Criminal Justice Act 1991. The guiding principle is 'just deserts': in other words, punishment should be in line with what is merited by the crime and should be as little and as inexpensive as is commensurate with maintaining public confidence.

But almost as soon as the ink was dry on the 1991 Act, the pendulum started to swing the other way. The middle and late 1990s saw the growth of 'what works'. Starting in North America and finding its way over the Atlantic, academics, prison managers and, especially, probation managers started to believe that, if the right programmes could be given to the right offenders, there was a good chance of reducing recidivism. Many of these programmes were cognitive-behavioural – i.e. designed to change the thought processes of offenders (e.g. to think before acting rather than doing so impulsively).

The upshot was that the 1991 Act's successor, the Criminal Justice Act 2003, is more balanced than its predecessor: while it does not abandon just deserts, it enables sentencers to look at the needs of the offender as well as the needs of the offence. For the first time, the purposes of sentencing are laid down in legislation. These are:

- the punishment of offenders;
- the reduction of crime (including its reduction by deterrence);
- the reform and rehabilitation of offenders;
- the protection of the public; and
- the making of reparation by offenders to persons affected by their offences.

Essentially, the sentencing framework remains one of three tiers: minor offences should be punished by fines; offences that are serious enough should be punished by community penalties; and offences that are so serious that no other punishment will suffice should be dealt with by imprisonment.

The 2003 Act takes a significantly different approach to imprisonment from its predecessor. At the bottom end, it provides supervision for all who are incarcerated. This was in response to concern by politicians, officials and practitioners at the particularly high reoffending rate of those sentenced to short terms of imprisonment. Hence the creation of 'custody plus', which combines a short period of imprisonment (no more that 13 weeks in respect of a single offence) with a longer period of supervision in the community of between 26 and 49 weeks, the total sentence not to exceed 51 weeks. This new sentence has the potential to make a real difference but, sadly, resource constraints mean that it has not yet been implemented.

The rest of the framework, which has been implemented, clearly demonstrates the government's concerns about public protection. The 1991 Act's artificial division between over and under four-year sentences has now been swept away. Instead, there is a distinction between 'ordinary' prison sentences and those focused specifically on public protection. A court considering the sentencing of an offender committing one of a very long list of sexual and violent offences contained in Schedule 15 to the Act is required to consider whether it thinks that the offender is likely in future to present a 'significant risk to members of the public of serious harm occasioned by the commission by him of further specified offences'. Where the court is so satisfied, it is required to pass one of the new public protection sentences. If the maximum for the offence of which he or she has been convicted (not, note, the appropriate sentence in his or her particular case) is less than 10 years, then the court must impose an extended sentence. This comprises the normal custodial term plus a period of extended supervision. The offender is eligible for release from the halfway point onwards but may be kept in custody beyond this if the Parole Board considers it unsafe to release him or her.

Where the maximum for the offence is 10 years or more and the court considers the offender to be dangerous, then it must pass a sentence of imprisonment for public protection (IPP) (unless the maximum penalty is life and the offence deserves life, in which case that is what it must impose). IPP works very like a life sentence in that the judge sets a minimum period to be served (colloquially known as a tariff) and, after that, release is at the discretion of the Parole Board depending on whether it thinks the risks the offender presents in the community are manageable. For all other offenders imprisoned under the 2003 Act, release is automatic at the halfway point and licence conditions apply until the end of the sentence, rather than at the three-quarter point as before. This change in length of licence, together with improved enforcement activity by the Probation Service, is good news for public protection but sets another challenge for the prison population through increasing recalls.

With high-profile cases of serious crimes committed by offenders on release on licence hitting the headlines in 2006, the current climate is increasingly punitive and risk averse. The pendulum is perhaps starting to swing again.

*Keir Hopley*

### Related entries

*Abolitionism; Alternatives to imprisonment; Custody plus and custody minus; Deterrence; Just deserts; Life-sentence prisoners; New punitiveness; Politics of imprisonment; Prison population; Public perceptions; Rehabilitation.*

#### Key texts and sources

Ashworth, A. (1997) 'Sentencing in the 80s and 90s: the struggle for power.' Eighth Eve Saville Memorial Lecture, 21 May, King's College London (available online at **http://www.kcl.ac.uk/depsta/rel/ccjs/eighties-sentencing.html**).
Ashworth, A. (2005) *Sentencing and Criminal Justice* (4th edn). Cambridge: Cambridge University Press.
Cavadino, M. and Dignan, J. (2007) *The Penal System: An Introduction* (4th edn). London: Sage.

# SEPARATE AND SILENT SYSTEMS

The separate and silent systems were two disciplinary regimes that became prominent in prisons during the early to mid-nineteenth century. Both systems were based on the idea of reforming prisoners either through isolation or through silent-associated labour.

The separate and silent systems were two disciplinary regimes used in prisons from the early to mid-nineteenth century. Both systems were based on the idea that prisoners could be prevented from becoming 'worse' by limiting their contact with others. Thus, communication between prisoners was prevented, and first-time and young offenders were protected from the 'contaminating' influence of more hardened criminals. These measures were set against a background of growing numbers of prisoners and increasing crime rates which, in turn, were put down to the inadequately reformed prison of the earlier nineteenth century (McGowen 1998).

The two systems employed different methods of achieving reform of prisoners. The separate system was based on a regime where prisoners were isolated from each other at all times, and they spent all their time in separate cells where they worked, slept and ate. Prisoners were only allowed out of cells for exercise and to attend chapel. Separate exercise yards were constructed to ensure prisoners remained isolated and, at chapel, each prisoner was placed in a separate stall and wore a mask to prevent recognition between inmates. The separate system was also based on religious ideas: isolated prisoners could reflect on their behaviour and could recognize their sinfulness and, through conversing with, and instruction by, the prison chaplain, their behaviour could be transformed (Forsythe 1987). In contrast, under the silent system, prisoners were able to associate during labour but were to be silent at all times. This regime was enforced by guards watching the prisoners to detect even the smallest of gestures (McGowen

1998). Each of the systems was seen to have its own merits. The separate system made the management of the prisons much easier in terms of controlling the prisoners, but it did require major alterations to prison buildings, which were costly. The silent system, on the other hand, was cheaper because no structural alterations were required, but space was needed between prisoners and higher staffing levels were necessary to watch the prisoners at work.

Both systems had their origins in America. The Quaker American Society for Prison Discipline opened the first penitentiary planned on the use of the separate system at Walnut Street, Philadelphia, in 1819. Ten years later, the Eastern Penitentiary at Cherry Hill, Philadelphia, started to confine life-sentence prisoners to three years or more in separate cells. The rival system ran in the state of New York, where at Auburn and Sing Sing Prisons the prisoners worked in association but in complete silence (Henriques 1972). In England, the Governor of Coldbath Fields House of Correction in Middlesex, Captain George Laval Chesterton, was one of the notable supporters of the silent system, believing that silence allowed prisoners to contemplate their guilt – a necessary precursor of reform. Yet in order to succeed in reform, the silent system also adopted a system of incentives and punishments. The latter would increase in severity the longer the defiance lasted, although prisoners who behaved well received financial rewards, badges and an occupation to interest the mind (Forsythe 1987).

William Crawford, one of the first prison inspectors appointed by the government, had visited the prisons in operation in America and reported on them in 1834. Both Crawford and then Inspector of Prisons, the Reverend Whitworth Russell, became strong advocates of the benefits of the separate system and promoted its use after their appointments in 1835. The separate system was written into the Prisons Act 1839 and, in theory, all prisons across the country were supposed to operate in this way, although the extent to which they did varied.

Pentonville Prison, a government-run penitentiary opened in 1842 to hold 520 prisoners, had been designed with the separate system in mind. The construction of the prison prevented any communication between the identical cells, which measured 13 ft long by 7 ft wide by 9 ft high (McGowen 1998). When Pentonville first opened, convicts were to spend 18 months in solitude. However, even before Pentonville took its first prisoners, concerns were voiced regarding the severity of the regime and the effects it would have on the mental health of prisoners. By the mid-1840s public opinion was hostile due to high rates of insanity among the prisoners, and the periods of solitude had to be reduced from 18 to 12 months, and then to 9 months. There was widespread criticism of the separate system in newspapers such as *The Times*, and by novelist and social commentator, Charles Dickens. Media reports of the day reveal conflicting concerns about the mental health of prisoners, on the one hand, and prisons being seen as too soft on the other, all of which were underpinned by the principle of less eligibility (Johnston 2006).

By the 1850s there was disillusionment with separation: commentators complained that precautions against recognition were useless; there was concern that magistrates abused the system, not understanding its real aims; and the criminal statistics did not show the 'promised mass reformation of criminals' (Henriques 1972: 85). The separate system had failed to deliver on most of its reformatory aims and, by the Prison Act 1865, although separate cells were still used, reformatory ideals had been replaced with a penal philosophy based on deterrence. Greater severity was introduced and prisoners were subject to long hours of hard labour, harsh conditions and strict diets in order to achieve the discipline that characterized the Victorian prison. However, the philosophy behind the separate system has never entirely disappeared, and traces of it are still to be found in prisons such as the American 'supermax'.

*Helen Johnston*

### Related entries

*Architecture; Discipline; Less eligibility; Mental health; Supermax prisons; Victorian prisons.*

**Key texts and sources**

Forsythe, W.J. (1987) *The Reform of Prisoners, 1830–1900.* Beckenham: Croom Helm.

Henriques, U.R.Q. (1972) 'The rise and decline of the separate system', *Past and Present,* 54: 61–93.

Johnston, H. (2006) '"Buried alive": representations of the separate system in Victorian England', in P. Mason (ed.) *Captured by the Media: Prison Discourse in Popular Culture.* Cullompton: Willan Publishing.

McGowen, R. (1998) 'The well-ordered prison: England, 1780–1865', in N. Morris and D.J. Rothman (eds) *The Oxford History of the Prison: The Practice of Punishment in Western Society.* Oxford: Oxford University Press.

## SEX OFFENDERS

Sex offenders are those who have been convicted of a sexual offence or those whose offence has a sexual element.

On 31 May 2006, 6,600 offenders were in custody in England and Wales who had an index conviction for a sexual offence. Approximately one third were serving sentences of less than two years and just 40 were women. This figure underestimates the true size of the imprisoned sex offender population as it does not include those convicted of non-sexual offences (e.g. violence, murder) where the offence had a sexual element. Neither does it include those with a current non-sexual conviction but previous convictions for sexual offences.

Many imprisoned sex offenders are accommodated in separate units, wings or landings with other vulnerable prisoners. The prevailing public attitude towards sexual offenders is hostile, and this is often reflected in the attitudes and behaviour of other prisoners and some staff. Once labelled a 'sex offender', it becomes more likely that an inmate will be assaulted by other prisoners (Ireland 2002). Those sex offenders who choose to serve out their time on 'normal location' often survive by 'passing' as non-sex offenders (Schwaebe 2005). Another common strategy for survival is to deny guilt.

While such denial is understandable, it is not a strategy to be encouraged as it may prevent the offender from accessing help and support that could be beneficial to him.

Sex offenders would ideally be transferred to a treatment site as soon as possible after sentencing. Treatment is voluntary, and offenders are most likely to be able to consider the value of treatment if they are in a prison where staff and other prisoners understand and can explain the nature of treatment. Sex offenders are regarded as a high risk of harm group, falling automatically under the multi-agency public protection arrangement (MAPPA) procedures. By the nature of their offence, sex offenders are ineligible for some privileges, such as intermittent custody and home detention curfew. However, recidivism rates for sex offenders are much lower than is usually believed. A Home Office study of all offenders released from custody in the first quarter of 2002, or commencing a community penalty in the same time period, found a two-year reconviction rate of 33.2 per cent (16.9 per cent for sexual offenders against children) (Cuppleditch and Evans 2005).

Sex offender assessment begins at the point of sentence. The Prison Service uses a specialized, static risk-assessment tool to measure risk of sexual recidivism: Risk Matrix 2000. This allows initial decision-making about likely treatment need and helps prioritize resources for the highest-risk men. (Static-99 is a similar tool used by many other jurisdictions for the same purpose.) For those offenders who go on to engage in treatment (and some who do not), a further specialized assessment of dynamic risk factors is recommended. In the Prison and Probation Services of England and Wales, the dynamic risk tool used is the Structured Assessment of Risk and Need (SARN). The use of common tools ensures a consistent approach to assessing risk, need and progress throughout both the custodial and community parts of the sentence.

The Prison Service offers six sex offender treatment programmes (SOTPs), which can be combined together in different ways according to risk and need. In 2006–7, 25 prisons (including two private sector prisons) provided between them about 1,200 treatment places. The SOTP employed is based on the best evidence of what works with this difficult and damaged group of offenders. The SOTP is fully accredited by the independent Correctional Services Accreditation Panel, indicating that it is likely to be effective in reducing reoffending. SOTPs have been shown to have a significant impact on sexual and violent recidivism, with a particularly marked effect on medium-risk offenders (Friendship *et al.* 2003). Since this first evaluation was completed, additional treatment has been developed for higher-risk offenders, and the early indications are that the current approach significantly impacts on a range of dynamic risk factors for sexual offending.

Treatment programmes offered in English and Welsh prisons include the Rolling SOTP (for low-risk offenders); the Core SOTP (for medium-risk offenders); the Extended and Healthy Sexual Functioning programmes (additional to the Core for high-risk offenders); the Better Lives Booster programme (for all medium+ risk groups); and the Adapted SOTP (for offenders with an intellectual disability). The SOTPs adhere to all three of the risk, need and responsivity principles that form the basis of effective offender rehabilitation (Andrews and Bonta 2003). Accredited treatment programmes currently only exist for male sex offenders. Female sex offenders may receive one-to-one counselling or treatment, but cases of female recidivists are extremely rare.

It is vital to plan carefully for release, as sex offenders are a high risk of harm group and they are often not welcomed back into society. Experiences of hostility or alienation after release may increase risk. Six months before release, or at the first parole hearing, the offender manager will take an offender's case to a multi-agency public protection panel (MAPPP). The MAPPP assigns each offender a level, which corresponds to the number of agencies involved in risk management and the level of restriction which might be enforced on the offender. Level 1 offenders are managed by a single agency and would not be heavily restricted. Level 2 offenders are managed by two agencies, usually the police and the Probation Service. Level 3 is reserved for the 'critical few' offenders who are thought to represent an immediate and imminent risk of serious harm. The offender manager liaises with both the MAPPP and the Parole Board to ensure that an offender's licence conditions provide appropriate restrictions and controls, such as requiring registration with the police, directing residence in a controlled environment such as a hostel or defining geographical areas or locations which the offender cannot enter.

The number of sex offenders in prison is increasing, as sentences lengthen and release procedures become more demanding. At the same time, our knowledge of how to assess and treat imprisoned sex offenders is developing fast. It is encouraging that so many imprisoned sex offenders are willing to engage in treatment, especially as this requires disclosure of the details of the offending and other painful forms of self-examination.

*Ruth Mann*

### Related entries

*Child protection; Multi-agency public protection arrangements (MAPPAs); Offending behaviour programmes; Parole; Rehabilitation; Risk.*

### Key texts and sources

Andrews, D.A. and Bonta, J. (2003) *The Psychology of Criminal Conduct* (3rd edn). Cincinnati, OH: Anderson Publishing.

Cuppleditch, L. and Evans, W. (2005) *Re-offending of Adults: Results from the 2002 Cohort. Home Office Statistical Bulletin* 25/05 (available online at **www.homeoffice.gov.uk/rds**).

Friendship, C., Mann, R. and Beech, A. (2003) *The Prison-based Sex Offender Treatment Programme: An Evaluation.* London: Home Office.

Ireland, J. (2002) *Bullying among Prisoners: Evidence, Research and Intervention Strategies.* Hove, NY: Brunner-Routledge.

Schwaebe, C. (2005) 'Learning to pass: sex offenders' strategies for establishing a viable identity in the prison population', *International Journal of Offender Therapy and Comparative Criminology,* 49: 614–25.

# SHORT-TERM PRISONERS

**Short-term prison sentences are those of less than 12 months.**

Short-term prisoners are those serving less than 12 months' imprisonment. Of the 92,452 prisoners being received under sentence in 2005, 51,817 (56 per cent) were serving six months or less, and 7,983 were serving more than six months but less than 12 months (9 per cent). Overall, this means that almost two out of every three sentenced prisoners received into custody are serving short-term sentences. At any one time, these prisoners make up approximately 11 per cent of the total prison population (Home Office 2006). Since 1996, the growth in the numbers of people being sent to prison has been mirrored by a rise in the number of short-term sentences, particularly those serving less than six months.

The offences committed by those serving short-term sentences are theft and handling (25.7 per cent), motoring offences (19.1 per cent) and violence against the person (17.3 per cent); 'other' offences account for 22.6 per cent. However, some offences are more likely to attract short-term sentences. For example, 93 per cent of those convicted and sentenced to imprisonment for motoring offences were sentenced to less than 12 months. The evidence suggests that these sentencing policies are largely ineffective, and current plans for reform are unlikely to lead to any significant reduction in their use or improvement in their effectiveness. Other groups with a high density of short-term sentences are theft and handling (86 per cent), violence against the person (62 per cent) and fraud (58 per cent). Those least likely to attract short-term sentences were sexual offences (17 per cent) and drugs offences (23 per cent) (Home Office 2006).

Short-term prisoners are usually held in local prisons that are close to their homes, but often have the most impoverished facilities. There is also limited follow-up on release. Those sentenced to less than 12 months are normally released unconditionally at the halfway point of their sentence, and can be released earlier under the home detention curfew scheme. This has led to public criticisms of the effectiveness and meaningfulness of short-term sentences (Home Office 2001). While attempts to improve these deficiencies in other countries have included strict limits on the use of short-term sentences, the plans in England and Wales involve a blurring of the lines between custody and alternatives to custody through 'custody plus' and 'custody minus'.

*Jamie Bennett*

### Related entries

*Alternatives to imprisonment; Custody plus and custody minus; Local prisons; Prison population.*

#### Key texts and sources

Home Office (2001) *Making Punishments Work: Report of a Review of the Sentencing Framework for England and Wales.* London: Home Office.
Home Office (2006b) *Offender Management Caseload Statistics, 2005: England and Wales.* London: Home Office.
See also the Home Office's website for information on the resettlement of short-term prisoners (http://www.homeoffice.gov.uk/rds/pdfs2/occ83pathfinders.pdf).

# SOLIDARITY

**Solidarity may be defined as a union of interests, goals or sympathies among members of a group, expressed through forms of loyalty and mutual support.**

Sykes (1958) argues that prisoners espouse solidarity through the 'inmate code' but, in practice, this ideal of cohesion is frequently breached. None the less, many early studies of prison life report that prisoners share a collective identity, are bonded by their shared position of subordination and support each other in activities that are oppositional to the prison authorities.

If solidarity is contingent on collective grievances, and on relatively homogeneous experiences of incarceration, it is unsurprising that, in the USA in the 1970s, as prison conditions improved, as prisoner rights were progressively recognized and as prisons became more porous to the outside world, ethnic, racial, religious and criminal identities began to supersede a collective inmate identity as the main basis of affiliation and support (Carroll 1974). As they did so, and the prisoner community splintered into mutually hostile groups, the notion of general solidarity became less apposite. As Mathiesen (1965) notes, there is an important difference between 'peer cohesion', which exists within groups, and 'rank cohesion', which exists throughout an entire category of people (i.e. among all prisoners), and the latter may vary independently of the former. Thus, the prisoner world may consist of numerous subgroups which are internally highly cohesive but which express and exhibit little solidarity with each other. Indeed, in-group solidarity may be a source of exploitation for outsiders.

Expressions of solidarity need not take the form of collective action – indeed, it is during such incidents that the violent targeting of some prisoners, such as sex-offenders, belies the notion of rank cohesion – but these are often seen as the ultimate expressions of prisoner solidarity. In the past, disturbances in English prisons have been caused by a range of factors, including the prisoner population mix, overcrowding, low staff-to-prisoner ratios, restricted or harsh regimes, poor conditions and treatment, and staff industrial action. Recent years have seen improvements in prison conditions, grievance procedures and declining staff brutality and disrespect, and alliances of prisoners over common grievances are now relatively rare.

The apparent dissolution of solidarity can also be attributed to the individualization of the prisoner community, caused by a number of factors (Crewe 2005). The first is the introduction of policies designed to differentiate prisoner interests, in particular, the incentives and earned privileges (IEP) scheme. A second is the presence of hard drugs in prisons, particularly heroin, which leads to debt, exploitation and distrust, and which focuses users and dealers on personal rather than collective interests.

A third factor is the crime of 'prison mutiny', introduced following the prison disturbances of 1990, which has discouraged prisoners from taking collective action. Prisoners may express emotional solidarity towards each other and often empathize with the misfortunes of their peers, but few are keen to stand up for each other against prison officials in ways that are visible or involve personal sacrifice.

Political convictions appear to be the most effective basis for group solidarity. McEvoy's (2001) account of paramilitary imprisonment in Northern Ireland illustrates how staunchly and effectively prisoners were able to organize themselves when bound by ideology and when supported by networks and in the community. For prison authorities, such powerful solidarities may be highly challenging yet, as Sykes (1958) highlights, a degree of solidarity may be beneficial in preventing the prisoner community from collapsing into a Hobbesian state of nature.

*Deb Drake and Ben Crewe*

### Related entries

*Deprivations/'pains of imprisonment'; Friendship; Identity and self; Inmate code; Subcultures.*

### Key texts and sources

Carroll, L. (1974) *Hacks, Blacks and Cons: Race Relations in a Maximum Security Prison.* Lexington, MA: D.C. Heath.

Crewe, B. (2005) 'Codes and conventions: the terms and conditions of contemporary inmate values', in A. Liebling and S. Maruna (eds) *The Effects of Imprisonment.* Cullompton: Willan Publishing.

Mathiesen, T. (1965) *The Defences of the Weak: A Sociological Study of a Norwegian Correctional Institution.* London: Tavistock.

McEvoy, K. (2001) *Paramilitary Imprisonment in Northern Ireland.* Oxford: Clarendon Press.

Sykes, G. (1958) *The Society of Captives: A Study of a Maximum-security Prison.* Princeton, NJ: Princeton University Press.

# SPECIAL SECURITY UNITS

Special security units are designed to hold exceptional-risk category A prisoners who present the highest risk to the public and the highest risk of escape.

Special security units (SSUs) are designed to house exceptional-risk category A prisoners. These are the prisoners who not only present the highest levels of risk to the police, the public or the security of the state but also present a higher risk of escape by virtue of their access to resources or their personal resourcefulness. SSUs are effectively a prison within a prison, being small units with their own additional security measures, including a perimeter wall, housed within a high-security prison. The units were first created in the mid-1960s to address some of the problems that led to the creation of high-security prisons. They were initially considered a temporary measure but, with the emergence and expansion of paramilitary prisoners in the 1970s, it was recognized that special units needed to be built to house relatively small numbers.

The first purpose-built SSU was opened at Full Sutton Prison in 1988. It was recognized that the older units would have to close as they were not purpose built and were no longer suitable. A second SSU was opened at Whitemoor Prison in the early 1990s. There is also a third unit at Belmarsh Prison, which can be used for this purpose. These units became particularly high profile in 1994, when six prisoners, including five IRA paramilitary prisoners, escaped from the SSU at Whitemoor. This incident led to a highly critical report (Woodcock 1994) that identified extensive conditioning and complacency among staff in the unit and weaknesses in the security arrangements which, in turn, led to significant changes in the operation of these units.

As the peace process in Northern Ireland progressed, there were fewer prisoners requiring the levels of security the SSU entailed. Additionally, the conditions and psychological impact of detention in these units also came in for criticism from HM Inspectorate of Prisons (2001). For example, prisoners' movements were closely controlled, all visits were behind a glass screen and prisoners were subject to extensive searching and observation. By 2004, there were no longer any exceptional-risk Category A prisoners and the units were mothballed or put to alternative uses, although they can be brought into operation again if required.

Although there are increasing numbers of prisoners being detained in connection with terrorist offences, they do not belong to highly organized, paramilitary organizations such as those formerly associated with Northern Ireland and do not present the same level of escape risk. As a result, the SSUs have not yet been called back into operation. However, this is a situation that may change in the future.

*Jamie Bennett*

## Related entries

*Category A prisoners; High-security prisons; HM Inspectorate of Prisons; Official reports; Order and control; Paramilitary prisoners; Political prisoners; Searching; Security; Visits and visiting orders.*

### Key texts and sources

HM Inspectorate of Prisons (2001) *A Full Announced Inspection of HM Prison Whitemoor, 6–15 November 2000.* London: Home Office.

Woodcock, J. (1994) *Report of an Enquiry into the Escape of Six Prisoners from the Special Security Unit at Whitemoor Prison, Cambridgeshire, on Friday 9th September 1994.* London: HMSO.

For Amnesty International's report on special security units, see http://web.amnesty.org/library/pdf/EUR450061997ENGLISH/$File/EUR4500697.pdf.

# STAFF (PRISON)

The Prison Service in England and Wales employs almost 50,000 people in a wide variety of roles.

At the end of 2005, the Prison Service in England and Wales employed 48,425 staff. Of these staff, 25,971 were in the unified grades (prison officers and managers, including prison governors),

**Table 2** Staff employed by the Prison Service, 2005 (per cent)

| Staff group | Per cent |
|---|---|
| Officers (including senior and principal officers) | 50.7 |
| Operational support grades (carry out support work, such as staffing the gate and control room and escorting vehicles) | 15.2 |
| Administration | 15.3 |
| Healthcare | 2.2 |
| Chaplaincy | 0.6 |
| Psychology | 1.9 |
| Industrials (i.e. workshop instructors) | 7.0 |
| Other | 4.0 |
| Operational managers (i.e governor grades) | 2.8 |

working directly in prisoner management. A breakdown of staff employed by group is shown in Table 2 (HM Prison Service 2006).

Although some progress has been made over time, in terms of staffing, the prison system continues to be largely a white, male occupation. In total, 34 per cent of staff are female, although this is more concentrated in non-operational posts such as administration, healthcare and psychology. Only 21 per cent of officer grades are female. There are fewer than 6 per cent of staff who are black or from minority ethnic communities.

The prison staff group is largely stable. In total, there is a 6 per cent turnover rate, with only 3.5 per cent in the unified staff. There are approximately 5,000–6,000 new recruits to the Prison Service annually, with around 1,500 of those being new prison officers. The pay and benefits are competitive, particularly the pension arrangements. Pay for operational staff is set by an independent pay review body, established in 2001. Over the last 15 years, there have been some significant changes that have affected prison staff (Bennett *et al.* 2007). In particular, there have been movements that can be described as specialization, professionalization and decentralization. These have largely been informed by the development of the practices of new public management, which seeks to introduce private sector practices into the public sector in order to improve efficiency and effectiveness.

In terms of specialization, there has been a greater focus on the core role of particular grades. The most significant example is the growth of the operational support grade, which carries out tasks formerly carried out by prison officers, but not requiring the full range of prison officer skills (for example, working in the gate or control room, or escorting vehicles). Another example is the national review of works departments, which resulted in changes to the way staff in such departments are employed. Previously, they were officer-trades people, having both skills. However, it was generally recognized that the prison officer skills were superfluous in the role. Therefore the works departments were changed to trade specialists, and all those who wished to retain their prison officer role had to revert to mainstream duties. A similar change has happened in prison catering. These changes have enabled the Prison Service to recruit staff at lower cost to carry out these tasks, while ensuring that prison officers focus on their specialist roles of working with prisoners and that those other roles (trades, catering) focus on their own specialization.

Professionalization can be seen both in the increase in the number of professional staff, such as psychologists, and in the changing requirements placed on specific staff. An example of this is that heads of finance are now required to gain accountancy qualifications, and heads of human resources must gain qualifications in personnel management. However, this is in contrast to prison officers, who do not require any qualifications. For a period, it was an entry requirement that they had five GCSEs, but this led to significant shortfalls in recruitment and was rescinded. Instead, for prison officers, there has been a move to base professionalization on more practical, competency-based approaches. Competency criteria are widely used to inform recruitment, selection and appraisal. In addition, a national vocational qualification in custodial care has been developed and supported, and this will be mandatory for new prison officers from 2007.

Decentralization refers to the increasing move to contract prison work to private or other public sector providers. The largest examples of this are in education and healthcare. The provision of teaching is subject to competitive tendering, with teachers being employed by the contractor rather than directly by the prison. Healthcare services have transferred to local primary care trusts and, as a result, many staff have transferred to those organizations. This accounts for the reduction in directly employed health staff in recent years. There are also many other examples of this. For example, prison shops ('canteens') have been contracted out, and probation staff are employed by their probation services rather than the prison.

The Prison Service is an employer of a large workforce carrying out a wide variety of roles. It is recognized as a stable employer, although there are challenges in increasing the diversity of the workforce. Changes in prisons more generally, particularly the development of new public management, have led to new requirements among the workforce and have altered the organization's relationship with that workforce.

*Jamie Bennett*

### Related entries

*Cost of prisons; Governors; Healthcare; HM Prison Service; Industrial relations; New public management (NPM); Prison officers; Psychology in prisons.*

**Key texts and sources**

Bennett, J., Crewe, B. and Wahidin, A. (eds) (2007) *Understanding Prison Staff.* Cullompton: Willan Publishing.

HM Prison Service (2006) *HR Planning Staff Profiles and Projections Review – January 2006.* London: Home Office.

See also the website of the Prison Reform Trust (**http://www.prisonreformtrust.org.uk/subsection.asp?id=275**).

## STANFORD PRISON EXPERIMENT

The Stanford Prison Experiment was conducted in 1971 by a group of Stanford University research psychologists, led by Professor Phillip Zimbardo and his two graduate students, Curtis Banks and Craig Haney. The experiment was designed to control for the individual personality variables that were often used at that time to explain behaviour in prison and other institutional settings.

The Stanford Prison Experiment was designed to control for the individual personality variables that were often used at that time to explain behaviour in prison and other institutional settings. That is, the researchers neutralized the explanatory argument that pathological traits alone could account for extreme and abusive behaviour by 1) selecting a group of participants who were psychological healthy and who had scored in the normal range of the numerous personality variables they measured and selected for; and 2) by assigning participants to either the role of prisoner or guard on a completely random basis. The behaviour that resulted when these otherwise healthy, normal participants were placed in the extreme environment of a simulated prison would have to be explained largely, if not entirely, on the basis of the characteristics of the social setting or situation in which they had been placed.

The setting itself was designed to be as similar to an actual prison as possible. Constructed in the basement of the Psychology Department at Stanford University, the 'Stanford County Prison' had barred doors on the small rooms that served as cells; beds on which the prisoners slept; a hallway area that was converted to a prison 'yard' where group activities were conducted; and a small room that served as a short-term 'solitary confinement' cell that could be used for disciplining unruly prisoners. The prisoners wore uniforms that were designed to de-emphasize their individuality and to underscore their powerlessness. The guards, on the other hand, donned military-like garb, complete with reflecting sunglasses and nightsticks. The guards generated a set of rules and regulations that, in many ways, resembled those in operation in actual prisons, and the prisoners were expected to comply with their orders. However, the guards were instructed not to resort to physical force in order to gain prisoner compliance.

Despite the lack of any legal mandate for the 'incarceration' of the prisoners, and despite the fact that both groups were told that they had been randomly assigned to their roles (so that, for example, the guards knew that the prisoners had done nothing to 'deserve' their degraded prisoners status), the behaviour that ensued was remarkably similar to behaviour that takes place inside actual prisons and surprisingly extreme in intensity and effect. Thus, initial prisoner resistance and rebellion were met forcibly by the guards, who quickly struggled to regain their power and then proceeded to escalate their mistreatment of prisoners throughout the study, at the slightest sign of affront or disobedience. In some instances, the guards conspired to mistreat prisoners physically outside the presence of the experimenters and to leave prisoners in the solitary confinement cell beyond the one-hour limit the researchers had set.

Conversely, the prisoners resisted the guards' orders at first but then succumbed to their superior power and control. Some prisoners had serious emotional breakdowns in the course of the study and had to be released; others became compliant and conforming, rarely if ever challenging the 'authority' of the guards.

Despite the fact that the researchers could not keep the prisoners in the study against their will (and they had been informed at the outset of the study of their legal right to leave), as the study proceeded they 'petitioned' the prison 'administrators' for permission to be 'paroled' and they returned passively to their cells when their requests were denied. By the end of the study, they had disintegrated as a group. The guards, on the other hand, solidified and intensified their control. Although some of the guards were more extreme and inventive in the degradation they inflicted on the prisoners, and some were more passive and less involved, none of the guards intervened to restrain the behaviour of their more abusive colleagues. Although the study was designed to last for two full weeks, the extreme nature of the behaviour that occurred led the researchers to terminate it after only six days.

Controversial from the outset and widely discussed and cited since it was conducted, the study has come to stand in psychology and related disciplines as a demonstration of the power of situations – especially extreme institutional settings such as prisons – to shape and control the behaviour of the persons placed inside them. Its results give lie to the notion that extreme social behaviour can only – or even mostly – be explained by resorting to the extreme characteristics of the people who engage in it. The experiment counsels us to look instead to the characteristics of the settings or situations in which the behaviour occurs. It also stands as a challenge to what might be termed the 'presumption of institutional rationality' – that is, the tendency to assume that institutions operate on the basis of an inherent rationality that should be abided rather than questioned. Instead, the Stanford Prison Experiment (itself the most 'irrational' of prisons, in the sense that the guards had no legal authority over the prisoners who, in turn, had committed no crimes that warranted their punishment) suggests that a kind of 'psycho-logic' may operate in these settings that controls role-bound behaviour, whether or not that behaviour actually furthers legitimate goals.

*Craig Haney and Phillip Zimbardo*

*Related entries*

*Order and control; Power; Prison officers; Security; Structure/agency ('resistance'); Total institutions.*

**Key texts and sources**

Haney, C. (1999) 'Reflections on the Stanford Prison Experiment: genesis, transformations, consequences ("the SPE and the analysis of institutions")', in T. Blass (ed.) *Obedience to Authority: Current Perspectives on the Milgram Paradigm.* Hillsdale, NJ: Erlbaum.

Haney, C. (2006) *Reforming Punishment: Psychological Limits to the Pains of Imprisonment.* Washington, DC: American Psychological Association Books.

Haney, C., Banks, C. and Zimbardo, P. (1973) 'Interpersonal dynamics in a simulated prison', *International Journal of Criminology and Penology,* 1: 69–97.

Haney, C. and Zimbardo, P. (1977) 'The socialization into criminality: on becoming a prisoner and a guard', in J. Tapp and F. Levine (eds) *Law, Justice, and the Individual in Society: Psychological and Legal Issues.* New York, NY: Holt, Rinehart & Winston.

Haney, C. and Zimbardo, P. (1998) 'The past and future of US prison policy: twenty-five years after the Stanford Prison Experiment', *American Psychologist,* 53: 709–27.

See also http://www.prisonexp.org/.

# STRUCTURE/AGENCY ('RESISTANCE')

The tension between structure and agency is arguably best resolved in Giddens' (1977) theory of 'structuration', which is an important counter to the notion of prison 'deprivations', arguing that subordinates are never entirely powerless even in the most 'total' of total institutions. While riots, disturbances, homicide, suicide and self-harm are all extreme examples of the assertion of agency within the relatively rigid structures of incarceration, small but significant acts of 'resistance' are common.

Traditional sociology arguably has tended to adopt an 'over-socialized' image of the human subject as a passive conformist who co-operates with others. However, most sociologies of imprisonment have emphasized that actors frequently behave unpredictably, impetuously and, sometimes, confrontationally and that, despite the inevitable erosion of agency and identity that imprisonment entails, the majority of prisoners are able to maintain a self-identity as active, reasoning agents. In other words, the requirements of social conformity and discipline which confinement inevitably demands constantly jostle with prisoners' individual impulses and inclinations towards resistance. For example, Sparks *et al.* (1996) discredit the notion that people are basically 'acceptance seekers' passively conforming to an imposed regime, and highlight the balance that prison authorities must achieve between situational and social control methods. If all forms of imprisonment implied the unrelenting use of force, as some commentators suggest, prisons would have no genuine internal sense of order and little sense of legitimacy on which to base the maintenance of order. Either scenario – a muted and fragile order sustained by an enforced compliance or a bedlam of violent and desperate prisoners with nothing to lose – is too crude an analysis and places undue focus on the processes of structure and agency working as independent forces (Sparks *et al.*, 1996).

The project to integrate structure and agency is usually associated with Anthony Giddens (1977), whose attempt to demonstrate the link between social production (the way in which social life is produced by people as they go about their day-to-day activities) and social reproduction (the way in which social life becomes patterned and social institutions are reproduced over time, providing order and continuity in society) is known as 'structuration theory'. In brief, structuration theory attempts to show how social structures are constituted *by* human agency and yet, at the same time, are the very *medium* of this constitution – what Giddens terms a 'duality of structure' (Giddens 1977: 121). Thus, the prison system is both the medium in which the practices of prisoners and staff are shaped and the (partly unintended) outcome of those human, minded practices as they act back on, and shape, future environing processes. While Foucault (1977) demonstrated that people in all areas of everyday life are subject to the patterns, discourses and logic of organizations and institutions, Giddens' theory enables us to understand that the reverse is also true, and life (in any sphere, but not least the prison), although immensely routinized and structured, only 'happens' because 'real-life, flesh-and-blood people make it happen' (Sparks *et al.*, 1996: 72).

Giddens' attempt to account for human agency in even the most restricted structural environments is a significant theoretical breakthrough. Its rejection of the implicit (and sometimes explicit) portrayals of prisoners as having been 'mortified' is an important development because the majority of prison research characterizes power in prisons in a rather crude, one-dimensional way, and has arguably been guilty of the very thing that it has accused the prison system itself of – that is, stripping inmates of their personalities and individual identities, and replacing them with crude typologies which lump them all together in stereotyped categories of predictive behaviour. Even though Giddens devotes little attention to the prison *per se*, his criticism of Foucault is relevant. Foucault's conceptualization of the power of carceral organizations is arguably rigid and mechanistic, and those who are subject to forms of discipline are rendered acquiescent and anonymous. As Giddens says, 'Foucault's bodies do not have faces' (1984: 154). Even the most rigorous forms of discipline cannot dissipate human agency altogether. Although there are circumstances in which autonomy is severely limited, it is 'rarely negated entirely' (Giddens 1984: 156). 'Resistance' thus encompasses small, personal acts of defiance, assaults on the self (including suicide) and, more rarely, large-scale eruptions of disorder.

Cohen and Taylor (1972) are among the prison scholars who graphically illustrate that prisoners do not passively experience imprisonment: they live, negotiate and resist it even if, in doing so, they sometimes suffer predictable but undesirable consequences which merely reproduce the situation in which they find themselves. For example, a relatively minor act of defiance, intransigence or resistance may lead to punitive measures, such as the withdrawal of privileges or temporary removal of the prisoner into segregation. But as a means of 'keeping one's head above the mire of institutionalisation', transgressing rules becomes 'part of the survival kit' (Caird 1974: 62). Resistance among women prisoners is a relatively neglected area of study, although Bosworth (1999) argues that the restrictions placed on women's choice, autonomy and responsibility in prison (which, she argues, are greater than those faced by men in confinement) do not entirely disempower them. Women prisoners manage to resist full institutional control, which is always contingent and incomplete, not least because there are significant continuities between women's experiences of imprisonment and their lives outside.

Agency, in the form of resistance, is by its very nature a dynamic and active strategy requiring insight into the structural constraints being resisted. In other words, the violation of a rule does not in itself constitute resistance, unless committed by someone who sees through the institutional ideology and knowingly acts on that basis. An example is given by Jewkes (2002), who notes that some prisoners resisted in-cell television when it was introduced in the late 1990s because they believed it to be part of a 'carrot-and-stick' ideology being implemented to mask more punitive and security-orientated policies that were being introduced simultaneously. It is this knowingness and sense of being wise to the ideological structures of the prison that help many prisoners to maintain a stable sense of identity inside.

*Yvonne Jewkes*

### Related entries

*Coping; Deprivations/'pains of imprisonment'; Discipline; Discretion; Grievances; Identity and self; In-cell television; Legitimacy; Order and control; Power; Prison Rules; Riots (prison); Security; Self-harm; Suicide in prison; Typologies of prisoners.*

**Key texts and sources**

Bosworth, M. (1999) *Engendering Resistance: Agency and Power in Women's Prisons.* Aldershot: Ashgate.

Caird, R. (1974) *A Good and Useful Life: Imprisonment in Britain Today.* London: Hart-Davis.

Cohen, S. and Taylor, L. (1972) *Psychological Survival: The Experience of Long-term Imprisonment.* Harmondsworth: Penguin Books.

Foucault, M. (1977) *Discipline and Punish: The Birth of the Prison.* London: Allen Lane.

Giddens, A. (1977) *Studies in Social and Political Theory.* London: Hutchinson.

Giddens, A. (1984) *The Constitution of Society.* Cambridge: Polity Press.

Jewkes, Y. (2002) *Captive Audience: Media, Masculinity and Power in Prisons.* Cullompton: Willan Publishing.

Sparks, R., Bottoms, A.E. and Hay, W. (1996) *Prisons and the Problem of Order.* Oxford: Oxford University Press.

# SUBCULTURES

Prisoner subcultures – or social relations and hierarchies – comprise the everyday relationships between individual prisoners and prisoner subgroups, and the terms of status and stigma within this community.

Although some early studies of the prisoner world suggested a relatively organized community of prisoners, most accounts emphasize a society of conflict, disorganization and isolation. For most prisoners, the prison provides few friendships and is 'an atomized world' characterized more by 'trickery and dishonesty' than 'sympathy and cooperation' (Clemmer 1940/1958: 297). Relationships between prisoners tend to be instrumental and defensive, based on fear and self-interest as much as trust and affection. Prisoner groups offer material, social and physical support, but emotional support is less common, except in certain circumstances (for example, when prisoners are bonded by strong political or religious convictions). In-group cohesion is generally limited.

The majority of studies have described the prisoner community as being characterized by interlocking and somewhat fluid groups, based on locality, religion, age, lifestyle and criminal identity, with little formal leadership or organization (Irwin 2004; Crewe forthcoming). In men's prisons in the USA, race has been the primary axis of the social world, with prisoners split into ethnically homogeneous and often antagonistic cliques. The importance of racial identity and gang affiliation has diminished somewhat in recent years (Irwin 2004). In UK prisons, despite frictions and prejudice, race relations have been far more harmonious. Where social groups are defined by ethnicity, these groupings reflect shared cultural identifications rather than explicit attempts at ethnic segregation, and prisoners work, trade and socialize across ethnic lines. On the whole, in the UK, locality is more significant than ethnicity in defining prisoner affiliations – though the two are often related – and social groups are formed around networks imported from outside communities. In most prisons, the informal prisoner economy is dominated by groups from large urban centres but, with a multitude of interconnected cliques and networks, it is rare that the prisoner world is monopolized by a single social group. In higher-security prisons, where there are more prisoners with links to organized crime, group hierarchies are more apparent.

Prisoners also cluster to some degree according to their relative status and stigma. Such values partly relate to behaviour in prison. Thus, prisoners who are faithful to the inmate code tend to generate respect, while those who are naïve, 'weak', mentally unstable, unhygienic or disloyal to their peers are disparaged. Some prisoners achieve economic and physical power through exploitation and aggression. This power is not necessarily the same as admiration or credibility, although the two may be conflated. Indeed, scholars of US prisons describe the way that, as gang members and young, alienated, urban men flooded into prisons in the 1970s, the prison became a lawless social jungle in which sexual and physical violence were everyday occurrences and respect became equated with violence and victimization.

In almost all penal jurisdictions, kudos and contempt are also linked to certain criminal acts.

Thus, sex offenders are generally shunned and derided by other prisoners and petty criminals accorded little credibility, while professional criminals, armed robbers, terrorists and high-end drug dealers and fraudsters are normally given 'respect'. However, these terms are complex. Distinctions are made between different types of murder (e.g. spousal murder and contract killings) and different types of burglary (e.g. domestic and commercial). Meanwhile, there is no simple consensus about how to evaluate these differences morally, with petty criminals generally censorious about, rather than admiring of, serious violent offenders.

The terms of the prisoner hierarchy are also shaped by institutional factors and policies, and are subject to historical change. In lower-security prisons, the proximity of release is such that prisoners are less inclined to advertise or accumulate power. Power is bestowed upon some individuals, granting them a certain level of safety and recognition and giving them the capacity to intervene in wing issues, but few prisoners actively seek it. Crewe (forthcoming) argues that the clearest division in a medium-security establishment is a broad distinction between the minority of 'lads' and the mass of prisoners who have little means of or interest in asserting themselves. In more authoritarian prisons, the currency of violence among prisoners is likely to be higher than in prisons where there is less cause for and value in aggression. The introduction of anti-bullying strategies and efforts to eradicate staff brutality appear to have reduced the significance of violence in achieving status. Power and respect also accrue to prisoners who can provide scarce goods and services in the prison. In the current system of England and Wales, it is significant, then, that hard drugs, particularly heroin, have become central in the prisoner hierarchy. Drug dealers have considerable influence in prison, both because of the profit they can achieve and the desire that they can exploit. Meanwhile, by breaching a range of norms through their dependency and the acts of

stealing and manipulation that they normally carry out in order to feed their habits, drug users have become highly stigmatized.

Culture and social relations in women's prisons differ from those in men's prisons in a number of ways. Studies have repeatedly (and sometimes rather too pruriently) highlighted high levels of consensual sexual activity and the existence of pseudo-family units, which appear to provide women in prison with significant emotional support and with the familial roles that imprisonment otherwise denies them. Compared with men's prisons, trade networks are less developed, drug use is more medicinal and the hierarchy is less established. None the less, as in men's prisons, women who have offended against children are reviled, bullying is common and prisoner groups are based on friendships and acquaintances from outside prison (Owen 1998). In both men's and women's establishments, everyday culture is coloured by the combination of cynicism, misery, tales of personal demise, shame and misfortune, and wry humour, warmth and optimism about the future.

*Ben Crewe*

### Related entries

*Assaults; Bullying; Drugs; Economy; Friendship; Inmate code; Power; Sex offenders; Violence; Women in prison.*

**Key texts and sources**

Clemmer, D. (1940) *The Prison Community* (2nd edn 1958). New York, NY: Holt, Rinehart & Winston.
Crewe, B (2007) 'The sociology of imprisonment, in Y. Jewkes (ed.) *Handbook on Prisons*. Cullompton: Willan Publishing.
Crewe, B. (forthcoming) *Wellingborough: Power, Adaptation and the Everyday Social World of an English Prison*.
Irwin, J. (2004) *The Warehouse Prison: Disposal of the New Dangerous Classes*. Los Angeles, CA: Roxbury.
Owen, B. (1998) *In the Mix: Struggle and Survival in a Women's Prison*. Albany, NY: State University of New York Press.

# SUICIDE IN PRISON

Suicides in prison occur at a rate of about 120–140 per 100,000 prisoners per year in England and Wales. This means there are typically between 90 and 100 suicides in prison in any one year. This is higher than the rate in the general community, although the rate of suicide among offenders both before and after custody is surprisingly high. A disproportionate number of prison suicides occur among women and the young. Some prisons seem more prone to suicide than others.

The rate of prison suicide in England and Wales is high, and has been increasing. The suicide rate in 2005 was 125 per 100,000 prisoners. The rate in 1983 was 62 per 100,000 prisoners. There are difficulties in calculating prison suicide rates, as average daily population figures are used, where reception figures and length of stay may be more appropriate. The rate of suicide in the general population in England and Wales is around 11 per 100,000 for men and 3 per 100,000 for women. Rates are higher for the young (17 per 100,000 for men aged 20–39 and 3.5 per 100,000 for women aged 20–39). The rate of suicide for offenders under supervision in the community is about 100 per 100,000 (Sattar 2001). The prison population constitutes an 'at risk' group who bring into prison with them an elevated risk of suicide. It is likely that the prison experience contributes to their risk, however.

Explanations for the increase in prison suicides witnessed over recent decades include increases in population size, turnover and overcrowding; increases in the vulnerability of the prison population (e.g. offenders are drawn from increasingly high-risk groups in the community, for example, drug users); and problems relating to prison life and management. Around half to two thirds of prison suicides occur within the first month in custody. About half occur among prisoners on remand. Most official inquiries have more to say about the problems of prison life and management than they do about the vulnerability of the population. It is often difficult to identify individuals at risk and, arguably, prison factors are more amenable to change.

There have been numerous policy initiatives aimed at reducing the suicide rate in prisons, including the Caring for the Suicidal in Custody strategy launched in 1994. This was regarded at the time as a carefully researched and 'fundamentally sound' document, which required joint responsibility between healthcare and discipline staff for prisoners at risk. Following the 1994 strategy, the role of the Samaritans was developed in prisons and listener schemes were introduced (prisoners trained by the Samaritans to support their fellow prisoners). At the heart of this strategy was a collective approach, 'which encouraged supportive relationships' (HMCIP 1999: 46). It suffered from major problems of implementation, however (HMCIP 1999). That is, several important aspects of the policy were never fully brought into operation, so that there was little 'ownership of the strategy by senior managers', case reviews were infrequent, staff were insufficiently trained and there were no quality checks on 'vital documentation' (HMCIP 1999).

In January 1999 a working group was set up by the World Health Organization (WHO-Europe) in order to review suicide policy in prisons and to make improvements. A thematic review carried out by HM Chief Inspectorate of Prisons for England and Wales in 1998–9 (*Suicide is Everyone's Concern*) emphasized that 'suicide is everyone's concern' and outlined the broader objective of developing 'healthy prisons' – that is, institutions 'in which prisoners and staff are able to live and work in a way that promotes their well-being' (HMCIP 1999: 59). The four principles to be used as the 'test' of a healthy prison were as follows:

- The weakest prisoners feel safe
- All prisoners are treated with respect as individuals
- All prisoners are busily occupied, are expected to improve themselves and given the opportunity to do so
- All prisoners can strengthen links with their families and prepare for release (HMCIP 1999: 60).

In April 2001, the Prison Service's new Safer Custody Group proposed a strategy whereby 'an all-round pro-active approach will be developed which encourages a supportive culture in prisons based on good staff–prisoner relationships, a constructive regime and a physically safe environment. There will be improved identification and case arrangements for high-risk prisoners' (Safer Custody Group 2001). It was the broadest, the most generously resourced and the most determined strategy to date. The steps being taken formed part of the broader Safer Custody programme which aims to raise the standards of prisoner care and to make prisons safer places in which to live and work. The programme was supported by a team in Prison Service headquarters, the Samaritans and a wide range of prison interest groups. It involves, *inter alia*, providing full-time suicide prevention co-ordinators in high-risk local prisons, developing new screening procedures, improving mental health support and improving drug detoxification and treatment procedures. There is particular emphasis on the first phase of custody, with newly built (or converted) first-night centres forming part of this attempt to reduce levels of risk at this particularly dangerous time.

The new strategy was piloted in six 'high risk' prisons (Feltham, Winchester, Leeds, Eastwood Park, Wandsworth and Birmingham). Significant related interventions also took place in other establishments across the country. A Cambridge Institute of Criminology research team evaluated the strategy, finding that significant improvements could be made to the level of care for prisoners, to levels of prisoner distress and to cultural aspects of prisoner treatment. These improvements only occurred in two out of five prisons involved in the pilot, however, suggesting that implementation, and perhaps especially cultural change supporting implementation, is extremely difficult. Levels of vulnerability varied significantly between prisons of the same type. More significant, however, were the variations in prisoners' levels of distress, their perceptions of how safe they felt and the quality of their relationships with staff. In two of the pilot establishments, over a two-year period, improvements to the provisions of care, to staff culture

and to safety led to reductions in prisoner distress, and to fewer suicides (Liebling 2006).

*Alison Liebling*

### Related entries

*Discipline; First-night centres; Healthcare; HM Inspectorate of Prisons; Mental health; Overcrowding; Remand.*

**Key texts and sources**

HMCIP (1999) *Suicide is Everyone's Concern: Report of a Thematic Inspection on Suicides in Prison.* London: HMSO.

Liebling, A. (2006) 'Suicide and its prevention', in Y. Jewkes (ed.) *Handbook on Prisons.* Cullompton: Willan Publishing.

Safer Custody Group (2001) *Prevention of Suicide and Self-harm in the Prison Service: An Internal Review.* London: Home Office.

Sattar, G. (2001) *Rates and Causes of Deaths among Prisoners and Offenders under Community Supervision. Home Office Research Study* 231. London: Home Office.

See the various sections on suicide in prison at the Howard League's website (http://www.howardleague.org/).

## SUPERMAX PRISONS

Supermax (short for super-maximum security) prisons, or secure housing units (SHUs), are best understood as the highest-security accommodation in American state and federal prison systems.

The supermax – or secure housing units (SHUs) in prisons – is best understood as the highest-security accommodation (level VI) in American state and federal prison systems, although these prisons have been copied in other jurisdictions. According to the National Institute of Corrections' (NIC) definition, they typically provide accommodation that is physically separate from other units and in which a highly controlled and restrictive regime isolating prisoners both from each other and from staff is imposed upon prisoners who have been identified through an administrative rather than a disciplinary process as needing such control on the grounds of their violent or seriously disruptive behaviour. Although the accommodation is very secure, the main purpose is not to prevent escapes and absconds – which are largely factored out by the threat of the use of lethal force by armed guards – but control (and they are sometimes referred to as control prisons). The nearest equivalent in the Prison Service for England and Wales are the close supervision centres (CSC), although these are generally run on different principles.

Some commentators trace the origins of supermax back to the federal prison at Alcatraz, others to the Control Unit (H Block) at the federal penitentiary at Marion, Illinois. The term itself did not have much usage until the 1980s, when the federal authorities began to plan for a new administrative maximum (ADX) facility at Florence, Colorado, to replace Marion which, after intermittent lock-downs, had gone into permanent lock-down status following the killing of two officers in 1983. The federal system has comparatively few prisoners of its own who are extremely difficult to manage, but it has always provided a service for state prison systems by taking those prisoners which the states could not manage themselves. However, in 1982 Minnesota established an ingeniously designed 'new generation' maximum security prison at Oak Park Heights following extensive troubles at Stillwater, and soon found itself taking in boarders both from other states and from the federal system. In 1987, Arizona opened the first of its special management units, and the soubriquet of 'supermax' caught on as more and more states discovered that, in a harsh law-and-order climate, control prisons could attract funding, whereas those concerned with education and training or rehabilitation could not. Today, four fifths of all states, plus the Federal Bureau of Prisons, operate supermax facilities, and well over 20,000 prisoners are incarcerated in them. The federal system itself is a relatively parsimonious user with fewer than 0.5 per cent of its prisoners in supermax, but some states are much more profligate, with 5 per cent or more of their prisoners so confined (King 1999).

## Who goes to supermax and what happens when they are there?

To put it simply, in the populist vocabulary most frequently used, supermax is designed for 'the worst of the worst' and is predicated upon a rational choice model whereby 'bad behaviour gets you in: good behaviour gets you out'. There are (at least) three major issues with the use of supermax custody, which have attracted the attention of the courts and campaigners. First, who gets in and how? Transfer to supermax is by way of an administrative, not a disciplinary, procedure. There is no due process. In the 'best' systems there are reasonably clear criteria for entry and a reasonably careful process with central oversight which tries to ensure that strict criteria are employed (though these are few on the ground and none, except perhaps the federal system, appears to have the safeguards employed by the Close Supervision Centres Selection Committee in England and Wales). In the worst systems, wardens are able to refer more or less whom they choose to supermax. As a result, cases abound whereby juveniles and low-security prisoners are catapulted into supermax for trivial reasons, and many prisoners believe that they are in supermax simply to fill up the spaces.

Secondly, what happens when one is there? Supermax prisons vary in terms of the regimes they provide. At one extreme, for example, prisoners are completely isolated not just from fellow prisoners but also from staff who remain behind physical barriers. Prisoners do everything in isolation, including exercise in 'dog runs'. When out of their cells they may be handcuffed, leg ironed, belly chained, spit masked and accompanied by two or more officers. At Pelican Bay in California, armed guards supervise inside the prison, and the bleak living units or 'pods' are adorned with signs saying 'NO WARNING SHOTS'. At the other extreme things can be different. The NIC definition of supermax, for example, suggested that prisoners were physically separated both from each other and from staff. Oak Park Heights, more or less uniquely, has defied that, insisting not merely that prisoners can associate but that staff and prisoners share some spaces and that prisoners can benefit from programmes. Most states occupy a position on a continuum between these extremes, but skewed more towards the Pelican Bay model.

Thirdly, how does one get out? Some states operate fixed terms in supermax, but most link exit to reviews of behaviour. Although good behaviour is supposed to get you out, the periods of sustained good behaviour required vary from state to state and are often in excess of two years before consideration is given to transfer to lower-security settings. And what constitutes 'good behaviour' often depends upon discretionary judgements made by basic-grade officers with the result that prisoners may work their way towards release only to find themselves knocked back to the beginning of the evaluation process. Many prisoners spend much of their sentence in such facilities, from which they are eventually released to the street.

Since supermax facilities offer such scope for abuse and may be assumed to produce profound effects (King 2005), they have attracted the attention of both campaigners and the courts. After campaigns by Amnesty International and Human Rights Watch, Wisconsin has removed juveniles from its facility at Boscobel, and Virginia has downgraded Wallens Ridge to a level-5 facility. Increasingly, states have recognized the need to provide 'step down' units before transfer to normal location or release. In *Madrid* v. *Gomez* 889 F. Supp. 1146 (N.D. Cal. 1995), the Federal Court declined to find Pelican Bay in California in breach of Eighth Amendment protections against cruel and unusual punishment, despite conditions which 'hover on the edge of what is humanly tolerable', except in regard to prisoners with actual or potential mental health problems (see also Rhodes 2004). Few, if any, of these facilities would meet the more stringent criteria employed by the European Committee for the Prevention of Torture or HM Chief Inspectorate of Prisons. The NIC has tried to set out some principles of good practice, as have some of the more enlightened practitioners in their contributions to an American Correctional Association publication (Neal 2003). But there is little doubt that supermax is used more widely than can be justified, and there is an argument that acclimatization to 20 years of supermax custody for its own citizens paved the way for the American treatment of terrorist suspects at Abu Ghraib and Guantánamo Bay.

*Roy King*

## Related entries

*Close supervision centres; Death penalty; Escapes and absconds; European Committee for the Prevention of Torture and Inhuman or Degrading Treatment or Punishment (ECPT); HM Inspectorate of Prisons; New-generation prisons (NGPs); Rehabilitation.*

### Key texts and sources

King, R.D. (1999) 'The rise and rise of supermax: an American solution in search of a problem', *Punishment and Society*, 1: 163–86.

King, R.D. (2005) 'The effects of supermax custody', in A. Liebling and S. Maruna (eds) *The Effects of Imprisonment*. Cullompton: Willan Publishing.

Neal, D. (ed.) (2003) *Supermax Prisons: Beyond the Rock*. Lanham, MD: American Correctional Association.

Rhodes, L. (2004) *Total Confinement: Madness and Reason in the Maximum Security Prison*. Berkeley, CA: University of California Press.

See the US website **http://www.supermaxed.com/** for information about this variety of institution.

# T

## TEMPORARY RELEASE

In line with the so-called 'rehabilitative ideal', temporary release programmes are designed to prepare eligible prisoners for their eventual return to the community by releasing them under certain conditions for set periods of time.

First introduced by Captain Alexander Maconochie at the notorious prison colony of Norfolk Island back in the 1840s, the temporary release scheme, also known under such terms as 'release on temporary licence' and 'furlough', provides for short periods of authorized absence from the prison establishment, most usually granted when nearing the end of the custodial sentence or release on parole. The eligibility criteria usually vary with offence type and sentence duration. In most cases, the scheme takes the form of either a few days' home leave or work release, whereby prisoners undertake paid work in free-world settings during the day while spending non-working days and nights in custody. Study release is another form of temporary release, affording prisoners the opportunity to attend instructional programmes, including vocational and technical schools, high school, colleges and universities.

Temporary release programmes may be housed in either institutional or community facilities. In theory, temporary release is designed to ameliorate the practical and emotional harms of institutionalization (e.g. idleness, isolation, low self-esteem) and to facilitate prisoners' transition to civilian life, but it also helps them to abstain from criminal and other risk-prone activities (e.g. the use of illicit substances) in the period following permanent release. To this end, prisoners are given the opportunity to strengthen or re-establish family and social ties and to make arrangements for accommodation, work, education or training on final discharge. In the case of work release, prisoners may also make some modest savings, contribute to the financial needs of their dependants and maintain or acquire vocational skills, thus also enhancing their post-release employment prospects.

In tune with the 'liberalizing tradition' of the post-war period, the Criminal Justice Act 1948 was the first piece of legislation in England and Wales formally to provide for the release of prisoners on temporary licence, in the form of home leave. Paradoxically, however, the implementation of the scheme only realized noteworthy expansion of what has come to be seen as the demise of the 'rehabilitative ideal'. In 2002, for example, there was an all-time high of 287,732 temporary release grants, up from 164,521 in 1995, amounting to a rise of 75 per cent (Home Office 2003). Similar trends can be observed in Germany, France, Portugal, Greece and various other European jurisdictions. Unfortunately, little has been done to explore whether the expanded utilization of temporary release in recent years signifies a 'correctional renaissance' or, conversely, constitutes no more than an atheoretical response to practical problems of the moment, such as prison overcrowding and associated costs, and/or even masquerades another punitive turn in contemporary penality in alignment with urgent conservative control imperatives. It has been suggested, for example, that pre-release programmes such as temporary release are more often than not subordinated to a mixture of populist political motives and risk management considerations, while also being deployed as a surreptitious means to optimize institutional order. Under this prism, the authorities are inclined to disqualify those deemed to be high-risk offenders from such schemes, with a view to maintaining long-term custodial control over them and, consequently, achieving significant, albeit still temporary, reductions in crime rates – a practice often referred to as 'selective incapacitation'. By contrast, low-risk offenders are regarded as least prone to fail and thus more likely to shroud community-based programmes in a veil of success. At the same time, it is proposed, decision-makers often abuse their discretionary power, disproportionately favouring well behaved prisoners rather than targeting those in greater need of contact with the outside world, thereby turning pre-release measures into means of institutional control (see, further, Cheliotis 2006).

Outcome evaluation research not only provides rich data but also gives some more cause for optimism, though future analyses should incorporate more adequate controls for potential selection bias, either in the process of volunteering for participation in temporary release or in the risk assessment of licence applicants. With regard to prisoners' contacts, activities and accomplishments during temporary release, most licensees tend to spend their time constructively, contacting their families and partners with the aim of reaffirming emotional bonds or resolving relationship crises; seeking future employment or visiting an employer to firm up an existing offer; receiving training not available in prison; obtaining a driver's licence; and/or contacting the parole agent or some social agency. Dysfunctions, on the other hand, usually include intra-familial crises due to prisoners' unrealistic expectations and inadequate pre-release preparation for both them and their families; prisoners' difficulties in coming to terms with changes that have taken place to their families in the mean time; alienation from society and negative attention from civilians; and more practical concerns related to transportation, the avail-

ability of material resources and the duration of the leave. Work release participants may undergo frustration or resentment due to placement in an under- or over-structured setting; the non-availability of jobs fitting the prisoner's skills; frequent searches to prevent the smuggling of contraband into the institution; wage deductions disproportionate to the quality of accommodation and food supplied in the work release setting; and labour exploitation.

Seen through the lens of prisoners' families, temporary release appears to enhance family morale; to promote feelings of well-being for both husbands and wives; and to reaffirm marital and family commitments and to ease wives' own sense of imprisonment. Turning to programme rule violations and revocations – the most common outcome measures of temporary release effectiveness – previous research has consistently shown that late returns to the institution and escapes and absconds are rare. By the same token, and despite negative media coverage that only serves cynical market principles (often also political campaign interests), troublesome behaviour (e.g. alcohol consumption to the point of intoxication, fighting) and reoffending while on leave are observed in a tiny minority of cases. Similarly, against the 'nothing works' proposition, a recent comprehensive and systematic review of the literature showed that both home leave and work release schemes can be effective in reducing post-release recidivism rates, while work release may also enhance employment prospects (Cheliotis under review).

It remains to be seen whether or not the rehabilitative potential of temporary release will be sacrificed on the altar of 'administrative convenience' (on which, see Rothman 1980).

*Leonidas Cheliotis*

### Related entries
*Alternatives to imprisonment; Parole; Politics of imprisonment.*

**Key texts and sources**

Cheliotis, L.K. (2006) 'Demystifying risk management: a process evaluation of the prisoners' home leave scheme in Greece', *Criminology and Criminal Justice*, 6: 163–95.

Cheliotis, L.K. (under review) 'Reconsidering the effectiveness of temporary release: a systematic review of the literature.'

Home Office (2003) *Prison Statistics England and Wales, 2001.* London: HMSO.

Rothman, D.J. (1980) *Conscience and Convenience: The Asylum and its Alternatives in Progressive America.* New York, NY: Aldine de Gruyter.

See also the Home Office's website (http://www.ind.homeoffice.gov.uk/documents/oemsectiond/chapter38?view=Binary).

# THERAPEUTIC COMMUNITIES

Penal therapeutic communities work with offenders to address the root causes of their criminal behaviour. There are two types: democratic and hierarchical. Democratic therapeutic communities engage serious offenders in psychodynamic therapy in order to help them understand, and thus reduce, their challenging and anti-social behaviours. Hierarchical therapeutic communities offer a structured treatment programme for drug users.

Therapeutic communities are residential environments that utilize the social milieu and group process for their members' curative benefit. The two types, democratic and hierarchical (or concept based), share an encouragement of residents' active involvement in their therapy and the social learning that occurs naturally in the course of communal living, but differ in their theoretical orientation and value system. In English prisons, it is the democratic therapeutic community (DTC) which is most established; conversely, in the USA, only hierarchical therapeutic communities for drug users are currently supported.

The DTC owes its existence to innovations in the treatment of traumatized World War Two combat veterans. A handful of psychoanalytically orientated psychiatrists, most notably Tom Main and Maxwell Jones, developed a psychodynamic approach – emphasizing the (often unconscious) processes of change and personal development – to treat their patients' distress. In opposition to the 'medical model' of psychiatry, this new treatment modality was practised within a flexible, egalitarian organizational structure. Its key principles of democracy, communalism, permissiveness and reality confrontation, first identified by the social anthropologist Robert Rapoport (1960), promote a supportive 'culture of inquiry' and permeate all aspects of the daily regime. The community as a collective entity – which in prisons means the inmates *and* staff – therefore becomes the primary therapeutic instrument, based on the premise that social and psychological change can only evolve from the gradual accumulation of self-knowledge and insight into one's formative experiences and learnt maladaptive responses.

The original impetus to create a DTC for prisoners, however, can be attributed more to administrative pragmatism than ideological conviction. Reflecting the then hegemonic positivist paradigm, attempts in the 1930s to reduce recidivism focused on providing psychological treatment that would uncover offenders' allegedly causative 'mental disorder'. The subsequently recommended establishment of 'a penal institution of a special kind' (East and Hubert 1939: para. 172) was realized in 1962 when, facilitated by political support for the rehabilitative ideal, the first democratic, and still only 'whole', therapeutic community prison opened, Grendon in Buckinghamshire.

In the decades since, Grendon has specialized in treating violent offenders who predominantly suffer from psychopathy or personality disorder. Grendon's 235 'residents' volunteer for therapeutic community treatment and may elect to return to the mainstream system at any time. If assessed as suitable for therapy, inmates are assigned to one of five wings and to a fixed-membership small group, facilitated by a therapist, psychologist, probation officer or specially trained, uniformed prison officer. Largely non-directive and unstructured, these thrice-weekly groups enable inmates to explore their personal and offending history in considerable depth, to develop insight into their habitually problematic behaviours and attitudes, and, almost imperceptibly, through the development of attachment to and trust in others, to facilitate the broader, social therapy.

In addition, twice a week all residents and available staff attend their wing's community meetings. Chaired by an elected inmate, all matters relating to the functioning of the community – both the mundane and the substantial – are openly discussed and debated. Everyone is expected to assume collective responsibility for therapeutic and administrative decision-making, for the peaceful and efficient operation of the community and, through regular discussion, for their own and their peers' rehabilitative progress. Responsibility and communalism are further nurtured through the use of wing jobs and representative positions, approval for which must be sought first in the small group and then ratified by the whole wing community.

The community extends a high degree of tolerance towards its members, analysing rather than punishing the sort of unacceptable conduct and 'offence paralleling' (indicative of their characteristic offending behaviours) that in other prisons might result in adjudications. Such permissiveness, however, is balanced by the need to confront and benefit from these vicarious 'living-learning' opportunities. Acting as auxiliary therapists, residents must be prepared both to provide 'therapeutic feedback' on each other and to voice the detrimental effects of anti-social behaviour on them, rather than allowing their fellow inmates to rationalize or minimize their actions. Furthermore, any inmate who has repeatedly 'pushed boundaries' or broken one of the cardinal rules of abstinence – no violence, no alcohol or drugs, no sex – may face a 'commitment vote', by which the residents signify to staff (with whom the final decision always rests) their willingness or reluctance to allow that inmate to remain in therapy.

Grendon's status as 'the jewel in the crown' of the Prison Service, its creation of the 'gold standard' template for penal DTCs and the acknowledged need for expanded provision of DTC treatment for serious offenders (Maden *et*

*al.* 1994), all enabled the modest development of DTC units. These wholly or semi-contained wings in mainstream prisons are currently located at Gartree, Dovegate, Blundeston and Send Prisons. Dovegate, because of its comparable size, most closely 'rivals' Grendon for potential clientele. Blundeston is currently the only Category C prison to offer a DTC unit, while Send provides the only facility for women. Gartree's therapeutic community only accepts internal referrals of prisoners serving life sentences and, having been in operation since 1993, is now the longest surviving DTC unit. Conversely, three separate DTC units for young offenders have closed, most recently at Aylesbury Young Offender Institution, raising concerns about the fundamental suitability of such treatment for young prisoners. The DTCs at Barlinnie and Wormwood Scrubs also closed, having respectively failed to retain programme integrity and to protect against the operational intrusions and exigencies of the host prison. More positively, however, the offending behaviour programme offered by DTCs was approved by the Prison Service's Correctional Services Accreditation Panel in 2004, and all DTCs are now annually assessed for their adherence to this programme and core DTC principles and practices.

Research into the effectiveness of Grendon has produced largely positive results. Therapeutic community treatment has consistently and persuasively been found to improve inmates' psychological functioning, to lower levels of psychoticism, neuroticism, depression and hostility, and to inculcate greater self-esteem and self-confidence and pro-social interpersonal and communication skills. Additionally, after some initially discouraging results, recent Grendon reconviction studies have suggested that DTC treatment may reduce reoffending for older, motivated, serious recidivists who remain in therapy for at least 18 months, and who progress through the optimal five-stage 'therapeutic career model' (Genders and Player 1995). Such 'long stayers' have been found to be reconvicted less often both for any offence and specifically for violence, and to be less likely to be reimprisoned than control groups (Marshall 1997; Taylor 2000).

The time in treatment or 'dosage' effect has also been observed in successive American reconviction studies, following hierarchical therapeutic-community treatment for drug misuse. This model adheres to a set of explicit concepts about the psychological causes of addiction and its treatment and incorporates self-help and cognitive-behavioural techniques, group therapy and individual counselling, peer support and professional facilitation. Members must agree to abstain completely from using drugs in prison and accept a rigid, highly regimented and stratified social structure. It is thus more autocratic than democratic, and much closer to traditional penal culture. It was this multi-factorial model that the Prison Service in England and Wales adopted for its 1996 introduction of therapeutic community drug treatment and is now available in five prisons.

While hierarchical therapeutic communities excite little controversy, by contrast, Grendon and the nascent DTC units remain isolated penal anomalies. They continue to suffer from the erroneous belief, prevalent throughout the penal estate, that DTCs are only for 'nonces and grasses' or 'psychiatric cases' and, perhaps inevitably, the competing demands of security and therapy are not always successfully negotiated. With an interminably rising prison population, DTCs are also under considerable pressure to demonstrate cost effectiveness by working towards maximum occupancy. Nevertheless, they represent an ideologically important, if numerically insignificant, marriage between unashamed holistic rehabilitation and contemporary demands for evidence-based 'what works' interventions. Their 'special purpose' in conjoining therapy and demonstrable decency with coercive institutions of retributive punishment continues to be much admired by penologists, and much valued by those residents for whom it enables meaningful change.

*Alisa Stevens*

### Related entries

*Barlinnie; Life-sentence prisoners; New-generation prisons (NGPs); Offending behaviour programmes; Rehabilitation.*

### Key texts and sources

East, W.N. and Hubert, W. (1939) *The Psychological Treatment of Crime*. London: HMSO.

Genders, E. and Player, E. (1995) *Grendon: A Study of a Therapeutic Prison*. Oxford: Clarendon Press.

Maden, T., Swinton, M. and Gunn, J. (1994) 'Therapeutic community treatment: a survey of unmet need among sentenced prisoners', *Therapeutic Communities: The International Journal for Therapeutic and Supportive Organizations*, 15: 229–36.

Marshall, P. (1997) *A Reconviction Study of HMP Grendon Therapeutic Community. Home Office Research Findings 53*. London: Home Office Research and Statistics Directorate.

Rapoport, R. (1960) *Community as Doctor: New Perspectives on a Therapeutic Community*. London: Tavistock.

Taylor, R. (2000) *A Seven Year Reconviction Study of HMP Grendon Therapeutic Community. Home Office Research Findings* 115. London: Home Office Research, Development and Statistics Directorate.

For a review of therapeutic community treatment for people with personality disorders and mentally disordered offenders, see http://www.therapeuticcommunities.org/briefingpaper.htm.

## TIME

Time in the outside world is what men, women and children are forcibly deprived of when they are sentenced or remanded into prison. Whether the prison experience is long or short, research shows consistently that time remains a constant source of unseen and largely unacknowledged psychological suffering, as prisoners struggle with the pains of prison time.

'Doing time' has become a common metaphor in contemporary everyday speech for serving a prison sentence. The roots of this association lie in a historical transition in Western societies which saw, over centuries, the prison sentence of a certain length of time become the dominant form of punishment, as usage of the older forms of punishment (involving the gallows, chains, whipping posts and other instruments designed primarily to inflict physical damage) declined. This historical transition, from physical punishment to imprisonment for a length of time, is embedded in the larger transition to modern industrial societies, where time itself is economically, socially and culturally significant, both as a tool and as a commodity. Prison, and its seizure of a long, short or indeterminate slice of time from an individual's life, can be claimed, therefore, to be perhaps the most representative institution of industrial societies and modern states.

Perceptions of time inevitably altered after the invention of the pendulum clock in the seventeenth century and instruments to measure time proliferated as industrial capitalism began to flourish. Cyclical ideas about time, so suited to pre-industrial rural life that revolved around the repetitive experience of the four seasons, became overlaid in literature, culture and society with more linear ideas of time, where past, present and future are perceived internally as lying on a continuum. Ideas of progress and development became intrinsically bound up with notions of time: time was measurable, and 'lost' time had an economic cost.

Time discipline became the primary organizing principle in prisons and other institutions that confined large numbers of people in the post-Enlightenment period, just as in the factories of emerging capitalism. Although his history of the prison is considered somewhat partial, Foucault (1977) nevertheless shows convincingly the central historical importance of artifacts such as the timetable, where the object was to render bodies docile and wills compliant. The modern timetable in prison still has a central importance in producing compliance and conformity, but it is unfortunately determined by staff patterns of attendance that are, through custom and practice, less than flexible. It therefore revolves around the fixed rigidity of meals, staff coming on and going off duty, and lock-up times. These endless repetitions produce, for prisoners, flurries of noise and movement interspersed with long tracts of empty time. Constructive activities have to be fitted into the small window of time when the main group of prison officers are on duty and can supervise them, usually between 9 a.m. and 11.30 a.m.,

and 1 p.m. and 4.30 p.m. (Coyle 2005). Prisoners look forward to constructive activities to break the monotony of the day or week. Staff sickness and staff shortages, however, produce frequent cancellations, and the consequent disappointment is felt all the more painfully because of the rarity of positive events. In many large local prisons, inmates are confined in their cells for the majority of each day, often coming out for less than four hours. The last meal of the day may be as early as 4.30 p.m. The overnight lock-up period, when cells will not be opened for any reason other than dire emergency, is usually around 12 hours in duration but considerably more in some prisons.

We are now so acculturated to linear perceptions of time that we build them into the fabric of our lives, often unconsciously, and time is an important aspect of identity and self over the lifespan. In prison, however, the subjective experience of time as linear and progressive produces pain and suffering, precisely because the passage and development of the inmate's life have been forcibly arrested and must, for a passage of time, remain frozen in non-movement. It is the sheer eventlessness of prison life that produces discomfort, stress and enforced passivity (Toch 1992: 28). There are few markers to anticipate meaningfully, while prisoners remain painfully conscious that they are missing all the hitherto meaningful markers of time in the outside world – family birthdays, anniversaries, religious feast days, a child's first day at school, forthcoming matches in the football season and so on (Medlicott 2001: 135). All the chronology of birth, life and death flows on outside the prison, and prisoners remain bitterly aware of it all while forcibly prevented from participation. Their experience of time becomes more cyclical as the timetabled pattern of their days, weeks and months repeats monotonously. Internally, however, they are still emotionally and cognitively attached to the linear experience of their free lives. This fracture of their psychological time consciousness is an ongoing and punitive experience for all prisoners for the whole of their sentence, all the more painful because it is invisible and unacknowledged in the penal populism that sees prisons as holiday camps and prisoners as deserving of less eligibility. Even following release, prisoners are conscious of all they have missed and can never make up for, in terms of the temporal lived experiences of families and friends.

Research into the experience of prisoners shows that the personal management of the landscape of time is an agonizing challenge (Serge 1970; Cohen and Taylor 1972: esp. ch. 4; Medlicott 2001: esp. ch. 5). These texts, which span a hundred years of prisoner experience, show a remarkable consistency in the intensity of the pain experienced by prisoners in terms of their relationship with time. For the long-term prisoners in Cohen and Taylor's (1972) study, the chief deprivation/pain of imprisonment was the emptiness of their time, and their principle fear was of personal deterioration over the time-span of their sentence. They hardly dared to ask themselves if they would be the same person at the end of their long sentence, and they watched each other obsessively for signs of mental deterioration. They regarded Serge's (1970) fictional account, based on personal experience in early twentieth-century French prisons, as the most accurate with regard to the personal landscape of time. Serge (1970: 56–7) pointed out the agonies implicit in the very different relationship with time that dominates the psychological self in prison: 'There are swift hours and very long seconds. Past time is void. There is no chronology of events to mark it; external duration no longer exists.' He wrote of the terrifying insubstantiality of minutes, hours, day, months and years that must slip away before the prisoner can be released.

The prisoners in Medlicott's (2001) study, whether long-term or short-term prisoners, on remand or sentenced, confirm the terror of their obsessive relationship with the enemy of passing time. The length of sentence was not the deciding factor in their ability to cope: it was their capacity to adjust their individual time sense and to develop an appropriate *personal timeness* (2001: 141). They describe their strategies of denial, distortion and acceptance as they attempt to cope with time as an intangible and implacable enemy, struggling to define

it meaningfully: 'Literally, the seconds ticking away, that's the Chinese water torture of what it's like' (2001: 133). The best coping prisoners are those who have consciously decided to adopt a proactive attitude towards time, making small but positive choices about how to spend their time (2001: 135).

Prison Rule 3 enshrines the principle of encouraging and assisting prisoners to lead a good and useful life. This suggests full daily programmes to counter the many social, educational and employment deficits of prisoners, most of whom come from the margins of society. Yet the failure of the Prison Service to organize and fill prisoners' time appropriately has come under constant criticism from many quarters. One of the four key tests in the concept of the healthy prison, first set out by the World Health Organization and used as a basis for inspections by HM Chief Inspectorate of Prisons, has been purposeful activity. Reports from HM Chief Inspector of Prisons, whether thematic reviews or unannounced inspections of individual institutions, always emphasize the importance of meaningful activity, and usually conclude that the Prison Service is failing in its responsibility to fill prisoners' time in purposeful ways. Prisoners cannot be adequately prepared for release unless their time is used productively, with education and training, work, preparation for future employment, physical exercise and association with others. More fundamentally, the legitimacy of prison is undermined when prisoners are compelled to serve time in ways that do not attempt, through appropriate use of that time, to help them address their offending behaviour.

*Diana Medlicott*

### Related entries

*Deprivations/'pains of imprisonment'; Education and training; Employment and industries; HM Inspectorate of Prisons; Identity and self; Legitimacy; Less eligibility; Local prisons; Long-term prisoners; Physical education (PE); Total institutions.*

**Key texts and sources**

Cohen, S. and Taylor, L. (1972) *Psychological Survival: The Experience of Long-term Imprisonment.* Harmondsworth: Penguin Books.

Coyle, A. (2005) *Understanding Prisons: Key Issues in Policy and Practice.* Maidenhead: Open University Press.

Foucault, M. (1977) *Discipline and Punish.* Harmondsworth: Allen Lane.

Medlicott, D. (2001) *Surviving the Prison Place: Narratives of Suicidal Prisoners.* Aldershot: Ashgate.

Serge, V. (1970) *Men in Prison.* London: Gollancz.

Toch, H. (1992) *Living in Prison: The Ecology of Survival.* Washington, DC: American Psychological Association.

See also **http://inspectorates.homeoffice.gov.uk**.

# TOTAL INSTITUTIONS

'A total institution may be defined as a place of residence and work where a large number of like-situated individuals, cut off from the wider society for an appreciable period of time, together lead an enclosed, formally administered round of life. Prisons serve as a clear example, providing we appreciate that what is prison-like about prisons is found in institutions whose members have broken no laws' (Goffman 1961: 11).

The central feature of total institutions, as conceptualized by Erving Goffman (1922–82), can be broadly described as a breakdown of the barriers ordinarily separating three spheres of life: sleep, play and work. First, all aspects of life are conducted in the same place and under the same central authority; secondly, each phase of the member's daily activity is carried on in the immediate company of a large batch of others, all of whom are treated alike and required to do the same thing together; thirdly, all phases of the day's activities are tightly scheduled, with one activity leading at prearranged time into the next, the whole sequence of activities being imposed from above by a system of explicit formal rulings and a body of officials; finally, the various enforced activities are brought together into a single rational plan purportedly designed to fulfil the official aims of the institution.

Although the passage through the 'barrier' from the outside community into the total institution involves many necessary administrative procedures, its symbolic significance goes well beyond the bureaucratic requirements of the establishment. Described by Goffman (1961: 25) as a 'civil death', entry into the total institution involves being subjected to a series of social and psychological attacks, which undermine the sense of self:

*The recruit...comes into the establishment with a conception of himself made possible by certain stable social arrangements in his home world. Upon entrance, he is immediately stripped of the support provided by these arrangements...[and] he begins a series of abasements, degradations, humiliations and profanations of self. His self is systematically, if often unintentionally, mortified (Goffman 1961: 24).*

Goffman's work on total institutions extends our thinking about the ways in which the structural properties of institutions impact upon, and radically alter, the sense of identity and self held by their occupants. His studies of social interactionism were formulated in mental hospitals, and it was here that he first used the term 'total institution' to describe the kind of closed environment where time and space could be completely controlled by an authority. But although not specifically concerned with the prison as a social organization, Goffman believed that the experiences of inmates in any total institution, be it a prison, monastery, army barracks, boarding school, mental hospital (or even, contemporaneously, the total institution perhaps most familiar to many of us today – television's *Big Brother* house), would be similar and recognizable by their common components. Most fundamentally, total institutions are characterized by 'closure' so that, although not completely sealed off from the outside world, social intercourse between those inside the institution and those outside it is severely restricted.

But although the physical appearance of total institutions can be austere, many writers have criticized Goffman and his followers for placing too much emphasis on the 'totality' of total institutions, arguing that prison walls are inherently more permeable to external forces than Goffman implies. For example, one commentator argues that any total institution can be subverted or vanquished by individual 'escape attempts' or 'by journeys into the world of drugs, alcohol and "hard porn"' (Brittan 1977: 28). To these we might now add in-cell television. However, although some aspects of the definition of 'total institution' provided by Goffman might be deemed inappropriate in relation to modern prisons, the term conjures up an imagery whose topic is not really institutions but confinement (Sparks *et al.* 1996). In its evocation of the 'role-stripping' procedures of bureaucratization, the inherent deprivations of incarceration and the substitution of institutional values for human ones, 'total institution' thus remains a compelling empirical description (Jones and Fowles 1984: 22). Indeed, Goffman's model can be seen to have a wider application than a place where inmates are isolated from society, and an implicit motif of *Asylums* (1961) is that the whole of society is a total institution, an idea that has been developed in the notion of the *carceral society*.

*Yvonne Jewkes*

### Related entries

*Carceral society; Identity and self; In-cell television; Structure/agency ('resistance'); Time.*

#### Key texts and sources

Brittan, A. (1977) *The Privatized World*. London: Routledge.
Goffman, E. (1961) *Asylums: Essays on the Social Situation of Mental Patients and Other Inmates*. London: Penguin Books.
Jones, K. and Fowles, A. (1984) *Ideas on Institutions: Analysing the Literature on Long-term Care and Custody*. London: Routledge.
Sparks, R., Bottoms, A.E. and Hay, W. (1996) *Prisons and the Problem of Order*. Oxford: Oxford University Press.

# TRAINING PRISONS

Training prisons are those prisons that house medium- and long-term sentenced prisoners for the main part of their sentence. They provide a range of services to reduce reoffending and support resettlement. However, these services are not always consistently provided, and overcrowding reduces their potential effectiveness.

The term 'training prisons' is used in the official literature on categorization and allocation, but is not specifically defined. The term is used inconsistently in other literature, from broad usage where it describes all prisons, including high-security prisons and open prisons that hold sentenced prisoners for the main part of their sentence, to more narrow definitions that focus on prisons with a specific work-based training role, such as the industrial prison, Coldingley.

It is suggested here that, as high-security and open prisons can be described as separate categories, the term training prison should properly be used to describe those prisons where medium- and long-term prisoners spend the main part of their sentence. Using this definition, there are currently eight Category B and 36 Category C training prisons, holding just over 4,000 and 21,000 prisoners respectively (HM Prison Service 2006). For women, there are just over 1,000 places in five closed prisons, and there are just under 7,000 places in 14 closed young offender institutions. Training prisons thus account for just under half of the average prison population.

Training prisons are intended to provide activities aimed at reducing reoffending. They therefore provide 66 per cent of the offending behaviour programmes completed in prisons, 59 per cent of the work skills accreditations and over 50 per cent of the education accreditations. However, they contribute less significantly to resettlement targets, such as securing employment and accommodation, reflecting the fact that fewer prisoners are released from training prisons than other types of prison (e.g. local prisons). These figures, however, mask significant variations between the prisons. Some are specialist facilities, such as Gartree Prison (which is dedicated to managing life-sentence prisoners), Grendon (which is a therapeutic community) and Coldingley (described above). They also vary in the services they provide. For example, some prisons, such as Moorland and Buckley Hall, provide over 30 hours' purposeful activity per prisoner per week, while others (such as High Down) provide less than 20 hours. Four of the prisons delivered over 200 offending behaviour programmes each during 2005–6, but nine delivered none at all (HM Prison Service 2006).

Training prisons are also significantly less overcrowded than local prisons; however, they are often remote from the prisoner's home. This has led to some prisons taking on a mixed local and training role. This was the model for the multi-functional community prison proposed in the Woolf Report following the prison riots of 1990. Although the proposal was widely welcomed, the extensive building and reorganization work required has meant that it has not been widely realized. Population pressures also mean that it is not always possible to transfer prisoners to the training prison that would best meet their needs.

*Jamie Bennett*

### Related entries

*Activities; Education and training; Employment and industries; Long-term prisoners; Offending behaviour programmes; Woolf Report; Young offender institutions (YOIs).*

**Key texts and sources**

HM Prison Service (2006) *Annual Report and Accounts, 2005–2006.* London: HMSO.
See also the Ministry of Justice website (http://www.mojuk.org.uk/bulletins/hanson5.html).

## TRANSFERS

Transfers are the (sometimes enforced) movement of prisoners from one prison to another.

Transfer describes the movement of a prisoner from one prison to another. This may happen for a number of reasons, including meeting individual needs, managing population pressures or for disciplinary reasons. Prisoners may also undertake other movements outside the prison, known as escorts (for example, going to court, to police interviews or to hospital).

The Woolf Report, published following the widespread prison riots of 1990, recommended that prisoners be held close to their home area, in 'community prisons'. This is one of the principles that guides prison transfers, but not the only one. As a result, prisoners may still find themselves distant from their friends and relatives. Lord Woolf argued that transfers away from prisoners' home areas could result in individuals harbouring a sense of grievance and could fuel disorder in prisons.

Many transfers take place as part of the categorization and allocation system, which takes account of such issues as security, control and prisoners' rehabilitation. The aim of such transfers is to ensure that prisoners are located in a prison that best balances the competing demands of security, control and justice. However, due to overcrowding and the ever-growing prison population, it is not always possible to achieve a neat balance between needs and resources. It is therefore necessary at times to transfer prisoners to prisons that may not ideally match their needs. For example, the Prison Service Order on categorization and allocation emphasizes the importance of ensuring that available spaces in training prisons are filled. It is also occasionally necessary to transfer prisoners at short notice, usually between local prisons. These are known as 'overcrowding drafts' and mean that prisoners can be moved or released hundreds of miles from home.

The transfer of prisoners can also be used as a disciplinary measure. In the past, prisoners could be temporarily transferred for up to 28 days, a system sometimes known as the 'merry-go-round'. Although this has been formally abolished, prisoners still transfer between segregation units in a similar way. Another form of informal discipline is the transfer of prisoners for security or operational reasons to prisons that are distant from their homes (King and McDermott 1995; Sparks *et al.* 1996). Such measures form part of the informal control mechanisms of prison management.

Prisoners in all categories other than Category A can be informed in advance of their transfer. Category A prisoners, however, are not informed, due to the potential risk of escape. This is sometimes referred to as 'ghosting', although the term is also used to refer generally to transfers for disciplinary reasons. Transfers therefore meet a number of functions, ranging from meeting individual needs to logistical management and maintaining control.

*Jamie Bennett*

### Related entries

*Categorization and allocation; Category A prisoners; Discipline; Order and control; Overcrowding; Rehabilitation; Security; Segregation.*

### Key texts and sources

King, R. and McDermott, K. (1995) *The State of Our Prisons.* Oxford: Clarendon Press.
Sparks, R., Bottoms, A.E. and Hay, W. (1996) *Prisons and the Problem of Order.* Oxford: Clarendon Press.
See also the Prisoners Families' website (http://www.prisonersfamilieshelpline.org.uk/php/bin/readarticle.php?articlecode=9255).

## TRANSPORTATION

Prior to the 1830s, hanging was the statutory punishment for many offences, but mitigation could result in the release of potentially dangerous felons. The Transportation Act 1718, by establishing transportation as the courts' routine secondary punishment, ensured their removal, usually to America. Its availability also frustrated attempts to abolish most capital statutes as inhumane and to construct costly state-controlled prisons where felons would instead serve lengthy sentences under rigorous regimes.

By 1775, approximately 60,000 felons, two thirds male, had been transported to America, mainly from London and Bristol by merchant captains who recouped the cost by auctioning them off to southern plantation owners for the period of their sentence. From 1776, the now rebellious colonists refused to accept convicts, so some were sent instead to Africa or the West Indies. The courts continued to hand out transportation sentences so, as a temporary measure – which lasted into the 1850s – the Hulks Act 1776 permitted decommissioned warships to be located in the Thames and elsewhere to accommodate these convicts. They were then set to hard-labour tasks, such as dock construction and river dredging, which the authorities had earlier dismissed as degrading and 'un-British' when suggested by pro-prison campaigners. A reluctant government also passed the Penitentiary Act 1779, which sanctioned two penitentiaries (male and female), with hard labour, solitary confinement and sentences (long for the time) of up to two years. The prisons were never built, though the Act's salient provisions did feature in subsequent nineteenth-century penal practice.

The government's real intention was to recommence transportation, but the rebels won in 1783 so that other locations were sought, and, in 1786, came the decision to create a penal colony at Botany Bay (Sydney, New South Wales) in recently discovered Australia. Why Australia? Its distance from Britain virtually guaranteed that released felons would never return. Also, convict labour could more rapidly construct Australia's key infrastructures – harbours, roads, bridges – and so thwart the potential ambitions of other European nations. Between 1788 and 1868, around 120,000 males and 40,000 females were sent to Australia and worked there under government supervision. Convicts of all ages, married and unmarried, were transported, but the courts seem to have particularly targeted the young and the single, often for trivial or first offences, to prevent any future offending and possibly because of their greater use as workers.

There was no uniform convict experience. The regulations and regimes governing them varied according to time and place, and much depended on individual manual skill, literacy, personal behaviour, ingenuity and luck. At one period, newly arrived convicts were quickly assigned to free settlers for unpaid work in an agricultural, industrial or commercial capacity. Assignment also benefited the authorities who no longer had to accommodate or feed the convicts – who, on completion of their required day's work, were allowed to undertake further paid work. At other periods, complaints that convict regimes were too lax resulted in all males serving a mandatory period in labour gangs on public works before assignment. Women offenders, transported partly as partners for the men, were set to work in textile factories or assigned as domestic servants. Estimates vary on the harshness of convicts' treatment. Serious offenders could be executed. Possibly up to a quarter of male convicts, annually, were flogged for minor infractions in the settlements or on assignment. Frequent offenders could end up working in chain gangs in severe penal settlements, such as Norfolk Island. Sentences could be extended, but most convicts were released early on a revocable ticket-of-leave, and their wives and children could apply for a free passage to join them.

The virtual abolition of the death penalty in the 1830s saw transportation sentences peak. Significant numbers were still transported in the 1840s, but against a background of mounting dissatisfaction. The New South Wales free settlers, convinced that self-government was unattainable, refused to accept any more convicts who were sent, instead, to Van Diemen's Land (Tasmania) whose free settlers had similar objections. Moreover, the discovery of gold in New South Wales and Victoria (1851) brought in a flood of free labour, lessening the need for convict labour. In Britain, criticism grew over the unsanitary and immoral conditions in the hulks, which continued to hold convicts, ostensibly awaiting shipment to Australia. In practice, many of the shorter sentences were served entirely there. Up to the late 1840s,

Parliament and the judges still favoured transportation, questioning whether imprisonment was a sufficient punishment or whether the new penal ideas would prove any more successful. Officialdom had long argued that transportation effectively deterred; that convicts suffered the pain of separation, often for ever, from their families and friends; that convicts were subject to very punitive regimes; and that transportation remained the cheaper option. However, doubts continued to grow about transportation's deterrent value or its cheapness. Crime levels were continuing to rise. Some criminals allegedly preferred transportation to imprisonment, to be free of existing family ties and responsibilities.

By the 1850s Parliament favoured separate imprisonment for all convicts, and a number of new prisons had been built to accommodate the so-called separate system. Pentonville (adults) and Parkhurst (juveniles) were still intended as reformative first-stage prisons prior to transportation, but 16,000 convicts could now serve longer prison sentences more cheaply at home. In 1853, 1,864 convicts were sentenced to transportation and 504 to penal servitude. In 1855, 325 were sentenced to transportation and 2,048 to penal servitude. In 1856, Colonel Joshua Jebb, Surveyor-General of Prisons, was asserting that prison was cheaper, a more certain deterrent and free of any settlers' wishes. The last convicts sailed to Western Australia in 1868. For many transportees, poverty rather than innate criminality probably explains their offending, and so Australia's rapid change from a penal settlement into a prosperous colony offered greater opportunities for ticket-of-leave convicts on release. Most were simply absorbed into the workforce, merging into the mainstream of Australian life, some with considerable success. A proportion continued to offend. Very few returned to Britain.

*Laurie Feehan*

*Related entries*
*Death penalty; Victorian prisons.*

**Key texts and sources**

Ekirch, A.R. (1990) *Bound for America: The Transportation of British Convicts to the Colonies, 1718–1775.* Oxford: Oxford University Press.

Robson, L.L. (1976) *The Convict Settlers' Australia.* Melbourne: Melbourne University Press.

Shaw, A.G.L. (1964) *Convicts and Colonies: A Study of Penal Transportation from Great Britain and Ireland to Australia and Other Parts of the British Empire.* London: Faber & Faber.

# TYPOLOGIES OF PRISONERS

Typologies of prisoner roles within inmate society were a major preoccupation of prison sociology in the 1940s, 1950s and 1960s. They formed an integral part of analyses of prisoner subcultures, which was the dominant theme in prison sociology at this time. They seek to define, and in some cases explain or predict, prisoners' mode of adaptation to imprisonment.

Typologies of prisoners describe the roles played within prisoner subcultures and seek to explain how individuals adapt to imprisonment. Early typologies were broadly functionalist and influenced by deprivation models. They suggest that the problems of prison life generate more or less universal modes of adaptation, which together constitute a self-sustaining organic whole. Differing from classification systems, which merely list a set of variables and indicate how they might be combined, typologies explore the relationships *between* variables. Typologies thus propound sets of empirically testable hypotheses (Schrag 1944).

Schrag's ideas strongly influenced subsequent prison scholars. He identified four roles, which he described using their prison terms and a descriptor of his own: the *square john* (pro-social), with little criminal history who resists the inmate subculture and identifies with staff; the *right guy* (anti-social), who lives by the inmate code and has a strong sense of prisoner solidarity; the *con politician* (pseudo-social), who dominates roles of formal representation, apparently representing the prisoners but ultimately self-serving; and the *outlaw* (asocial), who subscribes to no code, shows little fixed loyalty and uses violence with no consideration beyond his likelihood of success. Although the typologies of prisoners that were produced over the following decades are too numerous to detail comprehensively (and often add little to those that have gone before), this basic scheme of pro-social, anti-social, pseudo-social and asocial is discernible in many.

Like Schrag's, Sykes's (1958) prisoner typology was based on a deprivation model of prisoner adaptation. He described a set of empirically observed roles that were sufficiently significant in the prisoner subculture to warrant a specific argot term. Sykes identified *rats*, who inform on others for personal gain; *centre men*, the equivalent of Schrag's *square johns*; *gorillas*, who take what they want from others by force to assuage their material deprivation; *merchants*, who selfishly 'sell when they should give'; *wolves*, sexual predators, not stigmatized by the inmates because they maintain their masculinity; *punks*, who are feminized and coerced into passive homosexuality in prison; *fags*, effeminate 'passive homosexuals' by orientation; *ball busters*, volatile and resistant to authority; *real men*, who embody the values of the inmate code; *toughs*, who are aggressive but not bullies because they will fight anyone; and *hipsters*, who posture and start conflict strategically, when they can gain from it.

Goffman (1961) outlines a typology of responses to incarceration by inmates of total institutions generally, not just those of penal institutions. These 'lines of adaptation' are ways of managing the tension between the home world and the institutional world. He describes *situational withdrawal*, where the individual withdraws attention from everything apart from 'events immediately around his body'; the *intransigent line*, where inmates refuse to co-operate with staff, which is typically a temporary initial reaction to the institution succeeded by another adaptation; *colonization*, whereby inmates build a relatively contented existence within the institution; and *conversion*, where inmates (like the *square john*) adopt the official or staff view of themselves. While these adaptations seem to offer coherent approaches to coping with incarceration, Goffman suggests that few follow a single line very far. In this he deviates from the more rigid typologies discussed above, suggesting that most inmates adopt a flexible, opportunistic approach to managing institutional life and to maximizing the chances of survival. Strategies for this include conforming to inmate culture when with inmates and concealing the extent of co-operation with staff.

In the 1960s, prison scholars began to question whether their predecessors were too impressed by the impact of institutionalization and ignored how individuals' responses are conditioned by prior experience. Irwin and Cressey (1962) were among the first to highlight continuities between prison and street culture, and the improbability that inmate subcultures were generated by institutional life in isolation (see Importation model). They located the origin of prison types in society at large: the *thief*, roughly corresponding with Schrag's *right guy*, who embodied an anti-authoritarian and solidaristic ideal, personifying the norms of the inmate subculture; the *convict*, who had spent a substantial time in institutions, utilitarian in outlook and intent on getting what he could from the prison system; and the *square*, who, with no prior criminal background, was equivalent to Schrag's *square john*.

Despite their claims to universality, few prisoner typologies refer to inmate cultures among women in prison. Giallombardo (1966) is one exception, and the inmate code and roles she identified differ significantly from those of male prisoners. Giallombardo argued that females' adaptations to prison are influenced by their prior socialization – in particular, the ways which popular culture teaches women to view one another as essentially rivals in the marriage market. Giallombardo's typology differs from typologies of male prisoners in two significant ways. First, it includes no equivalent of the 'right guy' because 'concepts such as "fair play," "courage," … consistent with the concepts of endurance, loyalty, and dignity associated with the "right guy" are not meaningful to the female'. Secondly, it is dominated by roles associated with women's sexual and pseudo-familial relationships with one another. This reflects a wider academic preoccupation with (homo)sexuality in women's prisons; Giallombardo views this as reflecting the paucity of social roles available to women in society generally. Others of the few similar studies of women's adaptation to prison have found types equivalent to the *real man* and *con politician*, although, as Pollock (1997) points out, these studies set out to map typologies of male prisoners on to groups of women inmates, so it is perhaps unsurprising that they found them. Importantly for the validity of Giallombardo's conclusions, the existence of the *right guy* has more recently been questioned, with the increasing suspicion that he was probably a product of prison researchers' collective imagination rather than a genuine type (Pollock 1997).

Cohen and Taylor (1972) explain adaptation to prison in terms of inmates' identities, biographies and ideologies. They tentatively link offenders' relationship with authority, their typical offence, underlying 'ideology' and style of adaptation to prison. Unlike some earlier scholars, they stress the limited and illustrative nature of their typology and its principal function as a means of exploring the adaptations to prison of a very specific group of maximum-security prisoners observed during their research. Their study describes five types. First are prisoners with *confrontational* relationships with authority. Typically convicted of armed robbery, they co-operate with others but do not have a regular group of companions and are the type most likely to lead riots and attempt escape. This is ascribed to an underlying ideology of *romantic anarchism*. In prison, they confront authority and resist 'adjustment' to the conditions of incarceration. A second type has a more *symbiotic* relationship with authority, engaging in semi-legal activities such as protection and fraud, which is linked to an ideology of *innovative capitalism*. The adaptation of this group is *campaigning*, using a familiarity with the law to lobby MPs and to generate support for their cause. The third group are professional career thieves, with a *trumping* or *outflanking* approach to authority. They enjoy a cat-and-mouse relationship with the police and are determined to win the game. These offenders usually live predominantly respectable lives outside prison, occasionally co-operating with a group of specialists to carry out a major job. Their ideology is one of *cool hedonism*. In prison, dissimilarity from more confrontational criminals means they are generally pushed into 'unhappy conformity to prison routines'. No common style of adaptation is ascribed to this group, but many 'gave in'. Fourthly, are *private sinners* – isolated persistent sex offenders. Their relationship with authority is difficult to characterize and their ideology is one of *inner-worldliness*. Their mode of adaptation is *mystical retreatism*: they remain solitary, have little contact outside prison and any aggression is likely to be directed at individuals rather than authority in general. Finally, *situational* criminals, driven to offend by circumstance, show no pattern of offending history, underlying ideology or adaptive style.

These later typologies illustrate a shift from the deprivation-focused, functionalist approach of the 1940s and 1950s to a more nuanced view of individuals' adaptations to prison as influenced by a much broader range of factors than the conditions of imprisonment. In recent years the value of prisoner typologies has been questioned, and criticisms have been voiced of quantitative methods of producing them (Pollock 1997). Most prison sociologists today would argue that general categories that claim

to encompass highly individuated human responses to the pressures of incarceration are very difficult to sustain.

*Abigail Rowe*

### Related entries

*Argot (prison); Homosexuality in prison; Importation model; Inmate code; Masculinity; Sex offenders; Solidarity; Subcultures; Total institutions; Women in prison.*

**Key texts and sources**

Cohen, S. and Taylor, L. (1972) *Psychological Survival: The Experience of Long-term Imprisonment.* Harmondsworth: Penguin Books.

Giallombardo, R. (1966) 'Social roles in a prison for women', *Social Problems*, 13: 268–88.

Goffman, E. (1961) *Asylums: Essays on the Social Situation of Mental Patients and Other Inmates.* New York, NY: Doubleday Anchor.

Irwin, J. and Cressey, D.R. (1962) 'Thieves, convicts and the inmate culture', *Social Problems*, 10: 142–55.

Pollock, J.M. (1997) 'The social world of the prisoner', in J.M. Pollock (ed.) *Prisons: Today and Tomorrow.* Gaithersburg, MD: Aspen.

Schrag, C. (1944) 'Social types in a prison community.' Unpublished master's thesis, University of Washington.

Sykes, G. (1958) *The Society of Captives: A Study of a Maximum Security Prison.* Princeton, NJ: Princeton University Press.

See **http://law.jrank.org/pages/2214/Typologies-Criminal-Behavior-Offender-typologies.html** for US typologies of prisoners and criminal behaviour.

# U

## USE OF FORCE (CONTROL AND RESTRAINT)

Force may be used by prison staff as a last resort. It must be reasonable in the circumstances, necessary and proportionate.

When violence occurs in prisons, staff must be capable of intervening safely in order to bring the situation under control. Under such circumstances, the Prison Rules state that 'An officer in dealing with a prisoner shall not use force unnecessarily and, when the application of force is necessary, no more force than is necessary shall be used'. In the UK, the use of force is based on simple, formalized techniques and drills that can be employed by all prison staff regardless of gender, race or age (HM Prison Service 2006). These are known as control and restraint techniques (C&R).

Training for staff is split into three areas. C&R basic (including personal safety) is training for the majority of staff and includes instruction on how to deal with immediate threats and how to manage relatively isolated incidents. C&R advanced is training for dealing with concerted indiscipline, such as riots. It consists of a series of drills and techniques that allow staff to regain control of prison buildings which have been lost through acts of concerted indiscipline. This training is delivered by national instructors to selected staff. The techniques allow staff to get safely into a position to take the surrender of prisoners or to arrest prisoners using C&R basic techniques, as necessary. Long and short shields of the type commonly used by many police forces and the British army are provided to protect against thrown debris or 'flak' and blunt instruments. Prison officers are also issued with an extendable baton, which replaced the old-style truncheon. This can be used defensively in extreme circumstances. Specialist training includes more complex incidents, such as hostage taking and incidents at height. Specialist use of force is usually conducted by national instructors. The techniques can be employed on all categories of prisoners (i.e. young offenders, female and adult prisoners). The only other force training in use is physical control in care (PCC), which was developed for use in secure training centres. These techniques are deployed on juveniles and involve control methods without the use of pain in order to gain compliance.

C&R is based on the use of a team of three officers, one controlling the head and the other two officers controlling the arms. Support staff can assist by supervising the incident and restraining the legs of a particularly violent prisoner. The techniques are based on *aikido* arm and wrist locks, whereby compliance can be achieved, with the gradual and controlled application of pain. Once compliance has been achieved, the pain can be eased off while still maintaining control.

C&R techniques have been deployed effectively and are an example of good practice in the minimal and humane use of force, particularly when compared with unstructured violence, the widespread use of chemical incapacitants or such technology as electric shock or stun devices.

*Andy Simpson*

*Related entries*

*Human rights; Prison officers; Prison Rules; Riots (prison); Secure training centres; Staff (prison); Violence.*

**Key texts and sources**

HM Prison Service (2006) *Use of Force Manual.* London: Home Office.

See also the Prison Service's website (http://pso.hmprisonservice.gov.uk/pso1600/ Sec%202.3%20CR.htm).

## VICTORIAN PRISONS

The 'Victorian prison' refers to prisons during the reign of Queen Victoria (1837–1901). The Victorian period is key to our understanding of prisons and imprisonment, not only in terms of the significant changes that were made in the administration of prisons and the treatment of offenders during that time but also because it continues to shape our ideas about prisons and imprisonment.

By the time Victoria came to the throne in 1837 there had already been over 60 years of change in the organization and running of prisons in England and Wales. From the 1770s, reformers such as John Howard and Elizabeth Fry had a significant impact on prison conditions. Prisons (at this time gaols and houses of correction or bridewells) were no longer characterized by the squalor, disease and disorder of the eighteenth century. The Gaols Act 1823 introduced a system of classified association where prisoners were placed into classes according to their offence and their gender, where alcohol was banned and where chaplains and doctors were appointed to each prison (McGowen 1998). The prisons of the nineteenth century were thus 'reformed' in the sense that they were cleaner and healthier, and conditions in general were undoubtedly better in some respects for prisoners, but what came with this reform was a different kind of misery.

During the 1820s and 1830s there was an ongoing debate between two different systems of punishment used in prisons: the separate and silent systems. One of the overriding effects of the 'reform' period had been to alter the aims of imprisonment. This signified a movement away from simply holding those awaiting trial, transportation or execution, or putting to work petty offenders, towards an objective concerned with the reform of the prisoner. Both the separate and silent systems offered methods to achieve this end, either through isolation or silent work. The intention was that a prison sentence would not merely be served but would fundamentally *change* an offender.

By the early part of the nineteenth century, the government had also become involved in running prisons. Millbank, the first government-run penitentiary, had opened in 1816, Inspectors of Prisons were established under the Prison Act 1835 and, by the Prison Act 1839, the separate system had been adopted as the preferred method of reform for the whole country, at least in theory. The first Inspectors of Prisons, William Crawford and the Reverend Whitworth Russell, were both strong advocates of the separate system. By the 1840s the Millbank experiment had failed and the government turned its attention to Pentonville 'Model' Prison, which opened in 1842. Pentonville had been designed around the use of the separate system, although its demise, primarily due to concern about high rates of insanity, was relatively swift and, by the 1850s, it was, like Millbank, used as a convict depot. These changes signified another feature of Victorian imprisonment: the increasing role of the government in prison administration. Throughout this period the government urged the borough and county authorities who ran the gaols and houses of correction to standardize their policies and practices. The government, however, also became involved in the administration and running of its own prisons.

In 1850 the convict system was established. The main reason behind this was the dramatic decline in the number of prisoners that Australia would allow England to transport there. Thus, for the first time, the country was faced with a new problem: what should be done with the offenders who, in previous decades, would have been shipped off to the other side of the world? It was resolved that, after a period of imprisonment, prisoners should be put to labour on the public works. The Chairman of the Directors of Convict Prisons, Joshua Jebb (later Sir), estimated that four years would be the minimum sentence, one year in separate confinement and then three years on the public works. Over the next 20 years, five establishments were built or adapted: Chatham, Dartmoor, Portsmouth, Portland and Borstal. The Penal Servitude Acts 1853 and 1857 set out the guidelines – four to six years' penal servitude represented seven to ten years' transportation, and six to eight years' penal servitude represented ten to fourteen years' transportation. The first Act retained transportation for those offenders sentenced to fourteen years to life, but this was abolished by the second Act and the minimum sentence was reduced to three years' penal servitude (Tomlinson 1981).

Prisoners in the convict system experienced a regime of progressive stages and marks. After the initial period of separate confinement, they were put to work building or labouring in naval dockyards. There was then a three-stage system to proceed through in order to obtain early release (conditional on a 'ticket-of-leave' – an early form of parole), during which the convict's progress was recorded and marks were awarded. The prisoner was informed of the number of marks he needed to win release; each of the stages was denoted by conduct badges; marks were forfeited for bad behaviour and indifferent behaviour led to serving the whole of the sentence; and it was only through 'energy, commitment and complete submission' that early release could be obtained (McConville 1998a: 123).

Thus by the 1850s and 1860s the reformatory aims of the prison had been lost and, although the separate system was retained as a means of holding prisoners, any ideas based on the transformation of the prisoner were not. Instead, prison regimes and policies increasingly focused

on deterrence. The Prison Act 1865 embodied many of the recommendations of the 1863 Carnarvon Committee. The new regime in prison would be one of 'hard labour, hard board, hard fare', severity and discipline would be achieved through uniform practices, and the aims of imprisonment shifted from reforming the offender to a disciplinary regime based on deterrence (McConville 1998a). The Act also removed the use of the terms 'gaols, houses of correction and bridewells' and replaced them with the generic term 'local prisons' to distinguish them from the government-run 'convict prisons'.

In 1877 the control of local prisons was centralized, and the administration was transferred to the government under the control of the Prison Commission (until 1963, when it became the Prison Department of the Home Office), chaired by Edmund Du Cane. This change also signalled a process of rationalization in which smaller prisons were closed down, resulting in 112 local prisons by 1877, from an estimated 335 in 1819 (McConville 1998a). Although the most serious offenders remained in convict prisons, the majority of prisoners were dealt with by the local prison system. In 1877, there were around 20,000 prisoners held in local prisons, but the convict prisons held around half that number. These figures mask the reality of imprisonment at this time: there were more than 187,000 committals to local prisons in 1877, whereas in convict prisons the figure was around 1,900. Thus one of the most significant features of local prisons at the end of the nineteenth century was the high turnover of prisoners – the average length of sentence at this time was about ten days (McConville 1998b).

The Gladstone Committee Report in 1895 heralded a new direction for prisons at the end of the nineteenth century. The report combined both principles of deterrence and reform and focused on the individual characteristics of the offender, acknowledging the positivist influences of the time concerned with scientific principles of treatment and classification. Those considered 'reformable' (children, juveniles and first offenders), those deemed 'treatable' (inebriates and the feeble-minded) and those regarded as 'incurable' (habitual criminals and the mentally ill) were all removed from the prison, leaving behind a segregated prison population who remained due to the severity or frequency of their offences (Garland 1985).

The Victorian period is central to our understanding of prisons and imprisonment in terms of the significant changes that were made in the administration of prisons and the treatment of offenders, but it is also important for the distinctive mark it has left on our ideas about prisons. It was during this period that the prison was established as 'a place apart', and the prisoner as occupant of this 'other' world. As the prisoners were more closely controlled and observed, and the public became less familiar with the inside of the prison, the prison 'loomed even larger in the public's imagination as the prisoners disappeared from view' (McGowen 1998: 98). It is the austere Victorian prison, with its long wings and small windows, that remains a prominent feature of our prison system today and that provides an architectural style that symbolizes many people's ideas about the prison; the Victorian prison has left a particularly enduring mark (Jewkes and Johnston 2007).

*Helen Johnston*

### Related entries

*Chaplaincy; Discipline; Fry, Elizabeth; Howard, John; Less eligibility; Local prisons; Separate and silent systems; Transportation.*

#### Key texts and sources

Garland, D. (1985) *Punishment and Welfare.* Aldershot: Gower.

Jewkes, Y. and Johnston, H. (2006) *Prison Readings: A Critical Introduction to Prisons and Imprisonment.* Cullompton: Willan Publishing.

Jewkes, Y. and Johnston, H. (2007) 'The evolution of prison architecture', in Y. Jewkes (ed.) *Handbook on Prisons.* Cullompton: Willan Publishing.

McConville, S. (1998a) 'The Victorian prison, 1865–1965', in N. Morris and D.J. Rothman (eds) *The Oxford History of the Prison: The Practice of Punishment in Western Society.* Oxford: Oxford University Press.

McConville, S. (1998b) 'Local justice: the jail', in N. Morris and D.J. Rothman (eds) *The Oxford History of the Prison: The Practice of Punishment in Western Society.* Oxford: Oxford University Press.

McGowen, R. (1998) 'The well-ordered prison: England, 1780–1865', in N. Morris and D.J. Rothman (eds) *The Oxford History of the Prison: The Practice of Punishment in Western Society.* Oxford: Oxford University Press.

Tomlinson, M.H. (1981) 'Penal servitude, 1846–1865: a system in evolution', in V. Bailey (ed.) *Policing and Punishment in Nineteenth Century Britain.* London: Croom Helm.

## VIOLENCE

Violence in prisons can take the form of person-to-person encounters or collective (and sometimes organized) activity. Interpersonal violence has been defined as 'any incident in which a person is abused, threatened, or assaulted ... [in which] the resulting harm may be physical, emotional, or psychological' (HM Prison Service 2004).

Interpersonal violence between prisoners takes many forms and is shaped by different factors in different establishments (Bottoms 1999). Young men in custody may resort to violence in the belief that it will resolve their arguments, as suggested by the frequency of fights (many of which are prearranged as opposed to spontaneous) in young offender institutions. In contrast, adult men in local prisons tend to use violence mainly in retaliation or self-defence. Women in prison who are involved in assaults see violence as a means of punishment or of maintaining self-esteem or honour. On the whole, they do not view a fight as a means of resolving differences (Edgar *et al.* 2003).

There is no convincing single-cause explanation for violence between prisoners. However, from a practical perspective, it is useful to explore violence between prisoners as the outcome of a conflict or dispute. Conflicts are situations between two or more persons in which the key parties pursue competing interests in uncompromising ways. Conflict is endemic in prison, and how disputes are handled can determine whether these conflicts are resolved peaceably or lead to a fight or assault.

There are several key factors that contribute to the risk of physical violence in prison. The first is a clash of interests, which can be about material goods or about values. For example, a wing of 60 prisoners might have only three payphones available to prisoners for two hours each evening. Limited access to goods and services in prisons creates competition among prisoners, and the risk of being exploited is a widespread concern. Hence, the fear that someone might take advantage (e.g. by gaining a place in the queue for food) assumes special significance. Attitudes concerning honour, loyalty, fairness, respect or other values are involved in all conflicts. For example, a prisoner accused of cheating may fight to defend his personal honour, even when there is no material interest at stake.

The second factor is the way prisoners react to disputes and the techniques they use that may exacerbate the conflict. These reactions can include threats, accusations, verbal abuse, invading personal space or hostile gestures. A lack of conflict resolution skills increases the risk of violence when disputes arise.

A third determinant in prison conflicts is the relationships between prisoners and the importance of the power balance between them. Prison hierarchies in England and Wales tend to be fluid and unstructured, but each individual needs to be vigilant about the assessments made about him or her by other individuals. Any person-to-person conflict can quickly escalate into a test between two people to decide who can dominate the other. When prisoners believe that a counterpart is attempting to intimidate them, an aggressive response is likely.

Power contests are a particular type of conflict and a frequent contributor to fights. Such contests can feature mutual intimidation, a focus on the balance of dominance and control, a fear that compromise will give the opponent a permanent advantage and a belief that superior force alone determines who wins. Power contests show why some disputes become so important to prisoners. When a power contest is triggered by a dispute over a piece of property, there may be a temptation to trivialize the conflict as a fight over a pot of yogurt, one unit on a phonecard or a game of pool. But in prison these contests are fought to preserve self-respect and honour.

A final factor in prison violence is the nature of the prison setting. The institutional environment can allow prisoners to fight with impunity – for example, when corridors are out of sight of or not easily observed by prison staff. Other aspects of the prison environment that contribute to violence include loss of personal autonomy and a lack of non-violent routes for resolving conflicts.

Prisons typically exhibit a wide range of behaviours by which some prisoners are harmed by other prisoners or by staff. Many prisoners' everyday experience includes personal insults in the form of banter and the isolation of weaker prisoners through exclusion and threats. Such experiences of victimization provide the backdrop against which violent behaviour in prison appears to fulfil needs for self-protection. While perpetrators and victims of robbery in prison comprise separate groups, there is a substantial overlap of victims and perpetrators of assault (O'Donnell and Edgar 1996).

Prisoners accept that physical violence is a part of prison life. A fairly widespread belief among prisoners is that those who fail to stand up for themselves (among their peers) with force are likely to be targeted by others for future exploitation. When faced with a dispute that is becoming increasingly volatile, a prisoner is likely to be aware that the other party has the potential to use aggressive physical force. The interaction of the social setting with its pro-violence attitudes and high incidence of assault, and the ever-present threat of person-to-person conflict, leads some to define a violent response as justifiable and rational.

The need for strategies to reduce violence in custody has prompted a call for 'safer prisons'. The priorities for promoting safer prisons are to ensure personal safety, to provide opportunities to exercise personal autonomy and to build in mechanisms for prisoners to resolve conflicts. Safe prisons meet the basic human needs of both prison staff and prisoners, including a measure of privacy, a structure to the day, support and emotional feedback, activity and the freedom to make real choices (HM Prison Service 2004).

*Kimmett Edgar*

## Related entries

*Assaults; Local prisons; Power; Staff (prison); Women in prison; Young offender institutions (YOIs).*

### Key texts and Sources

Bottoms, A.E. (1999) 'Interpersonal violence and social order in prisons', in M. Tonry and J. Petersilia (eds) *Prisons.* Chicago: University of Chicago Press.

Edgar, K., O'Donnell, I. and Martin, C. (2003) *Prison Violence: The Dynamics of Fear, Power and Victimisation.* Cullompton: Willan Publishing.

HM Prison Service (2004) *Violence Reduction Strategy.* London: Safer Custody Group.

O'Donnell, I. and Edgar, K. (1996) *Victimisation in Prisons. Research Findings* 37. London: Home Office Research and Statistics Directorate.

# VIOLENCE REDUCTION

**Violence reduction is a Prison Service strategy aimed at improving the safety of staff and prisoners.**

The 'Violence reduction' strategy was introduced by the Prison Service in May 2004 (Borrill and Brigden 2005). This national policy provides a framework, guidance and principles that are constructive and restorative but that recognize the dynamic nature of violence and the need for local flexibility and responsiveness. Each establishment is responsible for developing a local strategy to reduce violence and to maintain personal safety for staff and prisoners, rather than a prescriptive 'one size fits all' model. The age, gender and profile of the prisons; the locality, age and layout of the building; the category and history of the establishment; and the experience of the staff working in it will all have a bearing on the interpersonal dynamics and the conflicts that arise.

The Prison Service definition of violence is: 'any incident in which a person is abused, threatened, or assaulted. This includes an explicit or implicit challenge to their safety, wellbeing or health. The resulting harm may be physical, emotional or psychological.' This definition is broader than physical violence and takes into account the impact that fear has on well-being. The links between fear and distress in a prison environment have been identified in recent research (Liebling *et al.* 2005). The definition and strategy also embrace bullying and give renewed vigour to previous anti-bullying work.

In each prison, a multidisciplinary group must consider an analysis of incidents, including knowledge of perpetrators, victims, location or circumstances and information from specific surveys. On the basis of this analysis, a plan to improve personal safety must be produced. This plan and the supporting policy statement should make clear everyone's responsibility in preserving personal safety and reducing violence.

The local strategy will unite a number of strands covered by other policies and instructions – for example, security, incident reporting, discipline, race and diversity, induction, incentives and earned privileges (IEP), drug strategy, multi-agency public protection arrangements (MAPPA's) and use of force. The focus is on a whole-prison approach, where all aspects of service delivery and prison life are considered as opportunities to create a safer environment. A combination of prevention, risk management and problem-solving is promoted, including changes in culture, behaviour, situational circumstances, the physical environment and organizational factors.

*Gill Brigden*

## Related entries

*Assaults; Bullying; Discipline; Incentives and earned privileges (IEP); Multi-agency public protection arrangements (MAPPAs); Security; Use of force (control and restraint); Violence.*

### Key texts and sources

Borrill, J. and Brigden, G. (2005) *Implementation of the Violence Reduction Strategy. Safer Custody Group Briefing Paper* 15. London: HM Prison Service.

Liebling, A., Tait, S., Durie, L., Stiles, A., Harvey, J. and Rose, G. (2005) 'An evaluation of the Safer Locals programme – final report to Prison Service, Safer Custody Group.' Unpublished.

# VISITS AND VISITING ORDERS

> The visits that prisoners are entitled to receive from family and friends represent a vital way of maintaining meaningful family relationships. For many families, however, visiting prisoners entails severe practical and financial difficulties which may ultimately prevent them from seeing their loved ones.

Visits are often thought to be the most important aspect of prison life and are certainly the preferred method of contact for both prisoners and their families. In England and Wales, convicted prisoners are entitled to two visits every four weeks, while those on remand may receive as many as they wish. The duration of each visit varies according to such factors as demand and available staff, but visits to convicted prisoners should last at least an hour. In order to arrange a visit, convicted prisoners need to send their prospective visitors a visiting order. This document states the visitors' names and personal details and is needed to book the visit and attend the prison.

Visits are increasingly being recognized as an essential part of the rehabilitative process, and they can perform several different functions (Shafer 1994). They provide protection against institutionalization by reminding prisoners of the outside world and can enable them to continue their role as family members, albeit to a limited degree, by giving them the opportunity to deal with home and family-related matters. Visits can also smooth the adjustment of both prisoner and family to release by allowing them to discuss their expectations of one another, and they may reflect a promise of continued support. Several research studies have found that receiving active family support during imprisonment in the form of visits is associated with a reduced risk of recidivism (Visher and Travis 2003). However, quite how and why visits contribute to reducing reoffending remain largely unexplored (Mills and Codd 2007), but their connection with positive resettlement outcomes may go some way to explaining this relationship. Prisoners who receive visits during their

confinement are more likely to have employment and accommodation arranged on release (Niven and Stewart 2005), both of which are known to promote successful resettlement and to reduce the risk of reoffending. Nevertheless, it is not clear whether visits act as a direct causal factor here, but they may signify a strong support network that is well equipped to provide assistance on release (Niven and Stewart 2005).

Despite these potential benefits, many prisoners do not receive their full entitlement to visits. This may be because they do not want their relatives to see them in prison, but it is also likely to be affected by the many practical challenges that visitors face when attending prisons (Mills and Codd 2007). Prisoners, particularly those in training prisons, are usually held some considerable distance away from their local area. Travelling to visit imprisoned relatives or friends in distant and often remote prisons is therefore time-consuming and expensive, and may be difficult with small children, especially if it involves several changes of public transport. Close relatives and partners who are in receipt of income-related state benefits can claim financial assistance for two visits a month through the Assisted Prison Visits scheme, but many do not apply as they struggle to cope with the complicated claims process and cannot pay for the costs of visiting up front as is required by the scheme.

Prison security procedures may also discourage family and friends from visiting. Rub downs and strip searches can be humiliating and distressing, and they can convey the impression that visitors occupy a low status, creating a sense of shame and making visitors feel like criminals themselves. Analogous to other forms of communication such as letters and telephone calls, visits suffer from a lack of privacy as they may take place in a crowded and uncomfortable visits hall where it is hard to discuss sensitive or personal issues, particularly if bored and fractious children are present. Finally, families frequently complain about the lack of available information on visiting rules and procedures which vary from prison to prison, and report problems booking visits on often engaged telephone-booking lines. Above all, such difficulties cast doubt on the value of visits for families and can make them feel that they are being punished along with prisoners because they are denied meaningful contact with their loved ones.

Various initiatives have been established in prisons to facilitate visiting and to help to maintain family ties, most of which are run by or in association with the voluntary sector. Of these, two are worthy of particular note. Visitors centres aim to reduce the stress and anxiety associated with visits by providing information and support to visitors and, in some cases, more extensive facilities, such as childcare and contact with various agencies. Children's visits, or 'extended visits' as they are sometimes known, enable imprisoned parents and their children to spend a longer time together in a more relaxed, child-friendly environment, with the aim of maintaining a positive parent–child relationship. Although they have obvious benefits, these initiatives vary drastically from one establishment to another and usually rely on volunteers and short-term funding, making their continued existence highly vulnerable. Despite the increasing recognition of the importance of family ties, little action has been taken by statutory bodies to encourage visits, and the difficulties that visitors face are likely to intensify further as the prison population continues to rise and prisoners are sent to wherever there is space for them.

*Alice Mills*

### Related entries

*Communication; Families of prisoners; Security; Training prisons.*

#### Key texts and sources

Mills, A. and Codd, H. (2007) 'Prisoners' families', in Y. Jewkes (ed.) *Handbook on Prisons*. Cullompton: Willan Publishing.
Niven, S. and Stewart, D. (2005) *Resettlement Outcomes on Release from Prison in 2003. Home Office Research Findings* 248. London: Home Office.
Shafer, N. (1994) 'Exploring the link between visits and parole success', *International Journal of Offender Therapy and Comparative Criminology*, 38: 17–32.

Visher, C.A. and Travis, J. (2003) 'Transitions from prison to community: understanding individual pathways', *Annual Review of Sociology*, 29: 89–113.
See also the website of Affect – Action For Families Enduring Criminal Trauma (**http://www.affect. org.uk/information/prison_visits.htm**) – and the Prison Service's website (**http://www. hmprisonservice.gov.uk/adviceandsupport/ keepingintouch/visitorsguide/**).

## VOLUNTARY SECTOR

The voluntary sector comprises non-profit-making, non-statutory organizations that usually have charitable status and that usually provide the services of people who work without remuneration.

### Origins of voluntary sector involvement in prisons

Voluntary organizations range from small community groups that may not be formally constituted to larger service providers, registered charities and social enterprises. They are generally non-profit making or distributing, non-statutory and autonomous, and usually have charitable status. They cover a range of activities and policy areas, and may or may not use volunteers. Collectively, they make up the voluntary and community sector.

Voluntary sector work has been undertaken in the Prison Service since the early nineteenth century. Elizabeth Fry was one of the first volunteer prison reformers. Her work, and that of Victorian charities and philanthropic societies, heralded the start of a long history of community engagement in prisons in England and Wales. Volunteer missionaries also worked in the police courts, giving advice and assistance to offenders, offering alternatives to custody and giving financial support to prisoners' families and those leaving prison. This work is now recognized as the foundation of the Probation Service.

The twentieth century saw voluntary organizations being given the main responsibility for running approved schools. The advent of the welfare state after the Second World War led to a brief decline in voluntary sector activity in prisons, but its involvement grew again in the latter part of the century in line with the changing social environment, with new groups emerging. Family members, victims and ex-offenders set up their own voluntary organizations based on their perceptions of the needs of prisoners and the causes of crime. Voluntary sector engagement in prisons flourished, and organizations assumed a significant role in contributing to some of the core prison functions.

Since the late 1990s, the Prison Service has recognized the positive input that the voluntary and community sector makes, valuing its contribution as a resource: 'Whatever the motivation, and despite differing cultures and ways of operating, the penal voluntary sector and the Prison Service overlap in their broad aims of seeking to aid resettlement and reduce re-offending' (Bryans *et al.* 2002).

### Recent developments

The National Offender Management Service (NOMS) was introduced in 2004 and put greater emphasis on working with the voluntary and community sector. The announcement of the three Reducing Re-offending Alliances in 2005 included the Faith and Voluntary and Community Sector Alliance, which recognizes the role of voluntary and faith groups in helping to reduce reoffending. It promotes the growth of voluntary work in the wider community by encouraging people to work collaboratively to tackle the causes of social exclusion and criminal activity. NOMS has made clear its intention to commission services from a plurality of providers to secure places in custody or on community sentences, based on quality, value for money and innovation. So, while many of the service providers are expected to be primarily from the National Probation Service and the Prison Service, it is anticipated that NOMS will also commission services from the commercial and not-for-profit or voluntary sector.

There are more than 960 voluntary sector organizations working with prisoners, their families and ex-prisoners, and over 12,000 individuals volunteering within the criminal justice system. These figures are set to grow in the coming years. In prisons, volunteers and voluntary organizations already provide a range of services, often in connection with resettlement activities. Areas of work include accommodation advice and provision, education and employment skills training, multi-faith support, drugs and alcohol treatment, suicide prevention, family relationships, healthcare and mentoring. Voluntary engagement brings specialist expertise, knowledge and commitment, increasingly working 'through the gate' to provide the main link between the prisoner and the wider community. Some organizations receive funding from the prison while others rely totally on charitable donations.

Prison Service Order 4190 was introduced in June 2002 following approval by the Prison Service Management Board of the *Strategy for Working with the Voluntary and Community Sector* (HM Prison Service 2002). It was designed to ensure a strong and consistently managed effective relationship between the Prison Service and the voluntary sector, and volunteers at headquarters, area and establishment level. It sets out mandatory requirements and gives guidance on good practice in working with the voluntary and community sector, calling for effective arrangements between the Prison Service and the voluntary and community sector to ensure that services are focused, relevant and support regime objectives. Further, it requires action to ensure that voluntary organizations and volunteers form an integral part of the delivery of constructive work in establishments and the community. It makes clear that prison governors must give responsibility to a member of their senior management team for oversight of voluntary and community groups and that this role should be written into his or her job description. It also encourages the creation of voluntary sector co-ordinator posts.

In 2005 a *Guide to Good Practice* for volunteering in prisons was published by the Home Office, which further emphasizes the government's commitment to working with volunteers and those in the voluntary and community sector (Home Office 2005).

*Carol Buckland*

## Related entries

*Fry, Elizabeth; Home Office; Listener schemes; Market testing; National Offender Management Service (NOMS); Probation Service.*

### Key texts and sources

Bryans, S., Martin, C. and Walker, R. (2002) *Prisons and the Voluntary Sector: A Bridge into the Community.* Winchester: Waterside Press.
HM Prison Service (2002) *Strategy for Working with the Voluntary and Community Sector* (PSO 4190). London: Home Office.
Home Office (2005) *Volunteering: A Guide to Good Practice for Prisons.* London: Home Office.
See also the following websites:
    http://www.prisonersadvice.org.uk/home.html;
    http://www.prisonreformtrust.org.uk/;
    http://www.prisonadvice.org.uk/;
    http://www.howardleague.org/;
    http://www.prisoners families.org.uk/.

# VOTING RIGHTS

Convicted prisoners in the UK are 'disenfranchised' by a blanket ban on voting in national and local elections.

The disenfranchisement of prisoners in the UK dates back to the nineteenth century. Linked to the notion of 'civic death,' the Forfeiture Act 1870 denied offenders their rights of citizenship. The current blanket electoral ban on sentenced prisoners voting is contained in the Representation of the People Act 1983 (amended 1985, 2000).

In 1998 the Prison Reform Trust (PRT) published *Prisoners and the Democratic Process,* arguing that voting rights help to develop a sense of social responsibility and should be extended to all UK prisoners (PRT 1998). It also presented evidence to the Home Affairs Select Committee report *Electoral Law and Procedure.* In 1999 the Home Office Working Party on Electoral Procedures identified the disenfranchisement of convicted but unsentenced and remand prisoners as being caused by electoral criteria that prevent the acceptance of penal institutions as places of residence (White and Rees 2006). It concluded that preventing remand prisoners from voting was accidental – that it had no argument of principle – and it recommended that remand prisoners be recorded without a fixed address. The 2000 amendment saw this implemented, but no recommendations or changes were made with respect to the enfranchisement of convicted prisoners.

Over the years there has been increasing pressure to change the law. On 2 March 2004 the PRT and Unlock (the National Association of Ex-offenders) launched the 'Barred from Voting' campaign. The key arguments were that the ban infringes human rights; further isolates people on society's margins, despite the link between social exclusion and crime; disproportionately affects ethnic minorities who are over-represented in prison; does not improve public safety; does not act as a deterrent or contribute towards rehabilitation; discourages political interest and debate on prisons and penal policy; encourages political and economic neglect of prisons and prisoners, which encourages reoffending; and removes the right to representation on issues such as human rights, living conditions and personal safety (Unlock and PRT 2004). Notable supporters of the campaign included former Conservative Home Secretary, Lord Douglas Hurd, Liberal Democrat President, Simon Hughes, and Labour Peer, Baroness Kennedy QC.

The UK is one of only eight European countries automatically to disenfranchise sentenced prisoners, the others being Armenia, Bulgaria, the Czech Republic, Estonia, Hungary, Luxembourg and Romania. The majority have no ban (18 states, including Denmark, Spain, Sweden and Switzerland) or a partial ban (13 states, including France, Germany and Italy). In Australia and New Zealand, the length of sentence determines voting rights. In 2002 the Canadian Supreme Court stated that denying the vote 'countermands the message that everyone is equally worthy and entitled to respect under the law'. In 1999 the South African Constitutional Court gave all prisoners voting rights, declaring: 'The vote of each and every citizen is a badge of dignity and personhood. Quite literally it says that everybody counts.'

In March 2004, the European Court of Human Rights (ECtHR) gave its judgment in the case of *Hirst* v. *The United Kingdom*, finding that the ban breached Article 3 of Protocol 1 of the European Convention on Human Rights, which guarantees 'free elections...under conditions which will ensure the free expression of the opinion of the people in the choice of the legislature'. The case was brought by John Hirst, a serving prisoner at Rye Hill Prison, after an unsuccessful challenge at the High Court. Much reference was made by the court to *Sauvé* v. *The Attorney General of Canada* (No. 2), which rejected Parliament's argument for denying the vote on social, philosophical or political grounds as being 'inappropriate on a decision to limit fundamental rights'. The court held that, in a democracy built on principles of inclusiveness, equality and citizen participation, elected representatives had no right to disenfranchise a segment of the population.

The Department of Constitutional Affairs responded: 'We have always argued that prisoners should lose the right to vote while in detention because if you commit a crime that is serious, you should lose the right to have a say in how you are governed...This judgement questions that position.' The government appealed, submitting that the ban was restricted to around 48,000 prisoners 'convicted of crimes serious enough to warrant a custodial sentence and not including those on remand.'

The debate became even more prominent, leading up to the 2005 general election. Liberal Democrat, Charles Kennedy, declared: 'We believe that citizens are citizens. Full stop...you have to have the entitlements that go with it in terms of voting.'

In October 2005, the Grand Chamber of the ECtHR rejected the government's appeal by a majority of 12 to 5, stating: 'Such a general, automatic and indiscriminate restriction on a vitally important Convention right had to be seen as falling outside any acceptable margin of appreciation.' The decision on how to secure these rights was left to the UK legislature.

The ECtHR ruling polarized political opinion. The Liberal Democrats welcomed the ruling, stating that: 'Telling offenders that they have no part to play in our democracy is no way to end the cycle of crime.' The Conservatives dismissed the human rights argument, with the Shadow Attorney General declaring that: 'Giving prisoners the vote would be ludicrous.' Lord Falconer, the Lord Chancellor, said:

> I can make it absolutely clear that in relation to convicted prisoners, the result of this is not that every convicted prisoner is in the future going to get the right to vote...We need to look and see whether there are any categories that should be given the right to vote.

> *Chris Bath*

### Related entries

*Citizenship; Human rights; Less eligibility; New punitiveness; Politics of imprisonment; Prison Reform Trust; Remand.*

---

**Key texts and sources**

Prison Reform Trust (1998) *Prisoners and the Democratic Process.* London: PRT.

Unlock and Prison Reform Trust (2004) *Barred from Voting: The Right to Vote for Sentenced Prisoners* (available online at **www.unlock.org.uk/campaign.aspx**).

White, I. and Rees, A. (2006) *House of Commons Standard Note SN/PC/1764: Convicted Prisoners and the Franchise.* London: Parliament and Constitution Centre, House of Commons.

The case of *Hirst* v. *The United Kingdom* (No. 2) Judgment, European Court of Human Rights Grand Chamber (2005) is available online at the HUDOC Collection (**http://cmiskp.echr.coe.int/**).

---

# VULNERABLE PRISONERS' UNITS (VPUs)

Vulnerable prisoners' units (VPUs) provide a safe living environment for those who would be vulnerable in the general prison population.

Under Prison Rule 45, prisoners can be removed from associating with other prisoners, either for the maintenance of good order or discipline or because removal is in his or her own interests. Rule 45 authorizes such prisoners to be placed in segregation units on a short-term basis. However, as there are large numbers of prisoners who would be vulnerable in the general prison population and therefore need to be separated in their own interests, special units have had to be established, known as vulnerable prisoners' units (VPUs). The Woolf Report published following the widespread prison disorder of 1990 noted that the phenomenon of a stable population of vulnerable prisoners was largely confined to the UK and North America, but was less of an issue in Europe.

Prisoners may be vulnerable for a range of reasons, including the nature of their offence (sex offenders, informants and convicted police officers being particularly targeted by fellow prisoners); their personality or ability to cope; and mental health and self-harm problems. Some prisoners may become vulnerable for reasons such as debt or being the victim of violence or bullying. Prison officers should attempt to identify prisoners who are potentially vulnerable on their reception into prison.

VPUs generally experience fewer incidents of disorder and assaults than ordinary wings, and this provides scope for improved staff–prisoner relationships. However, surveillance and control are evident, partly out of a desire to maintain equality but also due to particular risks, including that of sexual activity and the presence of 'super-vulnerable' prisoners who may struggle to cope even in these units (Hay and Sparks 1996). VPUs have been criticized because they confirm the stigmatization of certain groups, tacitly support prisoner subcultures and reduce the opportunities available to certain prisoners (Hay and Sparks 1996). It can also be argued that VPUs can make prisons more complex to operate as they effectively become separate prisons within a prison, and this can result in reduced facilities for all prisoners. As a result of these criticisms, some organizations have refused to work with such separation. Most notably, the chaplaincy in the majority of prisons is integrated, and the Samaritans have insisted that the prisoners they train as listeners attend mixed groups. In addition, some prisons have abolished VPUs and have integrated all prisoners (e.g., see HM Chief Inspector of Prisons 2003). However, they are unlikely to disappear in the near future as they form an integral part of the risk management of prison life (Hay and Sparks 1996).

*Jamie Bennett*

### Related entries

*Bullying; Inmate code; Listener schemes; Mental health; Risk; Segregation; Self-harm; Sex offenders; Subcultures.*

#### Key texts and sources

Hay, W. and Sparks, R. (1996) 'Vulnerable prisoners: the risk in long-term prisons', in J. Reynold and U. Smartt (eds) *Prison Policy and Practice: Selected Papers from 35 Years of the Prison Service Journal.* Leyhill: Prison Service Journal.

HM Chief Inspector of Prisons (2003) *Report on a Full Unannounced Inspection of HMP Durham, 18–22 August 2003.* London: Home Office.

# 'WAR ON TERROR'

Detention has played a central strategic role in the 'war on terror'. In the immediate aftermath of the 9/11 attacks, emergency legislation was adopted in both the UK and the USA which expanded powers of surveillance and permitted detention without trial of non-citizens. Hasty augmentations of the US prison estate began around the same time and, by early 2002, regular flights transported detainees to sites in Iraq, Afghanistan and Cuba which now resonate familiarly around the world: Abu Ghraib, Bagram, Guantánamo Bay.

Since its onset, the 'war on terror' has been propelled by a militaristic agenda that has sought to minimize external legal or political interference with a security-driven process. The tactics employed to this end include the physical exclusion of human rights monitors from penal sites, procedural exclusion of judicial oversight and attempted jurisdictional relocation of judicial responsibilities to military organs. An illustrative example is the energy invested in redefining war-on-terror detainees as something other than prisoners of war: a chore that required, *inter alia*, the construction of a complex military–legal architecture and the promotion of a nomenclature ('enemy combatant') of disputed legal meaning and significance. Such exclusionary tactics have been underpinned by practices designed to obscure the role of the state through the use of proxy actors (such as privately hired security companies) and processes of 'juridical othering' (Jamieson and McEvoy 2005).

The quintessence of juridical othering is the Central Intelligence Agency (CIA) practice known as 'rendition' or 'ghosting' detainees: the abduction and transportation of detainees to covert penal facilities known as 'black sites'. Although rendition as a procedure predates the war on terror, it has been massively expanded in recent years and is believed to encompass more than one hundred countries which are complicit in either handling or receiving covert CIA flights, or in hosting detention centres. The transnational and covert nature of rendition is paradigmatic of counter-insurgency in the war on terror. However, despite exhaustive and sophisticated attempts to control information regarding terror detainees, a constant flow of evidence has emerged detailing prisoner mistreatment and abuse. Some of this has been graphic and explicit, such as the extensive photographic evidence of detainee physical and sexual abuse at Abu Ghraib and Guantánamo Bay released to media outlets in 2004. Considerably more has been mundane and administrative, such as the millions of pages of official documentation obtained subsequent to Freedom of Information 2000 requests by human rights organizations and others, which trace the comprehensive administrative sanctioning of torture and its reconstruction as 'counter-resistance' or 'enhanced interrogation techniques' (Greenberg *et al.* 2005).

The pedestrian nature of this complicity in torture indicates a further leitmotiv of the war on terror. To date, comparatively little energy has been deployed by the US authorities in obfuscation or denial of tactics such as torture, humiliation and 'ghosting' prisoners. Instead, much of the state rhetoric has sought to normalize inhumane treatment, to bureaucratize it and to claim that it *works*. Methods of interrogation previously portrayed as illegal and redundant in 'civilized' nations have been reconstructed as necessary, procedural, even indispensable (Greenberg *et al.* 2005). The abrogation of human rights norms has been achieved with reference to a security narrative which explicitly justifies prolonged detention without charge, evidence of threat or intelligence value on the basis of preventing prisoners from taking up arms against the USA in the future. The US Supreme Court acknowledged in *Hamdi* v. *Rumsfeld* that, in the context of a 'war without end', this argument creates 'a substantial prospect of perpetual detention' for current detainees. Indeed, many of the most heated battles concerning the treatment of war-on-terror detainees have been waged in the courts. Prisoners, their lawyers, non-governmental organizations and others have made law perhaps *the* key strategy of resistance to the abuses perpetrated in these sites, with considerable judicial concurrence. The US Supreme Court rejected the proposition that detention in Guantánamo Bay could enable a legal vacuum beyond US judicial oversight, asserting that detainees may bring a habeas corpus suit in a US federal court and were entitled to have their case heard and decided by an impartial body (*Hamdi* v. *Rumsfeld*; *Rasul* v. *Bush*). The subsequent attempted relocation of the judicial role demanded by these rulings to military commissions was also rejected by the Supreme Court, which found that the Geneva conventions required 'a regularly constituted court' operating in accordance with due-process norms (*Hamdan* v. *Rumsfeld*).

However, the significance of such judicial activism has been all but eliminated by legislative redaction. *Hamdan* v. *Rumsfeld* was countered with the Military Commissions Act 2006, which explicitly prohibits the invocation of the Geneva conventions in a writ of habeas corpus. Similarly, in the UK, although the House of Lords has struck down provisions which permitted the indefinite detention of foreign nationals without trial and admissibility of evidence gained by torture, legislation has been introduced (such as the Terrorism Act 2006) removing traditional checks and balances and abrogating human rights and due-process norms.

Finally, although superficially war-on-terror detention policy appears to be unique and novel, the science or 'supermax mentality' of US corrections generally is highly prevalent in the penal approach (Gordon 2006). Concurrent themes are apparent in the fixation on the security, control and isolation of prisoners. Solitary confinement is used extensively against terror suspects and, for some detainees, has been almost unbroken for periods of up to 18 months. Policy convergences are even more apparent in the light of the practice of 'head-hunting' personnel from domestic maximum-security detention facilities to serve in Abu Ghraib or Guantánamo Bay, including prison officers with extensive records of violence against detainees (Gordon 2006).

Despite determined efforts to exclude all avenues of prisoner resistance, the evidence from Guantánamo Bay (the site about which most is currently known) is of continually escalating protest since 2001–2. However, hunger strikes were suppressed by brutal force-feeding practices and it appears that many of these protests have turned inwards, into acts of self-harm and attempted suicide. Such protest is indicative of the desperation and hopelessness that prisoners detained in such appalling conditions must feel. Of those individuals who have been 'renditioned' we know, as yet, nothing at all.

*Kirsten McConnachie*

### Related entries

*Foreign national prisoners; Human rights; Political prisoners; Supermax prisons.*

**Key texts and sources**

Gordon, A.F. (2006) 'Abu Ghraib: imprisonment and the war on terror', *Race and Class*, 48: 42–59.

Greenberg, K.J., Dratel, J.L. and Lewis, A. (2005) *The Torture Papers: The Road to Abu Ghraib.* Cambridge: Cambridge University Press.

Jamieson, R. and McEvoy, K. (2005) 'State crime by proxy and juridical othering', *British Journal of Criminology*, 45: 504–27.

McEnvoy, K., McConnachie, K. and Jamieson, R. (2007) 'Political imprisonment and the "War on terror"', in Y. Jewkes (ed.) *Handbook on Prisons.* Cullompton, Willan Publishing.

# WELFARISM

Welfarism is a particular strand of thought and practice in criminal justice that prioritizes the personal and social disadvantages of the offender as the focus for intervention, blurring the distinction between delinquency, neglect and other social needs. By contrast, the 'justice' perspective is concerned solely with the manifestations of criminal behaviour and has no concern for the offender's social circumstances.

The welfarist approach does not hold offenders responsible for their actions and seeks to respond constructively to those 'needs' that are seen as underlying causes, of which deviant behaviour is merely a symptom. The 'causes' of crime are located in adverse social conditions, such as poverty and family breakdown, and it is necessary to address these flexibly and sensitively, depending on individual circumstances, rather than to impose standardized forms of punishment or control.

Within 'welfarism', two strands can be identified: for some, it is disadvantage, social exclusion and oppression that are the primary factors associated with criminal behaviour; for others, the central focus is on individualized causes of problems, such as family conflict, substance misuse or prior victimization. However, both agree that the most appropriate response to offending behaviour is to tackle these underlying issues. Practical help, support, care and effective treatment are believed to be doubly justified, in that the consequent improvement in offenders' life chances and social functioning will also reduce the likelihood of future reoffending.

Welfarist ideas have been well established in criminal justice over a long period, and they have been particularly associated with concerns over children who get into trouble, whose propensity to offend may be attributed to a problematic upbringing or adverse circumstances. Thus, for example, a history of neglect or abuse may be seen to offer a degree of mitigation for any offence committed while also indicating the need for intervention based on principles of therapeutic intervention and support.

Modified penal sanctions for young offenders have been in place since at least 1854 when the Youthful Offenders Act was passed (Hendrick 2006). Since then, law and policy have consistently incorporated welfare principles into provision for young people, both within and outside secure settings. Borstals were legally established in 1908 to provide a more welfare-oriented regime for young delinquents (aged 15–21) than the adult prison. Interestingly, at the same time, a similar 'welfare' strand was introduced into the adult sphere with the Probation of Offenders Act 1907. There was a growing sense that offenders, of whatever age, could be 'rescued' from their unacceptable lifestyles, and thereby reformed. By the 1920s, neglect and delinquency became conflated in the minds of criminologists (Muncie 2004). Concerns about the relationship between social deprivation and offending have continued to influence penal thinking, notably during the 1960s and 1970s. This perspective heavily influenced the white paper, *Children in Trouble* (1968), and the Children and Young Persons Act 1969. Under this legislation, the distinction between the needs of young people and due process was blurred so that, for example, the s. 7 care order could be imposed in place of penal sanctions. At the same time, it was intended that young offenders under the age of 14 would be lifted out of the criminal justice system entirely and responded to by way of social services intervention. It was at this point that the Scottish Children's Hearing System was established too, also drawing heavily on 'welfarist' principles.

However, the Children and Young Persons Act was not fully implemented, and the consequence was a process of 'vertical integration' between the welfare system and conventional criminal justice processes. As a result, the number of young people sentenced to custody was unaffected (in fact, it increased), while the population 'in care' increased dramatically (Thorpe *et al.* 1980).

By the early 1980s, it was widely accepted that 'welfarism' had been a massive failure as an intervention strategy. It had infringed upon their civil rights, but it had not improved the life chances of young offenders, it had not reduced the use of custody and it had not contributed to a reduction in reoffending rates (Muncie 2004). Young people were the victims of a process of 'net-widening', which brought them into the ambit of the justice system on ostensibly 'welfare' grounds, and then accelerated them up the criminal tariff if they offended again. Thus discredited, 'welfarism' was displaced by other strategies, such as 'systems management', which focused almost exclusively on offending behaviour, with little concern for the social context of the offender's actions. The absence of a specific welfare orientation in youth justice was not seen as problematic, while other approaches appeared to be successful in decriminalizing and decarcerating young offenders. However, with the reversal of this trend and the increasing reliance on intensive penal measures during the 1990s, the implications became more significant. The political commitment of New Labour to be 'tough on the causes of crime' appeared to signify a readiness to reintroduce welfare considerations into the judicial process, but this did not materialize and, indeed, the focus on controlling behaviour alone was intensified.

Assessment tools (ASSET for young offenders and OASys for adults) provide little space for the welfare of offenders, epitomizing the refocusing of emphasis away from addressing need and towards the management of risk and control. This process is reflected, too, in the progressive separation of probation training and practice from that of social work.

Despite this apparent rejection of welfare principles in the justice sphere, there have been a number of signs that the connection has not been completely broken. For instance, the All-Wales Youth Offending Strategy (2004) seems to retain a central concern with the well-being of young people coming within the remit of the justice system; at the same time, the notion of 'vulnerability' has emerged as a trigger for modifying the treatment of young people in custodial settings. It has been suggested that the 'discarded ideas' of social work may be reasserting themselves (Raynor and Vanstone 2002), and that this is largely because practitioners find themselves having to engage with and respond to the adverse circumstances of those who offend.

*Roger Smith*

*Related entries*

*Borstals; Rehabilitation; Reoffending; Risk.*

**Key texts and sources**

Hendrick, H. (2006) 'Histories of youth crime and justice', in B. Goldson and J. Muncie (eds) *Youth Crime and Justice*. London: Sage.
Muncie, J. (2004) *Youth and Crime* (2nd edn). London: Sage.
Raynor, P. and Vanstone, M. (2002) *Understanding Community Penalties: Probation, Policy and Social Change*. Buckingham: Open University Press.
Thorpe, D., Smith, D., Green, C. and Paley, J. (1980) *Out of Care*. London: George Allen & Unwin.

# WOMEN IN PRISON

In 1995, the average number of women in prison in England and Wales was 1,998; by September 2005, this figure had more than doubled to 4,580. This constitutes roughly 6 per cent of the total prison population. Women offenders tend to be damaged and to suffer wide-ranging social exclusion, and prison is an expensive way of damaging them still further.

Although the nature and seriousness of offending by women have not increased, the overall picture of women in prison over the last ten years has seriously worsened, in terms of the rise in the female prison population, the prevalence of damage and vulnerability in women prisoners, the disproportionate number of black and minority ethnic prisoners and recidivism rates following release (Medlicott 2007).

The dramatic and disproportionate rise in the population of women in prison can be explained by the significant increase of severity in sentencing policy. Fewer than 10 per cent are charged with violent offences, and the commonest offences are theft and handling stolen goods and drugs offences. Most women in prison are serving very short sentences of six months or less. The remand population has seen a serious rise in the last ten years, and about one in five are on remand. The majority of women prisoners are under 40 years of age, and 66 per cent are already mothers. At least a third of these mothers are single parents, and frequently their children must be taken into care when they are incarcerated. Almost 18,000 children are separated from their mothers by imprisonment each year.

During 2004, 114 babies were born to mothers in prison: some of these would be forcibly separated from their mothers immediately following birth and either taken into institutional care or passed around a number of different carers. Such babies are less likely to be reunited with their mothers on release and, in turn, they inevitably suffer some of the deficits in care that are often the forerunner to subsequent offending. There are only about 80 places for babies to remain with their mothers in only seven women's prisons and there is no automatic eligibility. It is the demeanour of defendants, and how they measure up against gender stereotypes, that will assist court decisions about the disposal of pregnant women. Mother and baby units (MBU) at least spare women the anguish of separation from their newborns. They offer the opportunity for babies to bond properly with their mothers and to experience some continuity of care until they are taken from imprisoned mothers at 9 or 18 months of age. Advice and peer support are available in such units, and mothers have the opportunity to learn mothering in a protected environment. However, this protected environment is also highly charged with discipline and control, which can infantilize mothers and prevent them from maturing as autonomous carers. The lack of stimulation and of access to normal support networks in family and community can also result in impoverished early experiences for the child (Medlicott 2007).

The impact of prison produces great strain on families. Women tend to be the primary carers of young, old and vulnerable family members. Maintaining and strengthening family ties are widely regarded as the most important elements in preventing reoffending. However, the difficulty of maintaining close family ties is exacerbated by the fact that the chances of being imprisoned far from home are much greater for women because of the smaller number of women's prisons. At the end of September 2004, the average distance from home for female prisoners was 62 miles.

Following release, the poverty of most women will be increased. Having stable accommodation reduces reoffending by over 20 per cent, but more than a third of women prisoners can expect to experience homelessness. The majority of them will have depended on housing benefit prior to custody, but this entitlement ends for all sentenced prisoners in prison for more than 13 weeks. Upon release from prison, 38 per cent of women prisoners expect to be homeless. All this instability makes reoffending sometimes seem the only option. Ten years ago, 38 per cent of female ex-prisoners were reconvicted within two years of release, but 57 per cent of those released from prison in 2002 were reconvicted within two years.

Women on entry into prison tend to demonstrate characteristics of severe social exclusion, including unemployment, low educational attainment, physical and mental health problems, domestic violence victimization and addiction. They react badly to imprisonment, with behaviour that covers the whole spectrum from rebellion to extreme withdrawal. They do not tend to riot, to rebel collectively or to attempt to escape or abscond. Individually, however, they commit more disciplinary offences than men: it has been observed that these tend to relate to disobedience and disrespect – behaviour that would commonly be viewed as normal in male prisoners. More serious than these strategies, however, are the levels of low self-esteem and helplessness that lead to self-harm and suicide in prison. Women who have entered prison damaged, vulnerable, mentally ill and/or addicted to drugs find themselves in an environment that is seemingly almost designed to exacerbate their distress, with its bleak environment, its removal of personal choice and its insistence on conformity. Despite making up only 6 per cent of the total prison population, women account for 25 per cent of all recorded deliberate self-injury. Some 14 women killed themselves in prison in England

and Wales during 2003, and 13 during 2004. Interviews with women who have survived incidents of severe self-harm show the yawning need for specialist help in relation to mental health, and for improved support for women made vulnerable by stressful life events (Borrill *et al.* 2005).

Holloway Prison is the largest women's prison in England and Wales, and its chequered history shows how penal policy in relation to women has demonstrated clear failures in moral legitimacy. It was redeveloped in the 1980s, with comprehensive psychiatric, medical and general hospital facilities, and it embodied the long-standing notion that criminal women needed medicalization and care rather than punishment. Successive inspection reports have produced evidence of horrific and inhumane conditions. In 1995, for example, the Chief Inspector reported overcrowding, filth, the suspension of most educational and other classes, almost continual lock-up, rats, cockroaches and uncleared rubbish. There was evidence of racial discrimination, the wide availability of illegal drugs, neglect, high levels of self-harm, and physical and verbal bullying (Ramsbotham 2005). Successive independent inspections, concern expressed by experienced commentators, observers and researchers, and full awareness on the part of the Prison Service and the relevant ministers have failed to make the necessary improvements and bring Holloway up to appropriate standards of legitimacy. In 2002, a critical report by Anne Owers, the Chief Inspector, found that children under 18 were still being housed in Holloway, despite government and Prison Service commitments to abandon this practice.

Two contrary trends have been observed in the literature as typifying women's imprisonment since the middle of the nineteenth century, in which the principles of *sameness* and *difference* to men have combined to make women's prisons especially limiting and repressive. On the one hand, prison policy for women has echoed that of men's prisons, often by default because policymakers have only recognized the larger male prison population as significant. On the other hand, a repressive

patriarchy has always chosen to recognize women prisoners as doubly deviant: damned because they are criminals and doubly damned because they have departed from the natural standard of femininity (Carlen and Worrall 2004). It has been observed that this still produces erratic and subjective sentencing, sometimes based on childcare responsibilities, and judgements about the quality of mothering and the capacity of the accused to respond to normalizing regimes (Hedderman and Gelsthorpe 1997).

In 2000, the quantifiable financial costs to public bodies of imprisoning women were estimated at £118 million (Prison Reform Trust 2000). Impossible to quantify, however, are the failure to reduce recidivism, the loss of female prisoners' lives, the damage to their mental and physical health, and the overall social, economic and emotional costs to prisoners, families and wider society. Most women prisoners have been the victims of abuse, poverty, neglect and marginalization. It is sensible and just to implement radical reform of the arrangements for dealing with women offenders. Society needs another vision than the harsh disciplinary one if it is to keep open the conditions of possibility for real personal change and subsequent social, political and economic inclusion. Such a vision, for women, could appropriately be grounded in restorative justice (Medlicott 2007).

*Diana Medlicott*

### Related entries

*Black and minority ethnic (BME) prisoners; Drugs; Homelessness; Legitimacy; Mental health; Mother and baby units (MBUs); Prison population; Remand; Self-harm; Sentencing policy; Suicide in prison.*

### Key texts and sources

Borrill, J., Snow, L., Medlicott, D., Teers, R. and Paton, J. (2005) 'Learning from "near misses": interviews with women who survived an incident of severe self-harm in prison', *Howard Journal of Criminal Justice*, 44: 57–69.

Carlen, P. (ed.) (2002) *Women and Punishment: The Struggle for Justice.* Cullompton: Willan Publishing.

Carlen, P. and Worrall, A. (2004) *Analysing Women's Imprisonment.* Cullompton: Willan Publishing.

Hedderman, C. and Gelsthorpe, L. (1997) *Understanding the Sentencing of Women. Home Office Research Study* 170. London: Home Office.

Medlicott, D. (2007) 'Women in prison', in Y. Jewkes (ed.) *Handbook on Prisons.* Cullompton: Willan Publishing.

Prison Reform Trust (2000) *Justice for Women: The Need for Reform.* London: Prison Reform Trust.

Ramsbotham, D. (2005) *Prisongate: The Shocking State of Britain's Prisons and the Need for Visionary Change.* London: Free Press.

See also the website of Women in Prison (http:// www.womeninprison.org.uk/) and the Prison Service's website (http://www.hmprisonservice.gov.uk/adviceandsupport/prison_life/femaleprisoners/).

# WOOLF REPORT

The Woolf Report was the official report into the widespread prison disorder in England and Wales in April 1990.

## Background to the Woolf Report

The 1980s witnessed a spate of serious prison riots that reached its peak when, on 1 April 1990, prisoners at Manchester Prison (Strangeways) began the longest and most devastating riot in British penal history. The siege lasted for 25 days, during which time serious riots broke out in five other prisons and various disturbances occurred in more than 30 establishments. One prisoner died, 147 prison officers and 47 inmates were injured, and damage was estimated at £30 million. On the fifth day, then Home Secretary, David Waddington, announced his intention to open an independent public inquiry into the events under the direction of the then High Court judge, Lord Justice Woolf, who was subsequently invited to interpret the terms of reference of the inquiry as he saw fit. He chose to adopt a broad canvas approach, addressing questions concerned not only with what happened during the course of the riots and how they were handled but also with the underlying causes of the unrest and what lessons could be learnt for the future. His report, published just nine months later, has been widely acclaimed.

The demonstrations in the 1980s were not the first such disturbances in English prisons. But they were interpreted in a completely new, and much more liberal, light. Prior to the Woolf Report, prisons were prone to distinguish passive demonstrations, which involved large numbers of prisoners, from 'riots' that were blamed on a minority of exceptionally difficult prisoners. Such an approach effectively denied the influence of systemic factors arising from the ways in which prisons are organized and prisoners are treated. Hence prisoner unrest tended to be responded to punitively: the hard core of persistent troublemakers were housed away in special control units and, from the late 1970s, military-style riot squads were set up to intervene forcibly to quash prisoner protests.

The Woolf Report broke with the 'rotten apple' tradition, highlighting the contribution made by impoverished regimes and strained staff–prisoner relationships, openly acknowledging the part played by systemic factors. Although revolutionary in its approach, the inquiry was not so radical as to question sentencing decisions or the legitimacy of imprisonment. Woolf accepted the Prison Service's own *Statement of Purpose* as his starting point, yet he provided a critical perspective from which to reconceptualize the task of imprisonment. He noted that the *Statement of Purpose* imposed three key duties: 1) to keep secure those whom the courts put in its custody; 2) to treat those who are within its custody with humanity; and 3) to look after those in custody in such a way as to help them to 'lead law-abiding and useful lives' both while they are in custody and after release (Woolf and Tumin 1991: para. 10.11). With this in mind, Woolf made 12 key recommendations and a number of accompanying proposals.

## Key recommendations and the failures of implementation

A central theme running through the report was that stability in prisons rests on there being a proper balance between three elements: *security* arrangements, to prevent prisoners from escaping; measures of *control*, to prevent disruption and disorder within establishments; and procedures for *justice*, to ensure that all prisoners are treated with humanity and fairness. Woolf concluded that the failure of the Prison Service to convince prisoners that they were being treated fairly created difficulties for the maintenance of security and control. The answer, he claimed, was in better communication between prisoners and staff and for prisoners to be given a greater element of responsibility for the conduct of their lives in prison. Substantively, the report recommended that prisoner compacts (agreements) should be developed and that measures should be introduced to establish a greater degree of independence and fairness within adjudications and procedures for grievances. Recommendations were also made concerning the development of community prisons and the reduction of overcrowding.

The report struck a fine balance in its appeal. First, it gave hope and direction to those who aspired to reinforce the rehabilitation of offenders. Secondly, it avoided alienating the law-and-order lobby. And, thirdly, it struck a chord with the justice lobby. Accordingly, its central propositions were taken up by the government in its White Paper, *Custody, Care and Justice*, which claimed to chart 'a course for the Prison Service...for the rest of [the] century and beyond' (Home Office 1991: para. 3).

Penal reformers have described the Woolf Report as the most enlightened blueprint for improving the prison system presented to any post-war government. As Lord Woolf said, a decade later: 'There was undoubtedly a considerable feeling of optimism within prison circles. Prison numbers were falling. There appeared to be an opportunity for fundamentally improving the prison system. The Prison Service, supported by staff and officers at all levels, seemed determined to seize the opportunity this gave'

(2001). He pointed out that in almost every area covered by the report's recommendations the past decade had seen improvements: the physical conditions inside prisons had been transformed; slopping-out had virtually disappeared; and prisons were more just and more secure. Improved standards of justice, he admitted, was an area where there has been substantial progress in implementing the reforms. Indeed, there is now a Prisons and Probation Ombudsman; independent monitoring boards (boards of visitors) no longer have the disciplinary powers considered so inappropriate for a body responsible for being the public's watchdog; and there is also now an established grievance procedure.

Yet, in his speech, Lord Woolf claimed to be saddened that so much more could have been done were it not for the scourge of overcrowding. Added to this, the notorious Whitemoor and Parkhurst escapes and problems over temporary release had further pressurized an already overstretched system. These pressures resulted in a failure to develop innovative good practices and to maintain regimes. It was conceded that little progress had been made on prisoner compacts because the Prison Service could not deliver what the compact should provide. The concept of community prisons, too, remained unfulfilled. Finally, Lord Woolf revisited one of the major proposals of his report: that there should be a new Prison Rule that no establishment should hold more prisoners than provided for in its certified normal accommodation. On this, he remarked: 'My suggestion has been a total failure for two reasons, the first, it was not accepted, and second, even if it had been, it would have been insufficient to stem the flood.'

*Elaine Genders*

## Related entries

*Certified normal accommodation (CNA); Fairness; Grievances; Independent monitoring boards; Legitimacy; Official reports; Overcrowding; Prisons and Probation Ombudsman; Riots (prison); Sanitation.*

**Key texts and sources**

Home Office (1991) *Custody, Care and Justice: The Way Ahead for the Prison Service in England and Wales* (Cm 1647). London: HMSO.

Player, E. and Jenkins, M. (1994) *Prisons after Woolf: Reform through Riot.* London: Routledge.

Woolf, Lord (2001) 'The Woolf Report: a decade of change?' Address to the Prison Reform Trust, London, 31 January (available online at **http://www.judiciary.gov.uk/publications_media/ speeches/pre_2004/31012001.htm**).

Woolf, Lord Justice and Tumin, S. (1991) *Prison Disturbances, April 1990* (Cm 1456). London: HMSO.

# WORLD PRISON POPULATIONS

There are more than 9.25 million people in prison around the world. However, imprisonment levels and the composition of the prison population vary considerably between countries and states. Almost half of the world's prisoners are in the USA (2.19 million), China (1.55 million plus pre-trial detainees and prisoners in 'administrative detention') and Russia (0.87 million).

## *How many prisoners worldwide?*

The first estimate of the number of people held in prisons and other penal institutions throughout the world placed the total at over 8 million (Walmsley 1999). The *World Prison Population List* gave details of the number of prisoners held in some 180 independent countries and dependent territories, and estimated the number held in the other countries on the basis of the rate per 100,000 among their neighbours in the same part of their continents. The most recent (7th) edition of this list, which gives details of the number of prisoners in 214 countries, reports that the total has risen to more than 9.25 million (Walmsley 2007). The list is compiled using information from individual prison administrations (obtained from them directly), from their publications and websites, or from information they have supplied to international bodies, such as the

United Nations and the Council of Europe, and at international conferences. For some countries the information comes from the ministry responsible for prisons or from the national statistical office.

The world total is more than 9.25 million but, for various reasons, an exact figure is not obtainable. A very small number of countries do not publicize the full extent of their prison population, omitting those in pre-trial detention and, in the case of China, those held in 'administrative detention'. Another very small group do not publicize any figure at all, including countries where the number is unknown because of war or other disruption (including Afghanistan, Iraq and Somalia). Other factors that thwart attempts to put an exact figure on the world prison population are the impracticability of establishing the number of prisoners throughout the world on a particular date and differences in the definition of a prisoner. For example, people held in custody are usually omitted from national prisoner totals if they are not under the authority of the prison administration – such as pre-trial detainees held in police facilities, juveniles held in special separately run facilities and offenders compulsorily detained for psychiatric treatment.

## *The world prison population league table*

In order to compare prison population levels in different countries, prison population totals are generally expressed in terms of the rate per 100,000 of the national population. This is known as the prison population rate or, more rarely, the prisoner rate. (The terms 'imprisonment rate' and 'incarceration rate' are sometimes used but are ambiguous in that they could equally well refer to the proportion of offenders who, upon conviction, are sentenced to imprisonment.)

The USA has the highest prison population rate in the world, some 738 per 100,000 of the national population, followed by Russia (611), St Kitts and Nevis (547), the US Virgin Islands (521), Turkmenistan (*c.* 489), Belize (487), Cuba (*c.* 487), Palau (478), the British Virgin Islands (464), Bermuda (463), the Bahamas

(462), the Cayman Islands (453), American Samoa (446), Belarus (426) and Dominica (419). However, more than three fifths of countries (61 per cent) have rates below 150 per 100,000. The rate in England and Wales – 148 per 100,000 of the national population – is above the midpoint in the world list.

Prison population rates vary considerably between different regions of the world and between different parts of the same continent. For example, in Africa the median rate for western African countries is 37 whereas, for southern African countries, it is 267; in the Americas the median rate for South American countries is 165.5 whereas, for Caribbean countries, it is 324; in Asia the median rate for south central Asian countries (mainly the Indian subcontinent) is 57 whereas, for (ex-Soviet) central Asian countries it is 292; in Europe the median rate for southern European countries, is 90 whereas, for central and eastern European countries, it is 185; and in Oceania (including Australia and New Zealand) the median rate is 124.5.

The aforementioned increase in the world prison population total is a reflection of the fact that prison populations are growing in many parts of the world. The 2007 edition of the *World Prison Population List* reports that, compared with earlier editions of the list, prison populations have risen in 73 per cent of countries and that this trend is evident in all continents – 64 per cent of countries in Africa having registered increases, 84 per cent in the Americas, 81 per cent in Asia, 66 per cent in Europe and 75 per cent in Oceania.

There are considerable variations between countries in the proportion of the prison population who are pre-trial detainees/remand prisoners (International Centre for Prison Studies 2006). They generally (i.e. in more than 60 per cent of countries) constitute between 10 and 40 per cent of the total prison population. However, in 38 countries pre-trials/remands comprise more than half the total prison population, including 16 countries in Africa, 7 in South America and 4 in the Indian subcontinent. The highest percentages are in Haiti (where 89 per cent of prisoners are pre-trials/remands), Andorra (77 per cent), Bolivia and Sao Tome e Principe (both 75 per cent), Mozambique (73 per cent), Timor-Leste (71 per cent) and India (70 per cent). In England and Wales, 16.6 per cent of the prison population are pre-trials/remands.

More than half a million women and girls are held in penal institutions throughout the world, either as pre-trial detainees (remand prisoners) or as having been convicted and sentenced (Walmsley 2006). About a third of these are in the USA (183,400), 71,280 (plus women and girls in pre-trial detention or 'administrative detention') are in China, 55,400 in the Russian Federation and 28,450 in Thailand. No other country reports a female prison population as high as 15,000. Female prisoners generally (in about 80 per cent of prison systems) constitute between 2 and 9 per cent of the total prison population. Just 13 systems have a higher percentage than that. The highest is in Hong Kong–China (22 per cent), followed by Myanmar (18 per cent) and Thailand (17 per cent). The median level is 4.3 per cent. There are continental variations in the prevalence of women and girls in the total prison population. In African countries they constitute a much smaller percentage of the total (the median is 2.65 per cent) than in the Americas and Asia, where the median level is twice as high (5.3 and 5.4 per cent, respectively). The median levels in Europe and Oceania are 4.4 and 4.3 per cent, respectively. In England and Wales, 5.6 per cent of the prison population are women and girls.

Foreign prisoners generally (i.e. in 60 per cent of countries) constitute less than 7 per cent of the total prison population (ICPS 2006). However, in 28 countries they constitute more than a quarter of the prison population and, in 15 countries, including 8 in Europe (Andorra, Austria, Belgium, Cyprus, Gibraltar, Greece, Luxembourg and Switzerland), more than 40 per cent. The highest percentages are in the United Arab Emirates (87 per cent), Andorra (84 per cent), Luxembourg (75 per cent), Switzerland (70 per cent), The Gambia (67 per cent) and Qatar (60 per cent). In England and Wales, 12.5 per cent of the prison population are foreign nationals.

From an international perspective the number of young people under 18 who are included in prison population totals is unfortunately a poor guide to the number of such people who are held in custody as a result of criminal offences. This is because countries vary enormously in their legislation and practice in respect of offences committed by those who are underage. The lowest age at which a young person may be committed to a prison is 18 in some countries, in which case no person under 18 appears in prison population totals, but elsewhere it is 17, 16, 15, 14 or even younger. Naturally the lower the age, the greater the likelihood is of a country having more young people under 18 in the prison population. In many countries young people who are held in custodial institutions as a result of an offence are under an authority other than the prison administration. Thus they do not appear in national prison population totals. In England and Wales, 3.2 per cent of the prison population are young people under 18. This constitutes about 2,500 juveniles, in addition to which some 270 juveniles are held in secure training centres and 230 in local authority secure children's homes. UNICEF estimates that there are about one million children and adolescents (younger than 18) in detention worldwide.

### Overcrowding: a global phenomenon

Overcrowding in penal institutions is a serious problem in many countries. It is agreed to be a cause of, or contributory factor to, many of the health problems in prison, most notably communicable diseases and mental health, and it also contributes to health problems in the community since the vast majority of prisoners will return to the community in due course. This is why the international standards (e.g. Council of Europe 2006) insist that accommodation for prisoners must not only be adequately lit, heated and ventilated but must also provide adequate cubic content of air and sufficient floor space. If overcrowding is defined as having more prisoners than the official capacity of the prison system, then two thirds of the world's prison systems are overcrowded (ICPS 2006). And overcrowding is not just widespread, it is often severe: in 36 countries there is an occupancy level of over 150 per cent (more than three prisoners for every two spaces) and in 14 countries, 9 of them in Africa, the level is over 200 per cent (more than two prisoners for every space). The countries with the highest occupancy rates in the world are Zambia (331 per cent), Benin (307 per cent), Barbados (302 per cent), Cameroon (296 per cent), Bangladesh (288 per cent) and Kenya (284 per cent). In England and Wales the occupancy rate is 113 per cent, based on the uncrowded capacity (so-called 'certified normal accommodation'). As overcrowding has increased, more reference has been made to the 'operational capacity' – a level at which the prisons may be said to be 'overcrowded but manageable'.

For two reasons even the above analysis underestimates the extent of overcrowding: first, many countries whose prison systems have less than 100 per cent occupancy rates report overcrowding in some of their prisons, almost always in institutions for pre-trial and remand prisoners; and, secondly, in many countries the official capacities of institutions are higher than can be justified by the amount of space available, so that there is often evidence of overcrowding even in countries where the prison population is lower than the officially stated capacity.

*Roy Walmsley*

### Related entries

*Children in custody; Foreign national prisoners; Girls in prison; New punitiveness; Overcrowding; Prison population; Remand; Women in prison.*

## Key texts and sources

Council of Europe (2006) *European Prison Rules, Rec (2006) 2*. Strasbourg: Council of Europe Publishing.

International Centre for Prison Studies (2006) *World Prison Brief – Online Database on the World's Prison Systems*. London: International Centre for Prison Studies, King's College (available online at **www.prisonstudies.org**).

United Nations (2006) *United Nations Surveys of Crime Trends and Operations of Criminal Justice Systems*. Vienna: United Nations Office on Drugs and Crime (available online at **www.unodc.org**).

Walmsley, R. (1999) *World Prison Population List. Research Findings* 88. London: Home Office Research, Development and Statistics Directorate.

Walmsley, R. (2006) *World Female Imprisonment List*. London: International Centre for Prison Studies, King's College.

Walmsley, R. (2007) *World Prison Population List* (7th edn). London: International Centre for Prison Studies, King's College.

The Council of Europe's annual penal statistics (SPACE) are available online at **www.coe.int**. See also the Home Office's world prison population list (**http://www.homeoffice.gov.uk/rds/pdfs2/r188.pdf**) and the website of the International Centre for Prison Studies, King's College London (**http://www.prisonstudies.org/**).

# Y

## YOUNG MEN IN PRISON

Young men in prison are males aged 18–20, but include 21-year-olds who have been convicted while aged 20 or under and who have not been reclassified as part of the adult population; males convicted at the age of 21 are sent to an adult prison.

In January 2006 there were 8,031 young men aged 18–20 in prison, of whom 1,937 were on remand. Young men are accommodated in 16 young offender institutions (YOIs) and 42 adult prisons across England and Wales (Solomon 2004). Young men thus defined are located in prisons separately from those aged 15–17, who are overseen by the Youth Justice Board. These juvenile prisoners are often informally called young men, but this dictionary entry treats young men aged 18–20 separately, as does the Prison Service.

In 1999 a consultation paper called *Detention in a Young Offenders Institution for 18–20-Year-Olds* discussed abolishing the sentencing of these young men to a separate part of the prison estate. It proposed that the sentence of detention in YOIs for 18–20-year-olds was no longer justified on the grounds that these institutions did not cater for the particular needs among that age group and that it was a difficult system to enforce practically. In 2001 the Labour Party's election manifesto, *Ambitions for Britain*, pledged to improve conditions for this age group in prison, as did the command paper, *Criminal Justice: The Way Ahead*. However, these large-scale changes have not taken place, and less attention is paid politically to young men in prison compared with either adult males or those aged 15–17.

Young offender establishments vary in size, architecture and in their daily regime. Young men may be allocated a single cell or may share with their 'cellmate'. Young men are offered education and training and have the opportunity to apply for a job, which may be in the kitchens, as a cleaner or in one of the workshops. During the day there is 'association', often called 'sosh' – a period of time where they can socialize with one another, shower and make telephone calls to people outside. Managing this period of association is important for practical adaptation and so for psychological adaptation (Harvey 2007).

Young men import with them into prison a variety of difficulties which interact with the prison environment. Some enter prison with psychological problems, drug problems and a history of self-harming behaviour. In prison these young men have to adapt to a lack of freedom, to an environment with a high level of uncertainty and one that can induce concerns over personal safety. They also have to maintain whatever relationships they have beyond the prison walls. Yet various sources of support exist within the YOIs themselves: the chaplaincy (for all faiths), mental health professionals, medical staff and listener schemes (prisoners trained by the Samaritans). Prison officers may also be vital sources of practical and emotional support.

Policy-driven research has ensured that the position of young men in prison has not been forgotten (see, for example, Lyon *et al.* 2000; Nacro 2001; Solomon 2004; Farrant 2005). Academic research on young men in prison has considered a number of relevant areas (Harvey 2007). Research has focused on suicidal behaviour, coping and psychological distress, bullying behaviour, identity and self, the socialization of prisoners entering custody and the psychosocial experience of imprisonment.

*Joel Harvey*

## Related entries

*Bullying; Coping; Education and training; Identity and self; Listener schemes; Mental health; Remand; Self-harm; Young offender institutions (YOIs); Youth Justice Board (YJB).*

### Key texts and sources

Farrant, F. (2005) *A Sobering Thought: Young Men in Prison. Out for Good Research Briefing 1.* London: Howard League for Penal Reform.

Harvey, J. (2007) *Young Men in Prison: Surviving and Adapting to Life Inside.* Cullompton: Willan Publishing.

Lyon, J., Denison, C. and Wilson, A. (2000) '*Tell Them So They'll Listen': Messages from Young People in Custody.* London: Home Office.

Nacro (2001) *Young Adult Offenders: A Period of Transition.* London: Nacro.

Solomon, E. (2004) *A Lost Generation: The Experiences of Young People in Prison.* London: Prison Reform Trust.

See also the websites of the Howard League (http://www.howardleague.org/index.php?id=292) and the National Association for Youth Justice (http://www.nayj.org.uk/website/).

# YOUNG OFFENDER INSTITUTIONS (YOIs)

Young offender institutions (YOIs) are specialist penal facilities managed by the Prison Service and designed for prisoners aged 15–20 years. Male 'juvenile' prisoners (15–17 years) are normally detained separately from 'young adult offenders' (18–20 years), although exceptions to this 'rule' have been known to apply with regard to female 'juvenile' prisoners.

At the end of August 2006 the number of under 21-year-old prisoners in England and Wales – either sentenced or remanded – stood at 11,672, 2,528 of whom were children ('juveniles'). In the last ten years or more the number of children and young people entering penal custody in England and Wales has increased very significantly. Approximately 85 per cent of 'juvenile' prisoners – the remaining 15 per cent being held in secure training centres and local authority secure children's homes – and all 'young adult' prisoners are held in young offender institutions (YOIs) and, although there are specific Prison Rules governing these establishments, the regimes and conditions bear many similarities to those found in adult prisons.

For 'young adult' prisoners, an induction programme runs over the first few days following arrival in a YOI. This is designed to provide an opportunity for young prisoners to share any concerns that they might have with prison personnel (particularly their personal officer), to arrange education and training sessions and to settle the terms of a 'sentence plan'. There is greater regime differentiation from adult prisons for juvenile prisoners. Induction is ostensibly more 'child centred' and individually tailored. Juvenile prisoners are more rigorously assessed on arrival at the YOI and they are routinely provided with a 'first-night pack' that includes a telephone card and reading/writing materials. YOI staff are required to provide juveniles with an opportunity to contact their families/carers within two hours of arriving at the YOI. The more detailed attention that focuses on the younger prisoners in YOIs is derived from a recognition of their particular vulnerabilities.

Indeed, since 2000 the Youth Justice Board (YJB) and the Prison Service have together implemented a programme of substantial reform designed to improve the conditions and treatment of juveniles in penal custody. Institutional regimes must now be based on clear principles, and the YJB insists that there should be a structured and 'caring' environment in YOIs in order that 'juvenile' prisoners are kept safe and secure. As such, the YOIs that hold 'juveniles' have had centrally determined standards imposed upon them; are classified as 'authorized' or 'accredited'; must operate and deliver in accordance with 'contracting conditions'; are expected to provide placements that are then 'purchased' or 'commissioned' by the YJB; and are subjected to more rigorous forms of monitoring and inspection.

Despite such reforms, the best efforts of the most motivated prison staff and reports of considerable improvement, HM Inspectorate of Prisons continues to raise serious and consistent concerns about the practices and regimes in some YOIs with regard to 'juvenile' and 'young adult' prisoners. Furthermore, in 2002 the Children's Rights Alliance for England (CRAE) undertook a detailed analysis of the conditions and treatment experienced by juvenile prisoners, drawing on reports prepared by the Prisons Inspectorate. The results were problematic: widespread neglect in relation to physical and mental health; endemic bullying, humiliation and ill-treatment (staff-on-prisoner and prisoner-on-prisoner); racism and other forms of discrimination; systemic invasion of privacy; long and uninterrupted periods of cell-based confinement; deprivation of fresh air and exercise; inadequate educational and rehabil-itative provision; insufficient opportunities to maintain contact with family; poor diet; ill-fitting clothing in a poor state of repair; a shabby physi-cal environment; and, in reality, virtually no opportunity to complain and/or make represen-tations. According to the CRAE report, such negative and neglectful processes continue to define the conditions and treatment of many young prisoners in YOIs in England and Wales, irrespective of recent reforms.

Prison Service staff working in YOIs under-take enormously challenging jobs with minimal training: they are effectively required to provide a service (to young prisoners and the commu-nity) for which they are singularly ill-equipped. There is mounting evidence of the social prob-lems 'imported' into YOIs. 'Juvenile' and 'young adult' prisoners often experience damaged biog-raphies, and increasing concerns are being raised about the mental health of many young prisoners – male and female. Such problems are additionally compounded by overcrowding, the inevitable strain on staffing and the frequent movement of young adult and juvenile prison-ers around the YOI estate (unsettling young prisoners, fracturing relationships with staff, disrupting education and training programmes and producing inconsistent assessment, support and supervision). Furthermore, the Prison Reform Trust has reported that approximately 35 per cent of young adult and juvenile prison-ers are held in YOIs over 50 miles away from their home areas, making visits from family and friends difficult if not impossible.

Girls and young women, and young black and minority ethnic prisoners are particularly ill-served by YOIs. Despite repeated assurances from government ministers that all girls will be removed from YOIs, this has yet to be applied to 17-year-olds who continue to be held in five YOIs (Cookham Wood, Downview, Eastwood Park, Fosten Hall and New Hall). The limited number of specialist places for female juveniles in YOIs inevitably compounds the problems relating to distance from home. Furthermore, it is not unknown for female juvenile prisoners to be held on young adult wings. Racism also con-tinues to permeate both male and female wings in YOIs. The publication, in June 2006, of the report of the inquiry into the circumstances that led to the death of Zahid Mubarek – a young Asian prisoner murdered by his racist cellmate at Feltham YOI – highlighted the depth and breadth of institutionalized racism in YOIs (see Mubarek Inquiry; Official reports).

Against a backdrop of seemingly ever-increasing numbers of prisoners being held in YOIs in England and Wales, moribund condi-tions, human suffering and persistent failure when measured in terms of rehabilitation and recidivism, efforts to improve the treatment of society's youngest state prisoners and to enhance the 'performance' of YOIs seem as remote as ever.

*Barry Goldson and John Muncie*

### Related entries

*Black and minority ethnic (BME) prisoners; Bullying; Clothing; Education and training; HM Inspectorate of Prisons; Mental health; Mubarek Inquiry; Overcrowding; Prison Reform Trust; Prison Rules; Rehabilitation; Secure training cen-tres; Youth Justice Board (YJB).*

---

### Key texts and sources

Children's Rights Alliance for England (2002) *Rethinking Child Imprisonment: A Report on Young Offender Institutions.* London: Children's Rights Alliance for England.

HM Chief Inspector of Prisons (2006) *Annual Report of HM Chief Inspector of Prisons for England and Wales, 2004–2005.* London: HMSO.

Howard League for Penal Reform (2006) *Women and Girls in the Penal System*. London: Howard League for Penal Reform.

Prison Reform Trust (2006) *Bromley Briefings Prison Factfile*. London: Prison Reform Trust.

Youth Justice Board (2004) *Strategy for the Secure Estate for Juveniles*. London: YJB.

The website of Every Child Matters is at **http://www.everychildmatters.gov.uk/youthjustice/yoi/**. See also the Prison Service's young adult offenders web page (**http://www.hmprisonservice.gov.uk/adviceandsupport/prison_life/youngoffenders/**).

## YOUTH JUSTICE BOARD (YJB)

**The Youth Justice Board (YJB) has, since 1998, been responsible for overseeing the youth justice system for England and Wales. In 2000 it was also made responsible for commissioning custodial provision for juvenile offenders aged 10–17.**

The Youth Justice Board (YJB) is a statutory, corporate, non-departmental public body comprising 10–12 members. In the summer of 2006 it had a staff of just over 200. The board is sponsored and largely funded by the Home Office (it now comes under the remit of the Ministry of Justice). Its functions are to monitor the operation of the youth justice system and the provision of youth justice services in England and Wales; to advise the Home Secretary on the same; to monitor the extent to which the principal aim of the youth justice system – the prevention of offending – is being achieved; to collect and publish data on the operation of the system; to identify and promote good practice; to make grants to local authorities and other bodies; and to commission research (Crime and Disorder Act 1998, s. 41). In 2000 the Home Secretary added to these duties the commissioning of custodial provision for children and young people aged 10–17 years.

The board manages neither the 157 youth offending teams (YOTs) in England and Wales nor the more than 30 secure establishments it commissions to accommodate children and young people in custody. The YOTs are accountable to, and managed by, their local authority chief executives and elected councillors. Local authority secure homes, secure training centres and young offender institutions are managed by the local authorities, commercial companies and the Prison Service, who operate them subject to legal contracts or service-level agreements with the YJB. The only operational service the YJB performs is the initial placement of these young offenders: placement is according to their individual needs, as assessed by the YOTs, and the availability of suitable places.

Every YOT receives a core grant from the board plus such ring-fenced monies as the board distributes to develop programmes it considers effective. The latter have included intensive supervision and surveillance programmes for higher-risk offenders under supervision, early prevention schemes targeted at younger children deemed to be at risk and support schemes for young people leaving custody. All YOTs are required to return performance data to the YJB on a quarterly basis and, since 2006, these have been published in the form of a weighted scorecard. The board also employs a cadre of monitors, based regionally, to monitor YOT performance and, in the case of the closed estate, to monitor both performance and contract compliance.

The board undisputedly exercises considerable influence. Views differ as to whether that influence has been positive or negative and whether the board is able effectively to challenge, through the advice it offers, the direction of government policy (see Smith 2003; Audit Commission 2004). The board publishes an annual report and accounts as well as a series of effective practice guides, research reports, strategic plans and regular briefings and bulletins for practitioners. The annual report sets out the board's current targets and performance against them. These documents are accessible via the YJB website (www.youth-justice-board.gov.uk).

*Rod Morgan*

## Related entries

*Children in custody; Girls in prison; Home Office; Secure training centres; Young men in prison; Young offender institutions (YOIs).*

**Key texts and sources**

Audit Commission (2004) *Youth Justice 2004: A Review of the Reformed Youth Justice System*, London: Audit Commission.

Morgan, R. (2007) 'Children and young persons', in Y. Jewkes (ed.) *Handbook on Prisons.* Cullompton: Willan Publishing.

Morgan R. and Newburn T. (2007) 'Youth Justice' in M. Maguire *et al.* (eds) *The Oxford Handbook of Criminology*, Oxford: Oxford University Press.

Smith R. (2003) *Youth Justice: Ideas, Policy Practice.* Cullompton: Willan.

**www.youth-justice-board.gov.uk**

# References

Adams, M. (2007) 'Integrated offender management: aspiration or reality for the North West Pathfinder?', *Prison Service Journal*, 169: 42–9.

Adams, R. (1992) *Prison Riots in Britain and the USA*. London: Macmillan.

Aday, R.H. (2003) *Aging Prisoners: Crisis in American Corrections*. Westport, CT: Praeger.

Advisory Council on the Penal System (1968) *The Regime for Long-term Prisoners in Conditions of Maximum Security*. London: HMSO.

Aebi, M. (2005) *Council of Europe Annual Penal Statistics SPACE I: 2004 Survey on Prison Populations*. Strasbourg: Council of Europe.

American Correctional Association (1996) *Preventing and Managing Riots and Disturbances*. Lanham, MD: American Correctional Association.

American Friends Service Committee (1971) *Struggle for Justice: A Report on Crime and Punishment in America*. New York, NY: Hill & Wang.

Amnesty International (2006) *Amnesty International Handbook* (available online at **http://www.amnesty-volunteer.org/aihandbook/index.html**).

Andrews, D.A. and Bonta, J. (2003) *The Psychology of Criminal Conduct* (3rd edn). Cincinnati, OH: Anderson Publishing.

Anon (2006) 'Fewer life prisoners released on parole', *Guardian*, 6 November (available online at **http://www.guardian.co.uk/crime/article/0,,1940808,00.html**).

Armour, W. (2005) 'Weekend prison', *The Magistrate*, October.

Arnold, H., Liebling, A. and Tait, S. (2007) 'Prison officers and prison culture', in Y. Jewkes (ed.) *Handbook on Prisons*. Cullompton: Willan Publishing.

Ashworth, A. (1997) 'Sentencing in the 80s and 90s: the struggle for power.' Eighth Eve Saville Memorial Lecture, 21 May, King's College London (available online at **http://www.kcl.ac.uk/depsta/rel/ccjs/eighties-sentencing.html**).

Ashworth, A. (2002) 'Sentencing', in M. Maguire *et al.* (eds) *The Oxford Handbook of Criminology* (3rd edn). Oxford: Oxford University Press.

Ashworth, A. (2004) 'Criminal Justice Act 2003. Part 2. Criminal justice reform – principles, human rights and public protection', *Criminal Law Review*, July: 516–32.

Ashworth, A. (2005) *Sentencing and Criminal Justice* (4th edn). Cambridge: Cambridge University Press.

Audit Commission (2004) *Youth Justice 2004: A Review of the Reformed Youth Justice System*. London: Audit Commission.

Austin, J. (1986) 'Using early release to relieve prison crowding: a dilemma in public policy', *Crime and Delinquency*, 32: 404–502.

Barak, G. (ed.) (1994) *Media, Process, and the Social Construction of Crime*. New York, NY: Garland.

Baumgartner, M.P. (1992) 'The myth of discretion', in K. Hawkins (ed.) *The Uses of Discretion.* Oxford: Oxford University Press.

BBC News (2007) 'Woolf fears Home Office reforms' (available online at **http://news.bbc.co.uk/1/hi/uk_politics/6586437.stm**).

Becker, H.S. and Greer, B. (1960) 'Latent culture: a note on the theory of latent social roles', *Administrative Science Quarterly*, 5: 304–13.

Beckett, K. (1997) *Making Crime Pay: Law and Order in Contemporary American Politics.* New York, NY: Oxford University Press.

Beetham, D. (1991) *The Legitimation of Power.* London: Macmillan.

Behan, B. (1958) *Borstal Boy.* Berkeley, CA: Windhover.

Beit-Hallahmi, B. and Argyle, M. (1997) *The Psychology of Religious Behaviour, Belief and Experience.* London: Routledge.

Bennett, J. (2003) 'Winston Churchill: prison reformer?', *Prison Service Journal*, 145: 2–5.

Bennett, J. (2004) 'Jurassic Park revisited: the changing nature of prison industrial relations', *Prison Service Journal*, 156: 40–5.

Bennett, J. (2006) 'Undermining the simplicities: the films of Rex Bloomstein', in P. Mason (ed.) *Captured by the Media: Prison Discourse in Popular Culture.* Cullompton: Willan Publishing.

Bennett, J. (2007) 'Measuring order and control in HM Prison Service', in Y. Jewkes (ed.) *Handbook on Prisons.* Cullompton: Willan Publishing.

Bennett, J., Crewe, B. and Wahidin, A. (eds) (2007) *Understanding Prison Staff.* Cullompton: Willan Publishing.

Bennett, J. and Hartley, A. (2006) 'High security prisons as high reliability organisations', *Prison Service Journal*, 166: 11–16.

Bennett, J. and Wahidin, A. (2007) 'Industrial relations in prisons', in J. Bennett *et al.* (eds) *Understanding Prison Staff.* Cullompton: Willan Publishing.

Bernfeld, G., Farrington, D. and Leschied, A. (eds) (2001) *Offender Rehabilitation in Practice: Implementing and Evaluating Effective Programmes.* Chichester: Wiley.

Bhui, H.S. (2004) *Going the Distance: Developing Effective Policy and Practice with Foreign National Prisoners.* London: Prison Reform Trust.

Birmingham, L., Coulson, D., Mullee, M., Kamal, M. and Gregorie, A. (2006) 'The mental health of women in prison mother and baby units', *Journal of Forensic Psychiatry and Psychology,* 17: 393–404.

Black, J. (1995) 'Industrial relations in the UK Prison Service: the "Jurassic Park" of public sector industrial relations', *Employee Relations*, 17: 64–88.

Blunkett, D. (2003) *Civil Renewal: A New Agenda (the Edith Kahn Memorial Lecture).* London: Home Office.

Blunkett, D. (2004) *Reducing Crime – Changing Lives: The Government's Plans for Transforming the Management of Offenders.* London: Home Office.

Boards of Visitors (1998) *A Brief History of the Boards of Visitors, 1898–1998.* London: HMSO.

Borrill, J. and Brigden, G. (2005) *Implementation of the Violence Reduction Strategy. Safer Custody Group Briefing Paper* 15. London: HM Prison Service.

Borrill, J., Snow, L., Medlicott, D., Teers, R. and Paton, J. (2005) 'Learning from "near misses": interviews with women who survived an incident of severe self-harm in prison', *Howard Journal of Criminal Justice*, 44: 57–69.

Bosworth, M. (1999) *Engendering Resistance: Agency and Power in Women's Prisons.* Aldershot: Ashgate.

Bottoms, A.E. (1977) 'Reflections on the renaissance of dangerousness', *Howard Journal of Penology and Crime Prevention*, 16: 70–96.

Bottoms, A.E. (1980) 'An introduction to "the coming crisis"', in A.E. Bottoms and R.H. Preston (eds) *The Coming Penal Crisis: A Criminological and Theological Exploration.* Edinburgh: Scottish Academic Press.

Bottoms, A.E. (1999) 'Interpersonal violence and social order in prisons', in M. Tonry and J. Petersilia (eds.) *Prisons*. Chicago, IL: University of Chicago Press.

Bottoms, A.E. (2003) 'Theoretical reflections on the evaluations of a penal policy initiative', in L. Zedner and A. Ashworth (eds) *The Criminological Foundations of Penal Policy: Essays in Honour of Roger Hood*. Oxford: Oxford University Press.

Bottoms, A.E. (2004) 'Empirical research relevant to sentencing frameworks', in A. Bottoms *et al.* (eds) *Alternatives to Prison: Options for an Insecure Society*. Cullompton: Willan Publishing.

Bottoms, A.E. and Light, R. (1987) *Problems of Long-term Imprisonment*. Aldershot: Gower.

Boyle, J. (1977) *A Sense of Freedom*. London: Pan.

Boyle, J. (1984) *The Pain of Confinement*. Edinburgh: Canongate.

Bridgwood, A. and Malbon, G. (1995) *Survey of the Physical Health of Prisoners, 1994*. London: Office of Population Censuses and Surveys.

Bringing Rights Back Home (1997) (Cm 3782).

Brittan, A. (1977) *The Privatized World*. London: Routledge.

Brown, A. (2006) 'A brief early history of English prison riots: mutinies in Chatham Convict Prison 1861 and Dartmoor Convict Prison 1932', *Prison Service Journal*, 166: 45–9.

Brown, M. and Pratt, J. (eds) (2000) *Dangerous Offenders: Punishment and Social Order*. London: Routledge.

Bryans, S. (2000) 'Governing prisons: an analysis of who is governing prisons and the competencies which they require to govern effectively', *Howard Journal*, 39: 14–29.

Bryans, S. (2007) *Prison Governors: Managing Prisons in a Time of Change*. Cullompton: Willan Publishing.

Bryans, S. and Jones, R. (eds) (2001) *Prisons and the Prisoner: An Introduction to the Work of Her Majesty's Prison Service*. London: HMSO.

Bryans, S., Martin, C. and Walker, R. (2002) *Prisons and the Voluntary Sector: A Bridge into the Community*. Winchester: Waterside Press.

Bryans, S. and Wilson, D. (2000) *The Prison Governor: Theory and Practice* (2nd edn). Leyhill: Prison Service Journal Publications.

Burnett, R. (1992) *The Dynamics of Recidivism*. Oxford: Centre for Criminological Research.

Burnett, R. and Maruna, S. (2004a) 'So "prison works", does it? The criminal careers of 130 men released from prison under Home Secretary Michael Howard', *Howard Journal of Criminal Justice*, 43: 390–404.

Burnett, R. and Maruna, S. (2004b) *Prisoners as Citizens' Advisers*. London: Esmée Fairbairn Foundation.

Burnside, J., with Adler, J., Loucks, N. and Rose, G. (2005) *My Brother's Keeper: Faith-based Units in Prisons*. Cullompton: Willan Publishing.

Burnside, J. and Lee, P. (1997) 'Where love is not a luxury', *New Life*, 13: 36–54.

Burnside, J., Loucks, N., Adler, J. and Rose, G. (2005) *My Brother's Keeper: Faith-based Units in Prisons*. Cullompton: Willan Publishing.

Burton, F. and Carlen, P. (1979) *Official Discourse: On Discourse Analysis, Government Publications, Ideology and the State*. London: Routledge & Kegan Paul.

Butler, M. (forthcoming) 'Prisoner confrontations: the role of shame, masculinity and respect.' Unpublished thesis, University of Cambridge.

Caines, E. (2000) 'A predictable readjustment: politics and public management', *Criminal Justice Matters*, 40: 4.

Caird, R. (1974) *A Good and Useful Life: Imprisonment in Britain Today*. London: Hart-Davis.

Campbell, J. (2000) *The Masks of God. Vol. 1. Primitive Mythology.* London: Souvenir Press.

Cardozo-Freeman, I. (1984) *The Joint: Language and Culture in a Maximum Security Prison.* Springfield, IL: Charles Thomas Publishing.

Carlen, P. (1996) *Jigsaw: A Political Criminology of Youth Homelessness.* Buckingham: Open University Press.

Carlen, P. (ed.) (2002) *Women and Punishment: The Struggle for Justice.* Cullompton: Willan Publishing.

Carlen, P. and Worrall, A. (2004) *Analysing Women's Imprisonment.* Cullompton: Willan Publishing.

Carlile, Lord A. (2006) *An Independent Inquiry into the Use of Physical Restraint, Solitary Confinement and Forcible Strip Searching of Children in Prisons, Secure Training Centres and Local Authority Secure Children's Homes.* London: Howard League for Penal Reform.

Carrabine, E. (2004) *Power, Discourse and Resistance: A Genealogy of the Strangeways Prison Riot.* Aldershot: Ashgate.

Carrell, C. and Laing, J. (1982) (eds) *The Special Unit: Barlinnie Prison – its Evolution through its Art.* Glasgow: Third Eye Centre.

Carroll, L. (1974) *Hacks, Blacks and Cons: Race Relations in a Maximum Security Prison.* Lexington, MA: D.C. Heath.

Carter, P. (2003) *Managing Offenders, Reducing Crime: A New Approach.* London: Strategy Unit.

Cavadino, M. and Dignan, J. (2007) *Penal Systems: A Comparative Approach* (4th edn.). London: Sage.

Cavadino, M. and Dignan, J. (2007) *The Penal System: An Introduction* (4th edn.). London: Sage.

Chaplaincy Council (2003) *Prison Service Chaplaincy Handbook.* London: Prison Service.

Cheliotis, L.K. (2006a) 'Demystifying risk management: a process evaluation of the prisoners' home leave scheme in Greece', *Criminology and Criminal Justice*, 6: 163–95.

Cheliotis, L.K. (2006b) 'How iron is the iron cage of new penology? The role of human agency in the implementation of criminal justice policy', *Punishment and Society*, 8: 313–40.

Cheliotis, L.K. (under review) 'Reconsidering the effectiveness of temporary release: a systematic review of the literature.'

Cheliotis, L.K. and Liebling, A. (2006) 'Race matters in British prisons: towards a research agenda', *British Journal of Criminology*, 46: 286–317.

Children's Rights Alliance for England (2002) *Rethinking Child Imprisonment: A Report on Young Offender Institutions.* London: Children's Rights Alliance for England.

Clemmer, D. (1940/1958 2nd edn.) *The Prison Community* (2nd edn 1958). New York, NY: Holt, Rinehart & Winston.

Cohen, N. (2002) 'How Blair put 30,000 more in jail', *New Statesman*, 16 December (available online at **http://www.newstatesman.com/200212160011**).

Cohen, S. (1985) *Visions of Social Control.* Cambridge: Polity Press.

Cohen, S. and Taylor, L. (1972) *Psychological Survival: The Experience of Long-term Imprisonment.* Harmondsworth: Penguin Books.

Coleman, R. (2004) *Reclaiming the Streets: Surveillance, Social Control and the City.* Cullompton: Willan Publishing.

Collins, H. (1997) *Autobiography of a Murderer.* London: Macmillan.

Collis, R. and Boden, L. (1997) *Guidelines for Prison Libraries* (2nd edn). London: Library Association Publishing.

Commission for Racial Equality (2003a) *A Formal Investigation by the Commission for Racial Equality into HM Prison Service of England and Wales. Part 2. Racial Equality in Prisons.* London: Commission for Racial Equality.

Commission for Racial Equality (2003b) *Race Equality in Prisons: A Formal Investigation by the Commission for Racial Equality into HM Prison Service of England and Wales. Part 2.* London: Commission for Racial Equality.

Committee for the Prevention of Torture (2000) *11th General Report on the CPT's Activities.* Strasbourg: Council of Europe.

Committee of Inquiry into the UK Prison Services (1979) *Report* (the May Report) (Cmnd 763). London: HMSO.

Committee of Ministers (2003) *Recommendation of the Committee of Ministers to Member States on the Management by Prison Administrations of Life Sentence and other Long-term Prisoners (Adopted by the Committee of Ministers on 9 October 2003 at the 855th meeting of the Ministers' Deputies)* (Rec. (2003) 23E). Strasbourg: Council of Europe.

Committee of Public Accounts (2006) *The Electronic Monitoring of Adult Offenders. Sixty-second Report of Session 2005–6* (HC 997). London: HMSO (available online at **www.publications.parliament.uk/pa/cm200506/cmselect/cmpubacc/997/997.pdf**).

Council of Europe (1999) *Recommendation No. R (99) 22 of the Committee of Ministers to Member States Concerning Prison Overcrowding and Prison Population Inflation.* Strasbourg: Council of Europe.

Council of Europe (2006) *European Prison Rules, Rec (2006) 2.* Strasbourg: Council of Europe Publishing.

Coyle, A. (1996) *The Prisons We Deserve.* London: HarperCollins.

Coyle, A. (2002) *A Human Rights Approach to Prison Management: Handbook for Prison Staff.* London: International Centre for Prison Studies.

Coyle, A. (2003) *Humanity in Prisons: Questions of Definition and Audit.* London: International Centre for Prison Studies.

Coyle, A. (2005a) 'Imprisonment: the four Blair principles', *Prison Service Journal*, 161: 27–32.

Coyle, A. (2005b) *Understanding Prisons: Key Issues in Policy and Practice.* Maidenhead: Open University Press.

Coyle, A. (2007) *Prisons and the Ministry of Justice* (available online at **http://www.kcl.ac.uk/depsta/rel/icps/new.html**).

Coyle, A., Campbell, A., Neufeld, R. and Rodley, N. (2006) *Capitalist Punishment: Prison Privatization and Human Rights.* London: Zed Books.

Crawley, E. (2002) 'Bringing it all back home? The impact of prison officers' work on their families', *Probation Journal*, 49.

Crawley, E. (2004) *Doing Prison Work: The Public and Private Lives of Prison Officers.* Cullompton: Willan Publishing.

Crawley, E. (2005) 'Institutional thoughtlessness in prisons and its impacts on the day-to-day prison', *Journal of Contemporary Criminal Justice*, 21: 350–63.

Crawley, E. (2007) 'Imprisonment in old age', in Y. Jewkes (ed.) *Handbook on Prisons.* Cullompton: Willan Publishing.

Crawley, E. and Sparks, R. (2005) 'Older men in prison: survival, coping and identity', in A. Liebling and S. Maruna (eds) *The Effects of Imprisonment.* Cullompton: Willan Publishing.

Creighton, S., King, V. and Arnott, H. (2000) *Prisoners and the Law.* London: Butterworths.

Creighton, S., King, V. and Arnott, H. (2005) *Prisoners and the Law.* Haywards Heath: Tottel.

Crewe, B. (2005a) 'Codes and conventions: the terms and conditions of contemporary inmate values', in A. Liebling and S. Maruna (eds) *The Effects of Imprisonment*. Cullompton: Willan Publishing.

Crewe, B. (2005b) 'Prisoner society in the era of hard drugs', *Punishment and Society*, 7: 457–81.

Crewe, B. (2007) 'The sociology of imprisonment', in Y. Jewkes (ed.) *Handbook on Prisons*. Cullompton: Willan Publishing.

Crewe, B. (forthcoming) *Wellingborough: Power, Adaptation and the Everyday Social World of an English Prison*.

Crighton, D. (2006) 'Methodological issues in psychological research in prisons', in G. Towl (ed.) *Psychological Research in Prisons*. Oxford: Blackwell.

Cuppleditch, L. and Evans, W. (2005) *Re-offending of Adults: Results from the 2002 Cohort. Home Office Statistical Bulletin* 25/05 London: Home Office (available online at **www.homeoffice.gov.uk/rds**).

Davis, A. (2003) *Are Prisons Obsolete?* London: Open Media.

Davis, K.C. (1969) *Discretionary Justice: A Preliminary Inquiry*. Chicago, IL: University of Illinois Press.

Davis, M. (1990) *City of Quartz: Excavating the Future in Los Angeles*. London: Verso.

De Haan, W. (1991) 'Abolitionism and crime control: a contradiction in terms', in K. Stenson and D. Cowell (eds) *The Politics of Crime Control*. London: Sage.

Department of Health, HM Prison Service and National Assembly for Wales (2001) *Changing the Outlook: A Strategy for Developing and Modernising Mental Health Services in Prisons*. London: Department of Health.

Dodgson, K., Goodwin, P., Howard, P., Llewellyn-Thomas, S., Mortimer, E., Russell, N. and Weiner, M. (2001) *Electronic Monitoring of Released Prisoners: An Evaluation of the Home Detention Curfew Scheme. Home Office Research Study* 222. London: Home Office.

Donoghue, J. (2006) 'Antisocial behaviour orders and civil liberties: striking a balance', *Prison Service Journal*, 163: 8–12.

Downes, D. and Hansen, K. (2006) *Welfare and Punishment: The Relationship between Welfare Spending and Imprisonment*. London: Crime and Society Foundation.

DSPD Programme (2005) *Dangerous and Severe Personality Disorder (DSPD) High Secure Services for Men: Planning and Delivery Guide*. London: Department of Health, Home Office and HM Prison Service.

Dunbar, I. (1985) *A Sense of Direction*. London: Home Office.

Dunbar, I. and Fairweather, L. (2000) 'English prison design', in L. Fairweather and S. McConville (eds) *Prison Architecture: Policy, Design and Experience*. Oxford: Architectural Press.

Dwyer, C. (2004) 'The complexity of imprisonment: the Northern Ireland experience', *Cambrian Law Review*, 35.

East, W.N. and Hubert, W. (1939) *The Psychological Treatment of Crime*. London: HMSO.

Edgar, K. and Martin, C. (2004) *Perceptions of Race and Conflict: Perspectives of Minority Ethnic Prisoners and of Prison Officers. Home Office Online Report* 11/04 (available online at **http://www.homeoffice.gov.uk/rds/pdfs2/rdsolr1104.pdf**).

Edgar, K. and Newell, T. (2006) *Restorative Justice in Prisons: Making it Happen*. Winchester: Waterside Press.

Edgar, K. and O'Donnell, I. (1998) *Mandatory Drug Testing in Prisons: The Relationship between MDT and the Level and Nature of Drug Misuse*. London: Home Office.

Edgar, K., O'Donnell, I. and Martin, C. (2003) *Prison Violence: The Dynamics of Conflict, Fear and Power*. Cullompton: Willan Publishing.

Eigenberg, H.M. (2000) 'Correctional officers and their perceptions of homosexuality, rape, and prostitution in male prisons', *Prison Journal*, 80: 415–33.

Einat, T. (2005) '"Soldiers", "sausages" and "deep sea diving": language, culture and coping in Israeli prisons', in A. Liebling and S. Maruna (eds) *The Effects of Imprisonment*. Cullompton: Willan Publishing.

Ek, A. (2005) *Race and Masculinity in Contemporary American Prison Narratives*. London: Routledge.

Ekirch, A.R. (1990) *Bound for America: The Transportation of British Convicts to the Colonies, 1718–1775*. Oxford: Oxford University Press.

Elias, N. (1994) *The Civilizing Process*. Oxford: Blackwell.

Elliott, C. (1999) *Locating the Energy for Change: A Practitioner's Guide to Appreciative Inquiry*. Winnipeg: IISD.

Elliott, C. (2006) 'Speaking of performance improvement', *Prison Service Journal*, 163: 30–4.

Elliott, C. and Greaney, C. (2004) 'Improving performance through appreciative inquiry', *Prison Service Journal*, 156: 35–39.

Emsley, C. (2005) *Crime and Society in England 1750–1900* (3rd edn). Harlow: Longman.

Encinas, G.L. (2001) *Prison Argot: A Sociolinguistic and Lexicographic Study*. Laham, NY, and Oxford: University Press of America.

Evans, R. (1982) *The Fabrication of Virtue: English Prison Architecture, 1750–1840*. Cambridge: Cambridge University Press.

Fairweather, L. and McConville, S. (2000) *Prison Architecture: Policy, Design and Experience*. Oxford: Architectural Press.

Farrall, S. and Calverley, A. (2006) *Understanding Desistance from Crime: Theoretical Directions in Resettlement and Rehabilitation*. Maidenhead: Open University Press.

Farrant, F. (2005) *A Sobering Thought: Young Men in Prison. Out for Good Research Briefing* 1. London: Howard League for Penal Reform.

Farrant, F. (2006) *Out for Good: The Resettlement Needs of Young Men in Prison*. London: Howard League for Penal Reform.

Farrington, D.P. (1993) 'Understanding and preventing bullying', in M. Tonry (ed.) *Crime and Justice: A Review of Research*. Chicago, IL: University of Chicago Press.

Farrington, D.P., Ditchfield, J., Hancock, G., Howard, P., Jolliffe, D., Livingston, M. and Painter, K. (2002) *Evaluation of Two Intensive Regimes for Young Offenders. Home Office Research Study* 239. London: Home Office.

Farrington, D.P., Ditchfield, J., Howard, P. and Jolliffe, D. (2002) *Two Intensive Regimes for Young Offenders: A Follow-up Evaluation. Home Office Research Findings* 163. London: Home Office.

Farrington, D.P., Hancock, G., Livingston, M.S., Painter, K.A. and Towl, G. (2000) *Evaluation of Intensive Regimes for Young Offenders. Home Office Research Findings* 121. London: Home Office.

Faugeron, C. (1996) 'The changing functions of imprisonment', in R. Matthews and P. Francis (eds) *Prisons 2000 – an International Perspective on the Current State and Future of Imprisonment*. London: Macmillan.

Faulkner, D. (2006) *Crime, State and Citizen: A Field Full of Folk* (2nd edn). Winchester: Waterside Press.

Faulkner, D. and Flaxington, F. (2004) 'NOMS and civil renewal', *Vista*, 9: 90–9.

Fawcett Society (2004) *Women and the Criminal Justice System*. London: Fawcett Society.

Feeley, M. and Simon, J. (1992) 'The new penology: notes on the emerging strategy of corrections and its implications', *Criminology*, 30: 449–74.

Feeley, M. and Simon, J. (1994) 'Actuarial justice: the emerging new criminal law', in D. Nelken (ed.) *The Futures of Criminology*. London: Sage.

Ferlie, E., Ashburner, L., Fitzgerald, L. and Pettigrew, A. (1996) *The New Public Management in Action*. Oxford: Oxford University Press.

Ferm, V. (ed.) (1945) *An Encyclopedia of Religion*. New York: Philosophical Library.

Fitzgerald, M. and Sim, J. (1979) *British Prisons* (2nd edn 1982). Oxford: Blackwell.

Flanagan, T.J. (ed.) (1995) *Long-term Imprisonment: Policy, Science, and Correctional Practice*. Thousand Oaks, CA: Sage.

Floud, J. and Young, W. (1981) *Dangerousness and Criminal Justice*. London: Heinemann.

Flynn, N. (1998) *Introduction to Prisons and Imprisonment*. Winchester: Waterside Press.

Forsythe, W.J. (1987) *The Reform of Prisoners, 1830–1900*. Beckenham: Croom Helm.

Foucault, M. (1972) *The Archaeology of Knowledge*. London: Routledge.

Foucault, M. (1977) *Discipline and Punish* (trans. A. Sheridan). London: Allen Lane.

Foucault, M. (1980) 'Truth and power', in C. Gordon (ed.) *Power/Knowledge: Selected Interviews and other Writings, 1972–1977 by Michel Foucault*. London: Longman.

Fox, A. (1974) *Beyond Contract: Work, Power and Trust Relations*. London: Faber & Faber.

Friendship, C., Mann, R. and Beech, A. (2003) *The Prison-based Sex Offender Treatment Programme: An Evaluation*. London: Home Office.

Garland, D. (1985) *Punishment and Welfare*. Aldershot: Gower.

Garland, D. (1990) *Punishment and Modern Society*. Oxford: Clarendon Press.

Garland, D. (1996) 'The limits of the sovereign state: strategies of crime control in contemporary society', *British Journal of Criminology*, 36: 445–71.

Garland, D. (2001) *The Culture of Control: Crime and Social Order in Contemporary Society*. Oxford: Oxford University Press.

Garland, D. (2002) 'The cultural uses of capital punishment', *Punishment and Society*, 4: 459–87.

Genders, E. (2002) 'Legitimacy, accountability and private prisons', *Punishment and Society*, 4: 285–303.

Genders, E. and Player, E. (1989) *Race Relations in Prison*. Oxford: Clarendon Press.

Genders, E. and Player, E. (1995) *Grendon: A Study of a Therapeutic Prison*. Oxford: Clarendon Press.

Geyes, A. and Baumester, R. (2005) 'Religion, morality and self-control', in R. Paloutzian and C. Park (eds) *Handbook of the Psychology of Religion and Spirituality*. New York, NY: Guilford Press.

Giallombardo, R. (1966) 'Social roles in a prison for women', *Social Problems*, 13: 268–88.

Giddens, A. (1977) *Studies in Social and Political Theory*. London: Hutchinson.

Giddens, A. (1984) *The Constitution of Society*. Cambridge: Polity Press.

Gilbert, M. (1991) *Churchill: A Life*. London: Pimlico.

Gilligan, G. and Pratt, J. (eds) (2004) *Crime, Truth and Justice: Official Inquiry, Discourse, Knowledge*. Cullompton: Willan Publishing.

Goffman, E. (1959) *The Presentation of Self in Everyday Life*. New York, NY: Anchor.

Goffman, E. (1961) *Asylums: Essays on the Social Situation of Mental Patients and Other Inmates*. New York, NY: Doubleday Anchor.

Golden, R. (2005) *Mothers in Prison and the Families they Leave behind*. New York, NY: Routledge.

Goldson, B. (2002) *Vulnerable Inside: Children in Secure and Penal Settings*. London: Children's Society.

Goldson, B. and Coles, D. (2005) *In the Care of the State? Child Deaths in Penal Custody in England and Wales*. London: Inquest.

Gordon, A.F. (2006) 'Abu Ghraib: imprisonment and the war on terror', *Race and Class*, 48: 42–59.

Gormally, B. and McEvoy, K. (1995) *Release and Reintegration of Politically Motivated Prisoners in Northern Ireland: A Comparative Study of South Africa, Israel/Palestine, Italy, Spain, the Republic of Ireland and Northern Ireland*. Belfast: NIACRO.

Greenberg, K.J., Dratel, J.L. and Lewis, A. (2005) *The Torture Papers: The Road to Abu Ghraib*. Cambridge: Cambridge University Press.

Greer, C. (2006) 'Delivering death: capital punishment, botched executions and the American press', in P. Mason (ed.) *Captured by the Media: Prison Discourse in Popular Culture*. Cullompton: Willan Publishing.

Greer, K.R. (2000) 'The changing nature of interpersonal relationships in a women's prison', *Prison Journal*, 80: 442–68.

Grounds, A. (2005) 'Understanding the effects of wrongful imprisonment', in M. Tonry (ed.) *Crime and Justice: An Annual Review of Research. Vol. 32*. Chicago, IL: University of Chicago Press.

Hagell, A., Hazel, N. and Shaw, C. (2000) *Evaluation of Medway Secure Training Centre*. London: Home Office Research, Development and Statistics Directorate.

Hall, S. (1980) *Drifting into a Law and Order Society*. London: Cobden Trust.

Haney, C. (1997) 'Psychology and the limits to prison pain: confronting the coming crisis in the eighth amendment law', *Psychology, Public Policy and Law*, 3: 499–588.

Haney, C. (1999) 'Reflections on the Stanford Prison Experiment: genesis, transformations, consequences ("the SPE and the analysis of institutions")', in T. Blass (ed.) *Obedience to Authority: Current Perspectives on the Milgram Paradigm*. Hillsdale, NJ: Erlbaum.

Haney, C. (2006) *Reforming Punishment: Psychological Limits to the Pains of Imprisonment*. Washington, DC: American Psychological Association Books.

Haney, C., Banks, C. and Zimbardo, P. (1973) 'Interpersonal dynamics in a simulated prison', *International Journal of Criminology and Penology*, 1: 69–97.

Haney, C. and Zimbardo, P. (1977) 'The socialization into criminality: on becoming a prisoner and a guard', in J. Tapp and F. Levine (eds) *Law, Justice, and the Individual in Society: Psychological and Legal Issues*. New York, NY: Holt, Rinehart & Winston.

Haney, C. and Zimbardo, P. (1998) 'The past and future of US prison policy: twenty-five years after the Stanford Prison Experiment', *American Psychologist*, 53: 709–27.

Hannah-Moffatt, K. (2000) 'Prisons that empower: neo-liberal governance in Canadian women's prisons', *British Journal of Criminology*, 40: 510–31.

Harding, C., Hines, B., Ireland, R. and Rawlings, P. (1985) *Imprisonment in England and Wales: A Concise History*. London: Croom Helm.

Harding, R. (1997) *Private Prisons and Public Accountability*. Buckingham: Open University Press.

Harding, R. (2007) 'Inspecting prisons – prison inspection and accountability?', in Y. Jewkes (ed.) *Handbook on Prisons*. Cullompton: Willan Publishing.

Harvey, J. (2007) *Young Men in Prison: Surviving and Adapting to Life Inside*. Cullompton: Willan Publishing.

Hassine, V. (1999) *Life without Parole: Living in Prison Today* (2nd edn). Los Angeles, CA: Roxbury.

Hawkins, G. (1976) *The Prison: Policy and Practice*. Chicago, IL: University of Chicago Press.

Hawton, K., Fagg, J., Simkin, S., Bale, E. and Bond, A. (1997) 'Trends in deliberate self-harm in Oxford, 1985–1995, and their implications for clinical services and the prevention of suicide', *British Journal of Psychiatry*, 171: 556–60.

Hay, W. and Sparks, R. (1996) 'Vulnerable prisoners: the risk in long-term prisons', in J. Reynold and U. Smartt (eds) *Prison Policy and Practice: Selected Papers from 35 Years of the Prison Service Journal*. Leyhill: Prison Service Journal.

Hayward, D. (2006) 'Higher barriers: ex-prisoners and university admissions', in S. Taylor (ed.) *Prison(er) Education* (2nd edn). London: Forum on Prisoner Education.

Hedderman, C. and Gelsthorpe, L. (1997) *Understanding the Sentencing of Women. Home Office Research Study* 170. London: Home Office.

Hendrick, H. (2006) 'Histories of youth crime and justice', in B. Goldson and J. Muncie (eds) *Youth Crime and Justice*. London: Sage.

Henley, S. (2003) *The 21st Century Model Prison* (available online at **http://www. spacesyntax.net/symposia/SSS4/fullpapers/03Henleypaper.pdf**).

Hennessy, P. (1990) 'The political and administrative background', in M. Cave *et al.* (eds) *Output and Performance Measurement in Government: The State of the Art.* London: Jessica Kingsley.

Hennessy, P. (1991) *Whitehall.* London: Pimlico.

Hennessy, P. (1992) *Never Again: Britain, 1945–51.* London: Jonathan Cape.

Henriques, U.R.Q. (1972) 'The rise and decline of the separate system', *Past and Present,* 54: 61–93.

Hensley, C. (2001) 'Consensual homosexual activity in male prisons', *Corrections Compendium,* 26: 1–4.

Herman, D. (2003) '"*Bad Girls* changed my life": homonormativity in a women's prison drama', *Critical Studies in Media Communication,* 20: 141–59.

Hillyard, P., Pantazis, C., Tombs, S., Gordon, D. and Dorling, D. (2005) *Criminal Obsessions: Why Harm Matters more than Crime.* London: Crime and Society Foundation.

Hinsliff, G. (2005) 'US-style uniforms for yobs in new disorder crackdown', *Observer,* 15 May (available online at **http://observer.guardian.co.uk/politics/story/ 0,6903,1484282,00.html**).

HM Chief Inspector of Prisons (1996) *Patient or Prisoner? A New Strategy for Health Care in Prisons.* London: Home Office.

HM Chief Inspector of Prisons (1999) *Suicide is Everyone's Concern: Report of a Thematic Inspection on Suicides in Prison.* London: HMSO.

HM Chief Inspector of Prisons (2000a) *Inspection of Close Supervision Centres.* London: HM Inspectorate of Prisons.

HM Chief Inspector of Prisons (2000b) *Unjust Deserts: A Thematic Review by HM Chief Inspector of Prisons of the Treatment and Conditions for Unsentenced Prisoners in England and Wales.* London: Home Office.

HM Chief Inspector of Prisons (2003) *Report on a Full Unannounced Inspection of HMP Durham, 18–22 August 2003.* London: Home Office.

HM Chief Inspector of Prisons (2004) '*No Problems – Old and Quiet': Older Prisoners in England and Wales.* London: HM Inspectorate of Prisons.

HM Chief Inspector of Prisons (2006a) *Annual Report of HM Chief Inspector of Prisons for England and Wales, 2004–2005.* London: HMSO.

HM Chief Inspector of Prisons (2006b) *Extreme Custody: A Thematic Inspection of Close Supervision Centres and High Security Segregation.* London: HM Inspectorate of Prisons.

HM Chief Inspector of Prisons (2006c) *Report of an Unannounced Full Follow-up Inspection of HMP Pentonville, 7–16 June 2006.* London: Home Office.

HM Government (2006) *Working Together to Safeguard Children: A Guide to Inter-agency Working to Safeguard and Promote the Welfare of Children.* London: HMSO.

HM Inspectorate of Prisons (2001) *A Full Announced Inspection of HM Prison Whitemoor, 6–15 November 2000.* London: Home Office.

HM Inspectorate of Prisons (2005) *Juvenile Expectations: Criteria for assessing the conditions for and after treatment of children and young people in custody.* London: Home Office.

HM Inspectorate of Prisons (2005) *IRC Expectations: criteria for assessing the conditions for and treatment of immigration detainees.* London: Home Office.

HM Inspectorate of Prisons (2005a) *Parallel Worlds: A Thematic Review of Race Relations in Prisons.* London: Home Office.

HM Inspectorate of Prisons (2005b) *Report of a Full Announced Inspection of Yarl's Wood Immigration Removal Centre.* London: Home Office.

HM Inspectorate of Prisons (2006a) *Annual Report 2005–6.* London: Home Office.

HM Inspectorate of Prisons (2006b) *Expectations: Criteria for Assessing the Conditions in Prisons and the Treatment of Prisoners.* London: HM Prison Service.

HM Inspectorate of Prisons (2006c) *Foreign National Prisoners – a Thematic Review.* London: Home Office.

HM Inspectorate of Prisons (2007) *Annual Report 2005–6.* London: Home Office.

HM Inspectorate of Probation (2006) *An Independent Review of a Serious Further Offence Case: Damien Hanson and Elliot White.* London: Home Office.

HM Prison Service (1995) *Prison Discipline Manual.* London: HM Prison Service.

HM Prison Service (1997) *Prison Service Review.* London: HM Prison Service.

HM Prison Service (1999a) *Framework Document.* London: HMSO.

HM Prison Service (1999b) *Prison Rules 1999: The Young Offender Institution (Amendment) (No. 2) Rules 1999* (PSO 0100). London: HM Prison Service.

HM Prison Service (2000a) *Categorisation and Allocation* (PSO 0900). London: HM Prison Service.

HM Prison Service (2000b) *Voluntary Drug Testing Units and the Framework for Voluntary Drug Testing* (PSO 3620). (available online at **http://pso.hmprisonservice.gov.uk/ PSO_3620_voluntary_drug_testing.doc**).

HM Prison Service (2001) *Certified Prisoner Accommodation* (PSO 1900). London: HM Prison Service.

HM Prison Service (2002a) *Clinical Services for Substance Misusers* (PSO 3550). (available online at **http://pso.hmprisonservice.gov.uk/PSO_3550_clinical_services.doc**).

HM Prison Service (2002b) *Counselling, Assessment, Referral, Advice and Throughcare Services* (PSO 3630). (available online at **http://pso.hmprisonservice.gov.uk/ PSO_3630_carats.doc**).

HM Prison Service (2002c) *Strategy for Working with the Voluntary and Community Sector* (PSO 4190). London: Home Office.

HM Prison Service (2003a) *Regime Monitoring Guidance Notes, 2003–04* (PSO 7100). London: HM Prison Service.

HM Prison Service (2003b) *Segregation Units* (PSO 1700). London: Home Office.

HM Prison Service (2004) Order 0500: Reception (PSO 0500) London: HM Prison Service.

HM Prison Service (2004a) *Addressing Alcohol Misuse: A Prison Service Alcohol Strategy for Prisoners.* London: HM Prison Service.

HM Prison Service (2004b) *Category A Prisoners: Review of Security Category* (PSO 1010). London: HM Prison Service.

HM Prison Service (2004c) *HM Prison Service (Public Sector Prisons): Annual Report and Accounts, April 2003–March 2004.* London: HMSO.

HM Prison Service (2004d) *Mandatory Drug Testing* (PSO 3601) (available online at **http://pso.hmprisonservice.gov.uk/PSO_3601_mandatory_drugs_testing.doc**).

HM Prison Service (2004e) *Prisoners' Property* (PSO 1250). London: Home Office.

HM Prison Service (2004f) *Violence Reduction Strategy.* London: Safer Custody Group.

HM Prison Service (2005a) *Mother and Baby Units* (PSO 4801). London: Home Office.

HM Prison Service (2005b) *The Prison Discipline Manual: Adjudications* (PSO 2000). London: HM Prison Service.

HM Prison Service (2006a) *Annual Report and Accounts, April 2005–March 2006.* London: HM Prison Service.

HM Prison Service (2006b) *HR Planning Staff Profiles and Projections Review – January 2006.* London: Home Office.

HM Prison Service (2006c) *Key Performance Indicators, Key Performance Targets and Additional Measures: Sources and Calculations Guidance Notes, 2006–2007.* London: HM Prison Service.

HM Prison Service (2006d) *Race Equality* (PSO 2800). London: Home Office.

HM Prison Service (2006e) *Use of Force Manual.* London: Home Office.

HM Prison Service and Commission for Racial Equality (2003) *Implementing Racial Equality in Prisons: A Shared Agenda for Change*. London: Home Office.

HM Prison Service and Department of Health (2001) *Changing the Outlook: A Strategy for Developing and Modernising Mental Health Services in Prisons*. London: Department of Health.

HM Prison Service and Prison Reform Trust (2002) *Prisoners' Information Book*. London: HM Prison Service and Prison Reform Trust.

HM Prison Service/NHS Executive (1999) *The Future Organisation of Prison Health Care*. London: Department of Health.

Hollin, C. and Bilby, C. (2007) 'Addressing offending behaviour: "what works" and beyond', in Y. Jewkes (ed.) *Handbook of Prisons*. Cullompton: Willan Publishing.

Hollin, C. and Palmer, E. (2006) *Offending Behaviour Programmes: Issues and Controversies*. Chichester: Wiley.

Holloway, R. (1999) *Godless Morality: Keeping Religion out of Ethics*. Edinburgh: Canongate.

Home Affairs Committee (2005) *Rehabilitation of Prisoners. First Report of Session, 2004–5. Volume I*. London: HMSO.

Home Office (1979) *Report of the Committee of Inquiry into the United Kingdom Prison Services* (the May Report) (Cmnd 7673). London: HMSO.

Home Office (1984) *Managing the Long-term Prison System: The Report of the Control Review Committee*. London: HMSO.

Home Office (1991) *Custody, Care and Justice: The Way Ahead for the Prison Service in England and Wales* (Cm 1647). London: HMSO.

Home Office (1994) *Report of the Enquiry into the Escape of Six Prisoners from the Special Security Unit at Whitemoor Prison, Cambridgeshire on Friday 9th September 1994* (the Woodcock Report). London: HMSO.

Home Office (2001a) *Making Punishments Work: Report of a Review of the Sentencing Framework for England and Wales*. London: HMSO.

Home Office (2001b) *Review of the Boards of Visitors: A Report of the Working Group Chaired by Rt Hon Sir Peter Lloyd MP*. London: HMSO.

Home Office (2002) *Prisoners' Requests and Complaints Procedure* (PSO 2510). London: Home Office.

Home Office (2003a) *Prison Statistics England and Wales, 2001*. London: HMSO.

Home Office (2003b) *Prison Statistics: England and Wales, 2002*. London: HMSO.

Home Office (2005a) *The National Offender Management Service (NOMS): Strategy for the Management and Treatment of Problematic Drug Users within the Correctional Services*. London: NOMS.

Home Office (2005b) *Volunteering: A Guide to Good Practice for Prisons*. London: Home Office.

Home Office (2006a) *From Improvement to Transformation*. London: Home Office.

Home Office (2006b) *Offender Management Caseload Statistics, 2005: England and Wales* (available online at **http://www.homeoffice.gov.uk/rds/pdfs06/hosb1806.pdf**).

Home Office (2006c) *Population in Custody* (available online at **http://www.homeoffice.gov.uk/rds/**).

Home Office (2006d) *RDS Asylum Statistics, 2nd Quarter, April–June 2006*. London: Home Office.

Home Office (2006e) *Rebalancing the Criminal Justice System in Favour of the Law-abiding Majority: Cutting Crime, Reducing Reoffending and Protecting the Public*. London: Home Office.

Home Office (2006f) *Statistics on Race and the Criminal Justice System, 2005*. London: Home Office.

Hood, C. (1991) 'A public management for all seasons', *Public Administration*, 69: 3–19.

Hood, R. (1965) *Borstal Re-assessed*. London: Heinemann.

Hough, M., Jacobson, J. and Millie, A. (2003) *The Decision to Imprison*. London: Prison Reform Trust.

Howard, J. (1777b/1973) *Prisons and Lazarettos: An Account of the Principal Lazarettos in Europe*. London: Patterson Smith.

Howard, J. (1777a/1973) *The State of the Prisons in England and Wales*. London: Patterson Smith.

Howard League for Penal Reform (1997) *Lost Inside: The Imprisonment of Teenage Girls*. London: Howard League for Penal Reform.

Howard League for Penal Reform (2004) *Advice, Understanding and Underwear: Working with Girls in Prison*. London: Howard League for Penal Reform.

Howard League for Penal Reform (2006a) *Care, Concern and Carpets: How Women's Prisons can use First Night in Custody Centres to Reduce Stress*. London: Howard League for Penal Reform.

Howard League for Penal Reform (2006b) *Women and Girls in the Penal System*. London: Howard League for Penal Reform.

Howard, M. (1996) 'Protecting the public', *Criminal Justice Matters*, 26: 4–5.

Howe, A. (1994) *Punish and Critique: Towards a Feminist Analysis of Penality*. London: Routledge.

Hudson, B. (2002) 'Punishment and control', in M. Maguire *et al.* (eds) *The Oxford Handbook of Criminology*. Oxford: Oxford University Press.

Ignatieff, M. (1978) *A Just Measure of Pain: The Penitentiary in the Industrial Revolution, 1750–1850*. London: Macmillan.

International Centre for Prison Studies (2004) *Guidance Note 4 on Prison Reform: Dealing with Prison Overcrowding*. London: International Centre for Prison Studies.

International Centre for Prison Studies (2006) *World Prison Brief – Online Database on the World's Prison Systems*. London: International Centre for Prison Studies, King's College (available online at **www.prisonstudies.org**).

Ireland, J.L. (2002) *Bullying among Prisoners: Evidence, Research and Intervention Strategies*. Hove: Brunner-Routledge.

Ireland, J.L. and Ireland, C.A. (2003) 'How do offenders define bullying? A study of adult, young and juvenile male offenders', *Legal and Criminological Psychology*, 8: 159–73.

Irwin, J. (2004) *The Warehouse Prison: Disposal of the New Dangerous Classes*. Los Angeles, CA: Roxbury.

Irwin, J. and Clemmer, D. (1962) 'Thieves, convicts and the inmate culture', *Social Problems*, 10: 142–55.

Irwin, J. and Cressey, D.R. (1962) 'Thieves, convicts and the inmate culture', *Social Problems*, 10: 142–55.

Jacobs, J.B. (1977) *Stateville: The Penitentiary in Mass Society*. Chicago, IL: University of Chicago Press.

Jacobs, J.B. (1979) 'Race relations and the prisoner subculture', in N. Morris and M. Tonry (eds) *Crime and Justice*. Chicago, IL: University of Chicago Press.

James, A., Bottomley, A.K., Liebling, A. and Clare, A. (1997) *Privatizing Prisons: Rhetoric and Reality*. London: Sage.

James, E. (2003) *A Life Inside: A Prisoner's Notebook*. London: Atlantic Books.

James, W. (1897/1956) *The Will to Believe*. New York, NY: Dover.

Jamieson, R. and Grounds, A. (2005) 'Release and adjustment: perspectives from studies of wrongly convicted and politically motivated prisoners', in A. Liebling and S. Maruna (eds) *The Effects of Imprisonment.* Cullompton: Willan Publishing.

Jamieson, R. and McEvoy, K. (2005) 'State crime by proxy and juridical othering', *British Journal of Criminology*, 45: 504–27.

Jarvis, B. (2004) *Cruel and Unusual: Punishment and US Culture.* London: Pluto Press.

Jarvis, B. (2006) 'The violence of images: inside the prison TV drama *Oz*', in P. Mason (ed.) *Captured by the Media: Prison Discourse in Popular Culture.* Cullompton: Willan Publishing.

Jay, M. (1992) 'Scopic regimes of modernity', in S. Lash and J. Friedman (eds) *Modernity and Identity.* Oxford: Blackwell.

Jennings, A.F. (1996) 'A case for part-time imprisonment', *Prison Service Journal*, 108: 12–14.

Jewkes, Y. (2002) *Captive Audience: Media, Masculinity and Power in Prisons.* Cullompton: Willan Publishing.

Jewkes, Y. (2004) *Media and Crime.* London: Sage.

Jewkes, Y. (2005) 'Prisoners and the press', *Criminal Justice Matters*, 59: 26–9.

Jewkes, Y. (2006) 'Creating a stir? Prisons, popular media and the power to reform', in P. Mason (ed.) *Captured by the Media: Prison Discourse in Popular Culture.* Cullompton: Willan Publishing.

Jewkes, Y. (2007a) 'Prisons and the media: the shaping of public opinion and penal policy in a mediated society', in Y. Jewkes (ed.) *Handbook on Prisons.* Cullompton: Willan Publishing.

Jewkes, Y. (2007b) 'Prisons, public interest and the popular media', in Y. Jewkes (ed.) *Handbook on Prisons.* Cullompton: Willan Publishing.

Jewkes, Y. (ed.) (2007c) *Handbook on Prisons.* Cullompton: Willan Publishing.

Jewkes, Y. and Johnston, H. (2006) *Prison Readings: A Critical Introduction to Prisons and Imprisonment.* Cullompton: Willan Publishing.

Jewkes, Y. and Johnston, H. (2007) 'The evolution of prison architecture', in Y. Jewkes (ed.) *Handbook on Prisons.* Cullompton: Willan Publishing.

Johnson, R. (1998) *Death Work: A Study of the Modern Execution Process.* New York, NY: Wadsworth.

Johnson, R. (2005) 'Brave new prisons: the growing social isolation of modern penal institutions', in A. Liebling and S. Maruna (eds) *The Effects of Imprisonment.* Cullompton: Willan Publishing.

Johnston, H. (2006) '"Buried alive": representations of the separate system in Victorian England', in P. Mason (ed.) *Captured by the Media: Prison Discourse in Popular Culture.* Cullompton: Willan Publishing.

Jones, K. and Fowles, A. (1984) *Ideas on Institutions: Analysing the Literature on Long-term Care and Custody.* London: Routledge.

Jowell, R., Curtice, J., Park, A., Brook, C., Thomson, K. and Brough, C. (eds) (1997) *British Social Attitudes: The 4th Report.* Aldershot: Ashgate.

Jürgens, R. (2005) *HIV/AIDS and HCV in Prisons: A Select Annotated Bibliography.* Ottawa: Health Canada (available online in English and French at **http://www.hc-sc.gc.ca/ahc-asc/activit/ strateg/intactivit/aids-sida/hivaids-vihsida-pubs_e.html**).

Kauffman, K. (1988) *Prison Officers and their World.* Cambridge, MA: Harvard University Press.

Keith, Justice (2006) *The Report of the Zahid Mubarek Inquiry.* London: HMSO.

Kemshall, H. (2003) *Understanding Risk in Criminal Justice.* Maidenhead: Open University Press.

Kent, J. (1962) *Elizabeth Fry.* London: Batsford.

King, R.D. (1999) 'The rise and rise of supermax: an American solution in search of a problem', *Punishment and Society*, 1: 163–86.

King, R.D. (2000) 'Doing research in prisons', in R. King and E. Wincup (eds) *Doing Research on Crime and Justice*. Oxford: Oxford University Press.

King, R.D. (2005) 'The effects of supermax custody', in A. Liebling and S. Maruna (eds) *The Effects of Imprisonment*. Cullompton: Willan Publishing.

King, R.D. (2007a) 'Imprisonment: some international comparisons and the need to revisit panopticism', in Y. Jewkes (ed.) *Handbook on Prisons*. Cullompton: Willan Publishing.

King, R.D. (2007b) 'Security, control and the problems of containment', in Y. Jewkes (ed.) *Handbook on Prisons*. Cullompton: Willan Publishing.

King, R.D. and McDermott, K. (1995) *The State of Our Prisons*. Oxford: Clarendon Press.

King, R.D. and Morgan, R. (1980) *The Future of the Prison System*. Farnborough: Gower.

Koscheski, M., Hensley, C., Wright, J. and Tewksbery, R. (2002) 'Consensual sexual behavior', in C. Hensley (ed.) *Prison Sex: Practice and Policy*. London: Lynne Rienner.


Laming, Lord of Tewin (2000) *Modernising the Management of the Prison Service: An Independent Report by the Targeted Performance Initiative Working Group*. London: Prison Service.

Langan, P.A. and Levin, D.J. (2002) *Recidivism of Prisoners Released in 1994. Bureau of Justice Studies Special Report*. Washington, DC: US Department of Justice.

Lazarus, L. (2006) 'Conceptions of liberty deprivation', *Modern Law Review*, 69: 738.

Learmont, J. (1995) *Review of Prison Service Security in England and Wales and the Escape from Parkhurst Prison, Tuesday 3rd January 1995* (Cm 3020). London: HMSO.

Leech, M. (ed.) (2006) *The Prisons Handbook* (9th edn). Manchester: MLA Press.

Lewis, D. (1997) *Hidden Agendas: Politics, Law and Disorder*. London: Hamish Hamilton.

Liebling, A. (1991) 'Suicide in prisons.' Unpublished PhD thesis, University of Cambridge.

Liebling, A. (1992) *Suicides in Prison*. London: Routledge.

Liebling, A. (1999a) 'Doing research in prison: breaking the silence', *Theoretical Criminology*, 3: 147–73.

Liebling, A. (1999b) 'Prison suicide and prisoner coping', in M. Tonry and J. Petersilia (eds) *Prisons, Crime and Justice: An Annual Review of Research. Vol. 26*. Chicago, IL: University of Chicago Press.

Liebling, A. (2001) 'Whose side are we on: theory, practice and allegiances in prisons research', *British Journal of Criminology*, 41: 472–84.

Liebling, A. (2002) 'A "liberal regime within a secure perimeter"?', in A. Bottoms and M. Tonry (eds) *Ideology, Crime and Criminal Justice: A Symposium in Honour of Sir Leon Radzinowicz*. Cullompton: Willan Publishing.

Liebling, A, assisted by Arnold, H. (2004) *Prisons and their Moral Performance: A Study of Values, Quality and Prison Life*. Oxford: Clarendon Press.

Liebling, A. (2006) 'Suicide and its prevention', in Y. Jewkes (ed.) *Handbook on Prisons*. Cullompton: Willan Publishing.

Liebling, A. and Arnold, H. (2002a) 'Evaluating prisons: the decency agenda', *Prison Service Journal*, 141: 5–9.

Liebling, A. and Arnold, H. (2002b) *Measuring the Quality of Prison Life. Research Findings* 174. London: Home Office Research, Development and Statistics Directorate.

Liebling, A., assisted by Arnold, H. (2004) *Prisons and their Moral Performance: A Study of Values, Quality and Prison Life*. Oxford: Clarendon Press.

Liebling, A. and Bosworth, M. (1994) 'Incentives in prison regimes', *Prison Service Journal*, 98: 57–64.

Liebling, A. and Maruna, S. (2005a) 'Introduction: the effects of imprisonment revisited', in A. Liebling and S. Maruna (eds) *The Effects of Imprisonment*. Cullompton: Willan Publishing.

Liebling, A. and Maruna, S. (eds) (2005b) *The Effects of Imprisonment*. Cullompton: Willan Publishing.

Liebling, A., Muir, G., Rose, G. and Bottoms, A.E. (1999) *Incentives and Earned Privileges in Prison. Research Findings* 87. London: Home Office Research, Development and Statistics Directorate.

Liebling, A. and Price, D. (2001) *The Prison Officer*. Leyhill: Prison Service Journal.

Liebling, A., Tait, S., Durie, L. and Stiles, A. (2005) *The Safer Locals Evaluation*. London: Home Office.

Liebling, A., Tait, S., Durie, L., Stiles, A. and Harvey, J. (2005) 'Safer Locals evaluation', *Prison Service Journal*, 162: 8–12.

Liebling, A., Tait, S., Durie, L., Stiles, A., Harvey, J. and Rose, G. (2005) 'An evaluation of the Safer Locals programme – final report to Prison Service, Safer Custody Group.' Unpublished.

Lilly, J. and Deflem, M. (1996) 'Profit and penality: an analysis of the corrections–commercial complex', *Crime and Delinquency*, 34: 3–20.

Lindlof, T. (1987) 'Ideology and pragmatics of media access in prison', in T. Lindlof (ed.) *Natural Audiences: Qualitative Research of Media Uses and Effects*. Norwood, NJ: Ablex.

Lines, R., Jürgens, R., Stöver, H., Kaliakbarova, G., Laticevschi, D., Nelles, J., MacDonald, M. and Curtis, M. (2004) *Dublin Declaration on HIV/AIDS in Prisons in Europe and Central Asia*. Dublin: Irish Penal Reform Trust.

Livingstone, S. and Owen, T. (2003) *Prison Law* (3rd edn). Oxford: Oxford University Press.

Lloyd, C., Mair, G. and Hough, M. (1994) *Explaining Reconviction Rates: A Critical Analysis. Home Office Research Study* 136. London: Home Office.

Loader, I. (2006) 'Fall of the "Platonic guardians": liberalism, criminology and political responses to crime in England and Wales', *British Journal of Criminology*, 46: 561–86.

Logan, C. (1990) *Private Prisons: Pros and Cons*. New York, NY: Oxford University Press.

Loucks, N. (2000) *Prison Rules: A Working Guide*. London: Prison Reform Trust.

Lyon, J., Denison, C. and Wilson, A. (2000) *'Tell Them So They'll Listen': Messages from Young People in Custody*. London: Home Office.

MacDonald, D. and Sim, J. (1978) *Scottish Prisons and the Special Unit*. Glasgow: Scottish Council for Civil Liberties.

Maden, T., Swinton, M. and Gunn, J. (1994) 'Therapeutic community treatment: a survey of unmet need among sentenced prisoners', *Therapeutic Communities: The International Journal for Therapeutic and Supportive Organizations*, 15: 229–36.

Maguire, M. and Raynor, P. (2006) 'How the resettlement of prisoners promotes desistance from crime: or does it?', *Criminology and Criminal Justice*, 6: 19–38.

Maguire, M. and Vagg, J. (1984) *The Watchdog Role of Boards of Visitors*. London: Home Office.

Mandela, N. (1994) *Long Walk to Freedom*. London: Abacus.

Marshall, P. (1997) *A Reconviction Study of HMP Grendon Therapeutic Community. Home Office Research Findings* 53. London: Home Office Research and Statistics Directorate.

Martinson, R. (1974) 'What works? Questions and answers about prison reform', *The Public Interest*, 35: 22–54.

Maruna, S. and Immarigeon, R. (eds) (2004) *After Crime and Punishment: Ex-offender Reintegration and Desistance from Crime*. Cullompton: Willan Publishing.

Mason, P. (2000) 'Watching the invisible: televisual portrayal of the British prison, 1980–1991', *International Journal of the Sociology of Law*, 28: 33–44.

Mason, P. (2006) 'Hollywood's prison film: towards a discursive regime of imprisonment', in T. Serassis *et al.* (eds) *Images of Crime III. Representations of Crime in Politics, Society, Science, the Arts and the Media.* Freiburg: Max Planck Institute.

Mason, P. (2007) 'Prison decayed: cinematic penal discourse and populism, 1995–2005', *Social Semiotics.*

Mason, P. (forthcoming) 'Misinformation, myth and distortion: how the press construct imprisonment in Britain', *Journalism Studies,* 8.

Mathiesen, T. (1965) *The Defences of the Weak: A Sociological Study of a Norwegian Correctional Institution.* London: Tavistock.

Mathiesen, T. (1974) *The Politics of Abolition.* London: Martin Robertson.

Mathiesen, T. (1995) 'Driving forces behind prison growth: the mass media.' Paper presented at the International Conference on Prison Growth, Oslo, Norway, April (available online at **http://www.fecl.org/circular/4110.htm**).

Mathiesen, T. (1997) 'The viewer society: Michel Foucault's "Panopticon" revisited', *Theoretical Criminology,* 1: 215–34.

Mathiesen, T. (2000) *Prisons on Trial* (3rd edn 2006). Winchester: Waterside Press.

Mathiesen, T. (2001) 'Television, public space and prison population: a commentary on Mauer and Simon', *Punishment and Society,* 3: 35–42.

Mathiesen, T. (2003) 'Contemporary penal policy – a study in moral panics.' Paper presented at the European Committee on Crime Problems' 22nd Criminological Research Conference, Strasbourg.

Mathiesen, T. (2006) *Prison on Trial* (3rd edn). Winchester: Waterside Press.

Matthews, R. (2005) 'The myth of punitiveness', *Theoretical Criminology,* 9: 175–201.

McAlinden, A. (2001) 'Indeterminate sentences for the severely personality disordered', *Criminal Law Review,* February: 108–23.

McConville, S. (1981) *A History of English Prison Administration. Volume I: 1750–1877.* London: Routledge & Kegan Paul.

McConville, S. (1998a) 'The Victorian prison, 1865–1965', in N. Morris and D.J. Rothman (eds) *The Oxford History of the Prison: The Practice of Punishment in Western Society.* Oxford: Oxford University Press.

McConville, S. (1998b) 'Local justice: the jail', in N. Morris and D.J. Rothman (eds) *The Oxford History of the Prison: The Practice of Punishment in Western Society.* Oxford: Oxford University Press.

McEvoy, K. (2001) *Paramilitary Imprisonment in Northern Ireland: Resistance, Management and Release.* Oxford: Oxford University Press.

McEvoy, K., McConnachie, K. and Jamieson, R. (2007) 'Political imprisonment and the "War on terror"', in Y. Jewkes (ed.) *Handbook on Prisons.* Cullompton: Willan Publishing.

McGeorge, M. and Weber, H. (2001) 'Imprisonment for homicide: European perspectives concerning human rights', in D. Farrington *et al.* (eds) *Sex and Violence.* London: Routledge.

McGowen, R. (1995) 'The well-ordered prison: England, 1780–1865', in N. Morris and D. Rothman (eds) *The Oxford History of the Prison: The Practice of Punishment in Western Society.* Oxford: Oxford University Press.

McGowen, R. (1998) 'The well-ordered prison: England, 1780–1865', in N. Morris and D.J. Rothman (eds) *The Oxford History of the Prison: The Practice of Punishment in Western Society.* Oxford: Oxford University Press.

McGuire, J. (ed.) (2002) *Offender Rehabilitation and Treatment: Effective Programmes and Policies to Reduce Re-offending.* Chichester: Wiley.

McLaughlin, E., Muncie, J. and Hughes, G. (2001) 'The permanent revolution: New Labour, new public management and the modernization of criminal justice', *Criminal Justice,* 1: 301–18.

McNeill, F. (2006) 'A desistance paradigm for offender management', *Criminology and Criminal Justice*, 6: 37–60.

Medlicott, D. (2001) *Surviving the Prison Place: Narratives of Suicidal Prisoners*. Aldershot: Ashgate.

Medlicott, D. (2007) 'Women in prison', in Y. Jewkes (ed.) *Handbook on Prisons*. Cullompton: Willan Publishing.

Mehigan, J. and Rowe, A. (2007) 'Problematizing prison privatization: an overview of the debate', in Y. Jewkes (ed.) *Handbook of Prisons*. Cullompton: Willan Publishing.

Metraux, S. and Culhane, D.P. (2004) 'Homeless shelter use and reincarceration following prison release', *Criminology and Public Policy*, 3: 139–60.

Meyrowitz, J. (1985) *No Sense of Place: The Impact of Electronic Media on Social Behaviour*. Oxford: Oxford University Press.

Miller, J. (1991) *Last One Over the Wall: The Massachusetts Experiment in Closing Reform Schools*. Columbus, OH: Ohio State University Press.

Millie, A., Jacobson, J., McDonald, E. and Hough, M. (2005) *Anti-social Behaviour Strategies: Finding a Balance*. Bristol: Policy Press/Joseph Rowntree Foundation.

Mills, A. and Codd, H. (2007) 'Prisoners' families', in Y. Jewkes (ed.) *Handbook on Prisons*. Cullompton: Willan Publishing.

Mobley, A. and Terry, C. (2001) 'Guess who's coming to dinner? A prisoner perspective on the possibilities of re-entry.' Paper presented at the Bureau of Justice Statistics Program workshop on prisoner re-entry, Ann Arbor, Michigan.

Moore, R., Howard, P. and Burns, M. (2006) 'The further development of OASys: realising the potential of the Offender Assessment System', *Prison Service Journal*, 167: 36–42.

Morgan, R. (2002) 'Imprisonment', in M. Maguire *et al.* (eds) *The Oxford Handbook of Criminology* (3rd edn). Oxford: Oxford University Press.

Morgan, R. (2007) 'Children and young persons', in Y. Jewkes (ed.) *Handbook on Prisons*. Cullompton: Willan Publishing.

Morgan, R. and Evans, M. (2001) *Combating Torture in Europe*. Strasbourg: Council of Europe Publishing.

Morgan, R. and Newburn, T. (2007) 'Youth justice', in M. Maguire *et al.* (eds) *The Oxford Handbook of Criminology*. Oxford: Oxford University Press.

MORI (2001) *Public Attitudes towards Prisons: Report to Esmee Fairbairn Foundation*. London: Esmee Fairbairn Foundation.

MORI (2003) *Crime and Prisons Omnibus Survey*. London: MORI.

Morris, N. and Rotham, D. (1998) *The Oxford History of the Prison*. Oxford: Oxford University Press.

Morris, T. (1989) *Crime and Criminal Justice since 1945*. Oxford: Blackwell.

Morris, T. and Morris, P. (1963) *Pentonville: A Sociological Study of an English Prison*. London: Routledge & Kegan Paul.

Mountbatten, Lord of Burma (1966) *Report of the Inquiry into Prison Escapes and Security*. London: HMSO.

Muncie, J. (2001) 'Prison histories: reform, repression and rehabilitation', in E. McLaughlin and J. Muncie (eds) *Controlling Crime*. London: Sage.

Muncie, J. (2004) *Youth and Crime* (2nd edn). London: Sage.

Muncie, J. and Goldson, B. (eds) (2006) *Comparative Youth Justice*. London: Sage.

Muncie, J. and Wilson, D. (eds) (2004) *Student Handbook of Criminal Justice and Criminology*. London: Cavendish.

Murray, J. (2005) 'The effects of imprisonment on families and children of prisoners', in A. Liebling and S. Maruna (eds) *The Effects of Imprisonment*. Cullompton: Willan Publishing.

Nacro (2000) *The Forgotten Majority: The Resettlement of Short Term Prisoners*. London: Nacro.

Nacro (2001) *Young Adult Offenders: A Period of Transition*. London: Nacro.

National Audit Office (2003) *The Operational Performance of PFI Prisons*. London: NAO.

National Audit Office (2006a) *Serving Time: Prisoner Diet and Exercise*. London: HMSO.

National Audit Office (2006b) *The Electronic Monitoring of Adult Offenders*. London: HMSO.

National Institute of Justice (2003) *Correctional Boot Camps: Lessons from a Decade of Research*. Washington, DC: US Department of Justice.

National Offender Management Service (2006/2006a) *Office for Contracted Prisons: Statement of Performance and Financial Information: April 2005 to March 2006*. London: National Offender Management Service.

National Offender Management Service (2006, 2006b) *Population in Custody Monthly Tables: June 2006, England and Wales* (available online at **http://www.homeoffice. gov.uk/rds/pdfs06/prisjun06.pdf**).

Neal, D. (ed.) (2003) *Supermax Prisons: Beyond the Rock*. Lanham, MD: American Correctional Association.

Nellis, M. (2005) 'Electronic monitoring, satellite tracking and the new punitiveness in England and Wales', in J. Pratt *et al.* (eds) *The New Punitiveness: Trends, Theories and Perspectives*. Cullompton: Willan Publishing.

Nellis, M. (2006) 'Future punishment in American science fiction movies', in P. Mason (ed.) *Captured by the Media: Prison Discourse and Popular Culture*. Cullompton: Willan Publishing.

Newell, M. (1996) *The Open Prison Review*. London: HMSO.

Newsam, F. (1954) *The Home Office*. London: George Allen & Unwin.

Niven, S. and Stewart, D. (2005) *Resettlement Outcomes on Release from Prison in 2003*. *Home Office Research Findings* 248. London: Home Office.

Nobles, R. and Schiff, D. (2000) *Understanding Miscarriages of Justice*. Oxford: Oxford University Press.

NOMS (2006) *Population in Custody Monthly Tables: June 2006 England and Wales* (available online at **http://www.homeoffice.gov.uk/rds/pdfs06/prisjun06.pdf**).

NOMS (2007a) *Population in Custody Monthly Tables: March 2007 England and Wales* (available online at **http://www.homeoffice.gov.uk/rds/pdfs07/prismar07.pdf**).

NOMS (2007b) *Prison Population and Accommodation Briefing for 27th April 2007* (available online at **http://www.hmprisonservice.gov.uk/assets/documents/ 100029F327042007_web_ report.doc**).


O'Brien, P. (2001) *Making It in the 'Free World'*. New York, NY: SUNY.

Oddie, S. (2004) 'Exercise and drug detoxification', *Prison Service Journal*, 156: 21–4.

O'Donnell, I. (2004) 'Prison rape in context', *British Journal of Criminology*, 44: 241–55.

O'Donnell, I. and Edgar, K. (1996) *Victimisation in Prisons*. *Research Findings* 37. London: Home Office Research and Statistics Directorate.

Office for National Statistics (n.d.) *Census 2001: England And Wales* (available online at **http://www.statistics.gov.uk/census2001/profiles/727-A.asp**).

Office for Public Sector Reform (2003) *The Government's Policy on Inspection of Public Services*. London: Office for Public Sector Reform.

Owen, B. (1998) *In the Mix: Struggle and Survival in a Women's Prison*. Albany, NY: State University of New York Press.

Owers, A. (2007) 'Imprisonment in the twenty-first century: a view from the inspectorate', in Y. Jewkes (ed.) *Handbook on Prisons*. Cullompton: Willan Publishing.


Padfield, N. and Maruna, S. (2006) 'The revolving door: exploring the rise in recalls to prison', *Criminology and Criminal Justice*, 6: 329–52.

Parent, D.G. (1995) 'Boot camps failing to achieve goals', in M. Tonry and K. Hamilton (eds) *Intermediate Sanctions in Over-crowded Times*. Boston, MA: Northeastern University Press.

Parole Board (2006) *Annual Report and Accounts of the Parole Board for England and Wales, 2005–6.* London: HMSO.

Parry, J. (2004) *Prisoners Information Book – for Disabled Prisoners.* London: Prison Reform Trust/Prison Service.

Peters, E. (1995) 'Prison before the prison: the ancient and medieval worlds', in N. Morris and D. Rothman (eds) *The Oxford History of the Prison: The Practice of Punishment in Western Society.* Oxford: Oxford University Press.

Phillips, C. and Bowling, B. (2007) 'Ethnicities, racism, crime and criminal justice', in M. Maguire *et al.* (eds) *The Oxford Handbook of Criminology* (4th edn). Oxford: Oxford University Press.

Piacentini, L. (2007) 'Researching Russian prisons: a consideration of new and established methodologies in prison research', in Y. Jewkes (ed.) *Handbook on Prisons.* Cullompton: Willan Publishing.

Player, E. and Jenkins, M. (1994) *Prisons after Woolf: Reform through Riot.* London: Routledge.

Pollitt, C., Sirre, X., Lonsdale, J., Mul, R. and Summa, H. (2003) *Performance or Compliance? Performance Audit and Public Management in Five Countries.* Oxford: Oxford University Press.

Pollock, J.M. (1997) 'The social world of the prisoner', in J.M. Pollock (ed.) *Prisons: Today and Tomorrow.* Gaithersburg, MD: Aspen.

Pratt, J. (2002) *Punishment and Civilisation: Penal Tolerance and Intolerance in Modern Society.* London: Sage.

Pratt, J. (2007) *Penal Populism.* London: Routledge.

Pratt, J., Brown, D., Brown, M., Hallsworth, S. and Morrison, W. (2005b) 'Introduction', in J. Pratt *et al.* (eds) *The New Punitiveness: Trends, Theories, Perspectives.* Cullompton: Willan Publishing.

Pratt, J., Brown, D., Brown, M., Hallsworth, S. and Morrison, W. (eds) (2005a) *The New Punitiveness: Trends, Theories, Perspectives.* Cullompton: Willan Publishing.

Price, B. (2006) *Merchandizing Prisoners: Who Really Pays for Prison Privatisation?* Westpoint, CT: Praeger.

Prime Minister's Strategy Unit (2004) *Alcohol Harm Reduction Strategy for England.* London: Strategy Unit.

Prison Reform Trust (1998) *Prisoners and the Democratic Process.* London: PRT.

Prison Reform Trust (2000) *Justice for Women: The Need for Reform.* London: Prison Reform Trust.

Prison Reform Trust (2003) *Growing Old in Prison: A Scoping Study on Older Prisoners.* London: Centre for Policy on Ageing/Prison Reform Trust.

Prison Reform Trust (2004) *Forgotten Prisoners: The Plight of Foreign National Prisoners.* London: Prison Reform Trust.

Prison Reform Trust (2006a) 'Inside criminal justice', *Prison Report,* 69: 4.

Prison Reform Trust (2006b) *Bromley Briefings: Prison Factfile.* London: Prison Reform Trust.

Prison Reform Trust and National AIDS Trust (2005) *HIV and Hepatitis in UK Prisons: Addressing Prisoners' Healthcare Needs.* London: Prison Reform Trust (available online at **http://www.nat.org.uk/HIV_Testing_&_Care/Prisons_&_detention**).

Prison Research Action Project (1976) *Instead of Prisons: A Handbook for Abolitionists.* Syracuse, NY: Prison Research Action Project (available online at **http://www.prisonpolicy.org/scans/instead_of_prisons**).

Prisons and Probation Ombudsman (2006) *Annual Report* (Cm 6873). London: HMSO.

Prisons Ombudsman (1998) *Annual Report, 1997* (Cm 3984). London: Home Office.

Pryor, S. (2001) *The Responsible Prisoner: An Exploration of the Extent to which Imprisonment Removes Responsibility Unnecessarily and an Invitation to Change.* London: HM Prison Service.

Radzinowicz, L. and Hood, R. (1990) *The Emergence of Penal Policy*. Oxford: Clarendon Press.

Raine, J. and Willson, M. (1997) 'Beyond managerialism in criminal justice', *Howard Journal*, 36: 80–95.

Ramsbotham, D. (2005) *Prisongate: The Shocking State of Britain's Prisons and the Need for Visionary Change*. London: Free Press.

Ramsey, M. (2003) *Prisoners' Drug Use and Treatment: Seven Research Studies*. Home Office Research Study 267. London: Home Office.

Rapoport, R. (1960) *Community as Doctor: New Perspectives on a Therapeutic Community*. London: Tavistock.

Raynor, P. and Robinson, G. (2005) *Rehabilitation, Crime and Justice*. Basingstoke: Palgrave.

Raynor, P. and Vanstone, M. (2002) *Understanding Community Penalties: Probation, Policy and Social Change*. Buckingham: Open University Press.

Rethinking Crime and Punishment (2004) *The Report*. London: Esmee Fairbairn Foundation.

Rex, S. and Tonry, M. (eds) (2002) *Reform and Punishment: The Future of Sentencing*. Cullompton: Willan Publishing.

Rhodes, L. (2004) *Total Confinement: Madness and Reason in the Maximum Security Prison*. Berkeley, CA: University of California Press.

Richards, M., McWilliams, B., Allcock, L., Enterkin, J., Owens, P. and Woodrow, J. (1994) *The Family Ties of English Prisoners*. Cambridge: Cambridge Centre for Family Research.

Rideout (2006) *The Creative Prison: Creative Thinking within the Prison Estate*. Stoke-on-Trent: Rideout/Creative Arts for Rehabilitation (available online at **www.rideout.org.uk**).

Roberts, J. (2005) *The Virtual Prison: Community Control and the Evolution of Imprisonment*. Cambridge: Cambridge University Press.

Roberts, K. (ed.) (1993) *New Challenges to Understanding Organizations*. New York, NY: Macmillan.

Robson, L.L. (1976) *The Convict Settlers' Australia*. Melbourne: Melbourne University Press.

Rose, J. (1994) *Elizabeth Fry*. London: QHS.

Rothman, D.J. (1980) *Conscience and Convenience: The Asylum and its Alternatives in Progressive America*. New York, NY: Aldine de Gruyter.

Ruck, S.K. (1951) *Paterson on Prisons: Being the Collected Papers of Sir Alexander Paterson*. London: Frederick Muller.

Rutherford, A. (1984) *Prisons and the Process of Justice: The Reductionist Challenge*. London: Heinemann.

Ryan, M. (2003) *Penal Policy and Political Culture in England and Wales*. Winchester: Waterside Press.

Ryan, M. (2006) 'Red Tops, populists and the irresistible rise of the public voice', in P. Mason (ed.) *Captured by the Media: Prison Discourse in Popular Culture*. Cullompton: Willan Publishing.

Ryan, M. and Sim, J. (2007) 'Campaigning for and campaigning against prisons: excavating and re-affirming the case for prison abolition', in Y. Jewkes (ed.) *Handbook of Prisons*. Cullompton: Willan Publishing.

Ryan, M. and Ward, A. (1989) *Privatization and the Penal System: The American Experience and the Debate in Britain*. Milton Keynes: Open University Press.

Safer Custody Group/Prison Service (2001) *Prevention of Suicide and Self-harm in the Prison Service: An Internal Review*. London: Home Office.

Sainsbury Centre for Mental Health (2006) *London's Prison Mental Health Services: A Review. Policy Paper* 5. London: SCMH (available online at **http://www.mark walton.net/04/mdo/archives/London_prison_mental_health_services.pdf**).

Samaritans (2001) *Risk 1 Project – a Strategy for Higher Risk Prisoners.* Ewell: Samaritans.

Sandbrook, D. (2005) *Never Had It So Good: A History of Britain from Suez to the Beatles.* London: Little Brown.

Sattar, G. (2001) *Rates and Causes of Deaths among Prisoners and Offenders under Community Supervision. Home Office Research Study* 231. London: Home Office.

Schafer, S. (1974) *The Political Criminal: The Problem of Morality and Crime.* New York, NY: Free Press/Macmillan.

Schauer, T. (2004) 'Masculinity incarcerated: insurrectionary speech and masculinity', *Journal for Crime, Conflict and Media Culture*, 1: 28–42.

Schishor, D. (1980) 'The new criminology: some critical issues', *British Journal of Criminology*, 20: 1–19.

Schrag, C. (1944) 'Social types in a prison community.' Unpublished master's thesis, University of Washington.

Schwaebe, C. (2005) 'Learning to pass: sex offenders' strategies for establishing a viable identity in the prison population', *International Journal of Offender Therapy and Comparative Criminology*, 49: 614–25.

Scott, D. (2007) 'The changing face of the English prison: a critical review of the aims of imprisonment', in Y. Jewkes (ed.) *Handbook of Prisons.* Cullompton: Willan Publishing.

Scottish Executive (2006) *Prison Statistics* (available online at **http://www.scotland. gov.uk/Publications**).

Sechrest, L., White, S. and Brown, E. (1979) *The Rehabilitation of Criminal Offenders.* Washington, DC: National Academy of Sciences.

Selby, M. (1994) 'Goals for gaolers?', *Prison Report*, 98: 22–3.

Serge, V. (1970) *Men In Prison.* London: Gollancz.

Shafer, N. (1994) 'Exploring the link between visits and parole success', *International Journal of Offender Therapy and Comparative Criminology*, 38: 17–32.

Shaw, A.G.L. (1964) *Convicts and Colonies: A Study of Penal Transportation from Great Britain and Ireland to Australia and Other Parts of the British Empire.* London: Faber & Faber.

Shaw, J., Appleby, L. and Baker, D. (2003) *Safer Prisons: A National Study of Prison Suicides 1999–2000 by the National Confidential Inquiry into Suicides and Homicides by People with Mental Illness.* London: Department of Health.

Shaw, S. (2007) 'A specialist ombudsman for prisoners', in *International Ombudsman Institute* and Linda C. Reif (ed.) *The International Ombudsman Yearbook. Vol. 8.* Boston MA: Brill.

Shepherd, A. and Whiting, E. (2006) *Re-offending of Adults: Results from the 2003 Cohort.* London: Home Office (available online at **http://www.homeoffice.gov.uk/ rds/pdfs06/hosb2006.pdf**).

Sherman, L.W. and Strang, H. (2007) *Restorative Justice: The Evidence.* London: Smith Institute.

Sim, J. (1990) *Medical Power in Prisons: The Prison Medical Service in England, 1774–1989.* Milton Keynes: Open University Press.

Sim, J. (1994a) 'Reforming the penal wasteland? A critical review of the Woolf Report', in E. Player and M. Jenkins (eds) *Prisons after Woolf: Reform through Riot.* London: Routledge.

Sim, J. (1994b) 'Tougher than the rest? Men in prison', in T. Newburn and E. Stanko (eds) *Just Boys Doing Business.* London: Routledge.

Sim, J. (2002) 'The future of prison health care: a critical analysis', *Critical Social Policy*, 22: 300–23.

Sim, J. (2007) *The Carceral State: Power and Punishment in a Hard Land.* London: Sage.

Simon, J. (1995) 'They died with their boots on: the boot camp and the limits of modern penality', *Social Justice*, 22: 25–48.

Simon, J. (2000) 'The "Society of Captives" in the era of hyper-incarceration', *Theoretical Criminology*, 4: 285–308.

Singleton, N., Farrell, M. and Meltzer, H. (1999) *Substance Misuse among Prisoners in England and Wales*. London: ONS.

Singleton, N., Meltzer, H., Gatward, R., Coid, J. and Deasy, D. (1998) *Psychiatric Morbidity among Prisoners in England and Wales*. London: ONS.

Singleton, N., Pendry, E., Simpson, T., Goddard, E., Farrell, M., Marsden, J. and Taylor, C. (2005) *The Impact of Mandatory Drug Testing in Prisons*. London: Home Office.

Smart, B. (1983) 'On discipline and social regulation: a review of Foucault's genealogical analysis', in D. Garland and P. Young (eds) *The Power to Punish*. London: Heinemann Educational.

SmartJustice (2006) *Crime Victims Say Jail Doesn't Work* (available online at **http://www.smartjustice.org/**).

Smith, P. and Goddard, M. (2002) 'Performance management and operational research: a marriage made in Heaven?', *Journal of the Operational Research Society*, 53: 247–55.

Smith, R. (2003) *Youth Justice: Ideas, Policy, Practice*. Cullompton: Willan Publishing.

Snow, D., Baker, S. and Anderson, L. (1989) 'Criminality and homeless men: an empirical assessment', *Social Problems*, 36: 532–49.

Snow, L. (2002) 'Prisoners' motives for self-injury and attempted suicide', *British Journal of Forensic Practice*, 4: 18–29.

Social Exclusion Unit (2002) *Reducing Re-offending by Ex-prisoners*. London: Social Exclusion Unit.

Social Inclusion and Offenders Unit (2006) *The Offender Library, Learning and Information Specification*. London: Social Inclusion and Offenders Unit.

Solomon, E. (2004) *A Lost Generation: The Experiences of Young People in Prison*. London: Prison Reform Trust.

Solomon, E. (2006) 'Crime sound bites: a view from both sides of the microphone', in P. Mason (ed.) *Captured by the Media: Prison Discourse in Popular Culture*. Cullompton: Willan Publishing.

Sparks, R. (1996) 'Penal "austerity": the doctrine of less eligibility reborn?', in R. Matthews and P. Francis (eds) *Prisons 2000: An International Perspective on the Current State and Future of Imprisonment*. Basingstoke: Macmillan.

Sparks, R. (2003) 'States of insecurity: punishment, populism and contemporary political culture', in S. McConville (ed.) *The Use of Punishment*. Cullompton: Willan Publishing.

Sparks, R. (2007) 'The politics of imprisonment', in Y. Jewkes (ed.) *Handbook on Prisons*. Cullompton: Willan Publishing.

Sparks, R. and Bottoms, A.E. (1995) 'Legitimacy and order in prisons', *British Journal of Sociology*, 46: 45–62.

Sparks, R., Bottoms, A.E. and Hay, W. (1996) *Prisons and the Problem of Order*. Oxford: Clarendon Press.

Sparks, R.F. (1971) *Local Prisons: The Crisis in the English Prison System*. London: Heinemann.

Starmer, K. (1999) *European Human Rights Law*. London: LAG.

Steele, J. (2002) *The Bird that Never Flew*. Edinburgh: Mainstream.

Stenson, K. and Sullivan, R. (eds) (2001) *Crime, Risk and Justice: The Politics of Crime Control in Liberal Democracies*. Cullompton: Willan Publishing.

Struckman-Johnson, C., Struckman-Johnson, D., Rucker, L., Bumby, K. and Donaldson, S. (1996) 'Sexual coercion reported by men and women in prison', *Journal of Sex Research*, 33: 67–76.

Sykes, G. (1958) *The Society of Captives: A Study of a Maximum Security Prison*. Princeton, NJ: Princeton University Press.

Sykes, G. and Messinger, S. (1960) 'The inmate social system', in R.A. Cloward *et al.* (eds) *Theoretical Studies in the Social Organization of the Prison.* New York, NY: Social Science Research Council.

Tartaro, C. (2006) 'Watered down: partial implementation of the new generation jail philosophy', *Prison Journal,* 86: 284.

Taylor, R. (2000) *A Seven Year Reconviction Study of HMP Grendon Therapeutic Community. Home Office Research Findings* 115. London: Home Office Research, Development and Statistics Directorate.

Teague, M. (2002) 'Public perceptions of probation', *Criminal Justice Matters,* 49: 34–5.

Thomas, C.W. and Foster, S.C. (1972) 'Prisonization in the inmate contraculture', *Social Problems,* 20: 229–39.

Thomas, J.E. (1972) *The English Prison Officer since 1850*: A Study In Conflict. London: Routledge & Kegan Paul.

Thorpe, D., Smith, D., Green, C. and Paley, J. (1980) *Out of Care.* London: George Allen & Unwin.

Tilt, R. (1998) *Howard League Magazine,* November: 13.

Toch, H. (1992) *Living in Prison: The Ecology of Survival.* Washington, DC: American Psychological Association.

Tomlinson, M.H. (1981) 'Penal servitude, 1846–1865: a system in evolution', in V. Bailey (ed.) *Policing and Punishment in Nineteenth Century Britain.* London: Croom Helm.

Tonry, M. (2004) *Thinking about Crime: Sense and Sensibility in American Penal Culture.* Oxford: Oxford University Press.

Towl, G. (2004a) 'Applied psychological services in HM Prison Service and the national Probation Service', in A. Needs and G. Towl (eds) *Applying Psychology to Forensic Practice.* Oxford: Blackwell.

Towl, G. (2004b) 'Applied psychological services in prisons and probation', in J. Adler (ed.) *Forensic Psychology: Concepts, Debates and Practice.* Cullompton: Willan Publishing.

Towl, G. (2006) 'Introduction', in G. Towl (ed.) *Psychological Research in Prisons.* Oxford: Blackwell.

Towl, G. and Forbes, D. (2000) 'Working with suicidal prisoners', in G. Towl *et al.* (eds) *Suicide in Prisons.* Leicester: British Psychological Society.

Travis, J. and Waul, M. (2003) *Prisoners Once Removed: The Impact of Incarceration and Reentry on Children, Families and Communities.* Washington, DC: Urban Institute Press.

Tyler, T.R. and Boeckmann, R. (1997) 'Three strikes and you are out, but why? The psychology of public support for punishing rule breakers', *Law and Society Review,* 31: 237–65.

Tyler, T.R. and Huo, Y.J. (2002) *Trust in the Law: Encouraging Public Cooperation with the Police and Courts.* New York, NY: Russell-Sage Foundation.

Umbreit, M. (1996) *Responding to Important Questions Related to Restorative Justice.* St Paul, MN: Center for Restorative Justice and Peacemaking, School of Social Work, University of Social Work.

United Nations (2006) *United Nations Surveys of Crime Trends and Operations of Criminal Justice Systems.* Vienna: United Nations Office on Drugs and Crime (available online at **www.unodc.org**).

Unlock and Prison Reform Trust (2004) *Barred from Voting: The Right to Vote for Sentenced Prisoners* (available online at **www.unlock.org.uk/campaign.aspx**).

UN Office on Drugs and Crime (2006) *HIV/AIDS Prevention, Care, Treatment and Support in Prison Settings: A Framework for an Effective National Response.* New York, NY: United Nations, co-published with the World Health Organization and the Joint United Nations Programme on HIV/AIDS.

Useem, B. and Kimball, P. (1989) *States of Siege: US Prison Riots, 1971–1986*. Oxford: Oxford University Press.

Van Kesteren, J., Mayhew, P. and Nieuwbeerta, P. (2000) *Criminal Victimisation in Seventeen Industrialised Countries*. Dutch Ministry of Justice.

Van Ness, D. and Heetderks, K. (2001) *Restoring Justice* (2nd edn). Cincinnati, OH: Anderson Publishing.

Vanstone, M. (2004) *Supervising Offenders in the Community: A History of Probation Theory and Practice*. Aldershot: Ashgate.

Visher, C.A. and Travis, J. (2003) 'Transitions from prison to community: understanding individual pathways', *Annual Review of Sociology*, 29: 89–113.

Von Hirsch, A. (1993) *Censure and Sanctions*. Oxford: Oxford University Press.

Von Hirsch, A., Bottoms, A., Burney, E. and Wikestrom, P.-O. (1999) *Criminal Deterrence and Sentencing Severity: An Analysis of Recent Research*. Oxford: Hart Publishing.

Wacquant, L. (2002) 'The curious eclipse of prison ethnography in the age of mass incarceration', *Ethnography*, 3: 371–98.

Wahidin, A. (2004) *Older Women in the Criminal Justice System: Running Out of Time*. London: Jessica Kingsley.

Walker, N. (1983) 'Protecting people', in J.W. Hinton (ed.) *Dangerousness: Problems of Assessment and Prediction*. London: George Allen & Unwin.

Walmsley, R. (1999) *World Prison Population List. Research Findings* 88. London: Home Office Research, Development and Statistics Directorate.

Walmsley, R. (2006) *World Female Imprisonment List*. London: International Centre for Prison Studies, King's College.

Walmsley, R. (2007) *World Prison Population List* (7th edn). London: International Centre for Prison Studies, King's College.

Wheatley, M. (2007) 'Drug misuse in prison', in Y. Jewkes (ed.) *Handbook on Prisons*. Cullompton: Willan Publishing.

Wheatley, P. (2005) 'Managerialism in the Prison Service', *Prison Service Journal*, 161: 33–4.

Wheeler, S. (1961) 'Socialization in correctional communities', *American Sociological Review*, 26: 697–712.

White, I. and Rees, A. (2006) *House of Commons Standard Note SN/PC/1764: Convicted Prisoners and the Franchise*. London: Parliament and Constitution Centre, House of Commons.

Whitehead, P. and Statham, R. (2006) *The History of Probation: Politics, Power and Cultural Change, 1876–2005*. Crayford: Shaw & Sons.

Whitman, J. (2003) *Harsh Justice: Criminal Punishment and the Widening Divide between America and Europe*. Oxford: Oxford University Press.

Wilson, C. (2006) 'The ECHR: bringing rights home', in M. Leech (ed.) *The Prisons Handbook 2006*. Manchester: MLA Press.

Wilson, D. (1995) 'Against the culture of management', *Prison Service Journal*, 98: 7–9.

Wilson, D. (2005a) 'Book review: Alison Liebling, assisted by Helen Arnold (2004), *Prisons and their Moral Performance: A Study of Values, Quality, and Prison Life*, Oxford: Oxford University Press, Michael Tonry (ed) (2004), *The Future of Imprisonment*, Oxford: Oxford University Press', *Howard Journal*, 44: 229–31.

Wilson, D. (2005b) *Death at the Hands of the State*. London: Howard League for Penal Reform.

Woodcock, J. (1994) *Report of an Enquiry into the Escape of Six Prisoners from the Special Security Unit at Whitemoor Prison, Cambridgeshire, on Friday 9th September 1994*. London: HMSO.

Woolf, Lord (2001) 'The Woolf Report: a decade of change?' Address to the Prison Reform Trust, London, 31 January (available online at **http://www.judiciary. gov.uk/publications_media/speeches/pre_2004/31012001.htm**).

Woolf, Lord Justice and Tumin, S. (1991) *Prison Disturbances, April 1990* (Cm 1456). London: HMSO.

Worrall, A. (2001) 'Girls at risk? Reflections on changing attitudes to young women's offending', *Probation Journal*, 48: 86–92.

Wright, M. (1982) *Making Good: Prisons, Punishment and Beyond.* London: Burnett Books.

Youth Justice Board (2004) *Strategy for the Secure Estate for Juveniles.* London: YJB.

Zamble, E. and Porporino, F.J. (1988) *Coping, Behaviour and Adaptation in Prison Inmates.* New York, NY: Springer-Verlag.

Zehr, H. (1990) *Changing Lenses: A New Focus for Crime and Justice.* Scottdale, PA: Herald Press.

# Index